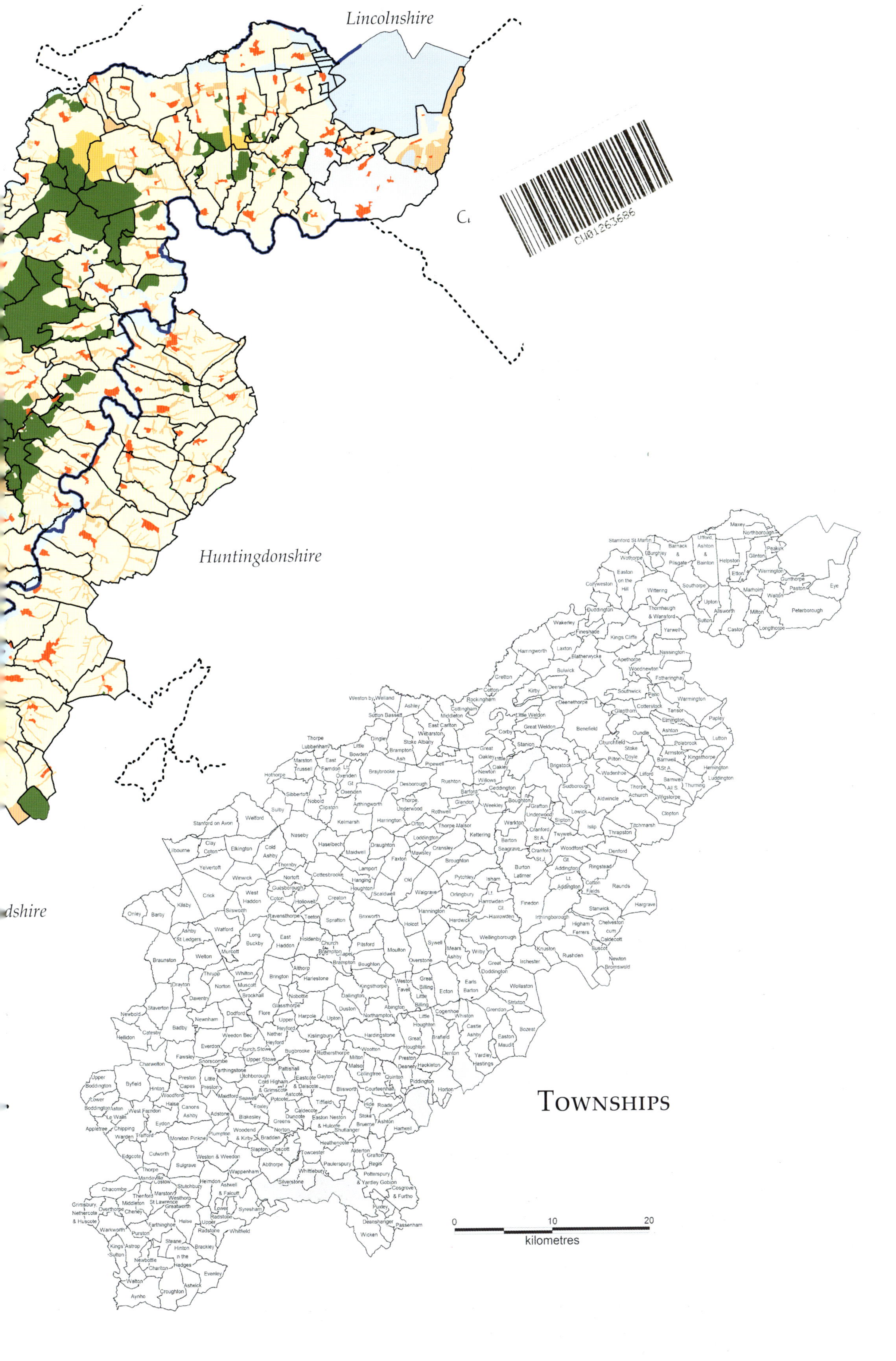

Lincolnshire
Huntingdonshire
dshire
TOWNSHIPS
0
10
20
kilometres
Stamford St Martin
Maxey
Northborough
Burghley
Barnack & Pilsgate
Ufford, Ashton & Bainton
Helpston
Glinton
Peakirk
Wothorpe
Easton on the Hill
Etton
Werrington
Gunthorpe
Collyweston
Wittering
Southorpe
Marholm
Paston
Eye
Walton
Duddington
Thornhaugh & Wansford
Upton
Ailsworth
Milton
Peterborough
Sutton
Castor
Longthorpe
Wakerley
Fineshade
Kings Cliffe
Yarwell
Harringworth
Laxton
Blatherwycke
Nassington
Apethorpe
Bulwick
Woodnewton
Gretton
Fotheringhay
Kirby
Deene
Southwick
Cotton
Rockingham
Perio
Warmington
Weston by Welland
Ashley
Cottingham
Deenethorpe
Cotterstock
Tansor
Sutton Bassett
Middleton
Little Weldon
Glapthorn
Elmington
Papley
East Carlton
Great Weldon
Benefield
Oundle
Ashton
Lutton
Dingley
Stoke Albany
Corby
Churchfield
Polebrook
Brampton Ash
Stanion
Stoke Doyle
Armston
Kingsthorpe
Thorpe Lubbenham
Little Bowden
Pilton
Barnwell St A
Hemington
Marston Trussell
East Farndon
Braybrooke
Pipewell
Brigstock
Wadenhoe
Lilford
Luddington
Hothorpe
Desborough
Rushton
Newton
Willows
Geddington
Sudborough
Thorpe Achurch
Barnwell All S
Thurning
Sibbertoft
Nobold
Clipston
Arthingworth
Thorpe Underwood
Barford
Glendon
Weekley
Boughton
Aldwincle
Wigsthorpe
Sulby
Rothwell
Grafton Underwood
Lowick
Clopton
Welford
Kelmarsh
Harrington
Orton
Slipton
Islip
Titchmarsh
Stanford on Avon
Naseby
Loddington
Thorpe Malsor
Kettering
Warkton
Cranford St A
Twywell
Thrapston
Haselbech
Draughton
Barton Seagrave
Cranford St J
Woodford
Denford
Clay Coton
Elkington
Cold Ashby
Maidwell
Mawsley
Cransley
Lilbourne
Faxton
Broughton
Yelvertoft
Thornby
Lamport
Burton Latimer
Gt Addington
Ringstead
Winwick
Nortoft
Cottesbrooke
Hanging Houghton
Old
Pytchley
Isham
Lt Addington
Cotton Fields
Raunds
Crick
West Haddon
Guilsborough
Coton
Hollowell
Creaton
Scaldwell
Walgrave
Orlingbury
Lt Harrowden
Gt Harrowden
Finedon
Kilsby
Ravensthorpe
Teeton
Spratton
Brixworth
Hannington
Irthlingborough
Stanwick
Hargrave
Onley
Barby
Silsworth
Hardwick
Higham Ferrers
Chelveston cum Caldecott
Ashby St Ledgers
Watford
Long Buckby
East Haddon
Holdenby
Church Brampton
Chapel Brampton
Pitsford
Holcot
Sywell
Wellingborough
Murcott
Moulton
Mears Ashby
Wilby
Knuston
Rushden
Buscot
Braunston
Welton
Overstone
Great Doddington
Irchester
Newton Bromswold
Althorp
Boughton
Thrupp
Whilton
Brington
Harlestone
Kingsthorpe
Weston Favell
Great Billing
Little Billing
Ecton
Earls Barton
Wollaston
Drayton
Norton
Muscott
Daventry
Brockhall
Nobottle
Dallington
Strixton
Glassthorpe
Abington
Cogenhoe
Whiston
Grendon
Staverton
Newnham
Dodford
Flore
Harpole
Duston
Upton
Northampton
Little Houghton
Newbold
Badby
Catesby
Weedon Bec
Upper Heyford
Nether Heyford
Kislingbury
Hardingstone
Castle Ashby
Bozeat
Hellidon
Everdon
Great Houghton
Brafield
Easton Maudit
Church Stowe
Bugbrooke
Rothersthorpe
Wootton
Fawsley
Snorscombe
Upper Stowe
Milton Malsor
Preston Deanery
Hackleton
Denton
Yardley Hastings
Charwelton
Farthingstone
Pattishall
Collingtree
Quinton
Piddington
Upper Boddington
Byfield
Preston Capes
Little Preston
Litchborough
Cold Higham
Grimscote
Eastcote
Dalscote
Gayton
Blisworth
Courteenhall
Horton
Hinton
Woodford
Maidford
Seawell
Potcote
Astcote
Tiffield
Lower Boddington
Aston le Walls
West Farndon
Halse
Canons Ashby
Adstone
Foxley
Caldecote
Hide
Roade
Appletree
Chipping Warden
Trafford
Eydon
Blakesley
Duncote
Greens Norton
Easton Neston
Hulcote
Stoke Bruerne
Ashton
Hartwell
Moreton Pinkney
Plumpton
Woodend & Kirby
Bradden
Shutlanger
Heathencote
Edgcote
Culworth
Weston & Weedon
Slapton
Foscott
Towcester
Alderton
Grafton Regis
Thorpe Mandeville
Sulgrave
Wappenham
Abthorpe
Paulerspury
Whittlebury
Potterspury
Yardley Gobion
Cosgrove & Furtho
Chacombe
Helmdon
Silverstone
Astwell & Falcutt
Thenford
Marston St Lawrence
Costow
Stutchbury
Westhorp
Greatworth
Grimsbury
Nethercote & Huscote
Middleton Cheney
Overthorpe
Lower Radstone
Upper Radstone
Syresham
Whitfield
Puxley
Deanshanger
Passenham
Warkworth
Farthinghoe
Halse
Wicken
Kings Sutton
Astrop
Purston
Steane
Hinton in the Hedges
Brackley
Newbottle
Charlton
Evenley
Walton
Astwick
Aynho
Croughton

An Atlas of

NORTHAMPTONSHIRE

The Medieval and Early-Modern Landscape

This volume has been published as part of the Rockingham Forest Trust's '*Rose of the Shires*' project, supported by the Heritage Lottery Fund.

An Atlas of

NORTHAMPTONSHIRE

The Medieval and Early-Modern Landscape

Tracey Partida, David Hall and Glenn Foard

Oxbow Books
Oxford and Oakville

Published by
Oxbow Books, Oxford, UK

ISBN 978 1 84217 511 8
A CIP record for this book is available from the British Library

This book is available direct from

Oxbow Books, Oxford, UK
(Phone: 01865-241249; Fax: 01865-794449)

and

The David Brown Book Company
PO Box 511, Oakville, CT 06779, USA
(Phone: 860-945-9329; Fax: 860-945-9468)

or from our website

www.oxbowbooks.com

Library of Congress Cataloging-in-Publication Data

Partida, Tracey.
An atlas of Northamptonshire : the medieval and early-modern landscape / Tracey Partida, David Hall and Glenn Foard.
p. cm.
Includes bibliographical references and index.
ISBN 978-1-84217-511-8
1. Northamptonshire (England)--Maps. 2. Northamptonshire (England)--Historical geography. I. Hall, David. II. Foard, Glenn. III. Title.
G1818.N5P3 2012
911'.4255--dc23
2012042971

Front Cover: Ridge and furrow at Cottesbrooke © Glenn Foard
Back Cover: top left: Early enclosure at Cransley in 1598 (NRO Map 1430); top right: The enclosed landscape at Brampton Ash © Tracey Partida; bottom right: Village earthworks and ridge and furrow at Marston Trussell © NCC; bottom left: Enclosures replacing open field furlongs at Braybrooke in 1767 (NRO Map 6393)

Printed by
Gomer Press, Llandysul, Wales

Contents

Acknowledgements

We would like to thank the owners of maps and archives for providing access to their collections and permission to reproduce some of the images. His Grace, The Duke of Buccleuch for kind permission to study the maps held at Boughton House and for permission to reproduce an extract of the Armston map. The Most Honourable, The Marquess of Northampton for kind permission to study the maps held at Castle Ashby House and for permission to reproduce extracts from the Denton map. Jon Culverhouse, Curator of Burghley House, the Burghley House Preservation Trust, and Dr Rosemary Canadine, archivist, for access to the Exeter maps and muniments held at Burghley. Sarah Bridges, County Archivist, and the staff of the Northamptonshire Record Office for access to the Sites and Monuments Record and for permission to reproduce aerial photographs; for access to documents; for permission to use extracts from manuscript maps as acknowledged. Of these the St Andrew's map of 1632 is reproduced by kind permission of QualitySolicitors Wilson Browne; The Papley map of 1632 is reproduced by kind permission of the Rockingham Castle Estate; Haselbech map of 1598 is reproduced by kind permission of the Trustees of Lamport Hall; the Woodcroft map by courtesy of Milton (Peterborough) Estates Company. The British Library for permission to reproduce maps of Nobottle and Naseby. The National Archives for permission to use an extract from the map of Pipewell Plain. The Ordnance Survey for permission to reproduce relief data. The British Geology Survey for permission to reproduce geology data. Tom Williamson of the University of East Anglia for the AHRC Project that enabled the Northamptonshire archaeological and historical data to be placed on GIS, and for access to the digital data. Stehen G. Upex and the Nene Valley Archaeological Trust for permission to use the air photograph of King's Cliffe. Mrs Emma Goodrum, Archivist, and the Provost and Fellows of Worcester College, Oxford; Dr Robin Darwall-Smith, Archivist, and the President and Fellows of Magdalen College, Oxford; Mr Christopher Jeens, Archivist, and the Principal and Fellows of Jesus College, Oxford, for access to College Archives. Judith Hodgkinson for kind permission to use the photograph of the Banbury Lane.

List of Figures

LIST OF TABLES

1 Introduction

The present volume complements the *Rockingham Forest Atlas* published in 2009.[1] It covers the remaining 1,999 square kilometres (772 square miles) of the historic county of Northamptonshire, which includes the Soke of Peterborough (see Figure 2 and Key Maps). The two volumes present in map and essay form the results of fieldwork and documentary research undertaken since the mid-1960s to map the landscape of the whole of Northamptonshire prior to enclosure by parliamentary act. The methodology of integration and analysis of the data in digital form, using a Geographical Information System (GIS), was developed by the authors in the 1990s in work for Northamptonshire County Council.

The county

A discussion of the topography and geology of the Rockingham area has been given in the previous atlas.[2] A brief outline is given here for the remainder of the county but it is not intended to give a full discussion as it is given in Williamson *et al.* 2012.[3]

Northamptonshire is dominated by the valley of the river Nene, which flows eastward, passing through the fen into the North Sea. The Welland, which also flows east through the fen, forms much of the northern boundary of the county. In the south-west the county also encompasses a small part of the Ouse catchment, particularly that of its tributary the Tove (Figure 2).

The geological strata dip gently to the south-east. Extensive areas of the gently sloping plateau have been overlain with drift deposits of boulder clay. There are a large number of relatively thin geological strata including various clays, limestones and ironstones. The east, central and south-eastern areas of the county are dominated by a gently dipping boulder clay capped plateau which has been only relatively lightly dissected by the rivers and streams. Where these have cut down through the strata an often bewildering array of strata come close to the surface across relatively short distances as one moves up the valley sides. It is here that the permeable geology is normally found.

In a few areas, notably in the far south-west and north-east there are areas of limestone plateau. In the north-west of the county the plateau has been heavily dissected with relatively small areas of higher ground where the permeable geology is usually found, separated by wide vales which are largely of clays (Figure 3). On the very eastern edge the county encompasses a small section of the fen.

This broad pattern of relief and geology, the latter working principally through the soils, has been a dominant influence of land use and settlement across the county throughout its history.

Administrative units

Whilst physical geography was a significant influence underlying landscape character, the way in which the landscape was managed and organised could be equally influential. Detailed discussion of these influences upon particular places is given within the following chapters but a brief overview is given here.

County

The historic county of Northamptonshire included all the townships within the Soke of Peterborough and those of Little Bowden (now in Leicestershire), Stoneton (now in Warwickshire), Nethercote and Grimsbury (now in Oxfordshire) and parts of Thurning, Lutton and Luddington (now in Cambridgeshire). With the exception of Stoneton (for which no data was available) all the townships now within adjacent counties are included. The county boundary is based upon the township boundaries as given in the historic map sources. The exceptions are Thurning, Lutton and Luddington which are particularly complex as they lay in two counties and map sources give different boundaries at different dates. For example Thurning is shown on the Ordnance Surveyors' Drawings (OSDs) of 1817 to be wholly in Huntingdonshire, the enclosure award and map of 1839 refer to it as being in both Huntingdonshire and Northamptonshire but the map does not mark the boundary, whilst the Ordnance Survey (OS) First Edition 1:10,560 scale mapping from the 1880s puts it in both with the boundary dissecting the village. However, it is possible that the later

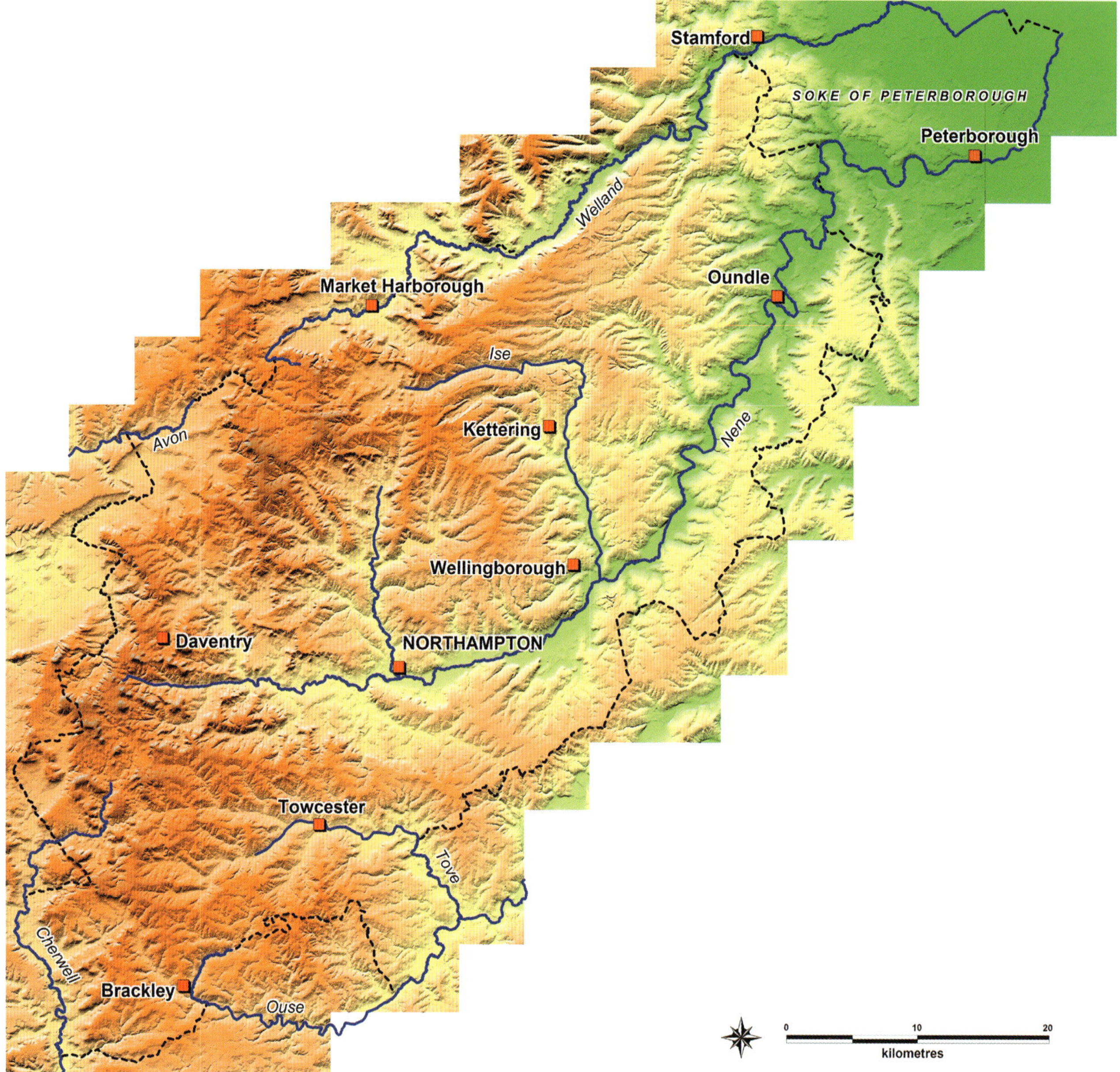

Figure 2. Northamptonshire relief, rivers and major towns. (Crown Copyright, Ordnance Survey licence no. 100026873).

boundary from the 1880s is an enclosure imposition. Similarly at Lutton and Luddington none of the maps mark the county boundary, though the enclosure map for Luddington refers to the parish as being in both Northamptonshire and Huntingdonshire 'or one of them'.[4] The boundary for all three has therefore been taken from the OSDs with reference to all other maps (Figure 4).

Other anomalies occur around Whittlewood and Salcey forests. It is known that both forests crossed the county boundary and data has been mapped to the extent shown on the 1608 map at Whittlewood and the 1826 enclosure map at Salcey, with a small area of additional data taken from the OSD of 1814 to complete Salcey Green.[5] For this section of the county boundary all the forest and relevant township maps were consulted and it was determined that the OSDs were the most accurate that pre-dated enclosure and thus have been used.

The county was divided up into smaller administrative units of hundreds (Figure 5), and townships. Parishes were at this date (pre-1880) ecclesiastical units and, although in Northamptonshire the parish and township were often the same unit of land, the parish did not influence the way the landscape was organised and managed, and they are not discussed here. Data were collected and analysed by the most influential administrative unit, the township.

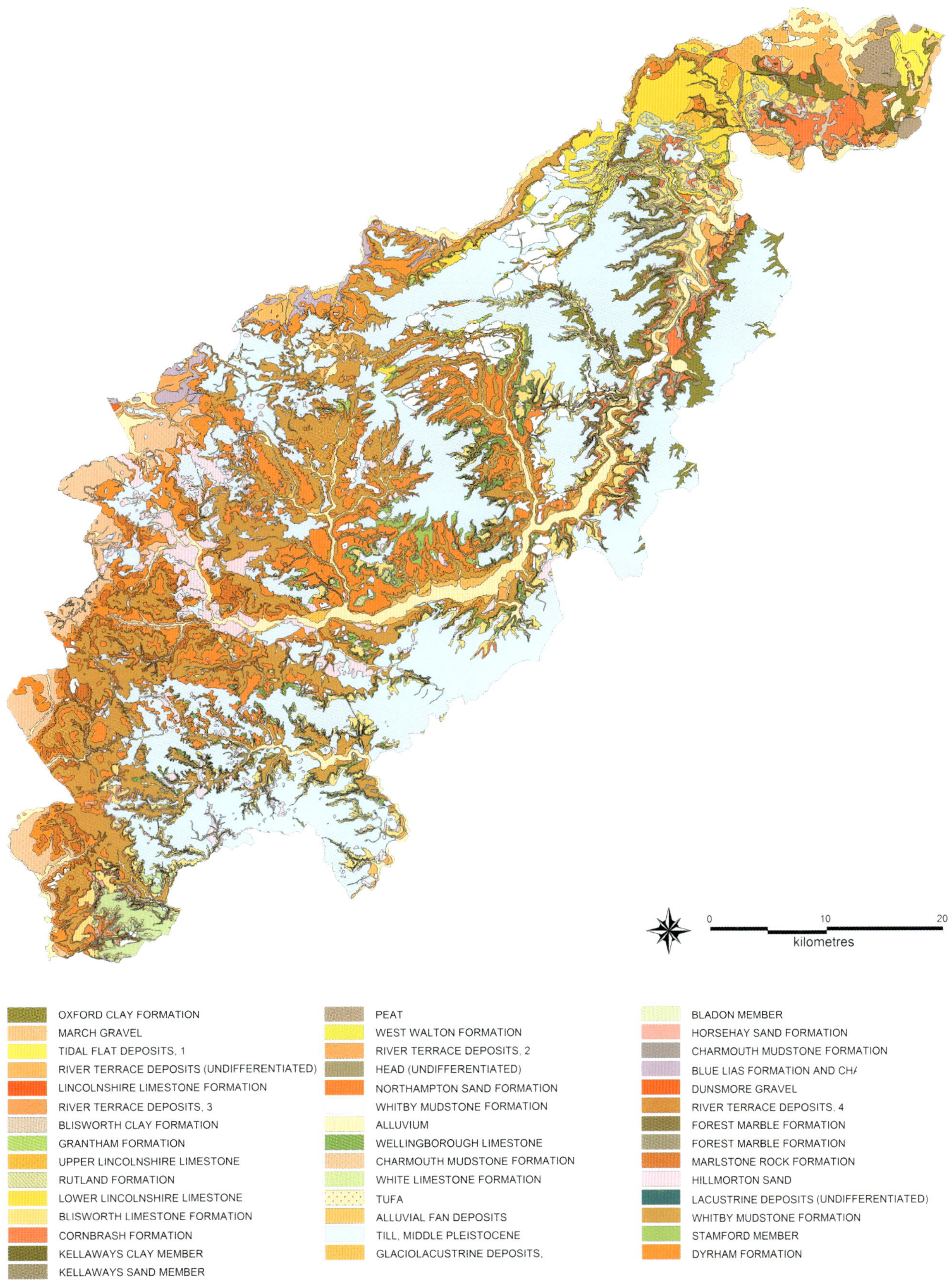

Figure 3. Northamptonshire geology.

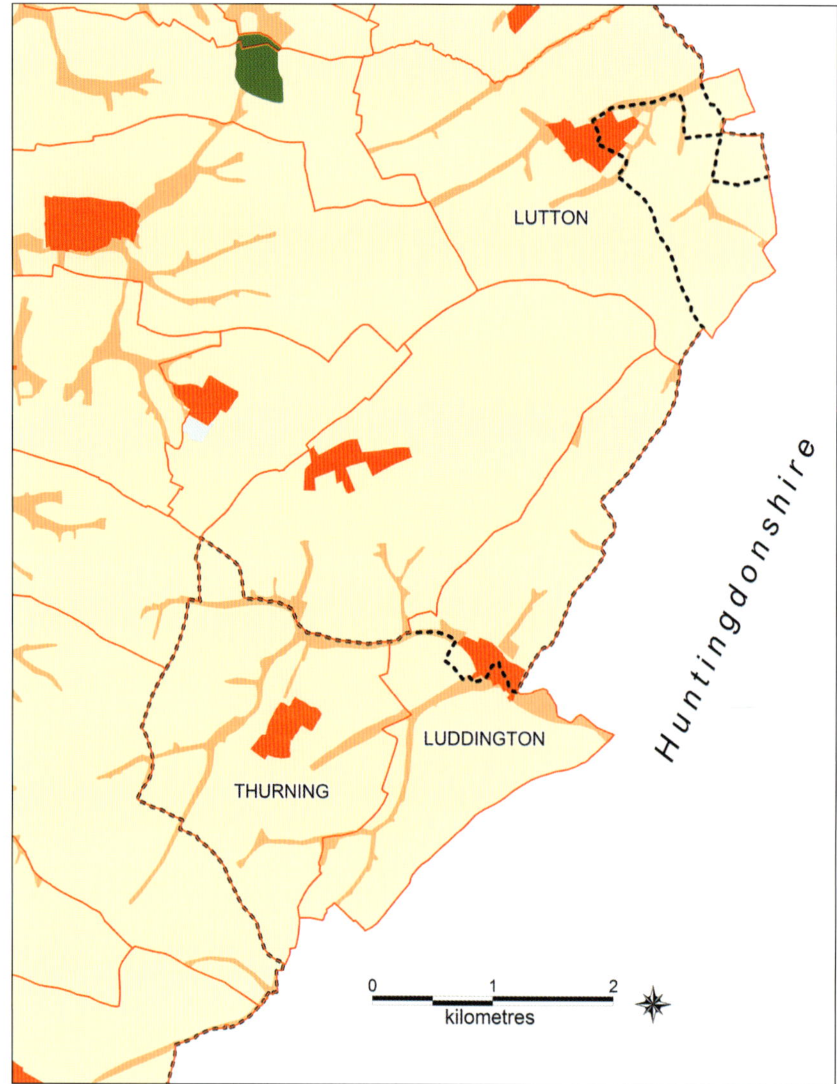

Figure 4. The pre-modern county boundary is shown as a dotted black line with the township boundaries in red. Thurning was in both Northamptonshire and Huntingdonshire but no map shows the boundary. Lutton and Luddington can be seen to lie in both counties with the boundary dissecting the villages.

Township

Townships were the primary unit of administration, within which communities and their resources were organised from the medieval period to the late 19th century, when they were reorganised into civil parishes. The township also forms the basic unit by which most of the earlier written sources for the landscape are organised and was normally the unit within which enclosure took place (see Chapter 4). They appear to have been formed to allow each community to have a balanced range of resources. In some instances they have detached blocks of land, often meadow or wood, which may be the result of manorial links or the division of earlier estates. Some township boundaries are known to be ancient and follow the same course as Saxon charter boundaries as at Oundle, Kettering and Badby.[6]

The range of resources within, or accessible to, each township were typically arable, pasture, meadow and woodland. The type and amount of each resource was highly influenced by the location of the township and its administrative structure. Those located adjacent to the Nene or Welland had a greater proportion of grass in the form of rich alluvial meadows than those in the 'champion' regions in the heart of the county. Similarly those within the forest perambulations had access to pasture within the woodland which, though highly regulated and linked to particular tenures, gave access to additional resources than those available to the champion townships (see Figure 1 and below).

It is likely that prior to the formation and fixing of township boundaries that some resources, particularly grazing, were shared among multiple townships. Figure 6 shows the location and extent of heath that it has been possible to plot, as well as heath related names. Where the location of the heath is known it can be seen to be on the periphery of the townships. The small blocks within each township represent the allocation of a once shared resource. For most places the date such divisions were made is not known but for others they are recorded and mapped as at Pipewell in 1518 (see 'estate maps' below). At Easton on the Hill part of the heath is shared with Wittering and allocations to each place are only made when Wittering is enclosed in 1759. An undated map of *c*.1780 marks the closes that now occupy the shared area as 'intercommoned farm'.[7]

The data in Figure 6 are presented with the early-modern heath underneath that of the medieval. Some of the medieval heath had gone by the early-modern. Conversely that shown as additional to the medieval is a reversion to heath on the poorer lands, notably still on the township periphery, but was not originally heath. Some had been part of the open field arable whilst other was woodland (see atlas pages 3 and 7 for examples).

Methodology

The open fields, woodland, settlement, communications and administrative organisation of the county in the medieval and early-modern periods have been mapped in so far as our data allowed. In the essays that precede the atlas proper the patterns revealed in the data have been related to the physical geography, comprising relief, drainage and geology. Geological information has been used here as a proxy for soil types, which have yet to be mapped at a high resolution for the county.

The GIS data have been created in two stages. Work on the Rockingham Forest area, comprising the northern quarter of the modern county, was undertaken in 2006–7 on behalf of the Rockingham Forest Trust, in a project managed for them by Stuart Storey-Taylor and funded mainly by a grant from the Heritage Lottery Fund. Digital data for the remainder of the historic county were created in 2007–10 on behalf of the University of East Anglia, in a project managed by Tom Williamson and funded by a grant from the Arts and Humanities Research Council. The digital data created in both projects are available to view and will be available for download online by the Archaeology Data Service (ADS) following publication of the present volume.[8]

There are many potential ways of presenting and analysing the information acquired. The approach in the present work, together with the *Rockingham Atlas* is to publish detailed maps at the 1:25,000 scale for the whole county, so that the principal evidence is available in an accessible format that can be used in the future for a variety of research purposes. Both volumes are accompanied by an introduction that explains the geographical and historical context of Northamptonshire, including chapters that deal with key aspects of landscape development. In preparing this introduction we have also drawn upon the large quantity of historical information which has been assembled by the authors over many years. The introduction to this volume presents an interpretation of the results of all this research as we currently see them.

Tom Williamson and his co-authors have approached the GIS data in a different way, discussing primarily the development of the landscape at a county level without the detail of parish by parish maps. While one of us has contributed on enclosure in both volumes, for some other topics the present volume presents an interpretation different from that given by Williamson. The two volumes both use GIS generated maps based on the same source data, while a draft on settlement which used some of the data and ideas presented here was provided to Williamson when he was compiling his volume in 2009. In all other respects the interpretations presented in the two volumes are quite independent. Doubtless other workers will make re-assessments in the future, drawing upon the published maps and GIS data and these are to be welcomed.

In this volume, chapters attributed to individual authors are indicated within the text. Chapter 2 *Forests and Woodland* and Chapter 3 *Open Fields*, by David Hall; Chapter 4 *Enclosure* by Tracey Partida, Chapter 5 *Rural Settlement* by Glenn Foard.

Our digital mapping of the historic landscape for the whole county was created to a uniform standard, but for case studies additional information was collected in much greater detail. The Ordnance Survey (OS) 1st Edition 1:10560 scale maps of the 1880s, warped and registered in GIS, formed the base for all digital mapping of the early-modern landscape. The accuracy of digital mapping from manuscript map sources is dependent on the accuracy of the scanned Ordnance base-maps, as well as being influenced by the difficulties of transcription of estate, enclosure and other source maps that are typically planimetrically inaccurate. Whilst we have sought to register the 1880s maps as accurately as possible, a few have internal inconsistencies of scale, but an overall accuracy in the mapping of ±5 metres has been attempted. The OS 1880s mapping was chosen as the base because they provide the first systematic accurate large scale mapping for the whole county which in turn allows systematic recording of data. Many of the features shown on the historic maps used for the base data still survived in the 1880s which enabled accurate location of features and some remnant features identifiable, again assisting accuracy and interpretation. Where appropriate data was also drawn from the smaller scale and far less accurate Ordnance Surveyors' Drawings (OSDs), held by the British Library, which

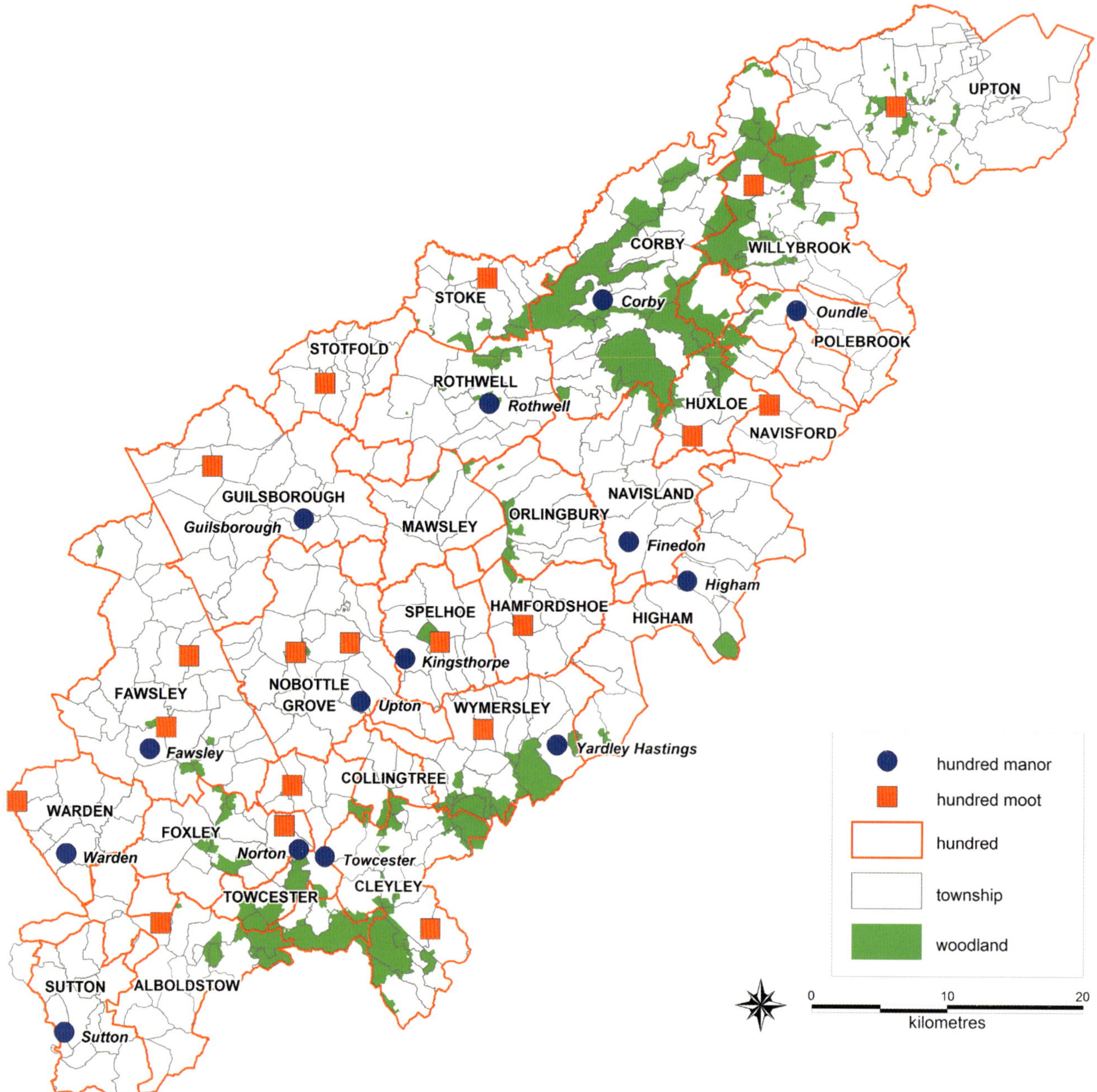

Figure 5. Map of Northamptonshire Hundreds showing the location of known hundredal manors and moots.

for Northamptonshire date from 1811 to 1819, but this data was again digitised to the 1880s map base.

The introductory chapters outline the major themes for which digital mapping has enabled analysis not previously possible. The atlas maps themselves represent two key phases of landscape development: the height of the medieval expansion, circa 1300; and the period of parliamentary enclosure, principally spanning the period 1727 to 1901 but focussing on the mid-18th to early 19th century. The sources and methods of recording for these two periods, which were quite different, are discussed below. Other data sets, utilised in case studies within the text, are explained as necessary. A list of the map sources is given in Appendix 2.

The base data has been supplemented by three other relevant pieces of evidence: digital mapping of the historic landscape previously undertaken by Glenn Foard; pre-medieval settlement and other archaeological evidence recorded during the last 40 years by David Hall and Paul Martin;[9] and information on the medieval and later taxation returns drawn from data compiled by, and unpublished analysis conducted by, the late Stephen Mitchell in the late

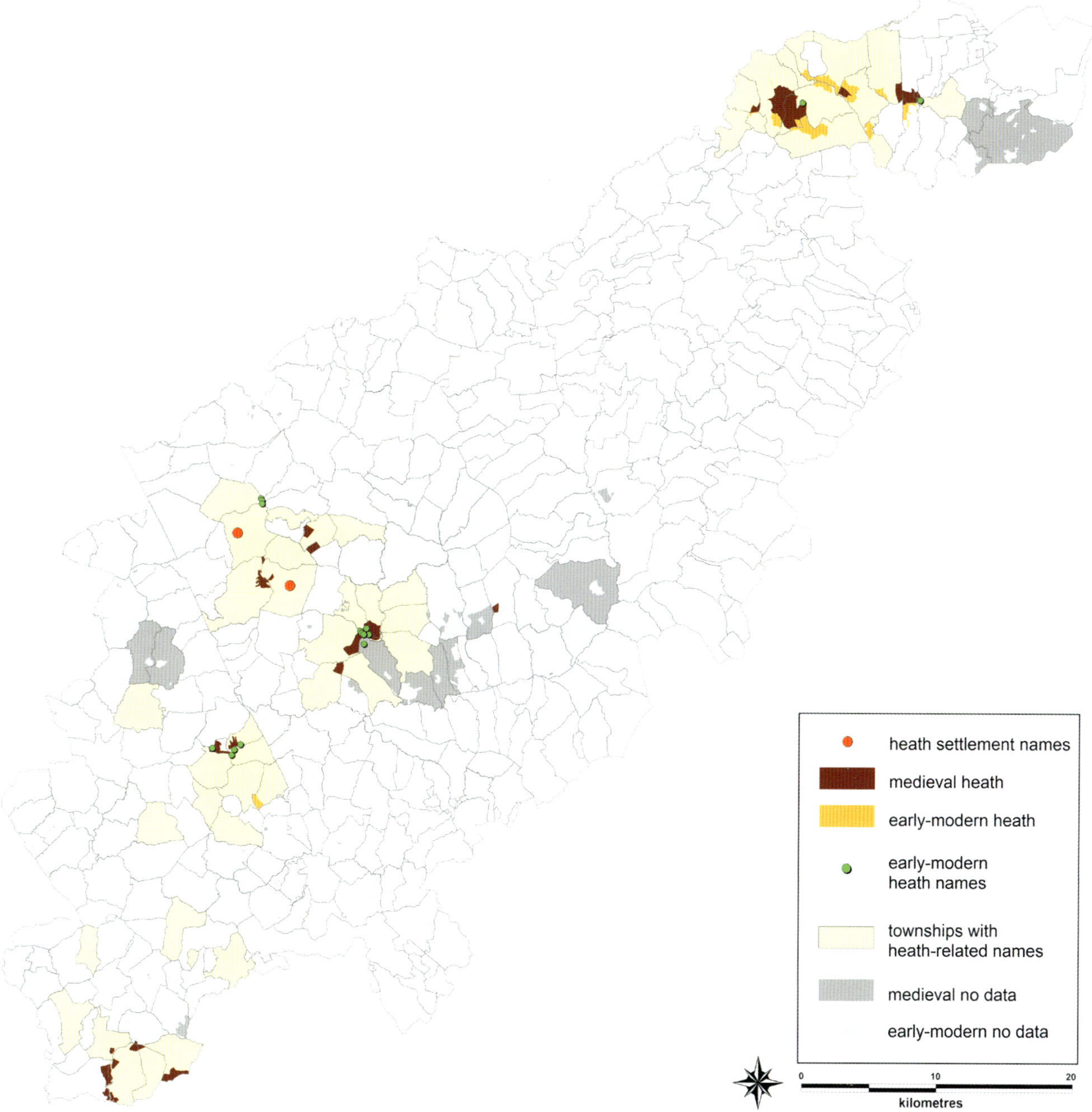

Figure 6. The location of heaths from mapped locations and names from other documentary sources. Note the location of the mapped areas and early-modern names on the periphery of townships indicating a once shared resource.

1970s when he was working for Northamptonshire County Council.

Medieval data sets

The field survey of Northamptonshire by David Hall began in 1961 looking for 'ancient sites' identified by pottery scatters and at the same time mapping the soil banks of furlong boundaries (headlands). One parish was surveyed at a time during winter months, when the land surface was weathered and slight earthwork remains and the dark soil stains, often associated with former settlement, could be discerned.

The area studied initially was the 29,000 acres of the Higham Ferrers Hundred, completed in 1969. Parish furlong patterns drawn up at the 1:10560 scale was achieved for Wollaston and Strixton in 1964. A wider area of survey was undertaken in the 1970s in response to the threatened expansion of Wellingborough, Northampton and Peterborough urban areas. At that stage it was estimated that the whole county could be completed during 'spare-time' fieldwork by the year 2000 (it was not then called a 'millennium project'). The total county area was substantially complete by 2000, but it took time to fill in some omissions for various logistical reasons. The final parish to be completed was Edgcote in 2011. So, including the early beginnings which were much concerned to locate pre-medieval sites, the whole project took 50 years. Woods were included in the survey to record surrounding banks and any other earthworks within them.

In order to present the accumulated data in a format suitable for digitisation and transfer to GIS, all the parish maps needed re-drawing. This was done manually and took six years to prepare. The open-field data were converted into digital form by Tracey Partida.

Medieval woodland is a single data set that includes wood, assarts and adjacent wood pasture. However, for Whittlewood and Salcey Forests, coppice boundaries have been added from the early-modern data and superimposed on the medieval atlas to assist location. Many coppices are known to have been in existence in the Middle Ages.

The water courses shown on the medieval atlas pages are comprised of the streams and slades recorded as part of the survey base data complemented with data edited from the early Ordnance maps. Late (straight) channels and drains have been removed. No water is shown in the region of Borough Fen as it is uncertain what water courses or drainage were there in the Middle Ages.

The settlement plans analysed here, by Glenn Foard, derive from the earliest or most useful historic mapping digitised for the atlas, enhanced by examination of further maps and other documentary sources and, where relevant, by earthwork, crop and soilmark evidence.[10] The extent of ancient enclosures is usually taken from historic maps but occasionally comes from reconstruction of the enclosure awards.[11] Together with furlong evidence from archaeological and historic map sources, these data have also been used to define the likely maximum extent of medieval settlements, though for most settlements great uncertainty remains over this. A good example is Long Buckby, where Cotton was almost certainly in origin a separate settlement but it is not clear when occupation extended from the main village to encompass it.

Because of the uncertainties of extent there are also small blocks of 'no data' shown around some of the settlements. While most of these were probably open field, whether arable, pasture or meadow, in some cases they might include part of the settlement.

There are a few small settlements and isolated sites such as castles where it has been impossible to suggest an extent of occupation, so these are represented on the mapping as a point location. The symbol used indicates where uncertainty remains over location.

The locations of churches and chapels within settlements are individually indicated with a symbol as these are discussed in the text. Monastic sites have not been indicated, except where they were wholly isolated settlements in their own right.

Existing data were found to be far too piecemeal or specialised to enable a reconstruction of the medieval road network to be presented on the atlas maps. Examples include small scale but detailed studies, such as Brown's work on the Anglo-Saxon charters for Stowe Nine Churches and Goodfellow's catalogue of medieval bridges of the county.[12] This is one of many avenues for future research which the present maps should now make possible, to some degree, by providing a base for analysis of evidence from written sources. Within settlements roads have been depicted by white lines, which also indicate greens, which are presented as there appears to be a high degree of stability of road network within settlements, though in some cases this data may be shown by future research to be in error.

Early-modern data sets

The data for the early-modern period have been collected, analysed and digitally mapped by Tracey Partida. The intention when collecting the base data was to map the landscape at, or closest to, the date of enclosure. For those places enclosed during the parliamentary period this is the *pre*-enclosure landscape as it was immediately before enclosure. For those places wholly enclosed prior to the first parliamentary act in the county, in 1727, the landscape shown is the pattern of ancient enclosure at a time closest as possible after the date of enclosure.

The atlas maps thus generally represent the landscape as it was in the mid-18th to earlier 19th century, the transitional period when enclosure from open field systems by parliamentary act was at its peak. Therefore some townships are seen to be wholly enclosed, some wholly open except for the settlement core, while others have a combination of ancient enclosure and some open fields still functioning. The data presented in the atlas are those derived from the map sources. Some features that are known to have existed or have been identified from further research, but for which there is no map evidence are not recorded on the atlas pages; though they may be considered within the essays. Data for the whole county are shown in Figure 94.

Historic maps including estate maps, enclosure maps and tithe maps are the primary source for these data, enhanced by 19th century Ordinance Survey mapping and other digital and documentary sources.[13] The features shown on the historic maps are largely dependent on the type of map (see below). Each land use feature commonly shown on the maps has been recorded to a separate data set. The primary features are: enclosures, either individual enclosed plots or, where the individual plots are not shown, then the extent of enclosure; buildings; wood, with individual named coppices distinguished where possible; wood pasture such as lawns, ridings, plains and greens; heath; fen; and open field. The 'open field' shown is the extent still functioning at the time of parliamentary enclosure, which will include arable and pasture. These individual types of open field land use are rarely shown on the source maps and so are not depicted in the atlas. Similarly, the strips occasionally indicated on the source maps have not been recorded here; that shown on the atlas pages is all taken from the medieval data set. Though it is uncertain how much of the arable furlongs had been converted to pasture by the time of enclosure, the strips that remained in use are unlikely to have been reorganised, therefore it was considered that the depiction of the medieval strips was valid.

Meadows too are rarely depicted on historic maps, at least in a way that would enable a discrete area to be recorded. Often it is simply a name against an allotment with no clear pre-enclosure boundary. Moreover, it is often unclear from the maps whether it was then still functioning as meadow or retained as a name only. For those reasons meadows have not been recorded on the atlas. However, for those townships where there were still functioning open fields, the meadow from the medieval period has been used for the early-modern atlas pages. Similarly the extent of landscape parks is not always shown on maps, though parkland features such as avenues and ponds usually are, while their bounds are often fluid, changing rapidly over a short space of time. Therefore landscape parks are not recorded on the atlas pages, though they may be considered within the essays.

The names given to places and features are those shown on the source map. Many do not record specific names, for example of heathland, therefore where no name is given it does not imply that the feature never had a name, simply that the source map did not give it. In addition the spelling of places and features is that given on the source map though we are aware that spelling and indeed some names, changed over time.

In seventy-nine townships enclosed by parliamentary act no pre-enclosure or enclosure map has been identified. For all of these places the OS 2-inch Surveyors' Drawings were consulted for the non-agrarian land use types of wood, heath and fen. It was considered valid to do this as the features shown on these maps were likely to have been in existence at the time of enclosure. There is little evidence for large scale planting immediately after enclosure, rather the reverse, while heath and fen are almost always lost at enclosure and certainly did not subsequently expand. For settlement layout in these places the OS First Edition, 1:10560 scale mapping from the 1880s was used in preference to having no data. The criteria adopted for mapping the settlement area from the 1880s OS maps was to include closes with buildings but with reference to the OSDs 2-inch maps to exclude post 1810s expansion. In addition earthwork data were used to establish if vacant closes in the 1880s may have formerly had occupation.

Township boundaries

Township boundaries were one of the most important features to be identified and digitised from historic map sources. It was essential to construct accurate township boundaries from the earliest possible source. All map sources for each township were consulted, as well as all maps for places within the county abutting that township (see Appendix 1). Earthwork and other survey data were also consulted, where necessary, in order to establish the most accurate and earliest version possible for the boundaries. It was of particular importance not to rely solely on enclosure maps as boundaries were often realigned at enclosure, where land was allocated to adjacent townships in lieu of particular rights and especially when intermixed land was divided up. This happened at the enclosure of Helpston with Glinton, Etton, Maxey, Northborough and Peakirk and most notably at Borough Fen, which didn't exist as a township until enclosure in 1812.

Occasionally townships lay partly in an adjacent county (see above) and where this happens data have been mapped and all analysis made on the whole township. Some townships are presented here as a single unit though we understand them to have functioned separately. Examples are Ufford, Ashton and Bainton; Easton Neston and Hulcote; Astwell and Falcutt, where no source, so far identified, has enabled the discrete townships to be identified. All townships are labelled with their name, which also usually applies to its village. Where there is also a hamlet within the township as with Syresham and Crowfield, then both settlements are named in addition to the township. In a few examples the village had been lost by the early-modern, as at Easton Neston, but the surviving hamlet of Hulcote is named. Where the secondary settlement is deserted or just a single farm by the time of the map as at Green's Norton and Caswell then only the township is labelled.

Some townships had detached blocks of land. Where we have been able to identify these they have been mapped and labelled, e.g. Wootton (det.) on Map 70. However, they are only named on the early-modern atlas pages as it cannot be said, without further research, whether they existed in the same form in the Middle Ages. It is possible that some are later allocations for shared rights, particularly in relationship to woodland and meadow.

The township boundaries are derived from early-modern maps and therefore have a direct relevance only to that period. The boundaries did not always remain static over time, so the same level of confidence cannot be given to these boundaries when they are shown on the medieval atlas pages. However, most of these townships are known to have existed in the medieval and, it appears likely, from documentary research already conducted on the open field landscape that many, probably most, ran along the same course in the medieval as they did when depicted on the early-modern maps. These units have therefore been used as the framework for presenting and analysing data from the medieval as well as the early-modern periods.

Water

Water courses are not always depicted on historic maps and, where they are, the recording may not always be consistent. Only major rivers might be depicted whilst lesser streams and tributaries might not, or the water course shown might be a post enclosure realignment. In order to provide a consistent data set for the whole county, water has been recorded from the OS 1:10,560 scale mapping of the 1880s but with reference to the earlier maps to exclude post enclosure channels.

The water as shown in the 1880s for the Soke is problematic in that much of it is known to be post enclosure drainage, particularly in and around the fen. The data for water in the fen townships; Helpston *et al.*, Eye, Peterborough and hamlets and part of Borough Fen has therefore been taken from the enclosure maps. For the northern part of Borough Fen no pre OS 1880s map has been identified and so, as it is impossible to know which of the drains shown are pre-enclosure, the water in this area has not been mapped.

Only large bodies of water of 500 metres and above in length have been recorded. Reservoirs, canals, industrial ponds associated with brick works, tramways and quarries and any feature interpreted as post enclosure drainage has not been recorded.

Roads

The recording of roads on historic maps is often, like water, both inconsistent and incomplete. A greater problem is that often it is the post enclosure route that is being shown, which may include realignment of earlier roads or wholly new routes. In order to provide a consistent data set for the county the roads depicted on Eayre's map of the county have been used. Eayre's map, made to accompany Bridges' County History, was begun around 1720 though not published, including additions, until 1791.[14] It shows major routes as well as some of the lesser ones and indicates junctions to other minor roads. The network of small routeways within each township is not shown. It only proved possible to map the roads from Eayre for the eastern part of the county because only there did sufficient historic maps survive to enable the significant inconstancies in scale in Eayre's map to be resolved with reference to large scale early maps.

Historic maps[15]

The features recorded on historic maps, or indeed any map, are largely dependent on the type of map being produced. This in turn depends on who has commissioned the map and for what reason. The three main types of historic map produced for the period of this study were estate maps, enclosure maps and tithe maps. It was not until the Ordnance Survey national mapping in the 19th century that a systematic and standardised survey was undertaken. Until that time maps were made by individuals, be they private or institutional, for varying reasons. All varied widely, contained different information and all have different advantages and caveats for the landscape historian.

Furthermore, the condition of the map can affect the accuracy of our interpretation. Maps might be large and unwieldy, dirty, faded, overwritten, damaged, torn, or even rat nibbled. The use of digital photography and software programs that enable enhancement of images has greatly improved the potential for analysis. But the map might also be a copy made many years after the original, in which case it is often impossible to know which features are original and which updated.

Historic maps of Northamptonshire range in date from the 16th century to the 19th and, as far as practicable, all were identified and significant maps photographed for analysis. Most are held at the Northamptonshire Record Office, some at other county record offices, in college and national archives and some in private collections; including estate archives. Over 1,000 historic maps have been seen and examined for the whole county, with data recorded from 740 individual maps. The data presented in the atlas pages utilises 461 of those maps. In view of the complexity of the maps a brief discussion of the various types is given here.

Estate maps

Estate maps are the most numerous type comprising some 400 of the 740 maps studied here in detail. They range in date from the early 16th to the mid-19th century; in size from a small scrap of paper, to several feet across; in coverage from a plot of a few acres to an area covering many thousands of acres. They also vary significantly in survey scale, the material on which they are drawn and in the amount of detail they record. Some are simple sketches, others works of art in their own right (Figure 7). The 1632 map of the St Andrew's Priory lands in Northampton is particularly fine and as well as depicting the landscape it includes numerous vignettes of labourers at various tasks in the fields (see Figure 21).[16]

Estate maps are the least standardised of all the map types and might be said to be typically atypical. In short, estate maps are as diverse as the people who commissioned them, and the surveyors who

Figure 7. Extract from the 1632 map of St Andrew's Priory lands in Northampton showing the priory precinct with enclosed lands, buildings and substantial fishponds. (NRO Map 4671).

drew them. The fundamental influence on the content of an estate map was the purpose for which it was commissioned. The earliest map identified was made in *c.*1518 and covers parts of Pipewell, Desborough and Rushton (Figure 8).[17] In 1518 the Abbot of Pipewell enclosed part of Pipewell Plain and the map was made in response to the resulting dispute over the loss of common rights. It gives very little detail of the landscape but enough to enable the location of the land in question and the areas which bounded it. Several similar maps show the division of land shared between townships. At Whistley wood the map of 1590 shows the parcels belonging to Brackley, Astwell, Radstone and Syresham.[18] In the Brand, maps dated 1610 show wood pasture on the edge of Geddington Chase which was commonable to Geddington, Stanion, Brigstock and Little Oakley.[19] Both maps are very detailed and give a wealth of information regarding the landscape. This type of map is particularly interesting, not only for the landscape evidence contained but also because it enables the process of the division of shared land to be seen and the land involved to be located.

Disputes commonly arose where there were, or had been, shared rights between places or where ownership was contentious. Such cases are most likely to be found in and around the forests. The dispute between Weldon and Brigstock over shared rights on Weldon Plain beside Farming Woods raged for centuries.[20] And perhaps the most significant of all in Northamptonshire was that caused by the attempt by Charles I to impose ancient perambulations within the Forests of Whittlewood and Rockingham. Detailed maps showing the perambulations and details of the landscape within and around the forest were made for the Cliffe Bailiwick in Rockingham, and for Whittlewood.[21] Unfortunately, the map that survives for Whittlewood is a copy made in early 18th century which omits much of the detail seen on the Cliffe

Figure 8. Extract from the monastic map c.1518 showing the enclosure and division of Pipewell Plain by the Abbot of Pipewell. The enclosure led to a dispute between the Abbot and the King's tenants of Desborough. (© National Archive, reproduced by permission, MPC 1/142).

map, which survives in the original.[22] Most notable with the Whittlewood map is the omission of the perambulations, which is a significant loss as they assist in the understanding of how landscapes were managed, particularly shared landscapes.

Estate maps are rarely concerned with administrative boundaries as their chief concerns are the boundaries of ownership. This might be a small group of closes, a short stretch of road, a park, or a whole township or more. The detail shown on maps of any size might be equally precise but is usually of less use for the present purpose when it covers just a small area. Lands belonging to other people or within a different township or manor are often marked by name only, without a definite boundary or other detail. At Ecton a particularly fine map dated 1759 is unusual in that it depicts hides rather than 'lands' or ridge and furrow strips (Figure 9). It is also a rare example of where such early features on a map can be identified with surviving archaeology (Figure 10). A similar example can be found at Brington where each individual strip is marked on the draft enclosure map and can be matched to those surviving on the ground.[23]

Estate maps also often continued as working documents so can have changes added. This is seen with the copy of the map of Roade, Ashton and Hartwell, where the original *c*.1725 map survives but in such poor condition as to be virtually unusable, due to exceptional water damage. The *c*.1760 copy has remarkable additional detail regarding the agricultural regime, however whether this detail is from 1725 or 1760 is unclear.

Enclosure maps

Enclosure maps might be supposed to give the most useful information regarding the landscape as it was at enclosure. This is a misapprehension, for enclosure maps omit as much data as they record. As well as the allotments being allocated to the various landowners and institutions as detailed in the award and the alignment of roads and footpaths, water courses and stone pits, typically they will record the detail of the settlement, closes and buildings and any dispersed buildings such as mills. Yet they rarely provide any detail of the landscape being replaced. What they are in fact showing is the landscape that is being imposed

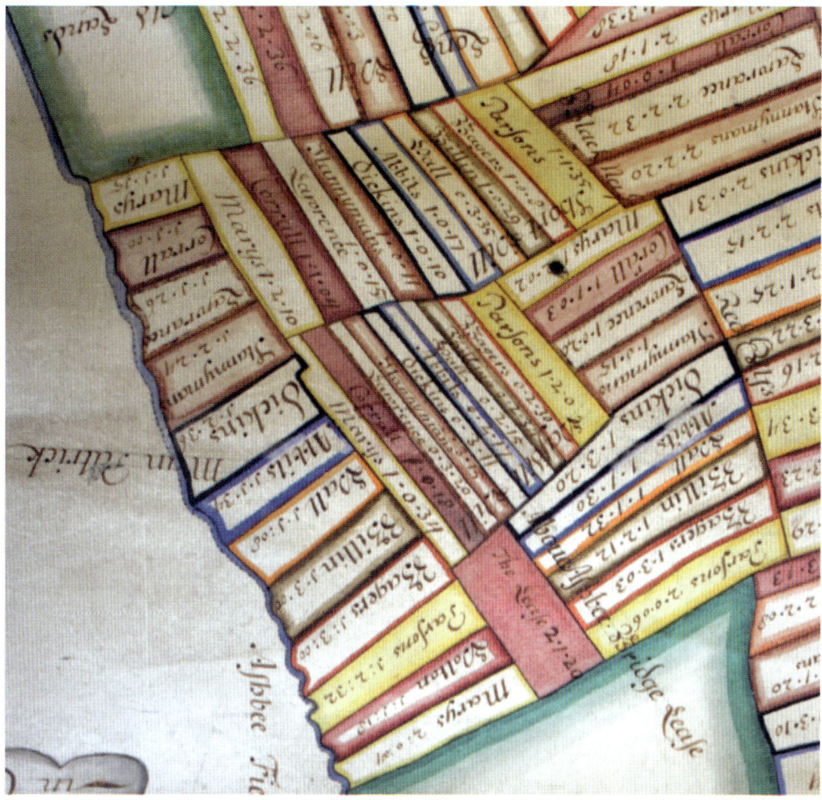

Figure 9. An extract from the estate map of Ecton dated 1703. This map is unusual in that is it recording not 'lands' but 'hides'. It can be compared with the air photograph, Figure 10, which shows the surviving strips with the distinctive hide baulks that can be identified with those on the map. The map has been rotated to compare with Figure 10 and north is at the bottom. (NRO Map 2115).

Figure 10. Surviving ridge and furrow with headlands and hide baulks at Ecton. In spite of the addition of new hedges across the earthworks many of the early features can be identified and matched to those on the 1703 map in Figure 9. (NMR NHC 2221/31 © Northamptonshire County Council).

by the enclosure process – in other words the post enclosure landscape. It is possible to reconstruct the extent of open fields from this information, but not the details such as the disposition of arable, pasture and meadow. Much of the open field may already have been put down to grass during the previous centuries, but the map gives no indication of this. Roads too were often altered at enclosure and, while the fact of alteration will sometimes be clear from the attached award, the details of the change are usually unclear (see Chapter 5).

Moreover, the post enclosure landscape shown on the maps is that initially created by enclosure i.e. the framework of a new landscape. The reorganisation that takes place after enclosure, in particular the sub-division of allotments and dispersal of buildings from the village, is not shown.[24] Enclosure maps are depicting the landscape in transition; any pre-enclosure features depicted are being replaced and the most significant of the post enclosure features are only partly given. That is not to say that enclosure maps are not useful. The detail they contain for the ancient enclosure can be very useful and the information regarding landownership is invaluable.

Of more use for landscape study are the draft enclosure maps. These are not as numerous as the enclosure maps, with only thirty-eight identified for the county compared to approximately one hundred enclosure maps. They can be extremely difficult to analyse as they can contain very complex data, because they are showing two landscapes (Figures 11 and 73). The existing landscape is drawn in great detail, with the intended new landscape superimposed above. Figures 11 and 12 show the same piece of landscape at Cold Higham from the draft enclosure and enclosure maps dated 1812 and 1813.[25] In the first the open field furlongs are shown and named, as are old enclosures, roads and footpaths. To this are added the red boundaries of the new allotments with the names of allottees and size of each parcel. The enclosure map in comparison is very simple, showing only boundaries of ownership with no detail of the landscape, or the alterations made to it by enclosure.

Other features that draft enclosure maps typically show that are omitted from enclosure maps are field closes, greens, open field pasture, cow pastures and meadows. As with all types of map there are certain caveats to their usefulness in addition to the complexity of the data. For example, some map only the land being enclosed and ignore the ancient enclosure, as at Greens Norton, or omit the village, as at Upper Boddington.[26]

Tithe maps

Tithe maps were created for a specific purpose. They therefore all record the same classes of information, though they do not always present it in the same way. The Tithe Commutation Act of 1836 abolished the tithe rate on agricultural products, the tax payable to the Church and replaced it with a yearly monetary payment. To achieve this it was necessary to assess the land subject to tithe payments, which was done systematically across England and Wales. The tithe apportionment was the legal document that detailed each parcel of land: the name and description; state of cultivation (pasture, arable, meadow etc.); measurement (in acres, roods and perches); and the rent charge (new tithe tax) payable on each parcel. They also record the owner and the tenant of each piece of land.[27] These are important documents in their own right, but taken together with the maps they are invaluable to the landscape historian.

Their record of field names, the most comprehensive for the county before the 1932 field names survey, can enable the identification of former land use. Unremarkable fields bearing park names can indicate a long abandoned function, just as 'stocking' and 'dibbings' indicates former woodland. Field names can also be indicative of previous settlement such as 'Great Chilcotes' and 'Little Chilcotes' in Thornby which indicate the area in which the deserted settlement lay.

The tithe maps record each land parcel with a number corresponding to that in the apportionment. It is therefore possible to reconstruct the layout of fields and settlements, as well as land use and patterns of tenure. This is particularly useful where the whole township was being assessed. But often in Northamptonshire it was a portion only and sometimes a very small area of the township, as at Alderton where only three closes comprising less than 50 acres were assessed and mapped.[28] At Alderton this is not problematic as there is a series of other maps including pre-enclosure estate maps and a draft enclosure map.[29] Unfortunately for many other places the small area covered by the tithe map is the only large scale historic map before the Ordnance Survey.[30]

In Northamptonshire parliamentary enclosure *usually* extinguished the tithes, giving the tithe owner a plot of land in lieu, which is why some tithe maps record just a small area and in many places no tithe commutation was necessary. Moreover, the apportionments and maps are concerned with titheable land, which some land such as the glebe, owned by the church, was not. Consequently this land is often omitted from the maps, or shown only as an extent with no internal features. Arguably the main disadvantage of tithe maps is their late date (1836–1858). By this time almost all the townships in Northamptonshire had been enclosed, some hundreds of years before and the landscape they depict may thus bear little resemblance to that which was created when originally enclosed from the open fields. Charwelton, for example, was enclosed circa 1480 but the earliest map found is the tithe dated 1847. Here and in other places like it, even with additional information from

Figure 11. An extract from the Cold Higham and Grimscote draft enclosure map showing both the pre-enclosure landscape, (in black), and the new landscape that is replacing it, (in red). Note also in the bottom right corner is marked 'part of Pattishall', this is the edge of a detached piece of Pattishall lying in Cold Higham (NRO MAP 2913).

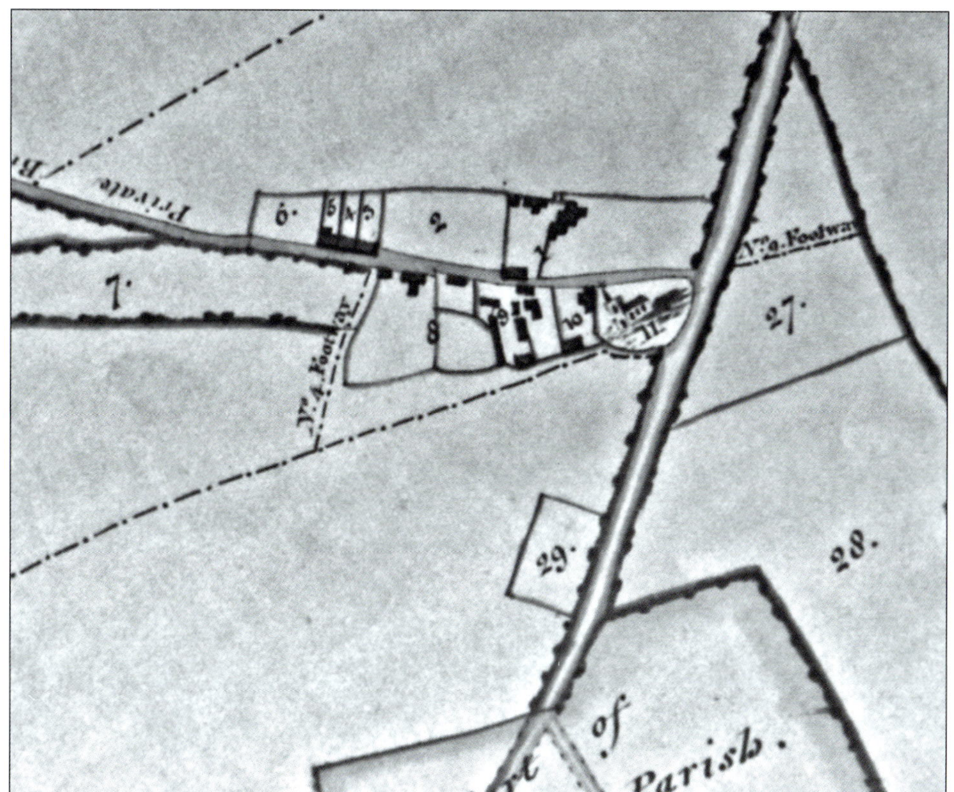

Figure 12. An extract from the Cold Higham and Grimscote enclosure map. Note the simplicity of the data contained compared to the draft enclosure map in Figure 9 (NRO MAP 2868).

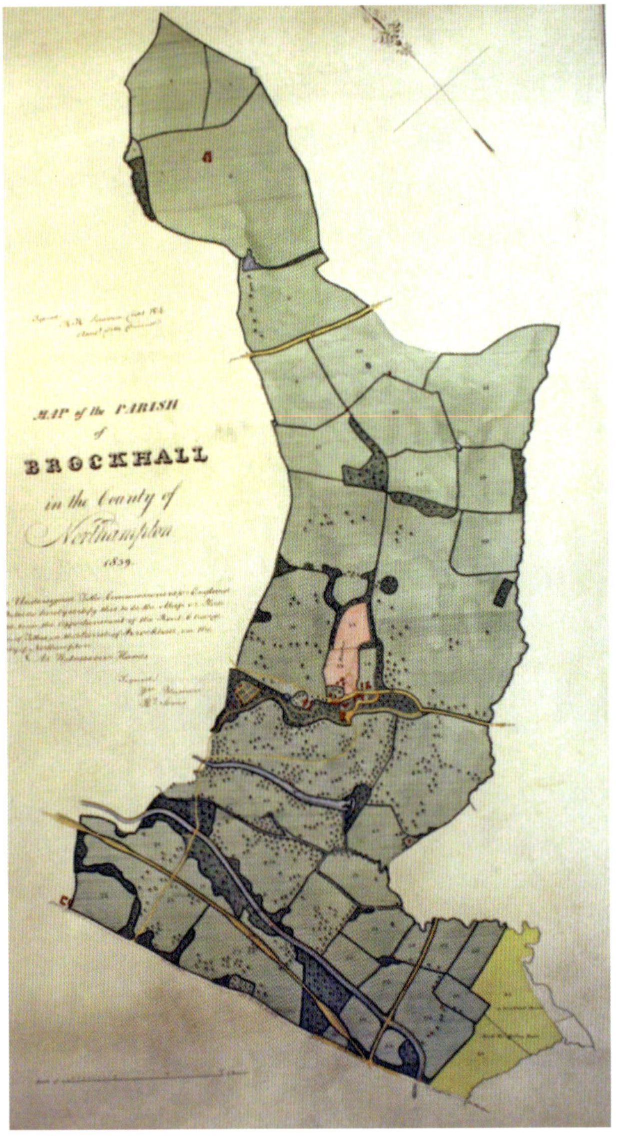

Figure 13. Brockhall tithe map 1839. The attention to detail, particularly in the depiction of trees, is entirely superfluous to its function but of great value to the landscape historian. (NRO T31).

earthwork data and documentary sources, we can learn little of the process of landscape evolution prior to first half of the 19th century.

The tithe maps' main advantage is that they were surveyed to nationally accepted standards, allowing precise location of features to a modern map base. Moreover, as these are legal documents we can have confidence that the boundaries they depict are accurate and not the result of artistic licence. However, unlike the Ordnance Survey mapping, which had standardised scales and conventions, fonts and styles, the instructions from the Tithe Commission to the surveyors allowed a great deal of leeway in how they depicted the required features (titheable land), and how much extraneous detail they could include. They might be in full colour, show water courses, indicate slope, footpaths, distinguish osier beds, park features and so on. They might be highly decorative or very plain, and they might even be a re-used estate map. Some surveyors were content to use decorative styles only for particular features, usually woods. This can be seen in the maps by Thomas Mulliner for Cottesbrooke, Sibbertoft and Faxton cum Mawsley, by R. P. Coles at Preston Deanery, on the unsigned map for Easton Maudit, on the Thenford map 'copied' by Davis and Saunders and on the Wicken map by John Bromley.[31] Occasionally decorative features are added to the borders of the map, as at Easton Maudit which exhibits a coronet above the title, and at Collyweston which sports a particularly elaborate north arrow.[32]

By far the most lavish is that for Brockhall (Figure 13), which is a match for many of the fine estate maps made elsewhere and is the finest of the sequence of maps made for Brockhall from 1614 onwards. Little Preston, Harrington and Preston Deanery are similarly colourful but don't have as many woods or park features.

2 Forests and Woodland

David Hall

Land use

The next two chapters describe the character of woodland and open-field arable. Both are complicated subjects having a wide range of related topics with abundant historical records. This account will outline the characteristic features of both woodland and arable landscapes. Worked examples will be used to illustrate the scope of the historical record when integrated with information provided by the atlas mapping. After woodland has been described, Chapter 3 will study the arable open-field, including comment on the various types of pasture resources that were intimately related to open-field operation.

Firstly, it is instructive to examine the overall county land use, which can be conveniently measured using the GIS mapping. The county size is 636,543 acres taking into account the problems of mapping the boundary in a few cases, where the strips of a single township were intermingled with those of a neighbouring county, as explained above for Thurning. In calculating the medieval land use type by percentages, areas not surveyed have been excluded. These are primarily the urban areas of Daventry, Northampton, Wellingborough and Peterborough, amounting to 25,801 acres leaving the effective total for calculation at 610,742 acres. The county totals and percentages then become:

Land use Type	Area Acres	Area Hectares	%
Arable	419,370	169,710	69
Pasture	71,594	28,973	12
Meadow	25,505	10,321	4
Heath	3,797	1,537	1
Woodland	63,499	25,697	10
Fen	8,971	3,630	1
Settlement	19,808	8,016	3
Total	610,742		100
Modern Urban	25,801		
Grand Total	636,543		

Table 1. County land use types and acreages.

These values confirm the long-held view that Northamptonshire, like other East Midland counties was predominantly arable in the Middle Ages, in spite of its wooded forest areas.

Although of considerable interest, the average values do not apply to many particular townships and across the county there is considerable variation according to the resources immediately available. Townships with significant areas of woodland or meadow had correspondingly smaller percentages of arable. Table 2 groups sample townships selected for a particular land use type, although most of them have resources additional to that chosen. The selected townships are located on Figure 14.

From which it is seen that the **arable percentages** for the chosen samples of six and seven townships are:

those with little other resource than arable had	79–91% arable
those with heathland in the range 8–16%	49–72% arable
meadows in the range 11–28%	62–77% arable
pasture ranging 13–39%	49–86% arable
townships with 9–38% wood	47–78% arable

The values further emphasise the predominantly arable nature of the county in the Middle Ages, in spite of appreciable areas of woodland, heath and pasture in some townships.

To place these land use measurements in a national context, some comparisons will be made with other counties. Several samples of other regions have been surveyed applying the same fieldwork techniques as used for Northamptonshire. In Leicestershire, the five parishes connected with the Battle of Bosworth site (1475) produced a plan with extensive arable dissected by a drainage-network of streams.[1] The 6,771 acres contained 5,338 acres of arable, or 79%. The somewhat different landscape of the Yorkshire Wolds had a high proportion of arable on planar areas with pasture lying in the small dales and steep scarps that dissect it.[2] The five townships in Wharram Percy parish, *c.*7000 acres, had arable ranging from 69 to 86%. At the parish level, Hinton St Mary, Dorset, lying on limestone, had a typical 'midland type' plan with arable amounting to about 84%.[3]

Township name	Selected land use	Area (acres)	Arable	Meadow	Pasture	Wood	Heath
Clopton	arable	1940	88	0	7	0	0
Farthinghoe	arable	1511	83	0	13	0	0
Lutton	arable	1510	90	0	7	0	0
Newton Bromswold	arable	830	91	0	7	0	0
Thornby	arable	1227	79	0	19	0	0
Watford	arable	2249	81	0	16	0	0
Weston & Weedon	arable	2303	82	0	15	0	0
Aynho	heath	2529	63	19	8	0	8
Church Brampton	heath	1195	69	0	17	0	12
Easton	heath	3238	49	4	2	27	16
Evenley	heath	1830	72	6	6	0	12
Helpston	heath	1852	68	8	4	7	10
Ravensthorpe	heath	1492	65	0	24	0	8
Chacombe	meadow	1717	66	17	13	0	0
Denford	meadow	1744	77	11	10	0	0
Ecton	meadow	2291	62	28	8	0	0
Grendon	meadow	1722	72	15	8	0	0
Maxey	meadow	2477	63	30	0	0	0
Sutton Bassett	meadow	747	68	20	10	0	0
Warmington	meadow	3218	70	16	9	0	0
Badby	pasture	2290	49	0	39	8	0
Charwelton	pasture	2431	70	0	28	0	0
Church Stow	pasture	821	55	0	32	0	9
Halse	pasture	1795	86	0	13	0	0
Kelmarsh	pasture	2854	74	0	24	0	0
Sulgrave	pasture	2028	81	0	15	0	0
Aldwincle	wood	2872	49	10	6	32	0
Benefield	wood	4284	50	1	9	38	0
Denton	wood	1082	73	0	7	14	0
Maidford	wood	1051	64	0	14	19	0
Piddington	wood	1078	47	0	8	42	0
Stoke Albini	wood	1722	67	2	18	11	0
Stoke Doyle	wood	1559	78	7	3	9	0

Table 2. Land use of selected townships.

Historical information relating to land use can be derived from surveys and field books, although there is often difficulty in knowing whether land already enclosed was once open field. In southern Dorset, Chilfrome, 940 acres (SY 55 99), lying on the edge of chalk downs, has a map of *c.*1823 showing there were open downland pastures extending to 50.5% of the township area.[4] The remainder consisted of open-field arable 29.2%, settlement 2.8%, meadow 2.9% and old enclosure 14.6%. Another chalk downland example is Iford, south of Lewes, Sussex (TQ 40 07). In 1842 it was largely open and the land use of its 2,175 acres was 51% downland pasture, 12% open-field, 13% old enclosure and 24% meadow.[5] In Derbyshire, Sheldon township, 2,068 acres, lying in Ashford parish in the White Peak, had much moorland pasture. It was mapped and surveyed by William Senior in 1617 for the Earl of Devonshire.[6] The area of settlement, closes and open-field arable amounted to only 601 acres or 29%. These examples contrast with the Midlands, having much less arable.

A useful insight into early land use is given by the distribution of furlong names relating to clearance or the breaking up of pastures for arable. The following name-forms and related variants have been collected from Northamptonshire terriers of various dates:

assart/sart
breach/breche
dibbing/dyb'
heath/hethe,
moor
stocking/stok'
stubb/stibbing
wold/wild/wald/old

The county distribution of each element is plotted on Figures 15–17.[7] The elements, *heath*, *moor* and *wold* are shown in Figure 15. *Heath* occurs only in locations at or in close proximity to well drained ironstone or sandy soils suitable for ericaceous species to develop. There is a complete absence of heath names on the clay and limestone soils east of Northampton, until Collyweston and the Soke in the north.

Wold occurs in a belt along the eastern county boundary, representing the former *bruneswald*, picked out by the place-names Warrington (Bromswold), Bucks, Newton Bromswold, Leighton Bromswold,

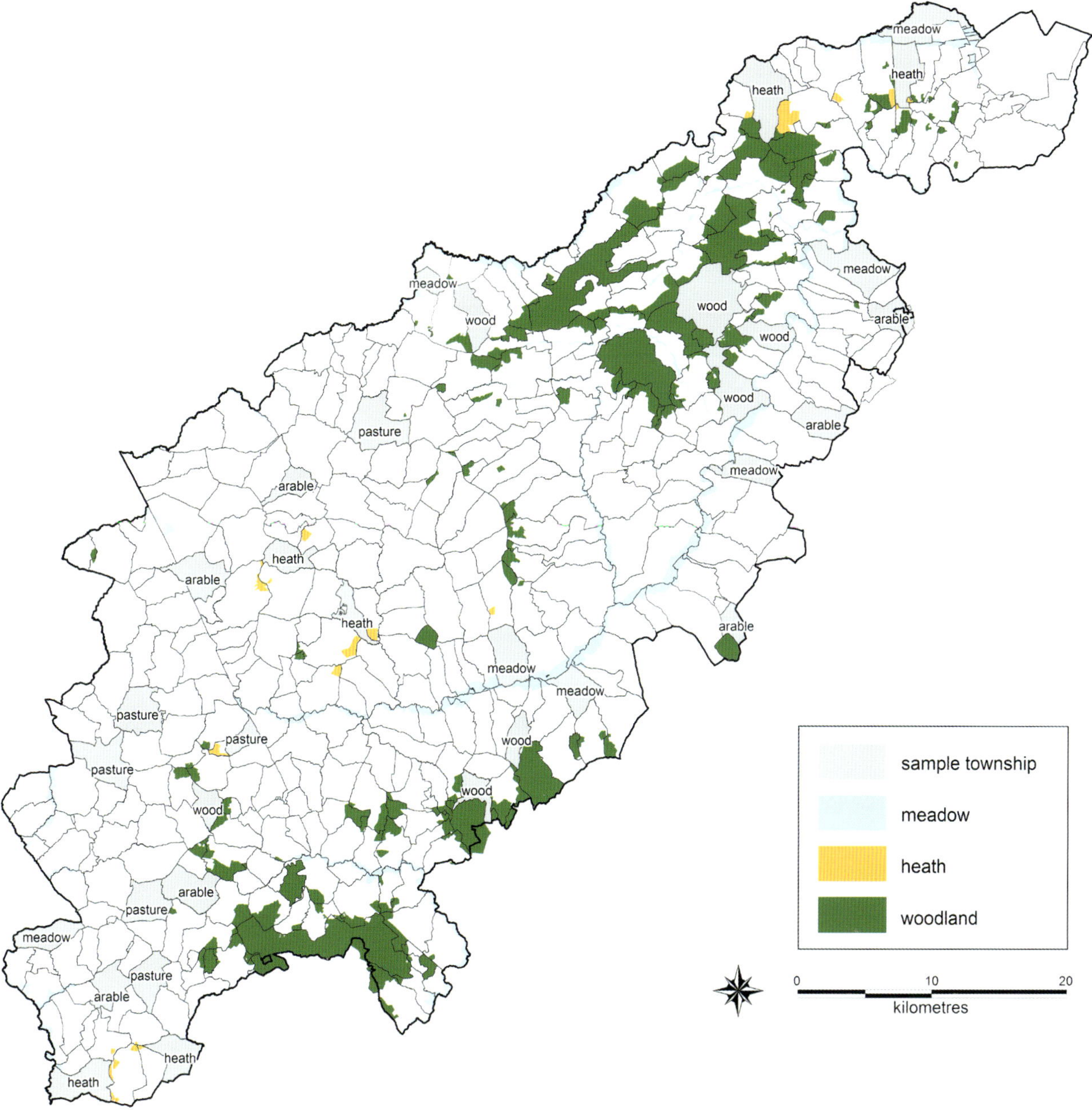

Figure 14. Location of townships with selected land use types.

Hunts and Luddington (Bromswold). Additional furlong names fill in the distribution in the Bruneswald region, but also show that the name is widespread throughout the county. It can occur wherever there is locally high 'marginal' clay, often on a level terrain. The small wold on the clay ground shared between Finedon, Burton Latimer, Woodford and the Addingtons has been mapped.[8] Fox has described various aspects of wolds in the East Midlands.[9] In Northamptonshire, the elements *wold* and *heath* are complimentary and the distributions do not overlap except in a very few townships. *Moor* is widespread throughout the county. No moors were very large and the name generally refers to marshy ground where a spring emerges, or to flat areas of clay with waterlogged 'sad' ground.

Figure 16 illustrates the Old English forms *breche*, *stubb* and *stocking*. All three elements are found countywide. The names represent 'clearing' in the sense of preparation for arable; there is no particular concentration near the forests, except perhaps for *stocking*. They probably mark clearance of small local areas, not necessarily 'woodland' at the time, but rough pasture and probably before the 11th century.

Sart, *dibbing* and *stibbing* distributions are shown in Figure 17. All three are strikingly associated with the three medieval forests and the Soke, which was reckoned 'forest' until 1215. *Dibbing* and *stibbing*

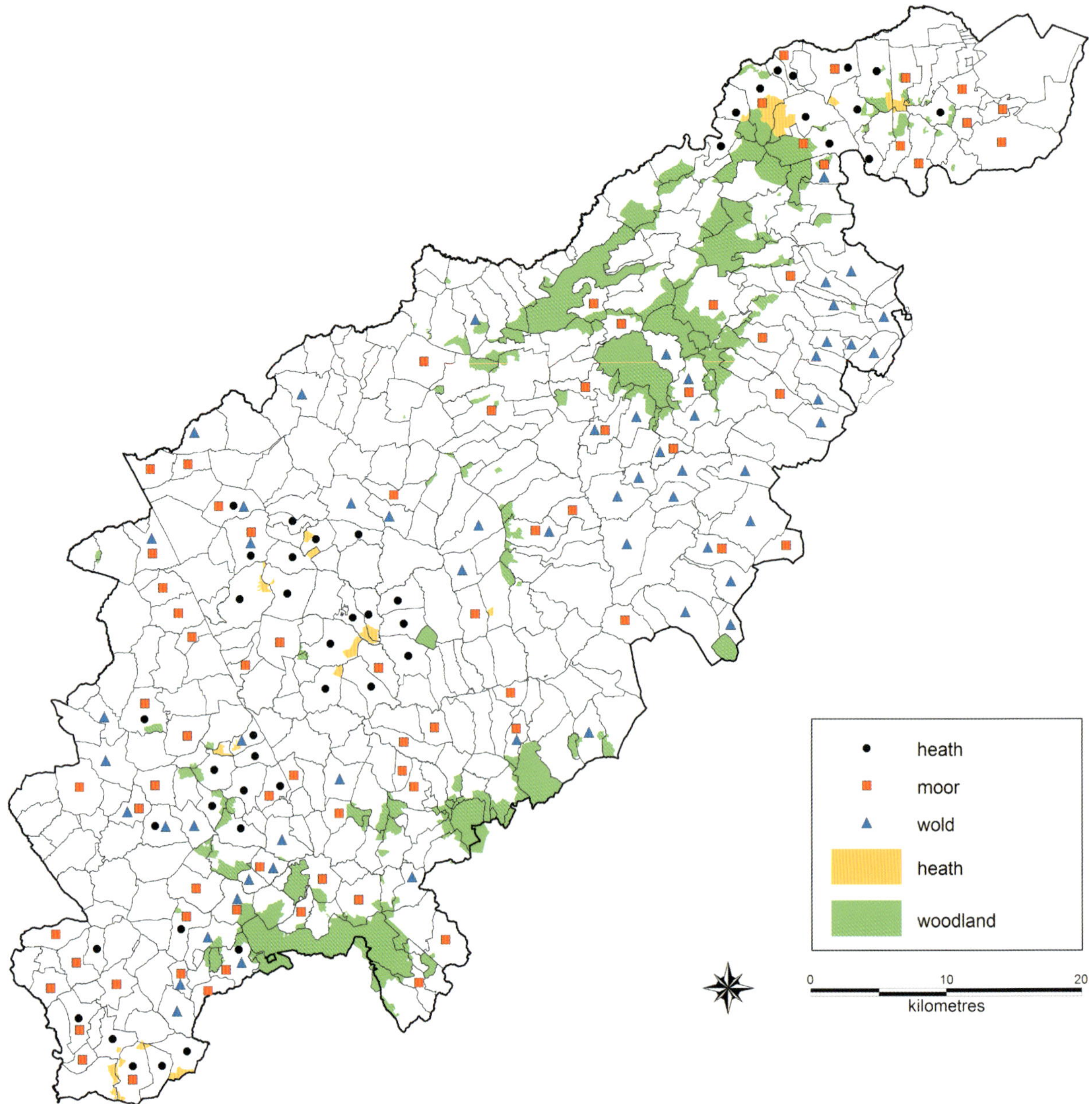

Figure 15. Distribution of furlong names with heath, moor and wold.

are found near Rockingham Forest only and are presumably local name-forms used instead of *stubbing* for clearance. There seems to be a subtle difference implied by the absence of *stibbing* from the south. *Sart* is a Norman-French term and would not have been used before 1066. Its close association with the medieval woods concords with the very numerous historical records of extensive assarting made at named, identifiable locations. What is most striking is the absence of *sart* from the medieval champagne parts of the county, with the implication that they were devoid of woods and largely opened up to arable before 1066.

The resources exploited and the resulting products available in the county during the Middle Ages are recorded in account rolls and court rolls. The Ramsey abbey manor of Elton, Hunts, lying across the River Nene near Fotheringhay, traded with Northamptonshire townships during 1307–14.[10] A ploughshare, 3 pairs of traces, wheels and horseshoes came from smiths at Oundle. Three jars of earthenware were bought for dairy milk. The source is not specified but it is likely to be Lyveden kilns near Oundle. Both iron and pottery production relied on charcoal readily available from nearby woods. Pigs were pannaged in Clyve (King's Cliffe) Park, which also provided a quarter of lime. Stone slates came from Southorpe for Elton grange porch and building stone was carted from Southorpe and Barnack to Gunwade, a hithe on the Nene near Castor. Barnack stone went farther afield; a stone was sent to Ramsey for an altar and another for

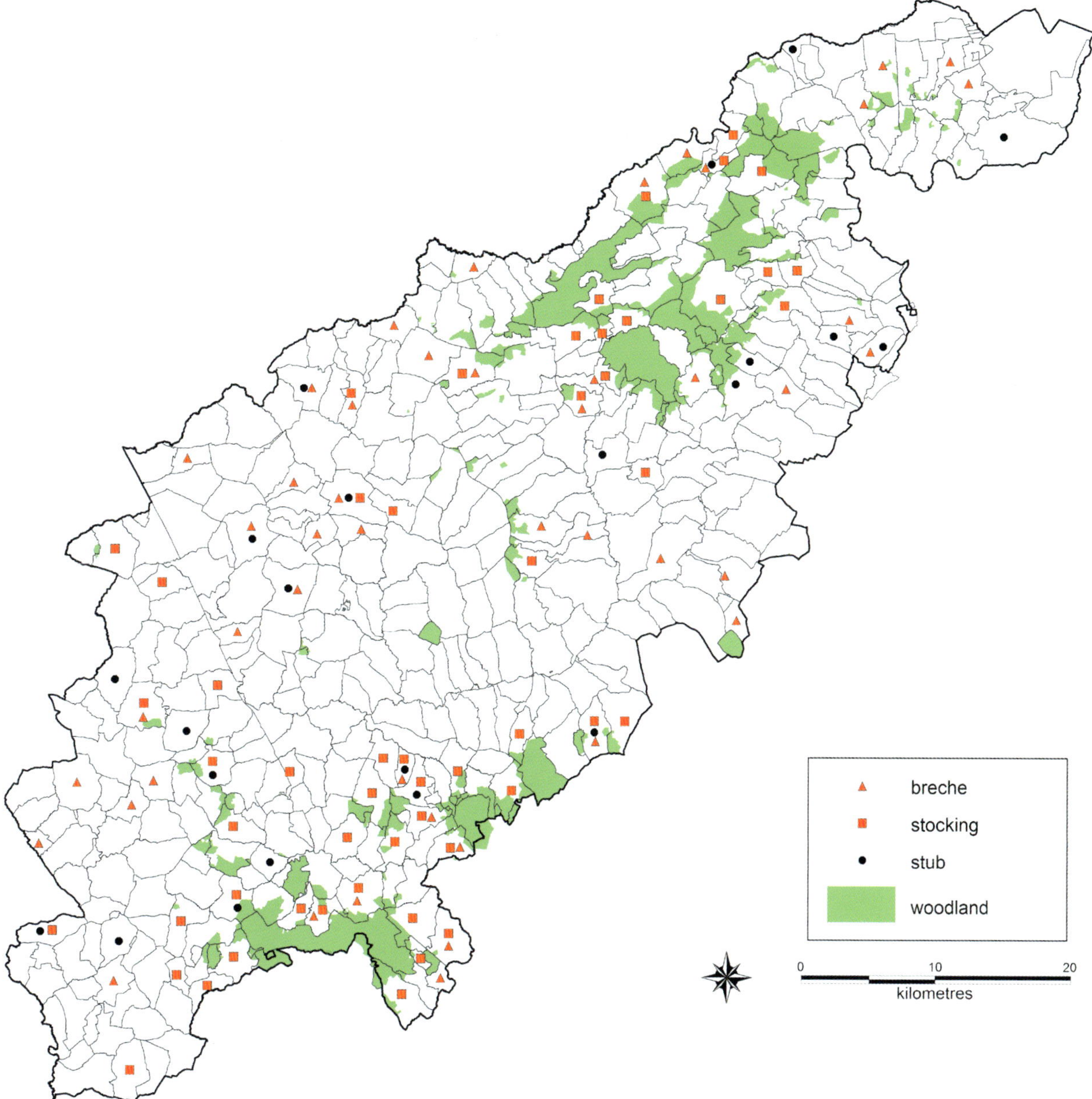

Figure 16. Distribution of furlong names with breche, stubb and stocking.

a lavatory in the abbot's hall. Large stones suitable for these purposes were discovered when Ramsey Mere was drained in 1853.[11] The accounts of Abbot Godfrey of Peterborough record 217,000 turves dug at Eye in 1301.[12]

Local woods provided Elton with faggots from Fotheringhay Park; timber for mills and plough beams came from Castor Wood and wood from Thornhaugh was used for making cogs; more timber came from Nassington and a rafter bought at Upton in the Soke was taken to Ramsey across the fenland waterways.

Forest and woodland

The physical structure and management of royal forests and woodlands have been described many times. Forest documentation as a whole is copious, there being the crown records at the National Archive, as well as numerous records accumulated by county landed families some of whom had been appointed crown officers and whose estates eventually acquired most of the woodlands. This account is concerned primarily to accompany the atlas and provide information relating to the development of the landscape. A few specific examples illustrate the wide range of records available.

Forest administration

Turner gives a full description of many aspects of forests in the 13th century and published examples of the records of courts of Eyre and Forest Inquisitions

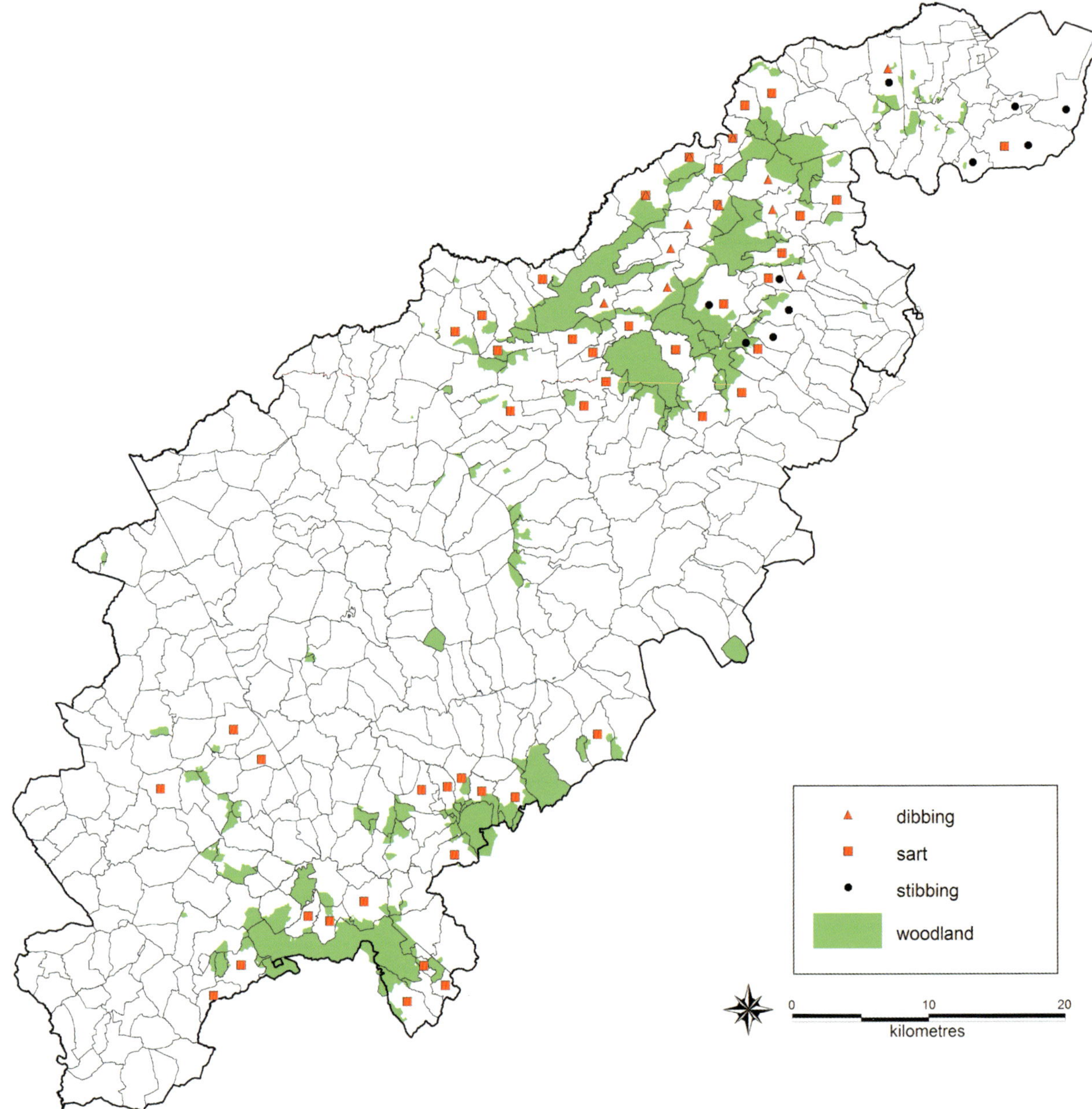

Figure 17. Distribution of furlong names with sart, dibbing and stibbing.

for several counties.[13] The legal bounds of the districts where forest law applied (which included much open ground as well as woods) were defined by metes and bounds called 'perambulations'. Surviving 13th-century perambulations were discussed and listed by Bazeley,[14] some are marked on Figure 18.

Pettit gives details of Northamptonshire forest administration in the 17th century[15] and a summary national view of the Royal Forests is given by the late 18th-century parliamentary *Woods Reports*.[16] commissioners were appointed primarily to obtain a supply of timber for the navy, since inland woods were then able to provide timber by means of canals and improved roads.[17] They were surprised to discover that no maps or detailed forest accounts had been kept since the Civil War and decided to make a separate report for each forest, because the rights of the crown and individuals varied so much in each of them and there had been many grants of fees and allowances (Third *Woods Report*, 1788, 559–61). The Report noted that in earlier times the chief forest officer had been a master forester appointed by the king who was responsible for:

Verderers (4) who were judges of the swanimote and directed all other officers.

Regarders (12) who went through all the forest every third year and enquired about offences, assarts, wastes etc.

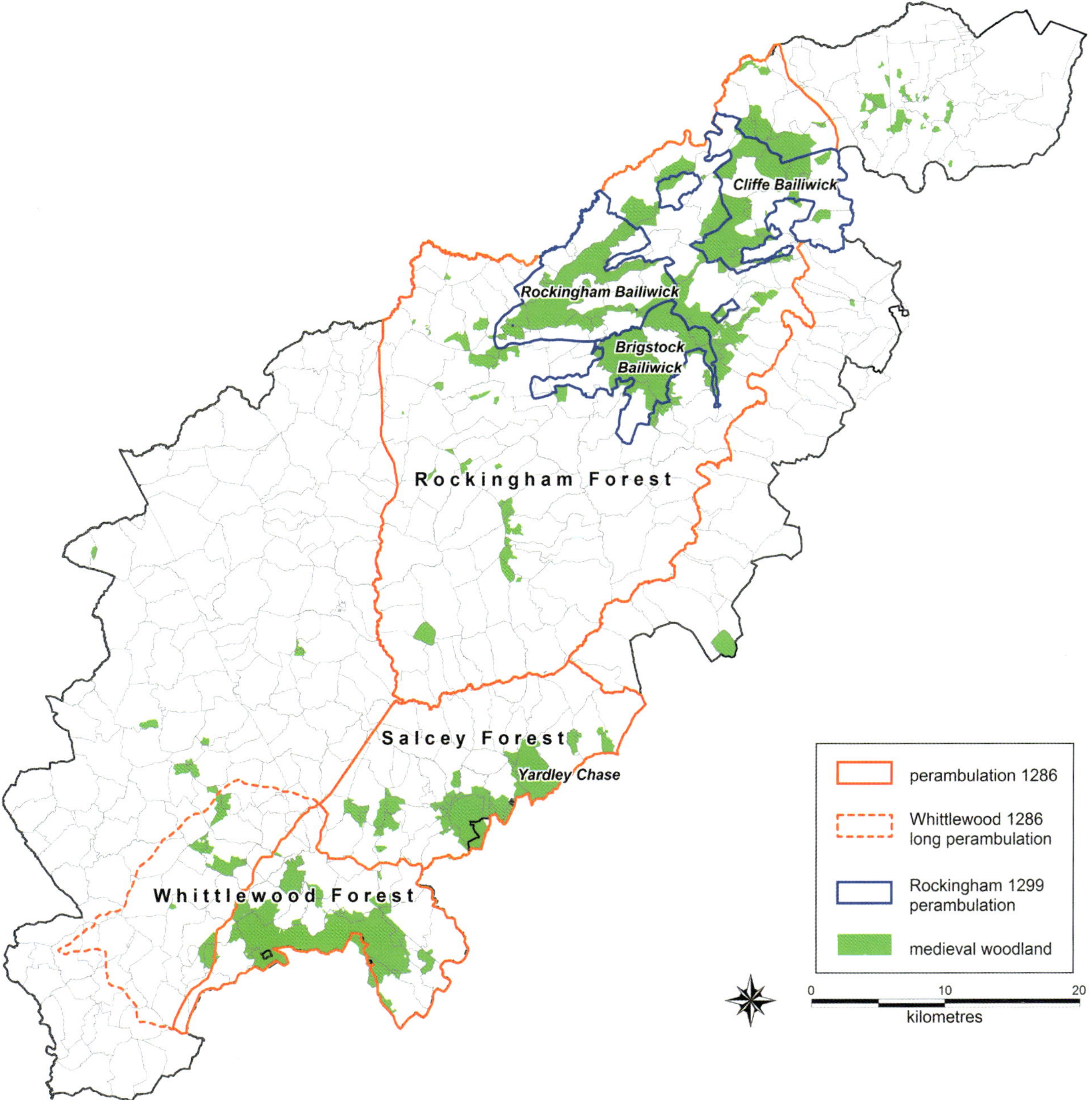

Figure 18. Northamptonshire Forests and woods.

Foresters who preserved the vert and venison and attached offenders, the number of them being at the discretion of the regarder.

Agistors (4) to receive and account for profits from herbage and pannage.

Woodwards to look after woods and present offences; the number was variable.

A steward to attend courts and assist the verderers.

There were three forest courts; the woodmote, that met every 40 days and presented to the swanimote. The swanimote met three times annually with all officers present, the verderers were judges. The chief court was the justice seat or court in Eyre that met once every 3 years. The court dealt with offences against the vert or game, ordered views of the game and gave licences for the sale of private woodlands.

Northamptonshire had three royal forests; Salcey, Whittlewood and Rockingham (Figure 18). Salcey Forest had a detached part consisting of woods lying towards Northampton at Courteenhall, Roade, Blisworth, Stoke Bruerne, Easton Neston, Tiffield and Gayton (Maps 68–9). The detached part of Wootton township was probably once woodland so explaining the name *Courteenhall* – 'Courta's hale' or 'corner', lying in a corner of the wood (Map 70 EM). Rockingham Forest similarly included detached woods on the locally high boulder-clay ground north-east of Northampton at Sywell, Pytchley, Mawsley (Map 36 M) and at Ashley.

Northampton Park *alias* Moulton Park was reckoned as part of Rockingham Forest.[18] The Soke was under forest jurisdiction before 1215.[19]

Figure 18 represents the woodland extent as recorded on maps of various dates from 1587 and verified by many written surveys of the 16th century and later. It does not differ greatly from the woodland recorded on Bryant's county map of 1827, made before there was large-scale grubbing up of woods. The earliest national source referring to woods is the Domesday Survey of 1086. It is not a woodland survey, but a record of the taxable assets of the major landowners that refers to woods somewhat inconsistently. Royal manors in the Rockingham region do not have particularly large amounts of wood assigned them, but at Greens Norton a wood '4 leagues long and 3 leagues wide' (probably 6 by 4½ miles) represents Whittlewood, with Silverstone and Whittlebury being chapelries of Norton church. Woodland at Yardley Hastings, 13 by 8 furlongs (1040 acres), belonged to Countess Judith, niece of William I and probably represents Salcey. She had interests in all the manors north of Salcey from Quinton to Grendon.

Darby and Terrett's plot of Domesday woodland shows that there is a close similarity to the medieval woodland distribution.[20] The similarity is greater when 'adjustments' are made, such as the wood of Earls Barton, a Nene Valley manor belonging to Countess Judith. The wood did not lie in the valley but was located near her major possession of Yardley Hastings, where the a coppice called Barton Broyle lying under Shortwood (Shortgrove) in Yardley Chase was recorded in the 13th century and later.[21]

The royal forests were created soon after 1066, judging from the 1086 Domesday entry for wood at Brixworth which states that it had been transferred into the (Royal) Forest.[22] Brixworth wood was likely to be on the high ground near the woods of Hardwick and Pytchley (Map 36 M). William II signed a charter at King's Cliff ('Clive') sometime during 1094–1100 when he was probably hunting at the royal manor,[23] which possibly was already established as the centre of the bailiwick. Rockingham Forest had taken its name from the royal castle of Rockingham by 1157.[24]

Salcey Forest is first recorded by name in 1206.[25] Many of the component woods and assarts were mentioned without identification in 1086 and are named later, such as Horn Wood in Easton Maudit in 1220[26] and Yardley Chase in 1233.[27] The earliest account of the whole is the description of the 'metes and bounds' of 1299,[28] which refers to Horn Wood and others near it, to the woods of Chadstone and to *schorte grave* and *childewode* belonging to the Ramsey Abbey manor of Whiston (Short Grove and Whiston Pike in Yardley Chase, (Map 61 EM)). Horton and Courteenhall are identifiable, as is Arno (assart) in Preston Deanery lying next to modern Salcey (Figure 19). A 17th-century version of this perambulation gives variant place-name spellings;[29] both are corrupt, thus *Pickelehacche* alias *Yerkelehatche* is likely to mean *Yerdelehatche*, especially as it is recorded after Hortonhatche. Within Yardley Chase some woods are recorded earlier; Arniss 1274, Grimpsey 1247 and Ravenstone Road 1247.[30]

Whittlewood Forest with its forest officers is first recorded by name as *Whitlewuda* in about 1130.[31] It was in the charge of a warden or master forester and Puxley was granted as a residence in about 1175.[32]

By 1792, much of what was once Royal Forest had been granted away, especially for Rockingham and Salcey, as found in the *Reports* made in 1791 and 1792.[33] New surveys and plans were made for those parts of Salcey and Whittlewood still reckoned to be crown woods. Detailed summary tables give the names and areas of all the coppices, open plains and ridings, enclosed lawns and lodges, with names of the officers and the value of their salaries and allowances.

Salcey consisted of 1,847 acres divided into 24 coppices grouped as three walks or bailiwicks; Hanslope, Piddington and Hartwell. Plains and ridings amounted to 471 acres, lawns 190 acres; there were 5 lodges. Whittlewood contained 5,424 acres almost surrounded by a ring mound consisting of 3,895 acres of timber and underwood in 69 different coppices, with 887 acres of open plains and ridings, 312 acres of enclosed meadow and 329 acres of enclosed lawns reserved for deer and for cattle belonging to the officers. There were five walks; Haselborough (of 17 coppices), Sholbrook 19, Wakefield 20, Hangar 8 and Shrob with 5 coppices. Both reports printed copies of the perambulations of 1299 and 1641 and gave a summary of a survey made in 1608, when Whittlewood had 51,046 oaks and 360 decaying trees. Rockingham Forest has already been discussed and mapped.[34]

Previous accounts of some Northamptonshire forests have been given. Baker described the history of Whittlewood,[35] and published the 1299 perambulation with its identification in 1841.[36] Page gives a good account of the early history of Whittlewood and its boundaries at different dates.[37] Wise provided much detail of Rockingham Forest, with descriptions of the local officers and their tasks,[38] and printed a perambulation of 1276.[39] In 1968 Pettit gave a full account of all three Northamptonshire royal forests in the 17th century and provided background information for the 16th century and earlier.

The physical structure of forests

There were two components to regions known as 'forests'. Legally the term 'forest' applied to an area belonging to the crown, partly extra-parochial, to which forest law applied. Physically it consisted of blocks of woodland with trees (usually called coppices) and equally important were open spaces, often consisting of considerable areas of land (called plains, lawns and shires), deer-parks, enclosures and assarts (woodland converted to pasture or arable). Officers and keepers resided in various forest lodges. The open-fields of some parishes lying within or near to the woods were also within the forest jurisdiction.

The three bailiwicks of Rockingham Forest were Clive (King's Cliffe), Brigstock and Rockingham, each based on a royal manor. The arrangement with foresters in charge was of early date, the 'forester of Clive' being referred to in 1198.[40] The bailiwicks were further divided into several parts called 'walks' for local administration purposes with keepers, woodwards and other forest officers. In 1300 the southern part of Brigstock Bailiwick was reckoned as a fourth bailiwick called Bulax.[41] It was held by Robert de Wauton who had four foresters whom he could remove at the swanimote.

Coppices, varied in area from about 30–80 acres. They were separated by access routes and spaces called ridings and plains, so forming a diapered plan. The coppice system was a carefully planned method of managing the forest for both hunting and timber production. Ridings and wide plains were suitable for chasing and hunting deer, leaving coppices as reserves for underwood and timber, as well as providing cover and breeding grounds. Hence both timber production and hunting could be effectively accommodated in the same forest.

Each coppice was surrounded by a bank and fence made to exclude deer during the early stages of the 'spring' – the natural re-growth after felling. Some banks had permanent hedges in parts and others were topped with a 'dead hedge' – a fence made of tree loppings. Cattle from open-field villages were allowed common grazing in the forest coppices and open plains, but the right did not often extend to swine, except for prescribed short periods. Any cattle over the allowed limit were impounded and fines imposed by the foresters. Animals were not allowed to graze the open areas called lawns, which were fenced off for the exclusive use of deer and the cattle of forest officers. Coppices were cut in rotation after about 21 year's growth and then enclosed for seven years to exclude deer and commoning cattle. The real value of grazing under coppices was probably not great, as noted for King's Cliffe Park coppices in 1593:[42] 'grasse growing under thicke coppice woods, is spire, flaggy and soure by reason of the continuall droping of the wood and ... little or no grasse [is] to be expected.'

Dating of the coppice arrangement is not known. Rackham has suggested sometime in the 13th century[43] but it is likely that the physical arrangement of the Forest is earlier. Northamptonshire woodland was certainly 'managed' at an early date because at Whittlewood there is a record of forest officers in about 1130.[44] Other foresters are named at Brackley in 1200–1210.[45] The earliest recorded foresters of Rockingham were Robert and Henry de Yarwell, who, in 1198, held the serjeanty of the forest in Cliffe Bailiwick.[46] It is therefore clear that the division into bailiwicks had occurred by that date.

At Oundle, the coppice system was described in 1360, when a ditch and hedge were placed around Hill Wood to exclude Glapthorn village herd from entering for seven years.[47] The wood was not called a coppice and it may well be that the term 'coppice' was not used before the 14th century, coppices merely being called 'woods'. Several wood-names, later recorded as 'coppices' occur in the Rockingham Bailiwick.[48] The earliest Whittlewood coppice-name is *loggecopis* (Lodge Coppice in Hazelborough) in 1367,[49] but 13 Whittlewood coppice names are recorded at an early date without the appellation 'coppice'. It is possible that since so many of the names are the same, then the fully developed system, as mapped in 1608, was in operation, by the 13th century and possibly earlier.[50] The existence of the bailiwick of Wakefield and of the name Hazelborough occurring in 1220 shows that these walks were established and likely, therefore, so was the whole system. The word, *coopertum*, 'cover', used in the 1299 perambulations to describe forest boundaries running between open fields and woodland may mean 'coppice' rather than being a general game-keeping term for any type of undergrowth 'cover'.

Once formed, the coppice system seemed to be physically stable. The only known example of a major redesigning of coppice banks occurred at the northern part of Salcey. Underlying the late-medieval coppices is another set of banks discovered by fieldwork that seem to make up an earlier stage of the lawn with other linear divisions, Figure 19. A 12th-century date is possible.

The woods and coppices marked on the early-modern atlas are as represented on maps of various dates from 1587. The medieval atlas has the same wood outline superimposed on a general area called 'wood pasture', which includes ground lying between open-field furlongs and the established woods as later mapped. The 'space' represents former woodland removed by assarting to form either enclosures or open commons. It cannot be known, without much historical analysis and reconstruction, what the state of this process was at the nominal date of '1300' assigned to the medieval atlas and hence assarts and commons cannot yet be mapped countywide. The coppices of later times have been assumed to take the same form in the Middle Ages – their names, as stated, can often be traced back to the 13th century and from the 1550s their acreages are given in wood accounts and surveys.

The field survey to record open-field furlongs included mapping woodland banks and other earthworks lying within them.[51] Generally there was a close correspondence between earthwork banks

Figure 19. Salcey Forest; early coppices and assarts. Surveyed coppice boundary banks are marked red and other earthworks black.

and the coppice boundaries. Of equal interest were the earthwork sites of former pounds and lodges. The large pound of Lowick has been described[52] and a small 13th century lodge site occurs in Horn Wood, near Easton Maudit.

A few earthwork sites of pre-medieval date were identified, the most spectacular being a Roman site in Thornhaugh Wood.[53] Two large ringworks at the south of Salcey (Figure 19), previously interpreted as Iron Age structures,[54] are more likely to be medieval pounds, judged from their remarkable state of preservation, similar to Lowick pound.

A stone surfaced trackway was found east of Stony Coppice in Salcey and continues as a stone spread in the arable field to the north. It is identified in 1337 as Preston Stoneway,[55] and in 1614[56] a crown rent was paid for 'Preston Stoneway alias Symonds Sarte'. It was probably a causeway to the lodge in Salcey Lawn, made across clay ground.

Some woods such as Abthorpe had dividing banks that probably relate to manorial divisions. Bucknell Wood near Abthorpe has a single bank around most of the outside, 4.5m wide and about 1m high. A well preserved part at the south-west has an internal ditch 2.3m wide. The wood is divided by an internal bank at the north-west, 4.5–5m wide which links to a natural stream. The bank and brook mark off the northern third of the wood. At the west, in the northern part of Thomas Wood, there is a well preserved medieval riding marked by parallel banks with internal ditches, separating Bucknell and Thomas Woods.

The management of the coppices in terms of underwood and timber production are recorded in detail from the 16th century onwards. Crown coppices have the earliest data. In the early-modern period the records of the country-house estates are very detailed,[57] sometimes including estimates of the volume of timber and payments to constables, church wardens, overseers of the poor and an allowance to provide drink for the game keepers and coppice keepers 'by my lord's order'. Much detail is available for the coppice management of Corby Woods during the 17th century and later.[58] Selected examples are given below.

For the Whittlewood region, a woodbook of *c*.1550, relating to the Honor of Leicester estate,[59] records sales of trees, presumably felled in Whistley Wood which had been assigned to the fee in 1235.[60] The names of each village, the recipient and the number of trees and price are recorded. Most people had 1–5 trees; prices varied from 2s to 5s per tree. The places served formed a block south-west from Helmdon including Culworth, Brackley, Thorpe (Mandeville), King's Sutton and Banbury.

In 1553, the two adjacent coppices of Fernelagh (Fernily) and Lady Quarter in the Haselborough Walk of Whittlewood were felled. An initial survey noted that within the hedges of the 60 acre coppices were 18 acres of 'waste' outside of the wood, lying in 'rydings heigh waies and grenes' as well as the 8 acres of ground under the hedges. Four acres of underwood were given to several forest officers – the justice of the forest, the master of the game, the lieutenant and the rangers and to the verderers – which left 30 acres of timber, out of which 400 timber trees were marked and reserved (to be left as standard trees). Sale of the remaining wood and underwood raised £99 4s 2d. The coppices were then ditched and quick-fenced, 13 men being paid for 100 days' work ditching. Three gates into the coppice were provided with ironwork and 1,050 yards of hedge were laid. A bridge was made for a carriage to take timber to Grafton (Regis). The total cost of these and other works (such as wages for selling the wood) came to £21 16s 10d, leaving £77 7s 3d. The wood sold went to local villages, some in North Buckinghamshire: Stratford (bought by 17 people, who were named and the money paid by each recorded), Potterspury 18 people, Houghton 2, Hulcot 1, Pattishall 4, Wick Hammond 2, Ashton 1, Bradwell 1, Shutlanger 2, Tiffeld 1, Grafton 1, Yardley 10, Cosgrove 2, Milton (Malsor) 2, (Rothers)Thropp 3, Castlethorpe 5, Furtho 2, Roade 1, Wolverton 1, Harsham (Haversham) 6, Alderton 1, Lathbury 12, Brafield 1, Yardley (Gobion) 5, Peyton 1, Northampton 1, Cotton End 1, Hanslope 1, Norton 1 and Lillingstone 2.[61] Pettit gives a distribution map of places receiving wood from crown coppices in all three forests.[62]

Long distance sales of Whittlewood timber were for bridge repairs at Henley on Thames (1691–1710).[63] In 1710 timber was provided for Blenheim and Woodstock Parks.[64] Wood was cut down by rioters in 1727 under the pretence of cutting coronation poles.[65] During 1727–34 rough timber from Whittlewood was used for the repair of the Great Lodge and outhouses at Wakefield Lodge.[66] The Woods in Rockingham Forest have been described.[67]

Manors neighbouring the royal woods often possessed pieces of it. Detached from Whitfield and Brackley was King's Hill and the assart of Litley (near Brackley Hatch). These were once seignurial woodland possessions, but had been given to Brackley Hospital in *c*.1210.[68] However the lord of Whitfield manor still had rights in Hazelborough Wood. This was disputed in 1672 and records were searched which established from a judgment made in the eyre of 1272, that the lord was to have 'reasonable estovers' in Hazelborough, which was specified in 1572 and 1620 to be 40 loads of wood taken by the view of the foresters and woodward.[69] Probably related to this search is a copy of an inquisition held in 1341 taken by John de Tinchewyk, forester of Whittlewood, as to whether Peter de Montibus and his ancestors (lords of Whitfield) used to have certain rights in Hazelborough Wood.[70]

Private woods

Horn Wood lying south of Eastern Maudit extends to 60 acres and once had a wall around it. Near the centre the remains of a lodge house, excavated in 1965 by Graham Clayson, revealed a small rectangular structure and pieces of 13th-century pottery. In 1086, a wood, 4 by 2 furlongs, belonging to the Easton Maudit and Strixton estate of Winemar,[71] is likely to be Horn Wood since the size is similar. Horn Wood and the adjacent assarts were granted to the abbey of St James, Northampton in 1255.[72]

When part of the wood was felled in 1515 the abbot's surveyor paid £6 13s 4d to the steward of Easton manor for access over his ground.[73] By 1544 the wood belonged to the Duchy of Lancaster, via appropriation from St James' Abbey. The Duchy tenant at Higham Ferrers felled the wood in 1572 and Easton lord, Christopher Yelverton, recalled that there should be 'paid unto the lord of this manor 1 acre of the wood as heretofor ... for passing out of the said wood over the ground of the lord of Easton'.

The Duchy made a survey of Horn Wood in 1623 and found it in poor condition with 'diverse and sondrye small runted spyer trees' only fit to make hovel parts and rafters for hovels.[74] In 1633 the wood was in the tenure of Christopher Yelverton who paid a rent of 43s yearly.[75] When he received licence to empark and disafforest Easton Maudit from Salcey Forest, Horn Wood was granted to him with the rest of manor and has belonged to it since.[76]

Other private woods were managed on a coppice system with regular felling of underwood for local use. Woods at Plumpton in 1606 consisted of Plumpton Great Wood, 173 acres, with three coppices in Oxehaie.[77] In *c.*1684, seven coppices were divided into 9 parts and one sold every year worth £65. It was managed by a woodman who was paid £11 yearly.[78] Woods lying away from the forests were usually small and belonged to particular neighbouring manors, such as the wood of Badby and the woods shared between Everdon, Farthingstone, Stowe and Dodford.

Forest management at the local level

Details of conditions in the Forests during the 13th century can be viewed from the returns of eyre courts and inquests, some published by Turner in 1899. They show that crown control was vigorously applied and punishments were severe. Not all those accused of offences were of lowly status.

In 1209 the forester of Cliffe found wet blood in the snow at Sibberton wood (Thornhaugh) which was traced to the house of Ralph Red of Sibberton, where the verderers found the flesh of a doe. Ralph was taken to Northampton prison where he died. In the same year a dead hart was found in the wood of Henry Dawney at Maidford, for which the whole village with the wood was 'seized in king's hand' (pp.3–4).

Simon of Overton, parson of Old, came into the field of Walgrave early on Easter Day, 1248 and took a roe. An inquiry made at Mawsley wood, by men from the four neighbouring villages of Old, Walgrave, Hannington and Faxton confirmed the offence. All such inquests required witnesses from four nearby villages to appear (p.89).

Men from Blisworth and Hanslope, Bucks, poached for 3 days at Rockingham in 1272. They caught 8 deer and carried venison in a cart to Stanwick, remaining there overnight and continued to Hanslope where it was eaten; several men were imprisoned. Four deer were taken from the park and warren of Northampton by Robert, count Ferrers, who broke the Park wall towards Moulton with dogs and greyhounds. Hares and rabbits were also taken from the same Park (pp.39–40).

Deer could be removed from the forests by royal sanction. William de Ferrers, Earl of Derby, received 15 live does and 5 live bucks from Rockingham Forest in 1251 to stock his park (Higham Ferrers Park near Newton Bromswold), which was the gift of the king (p.104).

Forest law slowly weakened over the centuries, until the brief imposition of early forest laws by Charles I. There were illegal depredations, often made by neighbouring villagers, manorial owners and forest officers.[79]

Some small woods were grubbed up before they were mapped and unless located by detailed historical reconstruction they do not appear on the atlases, being subsumed into the open field or pasture, through lack of knowledge. An example is Weedon Bec Wood which extended to 70 acres at SP 607 570, north of Everdon Stubbs. There had been more woodland at Weedon, probably lying near to the identified wood, because King John confirmed 48 acres of old assart and 2 acres of new assart in 1203.[80] The wood was referred to in 1528 and 1559 and disafforested soon after enclosure; in 1784 the site consisted of arable and pasture.[81] No map survives and its location was identified from field names and by reconstruction of the enclosure award.[82]

Assarts

Assarts were pieces of woodland taken out of royal control and converted to pasture or arable. The crown gave licence for these and charged fines or rents. Peterborough Soke was disafforested in 1215, removing it from forest law. First a survey of woodland was made recording 84 pieces totalling 1,600 acres. The abbot and convent, with the knights and freeholders agreed to make assarts and common rights were assessed. A list of assarts shows that many of them were small, lying at Cathwait, Woodcroft, Dogsthorpe and Walton.[83] Most of the surveyed woods were not grubbed up, many being left as a manorial resources and recorded in account rolls. For example 78 trees were felled at Castor (in *le hangende*, now Castor Hanglands Wood) to repair of the abbey grange there (Biggin) in 1301.[84]

Many assarts are detailed in 'assart rolls' of the 13th century and later.[85] Those made at Duddington next to Rockingham Forest have been discussed.[86] As well as the assart rolls, information can be obtained from crown rents. A rent roll made in 1337 lists 31 assarts in Salcey Forest totalling 445 acres.[87] Some of them still paid 'fee farm' rents to the crown in the early 17th century.[88] Most of the substantial assarts were made by local lords or monastic houses. The distribution of the name 'assart' shows it to predominate around the three royal forests, as explained (Figure 17).

Assarts were let by the crown for rents and not assigned to individual villages as an addition to their open fields. An inquest held at Puxley in Whittlewood Forest, in 1304, was part of a general enquiry about letting out to rent the wastes of forests, parks and woods south of the Trent.[89] In 1337, William Garet paid rent for 17½ acres of assart between Pokesleyrydyng and the Wykewey,[90] likely to be one of the closes west of Puxley (Maps 79–80).

The case-studies below describe assarts made next to Salcey and Whittlebury Forests which were seignurial enterprises and remained as enclosures in severalty ownership. The closes formed are indicated on the early-modern atlas maps where possible. Further work with field names and their acreages would yield accurate details of the area marked as amorphous 'wood pasture' around Salcey and elsewhere.

Piddington

The Hospital of St John, Northampton, founded *c.*1140, acquired interests at Piddington during the 13th century[91] and built a grange there. In 1299 William de Brampton granted to the Hospital assarts in Hartwell Wyk, Quinton, Courteenhall and Piddington.[92] The Hartwell Wyk land, called Bokardesley, had been held from the crown since *c.*1200 and the Courteenhall grant was specified as an assart held from the crown.[93] The master of St John's Hospital paid a rent to the crown for 8½ acres of assart near *flexley* and *thomesrydyng* In 1337.[94] Flexley lay near to the Grange.

The grange passed to the crown after the Dissolution of the Monasteries. In 1605 it was granted to Sir William Lane of Horton for £260, free of forest rights with licence to cut wood. It was described as a messuage and 220 acres of assart pasture called the Grange Pasture or St John's Closes, divided into several named closes abutting against the Forest of Salcey on the south and west, Piddington field north and on assarts called Parsons Sarts on the west, all formerly part of Salcey Forest.

William Lane also received a messuage and 121 acres of pasture, wood and wood ground, being assart lands and wastes called Laundons Sarte, Paulers Stockings, Ekeley alias Stoake Brand, Deadman close alias Kettelbush and Horton Hatchett Stockings lying within and near the Park of Horton in the parish of Horton.[95] Baldwyne Wake and John Wake paid rent for Dymarke alias Elkeny Sarte and Parsons Sarte in 1614.[96] The later descent of the Grange was sale by the Lane family in 1638 to Samuel Radcliffe, principle of Brasenose College, Oxford and it passed to in 1680 to Byron Eaton, principal of Gloucester Hall. Byron Eaton's two daughters gave the Grange to Worcester College, as Gloucester Hall was later named.[97]

Assarts along the north of Salcey were made to the west of Piddington Grange. The ditch of *Arno*, a named boundary of the 1299 perambulation, was referred to in 1432 as the close of *sherearnho* lying in Preston.[98] It is located on Preston Deanery tithe map as a close ('arnold') lying near to Salcey[99] (Figure 19). The close lay on a considerable spur, a 'ho', of land facing north. Next to it was Simons Sart, identified with 'waste' made at *meregrene* by Symon Carvell in 1337. Parsons Sart is probably to be associated with William de Brampton, parson of Piddington who paid rent for waste near Preston Wood held by Symon Carvell.[100] Meregrene and Flexley are named in the 1299 perambulation at the south of Piddington and Horton.

These documents describe a range of assarts and enclosures lying along the northern boundary of Salcey Forest. The enclosures contain no evidence of ridge and furrow on 1940s RAF photographs, nor are there any soil banks derived from ploughed-out furlongs to be seen on the ground. They were severalty holdings and never formed part of the open fields of either Horton or Piddington.

Helmdon Stockings

As well as the fields mapped in Figure 29 and described below, Helmdon had a detached piece of land called Helmdon Stockings lying next to Radstone and Whistley Woods (Map 74 M). A grange at Helmdon belonging to Biddlesden Abbey, Bucks included land 'in [the] wood' in 1227, further described as an assart lying between Radstone Wood and the assart of Simon de Turville (Helmdon manorial lord) and reaching to Banbury Way.[101] This shows that Biddlesden shared the seignurial assart, being part of the Stockings. In *c.*1230 Margaret de Quincey of Brackley confirmed rights to the monks lying near her chase of Whistley,[102] so confirming the location of the assart. Bridges[103] states that each of the three Helmdon manors had a portion of the 'innship' of Stockings in 1420. The abbot's Stocking was worth 30s in 1533.[104]

The Stockings ceased to be woodland and was converted to arable according to the fieldwork evidence of ridge and furrow and furlong boundaries (Map 74 M). By 1656 the Stockings consisted of pasture closes and the portion of it belonging to Overbury Manor amounted to 50 acres lying in three closes, with *hogerell feild* on the south.[105] This implies that the three manors shared 150 acres. The tithe map of 1846 gave the Stockings as 189 acres,[106] so the Biddlesden Stocking was perhaps 40 acres, or near a quarter. The stockings never became part of Helmdon open fields.

Parks

Deer parks were established next to many royal manors, such as Rockingham, Brigstock and King's Cliffe. They were presumably created for the more

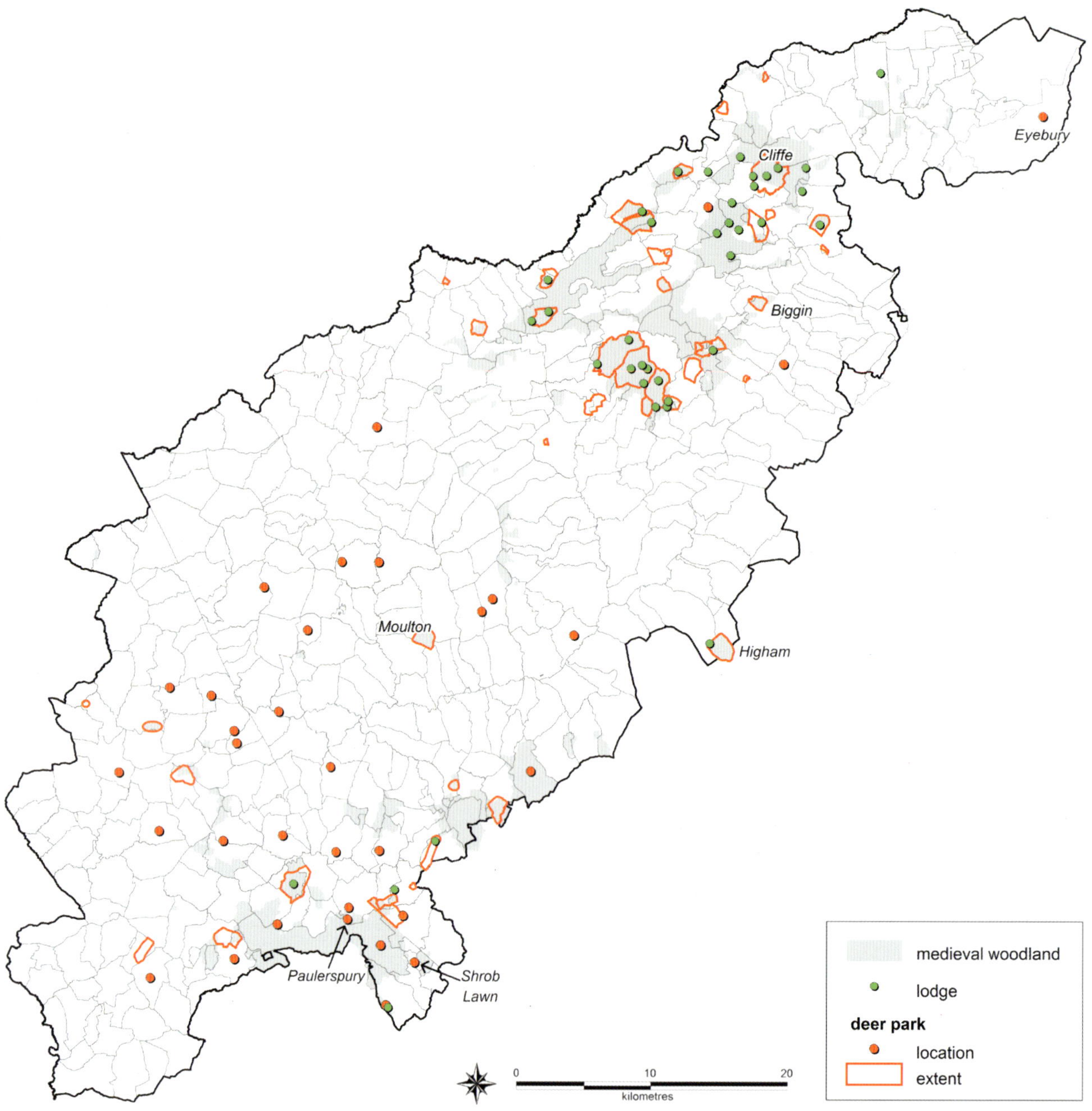

Figure 20. The medieval parks of Northamptonshire. Large deer parks (except Moulton and Higham Ferrers) lay next to the royal forests and are to be distinguished from the smaller enclosures called 'parks' located in the champion regions. These belonged to local manors and few were likely to have been used for deer.

convenient use of the king, the deer being confined to a limited space and easier to catch than in the open forest. Other magnates followed the royal example; William Peverel made a park near Higham Ferrers in the early 12th century and licences were given to manorial lords to make parks in the 13th and 14th centuries (many of them listed by Steane in 1975). Most were located next to the crown forests and some were large. Others were small and little more than manorial enclosures, such as Eyebury lying south of Eye (the large close south of Eye village on atlas map 10 EM), used to keep horses in 1301 and 1309.[107] The distribution of parks is shown on Figure 20.

To retain deer, the parks were encompassed by a ditch with an external bank surmounted by a timber pale, hedge or, occasionally, by a stone wall. An example can be seen at Biggin next to the A427 west of Oundle, created by Abbot Godfrey of Peterborough in 1307.[108] Late deer parks, such as Horton (1561), Holdenby (1587) and the enlarged Grafton Regis (1532) had no substantial earthworks, only a fence. Early large parks were managed like small forests with lodges, banked coppices, ridings and plains. The main open space for hunting purposes was called the lawn. Surveys were made of the woods in Cliffe Park in 1564 and 1593 giving the acreages and numbers of timber trees and their age, as well as the age and composition of the underwood.[109] Wadcrofte Coppice, 24 acres, was set with underwood of hazel, maple and thorn of 18 years growth and there were 120 oaks. One coppice had underwood 200 years old 'which dayly wasteth'. In 1593 the Park contained 600 oaks, 240 beeches and 140 ash trees and had 1000 deer.[110] Each park has its own particular history and two examples will be given.

Higham Park has been described by Kerr[111] and Hall and Harding.[112] It was first mentioned in 1166 when it was enlarged [113] and a record of 1200 refers to an exchange of land made between William Peverel and the king's great grandfather, Henry 1.[114] Hence a park was in existence before 1135. The first park created by William Peverel was identified partly by fieldwork that identified soil marks attributed to a levelled boundary bank and confirmed by the hedge lines on a 1794 map. From this evidence a plan of the two stages of the park were reconstructed;[115] see the hedge lines on atlas map 50 EM.

There is considerable detail relating to the park in account rolls, especially for the 15th century, which were studied by Kerr. A Great Lodge at the north of the park was surrounded by a moat and a small lodge lay at the south in Bedfordshire. Kerr described costs relating to the park paling and coppice management. There were at least two coppices in the park that were felled for poles and faggots as well as for timber. Loppings were used to burn lime.

Many oaks were felled at various times to repair the drawbridge over the moat surrounding the Great Lodge and for building works at Higham Castle and the mills. The Great Lodge had fish ponds, a dovecote, a chapel and other buildings roofed with stone tiles. Deer were taken to the park, some sent to other parks and carcases removed as venison from 1244 onwards. John of Gaunt paid for hounds and sent his falconers to the park in 1372–3. A final view of the park is given by a parliamentary survey of 1650.[116] There were then 6,654 trees of various quality. Soon after, the park was destroyed and converted to pasture closes. A list of them made in 1714 has names similar to those marked on the 1794 map.

Paulerspury Park had medieval origins, the old and new parks being united with 200 acres of fields and woods in 1409.[117] The 1409 enlargement had a straight boundary at the north, visible on 1940s aerial photographs showing that it cut across ridge and furrow. The small earlier parks are identifiable from curving hedge lines. A survey made in 1541,[118] noted that there were 176 deer in two closes. In four coppices there were 80 acres of wood (at 18 feet to the perch); Blakethycke (21 acres, with underwood 50 years old), Hawksnest (14 acres, 6 years), Asshe Coppice (12 acres, 2 years) and Barre Coppice (21 acres, 50 years old). Asshe Coppice had 440 large (standard) trees in it and Hawksnest 560 trees. There were also 354 acres of pasture and meadow.

Many additions were made to Whittlewood deer parks during the early 16th century by Henry VIII.[119] In 1532, Grafton medieval park was enlarged to about 1,000 acres taking in small medieval parks and open-field land. Hartwell Park took in three small medieval settlements (one of them being converted to a lodge) and part of the open-fields around them, cutting across arable lands. The surrounding bank is slight.

Another similar activity was a change in land use at Puxley by the creation of Shrob lawn. Shrob Lawn, as depicted on the 18th-century copy of a Forest map of *c.*1608, is not of medieval origin,[120] but was once the open field of Puxley, as previously noted.[121] Puxley had open-fields, the furlong boundaries of which were surveyed by fieldwork (Maps 77–78 EM). In 1356 Thomas Forester of Pouksley had a yardland there (15 acres of arable) and 'the fields of Pokesle' were referred to in 1413 proving there had been open-field land.[122] They were incorporated into a 'lawn' next to Shrob as marked the 1608 map. A similar activity took place to form Morehay Lawn in Cliffe Bailiwick taking in the fields of the deserted village of Hale.[123] No date for the formation of Shrob Lawn is known, but it was probably part of Henry VIII's enlargement of the nearby parks. The remainder of Puxley was entirely enclosed by the time of a survey made in 1566.[124]

This emparking and enclosing activity was a large-scale estate management presumably made to improve hunting. The enlarged Hartwell Park, with is odd, unusual linear shape and the enclosures made in Grafton Regis fields formed a connecting link between Salcey and Whittlewood Forests. There was then an unbroken tract of forest, royal parks, enclosures and forest from Syresham to Horton Woods (13 miles), available for hunting without any interruption by open fields or woods that had been granted away.

3 Open Fields

David Hall

The reconstructed medieval countryside has been compiled principally from archaeological fieldwork surveys, supplemented with information provided by RAF photographs taken during 1945–8 and maps dating from the early 16th century to the mid 19th century.[1] The nominal date ascribed to the 'medieval' maps is 1300. In the early 14th century, open fields were at their maximum extent before enclosures were made following a less intensive arable use, partly resulting from population decline after 1349.

Pasture and arable

The major component of the medieval countryside was arable land and various types of meadows and pastures which supported it economically. Figure 1 shows the county land use in the high Middle Ages. The categories mapped were settlements, arable, woodland, meadow, pasture and heath. Most townships located near to woodland had pasturing rights for village animals which contributed to the farming economy. Grassland will be discussed first.

Meadow

Extensive meadow occurs in the main river valleys of the Nene, Welland, Ise, Tove and Cherwell and at the fen-edge townships of the Soke; Maxey, Northborough and Eye. Winter flooding permeated the alluvial land with nutrients that encouraged a luxuriant growth of grass and hence an abundant hay crop (Figure 21). Meadows were kept free of animals until the end of hay-time after which they were used for common pasture. Places with limited amounts of meadow sometimes had detached pieces lying in the meadows of other townships. Weldon and Gretton examples have been described;[2] Croughton near Brackley had detached meadow at Aynho three miles away in the Cherwell Valley in *c*.1260[3] which was mapped on Aynho enclosure award of 1793.[4] At Bozeat, lying near the edge of Salcey Forest, the manor had 30 acres in the common meadow of Grendon in the Nene Valley in 1737.[5]

Townships located distant from rivers made use the narrow belts of alluviated or colluviated deposits lying in slades next to small brooks. These formed extensive networks of pasture between blocks of furlongs, their extent and form determined by the dendritic drainage pattern. Open-field maps of Twywell and Braybrooke specify that some slade-pastures were 'meadow'.[6] Very small pieces of slade ground at Helmdon were used as meadow. South of Alithorn Wood, customary holders of 1530 had '2 butts in the *lylmede* called *towne meyde* for each yardland' (north of furlong 71, Figure 29, below and see the end of Table 3 for other small meadow pieces at Helmdon).

Most meadows were divided into strips and were held in dispersed ownership exactly the same as arable lands. The meadow of *reynaldiswode* at Fineshade, divided into 11 parts, was schematically mapped in *c*.1200, by a linear pictorial diagram representing the width and the length of the strips, which are written on it.[7] The names of holders of strips of Harlestone Holm Meadow next to Brampton were listed in 1309.[8] Meadow strips are depicted on estate maps of Broughton 1728, Denford 1730, where they are called 'furlongs' and Castor, 1846.[9] Individual divisions are not visible on the ground because meadows were never ploughed and ridges or furrows did not develop to leave a physical record. At hay time, meadowmen measured out individual strips that were sometimes further marked by treading a line between each strip to flatten a narrow swathe of grass. Details of the process have been given for Wollaston and Warkworth.[10]

Some meadows had their strips let out each year by lottery and were called 'lot meadows'. Many examples are known. Cogenhoe[11] and Easton on the Hill maps of 1630 and 1820[12] mark several small 'lot meadows' lying in detached blocks throughout the meadows. At Norton by Daventry the method of allotting Pinchooke Meadow was described in 1635.[13] Its location was the far south-east of the parish next to the A5. The meadow was divided into 11 parts and a list of 11 names is given. Each person in turn took whatever lot was drawn 'as thees 11 lots doe aryse in order' as it was given in an earlier description made during 1548–1583. Lot meadows were used at Grimscote in the 15th century,[14] at Farthinghoe *c*.1612,[15] Hinton in the Hedges 1682,[16] and Woodend in 1778.[17] Bracken and furze were also subject to a lottery process at Badby in 1623.[18]

Figure 21. An extract from the St Andrew's Priory map of 1632 showing labourers scything, turning and gathering hay in the meadow. (NRO Map 4671).

A third, less common type of meadow tenure was that called 'parting meadows', where a few dispersed meadow strips were shared between two holdings. In any one year, one holder cropped half of the strips and in the next year he cropped the other half, so alternating annually with his partner. Aynho meadows operated this system which is fully described and explained in a 1720 fieldbook,[19] and a late 13th-century example is recorded at Pilsgate in Barnack.[20] Further examples are the doles of Callibridge Horsepoole Meadow at Milton Malsor, which were parted in 1675[21] and Fulwell Meadow in 1711.[22] The same sharing by 'parting' is found with leys at Aston le Walls in 1633[23] and in 1723 at Twywell.[24]

Pasture

Pasture occurred in several forms. Many steep hills and scarps could not be ploughed. The long line of spectacular scarps on the western and northern county boundary from Edgcote to Barby and Sibbertoft and along the Welland Valley to Stamford, provide many examples of rough pasture. Away from the county scarp were pastures on the hills near Daventry, Everdon, Weedon Bec, Harpole and on the Bugbrooke Downs, These pastures were commonly appropriated as part of the demesne. Pasture sometimes occurred in narrow belts or larger areas at the junction of permeable strata and clays. These were part of the open-field pasture of any particular system, as at Chipping Warden, Brixworth and on the east and north-east of Barnack.

Some townships in or near to Rockingham Forest had commons, greens and plains lying adjacent to the woods which were used for pasture (see Benefield Plain and Whining Green from Stoke Doyle to Wadenhoe).[25] They were most probably former woodlands pulled up at various dates but not used as private assarts nor taken into the common open fields. The other two forests did not have many greens or physical commons, most assarts being taken into severalty closes as described for Piddington and Horton. Salcey had a large green at the south (Map 70 EM) and another at the north. On the west, Hartwell 'modern' settlement lies in a green.

Small greens occurred within some villages, but the greens of Brafield and Evenley next to the settlements were large enough to be used for common grazing, similar to greens in many East Anglian villages. Great Brington Green lay a little west of the village and could have been used similarly. *Droves* linking vills to relatively distant resources of wood, pastures and heaths were a common feature of Rockingham Forest, as described.[26] They are rare in the remainder of the county. Paulerspury had a drove leading south into Whittlewood.

Heathland in Northamptonshire was not extensive comprising 0.62% of the total county area. Only two village names contain a 'heath' name element – East Haddon and West Haddon.[27] Morton described the three heathy regions of the county which lay in the north, centre and south-west.[28] Heaths formed on two types of geological exposure – decalcified limestone and Northampton Sands and Ironstone. The latter are very sandy near Northampton, especially on the west at Harlestone and Dallington, where considerable extents of heathy vegetation once grew, now entirely removed. There were small heaths at Farthingstone, Long Buckby, Church and Chapel Brampton and Ravensthorpe.

Elsewhere, the Northampton Sands and Ironstone has a much lower sand content and is known generally as 'ironstone' and agriculturally as 'red land'. Ironstone was used to smelt iron from Roman times to the early

Middle Ages, mainly in the Rockingham Forest area, with a little on the east of Salcey Forest at Easton Maudit and Bozeat. When iron smelting was re-introduced *c.*1870–1975, the ore was reckoned as low grade (because of the sand content) and latterly was mixed with Swedish ore.

Agriculturally, well-draining 'red land' was recognised as difficult, recent farmers quoting that it was good land provided it had a 'shower of rain every other day and a shower of manure on Sundays'. In other words if there was a dry summer, or the land had poor husbandry, it would yield little. In spite of this, the greater part of the ironstone-based soils were incorporated into open fields. That it was a potentially difficult soil was recognised at Newnham in the early 17th century when a two-field system was changed to five fields. Three fields with fertile soils based on limestone and clay were used for a three-course husbandry, the other two lay on red land and were run on a two-course system and used to grow rye, which is better suited to poor soil than wheat or barley. A similar difficulty with the red land accounts for the division of Finedon fields into as many as 11 parts during the 18th century, cultivated on a three-year cycle, but mixing up combinations of non-adjacent red land and heavy clay land in any one year, to even out the soil types.[29] Smaller outcrops of red land that had been incorporated into open-field furlongs, were often left to revert to grass 'leys' and were referred to in the early-modern period as 'heath'.

Heaths that developed on decalcified limestone are found at the north of the county near Wittering and Barnack and south-west of Brackley. The northern block has been described. It spread north into the Soke on the locally high ground of Barnack; a boundary description of Barnack, made in 1711, referred to the heaths of Ufford, Sutton, Wittering and Stamford St Martin's.[30] Much sandy land at Barnack was part of the medieval arable. The close proximity of acid and alkaline based soils in the Soke caused interesting contrasts of botanical species before modern ploughing.

The larger heaths were used as commons and had open-field grazing rights. Sheep grazed (untended) on Barnack Heath and a horse was left loose overnight in 1681.[31] Many heaths were sources of fuel as well as pasturing. Most provided furze and thorns that were used primarily for fuel. The large heath of Easton on the Hill accommodated far more grazing animals than found in most villages. In a survey made in 1818 prior to enclosure, it was noted that 90 sheep were allowed for each yardland and 23 for a cottage common.[32] Helpston Heath had a 'warren house' in *c.*1740.[33] At Little Stowe, south of Towcester, each yardland was allowed a piece of furze on the heath.[34]

Most of Harlestone Heath is now planted with conifer, as it was before 1829 and the remainder taken into modern arable. It is difficult to believe that in the 18th century it looked like the heathlands still surviving on the Breckland of East Anglia. However at Harlestone enclosure in 1766, there was a significant heath resource, since the allotments made allowance for rights of common and for '2 lots of brakes and 2 loads turf from the Heath' (yearly), that went with every yardland.[35] It was similarly valuable in the 13th and 14th centuries.

Harlestone Heath was probably once greater than shown (atlas map 44 M). A map of 1829 gives enclosed field-names that are mostly furlong names predating 1766, some with 'heath' indicators.[36] The size of the open-field yardland in the early 14th century, at 67–72 acres,[37] was much larger than normal (*c.*25 acres), suggesting that arable lands had encroached on a large area of 'waste' or heath.

William de Bray records various transactions involving heath in his Harlestone *Estate Book*. A purchase of 12 acres of heath made in 1329 states that it lay next to the royal way from Northampton to Lilbourne and next to the fields of Duston.[38] This can be identified precisely, located next to the A428 at SP 7142 6320. William also listed the heath held by St James' Monastery, Northampton.[39] It refers to heath at Wolvendale and Harlestone Frith, as well gifts by William de Staunton of 28 acres of heath and 1 rood called Pevereles Frith and a further 14 acres. Robert Kingesman gave 2 acres of heath. By good fortune the original charters of these transactions survive which give more detailed information. The one rood called Peverelesfrith lay between the heath of the canons and 14 acres of heath that belonged to William de Staunton's mother.[40] The 2 acres given (in *c.*1248) by Richard Kingesman of Harlestone to St James' lay between the heaths of William son of the priest and the heath of Margery Gobion (one of the manorial owners).[41] These grants specifying particular pieces of heath lying among parcels belonging to institutions or manorial lords were very probably part of a demesne block of heath.

Clayland pastures, formed by conversion of marginal arable to permanent pasture during the 15th to 18th centuries, grew furze and thorns which were used for fuel (Figure 22). These pastures, many lying on the alkaline soils of the clay wolds, are not to be confused with heaths formed on acid soils. Confusingly, the clayland gorse and bracken commons of Blakesley and Maidford were called 'heaths'. At Hackleton, in 1783, the clayland Cow Pasture Leys lay next to a 'heath ground' called Hackleton Furzes and reached to Denton Lane.[42]

There were thorns on the Wold at Catesby in 1389[43] and in 1461 *ridon* furlong was said to abut the Wolde Pasture[44]. The extensive Wold of Burton Latimer produced furze and thorns that were stinted, in 1635, allowing 120 faggots for a yardland, 60 for an ancient cottage and 30 for a newly erected cottage. Furze was cut from October to December in readiness for winter fires.[45] The furze growing on Crick Wold was assigned to named people in *c.*1640.[46] Denton court rolls of 1737

Figure 22. An extract from the St Andrew's Priory map of 1632 showing cattle grazing on the commons within the open fields. (NRO Map 4671).

Figure 23. An extract from the St Andrew's Priory map of 1632 showing labourers in the arable fields. The blocks of furlongs are delineated and in the foreground the strips are also shown with labourers ploughing, sowing and harrowing. (NRO Map 4671).

ordered that no one was to cut furze on the common except those who could show at a vestry what (stint) they may cut.[47] At Orlingbury it was noted in *c.*1808 that poor inhabitants immemorially had the privilege of cutting bushes, furze or thorns on 15 acres of land called the Wold and carried them 'on their backs and not otherwise,'[48] thus restricting the quantity taken.

Arable fields

The principal medieval land use away from the woods was an expanse of arable fields consisting of strips grouped into furlongs (Figures 23 and 25). Early-modern strips are, or were, familiar as ridge and furrow, preserved in some grass fields unchanged since enclosure. They are now largely erased by modern agriculture to the east of Northampton. Extensive examples are still to be found (2010) at Sutton Bassett, Weston-by-Welland and Braunston. More information on ridge and furrow of various types is given below.

The medieval atlas gives for the first time a record of the open-field pattern for a whole county (with the complimentary data from *Rockingham*) and provides an opportunity to study its physical form from a geographical viewpoint. The lay-out of township field systems are to a certain extent influenced by their boundaries (commonly streams or watersheds) and by the internal drainage pattern of slades and brooks (Figures 24 and 25). Drainage is determined by the relief, hence on the higher ground west of Northampton furlong patterns tend to be broken into small areas with groups of strips aligned in many directions to drain downslope. The fractured pattern is well illustrated by the hilly ground south of Daventry (details in the medieval atlas) and brought out by the absence of furlong alignments north of Northampton as well as south of Daventry (Figure 26).

East of Northampton, as the land-surface flattens out, furlong patterns are more regular, with near rectangular parts. Some planar landscapes have a fairly simple form, where strips of several furlongs lie in the same alignment (ignoring the slight 'reverse-S' curvature) draining to a river or dominant slade. This has been previously pointed out for Raunds and Wollaston.[49] Publication of the north-eastern quarter of the county showed that such alignments were widespread on the slopes in the Welland and Nene Valleys, with one example (at Wadenhoe) where 12 furlongs make up an alignment of 2,500m.[50] There are many more alignments discernible elsewhere in the county. Figure 26 illustrates the location of townships where there are more than three adjacent furlongs having their component strips in the same general alignment. In 10 townships there are as many as 8 to 13 such aligned furlongs. Some of them are nearly straight and others are curved (see the atlas pages for clearer detail at the 1:25,000 scale).

The conclusion to be drawn from these examples

would seem to be that large blocks of strips have been laid out on a single occasion before being divided into smaller units – the furlongs. It might alternatively be considered that such a pattern was achieved by first having a small set of inner furlongs and later adding blocks of strips, maintaining the same alignment. However, a model of this type would require a long-term manorial or communal control. The improbability of such a mechanism is indicated by those alignments that are curved, like Maxey or Astrop. Smooth curves running for up to 1000m created piecemeal could only be achieved by the use of surveying equipment, not available until many centuries after open fields developed. To the farmers who were ploughing strips in a given furlong, it mattered nothing what was the physical lay-out of the strips in adjacent furlongs, so long as it did not cause drainage problems; a series of furlongs lying in a curved line served no agricultural purpose.

Figure 24. An extract from the St Andrew's Priory map of 1632 showing the wide strip of pasture either side of the stream. The furlongs are also carefully delineated against the pasture. Sheep are grazing both the pasture and the fallow, closely monitored by a shepherd and dog. (NRO Map 4671).

Field systems with very long strips can be found elsewhere in the country, most notably Yorkshire.[51] Some can be conveniently viewed on satellite or photographic vertical images available on-line. The area around Pickering is a particularly striking, where long strip fields are preserved as present-day field boundaries, forming curves up to 1,200m in length.

Roman and earlier field systems, as recorded by cropmarks, generally have little relation to the furlong patterns. Early fields are not nearly so extensive and for the most part make up patterns more akin to the crofts of medieval villages than to the rolling acres of medieval furlongs. Furthermore, furlong patterns do not form coherent systems of fields in the sense of being a network of enclosures. The plan of Kislingbury and Rothersthorpe furlongs with the strips removed emphasises this (Figure 27). Completely enclosed 'rectangular' structures are very few and it is to be

Figure 25. Ridge and furrow, heads and headlands at Kilsby. The grouping of strips into furlongs is clearly seen and of note is the pasture associated with the stream in the centre of the picture which can be compared to that depicted on the map on Figure 24. (NCCAP SP5571/001 © Northamptonshire County Council).

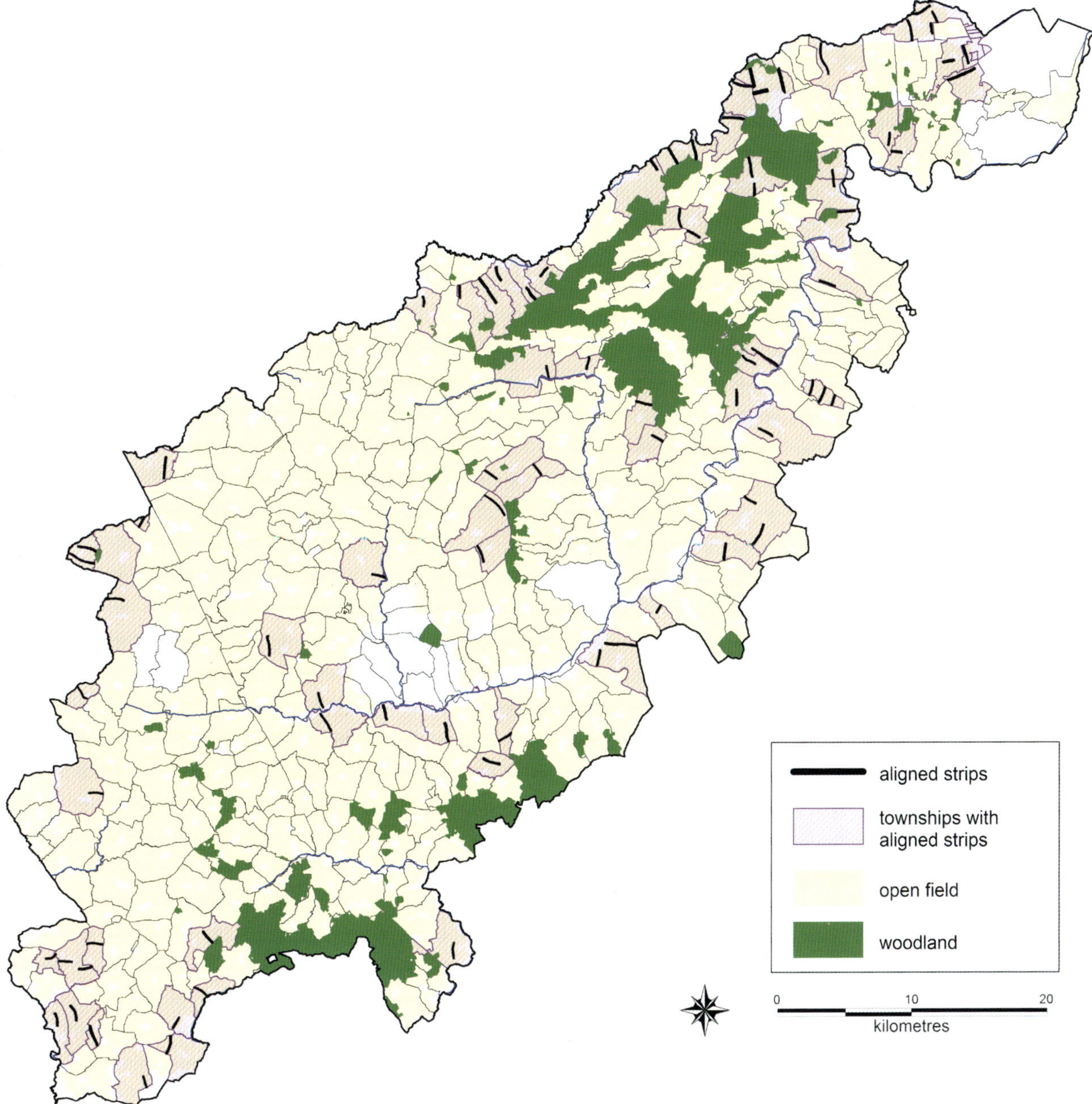

Figure 26. Location of townships having four or more adjacent furlongs with strips on the same alignment.

concluded that an 'enclosed' boundary system was not the objective of those who created furlongs.

One of the few cases where a furlong pattern does seem to be influenced by a Roman site, is at Lutton, TL 1119 8700. The near-flat landscape has furlongs with large blocks of strips, but by contrast, in one area where Roman pottery occurs on the surface, cropmarks of paddock ditches are coincident with a complicated set of small furlong boundaries (slight soil banks) in five instances (Figure 28).

Open-field farming operations and internal tenurial structure of Northamptonshire have been fully discussed (1995), with some updates given in 2009[52] and detailed studies made for Watford and Aynho.[53] Only a brief summary is necessary.

The smallest unit was a strip, called a *land* commonly of a rood or half an acre in area, set out in blocks called *furlongs*. Furlongs were grouped into areas called *fields*, which usually formed the basis of an agricultural rotation system. A farm was called a *yardland* and consisted of about 60 strips scattered throughout the field system. The county falls into Gray's 'classic' Midland area with two- and three-field systems, recorded from an early date.[54] A study of 270 townships made in 1995 showed that two or three fields were the predominant type. In the 15th century, there were 45 townships with open-field information, of which 12 were two-field (27%), 31 three-field (69%) and two had complex fields. By the 18th century, a total of 161 townships were still open

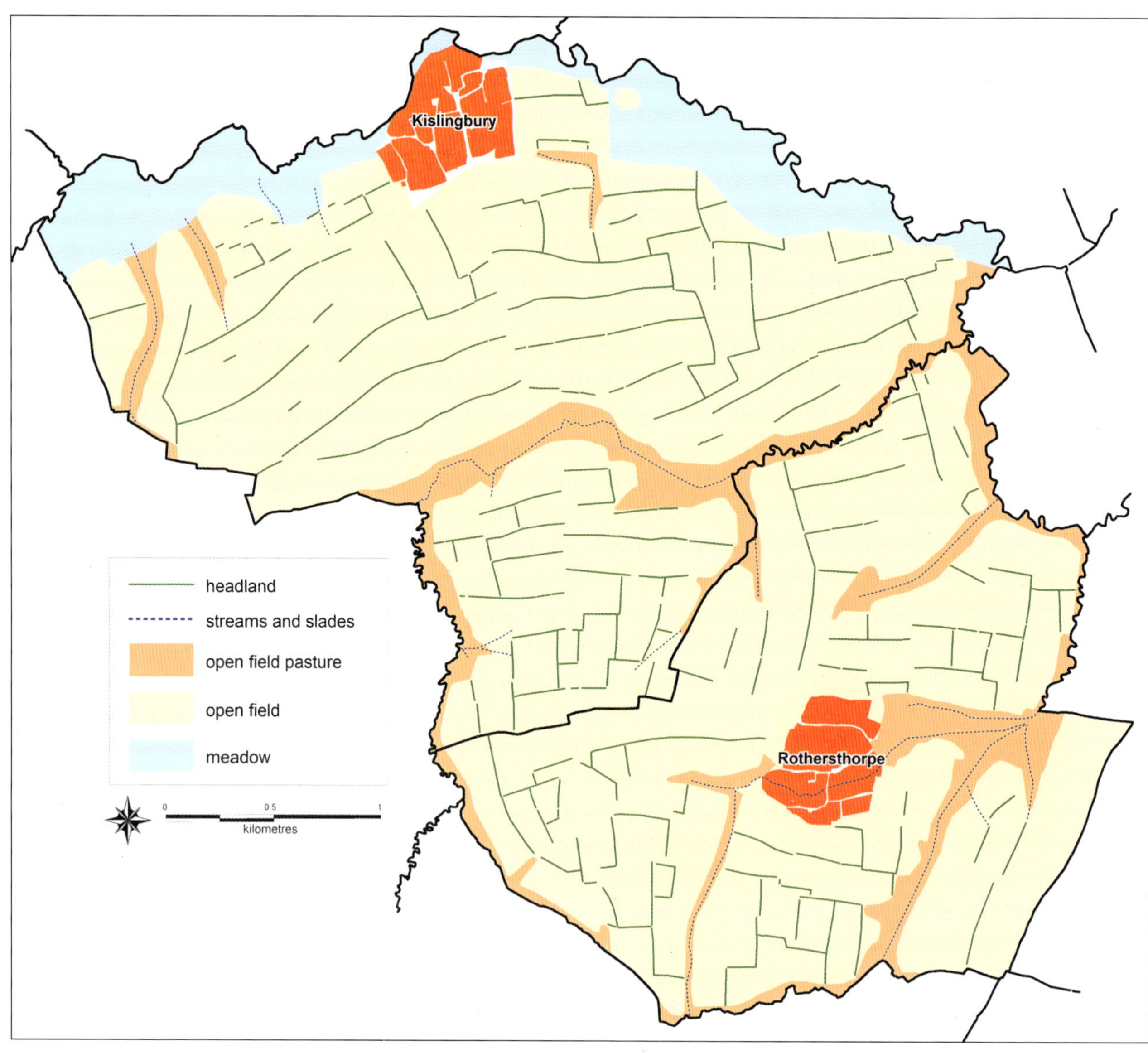

Figure 27. Kislingbury and Rothersthorpe furlong pattern.

and comprised 11 two-field systems (7%), 120 three-field (75%) and 30 with more than three fields.[55]

The fields were made up of the demesne (the manorial 'home farm') and the lands of the tenants, the former villeins or customary holders. Demesnes were mostly dispersed throughout a field system, but a third of them lay in a block near to the manor-house. The yardland farms of the tenants were always dispersed and in many cases there is ample evidence for a regular assignment of lands in the fields, so that each tenant would always have the same two neighbours. The agricultural operation of the fields, regulating important matters such as the date when a stubble field should be ploughed and the number of animals allowed for each yardland, was run by the manorial court. Where lordship was divided or when distant lords took no local interest, the fields were run by the village community, as the contents of several parish chests demonstrate.

A discussion of the dating and possible origins of intermixed, subdivided fields, as seen from the Northamptonshire evidence, was presented in 1995. The theme of open-field origins continues to be of much national interest and debate.[56] It has recently been further considered in a review of historical and other types of evidence collected from the whole country.[57]

The recent account does not need to be reiterated, except to say that among the many pieces of relevant evidence, this atlas provides two for Northamptonshire in detail, since they result directly from the fieldwork undertaken to map the medieval fields. First, the widespread occurrence of furlongs with aligned strips as explained above, has the implication that there had been an early initial layout of planned fields on the large scale. The second piece of fieldwork evidence is the identification of many Early and Middle Saxon sites, the locations of which are marked on the medieval atlas. It can be seen that many of

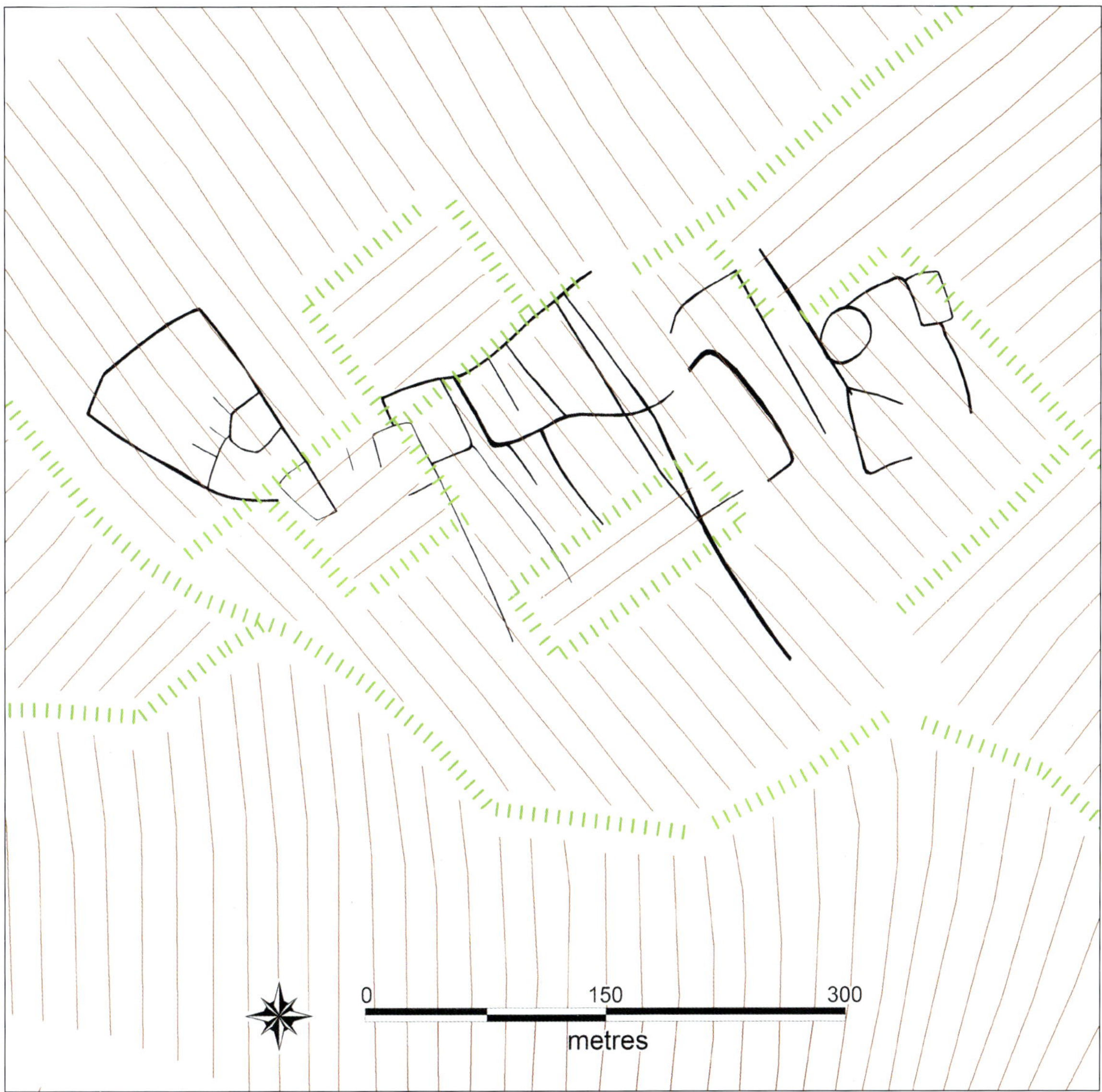

Figure 28. Lutton furlongs and coincident cropmarks (NMP). Headlands are green stippled lines, and cropmarks (of ditches) are black.

them lie away from the medieval villages and are overlain by open field furlongs and strips. It therefore follows that extensive medieval strip fields are not earlier than about the 7th century and may be as late as the early ninth century. These observations, taken with the numerical relationships often found to occur between the number of medieval yardlands in a township and Domesday taxation assessments, leads to the conclusion that many of the field systems date somewhat before 1066.

Field system case studies

The interesting overlapping field systems of Aynho have been published, adding to the information given in 1995.[58] Another complicated field system not described in the 1995 catalogue is that of Cosgrove and Furtho. The fields of the two settlements (plus the deserted Temple End) formed a single township, even though each had a church. The fields and strips that owed tithes to the two churches were intermixed, as proved by an analysis of furlong names. Potterspury church also received tithes from about a third of Furtho and Cosgrove fields, but Potterspury field system was quite separate. An area called Kenson Field, lying west of the A5 opposite to Potterspury, was part of the combined Furtho and Cosgrove township and probably in early times was a piece of woodland, being a larger Brownswood (Maps 77–78 M and 77–78 EM). Furtho and Cosgrove furlongs were arranged into three great fields by *c.*1290 and in 1364 and 1418.[59]

An area around Furtho village, mainly manorial demesne, was enclosed in 1571–2. The closes involved can be determined from Furtho Tithe Map of 1850.[60] The map is titled 'Furtho parish', but it is neither parish nor township. The parish boundary of the township against Passenham ran down the A5 to the River Ouse[61] and so included the eastern part of Old Stratford, which was never a separate parish or a township. After Furtho enclosure, Cosgrove maintained three equal-sized fields in the remaining open land.[62]

The medieval atlas provides a map for every township in the county, other than urban areas where the evidence has been destroyed. It has a wide variety of uses for landscape studies. The availability of furlong maps makes possible detailed analyses of historical documents. Only a few places have open-field maps, but many have copious historical records that describe fields – particularly useful are written surveys or fieldbooks.[63] The combined physical and written evidence can be used to elucidate detailed field and manorial demesne structure. The first stage in the process is to identify the furlongs, which is done by collecting their names and abuttals from terriers, compiling a list of enclosed field names and relating the information to the furlong plan. The procedure has been described elsewhere.[64]

Three worked examples of township field studies are given here to illustrate the potential of furlong plans and written data. Two have interesting block demesnes (Crick and Helmdon) and the third (Denton) shows the 17th-century disposition of intermixed estates referred to in the Domesday Survey of 1086, which indirectly demonstrates there was a dispersed demesne.

Helmdon

Helmdon has no contemporary open-field plan, but it does have a wealth of medieval and later historical records, most notably held by Magdalen[65] and Worcester Colleges, Oxford, the Biddlesden Abbey cartulary and the Ferrers Collection (Leicester CRO) which contains the archive of the Lovetts and Shirleys of neighbouring Astwell.

Helmdon manorial descent is complicated; the outline can be followed using the information given by Bridges and Baker[66] and from the muniments of Worcester College. The chief manor was Overbury near the church overlooking the village, still surrounded by a paddock with substantial banks.

Helmdon, assessed at four hides in 1086, descended to Simon de Montford and remained in the overlordship of the Honor of Leicester (later part of the Duchy of Lancaster). The family of Turville were local possessors in the early 12th century and until 1315 when Helmdon passed to the Lovett family by marriage. Nicholas de Turville granted property to his daughter Sarah, wife of Robert Lovett in 1315 and in 1317 granted 97½ acres of land,[67] which was demesne, as shown by the given furlong names. The manor was called Overbury by 1365 and remained with the Lovetts until about 1500. In 1513 it was in the hands of Thomas More and descended in about 1547 to his two daughters who sold it in 1548 to George Brown of Falcutt and his son John, although Alice Neale, daughter of Thomas More, held a manorial court in 1559.

Overbury remained with the Brown family. A George Brown held a court in 1628 and died in 1656. John, his son, married Catherine Morrell of Alston, Warks, in 1662 where they resided. He entered into many mortgages with London mercers and lawyers from 1657 to 1695, as well as with local people. He failed to pay interest and an early mortgager was Thomas Tite, a London merchant, who held a Helmdon court as lord in 1679. Thomas Lister of Whitfield was also involved by 1679 and John Gore, tailor, of Towcester, another mortgager, was described as lord in 1701, but he sold it to Thomas Lister in 1702. Charles Holt held the manor, purchased in 1721 from Barbara Lister who was married to his son Clobery and in 1723 his widow Anne Holt sold it to Worcester College, Oxford. The College sold the manor to C. A. Bartlett in 1908.[68]

Overbury manor became divided into three parts and the 11 virgates of land given to Biddlesden Abbey before 1227 made a fourth part; it was called a grange in *c.*1300. The grange had lands in *buryfeld*[69] and the abbot claimed a court at Helmdon in 1329. A court of survey of 1389 stated there were 3¼ free yardlands and 8½ villein, sum 11¾, agreeing with the 1227 grant.[70]

The manors called Middlebury and Netherbury were always subordinate to Overbury, there being no simple division into three or four equal parts. Middlebury, referred to in 1511, was held of Thomas More by Richard Crispe. In 1528 Augustin Crisp conveyed to one Brown (presumably the later the lord of Overbury) a capital messuage, 4½ yardlands and Crispe's Stockings. Netherbury or Copes manor, subordinate to the Turvilles was mentioned in 1420, held from Robert Lovett of Overbury. Anne Cope held it in 1518 (of Thomas More) and was the wife of Thomas Heneage in 1532. It was sold to John Fountaine in 1579 and passed to the Emily family of Helmdon.

The 1530 Biddlesden Abbey survey stated that 'Master Moor was lord of Overbury, Master Hennege lord of Netherbury and Master Gryfyn lord of the Minicourte'. Robert Gryfyn was one of the jury who made the survey and was probably tenant to Thomas Crispe, then stated to be 'of Northampton'. Robert was bailiff of Overbury in 1535.[71] A court of survey made in 1628 referring to Elizabethan court rolls noted that John Fountaine held 14 yardlands and Augustin Crispe 7 yardlands in *c.*1560.[72] The Biddlesden abbey land lying in the demesne had Messrs Crispe, Hennege and More as the chief possessors of neighbouring strips, confirming that the land was still in possession of the three manorial lords.

The Biddlesden Abbey survey of its possessions is the most useful single document relating to the fields, giving a long detailed terrier made in 1530.[73] It names all the furlongs with abuttal information, which have been supplemented by other abuttals and details from terriers of both earlier and later date. The results are plotted on Figure 29 and the furlong names and abuttals are given in Table 3.

Biddlesden owned both demesne (in Bury Field) and former villein fields (the Town Fields). In 1530 there were two great fields, the North and South with

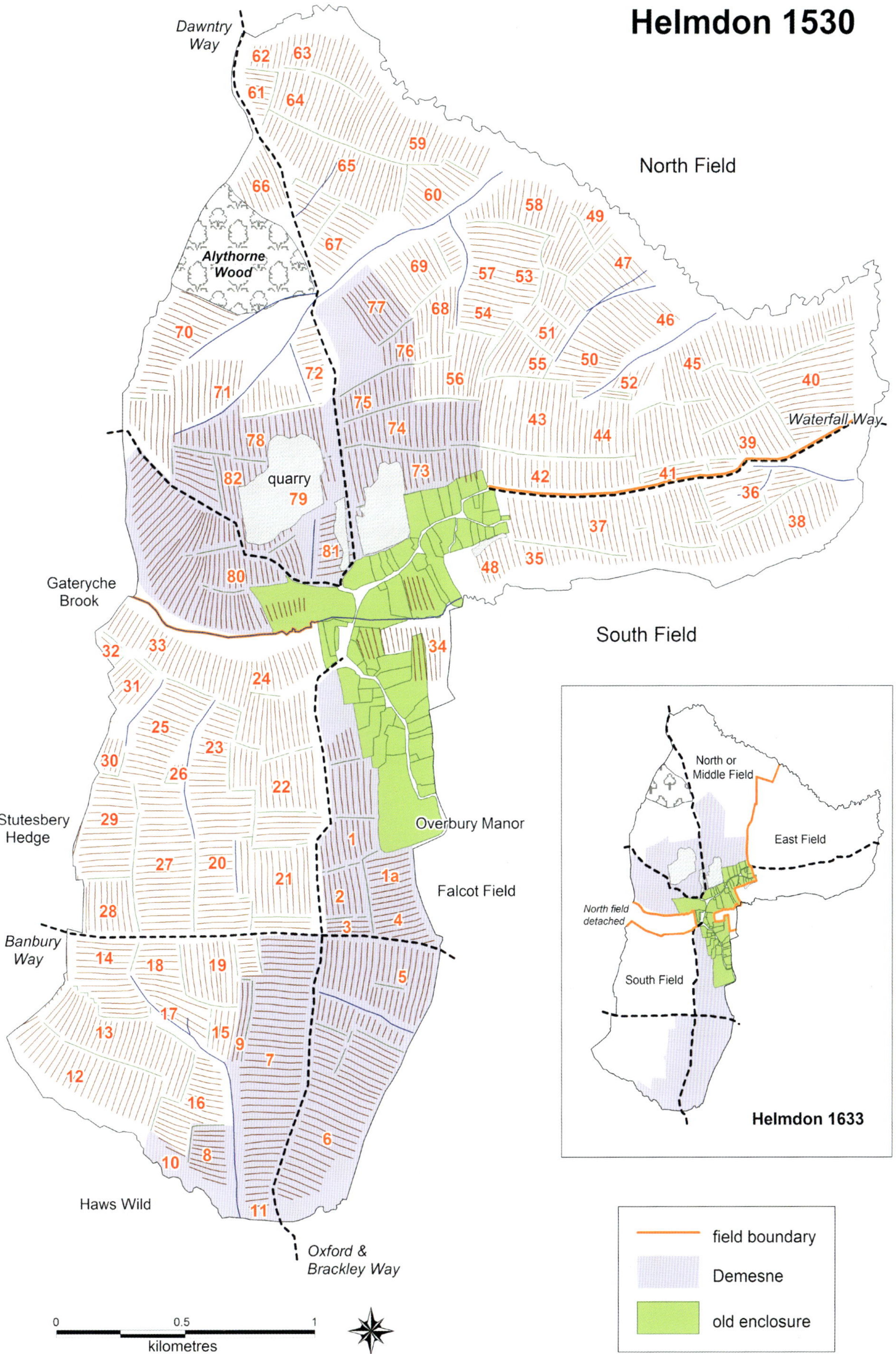

Figure 29. Helmdon open fields in 1530 showing the demesne. Broken black lines are roads; old enclosure and Alithorn Wood are as in 1759.

Beryfelde within Southfelde; Buryfeld ***c*****.1300** (Magd. Ch. Helmdon 26)	
1	Copedmore with lands lying north and south (NS).
1a	Under fatlande f[urlong], EW, next to copedmore.
2	Fattlande fg NS, abuts Falcott Feld [furlong], next to Oxford way.
3	Furlong at end of windmill hil, EW; binethewindmulne 1317; wynemylhylle next to Brackley way 1457.
4	Furlong shooting Falcot Feld, EW, begin at the hedge/boundary next Helmdon.
5	Wollan f. NS, near cross, abuts Banbury way, abuts a headland, has pikes.
6	Marsthill f. EW, abuts Oxford way; mersehulle next road to Banbury 1317.
7	Halywell f. EW, abuts Oxford way, abuts halywell meadow; aylwelleforlong 1317.
8	Farnhill f. EW, abuts a headland [HL], abuts farenslade; farnehulle 1317.
9	Fareslade f. NS, has HL of marsthill [*recte* halywell?] f. on E.
Meadow of Beryfeld in Southfelde	
10	Blackpitt NS, abuts Hawse Wild; black pits FN.
11	Halywell meyde, EW & NS to the brook.
Town Feld	
12	[no name], NS, near Hawse Wild, has thorotak [throughland?]; shooting into Haulse hedge & abuts hartwell 1664.
13	Longhertwell f. NS, near Stuttesbury hedge; hertwellelongge 1357 NS, abuts Halswelde [f.[12]]; 1396; longhertwell NS, abuts le yeldfeld and near Halse feeld 1457; G; short hartwell 1664; long hartwell FN.
14	Eynfeld f. EW, abuts Stuttesbury hedge next to Banbury way, has forschewter part rightly called scherterswell; helden feild G.
15	Town farnhill f. NS, on E a HL towards halowfareslade f.; townefarnehyll NS, G; farnill NS 1664.
16	Halowfareslade f. EW, at head of townfarnhill.
17	Under redland f. EW, HL on S; G.
18	Gorebrode f. EW, abuts eynfeld; gorebroad EW 1664; gores FN.
19	Redland f. NS, HL on west, abuts Banbury way; redelond 1317; redlands FN.
20	Helmdon feld f. EW, Banbery way S, abuts litelflatland; Helmdon hill EW,G &1664.
21	Litelflatland f. NS, HL of Helmdon feld fg W, abuts a forschewter [on Helmdonfeld f.]; G; fatlands FN.
	[South of 21] Windmill hill EW, Banbury way S, G.
22	Lowsymoor f. NS, abuts forschewter in Helmdon feld f.; losedonmor near the king's highway 1317.
23	Gorsse f. EW, forschewt S, abuts lowsymoor; gorse G.
24	Kulmeyde f. NS, abuts gaterychebrook; culls mead G; ? meadow on kane f. 1664.
25	Furlong between moors, EW; the moors FN.
26	Tow slade f. NS, abuts towslade; toweslade G; towslade NS 1664.
27	Middle f. EW; middle G; waterfurrows; 1664 and FN.
28	Awinstow f. NS, near awinstow way, abuts Banbury way; aunstowe G; haulmstraw FN.
29	Stowtnamfeld f. EW, abuts Stutesbery hedge; G; stoutmans hill FN.
30	Brodemoor f. NS, abuts forschewter in stowtnam feld.
31	Hassok f. NS, abuts brodemoor f., abuts gaterychbroke; hassocle G; gutteridge brook NS 1664; furze ground FN.
32	Mylne f. EW, abuts Stutesbery hedge, hedge also on S.
33	Stokwell f. NS, abuts HL on S; ? gutteridge brook NS 1664 (or 24); gateridge brook NS, G; gatteridge FN.
Townfeld in the eest side which is parcell of ye Southfeld	
34	First haste f. NS, part abuts Falcot feld, & part ryge way; ast forlong 1357; astforlong NS 1418; *id.* abuts le ridgewey & reaches estbroke 1457.
35	Followeth hast f. NS, abuts HL'between' waterfall way.
36	Whytmore f. EW, waterfall way N, HL of brodhalffacars fg S; long & short whitmore NS, G.
37	Brodhalffacars f. NS, abuts leydole meyde; broad half acres NS, G & 1664.
38	Fox holes f. NS, abuts leydole meyde, abuts the boundary/hedge of Astwell & Astwell park, ley teythe meyde E.

Furlongs west of 81 and 82 not named in 1530 terrier.

Sources. The table is based on Bittlesden terrier and survey of Helmdon, 1530 (Magdalen CP8/30), plus Magdalen Helmdon charters; 1317 ch. 68; 1357 ch. 49; 1407 ch. 48; 1418 ch. 75; 1457 ch. 46 (full abstracts of these charters are available on Helmdon village website).

1664 Terrier (two copies), Worcester College, Oxford, Helmdon Boxes 5 and 12.
G Glebe terriers at NRO dated 1633 and 1704, Box X588.
FN Fieldname map 1932, which gives locations, at NRO.

Table 3. Helmdon furlong names.

North Feld	
39	Beyn hill f. NS, buts wytmore, [*separate entry*], buts waterfall; south bean hill G; beane hill NS 1664; north beanland FN.
40	Waterfall f. EW, buts witmor.
41	Over waterfall EW, buts flyrtland; G.
42	Flyrtland NS, buts last; on W is the abbot's Ashcroft, near the village.
43	Longland f. NS, abuts flyrtland; G; langlands FN.
44	Womanland f. NS, abuts flyrtland; *id.* NS, G & 1664.
45	Northwell f. NS, abuts HL; northwell G, NS 1664.
46	Harepyttes f. NS, abuts northwell.
47	Northleyn hill f. NS, abuts meydeland.
48	Halffe yerdes f. NS, buts mylne dyckes, near village.
49	Styrt f. NS, butting on Weston brooke; stirts G.
50	Harpe or gormeyde f. EW.
51	Sheydeland f. NS; [*same as?*] shortland; schottelond 1401; shortland NS, G & 1664.
52	Lytele gryntall f. NS, last a HL at the head of womanland EW; little grintwell NS 1664.
53	Eyst breche f. EW; east breach G; bretch FN.
54	Hyll f. & hulle f. EW, 1st is a HL with greneway S; hill G.
55	Hangynge land f. NS, greneway W; hangere 1317.
56	Fyrst pytt f. NS, tursteputte 1317.
57	Weste breche f. EW; west breach G; breach EW 1664.
58	Stoke f. butting into Weston broke, NS; stoke f. EW & Weston brook NS,1664.
59	Long whytmore f. NS.
60	Dunstall f. EW; dunstable G; *id.* EW 1664.
61	Shorte whytemor f. EW.
62	Gyllruntre f. NS, last a HL at head of the same fg, Dawntre way W.
63	Swynsmore f. NS; le dene 1407; swynesworth abutted by deane NS & reaches stokebroke 1457; swinesmore G.
64	Whytlonde f. butt on swynsmore northwarde, NS, 3 lands are near to cattanger E.
65	Whytelond leys f. NS, land near to dunstall f. E.
66	Whytlond next alythorne, NS, 1st next alithorne, next Dawntree way.
67	The furlong under walworth buts into fleknell, NS; walworth 1401.
68	Walworth f. NS; under wallworth, breache f. E, G.
69	Hawtroghe f. NS, last land has furstpytway W; hawthorn G.
70	Under Alithorne f. EW & goodwynsthorne EW, abuts Sulgravefeld & reaches stayntwell f. 1418 &1457; under Alithorn G.
71	Steynwell alias lylmede longeland f. NS, stayntwellfurlong next goodwynsthorne EW; stantwell G.
72	Akermans hyll f. EW; ack'mans hill G. akermans hill EW 1664.
Bery felde in ye Northfelde	
73	Lytle fge buts on ye ashe closs of ye abbot, NS, ley hedge way E, furstpytway W; ?litiepece to scortehawetrourugwey 1317.
74	Eest quary f. NS; ?staindelf pece 1317.
75	Rugly knoll f. NS, next close of abbot, quary f. E; roweknolle 1317.
76	Bery walworth f. NS, furstpyte way E 1317.
77	Bery Halltrough f. NS; scortehawtrou next thorsputweye 1317; buryhavvetrough NS abuts havvetroughwey & reaches roughknolle 1457.
78	Thornetlete f. Dauntre way E; thorniled 1317.
79	Knoll hyll f. NS, 1st land abuts rygeway N; the furlong abuts rygway.
80	Marewell f. NS, last pieces are abbatts thornes; marewellehulle 1317.
81	marewellehulle 1317; marrowell FN.
82	Steyntwell f. NS, last land HL, stentwell butts E; ? stanwelleforlong 1317.
Meadow of beryfeld	
83	Milnedykes EW, doles; near 48.
84	Meydlande, NS, doles; near 47.
85	Northwell, EW, has a stone mete, doles, N of 45.
86	Gore meyde, near 50.
87	Catang EW, doles; 45.

Table 3. Helmdon furlong names continued.

both types of land divided equally between them. The large demesne was centred in a block on the Overbury manor next to the church. It ran to the southern township boundary and extended a long way towards the north. The quarries of Helmdon stone all lay within the demesne and reference to *furstpyte way* (1530) as *thorsputweye* in 1317 attests to the medieval date of the quarries.[74] The 1317 charter was a grant by Robert Lovett of 97½ acres and the 24 recorded furlong names, when related to the 1530 terrier, show it to be a grant of demesne. This is not stated in the document, but hinted at because some of the parcels consisted of groups of 6–13 selions whereas villein land would have lain in single strips.

Helmdon stone quarries and the buildings it served have been described by Parry[75] and there is a fine panel of stained glass in the church showing quarryman William Campiun wielding an axe to break stone in 1313.[76] Additional quarrying evidence comes from a grant of half an acre of land in 1699 to William Lord Lempster who paid £55 'for half acre of stone pitt or quarry in Helmdon ... for 7 years for the raising of stones with ingress and regress.[77] The stone was used to build Easton Neston House.[78]

Helmdon was the 'barony' seat for the south-western part of the lands of the Honor of Leicester in Northamptonshire. In the 17th century, business was mainly concerned with collecting fixed rents and recording the names of tenants owing suit of court in each village. A few open field items were noted. Each Helmdon yardland could have 4 cows and 20 sheep (1548) and the common pound needed mending (1551). In 1553 the Tove bridge needed repair and in 1674 a horse trespassed in the peas field and was impounded by the Hayward.[79]

The two fields described in 1530 had been divided into three by 1633 which remained until enclosure in 1759.[80] In 1633 they were called South Field, North or Middle Field and East Field. Leys had been introduced and amounted to 17% in 1744.[81] The named furlongs do not include any of the demesne furlongs, showing that the glebe was former 'town land'. A terrier of a half yardland made in 1664 referred to land in the North, Middle and South Fields,[82] was also 'townland' from the absence of demesne furlong names. The yardland size was 20 acres with 20% ley. The division of the Bury Fields after 1530 is not known.

The 1530 survey shows that the demesne was very elongated. The names of the three late manors suggest they lay one below the other and must therefore have been sited along Church Street, being restricted to the narrow belt of demesne. Hence the late manorial split is unlikely to account for the complicated village plan of Helmdon, with much of it lying along the Wappenham Road. It is probable that the two main parts relate to two adjacent settlements; one belonging to the manor and the other to the tenants.

Denton

The manorial structure of Denton was unusual in that one hide was stated to belong to Yardley Hastings in the Domesday Survey of 1086.[83] This hide was very probably given to the keeper of Yardley Woods by analogy with Bernwood Forest, Oxfordshire. The Bernwood forester had a hide of arable land called the 'derhyde' in 1252, lying in the fields of Boarstall, Bucks.[84]

Yardley land lying in Denton was still called the Yardley Hide in 1704 and owed tithe to the rector of Yardley. The other land in Denton, formerly belonging to Ramsey Abbey, paid tithes to the church of the abbey's chief local manor at neighbouring Whiston. A Denton survey of the mid 17th century[85] can be related to an open-field map of 1760.[86] With additional information from a Denton glebe terrier of 1704, which details the Yardley Hide, it is possible to map its location (Figure 30).

Both sources are incomplete for some of the furlongs to the south of the village. The survey lists 856 lands in the Yardley Hide lying in 93 pieces, plus 11 more pieces with the number of lands not stated. The number of lands per piece ranges from 1–29, but the average is 9.2 lands, which is sufficiently near 10 to suggest that there were originally 10 lands per hide piece and that the variation had arisen by exchanges. The 1:10 ratio of Domesday hides and medieval yardlands has been found for many places in the county. At an average of 0.33 acres per land (as has been used for Figure 30) the total area would be 285 acres for 856 lands.

What is certain is that the Yardley Hide consisted of blocks of strips (lands) dispersed in all the furlongs, many of them containing 8–12 lands. Figure 30 shows that there was a fairly regular disposition of pieces in the 17th century. Without medieval terriers it cannot be certain that this was always the arrangement, but the unchanging nature of the intermixed monastic and Yardley estates makes it very likely that Figure 30 substantially represents the situation in 1086.

The accuracy of the 17th-century data is not sufficient to determine whether the blocks of strips were, or were not, aligned through several furlongs, as possible at the north-west in Whiston Field. This is because the survey records the number of 'lands' in each piece, but not their areas, hence widths are unknown. It is probable that blocks were aligned, which implies that the layout was very early, if the tenurial arrangement pre-dates the subdivision into furlongs.

The dispersion of the Yardley Hide shows that the remainder of Denton lands owing tithe to Whiston were likewise dispersed; they were called 'Whiston Hides' in the Compton Survey. They can be traced back to a grant to Ramsey Abbey made before 1029.[87] An interpretation that, in 1086, the Yardley Hide lay in a small core of arable that increased in size as the field system expanded to occupy most of the township

Figure 30. Denton open fields in 1760 showing the Yardley Hide distribution.

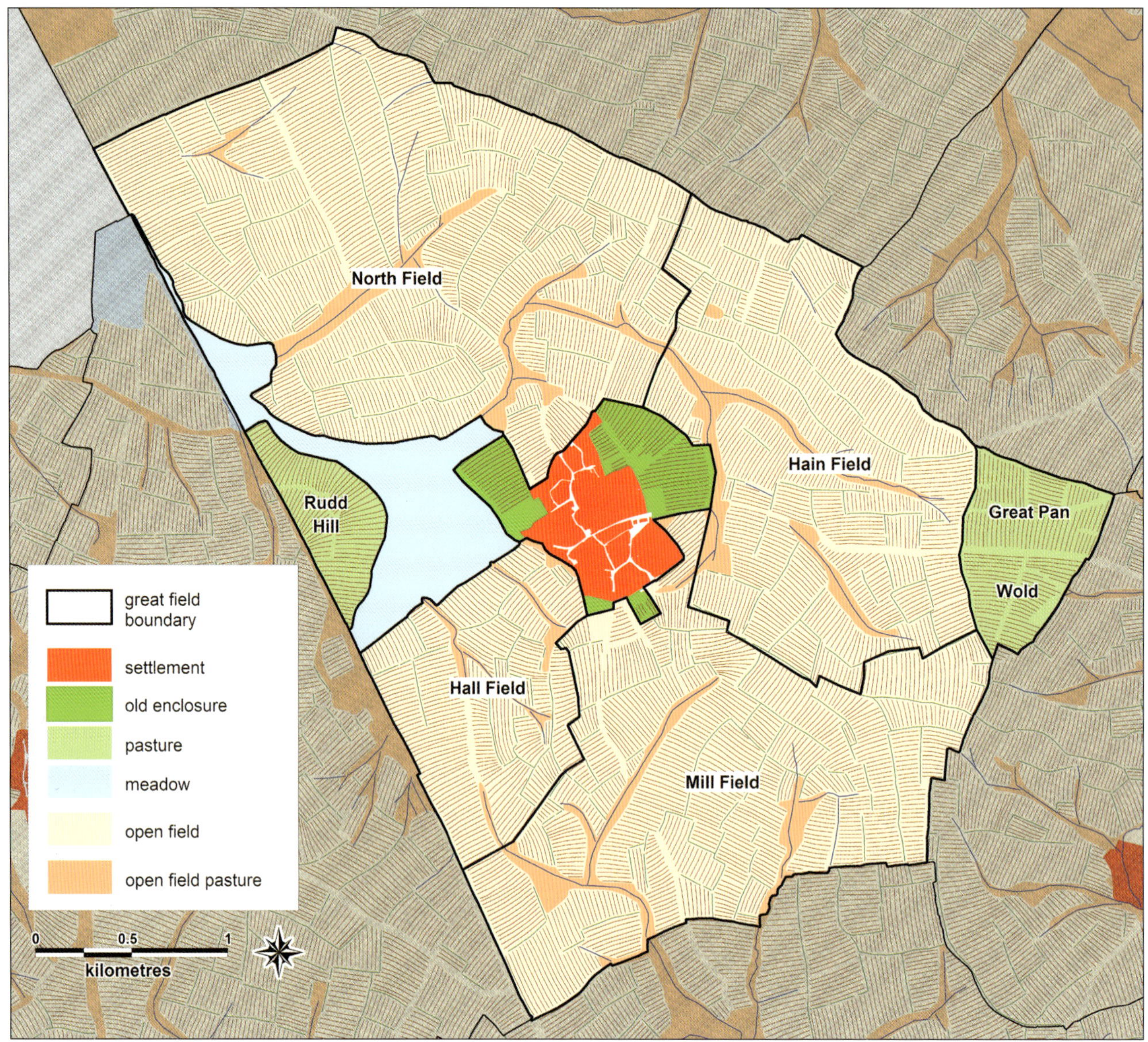

Figure 31. Crick open fields in 1776 showing the demesne and other great fields.

(Williamson *et al.* 2012), seems unlikely because intakes of the 12th century and later always seem to be severalty assarts, as discussed above. None of the Denton furlongs is named an assart.

Crick

Crick serves as another example of what can be deduced from documents, once a furlong map is available and the furlongs identified. It had a block demesne, the Hall Field and another discreet block of land called the Hain Field, i.e. the 'villeins' field' (Figure 31). Additionally there were two other open fields, making four in all, but they were run on a three-year cycle, as detailed in terriers from 1598 until enclosure in 1776.[88] There were two types of yardland, called Hall Land and Hain Land, in which the lands were restricted to only three of the four fields. The North and Mill Fields were common to both types of yardland and the third field was either the Hall Field or Hain Field, according to the type. The Hall and Hain fields are referred to in 1526 and the manorial structure shows that the arrangement can be traced to 1249. Crick has been used to develop a new theory of the open-field development in the Midlands and it is of interest to give a map showing the arrangement of these fields.[89]

Figure 31 shows the fields in 1776, reconstructed from data derived from terriers, the Quality Book, the reconstructed enclosure map and field names of 1839.[90] There was a nucleus of old enclosure around the village, meadows lying at the west and the four great open fields. A small area of furlongs called Rudhill on the far west had been put down as a common pasture before 1545; called a cow pasture in 1652.[91] High ground on the east, called the Wolds (by 1650) and Great Pen was also pasture in 1776. It is likely that the demesne originally included some of the village closes, since on the east there was a close called 'beddydike' (bury dike) and possibly Rudhill common had been demesne.

These three studies show the kind of detail that can be worked out for a township with extensive records. Each place yields one or more pieces of evidence that contributes to the national debate on the nature, origins and development of field systems and settlement.

Part of the Whittlewood area was investigated by Jones and Page.[92] It was primarily an investigation of settlement in part of the Whittlewood Forest region. The report comments on field systems, although no plans are given. Thus (p.94) 'there is nothing to suggest either the initial laying-out of long furlongs or their later subdivision'. Yet the atlas shows alignments of strips in several areas, for instance 6 furlongs east of Furtho and another 6 south of Deanshanger (Maps 78 M and 80 M) and smaller groups elsewhere.

The origin and extent of open fields was studied by the survival of pottery sherds in ploughsoil, assuming them to be derived by manuring (pp.92–3). This seems an uncertain method of assessment and makes the assumption that a), all the arable was manured with dung accumulated in byres, as well as by animals grazing freely and b), that domestic refuse containing pottery was consistently added to manure. Failure of either of these processes makes the procedure invalid. It is noted that St Neots Ware pottery sherds were not found out in the fields. This is as observed elsewhere in the county and beyond (Parry 2006, Fig. H compared with Fig. G). However, the soft shelly fabrics do survive winter frosts (sherds are found on many deserted village sites) and the conclusion is that in the 11th–12th century it was not the custom for domestic refuse to be added to manure heaps.

It is necessary to rectify an error about a small settlement lying south of Furtho identified as 'Knotwood'. The only reference given is the RCHM[93] where the source of the information is not given nor the place named. The stated location is at NGR SP 773 422. Jones and Page seem to have displaced this 500m to the south and claim it lay under a former Forest coppice called Knotwood (p.220). The extensive muniments of Furtho show that Knotwood was described as a coppice until grubbed up in the 17th century when it was converted to an enclosed pasture.

The settlement was actually called Temple End and lies in three main parts lying either side of a small brook and on a hollow way running from Furtho to Stony Stratford (Map 78 M) – called the 'great road' from Northampton to London which was 'stopped up' by Edward Furtho[94] when he made enclosures around Furtho in 1571–2.[95] The settlements lie at SP 7717 4236, SP 7715 4255 and SP 7730 4226, the first two not recorded by RCHM. In 1996 each had a dark area of soil yielding fragments of stone, domestic animal bone and much pottery of the 12–14th centuries. Temple End is named in many charters, such as one of 1334 dealing with a property transfer that refers to several messuages and gives a five-acre terrier of land and one acre of meadow 'in the fields of Cosgrove and Fortho'.[96]

Whiston Field	
1	Furlong under Hall hedge side
2	Furlong under Hall close hedge
3	Moor furlong
4	Flag doles
5	Barkers slade gate furlong
6	Spiney close furlong
7	Deep slade furlong
8	Furlong above deep slade on east side of Whiston way
9	Cross furlong
10	Furlong against Whiston hill
11	Whiston hill furlong
12	Whiston gate furlong
13	Furlong [at] end of the town headland
14	Brook furlong
15	Furlong from St Margaret's balk by Whiston way
16	Furlong east of the town headland
17	Long close pieces [two parts at right angles]
West Field	
18	Coopers hedge furlong
19	Banland furlong
20	Beryl mear furlong
21	Dale furlong
22	Fishers furlong
23	Brooks furlong
24	Little furlong
25	Cross furlong
26	Bartons hedge furlong
27	Spong furlong
28	Manse slade furlong
29	Mere slade furlong
Wood Field	
30	Carrian furlong
31	Books furlong
32	Whiston Pike furlong
33	Woodhill way furlong
34	Stone stile furlong
35	Hexley furlong
36	Furlong west of town headland
37	Stoney furlong
38	Moor hill furlong
39	Cross furlong
40	Foxholes furlong
41	Chadston Meer furlong

Source: Map and Survey 1760 by Eward John Eyre, Compton MS 1384, at Castle Ashby

Table 4. Denton furlong names.

Ridge and furrow

The survey that begat the mapping of all Northamptonshire medieval fields began with an interest

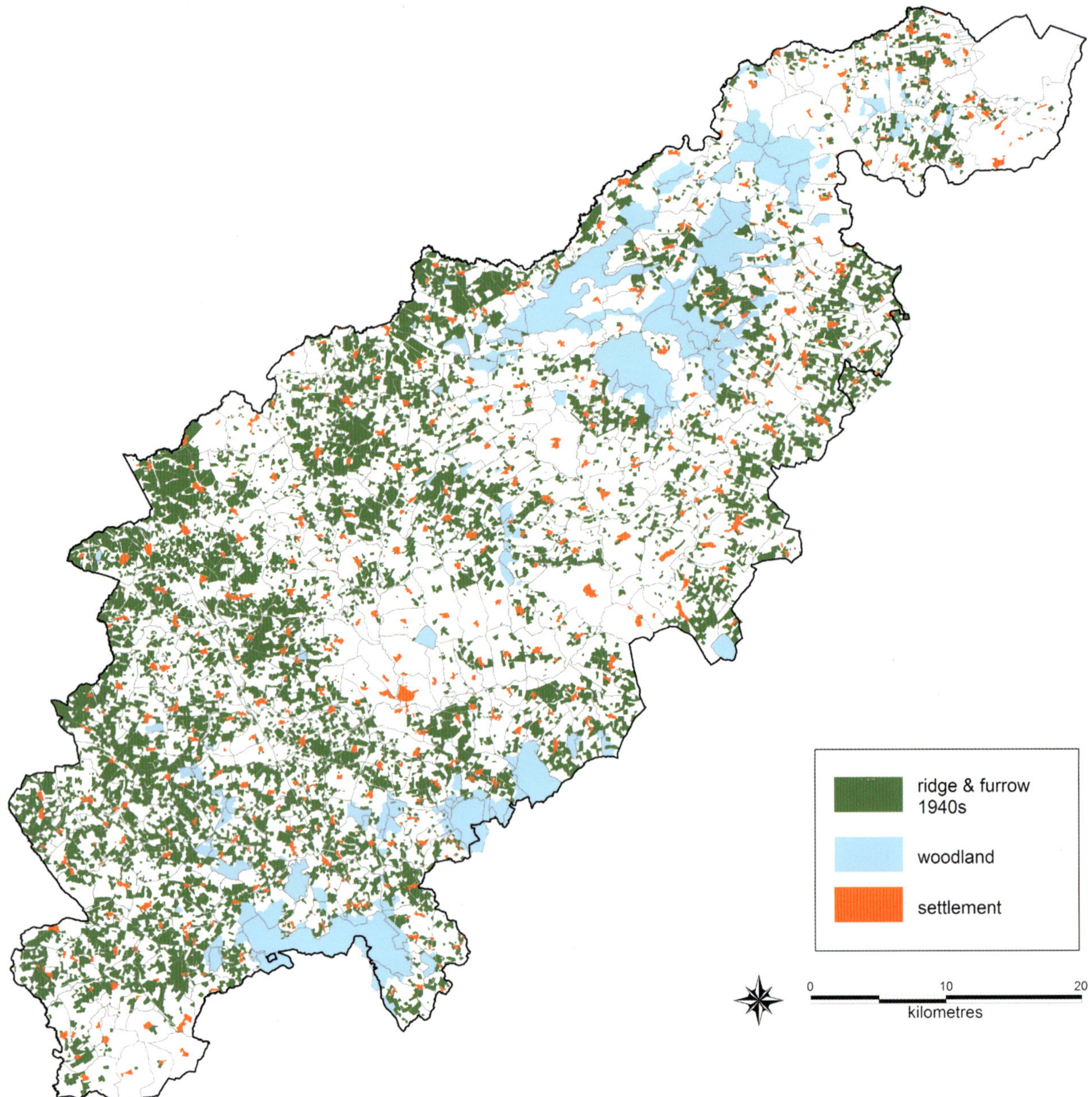

Figure 32. Ridge and furrow surviving in 1940, compiled from RAF vertical photographs.

in ridge and furrow – the 'fossilised' remains of late open fields abandoned at enclosure. In the course of the survey all surviving ridge and furrow was recorded. Early ridge and furrow is visible on vertical photographs taken in the late 1940s by the RAF.[97] Often, even clearer are the soilmarks of former ridges then recently ploughed-out under the auspices of the WarAg – the wartime authority that introduced a compulsory ploughing scheme to increase corn production. A combination of the two data types, supplemented in a few cases by field observation of ridges not visible on the 1940s photographs, has been made in Figure 32, giving the extent of ridge and furrow in 1940. Survival in the west of the county was extensive, especially at Crick, Lilbourne, Yelvertoft, Hellidon and Catesby. It shows that after enclosure large areas of the county were set down to permanent pasture, even though there had been much open-field arable during the early 18th century in unenclosed townships. The 1930s arable centred on good quality soils, especially those based on limestone at the north and far south and on the mixed soils north of Northampton and along the Nene and Ise Valleys. It must also have been the situation immediately after enclosure – the only difference possible being that there was even less arable in say 1830 than in 1930, but located in the same regions as here illustrated for the 1930s by the sparse amount of ridge and furrow.

In stark contrast is the small amount of ridge and furrow recorded on aerial photographs taken for

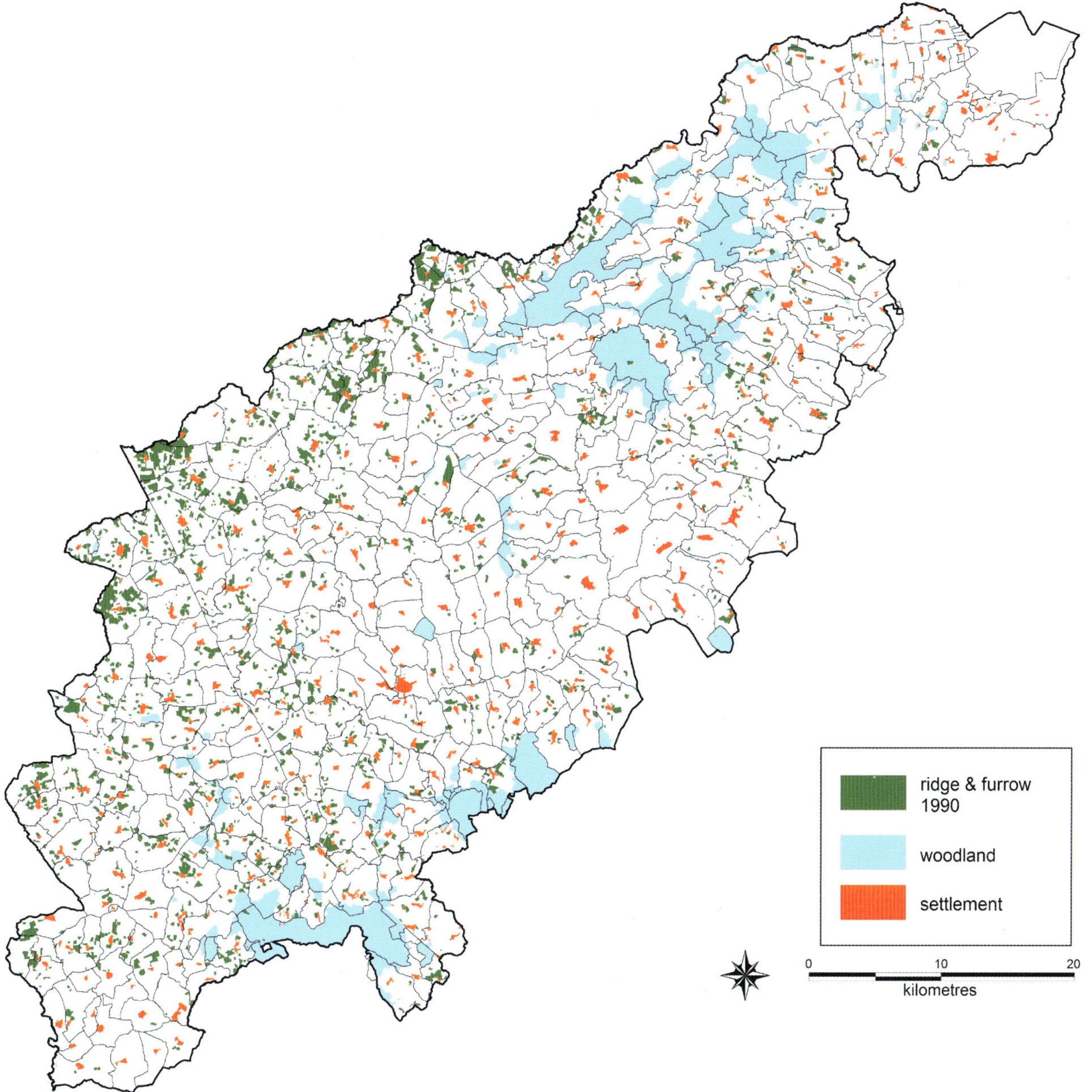

Figure 33. Ridge and furrow survival in 1990.

Northamptonshire County Council in 1990, Figure 33.[98] Yelvertoft, Braunston, Clipston and Sutton Bassett were then still good (and survived in 2000), but not many others. Ridge and furrow has no 'scheduled monument' protection rights and it is obvious from the immense destruction during the last 50 years that unless action is taken none will remain for future study. Farmers need making more aware – some have said they need not have ploughed out ridge and furrow, but they did not know it was of interest. Planners urgently need better training in conservation matters. One farmer sought planning permission for a new barn and the visiting officer asked why it was not to be placed next to the existing farm buildings. The owner explained that he expected destruction of ridge and furrow would not be allowed, to which the officer replied 'what's ridge and furrow?'

On the theme of ridge and furrow, it is necessary to distinguish between that which is remnant open-field strips held in dispersed ownership and cultivation ridges made by early-modern farmers as agricultural improvements. Ridges resulted when pastures were taken into arable before the development of underdraining with ceramic pipes (called 'tiles') in the 1830s. They were made for drainage, some ridges still being ploughed after 1830, since it was a cheap method. 19th-century cultivation ridges are typically straight and narrow, especially those made by steam ploughing, where a plough was winched across a field. Ridges newly ploughed in the 17th and 18th

Figure 34. Low profile 17th-century ridges in Handley Park, Towcester, dated after 1631 (© D. Hall).

Figure 35. 19th-century straight ridges at King's Cliffe, TL 011 992 in 1977 (now destroyed), dated after 1827 (Stephen G. Upex (Nene Valley Archaeological Trust, photo 1977/Y/23).

centuries can be wide and curved and so easily mistaken for open-field strips by the inexperienced.

Late cultivation ridges are still to be seen in northern counties at Durham, Teeside, Northumberland and Lancashire, where there were many large commons available for new arable intakes. Northamptonshire does not and did not have many examples of early-modern cultivation ridges, because, as the atlas shows, there were not many physical commons or wastes available. Further, the trend after 18th-century enclosures was to convert arable to pasture in many parts of the county, as proved by Figure 32. However several examples are of importance in that they can be dated.

Handley Park, Towcester (SP 67 47) was a detached part of Whittlewood Forest that had been converted to a park by 1236 and which had coppices and lawns until 1631 when it was sold, disparked and wood grubbed up.[99] Some of it was arable in the 1630s,[100] and Bridges[101] states that it had been arable before *c.*1720. By the time of the tithe map, made in 1849, the whole area was enclosed and used as pasture and arable (NRO, T134). Figure 34[102] shows broad, low-profile, curved ridges, datable to the 17th century.

Some wide straight ridges were made in the 19th century. A rectangular hedged-field at Naseby (SP 688 787) enclosed in 1820, is filled with straight ridges that do not conform with open-field ridge and furrow adjacent to it.[103] Figure 35 shows straight ridges 10m wide at King's Cliffe, TL 011 992, (now destroyed) on land that was part of a wooded coppice in Rockingham Forest in 1827 (marked on Bryant's county map), but pulled up before the Ordnance Survey map of 1885.

Narrow straight ridges near Thomas Wood (SP 636 443; visible on WEB images in 2011) lie on ground that was a seignurial coppice called Wappenham Wood, adjacent to Whittlebury Forest and still wooodland in 1761[104] but had been converted to agriculture by 1822.[105] At the deserted village of Onley (in Barby parish at SP 520 715), a published photograph shows narrow ridges lying over much of the village earthworks.[106]

The type of ridging described in the previous examples have profiles less than 'normal' open-field ridges and often the layout of blocks is disjointed, paying more attention to local microtopography for drainage purposes than to an organized overall plan. On the ground they 'look wrong'. The key physical indicator is the absence of soil transferred to heads and headlands, because they were ploughed for a short time compared to medieval ridges. Thus the 'headland' in the centre of Figure 34 is the same size as the other lands and the block of strips to its left has gaps at their ends, left for drainage. When ploughed flat late cultivation ridges survive as cropmarks and soilmarks for a few years and then disappear without trace.

4 Enclosure

Tracey Partida

Enclosed fields

The process of enclosure, whereby the open fields of the medieval period were gradually replaced by the patchwork of enclosures still evident today, began in Northamptonshire in the 15th century. The first township to be fully enclosed was Potcote in the south-west of the county in 1472. It took more than four hundred years to complete the process across the county with the final enclosure taking place at Sutton in the Soke of Peterborough in 1901.

A great deal has been written on the enclosure movement, both at a local and national level. Much academic debate generated over its consequences, particularly the social effects.[1] Whilst not disregarding this debate, the focus of this study is on the effects made on the landscape and on what survives in the landscape today. The process itself can be divided into two distinct phases; that which took place prior to the first act of Parliament in 1727, which is here considered as 'ancient', and that after 1727 which is described as the 'parliamentary period'. Enclosure, it has been suggested, created a man-made landscape.[2] But in Northamptonshire it can be argued that on the eve of enclosure there was not an inch of the county that was not already comprehensively managed. Management might differ between administrative units and landscape types, but all of the landscape had an economic value and was managed accordingly. This management applied to people as well as land, for movement within the landscape was controlled and prescribed according to who wanted to move where and for what reason.[3] It is important to consider these restrictions in order to understand the full impact that enclosure had on access to the land. It is especially important to remember that all land prior to enclosure was quasi-private in that it was owned by someone; communal farming did not mean communal ownership. Land that was open was not freely accessible. But before enclosure ownership of land did not necessarily entitle exclusive rights to it, whereas after enclosure it did. Prior to enclosure farming was communal and all proprietors had some say in how the system was managed. Enclosure ended the communal system and the dividing up and fencing of allotments was the ultimate communal activity in that it affected the whole community, even those with no landholding.

Ancient enclosure was achieved in three principal ways: piecemeal, where some but not all of the proprietors withdrew part of the land from communal farming; by unity of control, whereby all the land was held by a single owner who enclosed in one phase; or by general agreement whereby some or all of the land was enclosed by consensus of the majority. There is evidence of all these types in Northamptonshire and they do not entirely cease when, in the early 18th century, enclosure by Private Act of Parliament began to be used in the county.

The reasons for the transition to private acts have been described as the long-winded, protracted and complicated nature of the ancient method compared to parliamentary process of enclosure.[4] Also, the validity of earlier enclosures could be questioned, unless validated by a decree in Chancery.[5] In contrast, the act swept all before it once certain criteria were met, that is agreement of three-quarters or four-fifths of proprietors (by landholding not number), the lord of the manor, and the tithe holder.[6] Enclosure by Private Act of Parliament began in Northamptonshire in 1727 at Grafton Regis and Overstone. Both were acts ratifying agreements and were therefore the natural progression from the earlier type of enclosure to the new. Indeed the enclosures from the first half of the 18th century are more akin to agreements and in Northamptonshire the majority made in this period have acts and agreements but no award was made.[7]

The process of enclosure, whether it was within the 'ancient' or 'parliamentary' period, probably began long before any legal documentation was produced or the outcome achieved. Discussion amongst interested parties of the desirability and viability of such a course could take place over decades before formal measures were taken. Once the intent was established, however, the process within the two periods was somewhat different. In contrast, the outcome, in terms of the effects on the landscape, was to a large extent the same. Tracing the process within the different periods presents different challenges. For some of those places anciently enclosed there might not be any formal documentation, for others there may be an agreement and more rarely a map. Frequently only the date of enclosure can be determined, or in many cases just surmised, from indirect sources such as the glebe terriers or estate papers whilst the process remains unknown.[8] Fortunately some enclosures were made by substantial landowners who were important social and political figures who made and kept numerous records of estate management. For the parliamentary period there is a more prolific collection of sources from agreements or bills and subsequent acts, awards and numerous other documents such as commissioners and surveyors records. But they are not evenly distributed across the period or across the county. Some places might have an act but no award survives, in others there is an act and award but no map and so on. Examples of the varied sources for the process within the parliamentary and ancient periods are given below.

Of equal interest to the immediate effects of enclosure is the reorganisation that took place afterwards. Allotment boundaries were fixed but the subdivision of the land within them was at the choice of the individual owner. Hedged closes within the allotments could be at any size or shape, buildings of any type and in any location and plantations and woods planted wherever the owner desired. Similarly roads were set out at enclosure and, though not privately owned, they could be subtly altered after enclosure. The routes could not be changed without recourse to law but the roadside verges, features most substantial in early enclosures, could be altered. Some of these reorganisations occurred many years after enclosure and some, such as removing or adding hedges occurred repeatedly as the agricultural regime demanded.

There were in effect two landscapes subsequent to enclosure; that *created* by the process and that *resulting* from the process.

Ancient enclosure

Of the 129 townships wholly enclosed prior to 1727 it is possible to date 125 to a particular century, although 70 of these have a qualifier such as 'circa' or 'before'. Though establishing the exact date of enclosure can be problematic, ascertaining the process by which it occurred, in gradual steps or at a single stroke, is even more difficult. Enclosure agreements exist for at least fourteen places in Northamptonshire. Some refer to part of a township, typically one of the great fields or consolidation of the demesne lands, others comprise the whole township. Aynho, Litchborough, Loddington, Grafton Regis and Abthorpe are known to have been enclosed in phases and the agreement refers to one of these phases. At Haselbech and Greatworth the agreement refers to the whole township and in both cases is accompanied by a map. The existence of an agreement however is not proof that the enclosure occurred at that date. At Deenethorpe an agreement was made between the two principal landowners (see below) but was never carried out.[9] For some there is also a contemporary map, though this is rare. Given this dearth of detailed documentation, most of the discussion relating to anciently enclosed places concerns the final enclosure rather than the methods and process that achieved it.

There is no obvious pattern to the distribution of anciently enclosed places (Figure 36). They are slightly more common in the western half of the county and there are blocks with no enclosure in the centre of the county, for example in the Nene valley east of Wellingborough. There are also small clusters of contiguous enclosed places in the west and in the lower Nene. However, it is easy to over-analyse such tenuous spatial patterning and the question must be asked, if the patterns exist then to what do they relate?

The earliest ancient enclosures made in the 14th and 15th centuries are predominantly in the west of the county with only two outside of this region at Papley and Thorpe Underwood. Most were made in the 16th and 17th centuries, some 33 and 44% respectively. For these there is virtually no pattern except for the cluster along the lower Nene enclosed in the 17th century. Factors that may have affected the location of early enclosure are the size of township, topography and soils and tenure – both landownership and the type of tenancy.

The average size of Northamptonshire townships is 1,555 acres. It ranges from the tiny; 74 acres at Costow, 156 at Cotton, 180 at Hide and 188 at Perio, to some 5,000 acres at Peterborough.[10] Of the ten townships enclosed in the 14th and 15th centuries most are very small. Four have approximately 500 acres and another four have less than 1,000 acres. However, the other two are much larger; Easton Neston with Hulcote is some 1,745 acres, while Charwelton at 2,432 acres is one of the largest townships in the county. Of the eight smallest, seven are hamlets and might be expected to have small settlements making enclosure a simpler proposition. Easton Neston contained the hamlets of Hulcote and Sewardsley, whilst Charwelton had the two separate settlements of Church and Little or Lower Charwelton. That these larger townships did not have single settlements is of note as it is possible that they were enclosed in phases, with the hamlets or subsidiary settlements and their lands being enclosed in discrete blocks before final enclosure of the whole township. If that is so then they may have more in common with other townships enclosed during this period than a simple examination of size would suggest. A very similar pattern is seen in the enclosures of the 16th century, where 23 of the 43 township enclosed have less than 1,000 acres and nine have less than 500 acres. The others have between 1,000

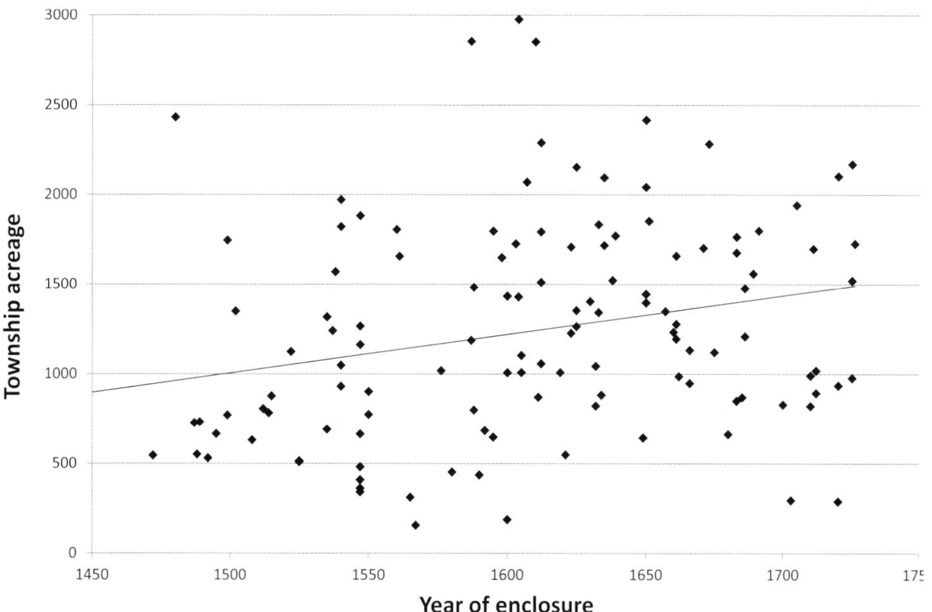

Table 5. The acreage of anciently enclosed townships relative to the date of enclosure.

and 2,000 with only Kelmarsh, with 2,854, exceeding that figure. There is, however, no correlation between the lowest acreages and actual date within the 16th century, as they are spread throughout (Table 5).

In the 16th century there does appear to be an association with size and status; 32 of the 43 places are hamlets and other small settlements like monastic granges, most of which are also the smallest in acreage. By the 17th century this pattern is lost, with only 10 of the 57 townships enclosed comprising less than 1,000 acres and none less than 500 acres. Most are between 1,000 and 2,000 acres with nine between 2,000 and 3,000 acres. Only five of the 57 are hamlets. From the first quarter of the 18th century of the 15 enclosures eight have less than 1,000 acres and two less than 300 acres, while four of the 15 are hamlets. The small places are predominantly in the west of the county and on the periphery of Rockingham Forest.

If the enclosures are plotted against the geology of the county there is some correlation between soil type and period of enclosure, with early enclosures tending to lie on impermeable geology. Furthermore the location of most of the 14th and 15th century enclosure is on the higher lands in the west of the county. But for the remainder the locations are as diverse as the geology. It has been suggested that early enclosures were often on poor soils that were difficult to cultivate. In Northamptonshire this does seem to be true where partial enclosure of a township is taking place. When examining enclosure of an entire township the causes are more complex and largely governed by the landowners and their particular preference of management. Indeed the way in which certain landscapes were managed was as influential on the inability to enclose as it was to its encouragement. For example there were three royal forests and a large expanse of fen within the county, all of it on poor or difficult soils and none of it enclosed before the 19th century.[11] Here it was the administrative framework that inhibited enclosure as the forests were Crown property. The fen belonged to Peterborough Abbey and it is likely that it was the lack of technological innovation required for drainage that inhibited its early enclosure.

The cluster of townships enclosed in the 17th century along the lower Nene (Figure 36) did not belong to a single landowner though Sir Edward Montagu owned and enclosed four of the eight townships.[12] All of these had come into the family's possession in the 15th century or following the Dissolution, as had Kingsthorpe, Luddington, Warkton and Weekley.[13] Boughton, which became the Montagu seat, was acquired earlier in 1528 when it was already at least partly enclosed as it had been imparked in 1473.[14] Kingsthorpe was enclosed *c.*1580 but Luddington, Warkton and Weekley not until 1807. There were other townships in which the family (later Dukes of Buccleuch) were the major landholders or held manorial rights (Figure 37).[15] It can be seen that there is no correlation between the amount of land they owned in a particular township and the date of its enclosure. The Montagus, it would appear, adopted a pragmatic approach to estate management, adapting to changes in agriculture practice place-by-place rather than adopting an 'enclosure ethos' as seen with the Spencers and the Treshams, who were both noted sheep farmers.

Estate influence on enclosure should not be

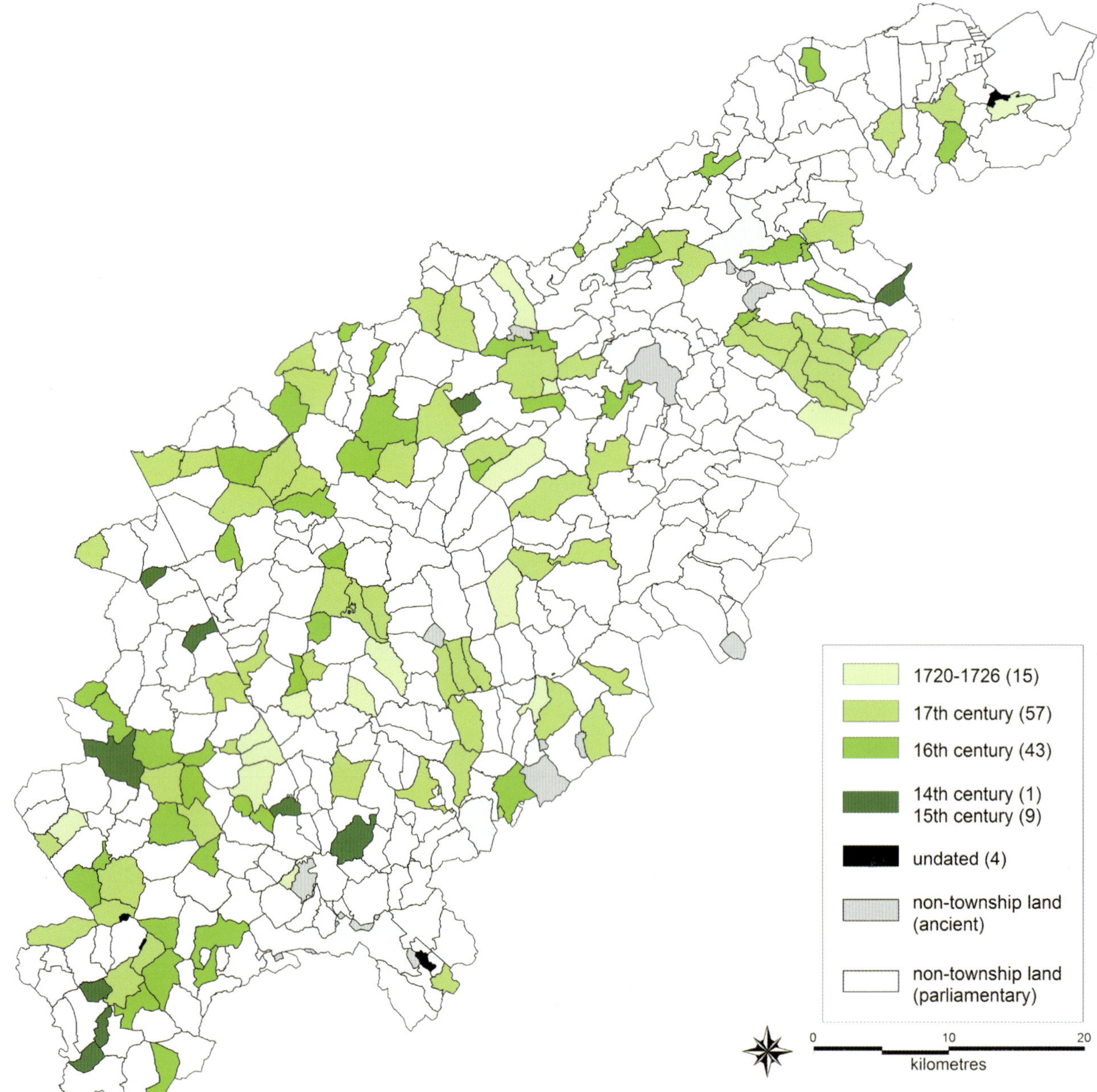

Figure 36. Townships that were wholly anciently enclosed. Most were enclosed in the 16th and 17th centuries. There is no obvious pattern to their location in the county though some do form clusters, notably those along the Nene valley.

underestimated and for individual places that were anciently enclosed the landowner was of course of primary importance. In many cases the single or largest landowner could enclose without needing to concern himself with the opinions of others, with the notable exception of the tithe holder. It is worth noting that after the Dissolution the landowner and tithe holder may well have been the same person.[16] Many of the early enclosures were made by estate owners who had land elsewhere that remained open. The land enclosed was often associated with imparking and/or sheep farming. Both influences were at work when Althorp was enclosed *c.*1520 by Sir John Spencer and at Fawsley which was enclosed before 1547 by Sir Edmund Knightley.

The purpose for some of the early enclosures could influence the method adopted to achieve it. This is most clearly seen where the lord of the manor consolidated his holding with a view to create or extend his park. This is seen at Deene, Kirby, Kettering, Wadenhoe ,[17] Aynho,[18] and Holdenby.[19] In none of these instances did full enclosure of the township take place at the same time as enclosure for the park.

It was not necessary to enclose an entire township simply to create a park or to lay out gardens around a country house and indeed most did not. Early

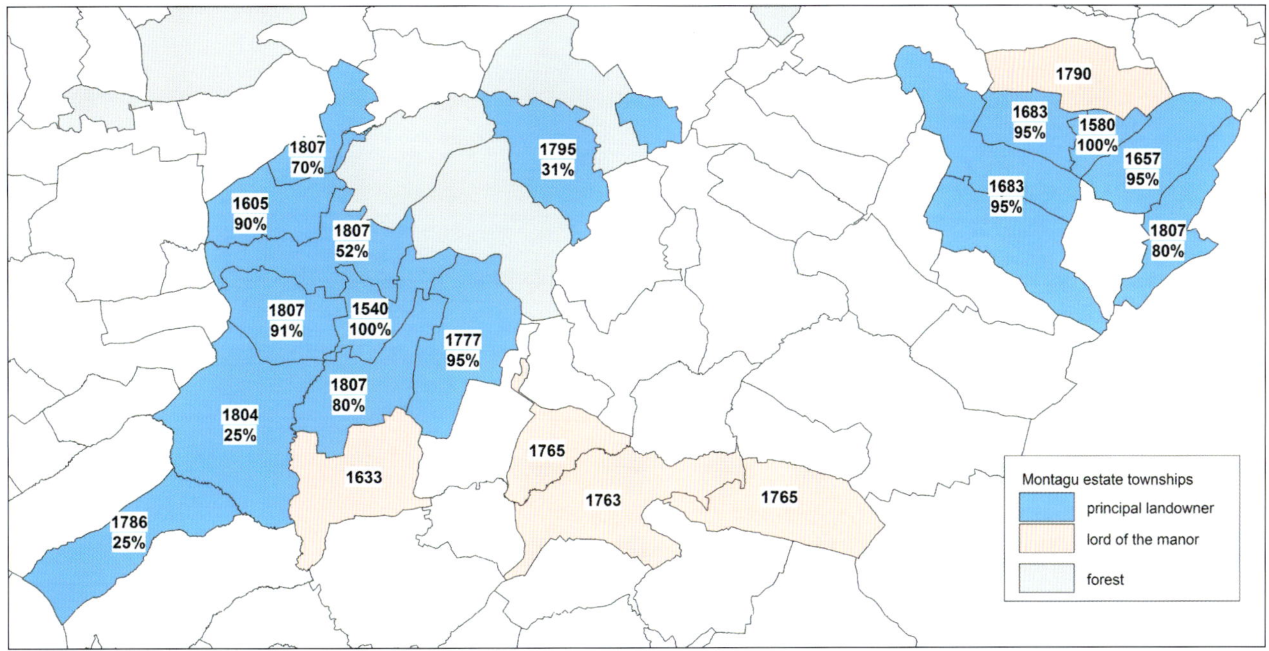

Figure 37. Map showing the townships owned by the Montagu family or in which they held manorial rights. There is no correlation between the amount of land owned and the date of enclosure.

deer parks were small and usually located away from the settlement. Later ones might be greater in extent but still often in peripheral locations. Few in Northamptonshire made the transition from deer park to landscape park, but even the largest of the newly created landscape parks did not encompass an entire township.

In the 1580s Sir Christopher Hatton, Chancellor to Elizabeth I had a series of maps made documenting the process of enclosure and imparking at his estates in Kirby and Holdenby.[20] At Kirby there is a series of three maps dated 1585, 1586 and 1587.[21] The first shows the township partly enclosed with large sheepwalks but also with open field furlongs complete with strips of ridge and furrow in the south. In the second map the strips have gone and their location is marked: 'Broke furlonge The ground latly inclosed'. In the third, enclosure is complete as is the laying out of new gardens that encompass the church. The village was already shrunken in the earliest plan but it had never been a large settlement.[22] This later phase though reorganising the land does wholly remove the village, though it does disappear in the next century.

At Holdenby he undertakes a similar programme and there are two maps dated 1580 and 1587. Here the objective is much more ambitious. He creates a large park to the side of the new house, extends the formal gardens and re-plans the village. But, as at Kirby, this was not the first re-design of the landscape as there was already a small park and earthworks around the church and site of the original house would suggest that part of the village had already been moved (Figures 38–40). In 1587, by the time the process was complete, the remainder of the township is still marked with the names of the great fields but they are shown with large ponds, plantations and in the north field a 'sheep penn'. Though the changes to the village are substantial and the park comprised a third of the township it is nevertheless the conversion of the rest to sheep farming that had the greatest effect on the wider landscape.

In order to achieve such reorganisation there had to be a single landowner or one sufficiently determined to expend much time and effort in exchanging or purchasing land from other landowners. At Holdenby Hatton was the only landowner.[23] At Kirby Thomas Brudenell, whose house and park were in the neighbouring township of Deene, also owned property. It was a happy coincidence that both wished to enlarge their parks at the same time and so exchanges were affected. Later in the 17th century the nephews of Hatton and Brudenell mentioned above and also named Christopher and Thomas, were negotiating exchanges of land in Deenethorpe. Here an agreement for enclosure was made and signed, but then Hatton reneged and sold his lands to his tenants 'and many others whosoever would buy'.[24] A map dated 1678 shows the township enclosed but the exact date and method is unknown.[25] Brudenell in particular was a keen encloser and was undertaking similar projects in his estates across the county and elsewhere in the country. His initial priority was enclosure of the demesne lands, but with the intention of reorganising the tenants' lands and their leases with

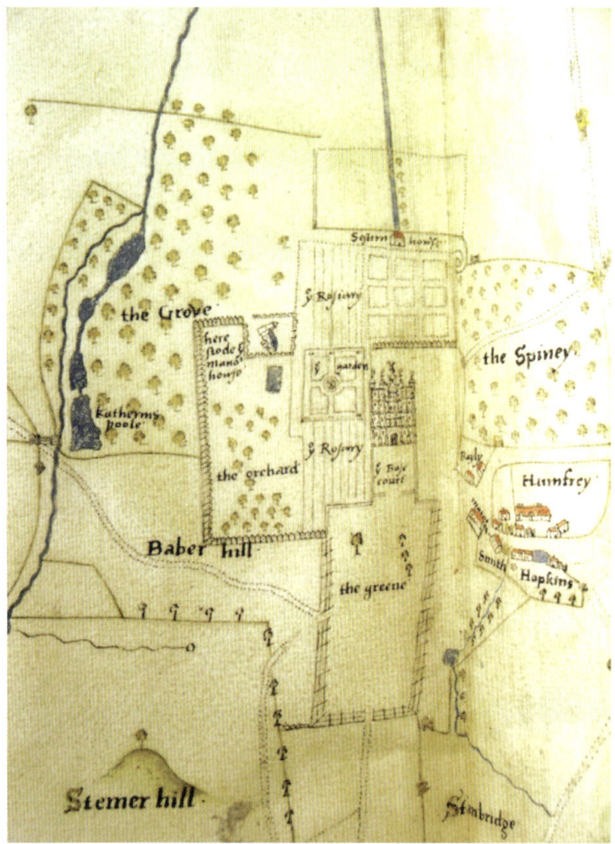

Figure 38. Holdenby in 1580 (NRO FH272). The site of the original house is to the east of the church and marked 'here stood the manor house'. The features on this map can be compared to those in Figure 39 and many can be identified on the air photo in Figure 40.

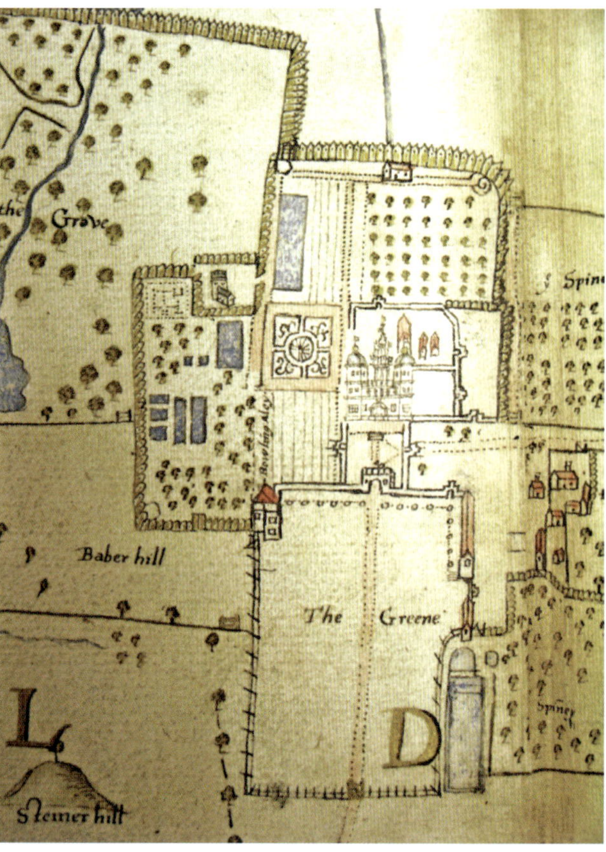

Figure 39. Holdenby in 1587 (NRO FH272). The village and gardens have been replanned and note the addition of a bowling green on the lower terrace of the 'roserry' to the west of the house. The features on this map can be compared to those in Figure 38. and many can be identified on the air photo in Figure 40.

Figure 40. Air photo of earthworks at Holdenby. The house seen in the photograph was almost entirely rebuilt in the 19th century with just a small wing from the 16th century building surviving. Many of the other features shown on Figures 38 and 39 can be identified as earthworks or standing structures. (© Glenn Foard).

Figure 41. Haselbech enclosure map dated 1598 is the earliest enclosure map in England and Wales. The allotments are shown but there is no landscape detail making it remarkably similar to later enclosure maps (compare to Figure 50). Of note are the few roads and the width of the 'Naseby Way' on the right. North is at the bottom. (NRO Map 561).

the aim of encouraging the more substantial tenant. In most cases this resulted in enclosure but Brudenell was nothing if not pragmatic and at Glapthorn, where enclosure was not possible due to tenants with life leases and other freeholders, he was content to reorganise his own lands by merging the demesne with the tenant lands, equalising the holdings and doubling the rents.[26]

The prime motivation for enclosure of a township would seem to be increased revenue from a change in agricultural regime or in the way the land was managed. Either the landowner would farm the land himself or would retain tenants, but on significantly increased rents and new leases. A dominant landowner, even if he was not the sole or majority landholder or was resident in the township, could have a significant influence on the decision to enclose if he had a vested interest in doing so. Haselbech was enclosed in 1598 and has an agreement as well as the earliest surviving enclosure map in England and Wales (Figure 41).[27]

Here there were 11 landowners including Sir

Thomas Tresham, who owned just over half of the land, most of which was let to tenants. He was lord of two of the three manors in Haselbech but resident at Rushton. His increasingly desperate financial situation, brought about by recusancy fines and a spiralling accumulation of loans and mortgages, meant his eagerness to enclose was largely due to the expectation of increased rents.[28] His negotiations with the other owners were clearly productive as Haselbech was enclosed and, on Tresham's land at least, converted to pasture. His plan backfired as tenants either could not or would not pay the increased rents and, as a result, in 1599 he was obliged to sell some of his land in Haselbech and did not recoup the cost of enclosure.[29] Haselbech village is shrunken and has good earthwork remains in the location of some of the buildings and closes shown on the 1598 map. It is likely that the depopulation occurred at this time, though there may have been other factors involved as the village was re-planned in the subsequent centuries.[30]

Enclosure of a whole township not only changed the landscape but also had a substantial impact on the people who lived and worked within it. At Church and Chapel Brampton, enclosed in *c.*1640 by the same Hatton involved in the agreement for the enclosure of Deenethorpe, many people lost not only their livelihoods but their homes. A petition made to Hatton by a number of his tenants protests at the enclosure:

> ... we do by way of grateful acknowledgment confess that we and our forefathers have lived happily for many years under your lordship and your right worthy ancestors until your lordships late Inclosures of the [open] fields which has plunged us into many great and pressing exigencies; some already being forced from the town (the place of their ancient abodes) and those who are left behind know not what course to take for present subsistence, or future livelihoods and maintenance....[31]

It is unclear from this whether the tenants were unable to pay increased rents, as had been the case at Haselbech, were unable to find work as sheep farming required fewer men, or were forcibly removed. There is evidence of shrinkage at Church Brampton seen on maps from the 16th and 18th century but the 18th century map for Chapel Brampton is incomplete and later development has obscured early features.[32]

The relationship between enclosure and settlement desertion or shrinkage is well recognised and has received considerable study.[33] There are some 91 known deserted settlements in Northamptonshire, most associated with ancient enclosure (Figure 42).[34] They are not, however, all associated with townships wholly anciently enclosed and indeed early enclosure did not inevitably entail settlement desertion, nor settlement desertion necessarily equate to early enclosure. In addition to those deserted there are the shrunken and migrated settlements, not shown on the map. Not least of the issues involved is the definition of desertion as opposed to shrinkage and migration or re-planning. Added to that are the problems of dating the settlement shrinkage – particularly problematic when enclosure of the whole township did not occur. Moreover, settlement desertion or shrinkage was arguably more a consequence of enclosure rather than the motivating force behind it.

The motives of very early enclosures appear to be associated with monastic establishments or other large landowners and sheep farming and imparking.[35] Sheep farming continued to influence enclosure throughout this period particularly in the 16th century.[36] There is ample evidence for sheep faming on maps from the period. Many have very large pasture closes from 50 to over 100 acres as at East Carlton (1723), Hardwick (1684), Newbottle (1621) and Catesby (1638).[37] Others are marked with 'sheep pasture' or 'sheepwalks', as at Hanging Houghton (1655) and on the splendid map of Armston (1716) (Figure 43).[38] Yet others are marked with 'sheep pens' as at Plumpton (before 1685) and on a particularly fine map of Papley (1632), which also has a 'ram close' (Figure 44).[39]

Places wholly enclosed prior to 1727 are only part of the total of ancient enclosure in the county, albeit the major part. Ancient enclosure within townships that achieved final enclosure in the parliamentary period is not insignificant (Figure 45). Nor does this map show all the land anciently enclosed. There are 61 townships enclosed in the parliamentary period for which no map has been identified but for which there are enclosure statistics from the awards. Most have very little ancient enclosure, but eleven have between 30 and 70% and that should be considered when assessing quantities and spatial patterning of enclosure from before the parliamentary period.

Parliamentary Period Enclosure

The process of enclosure in the parliamentary period is more widely understood than that of ancient enclosure. This is largely due to the volume of documentation it produced. Some, in particular the structure and language of the acts and awards, became increasingly formulaic so that certain documents can be said to be typically 'of the period'. Moreover, parliamentary enclosure has received more study than earlier periods.[40] Of the 261 places in Northamptonshire enclosed in this period (247 townships and 14 areas of waste i.e. forest and fen) some 93% were made by private act and award. The remaining 7% (19 townships) have no award and only eight have acts surviving. The enclosers in the other 11 townships, who felt no need for recourse to legal process, must have been very confident of their position. For these the date of enclosure can only be estimated from the glebe terriers or from map data. Most were enclosed in the first half of the 18th century, most had a single owner and the agreement

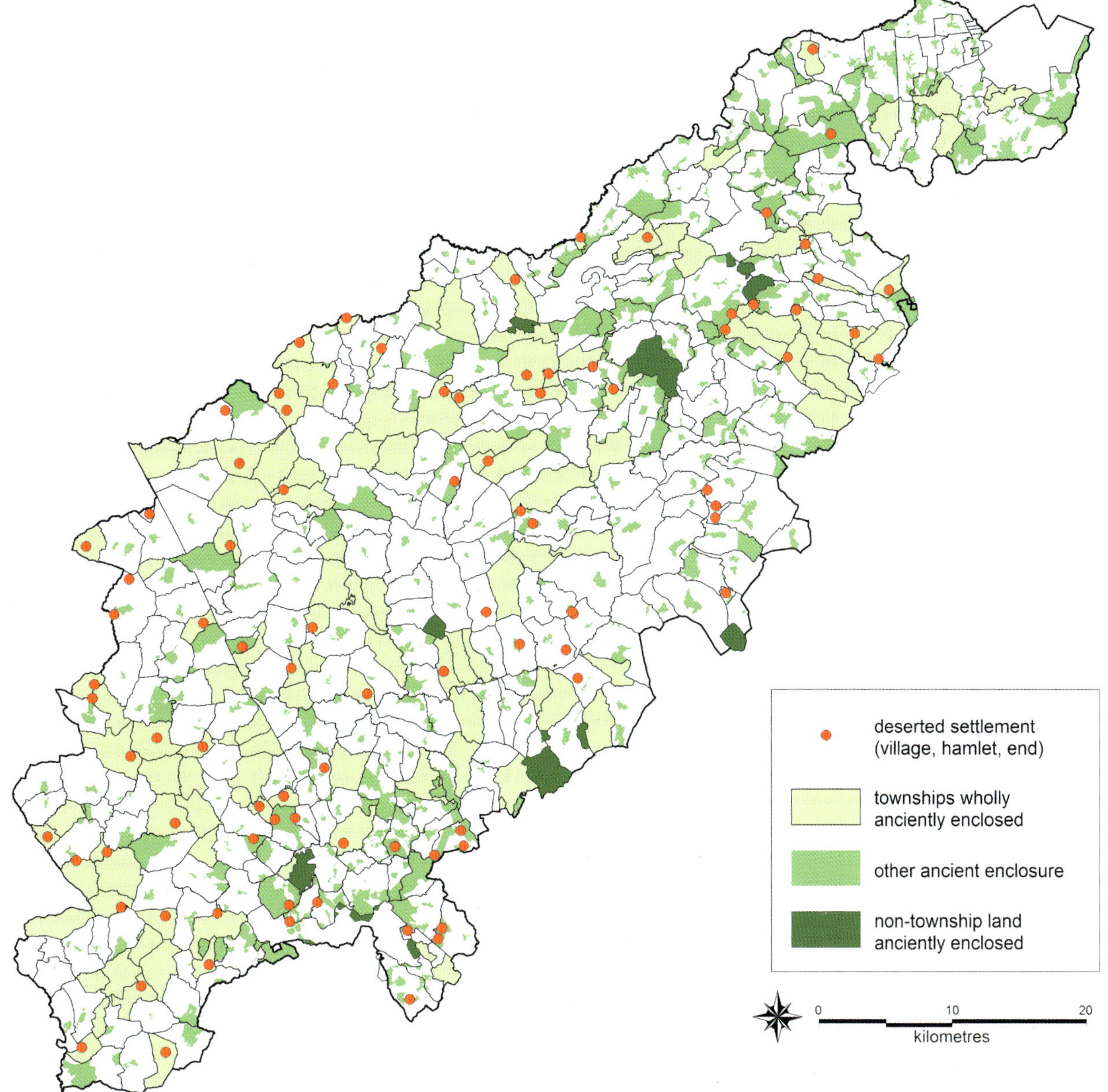

Figure 42. The location of deserted settlements in relationship to ancient enclosure.

was between them and the tithe holder. Also, where it is known, most had a significant part of the township already enclosed. These were in fact more akin to the ancient enclosures than the others of this period. Piecemeal enclosure also continued in this period. At Ashton (near Roade), part of the Duke of Grafton's estate, a map dated 1768 marks several plots of land as 'formerly common arable but now inclosed' while a map of 1727 shows this land as open. Final enclosure of Ashton took place in 1816, when the latter closes are marked as 'ancient'.[41]

For those that did seek recourse to Parliament, the process would have followed a predictable route. Discussion and agreement amongst the interested parties would necessarily have taken place prior to the first formal steps. Where there were few interested parties this was probably not a complicated or protracted undertaking. Where there were numerous interested parties and no dominant landowner it could be a long and involved business. In addition to the principle to enclose, there were issues relating to commutation of tithes and manorial rights to be considered, as well as the appointment of commissioners and the location of allotments. There was also the likelihood of protest. It was in everyone's interest to have as many of these issues as possible resolved in advance, in order to avoid costly interruption or delay to the formal process. In view of

Figure 43. An extract from the 1716 map of Armston showing the sheepwalk. Also of note is the rather fine armorial decoration.

Figure 44. An extract from the 1632 map of Papley showing sheep pens and ram close. (NRO Map 2221).

this meetings at all stages of the process were held in public and notices pinned to the church door and/or printed in local newspapers.

The next stage was a petition made to Parliament requesting the right to bring in a bill to enclose land in the said place, normally described as the 'Parish (Manor, Lordship, Liberty) of ..' and the land as 'open arable fields, Meadows, Pastures, Commons and Waste Grounds'. The petitioners would usually include the lord of the manor, the incumbent and other principal proprietors, described as the owners of 'Lands, Messuages, Tenements'. The lands were typically described as lying 'intermixed and dispersed in small parcels' and as such 'incapable of any considerable improvement' and if 'divided, inclosed and allotted' it would be to the advantage not only of the petitioners but to the 'Public'.[42] This formula of description continues throughout the process and is repeated in the act and in the preamble to the award, with care taken to include all types of land and description of place. Because intended as a catch-all such wording is not an exact description of the land concerned. In other words not every place would have contained arable, pasture common and waste. Nor, for that matter, would the 'public' necessarily have benefited from the enclosure, at least not in the same way as some proprietors might.

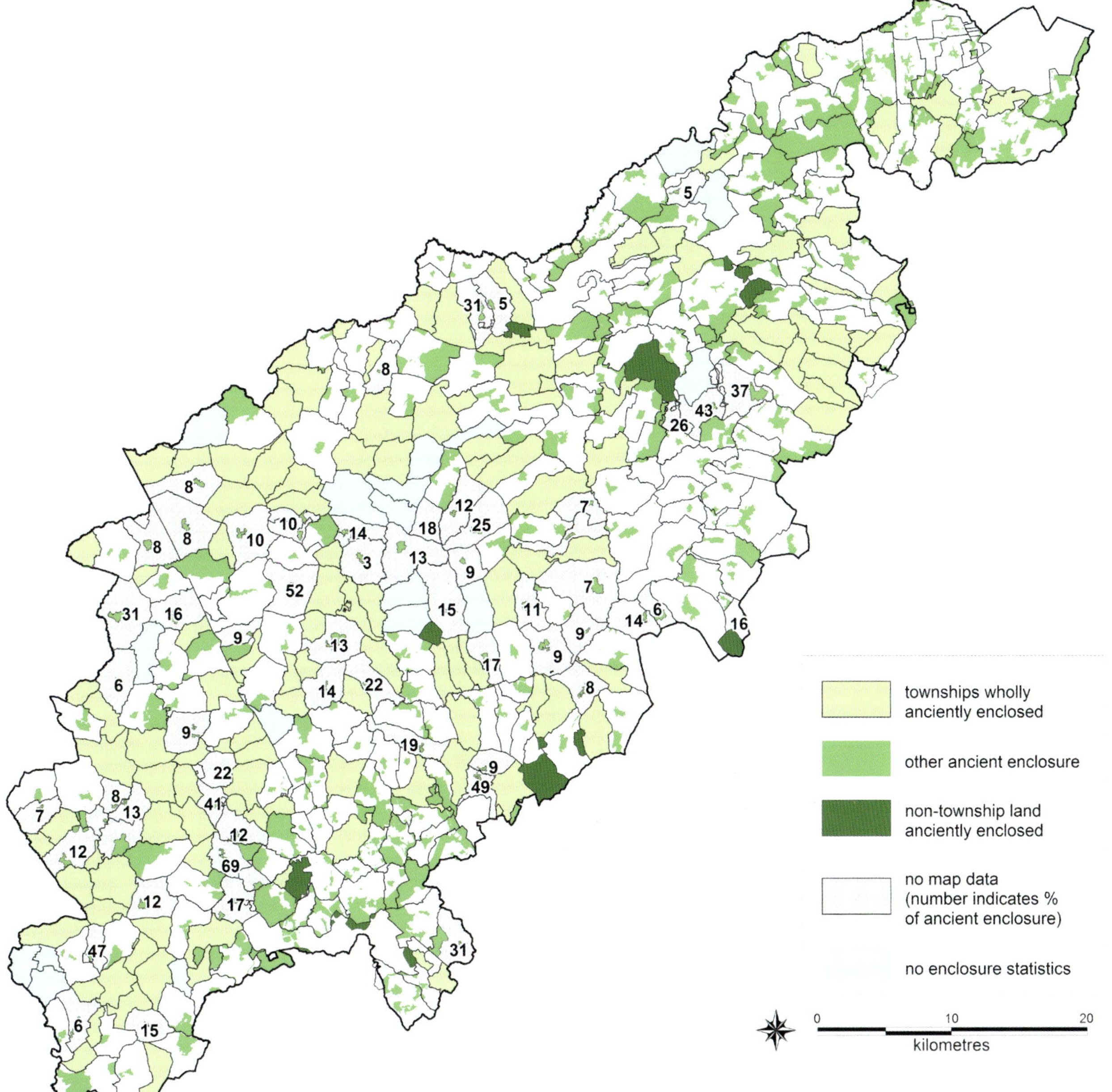

Figure 45. The total amount of ancient enclosure within the county. Some townships that were enclosed in the parliamentary period had very little enclosure outside of the village core, particularly those along the Nene valley. Others had substantial ancient enclosure in some places being a far greater proportion than the open land.

Once permission to submit the bill has been granted a local solicitor would be instructed to draw it up. At this stage opinion of all proprietors would not only be sought but recorded in a consent document in which they had to sign in one of three columns 'consent', 'dissent' or 'neuter'.[43] This was required by Parliament in order to ensure that the majority, in terms of landholding, were in agreement. The consent document for West Haddon survives and, of the 61 names that appear, 32 did not consent and their reasons are recorded. One or two regarded enclosure as a 'wicked thing', one as tending to 'ruin the nation' and two objected to the amount allowed in lieu of tithes. But most of them had no strong objections, citing their advanced age or lack of descendants as reasons for dissent and in general display apathy rather than outright opposition.[44] However, they were all smallholders and their numbers did not outweigh the landholding of the consenting group and the enclosure went ahead.

The submission of the Bill did not mean that enclosure was now inevitable, as opponents could bring a counter petition. However, if the Bill was successful it became a Private Act of Parliament.

At this stage the commissioners were appointed. They were usually chosen by the proprietors and were appointed with the intention of representing everyone's interests. By the second half of the 18th century there were normally three: one to represent the lord of the manor, one the tithe holder and the third for all other interests.[45] Earlier enclosures could have many more. At Brington, enclosed in 1743, the act appoints no less than ten commissioners, though does go on to state that 'any five' of them may conduct the process.[46]

It is from the date of the act that the communal system of farming in that locality ceased as the commissioners took charge, organising all stages of the process including 'ordering the husbandry' until the award was made. The act named the commissioners 'or their successors', should any refuse or be unable to undertake the role and gives the oath they are to swear, orders a survey to be made and authorises the commissioners to make allotments to the various parties. In so doing they have to take account not just of the quantity of land owned and allotted, but of its quality, location and convenience. They are responsible for appointing a surveyor, for hearing and adjudicating claims and for determining disputes arising from the process. The act also gives instructions as to the laying out of roads, gates, fences, trees, the provision of stone pits and of water and drainage. Very often a public sheep wash was also provided. Even the wayside herbage was allotted to someone, usually either the proprietor of the adjacent plot or the surveyors of the highways. The act also dealt with the costs of the process, the commutation of tithes if such were to be included, exchanges of land, the cessation of leases and compensation to the tenants, exonerated whoever was responsible for keeping the parish bull and boar (often the rector), and of course extinguished common rights. The subsequent awards were very detailed and no piece of land was unaccounted for.

The award begins by repeating the stipulations of the act, what is being done and why. It includes the signed oaths made by the commissioners and details the process of the various stages undertaken. It then goes on to describe the various allotments being made, who they are to and what they are for. It is clear from the description of costs and from the numbers in the schedule relating to the 'number on the plan' that it was usual for a map to be made to accompany the award. However, in Northamptonshire for seventy townships where an award was made no map has been located.[47] The award was the culmination of the legal process and set, if not in stone, then in law what the principal features of the new landscape would be. The physical changes to the landscape took somewhat longer, as the new allotments and roads that were staked out as part of the allotment process had then to be dug, fenced and drained.

Considering the complexity involved in all the tasks appointed to the commissioners, the process from act to award could be remarkably quick. In Northamptonshire of the 237 places for which acts and awards were made 133 were completed in just a year and another 57 took between two and three years. But some 12 places took ten years and another seven places took 11 years to complete. The majority of these lengthy enclosures were made in the late 18th and early 19th century and most involved enclosure of waste and/or intermixed townships. In these instances the number of claimants was often considerable, as was the size of the place being enclosed and the type of claim was complicated by varying tenures, manorial holdings and customs. When the draft award had been made proprietors had a final opportunity to object and request adjustments, which could further delay the process. A particularly unusual cause for delay was seen at Wellingborough, where the plan of the new allotments along with all the surveyors books were stolen from his house in January 1766, presumably by a person or persons particularly aggrieved at the situation.[48]

The chronology of parliamentary period can be traced very accurately for the 237 townships enclosed (Table 6). The enclosure of 'waste', or forest and fen as it might more precisely be described, is discussed separately below.[49]

The peaks of enclosure, seen firstly in the second half of the 1760s and the 1770s and then the early decades of the 19th century, accord with the national figures given by Michael Turner in his seminal work 'English Parliamentary Enclosure'. Nationally the early peak is primarily associated with the enclosure of open field arable and the latter, which coincided with the Napoleonic Wars, with enclosure of common and waste. Northamptonshire had very little waste, the forest and fen totalling only 6% of the county. Of that still unenclosed at this period some 17,000 acres, just over half, is enclosed during the Napoleonic period, but this is only 17% of the total enclosure in this period. The predominant type of enclosure in Northamptonshire was therefore of open fields. But although Northamptonshire was undoubtedly a 'champion' county in the medieval, by the parliamentary period the open fields were by no means predominantly arable.[50] In several townships that have a pre-enclosure or draft enclosure map that shows the land use the proportion of pasture is seen to be as significant a feature as the arable and in some cases the dominant one. At Polebrook where 91% of the 1,380 acres of the township was enclosed in 1790 some 500 acres were common pasture. Nor does that include the grass within the arable fields such as baulks and leys. Therefore at least 36% of the land enclosed was pasture, compared to some 9% in the medieval. At Southorpe the figures are even higher (Figure 46). Here it can be seen that by final enclosure

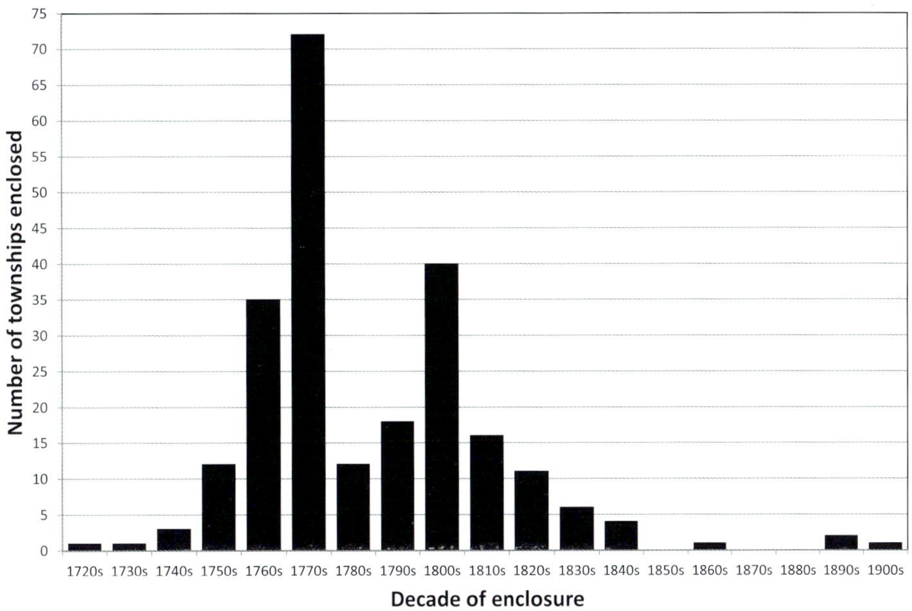

Table 6. The chronology of enclosure: the number of townships enclosed in each decade of the parliamentary period.

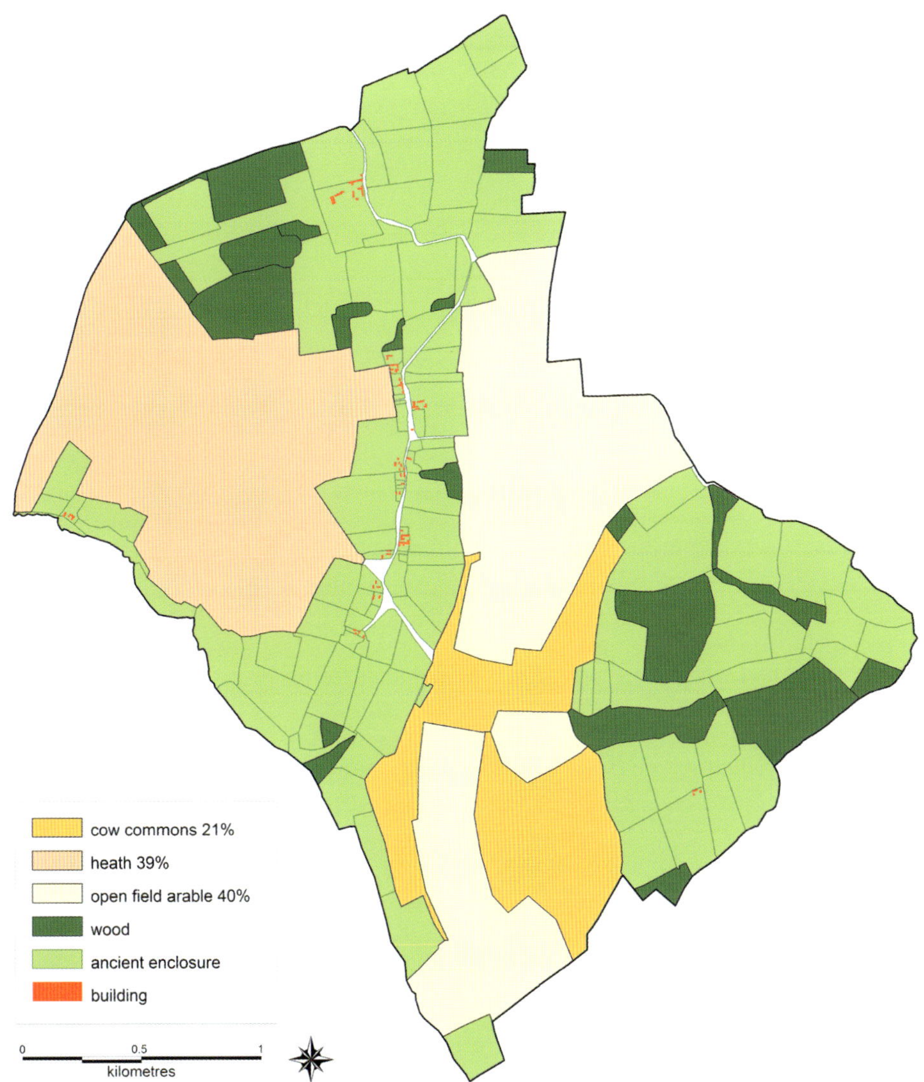

Figure 46. Southorpe in 1841 showing the proportion of open land that was permanent grass.

Figure 47. An extract from the 1760 map of Denton showing the freeboard against Brafield township. Note also the name of the adjacent furlong 'coopers hedge'. (Courtesy of The Marquess of Northampton).

in 1841 the township was already 55% enclosed and that of the remaining unenclosed land at least 60% was down to permanent grass; baulks and headlands are not included.

At Naseby, where 94% of the township was still open in 1820, the enclosure documents do not mention land use but other evidence indicates that at the time of enclosure two-thirds of the township was pasture.[51] Similarly at Rothwell the enclosure map gives no indication of land use but the award makes reference to the 'several sheep walks' and the allocation of land for tithes refers to the 'tithe hay', 'lambs' and 'wool'. All of which suggests that Rothwell had a considerable portion of the open fields (some 87% of the township was still open) down to grass.[52] Indeed pasture is not the only land use underestimated within the open fields for the idea that the arable was unrelieved by hedges or trees needs reconsidering. A series of exceptionally detailed pre-enclosure estate maps as well as a wide range of enclosure documents for some townships reveals not only hedges in the open fields but numerous trees.[53] Many awards refer to the removal of trees from allotments but do not specify the number or species. This may in fact be part of the formulaic language of awards in that all eventualities are covered regardless of whether the feature in question existed. However, it occurs sufficiently frequently to suggest that trees within the fields were not particularly uncommon. The most informative account is seen at Wilby where a survey of the trees on the allotments was made prior to enclosure and as well as a spinney there were 433 individual trees including oak, ash, elm and willow.[54] In addition to trees within the fields the township itself might be ring-fenced against some or all of its neighbours prior to enclosure. There is map and/or documentary evidence for this in many places including Brington, Wellingborough, Marston Trussell, Wilby and Denton.[55] In some cases the map will not depict a hedged boundary but will show gates on the roads indicating an enclosed township. At Denton the pre-enclosure map of 1760 is marked with neither but does mark a freeboard against the boundary with Brafield (Figure 47). Freeboards were narrow strips of land set along the outside of the hedge of either an enclosed townships or ring-fenced township which gave the proprietors access to the side of hedge in the neighbouring township for maintenance. As Brafield was not enclosed until 1827 and Denton in 1770 clearly there was a ring-fence and it belonged to Denton.

It is generally accepted that in Northamptonshire after enclosure most of the land was converted to grass.[56] But the evidence would suggest that the conversion of arable to pasture was an on-going process that in some townships had advanced to the point where the balance had tipped in the favour of grass, in some cases decades before enclosure. Enclosure was not then responsible for changing the agricultural regime so much as changing and reorganising its management.

In addition to the date of enclosure and its coincidence, or otherwise, with national trends it is possible, to examine the relationships between the date of enclosure, the amount of land enclosed and numbers of landowners (Tables 7–9), and to plot the spatial patterns of chronology (Figure 48).

This map raises interesting questions regarding the location of enclosure at particular periods. Those from the 1770s, the most prolific decade, form no significant pattern but are spread across the county. They are, however, notably absent from the Soke. Those pre 1770 are predominantly in the west of the county where there is also the greatest concentration of anciently enclosed townships. The two exceptions to this are Wittering and Thornhaugh on the edge of the Soke. Those that do form clusters are from the 19th century and can be seen to the north-east of Whittlewood where they are almost all part of the Duke of Grafton's estate; in the Soke where they are predominantly part of Earl Fitzwilliam's estate; and either side of the Nene by the Northamptonshire Wolds, where there is no dominant estate and for most townships no dominant landowner.

The relationship between the chronology of enclosure and the percentage of the township enclosed displays no correlation (Table 7). Nor is there any obvious link between the numbers of landowners and percentage enclosed (Table 8) or decade of enclosure (Table 9). A township enclosed in 1810 is no more likely to have more or less land enclosed, or more or fewer landowners than a township enclosed in 1770. In other words it is not possible to state that the date of enclosure is likely to reflect the amount of land enclosed or numbers of landowners involved, or indeed that any one of the factors had any significant influence on any of the others.

However, whilst the total number of landowners

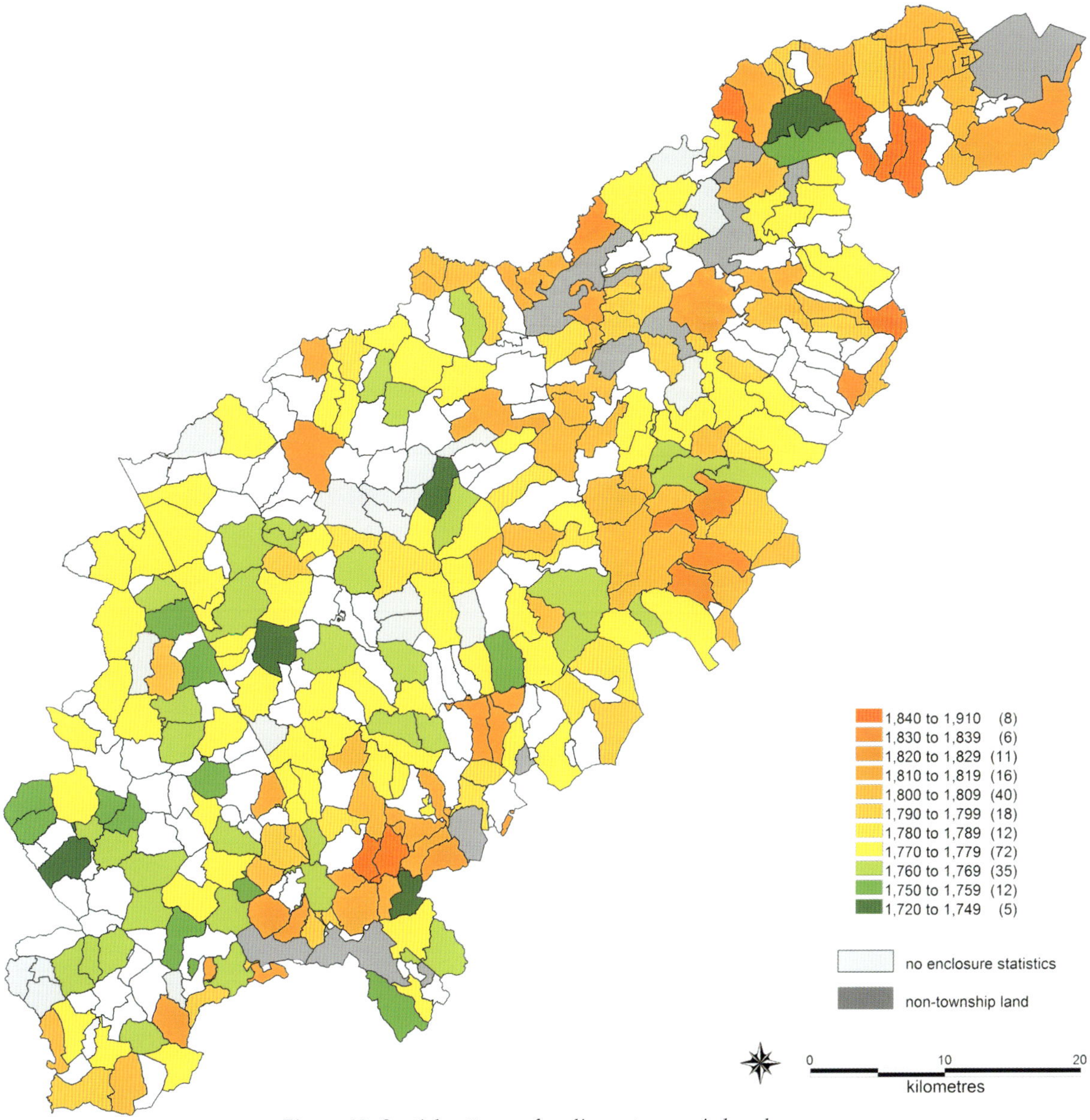

Figure 48. Spatial patterns of parliamentary period enclosure.

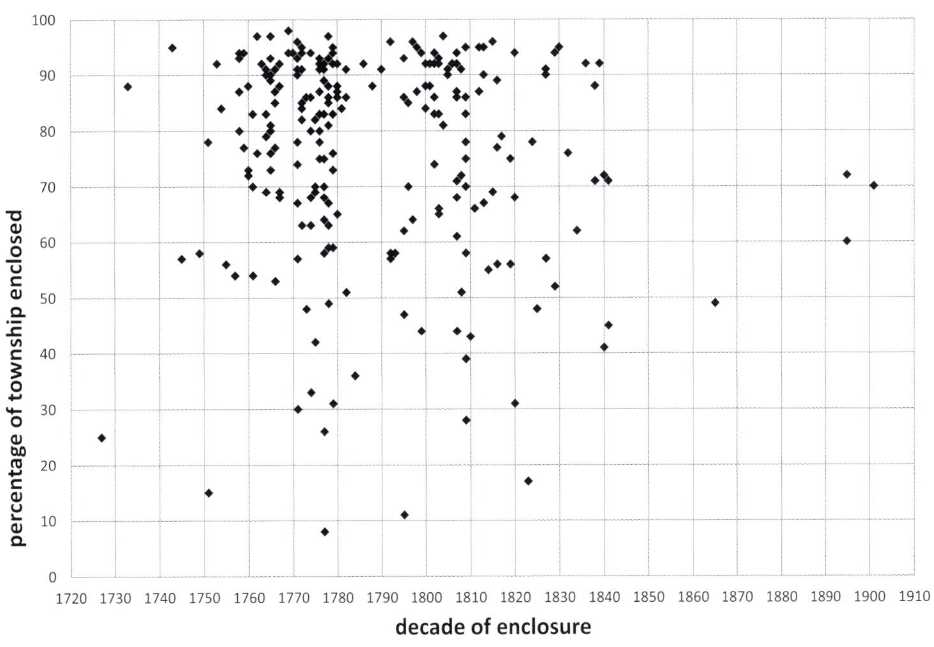

Table 7. The percentage of each township enclosed by decade in the parliamentary period.

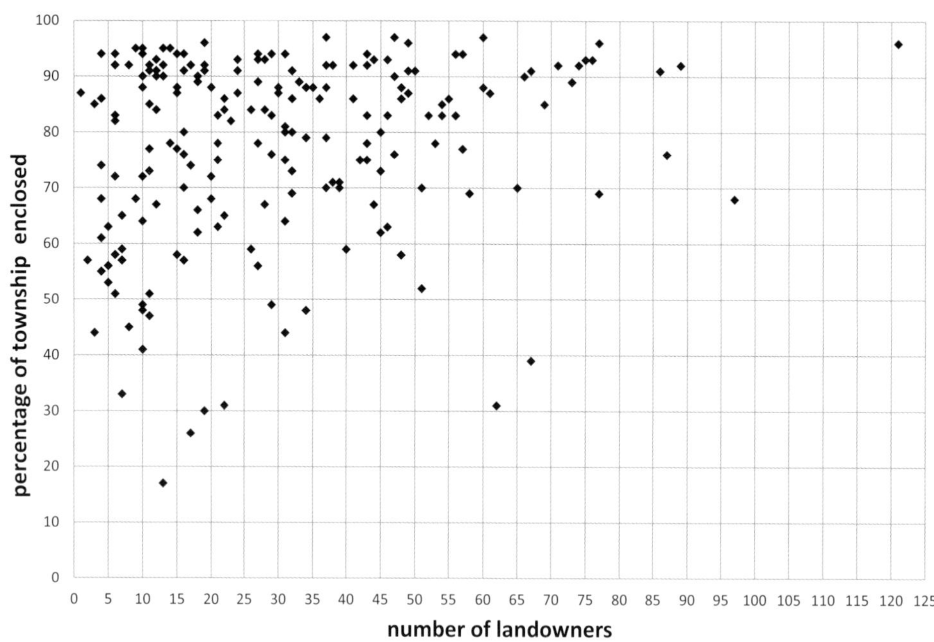

Table 8. The percentage of each township enclosed relative to the number of landowners/allottees in the parliamentary period.

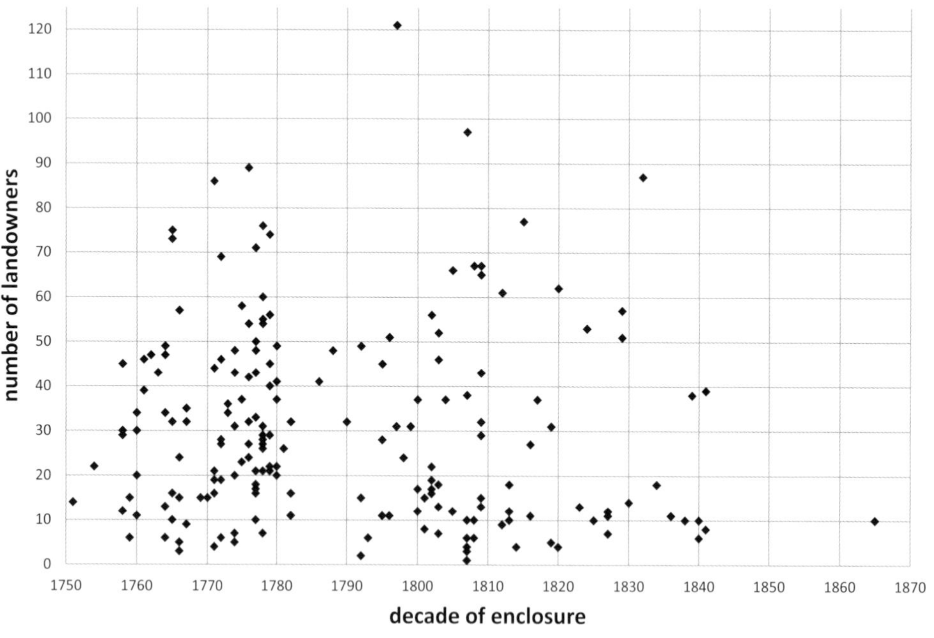

Table 9. The number of landowners/allottees in each township relative to the decade of enclosure in the parliamentary period.

within a particular place does not seem to have affected chronology of enclosure across the county, if there were a few or a single dominant owner within a group of townships they could be highly influential. This can be seen where a dominant estate managed the land with two or more townships having intermixed holdings. For example at Stoke Bruerne with Shutlanger; Glapthorn with Cotterstock; Ashton with Roade and Hartwell; Weekley with Geddington; and Helpston with Maxey, Deeping Gate, Peakirk, Glinton and Etton. In some cases the holdings are so intermixed that certain of the township boundaries are only fixed or indeed created at enclosure, as at Helpston *et al.* Another factor may have been cost and the principal owner/s might bring an act for more than one township even though there was no complicated intermixing of holdings. Warkton is some 6km from Little Oakley and some 21km from Luddington[57] but all were enclosed under a single act and all were part of the Buccleuch estate.[58]

The date of enclosure is unequivocal as it is that of the act.[59] The amount of land enclosed and numbers of landowners are taken from the award and require some clarification. The awards often include exchanges of land, sometimes involving ancient enclosure, whereby owners use the enclosure process as a means of reorganising their holdings into more convenient blocks. Possibly the most extreme example of this was at Ecton where Ambrose Isted, the lord of the manor, used the enclosure process to exchange land and acquire Little Ecton which he promptly demolished to extend his park.[60] But even where the exchanges were numerous, as for example at Paulerspury, they usually only involved very small plots and an examination of the database suggests this typically to be the case and the numbers of exchanges would not significantly skew the overall statistics of amount of land enclosed.

The numbers given for *landowners* are actually the number of *allottees* in the enclosure award. They include all landowners at the time of enclosure but importantly include some others who were not, or who were given additional land for rights rather than ownership. Allotments could be made to certain persons and institutions for non-landowning rights: to the tithe holder if tithes were being extinguished; to the lord of the manor for his rights in the soil and as compensation for enfranchisement of copyholds; to churchwardens; overseers of the poor; overseers of the highways; other parish officers; and to individuals for loss of common right. With the exception of the tithe allotments these allocations were usually very small. The lord of the manor was typically allocated less than one half a percent of the total amount enclosed for his rights in the soil. The churchwardens could be allotted land for the upkeep of the church, or where there were no separate overseers of the poor within the parish they could also be allocated a poor allotment. In either case the plot would be small usually less than 20 acres. That allotted for the poor often came with stipulations as to its management. Rarely were the poor allowed access to the land allotted them, rather it was to be rented out by the overseers and the income used in poor relief. At Clipston the income was to be used for fuel, meat, corn or apparel given out on the 24 December each year; Aldwincle was similar though distributed on January 1st. Most poor relief came with a similar proviso to that at Tiffield where only the 'most necessitous, industrious and honest poor persons who were not receiving collections from the parish' could receive benefit. At East Haddon in addition to buying fuel for the poor the churchwardens were to use the rent to 'teach poor children to read and write'. And at Ecton the income was to be used for 'putting out poor children as apprentices and other charitable purposes'. Orlingbury was unusual in that the land allotted to the poor was still accessible to them to 'carry away on their backs, but not otherwise, the bushes, furze and thorne for fuel'.[61] And at Naseby one of the plots awarded to the churchwardens is now the village allotment gardens and as such is still the communal property of the village (Figure 50).

Figure 49. Stone pits existed prior to enclosure as maintenance of the roads was a responsibility of each township. This map of the St Andrews Priory lands in Northampton in 1632 shows the town's stone pits to be a substantial quarry and likely to have been used for building stone as well as for road maintenance. (NRO Map 4671).

The overseers of the highways probably received the smallest allotments of all, generally less than one acre often in several very small stone pits (Figures 49 and 50). Similarly where people who did not own land in the open fields but received an allotment for common rights attached to other property, such as a cottage, the allocation was usually less than one acre. But cottage commons were very complex and not only varied from township to township but also in different manors within the same township, and are further complicated where the township or manor had rights of common in one of the forests or the fen.[62] Other parish officers such as the constables might receive a small plot, as at Towcester to 'defray the expense of their office'. And in the later enclosures an allotment might be made to parish overseers for 'a place of exercise and recreation

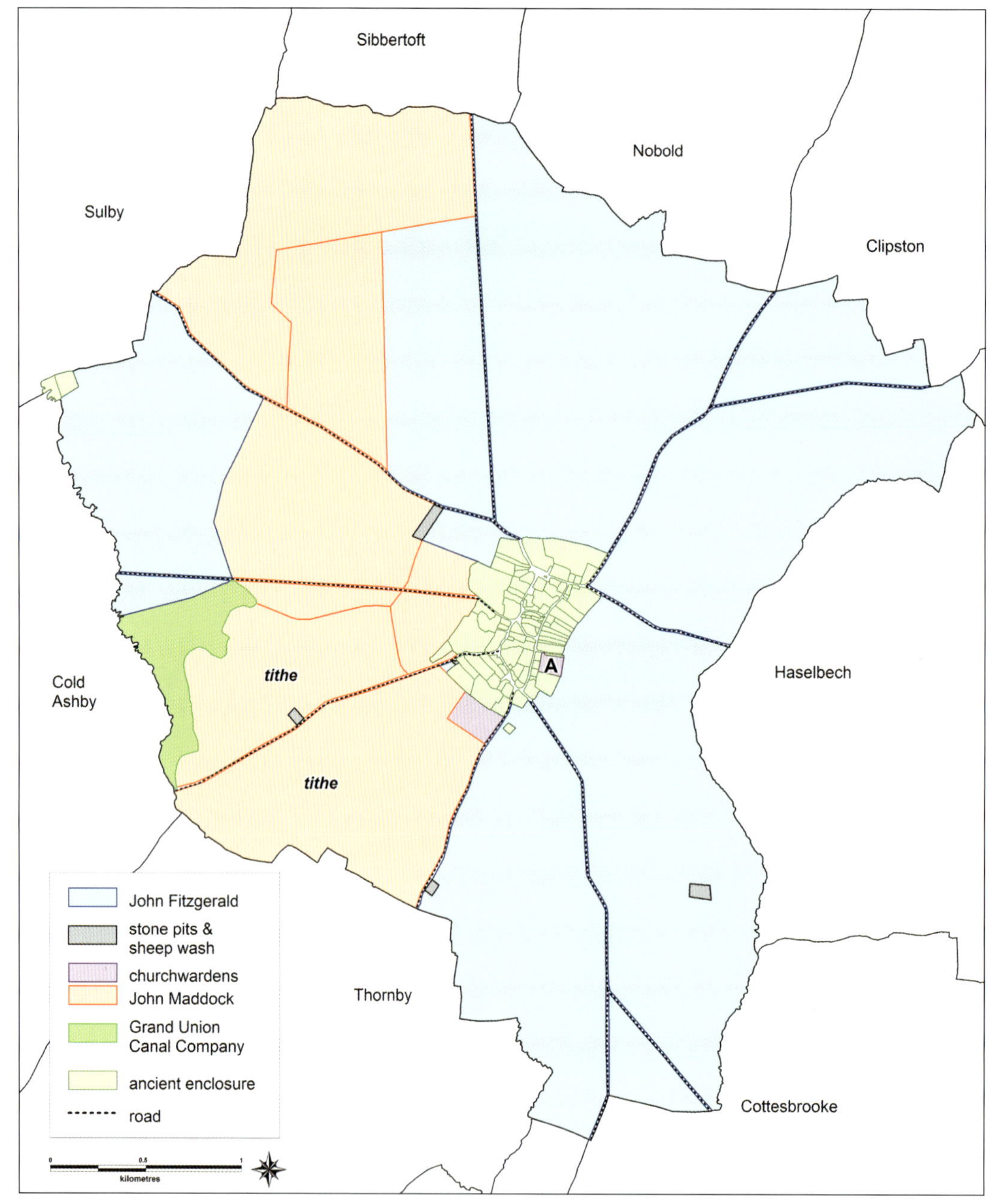

Figure 50. Enclosure allotments at Naseby taken from the enclosure map 1822. 'A' marks the plot that is now the village allotment gardens.

for the inhabitants of the parish' as at Collyweston where the plot of ground allotted remains the village playing fields to this day.[63]

By far the largest proportion of land allotted for non-landowning rights was that given for extinguishment of tithes. It was not a requirement of enclosure that tithes be extinguished but in the majority of Northamptonshire enclosures they were. Indeed when the Tithe Commutation Act was introduced in 1836 (whereby tithes were substituted by a money payment) only 23% of the county remained titheable.[64] As with most issues relating to enclosure there was no standardised approach and the methods adopted varied between places. In some places only the land being enclosed was exempted from tithe payments, with a plot of land allocated in lieu (for example Isham, Newnham, Norton, Northampton, Spratton and Islip); in other places the titheable ancient enclosure was also included and in yet others some but not all of the ancient enclosure might be included. If the owners of ancient enclosure also had land in the open fields the tithes on their ancient enclosures could be exempted with a subsequent reduction in their open field allotment which was given to the tithe holder. If, however, they did not own any open field land their tithes would remain payable or be commuted to a fluctuating corn rent based on the price of wheat. At Easton on the Hill the lord of the manor became the sole payer of a corn rent to the rector but received an allocation of land from all the other proprietors as compensation.

The amount of land allocated for tithes depended on whether it was for great or small tithes and the type of land in question i.e. open field arable, pasture or meadow; woodland; ancient enclosure, orchards, gardens and so on. Put simply the great tithes (including hay, grain and wood) were payable to the rector and the small tithes (all others) to the vicar. The reality was anything but simple.[65] The whole question of tithe payments was a very vexed one to all parties not least because it had become extremely complicated over the centuries, altered by custom, ignorance, evasion or avarice. One reason for resentment, on the part of the tithe payers, was that after the Dissolution of the monasteries many of the great tithes had devolved to lay hands and what was once considered to be a payment for the support of the church was now seen as a simple tax to private individuals. The small tithes that went to the vicar were objected to for a variety of reasons not least because any investment by the farmer resulting in increased yields was given to the vicar who had made no contribution to the improvements. It should be noted that the tithe recipients were generally equally dissatisfied with the state of affairs due to the difficulties of establishing what was due to them and then the problems of collecting their dues.

All tithes were a tenth of the produce but the amount of land allocated in lieu of tithes at enclosure was much greater than this. National studies have shown that by the end of the 18th century one fifth of arable and one ninth of pasture land were normally allocated.[66] In Northamptonshire this was also the usual amount allocated as at Wadenhoe and Raunds where it equated to 24% and 20% of the land enclosed respectively. The allotments given for tithes at Naseby can be seen in Figure 50. An examination of the data from the awards shows that a tithe allotment of 20% of the land being enclosed was not unusual and at least 43 places had more than this. At Walton no less than 41% of the land enclosed was allotted to tithe holders.[67] From this it can be seen that enclosure could enable non-landowners, either ecclesiastical or lay, to become quite substantial landowners or significantly increase their existing holdings.

Conversely landowners with very small holdings may have found themselves worse off after enclosure. They would have received an allotment equivalent in value to what they owned with an additional allowance for loss of common rights but they would also have lost a proportion of land for manorial, tithe and other institutional allotments discussed above and then had to share the costs. The gain and loss might have balanced out but the costs to a small owner could be crippling.[68] Costs for procuring the bill, act and award as well as commissioners, surveyors and labourers fees, equipment and victuals were usually met by all proprietors and paid proportionally to the amount of land owned; the greater the landholding the greater the proportion of the costs paid. But the cost of fencing was met by each individual for his own plot/s. Enclosure required all allotments to be ring-fenced and many of the maps indicated which owner has responsibility for fencing shared boundaries. Fences were initially post and rail as a protection for the 'quick sets' (hawthorn and blackthorn, the commonest species in the Midlands) and were proportionally more expensive the smaller the plot. Moreover, the rector and vicar's costs and those of the Crown if there were any, were generally met by the rest of the proprietors.[69]

The commissioners were aware of the adverse effects of costs to the small holders and not infrequently attempted to alleviate them. At Mears Ashby proprietors of less than one acre were exempt from costs, at Arthingworth the same applied to those with no more than 6 acres. At Raunds those with common right but no land or no more than ten acres in the open fields could apply to have their costs and fencing met by the other proprietors, providing the commissioners 'deemed them proper subjects for their benevolence'. Interestingly also at Raunds the cottagers could have a common pasture if six or more requested it. The commissioners presumably acknowledging that the tiny individual plots allowed for cottage commons were more useful if grouped into a shared larger plot. Small allotments made to the churchwardens for the church fabric or poor relief could also be exempt from costs, though this seems to be less frequent. At Apethorpe the costs of ring fencing the land allotted to trustees of church and town land were to be shared by the other proprietors and at Twywell where the 3 roods allotted to the churchwardens 'would not bear the cost of fencing' the commissioners could add the plot to 'any person they saw fit' who would then be responsible for paying an annual fee for 'beautifying the church'.[70]

The number of allottees could have a very significant effect upon the landscape created at enclosure. At Naseby there were only five allottees and only two of them were landowners; the others were made for stone pits, to the churchwardens and to the Grand Union Canal Company (Figure 50). Here the newly enclosed landscape is very simple with large blocks of contiguous land in single ownership. The only divisions are the roads and the few allotment boundaries on the western side of the township.

In contrast Kislingbury had 74 allottees creating a very different landscape (Figure 51). Here the patchwork of regular blocks familiar in the modern landscape was created at enclosure, but note the varied size of the plots reflecting the large number of

Figure 51. Kislingbury enclosure map 1779. North is at the bottom. (NRO Map 2853).

allottees. However, after enclosure owners were free to reorganise their allotments and in both places they did, resulting in very similar landscapes. An example of the comparable post enclosure landscapes in three townships with very different numbers of allottees at enclosure is given in Figure 52 and see also Figure 54 which shows the very similar modern landscape at Naseby.

Roads

Although the introduction of hedged enclosures was arguably the greatest change in the landscape at enclosure another fundamental change could be seen in the roads. Roads were one of the most standardised of features from the enclosure process; route, width, fences, gates and use of roadside herbage were all prescribed in the awards and new roads were often very straight; as such they are the most recognisably 'parliamentary' feature.

The road network created by parliamentary enclosure was prescribed by the conditions stipulated in the act and refined by the commissioners in the award. It has been suggested by Turner that the width of major roads created at enclosure decreased over the 18th century and that prior to 'about 1790' they were 60ft wide with only a 20ft central carriageway and equally wide grass verges to either side. After that date the width generally reduces to 40ft possibly as an attempt by the local parish officers to discourage undesirable elements, i.e. potential criminals and anyone who might at some point attempt to claim a settlement, from camping.[71] There is some suggestion

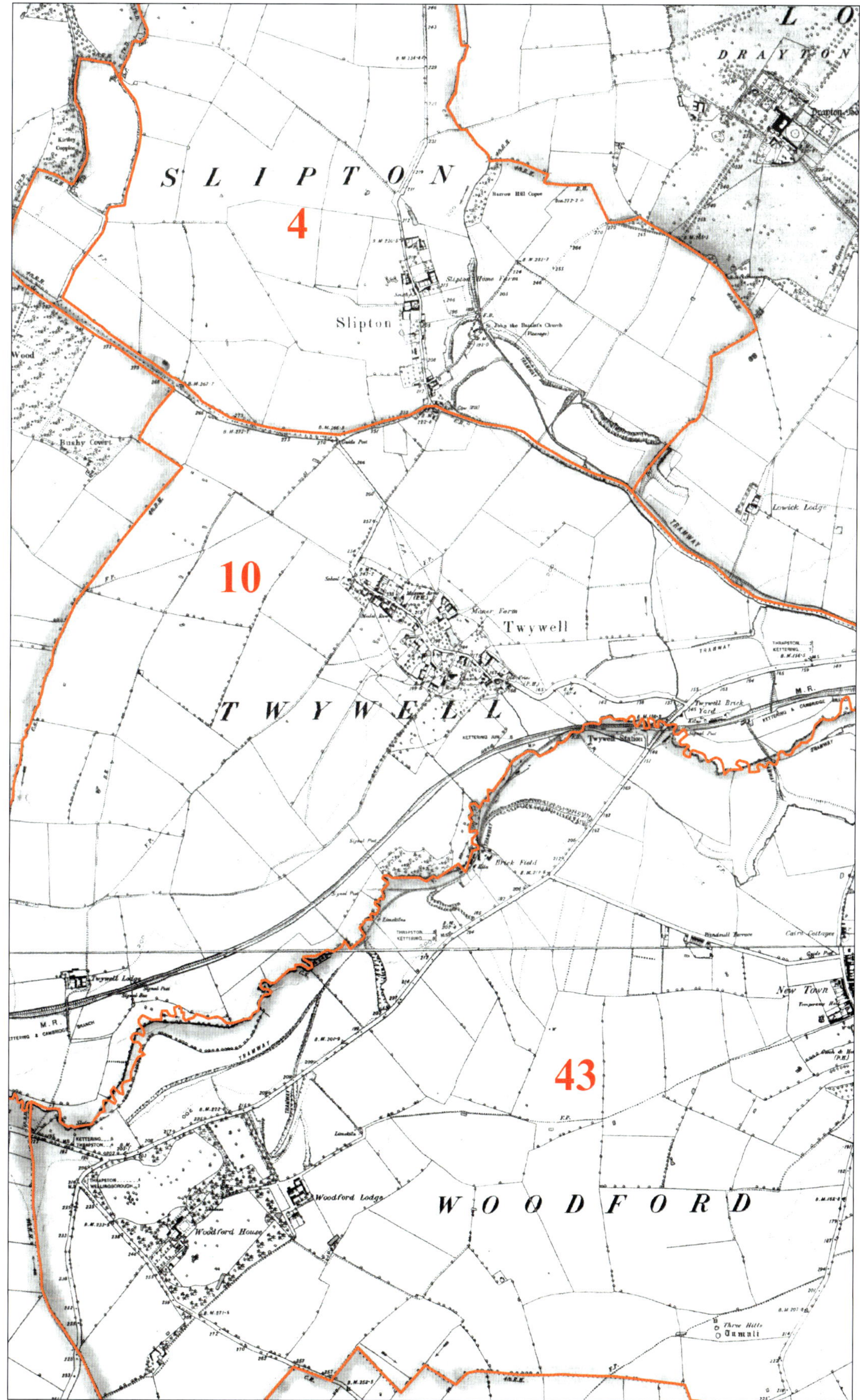

Figure 52. Slipton (1771), Twywell (1765) and Woodford (1763) in the 1880s showing the number of allottees at enclosure. Compare to Figures 50, 51 and 54.

Figure 53. The northern half of Naseby township in 1817. The township is ringed by ancient enclosure. Note the wholly open fields with no woods or enclosure outside of the village, and the meandering nature of the roads.This map provides some landscape detail with streams and topography indicated but no open field detail. (© British Library. Reproduced by permission, OSD 261).

that in Northamptonshire the width of roads did decrease over the period but no reasons are given for this and as with other issues connected to enclosure there is no standardisation across the county.

The act would normally give broad directions as to the width of the roads such as that at Brington (enclosed 1743) which stipulates '*all public roads to be made shall be and remain forty feet broad at the least between the ditches*'.[72] This varied between places some specifying a width of 60ft 'at the least' and some as little as 30ft.[73] The award specified each road, bridleway and footpath giving specific instructions to the width as decided by the commissioners. It did not however specify how much of the road was to be metalled nor did it give a precise description of the route the road was to take. Usually the start and end points are given with the route in between disappointingly vague; for example 'proceeding in a north-easterly direction'. A written description was probably considered unnecessary as the map made to accompany the award would define the route. The commissioners could alter the course of existing roads or extinguish them altogether as well as lay out wholly new routes. The lack of a written description is therefore particularly problematic for the 61 places where no map has been found and the exact road network created at enclosure is impossible to establish. Moreover, an enclosure map alone is of limited use as it will depict the new roads being established with no indication of pre-existing features. Turnpike roads are the exception to this as they were exempted from the award; it being specified that the commissioners had no authority to alter their route. They could, however, allocate small plots alongside the turnpikes as long as the enclosure did not encroach upon the specified width of the turnpike or inconvenience road users. In addition to route and width other factors affecting roads were also given in great detail. The allocation of roadside herbage, grazing of stock, gates and fencing, stone pits for making and maintenance were all covered in the award. Given this wealth of detail it is possible to examine many of the county's roads and the effects of enclosure upon them, particularly where there are pre-enclosure maps in addition to the enclosure map itself. An example of enclosure roads from the parliamentary period follows for Naseby which has a sequence of maps.

Naseby was enclosed in 1820. The award and map were made in 1822.[74] There is no draft enclosure map giving pre-enclosure detail but the extent of open field on the enclosure map matches that on an estate map of 1630.[75] Though the land use had changed significantly in the intervening period (see above) the road network remained largely the same. This can be verified by the Ordnance Surveyors Drawings dating 1817 which shows the pre-enclosure landscape at Naseby (Figure 53).

The network of pre-enclosure and enclosure roads has been mapped in Figures 54 and 56. Without the benefit of the pre-enclosure maps it would not be possible to plot the early routes of the roads from just the descriptions given in the award or from the roads shown on the enclosure map. For example the road from Naseby to Welford (via Sulby) is described as '*beginning at the North end of the village of Naseby and proceeding Northwestwardly over Spinney Field to the end of a road in the parish of Sulby at Hackney Hill Gate*'.[76] It is impossible to say from this description whether this is a new road, an existing road or slightly modified existing route.

However, when data from the early maps is overlaid on a modern OS Explorer background (Figure 54) it can be seen that the enclosure road to Welford ignores both existing roads, plotting a much straighter course between the two. All three come together some 500m before reaching the gate into Sulby. It is of note that Naseby is ringed by anciently enclosed townships and Clipston which had been enclosed in 1776, therefore the access points into these places were already fixed. The routes leading to these points however were not fixed and given the lack of any obstructing feature, such as ancient enclosures or woods, the new roads could take a winding or straight course. It can be seen in Figures 54 and 56 that the roads are very mixed; some following existing routes and others completely new. And of note is the lack of uniformity in the alignment of the new routes. The road to Welford, though reasonably straight, does curve slightly; the road to Cottesbrooke is not direct but has angular rather than curved bends; the roads to Cold Ashby on the east and Sibbertoft in the north are by contrast straight as a die (Figure 55).

The reasons for the different roads within what was, to all intents and purposes for the commissioners, a blank canvas is unclear. It does not appear to be related to the number of landowners or allotments made. There were very few allotments and only two principal owners and with the exception of the Thornby road, which was an existing route, the roads do not separate ownership (Figure 50). It may, however, be partly explained by the land use at the time of enclosure.

If the roads are viewed against the pattern of furlongs, as they would have been when at the height of the arable open field system, it can be seen that the enclosure roads on the same alignment as earlier ones fit within the furlongs (Figure 56). Similarly the roads to Welford and Cottesbrooke, though new, also fit within the furlongs. The particularly straight roads to Cold Ashby and Sibbertoft ignore the furlong pattern crossing the strips directly. There is no obvious reason why all of the new roads could not be as straight. But making new roads was expensive, which is arguably one of the reasons that existing alignments were retained. And it might also be why existing features within the furlong pattern such as headlands and baulks were used for convenience rather than crossing the ridge and furrow. At the time of enclosure two thirds of the open fields were pasture and perhaps in these areas it was simpler to create a direct route. If so the pattern of roads may represent, at least in part, the land use at the time of enclosure. Also of note is the meandering course of several of the early roads that take no account of the furlong pattern. However, this road pattern though pre-enclosure is not necessarily medieval and should not be taken as representative of the road system that existed at the height of the open field system. Nor does it indicate that prior to enclosure roads could take any route across the furlongs with no account of the crops. Indeed, field orders from 1803 specify '*that divers gates had been improperly erected and roads made across the fields*'. This was to cease and '*no cattle or carts or waggons be allowed to go over the field except in the regular established roads*'.[77]

All of the roads listed in the award are stipulated to be laid out at 30ft wide. There is no mention of who is allotted the herbage, the grass alongside each road, as is usually the case. Sometimes this is given to the owner of the adjacent plot or to the overseers of the highways to rent out for grazing using the income for upkeep of the roads. At Naseby the roads are so narrow that this was perhaps considered unnecessary. Interestingly there is no provision for footpaths in the award and Naseby is singularly lacking in footpaths today, having only one. This is remarkable, even amongst Northamptonshire townships.

Roads within anciently enclosed townships differ to those from the parliamentary period in several ways; they are more likely to retain the existing network, follow existing routes and many would have only been hedged on one side or not hedged at all. But perhaps where they differ most is in their width. Early roads were generally much wider than later ones both local routes as well as major thoroughfares. Such roads did not usually remain at this width – a rare surviving example is at Clopton in East Northamptonshire. In most cases they were absorbed into the closes which

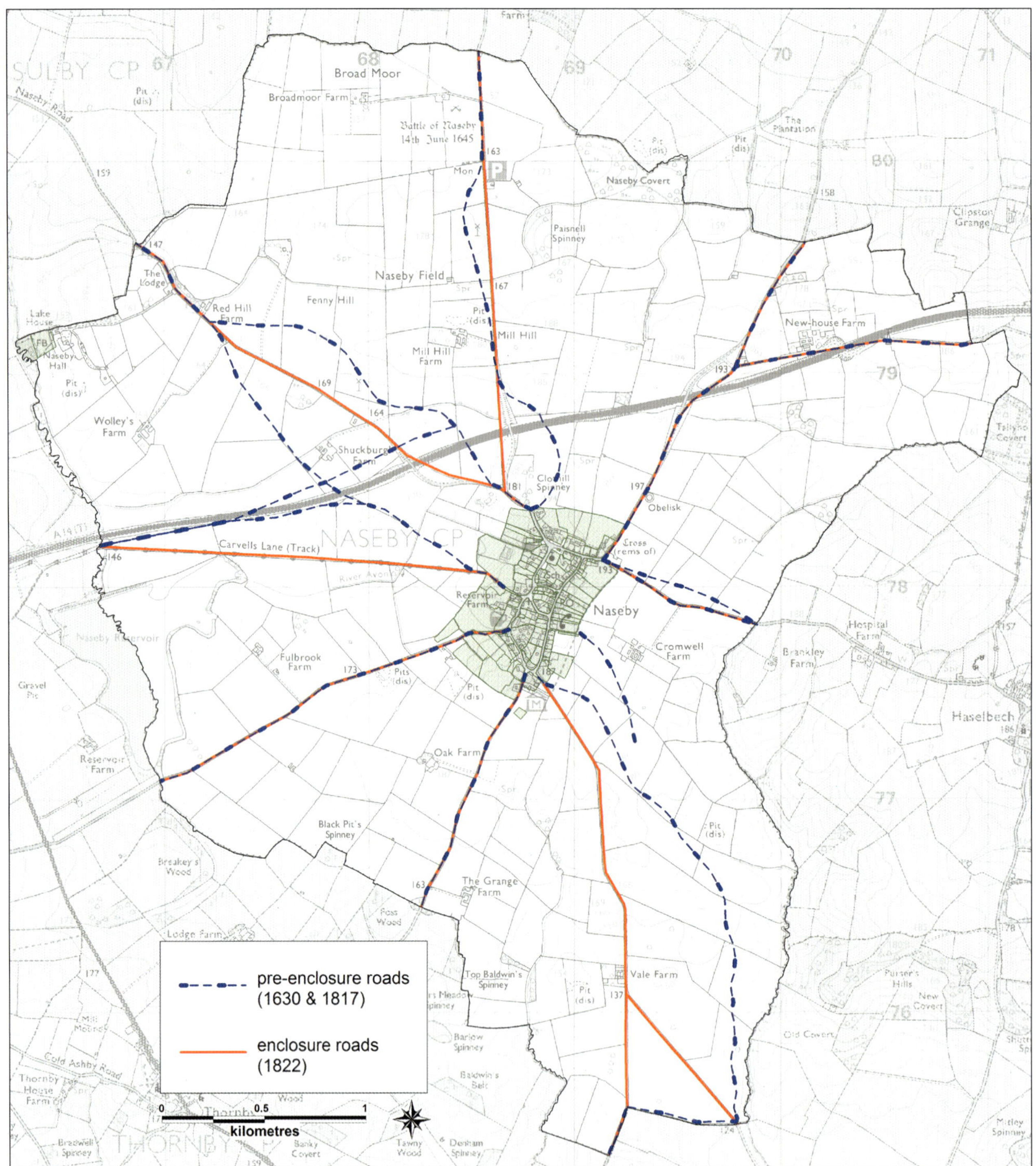

Figure 54. Naseby roads on the Ordnance Survey Explorer background. From this it can be seen which of the early roads were replaced and which are wholly new. Two of the enclosure roads were subsequently realigned to make way for another new road, the A14. (Crown Copyright, Ordnance Survey licence no. 100026873).

lay on either side so narrowing the width of the road. But they might also be encroached upon by new small plots being laid out along them. Wide verges alongside roads were generally described as 'waste' i.e. they were not cultivated. That does not mean that the land was not used as it provided valuable grazing particularly in townships with little other pasture. In the medieval period this waste was the property of the lord of the manor. At enclosure it was included in the allotment process and the lord of the manor received compensation. For many of the anciently enclosed townships some of the roads were left very wide at enclosure; at Charwelton (enclosed *c.*1480) up to 110ft, Thornby (enclosed 1623) 100ft, Clopton (enclosed before 1705) 140ft, Maidwell (enclosed *c.*1691) 120ft and at Haselbech (enclosed 1598) the road was at its widest 200ft across.[78] The obvious reason for this width is to facilitate the movement of stock and waggons on poorly constructed roads that rapidly became mired, especially in winter. This was particularly problematic on the major roads that passed through a township and upon which much more than local traffic would be travelling. Once turnpikes were introduced (the first in the county was 1706) these major routes were maintained separately; indeed in all but one of the townships discussed above the wide roads became turnpikes.

The exception is Haselbech which had only local roads, but due to the survival of a series of maps and other documents as well as particularly good archaeological features it is possible to trace

Figure 55. Naseby to Sibbertoft road facing south. (© Tracey Partida).

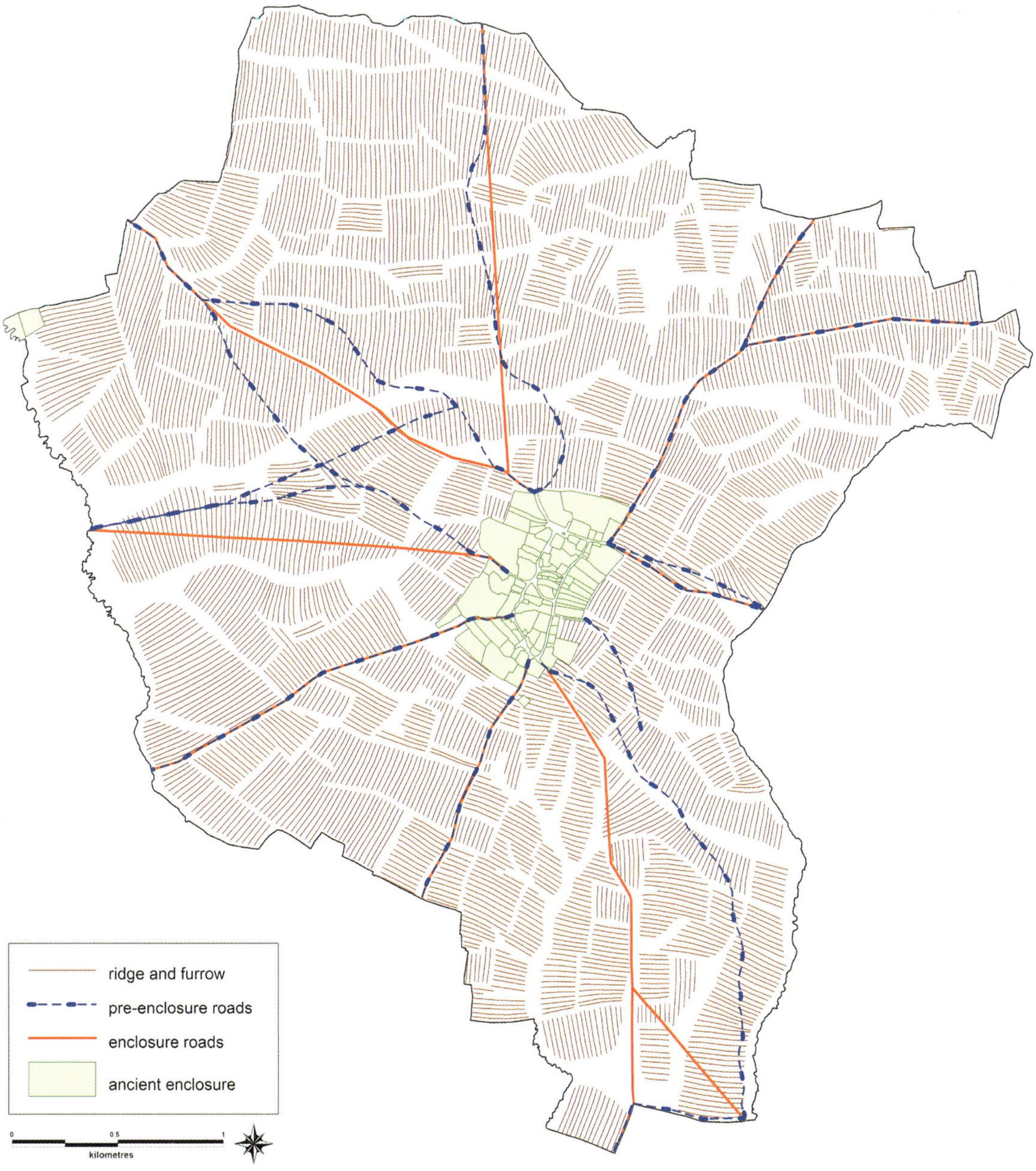

Figure 56. Pre and post enclosure roads at Naseby in relationship to the open field furlongs.

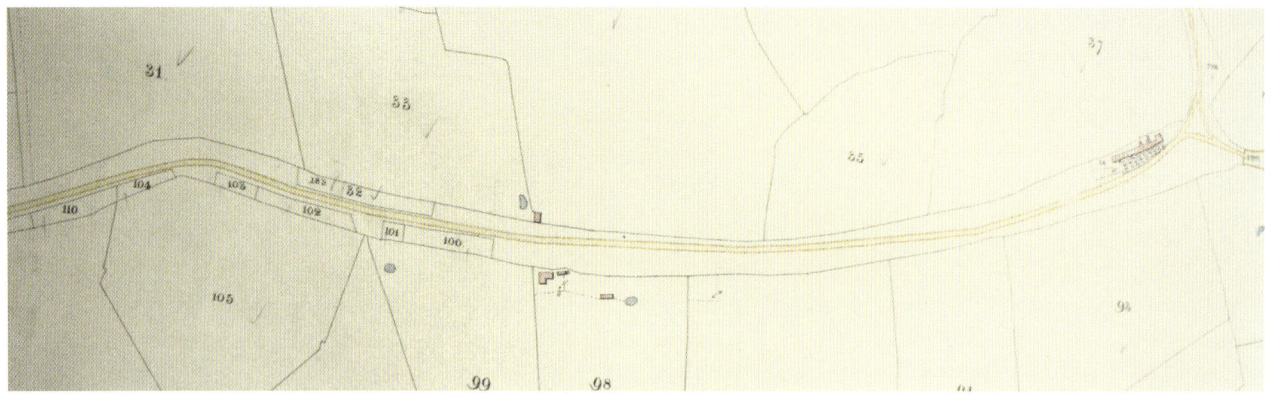

Figure 57. The 'Naseby Way' in Haselbech 1840, showing the 'gardens' that have been taken out of the road. (NRO T231).

the evolution of the roads. The first map is that accompanying the agreement dated 1598 which shows that most of the roads were hedged on one side only at enclosure. The exception is the road running to Naseby called the 'Naseby Way'. It is this road that is the widest being over 100ft broad for most of its length. The next map dated 1750 is incomplete but shows the eastern end of the road next to the village.[79] By this date the road has been narrowed with the close on the southern side taking in part of the road and a single plot with a building added to the northern side. Earthworks of the former edge of the road can be seen in the close on the southern side. Further along the road towards Naseby the road has also narrowed but in a very different way. Here the road has been encroached upon by small plots along either side, first seen on the tithe map dated 1840 (Figure 57).[80]

An undated map (but post-dating the tithe map) marked 'enclosure of waste' shows further plots being added to the northern side of this road.[81] The tithe schedule describes these plots as 'gardens'. Similar plots are seen on the tithe maps for Charwelton and Thornby where they are also described as 'gardens'.[82] At Maidwell an undated estate map also shows the same type of plots but has no accompanying schedule.[83] None of these places has a sequence of maps enabling dating of these features and even at Haselbech the date of all but the later ones are uncertain. These features do seem to be most commonly found in anciently enclosed townships where the roads were very wide, but not exclusively so.

At Paulerspury similar plots can be found alongside Watling Street (the modern A5) a major thoroughfare in the county and a turnpike. These were created at enclosure in 1819 when they were allotted to the Duke of Grafton.[84] By the time the tithe map is made in 1839 these plots have been further subdivided and are described as 'potato gardens'.[85] This description gives some clue as to their purpose, as does the size of the plots and fact that they were not occupied by owners but let to numerous people, indicating that they were intended for labourers to provide additional land for crops. Moreover, there is additional evidence in Paulerspury vestry minute book dated 19th February 1834 *'that a plan to obtain potato grounds for the poor be taken into consideration at the next vestry'*.[86] There is no further mention of this in the vestry minutes but clearly provision was made, albeit not managed by the parish officers. This example from Paulerspury is indicative of a process underway nationally. Towards the end of the 18th century there were various measures taken across the country to provide additional land to the poor as a response to increasing poor rates resulting from high grain prices and unemployment, aggravated by a succession of poor harvests and the Napoleonic Wars. Potato grounds and later allotment gardens were two of the methods introduced to provide land to the poor to grow crops. Potato grounds were plots of land let by farmers on a temporary basis to grow potatoes. They might be on the fallow in which case the tenant would benefit from land that had been ploughed and manured, or on uncultivated land such as the corners of fields and, significantly, roadside verges. In either case they were temporary arrangements the land reverting to the farmer, or the waste, once the crop was harvested. Allotment gardens differed in that were let annually by landowners, rather than farmers who might themselves be tenants, or parish officers. [87]

There are numerous places in Northamptonshire with these roadside plots in addition to those mentioned above. At Greatworth they are described as 'garden[s] in Welsh Lane', at Farthinghoe, Gayton and Watford as 'gardens taken from the waste' and at Sudborough, Stowe Nine Churches, Dingley and Moreton Pinkney simply as 'gardens'.[88] They are almost certainly evidence of provision for the poor in the form of potato grounds, or at least a variant of the type described by Burchardt. What is particularly interesting about them is that although they were intended as temporary measures they have become fossilised in the landscape and are a common feature in the county, if mostly overgrown and concealed. Also of interest are those that can be found along

Figure 58. An enclosed roadside strip in the Banbury Lane which may have been utilised by drovers, but was probably enclosed to create potato gardens for the poor. (© Judith Hodgkinson).

the Welsh Lane (or Road) and the Banbury Lane, both noted drovers' routes (Figure 58). It might be supposed that these in particular are most likely associated with pasturing cattle *en route* to market, and whilst convenient enclosed plots within wide verges may well have been utilised by drovers they weren't necessarily created by or for them. Indeed whilst wide roads were necessary for transporting cattle it is unlikely that drovers could have pastured their beasts wherever they thought fit and certainly not overnight. Grass within each township, enclosed or otherwise, was managed just like any other resource as has been discussed above. It is therefore doubtful that parish officials would have allowed large numbers of cattle belonging to 'foreigners', (as anyone not of the parish was referred to) to avail themselves of such a valuable resource, not at least without agreement and some form of payment. In the parish records viewed so far I have found no record of any such arrangement and where drovers' records have been studied they were clearly using taverns with grazing facilities and, equally importantly, water, as stopping places.[89]

The wide roadside verges may have served multiple functions over the centuries but the strongest evidence for the small enclosed plots along them is that they are the archaeological remains of late 18th and early 19th century poor relief.

Two other post enclosure features require some brief discussion and they are dispersed buildings and unenclosed land. Prior to enclosure there would have been few buildings outside the settlement core. The exceptions were mills, warren houses and lodges associated with hunting. After enclosure when land was organised into discrete blocks of ownership it was possible to locate farms and their buildings within the fields. This was the case whether the land was farmed by an owner/occupier or by an owner for tenants. And it explains why the landscape seen in the 1880s (when it is possible to compare the whole county from a single source) is remarkably similar. The extent of dispersal varied from place to place depending on the number of landowners, size of holdings and agricultural regime. Building investment was expensive so many smaller farmers would have remained in the village, as can be seen Clipston where in the 1880s there were only about four farms in the landscape but several in the village where many of the buildings survive to this day. There were 24 allottees at enclosure in Clipston most having small allotments. In the census returns from 1881 there are nine farmers and one farm bailiff, but significantly there are also six graziers and five shepherds. At Naseby there were about ten farms and several barns in the landscape.[90] Here there were only two owners but they had 35 tenants between them at the time of enclosure.[91] In the 1881 census for Naseby there are 11 farmers and five farm bailiffs but no graziers and only three shepherds. The agricultural regime at Clipston may explain, at least in part, why there were so few farms in the landscape; graziers rented land so did not need to live outside of the village, similarly shepherds did not require a permanent dwelling in the fields. Whilst at Naseby they may have been operating a different agricultural regime, but the fact that the majority of farmers were tenants may also partly explain why there were more farms built outside of the settlement. Building investment by large landowners and estates in both the village and wider landscape was the norm in the 19th century, partly because of the increased rents it produced. Evidence of which can be seen across the county especially as many estates adopted a 'house' style of architecture which is immediately recognisable. The grandest of the farm buildings are those on the Grafton estate where several model farms were built in the 19th century. This significant investment was seen partly as a means of advertising personal wealth and status but was also intended to attract a 'better class of tenant'.

There was very little land in Northamptonshire that was left unenclosed by an enclosure act. The notable exception is Ailsworth Heath. Ailsworth was enclosed with Castor in 1895 and the heath was specifically excluded from enclosure. At that date it was some 185 acres and the only substantial area of land unenclosed in the county. Other smaller blocks of unenclosed land are village greens many of which survive across the county. Some were lost, either partially or wholly, at enclosure when they were divided up and allotted, sometimes being added as front gardens to existing houses, as at Barby and Glinton.[92]

The landscape created by enclosure reflects the reasons behind it and the numbers of people involved. This is particularly relevant to early enclosures which are associated with parks and sheep farming creating distinctive landscapes. With later enclosures it is the number of landowners, or allottees, that arguably has the most significant effect upon the landscape. However, regardless of period or motive or numbers of landowners it is the changing agricultural regime and the modifications made in the landscape to accommodate it that has the most lasting effect upon the landscape. There are some features that are purely aesthetic, even outside of park boundaries, such as plantations on hills giving pleasing views from a country house or marking the boundary of an estate. Similarly some features are created for recreational purposes such as shooting or hunting where again plantations might be used. But these still exist within a working agricultural environment and those created for shooting might justifiably be considered working environments in themselves. Therefore the landscape we see in the county today is that created by an evolving agricultural regime.

The modern landscape developed from the enclosure process. But post-enclosure reorganisation means much of the original landscape is lost or obscured. There were features that might be said to be typical of a period; large closes, or very wide roads are indicative of early enclosures; whilst regular fields and straight roads are more common to later enclosures. But it is too simplistic to suppose that the modern landscape can be dated or understood simply by examining shapes and patterns. For example, regular features are not always from late enclosure. At Plumpton, enclosed in 1515, the first map is dated 1604 and shows remarkably regular plots with straight boundaries on the north side of the village. Similarly at Nobottle, enclosed *c.*1680, a map dated 1715 shows what is arguably one of the most regular landscapes in the county.[93] Nobottle was owned by Earl Spencer at neighbouring Althorp and at enclosure the landscape was clearly organised for the convenience of the tenants. Here there has been no dispersal of farms into the landscape, perhaps unnecessary in such a small township, rather each farm in the village has a contiguous group of closes radiating out like the spines of a fan. Each 'spine' has been arranged in such a way to allow the farms access to their land without crossing another property.

Similarly, some very large closes might be supposed to be early but are the result of hedgerow removal. Where there is good map evidence it is possible to identify particular features even when the remainder of the landscape has changed beyond recognition. For example at Abthorpe enclosure took place in stages, some of it documented in 1610, with final enclosure in 1823. The landscape has changed dramatically since as most of the early boundaries have been removed. But of note are the two lanes to the south-west of the village leading through the closes to barns and then stopping. These almost certainly represent the access ways created as part of the early phases of enclosure and now fossilised in the landscape.[94] Without maps it is impossible to do this, as at Charwelton enclosed in *c.*1480 but where the first complete map is the tithe dated 1847. We can learn a great deal about the landscape in 1847 but have no idea how it evolved in the preceding 367 years.

The implications for conservation and management cannot be underestimated. In order to understand how the landscape evolved and what particular features represent and when they first appeared it is necessary to examine all available maps. From this it is possible to reconstruct the landscape from different periods and trace its evolution.

Enclosure of the forests

An account of forest administration and rights of various communities is given in Chapter 3. What follows is a very brief discussion of the enclosure and immediate aftermath, of the forests.

Rockingham, Whittlewood and Salcey forests were enclosed between 1795 and 1853.[95] In Rockingham and Whittlewood there were separate acts for the various walks and bailiwicks within the forests, only Salcey was enclosed in its entirety by a single act. In some cases walks or bailiwicks were enclosed with the open field land in adjacent townships; Rockingham bailiwick was enclosed with Gretton, Brigstock bailiwick with Brigstock and Stanion and

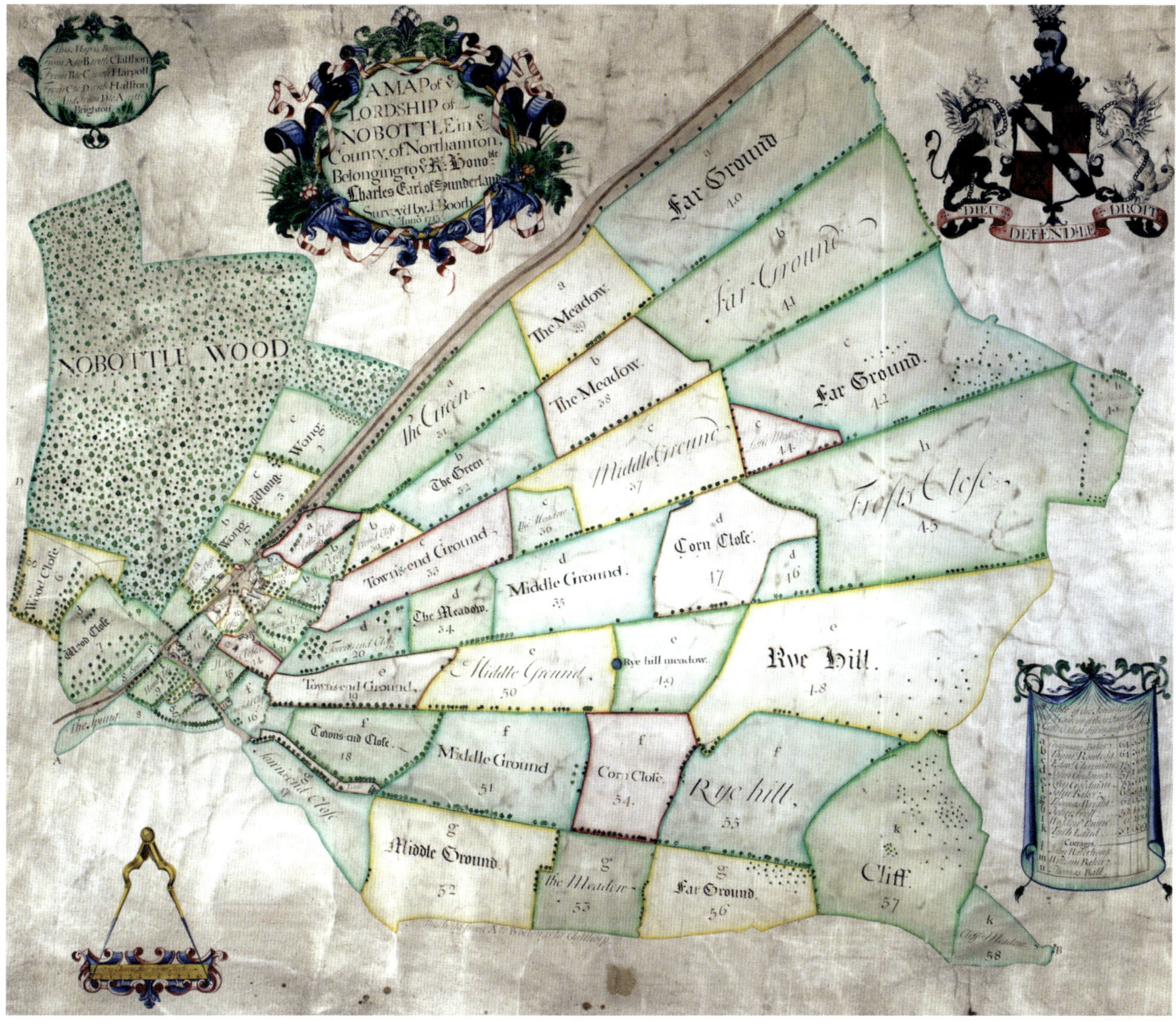

Figure 59. Nobottle in 1715. Of note is the regular pattern of closes. Each set of closes is organised to give the individual farms in the village access to their land without crossing another property. (© British Library. Reproduced by permission, ADD.78143).

in Whittlewood Hazelborough Walk was enclosed with Silverstone. In Rockingham the woods had been alienated by this date (see Chapter 2) though the Crown still retained certain rights. Both Whittlewood and Salcey were still the property of the Crown. All three were still subject to forest law and to various common rights within neighbouring townships and manors.

The acts to enclose the forests were similar to those for enclosing open field land in that they cite the need for improvement as the motivation for enclosure. But they also state the 'injurious' nature of common rights and in particular the abuse of such rights, including nut gathering, upon the growth of timber and wellbeing of the deer thus compounding the need to enclose.[96] Common rights could be and were, held by individuals and institutions from the Crown to the poor. As such they varied enormously depending on the affiliation of the holder. The Crown might hold mineral rights, rights in the soil and of course rights to the deer, as well as common rights attached to manorial holdings in forest townships. Other owners of woods, or township property, or manors, or forest offices could also hold rights, as could the landless poor.

Untangling the validity of claims to various rights was an unenviable task given the complex granting out of lands and privileges over the preceding centuries. For example at the enclosure of Rockingham bailiwick the numerous claims included the king who claimed 'sole right' in the deer as well as their 'herbage and feed', yet the Earl of Winchelsea also claimed 'all the deer', except those supplied annually to the king's larder, as well as the herbage. Moreover, Sir Arthur de Capell Brooke owned a significant number of coppices and woodland around Beanfield Lawn as well as purlieu woods and rights as lord of the manor of Great Oakley. The Earl of Winchelsea and

Nottingham owned Beanfield lawn and various forest offices. He also owned substantial woods in and was lord of the manor of Gretton.[97] Lord Sondes claimed to be sole proprietor of forest land in the parish of Rockingham and also the rights as lord of the manor of Rockingham. The Earl of Cardigan owned woods in and was lord of the manor of Corby. Other aristocratic claimants held rights but not woodland: the Duke of Buccleuch as lord of the manor of Little Oakley and for privileges granted to a predecessor; the honourable Barbara Cockayne Medlicott as lady of the manor of Cottingham with Desborough. There was a further claim on this last manor by the 'Lords of the Manor of Cottingham with Desborough in trust for the copyholders of the same manor'.[98] There were then claims by various forest officers and the rectors and vicars of the several parishes concerned; Rockingham, Cottingham cum Middleton, Great Oakley, Little Oakley, Gretton and Corby. Lastly claims for common rights relating to individual properties in the different parishes including those belonging to the aforementioned manorial holders and over two hundred smallholders.

The claims documents for Brigstock bailiwick are particularly useful in that they specify what the claim is e.g. a cottage and what rights are attached to the holding.[99] For example Adam Bellamy claims the rights for two copyhold cottages which include '2 acres of hedgerow and freeboard as part of the ring fence of farming woods' and for 'horses and neat cattle' on Lords Walk and in Geddington Chase.[100] Many of the claims include a section of hedge and most specify the number of different stock they are entitled to common including 'hogs in the time of acorns'. The less specific 'according to the usual custom' claims were generally disallowed. In addition to stocking animals in the woods some claims were also made and allowed, for gathering 'grass with a hook out of the coppices ... to bring home to give to cattle in the stable' thus giving additional feed when the woods were not open.[101]

Once the claims had been heard and made public it was possible for objections to be made before the commissioners made their decision. The published objections to the claims in Rockingham bailiwick show that the Crown objected to some or all of every one of the aristocratic and manorial claims as well as the unstinted right of common of all claimants. They and the rector of Cottingham cum Middleton in turn objected to the Crown's and each others' claims. No objection was made, or at least recorded here, by the numerous smallholders.[102]

The enclosure of Whittlewood and Salcey were less complicated as the Crown was the sole owner. But allotments were made to the Duke of Grafton who had certain rights in the underwood as well as holding the offices of Warden, Master Forester or Ranger and Master of the Game in Whittlewood, whilst his son the Earl of Euston was Warden at Salcey.[103] Compensation also had to be made to the commoners of the forest villages. At Salcey the villages of Hartwell, Ashton, Quinton, Piddington and Hackleton, and Hanslope in Buckinghamshire claimed rights of common in the forest. After the Crown's and Duke's allotments had been made the proprietors from the aforementioned villages received allotments in the residue, though each block was situated as close to the township in question as was possible.[104] It is of note that all trees on these allotments, including 'underwood, bushes, hollies and thorns and standels' remained the property of the Crown and the duke, though the new proprietors could purchase them if they wished. Similarly in Whittlewood the townships of Whitfield, Silverstone, Syresham with Crowfield, Wappenham and Slapton had right of common in Haselborough walk; and Whittlebury, Potterspury with Yardley Gobion, Passenham with Deanshanger, Paulerspury with Heathencote, Alderton, Grafton Regis, Wicken and Lillingstone Lovell and Lillingstone Dayrell (the latter two in Buckinghamshire) over Wakefield, Hanger, Sholbrook and Shrob walks.[105] General allotments were made to each of these townships in lieu of common rights.

Allotments were also made as compensation to the poor for loss of the right 'to gather sere and broken wood'[106] which would be vested in the churchwardens or overseers of the poor. At the later enclosure of Whittlewood there was no allotment of land but the commissioners purchased annuities, dividends from this to be used to buy coal to be distributed at Christmas.[107]

After enclosure those woods that were Crown property or remained in private hands continued, mostly, wooded. And it is of note that at Whittlewood and Salcey the allotments made to the Crown and the Duke of Grafton were to be 'best adapted, from the nature of the soil and other circumstances, for the growth and cultivation of timber' suggesting the intention was to retain the woods after enclosure.[108] Furthermore, where the woods were in the hands of a single owner he often took pains to allot plots in lieu of common right in other land that he owned rather than lose any of the woods. At Farming Woods and Geddington Chase in Brigstock bailiwick all allotments made for common right were outside of the privately owned woods.[109] And at King's Cliffe the Earl of Exeter gave up part of his park (which hadn't functioned as a park since at least the 1640s) to keep Westhay Walk intact.[110] Sulehay and Shortwood in Cliffe, owned by the Earl of Westmoreland also remained wooded. Morehay also owned by the Earl[111] was grubbed up before the 1880s, though some has been replanted. Rockingham bailiwick was grubbed up, physically enclosed and converted to farm land. Though this proved less favourable than had been anticipated as the land proved to be 'poorly draining, unproductive and inferior'.[112]

5 Rural Settlement

Glenn Foard

This study of rural settlement in medieval and early-modern Northamptonshire is intended to complement and extend that published in 2009 for Rockingham Forest, where the background to and methodology for our analysis is described. In the present chapter we have considered all 636 medieval settlements in the county, including ends and isolated sites, but the primary focus is on the 465 villages and hamlets. Using GIS we have compared the distribution of settlement with the underlying physical geography and with aspects of the county's medieval and early-modern landscape presented in this and the Rockingham atlas. At a more detailed level we have also compared the plan forms of each village with these same factors, though plans of only a few examples can be presented here to illustrate that analysis. The present chapter also brings together more tenuous evidence, to develop speculative hypotheses for village origins and development which could be tested by further documentary and archaeological research.

The settlement plans analysed here derive from the earliest or most useful historic mapping, enhanced by examination of further maps and other documentary sources and, where relevant, by earthwork, crop and soilmark evidence.[1] The extent of ancient enclosures is usually taken from historic maps but occasionally comes from reconstruction of the enclosure awards.[2] Together with furlong evidence from archaeological and historic map sources, these data have also been used to define the likely maximum extent of medieval settlements, though for most settlements great uncertainty remains over this.

Various difficulties were encountered in the study. Problems arose from the variable level of detail on historic maps and, because it was a countywide survey, the resolution at which the open field mapping was undertaken. Thus, for example, definition of the extent of greens on the periphery of villages has usually been possible only where pre-enclosure or draft enclosure maps survive (Figure 86). Other difficulties arose because so many of the sources were from the 18th and especially 19th century. Indeed, for 17% of sites (77 of 465 villages and hamlets) the earliest usable mapping was the first edition 6 inch Ordnance Survey of the 1880s. By this time key elements of medieval plan form will often have been lost or obscured through decay of tenement rows, as a result of desertion, engrossing, accretion and subdivision.

The earlier the available mapping the greater is the chance of recovering a plan form which more closely reflects the medieval situation. Where decline, re-planning or growth has confused the earlier plan of a village, the survival of early maps has sometimes enabled much of the original pattern to be recovered. In other cases major plan form change predates even the earliest of maps. For example, at Holdenby there are maps from the late 16th century which show elements of the village which were lost in later re-planning, yet the first stage of removal of tenements, for the laying out of the great house and its gardens, predates even these maps (Figures 38–40).[3] Earthwork, soil or cropmark data have also occasionally enabled recovery of plan forms where major changes pre-date the earliest map. While at Holdenby any such traces of the earlier settlement, apart from the original manor site, have been overwritten by the garden earthworks, at Hulcote earthworks show the layout before the hamlet was replanned around a new rectangular green in the 19th century. Similar evidence has also been has been discussed by Taylor for a number of other wholly deserted and heavily shrunken settlements.[4] However there are difficulties with many such sites in recognising the full pattern of roads, houses and tenements from such archaeological evidence. Only in a few exceptionally well documented settlements, most notably the small towns of Oundle and Kettering and the village of Irthlingborough, do written sources enable the late medieval plan form to be mapped with a high degree of confidence. Analysis of these settlements shows the true nature and scale of late medieval and early-modern changes in plan form, which has major implications for the analysis of the plan form of those settlements where all we have are much later maps.[5]

Surface geology, which is mapped countywide at 1:10,000 scale, proved the most significant of all the data sets with which we compared settlement distribution and plan form. For this analysis the geological strata were grouped into related permeable and impermeable types, both to simplify maps and, for tables and graphs, to reduce biases where some geological types are of small extent. It seems likely that the influence of surface geology works principally through its impact on soils. The present analysis would therefore have been greatly enhanced if comparison had been made to soil type, for the influence of the underlying parent geology on the soil is mediated by other factors such as slope, through its impact on drainage. Unfortunately the soils of Northamptonshire are only mapped at sufficient detail for one 10km square in the county. The value of the 1:250,000 scale soils mapping was assessed, but it is such a coarse data set that it only proved useful to reveal the broadest of patterns. The best example is the association of woodland surviving in *c.*1300 with the distribution of boulder clay. When comparison is made to the soils data this correlation is refined, for the woodland is seen to focus particularly on the Hanslope soils series but to be largely absent from the better drained Ragsdale series.

Several data sets we have used exclude the Soke of Peterborough, because they were originally produced for the Northamptonshire SMR and so covered only the modern county. These include the data on Saxon and medieval estate and ecclesiastical dependencies, and Stephen Mitchell's unpublished study of medieval and early-modern taxation and related data.[6]

Despite having one of the most nucleated of medieval settlement patterns, Northamptonshire still had some villages which display distinct 'ends', a small number of hamlets and a few isolated sites such as granges.[7] The distribution map of medieval settlement presented here is based on documentary evidence from the county place names volume and the county histories, complemented by archaeological evidence from the SMR and NMP and by examination of all relevant historic maps (Figure 60).[8] Settlements known only to be of early-modern date, such as Foster's Booth, Oakley Bank and Road Weedon, have been excluded but uncertainty remains over a few other sites. For example, Brackley Hatch has been excluded, despite the presence of embanked enclosures, because no early occurrence of the settlement name has been identified. While towns, suburbs and market villages are shown in the distribution maps, for all other aspects of our settlement analysis market villages are not distinguished from other villages.

We believe that the present analysis has identified all substantial nucleated settlements that existed in medieval Northamptonshire. Relatively few isolated medieval sites, including individual 'farms' (sometimes moated), granges, castles, monastic establishments (mainly hospitals and hermitages) and churches are known in the county. Where extensive fieldwalking and documentary research has been undertaken such isolated sites have rarely been discovered, suggesting that few such sites remain to be identified.[9] Just a handful of hamlets or isolated sites were newly identified in our historic map analysis. These include Coates on the edge of Newnham – taken to be a former hamlet – and Hale in Preston Deanery – previously known from documents but now accurately located from map evidence.[10] One or two other hamlets, such as Westhorpe immediately east of Bainton and Descote in Pattishall, known as place names from documentary evidence and broadly located, have now been accurately positioned from earthworks revealed in our search of aerial photographs.[11] Such sites are least likely to have been missed in well recorded areas of parliamentary enclosure, as the present study would normally have identified isolated areas of ancient enclosure. They are far more likely to have been missed in areas of ancient enclosure or where, as at Newnham, an early hamlet has apparently been enveloped by a village. New sites are most likely to be found in woodland areas, as that is where the majority of small hamlets and isolated farms are known.

There are several place names that are indicative of lost settlements where we still lack archaeological confirmation of the site. Examples are Luscotes, which lies within an area of assarts in the detached portion of Brigstock township; Nortoft, in the detached portion of Barby township; and Buscot, which lay in a small land unit shared between Higham Ferrers and Newton Bromswold. Such sites have normally been classified here as 'farm' but may prove to be small hamlets.[12] There is also medieval documentary evidence for several other cot, toft and related names where we have failed to establish even the general area of the site within a township, such as Isworth in Cosgrove.[13] Several other names can be placed but it is uncertain if a medieval settlement ever existed there, as with Sultoftes in the west of Kirby township in Rockingham Forest. Some of these names may relate to abandoned Saxon settlements, as seems likely with Sharlecotes which lies far beyond the well documented ancient enclosures in Kettering township. Even where there is confirmation of a site and its medieval date, it is not always clear whether the settlement was a hamlet or an isolated 'farm', as at Coton in Gretton where the documentary evidence seems to conflict with the archaeological data.[14]

The known deer park lodges lie principally on boulder clay in the heart of the woodland (Figure 20). They have not been added to the settlement map as, in the absence of further documentary or archaeological research, it is often uncertain whether the site is medieval or later. Classification of sites on archaeological evidence alone is equally problematic, as with the 'farm' identified in Morehay by the RCHM which is more likely from its location to be a lodge.[15] Mills are also excluded as they represent a specialist topic beyond the scope of the present study.

We have applied a simplistic classification of nucleated settlement into three main groups: village, end and hamlet (Figure 60). Northamptonshire's medieval villages were typically the only or the principal settlement in a township, were of substantial extent and had a medieval church.[16] Hamlets were normally subsidiary settlements within a township, of small size, lacking a church and were often manorially dependent (Figure 61). Ends have been identified where named as such in the place-name volume, on OS 1st edition 6 inch mapping and other historic maps or, in the Rockingham area, where identified from additional documentary research.[17] A few other ends have been identified where plan form suggests a loose association with the main part of the village. Most of the semi-dispersed areas of settlement in Hartwell are classified as ends, not hamlets, because of the straggling nature of the occupation (Figure 91).

While in most cases the classification was straightforward, there are a few cases which highlight the somewhat arbitrary nature of the boundary we have drawn between village and hamlet. For example, a number of complex settlements of similar form have been differently categorised, depending on whether or not the components gained separate township status – though it must also be noted that our record of medieval townships is not definitive. Thus the two Cranfords, which are in the form of paired settlements set on either side of a stream, are classified here as separate villages. In contrast the similarly paired and loosely joined settlements of Upper and Lower Glapthorn did not become separate townships and so are classified here as a village with an end. The two nucleated settlements in the single township of Benefield, which are 1 km apart, are classified as a village (Lower Benefield, in the valley, which contained the castle and church) and a hamlet (Upper Benefield, which lies on the boulder clay plateau).

Further complications arise where township organisation was complex or is not fully understood. This is particularly true in parts of the Soke. Elsewhere we find some extremely small, separate land units. Thus the hamlet of Coton, a dependency of Gretton, has its own land unit which apparently comprised just 156 acres (63 ha), while Gretton village itself had a township comprising 2081 acres (842ha). Further problems arise where medieval sources show overlapping groupings for different purposes. Thus in part of the Peterborough Abbey estates in the 13th century it is stated that the '*vills of one lordship are united as one vill, to wit: Polebrooke, Armston and Kingsthrope and a certain portion of Thurning ... In like manner Clapton pays annually ... with Catworth, which is joined to it in [one] vill ... Likewise Hemington, Littlethorpe (parcel of Luddington) and a part of Winwick are one vill ...*'.[18] Groupings also changed over time, as with the apparent fragmentation after 1086 of a single land unit centred on Wadenhoe to form three separate townships: Wadenhoe, Pilton and Stoke Doyle.[19] In some cases these changes may reflect the very process of village development. That many subsidiary settlements gained greater independence in the late Saxon or earlier medieval period is suggested by the place name evidence. For example, the *thorpe* element of Ravensthorpe indicates an originally dependent status, while at Thornhaugh this is implied by its silent inclusion with Wittering in 1086.[20] A similar process presumably occurred where townships have been subdivided, as with Great and Little Brington or Upper and Lower Boddington.

At the other extreme are the problems posed by polyfocal settlements. In some cases the ends originated in separate hamlets, which were later enveloped by the expansion of the principal settlement. This has been demonstrated in the case of Thorpe End in Raunds by extensive archaeological work, showing it was encompassed by the late Saxon and earlier medieval expansion of the village.[21] Other examples are implied by the settlement name, as with Cotton in Long Buckby and Scanthorpe in Rushden. At Little Ecton, which lay on the eastern edge of Ecton village, systematic fieldwalking has provided ephemeral evidence which seems to confirm a Saxon origin.[22] For most polyfocal settlements, in the absence of place name or archaeological data, we do not know which ends originated as separate settlements and which represent expansion from a single focus.

Occasionally there is more than one name recorded for a settlement, which might suggest the village originated as two separate sites. For example, what we now know as the shrunken village of Kelmarsh is recorded in 1086 as *Keilmerse* and *Cailmarc* (presumably the same place), but there is another entry in the same hundred for a place called *Calme*, which also probably relates to Kelmarsh. It is possible that the latter represents the area of occupation at the east end of the medieval village, beside the major road, while Keilmerse was the low lying western part of the settlement, which lay beside Calme marsh.[23] Other examples, usually assumed to related to a single place but perhaps reflecting origins as two discrete settlements, include Wittering, which also appears as Witteringham, and Drayton (in Daventry) which also appears as Drayham.[24]

The study of medieval and early-modern settlement in England by Roberts and Wrathmell, which was based principally on early 19th century mapping, considered the size and frequency of nucleated settlement together with degrees of dispersal. Their analysis, elaborating that presented in various earlier works, places Northamptonshire within a Central Province in 'the heart of village England'. This is a landscape dominated by village and hamlet and by open field systems. Only the fen edge settlements in the Soke of Peterborough extend into their Eastern province (Figure 62).[25] The county lies within their Midland sub-provinces, which have the highest concentration of nucleation in England and an extremely low density of dispersal. This, they noted

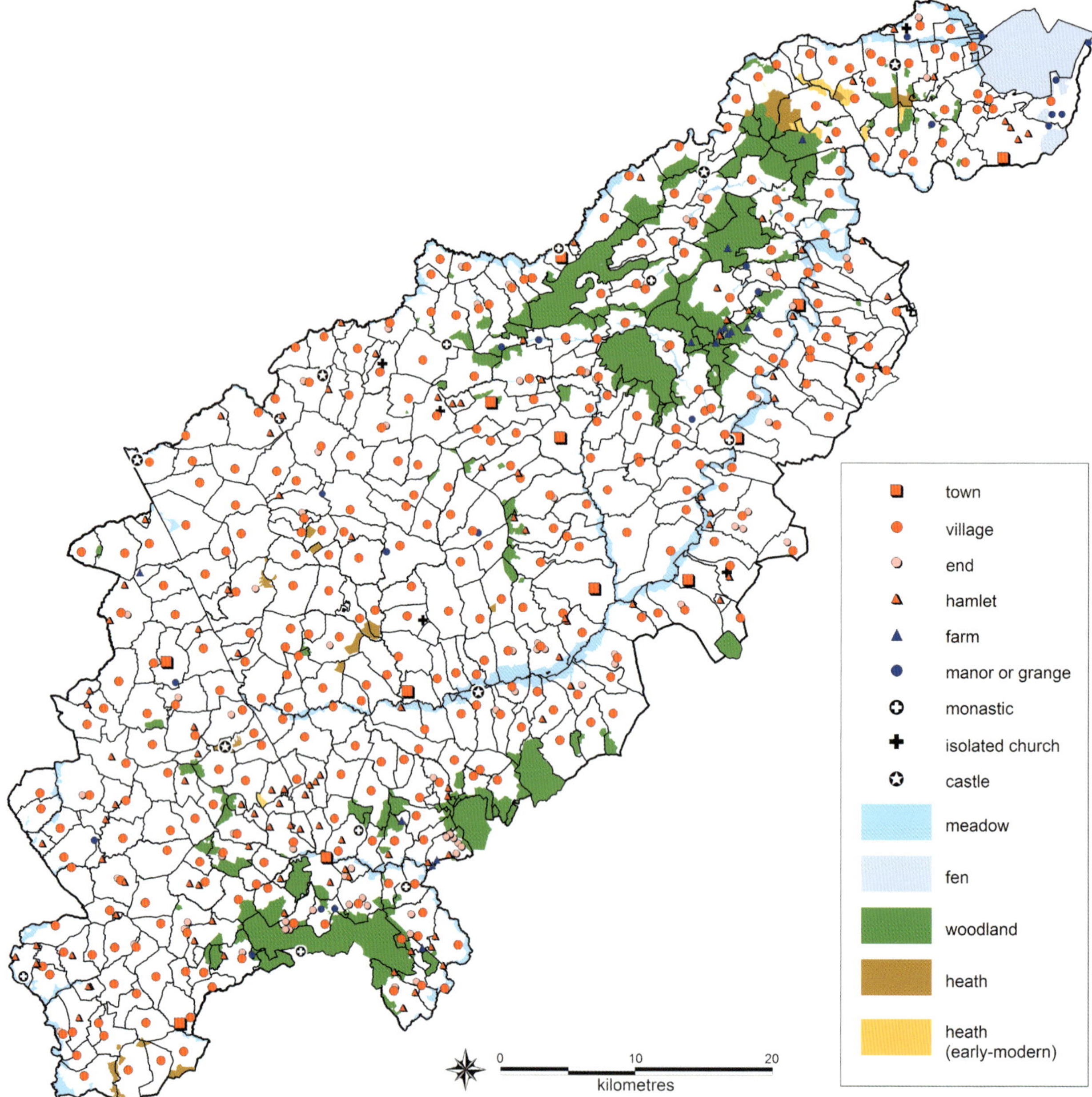

Figure 60. Map showing the pattern of medieval settlement in Northamptonshire, viewed against a background of townships and medieval land use.

with surprise, was even true of the woodland areas. They also remarked upon the difficulties encountered in defining local regions within this zone, which they had to do simply from the density of nucleation. Even the sub-province boundary, between the Inner Midlands and East Midlands, proved problematic. It was defined from the slightly lower degree of intercalated dispersal in the east, although Roberts and Wrathmell admitted that here post enclosure dispersal might have compromised their data. Comparison of our settlement map with their boundaries shows some correlation, as with the degree of dispersal in Rockingham Forest (area 2a). However, the majority of the settlement dispersal we have identified in the Tove valley/Whittlewood and Salcey area is omitted by their areas 5 and 6.

Physical geography appears to have been the principal determinant of the distribution and varying character of settlement in Northamptonshire. In part this acted directly through availability of water or of well-drained sites suitable for occupation. However, far more important for settlement location was its impact upon land use, mediated by administrative and estate organisation. Different regions of the county have distinct combinations of surface geology in particular topographical situations. As a result, in

Figure 61. Map indicating the extent of each medieval settlement, in so far as it can be estimated with existing data, together with the distribution of medieval churches, set in a context of townships. Settlements lacking an estimated extent are typically isolated farms or small hamlets.

different regions the preferred settlement locations vary in their topographical position and the geological formation they occupy.

Agricultural land use capability also varied according to the extent and topographical position of the types of surface geology, creating distinctive patterns of core and periphery in each region of the county. This is reflected in the distribution of wealth and population which, from 1086 to 1801, can be mapped from taxation and related data.[26] The example used here is the 1334 Lay Subsidy, which is Northamptonshire's most complete data set pre-dating the plagues (Figure 63). These data reveal a clear association of wealth (and, with other data sets such as the 1377 poll tax, population levels) with the core areas of intermixed permeable and impermeable geology, particularly along the main river valleys. In contrast the peripheral areas tend to have lower wealth (and population) or at least a tendency towards lower per capita wealth. The peripheral areas tend to lie in the extensive tracts of clay – on mudstones in the vales and on boulder clay across the plateau – or in the areas of permeable geology seen on limited parts of the plateau – such as that in the north-east around Wittering and that in the south-western tip of the county. The lower agricultural potential in the

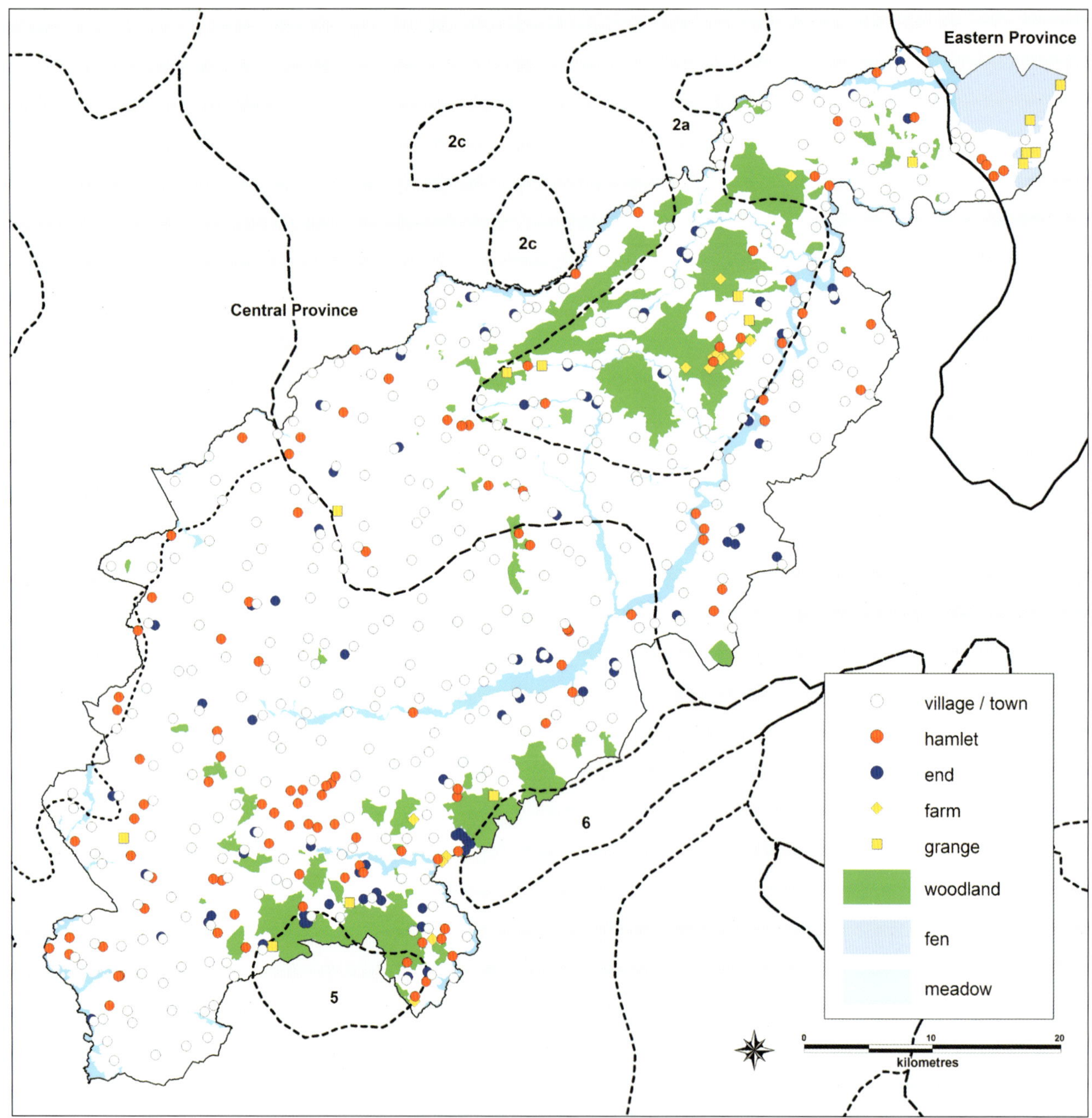

Figure 62. Map showing the pattern of medieval settlement, emphasising the distribution of dispersed and semi-dispersed elements, viewed in the context of the main medieval land use types and also the national settlement zones defined by Roberts and Wrathmell (2000).

periphery is also reflected in the retention of woodland on substantial parts of the boulder clay and of heath on the much smaller area of permeable plateau. The zoning also influences the pattern of Saxon estates, with estate centres usually lying in the core while dependencies tend to lie in the periphery.[27]

The graphs presented here and in the Rockingham atlas demonstrate this strong influence of geology on the distribution of medieval and earlier rural settlement (Table 10). The percentage of early-middle Saxon settlement on each geological grouping, relative to the percentage of the county covered by that geology, demonstrates the high preference for permeable and aversion to impermeable geology – especially boulder clay.[28]

From their often close association with the principal manor sites, medieval churches are likely to provide a good guide as to the location of the late Saxon core of medieval villages. Indeed they are a more secure data set than the distribution of manors themselves, which were far more likely to have been lost or to have moved. For example, well before the first map

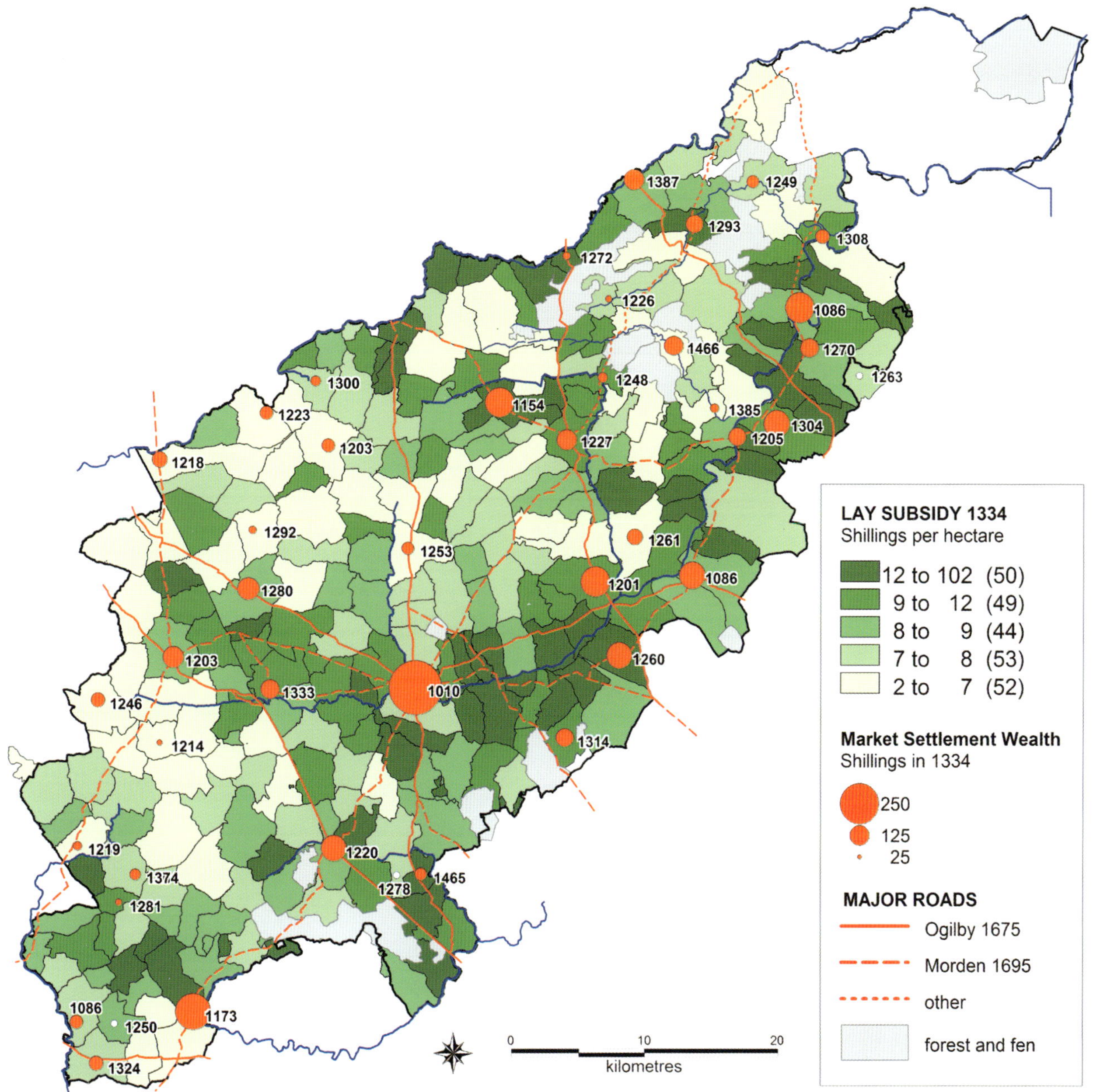

Figure 63. Map of the distribution of wealth by township and for medieval market settlements (indicating their foundation or earliest recorded date), as indicated by the Lay Subsidy of 1334. The data is provided here for the modern county of Northamptonshire only, and is shown in relation to the major elements of the medieval road network, in so far as it can be suggested from 17th-century sources.

of Oundle was prepared in 1810 the principal manor, known as Burystead, was transferred from its medieval site close to the church to a location in the east of the town.[29] This is not to suggest that most churches are primary features. There are various examples of parochial status being acquired during the medieval period, as at East Carlton which had been a chapelry of Cottingham but had acquired parochial status by 1254. This process may, in some cases, have involved the construction of a new church.[30] Churches show an even stronger bias towards permeable geology than do early-middle Saxon settlements. This may be a result of the nucleation process in the middle Saxon period focussing occupation even more strongly onto the most suitable locations.

There is a clear correlation between the pattern of distribution of early-middle Saxon sites and that of nucleated medieval settlements. The Saxon sites cluster along the same preferred geological zones as the medieval, avoiding the same wide tracts of clay and of permeable geology (Figure 64).

Assessment of the geological types encompassed

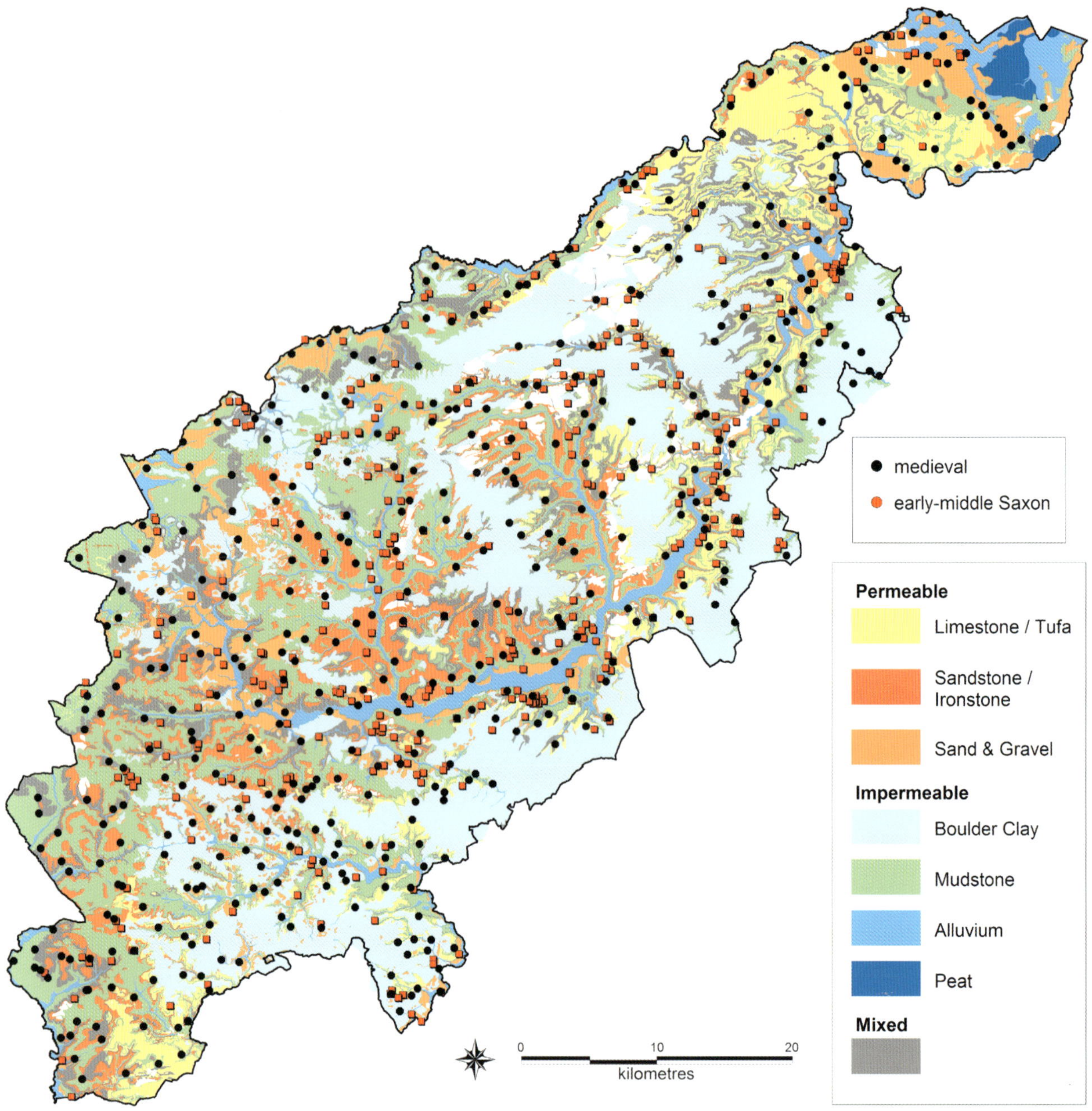

Figure 64. Map showing the distribution of early-middle Saxon and medieval settlement in relation to simplified surface geology (white areas indicate no geological data).

by whole villages reveals a weaker preference for permeable geologies than is shown by both churches and early-middle Saxon sites (Table 11). This is likely to result from village expansion during the medieval period, with occupation being forced into less favourable locations adjacent to the original core, thus reducing the percentage of the site lying on permeable geology. Hamlets show an even weaker bias towards permeable geology. This may result, in part, from their original sites lying on smaller islands of permeable geology, which meant that expansion resulted in a higher percentage of the site being forced onto impermeable strata.

Administrative and tenurial organisation was another important influence on the pattern of settlement, for these were the units within which land use potential was exploited. The way in which this potential was distributed, within early estates and within medieval townships, had an influence on the position of settlements and how they functioned – though it might be argued that the original delineation of the townships themselves was determined, at least in part, by the location of settlements. Large Saxon estates, such as Oundle, appear normally to have been centred on a river catchment or part thereof, with their boundaries lying at or close to the watershed.[31] The

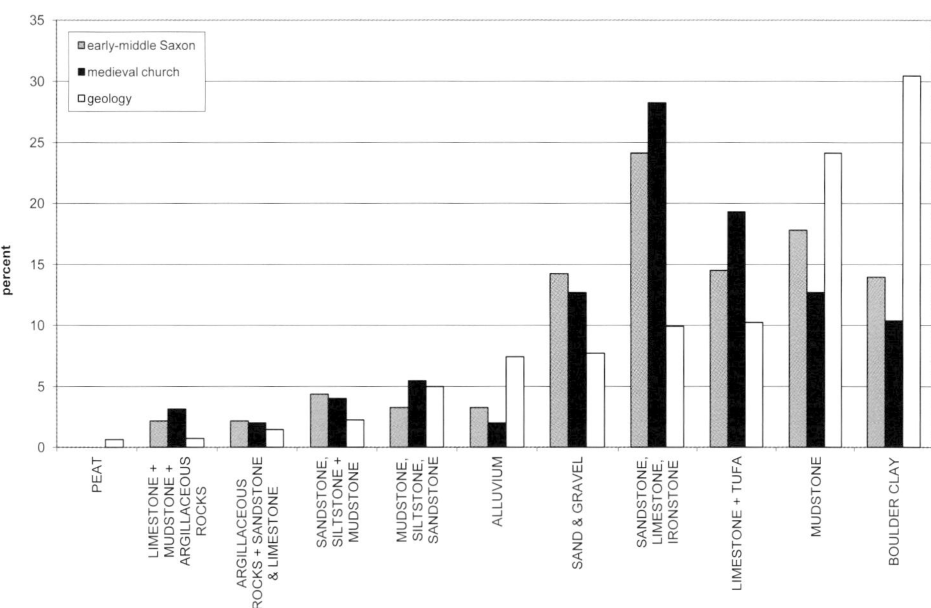

Table 10. Graph showing the percentage of early-middle Anglo-Saxon sites and (as a proxy for late Saxon settlement cores) of medieval churches on each of the main geological groupings, compared to the percentage of the county covered by that geology.

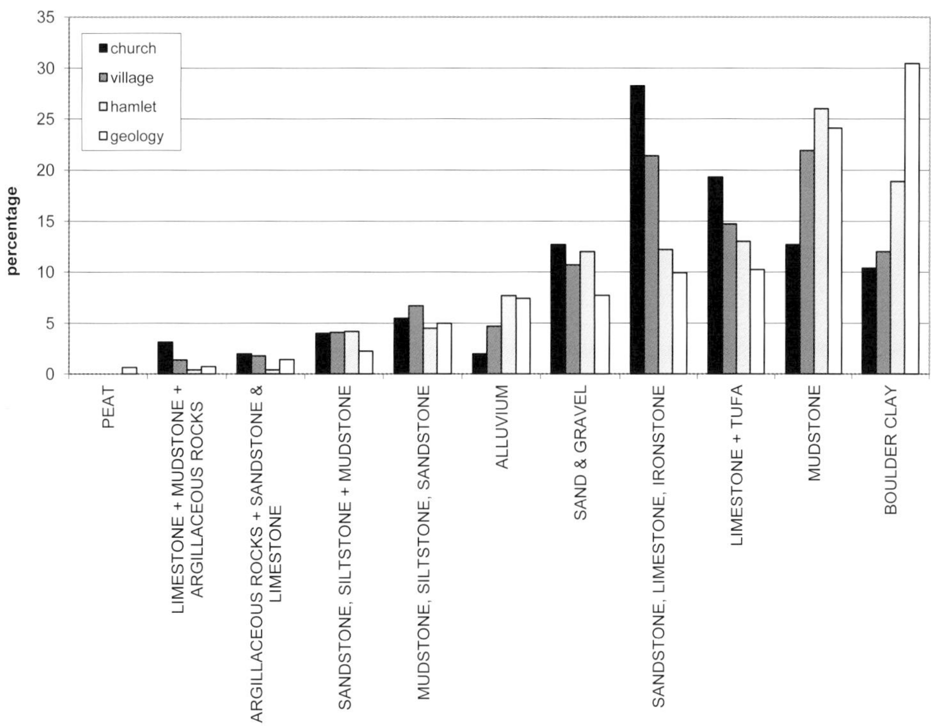

Table 11. Graph of average percentage of nucleated settlement area and of point location for churches relative to geology.

main exceptions are those which lay at the head of river networks, as with Kings Sutton, where estates might span two catchments (Figure 70).[32]

As we have seen, the best agricultural land generally lay on permeable geology in the river valleys. The areas of low agricultural potential, often occupied by woods, wolds and heaths, lay mainly on the watersheds, which were also frequently the boundaries of early estates. Where river and watershed were in close proximity then individual townships might provide a complete transect of this zone. Where they were more distant then there might be two or even three townships lying between river and watershed (Figure 65). In some cases, such as Earls Barton these townships were originally

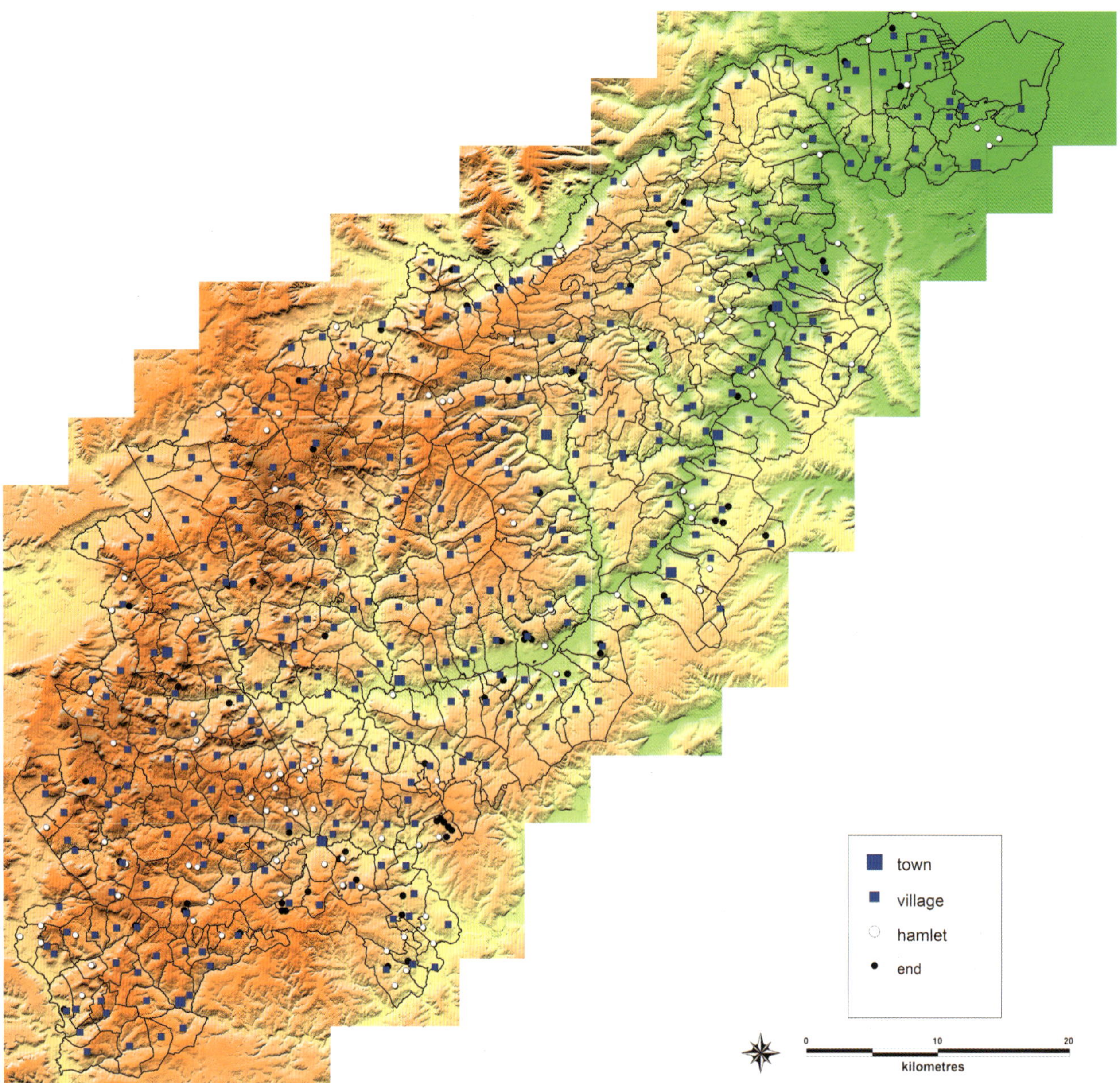

Figure 65. Map showing the pattern of townships and medieval settlement in relation to relief. (Crown Copyright, Ordnance Survey licence no. 100026873).

grouped into a single late Saxon estate which stretched from river to watershed.[33]

Settlements typically lay on permeable geology, providing a well drained site for occupation, but in close proximity to a water supply from stream or springs. The sites are normally at or close to geological boundaries, which often determine the location of springs. Unfortunately we have not been able to undertake a systematic analysis of this association. This is because of the inadequacy of data on spring location, even in the mapping of the 1880s, and the difficulty of predicting with sufficient consistency their location from geological boundaries.

Occupation normally avoided broad expanses of any geology, because it was too wet or too dry and thus had lower agricultural potential (Figure 64). This is generally the case with the woodland zone on the boulder clay plateau, the plateau limestone and ironstone, and the expanses of mudstone in the vales of the north-west. Water supply will also often have been difficult on the plateau, though it was not impossible as is shown by the presence of extensive Roman settlement and a few medieval villages, such as Brafield on the Green and Upper Benefield. Only in a few extreme areas was settlement almost impossible, most notably on the limestone plateau around Wittering where almost no water existed away from one or two streams.

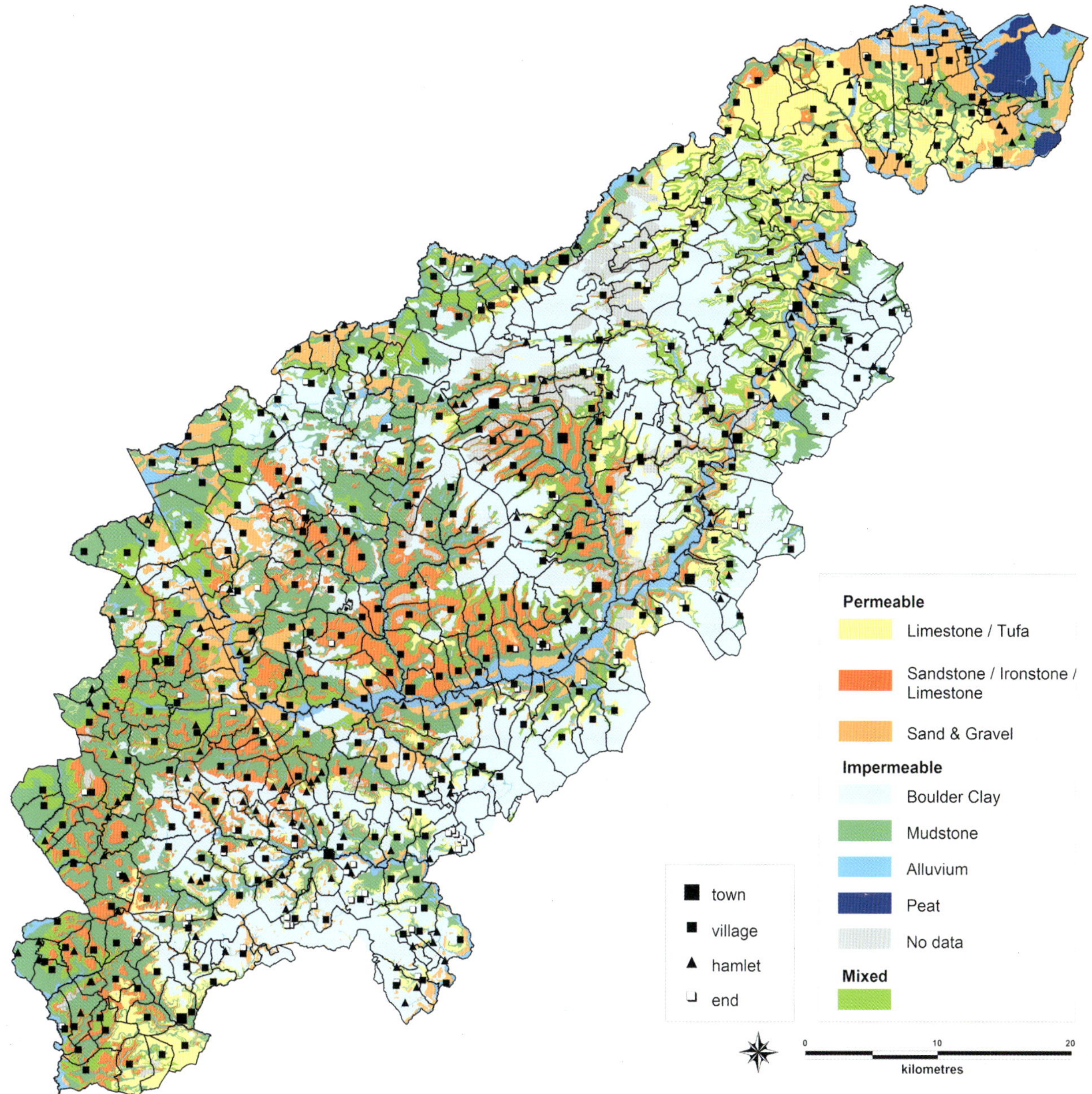

Figure 66. Map showing the pattern of townships and medieval settlement in relation to simplified geology.

Within most catchments there were two or three preferred types of medieval settlement location, set at different heights, which correspond closely with exposures of particular permeable strata. Early-middle Saxon settlement shared similar preferences. In the Upper Avon the lower preferred locations were typically on gravels beside water courses, whereas the higher locations were on the scarp edges on marl or limestone. Occupation was largely absent from the wide tracts of mudstones in vales and the smaller areas of boulder clay on the hilltops. In the Nene valley the lower position was often on gravel on the edge of the valley floor, and the next on the scarp edge on limestone or ironstone. Sometimes there was a higher location set back on another limestone or ironstone band, immediately below the wide boulder clay plateau. The exact location of settlement along each of these preferred zones appears to be determined primarily by availability of water, something very clearly seen in the upper Welland valley.[34]

Judging from the geology, the different preferred locations had hinterlands with differing agricultural potential. For example, in the Nene the intermediate location tended to be the most desirable as it lay at the heart of the broadest area of mixed geology. This is reflected in the distribution of wealth seen in the medieval taxations; the location of central places and dependencies recorded in Domesday and later sources;

and in the position of principal versus subsidiary place names.[35] Between Wellingborough and Northampton it is in exactly this intermediate location that one finds the major villages, including the Saxon estate centre at Earls Barton. A few subsidiary settlements lay on the lower level, such with Barton Thorpe and Little Billing. Set back at the highest level, often close to the heads of tributary streams, were villages such as Wilby and Mears Ashby which, from documentary and/or place name evidence, appear often to have been dependent settlements. In some parts of the Nene there were just two levels of preferred location and in others just one, depending on the distance between river to watershed. This will often be a response to the degree to which permeable geology extends back from the river. This is determined by the size of tributary streams and thus the extent to which they have cut back into the plateau to expose the underlying strata. Occasionally the principal location is found very close to the river, especially where the scarp of the plateau edge approaches close to the Nene, as at Higham Ferrers.

Geology also assists in the interpretation of individual settlement plans. Extensive archaeological investigation in Raunds village has shown several early foci of occupation which are set mainly on limestone. During the medieval these expanded for more than 500m along the narrow valley, mainly on permeable geology.[36] In the absence of the sort of work undertaken at Raunds, for most villages we cannot securely distinguish the early core from areas of medieval expansion. However, given our knowledge of the distribution of Saxon settlement, reasonable conjecture is often possible, based on the distribution of permeable geology and – to minimise the danger of circular argument – the location of church and principal manor. Such analysis suggests that many other settlements expanded during the medieval period, from one or more early foci on permeable geology, to create villages which extended across a wide area of the preferred zone. Yet there are others, such as Lilbourne, which appear to have expanded from a core in the preferred zone out across adjacent clayland. Only occasionally do villages lie wholly away from the preferred zone and these are typically subsidiary settlements in what are probably late townships. An example is the village of Newbold which, in addition to its 'new' name, is documented as a dependency of Catesby. Yet even here, thanks to systematic fieldwalking, we know that Newbold had an early-middle Saxon precursor. It lay on the periphery of the medieval settlement on a tiny patch of limestone in an otherwise extensive area of impermeable geology.[37] There are just a handful of substantial villages which lie wholly on the clay, such as Brafield on the Green which is discussed below.

Northamptonshire can be divided into four broad regions based on physical geography. Each had a distinctive pattern of medieval land use, as defined in the present atlas (Figure 1), and each had its own distinctive distribution and forms of settlement. The largest is the central region. This is dominated by a boulder clay capped plateau which has been cut through by valleys of varying size, exposing mixed but predominantly permeable geology, with gravels and alluvial clays on the valley floor. Typically the boulder clay plateau seems to have been wood, wood pasture or wold in the Saxon period, although by 1300 much of this had been replaced by arable. The early core of open field systems are expected on the mixed geologies of the valley sides while, in the medieval, meadow was situated on the alluviated valley floor. Settlement typically avoided the plateau, except for granges and other isolated settlement, created through medieval assarting in the forests, and lodges in medieval deer parks. Villages, and before them dispersed early-middle Saxon settlement, concentrated largely on the permeable geology along the valleys. This pattern is clearly exhibited in the Oundle area, where the bounds of a Saxon charter broadly confirms the pattern of land use noted above.[38] The Tove catchment forms a sub-region, with a more fragmented boulder clay plateau and narrower valleys dominated more by mudstones than limestone or ironstone. Here a somewhat more dispersed pattern of medieval settlement is seen, with many more hamlets.

Second is the north-western region, where the landscape is far more heavily dissected. Here there are broad valleys, occupied by relatively small streams, which are dominated by mudstones. The permeable geology is largely restricted to fragmented areas of higher ground, which contained areas of heathland, indicated mainly by field and furlong names (Figure 6). Particularly in the north of this region there are areas of boulder clay capping small areas of the high ground. There is a correlation between this zone and the distribution of early-modern cob buildings, perhaps in part because of a dearth of good building stones, which are widely available across most of the rest of the county.[39]

The third region is the far south-west. Here the plateau is largely of limestone, which in places had substantial areas of heath, whereas in the valleys of the Cherwell and Upper Ouse the geology is mainly of mudstones. While much of this plateau was not ideal for settlement, it was sufficiently dissected by streams to create locations favourable to the development of villages.

The Soke of Peterborough is the final region. In the west lies the extensive limestone plateau, much of which during the last millennium appears to have havered between heath and woodland. Further east the plateau is more fragmented creating a situation where limestone and mudstone are intermixed, resulting in a mosaic of wood, heath and arable on the higher ground. However, in both east and west, the plateau was largely avoided by settlement. The majority of villages are found on the lower lying ground, which has extensive gravels, extending into wide alluvial deposits beside the Nene and especially the Welland. Pastures, meadow and small moors lay on the wet parts of the low lying gravels and alluvium. To the east there was an abrupt change, where the Car Dyke forms the western boundary of Northamptonshire's small segment of the peat and silt fen. Within this area the place name evidence indicates the former presence of several 'islands': two larger ones at Maxey and Eye and a small one at Oxney.[40] The Soke presents a distinctive landscape where the form and distribution of settlement was subtly different to the rest of the county, both in the character of its villages and in the presence of a more dispersed pattern of occupation. In this same area Domesday shows an unusual degree of grouping of settlements under a few manors, This is, in part, because the area – the double hundred of Upton (Figure 5) – remained in the hands of a single lord, the Abbot of Peterborough.[41] In the rest of the county the royal estates seem to have been split between different lords and the sokes divided into two separate hundreds.[42]

Where villages have seen extensive investigation, such as Raunds, Wollaston and Warmington, there were typically several foci of occupation in the early-middle Saxon period. But, as these are all relatively large villages lying in the Nene valley, they are unlikely to be representative of all the county's villages.[43] Documentary evidence also hints that some Nene valley villages may already have had most of their virgate tenements in place by the late 11th century. At Fotheringhay in 1548 the number of virgates seems to correlate with the number of hides recorded in 1086. These virgates were distributed throughout the village, suggesting that it may already have been close to its present extent by 1086. However, we cannot be certain that all the tenements were already single virgates or that the pattern seen in 1548 has not been influenced by subdivision and/or redistribution of virgates during the intervening centuries.[44]

In contrast to the large villages of the Nene valley, fieldwork in Whittlewood has suggested that townships in peripheral areas may have had far less early-middle Saxon occupation. This is not the case throughout the county for at Hargrave, which lay on Bromswold, the medieval village developed where there had been an agglomeration of at least three early-middle Saxon sites.[45] Place name evidence at Bulwick suggests a similar process may have occurred there, where three *wic* names lie in different parts of this large but somewhat loosely nucleated settlement.[46] It is not clear when such early foci coalesced to form villages, but investigations at Silverstone suggest it may have been later than in core areas like Raunds.[47] If Hall is correct, in arguing that extensive area of Saxon woodland and pastures in these peripheral zones were replaced by extensive open fields, then the villages here may have seen even greater expansion in the late Saxon and earlier medieval periods than those in core areas.

The suggestion that large areas of peripheral land were under pasture, heath or woodland in the Saxon period is supported by the high frequency of settlements with pastoral names, especially in the boulder clay zones. These elements include *leah*, *feld*, *wold* and *mor*, as well as others which may indicate pastoral activity, such as *ham* and *wic*. *Wold* and *leah* also appear in various furlong and related names on the boulder clay. In many cases such land use and names, where they can be located, lie on the periphery of and often straddling the boundaries of townships.

Wold may be used in the sense of open wood pasture and, significantly, it tends to exist in discrete zones, set on the boulder clay adjacent to the woodland (Figure 67). The major exception is Bromswold, which occupies a quite separate boulder clay zone on the eastern watershed of the Nene downstream from Higham Ferrers, where it complements Rockingham Forest on the western watershed. *Wood* and *grove* names are also found on boulder clay on the periphery of the woodland, particularly in Whittlewood.[48] So too are some tree names, thought they have a less consistent association, whereas others such as Plumpton, Paulerspury and Potterspury, simply refer to fruit trees. In the far north-east there is a distinct grouping of names suggesting a small area of distinctive fen edge woodland. They include the element *holt*, a specialised woodland possibly of one tree type, *sallow* names in Dogsthorpe and a number of closes named wood on the edge of Eye.[49]

The three heathland zones, in the north-east, north-west and far south-west, may have functioned in a pastoral role equivalent to that of woodland, wold and fen seen elsewhere in the county (Figure 6). Another name with pastoral implications is marsh (*mersc* or *mor*), though as Hall has noted above, these were probably all relatively small areas within any township and thus of only very local significance.

Leah is the most common of topographical settlement names, found mainly on the periphery of woodland zones (Figure 67). Interestingly they tend to lie in distinct zones adjacent to, but separate from, the wold and woodland. Many more *leah* names are found within the woodland, while others occur as furlong and pasture names in the open fields, probably indicating that woodland lay much closer when the name was established. While *leah* can be interpreted in place names as either wood or open pasture within woodland, the leys surviving on early-modern mapping in Northamptonshire woodlands are typically discrete areas of pasture. The term also seems to be used for open ground within or beside woodland in the 10th century charter of Oundle.[50] In contrast the *feld* names, discussed below, may relate to

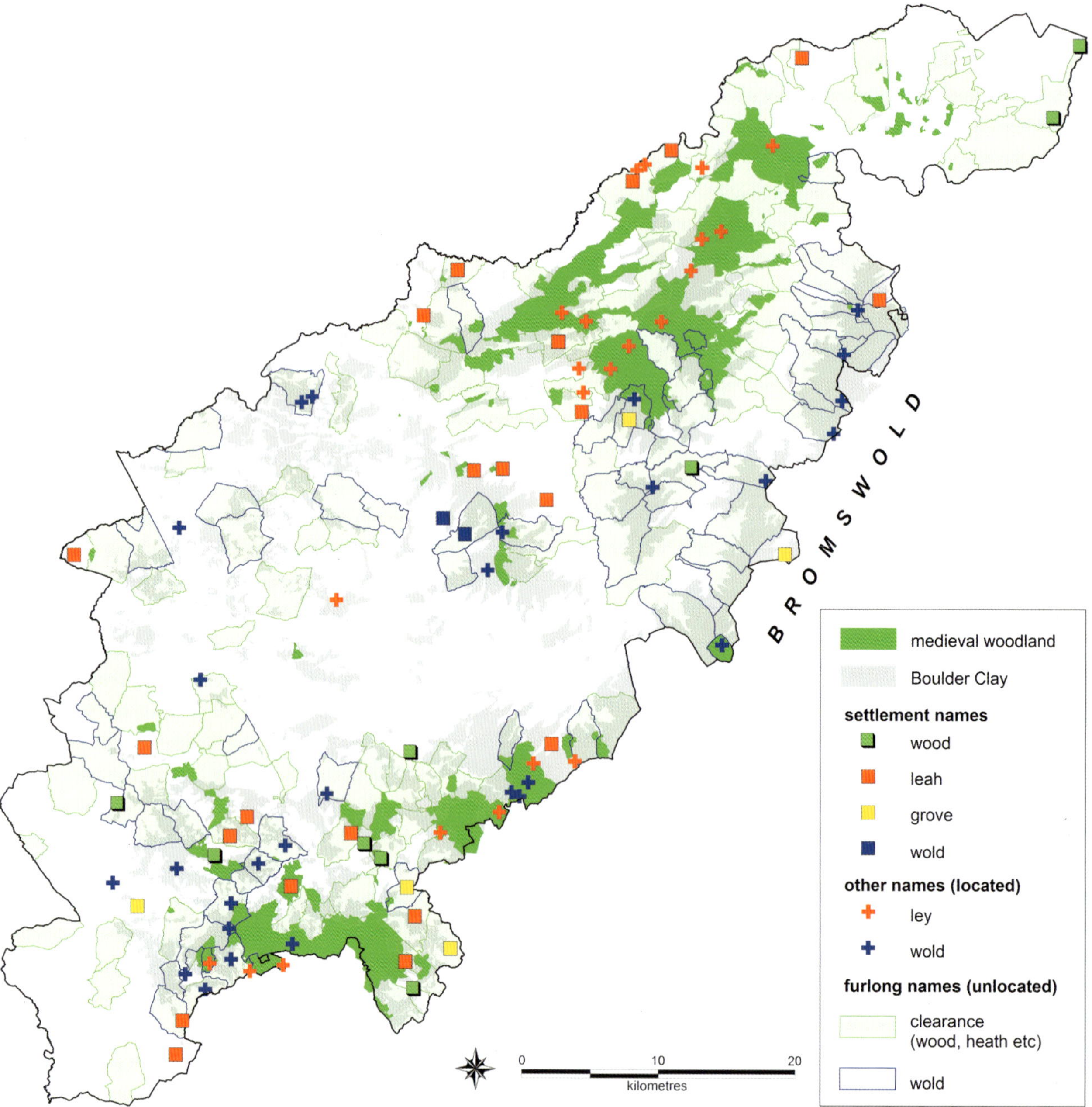

Figure 67. Map of the distribution of settlements with woodland and wold related names, viewed against a background of medieval woodland and of wold and woodland related furlong and field names. Wold and woodland appear in most cases to exist as discrete zones, closely associated with the distribution of boulder clay.

somewhat broader areas of pasture in the woodland zone, especially if the identification of some with later forest lawns is an indication of their original extent.

Some *ham* names are associated with woodland, but others are in core areas far removed from woodland (Figure 68). An explanation may lie in the suggestion, from at least one place name scholar, that *ham* could relate to man-made pastoral enclosures.[51] The association of a middle Saxon oval stock enclosure with adjacent high status occupation at the Saxon estate centre of Higham Ferrers (*high ham*), discussed below, may support this interpretation. So too may the *ham* names of other Saxon estate centres: Northampton, Passenham and Medeshamstede (Peterborough). Several more seem once to have had *ham* names, as at Witteringham (Wittering) and Drayham (possibly Daventry).[52] Dependent settlements with *ham* name elements may also contain man-made pastoral enclosures, such as Syresham, though the suggestion of such enclosures from village plan form alone is fraught with difficulties.

Wic names, some of which include stock related elements, as in Bulwick and the two Hardwicks, may all have had a pastoral function. They tend to lay in

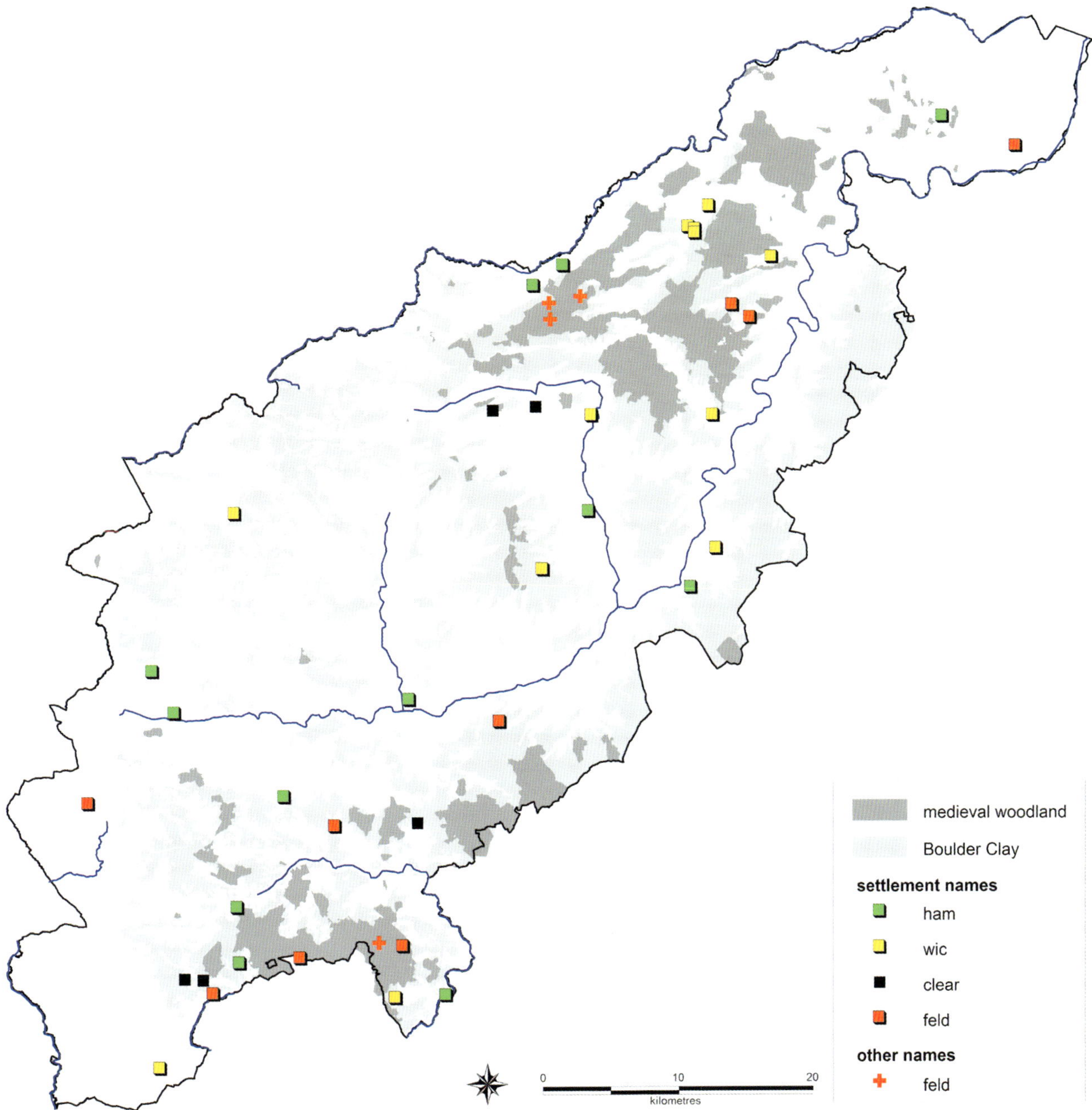

Figure 68. Map showing the distribution of ham, wic, clear and feld place names. They are depicted in relation to the distribution of medieval woodland and of bounder clay, which indicates the broad zones where wold and other woodland probably lay in the Saxon period.

peripheral zones, particularly woodland or boulder clay areas, although examples are also found in zones with heathland, at Astwick and possibly Winwick. They may have been single farms or small hamlets which later grew to form villages. The most complex example is that of Bulwick, which grew from three *wics*. Some appear related to valley pastures, as at Lowick and Southwick. A clear plan form association has not been found, although a putative wide drove leads directly into Lowick.[53] Stanwick also sits along either side of a pasture strip, set along the floor of a small valley, this is a common village plan form which, as discussed below, may have a simple geological explanation.

The names of other hamlets and farms suggest dependency, but without a land use implication (Figure 69). Most common are *cot* and *thorp*. *Thorps* are sparsely spread across the county while *cots* appear more concentrated. *Toft*, which may represent Danish names with a similar significance to *cot*, have a very discrete distribution, closely related to that of the *by* names discussed below. These dependent places generally occupy a preferred settlement area but often lie in peripheral zones. This contrasts with *tun*

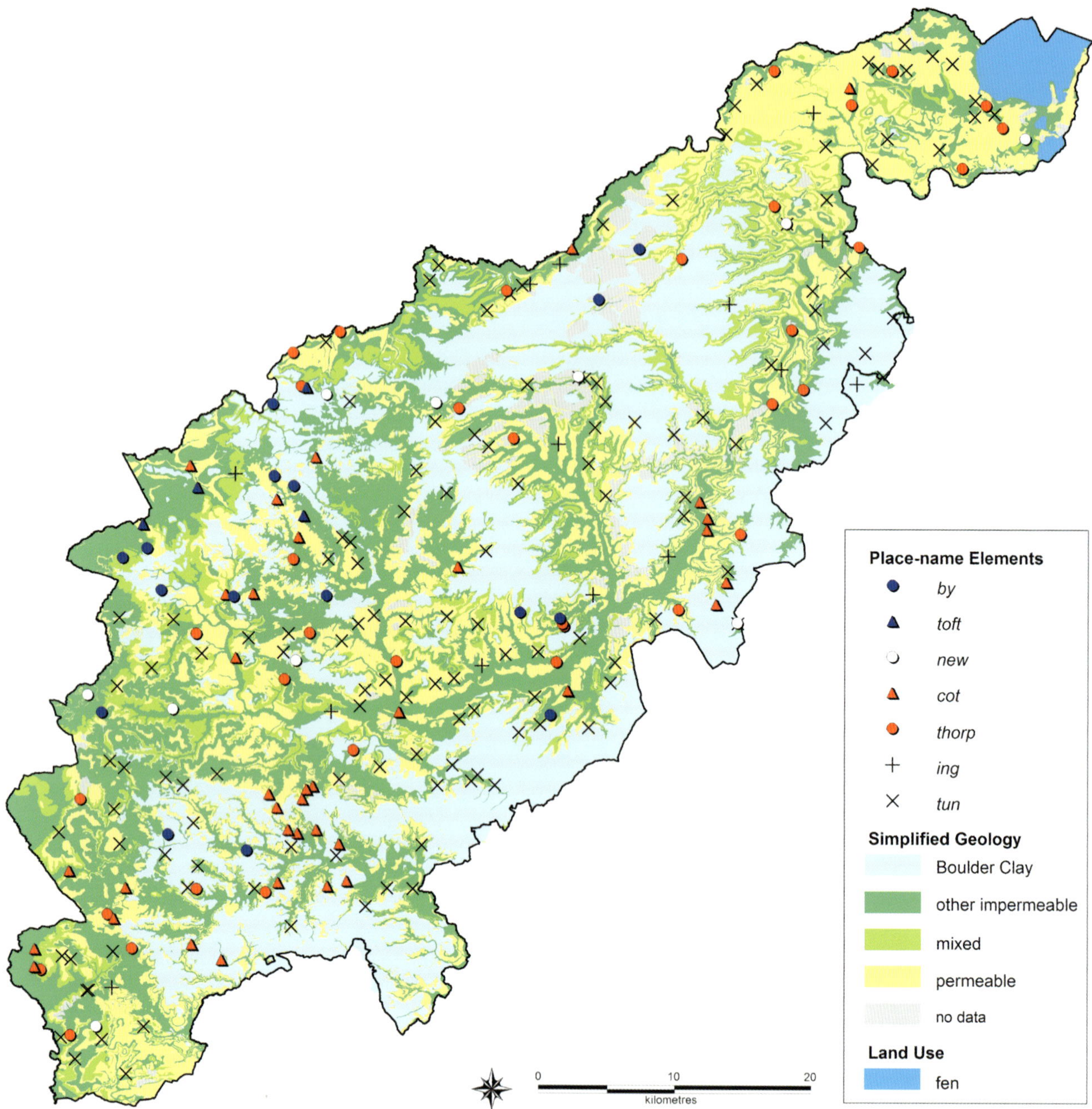

Figure 69. Map showing the distribution of Danish and other subsidiary settlement names, compared to key names elements associated with principal settlements, viewed in relation to simplified geology.

and especially *ing* names which tend to concentrate in core areas and to shun peripheral zones, except in *Bromswold* (Figure 69).

Early-middle Saxon occupation has been found in close association with Thorpe End and West Cotton in Raunds and Coton in Gretton. This might indicate that the *cots* and *thorps* are remnants of the more dispersed early-middle Saxon settlement pattern which survived the middle Saxon process of nucleation.[54] This is supported by the apparent association, outside the woodland zones, of dependent settlements and ends. The most notable groupings are seemingly linked to particular Saxon estates, such as Earls Barton/Yardley Hastings, Higham Ferrers/Irthlingborough and Oundle (Figure 62). There is also a very distinct grouping of *cots*, most with their own small township, associated with the Towcester/Greens Norton royal estate of 1086. It is such a distinctive pattern that it may indicate the process of nucleation in the Tove was less complete than in other river valleys in the county.

Cots and *thorps* were most often small subsidiary settlements which lay within the township of a larger village. Many lack plan form evidence, as they proved very vulnerable to late and early-modern desertion, but where a plan is visible, as with Thorpe in Earls Barton, it tends to be simple.[55] A few *thorps* grew substantially, as with Barton Thorpe, or merged to form a larger single village, as noted below for Abbotsthorpe and Southorpe in Warmington. A few even grew into substantial villages that acquired their own township, as with Ravensthorpe.

Several small hamlets appear to originate as (or have been reorganised to comprise) a single hide of land. Thus Coton in Gretton consisted of 120 acres in one medieval source; Eaglethorpe in Warmington seems to have comprised two messuages of 60 acres each; while in Roade the actual name of the dependent hamlet is Hide.[56]

Where identifiable, the land units of such hamlets are also usually very small, as at Coton in Gretton. Another example may be Doddington Thorpe, for this deserted hamlet lay within an area later known as Thorpe Field, the fourth and by far the smallest of the open fields in Great Doddington township.[57] Cursory fieldwalking of a small part of the site produced two early-middle Saxon sherds, in addition to medieval occupation deposits. The medieval occupation extends into an adjacent old enclosure in Wilby township, where it may represent Wilby Thorpe which is mentioned in 1251. If this indicates an early-middle Saxon settlement, then this thorpe may provide a clue to the origin of various villages in peripheral locations. It appears to be one half of a paired settlement, the other – now a village called Wilby – lies in a similar location on the opposite side of a small valley.[58] As discussed below, such paired sites are a common settlement form in both the early-middle Saxon and the medieval period. Judging from its dependent relationship in the Earls Barton estate in 1086, its peripheral location and its *by* place name, Wilby may have been raised from hamlet to village. The *by* name, because of Danish origin, suggests this occurred at some time after 850 and before 1086, when it is recorded in Domesday. The spatial relationship of its township to that of Great Doddington may indicate it was taken out of the land of that settlement. In contrast, Doddington Thorpe hardly grew, presumably stifled because it was left with such a small land unit within a township dominated by the main village. Buscot, which is discussed below, may be another example of this process of township formation. The hamlet, within the land unit of Higham Ferrers, was left with a tiny land unit split between Higham and the new township of Newton Bromswold.

This putative growth of Wilby and appearance of Newton may have been driven by the process of late Saxon open field expansion suggested by Hall. This may have led to the creation of a large number of such new townships in some areas. Also in the Earls Barton estate there is Mears Ashby township, which may have been taken out the land of the estate centre itself, and others along the Nene could have developed in the same way.[59] For example, the dependent hamlet of Wigsthorpe lies in a poor geological context in a peripheral location relative to Lilford, which is on permeable geology beside the river. The pattern is repeated in the Ise, where the hamlets of Badsaddle and Wythmail lie on the clay, above and dependent upon Orlingbury, which itself sits back from the main valley, which is occupied by Isham.

The *by* villages in the north-west of the county, such as Barby and Kilsby, may all represent expansion onto clay from small original foci sited on permeable geology. They are grouped with other subsidiary names, including *wic* and the only grouping of Danish *toft* names. This might indicate development of new townships and promotion of farms or hamlets to villages in this peripheral area in the period after 850. The distribution of *by* and *toft* names might thus prove to have as much to do with the chronology of township formation as it does with the distribution of Danish occupation and ownership. Apart from this grouping in the north-west, most *by* names are associated with specific Saxon estates (Earls Barton/Yardley; Corby/Weldon and Greens Norton), but significantly they seem to lie in the periphery not the core of the estate.[60]

New settlement names are also found in a peripheral context. These may also be settlements elevated from subsidiary sites, for archaeological surveys on the villages of Newton Willows and, as noted above, at Newbold beside Catesby, have produced evidence of early-middle Saxon settlement.[61] Some of the *new* settlements show intermixing of township or parochial land with an adjacent settlement, suggesting incomplete separation from a primary township. Examples are Woodnewton, which has land (in Hale) intermixed with Apethorpe; Newnham with Badby; Newbottle with Astrop and Charlton; and Newton Bromswold which, as we have seen, shared land in Buscots with Higham Ferrers.[62] In other cases the raising of subsidiary settlements to township status is suggested by *little*, *chapel* and other prefixes to the township name, as with Chapel Brampton and Little Billing.

The pattern of core and periphery seems to have been exploited by the Saxon estates, which generally encompassed a balance of different types of land. The resulting variation in land use across the estates is sometimes reflected in place name elements. If peripheral resources were a long distance from the core then this might result in sharing of detached rights – most often woodland – between the estate's component settlements. A settlement's position in the estate hierarchy, as well as spatially relative to core and periphery, is likely to have influenced the chronology and character of its evolution, which may be reflected in its plan form. Using a range of evidence, including paired Domesday hundreds and dependent tenurial and ecclesiastical relationships, a partial reconstruction of the Saxon estates has been suggested.[63] Several span the Nene valley, from wood to wold on either

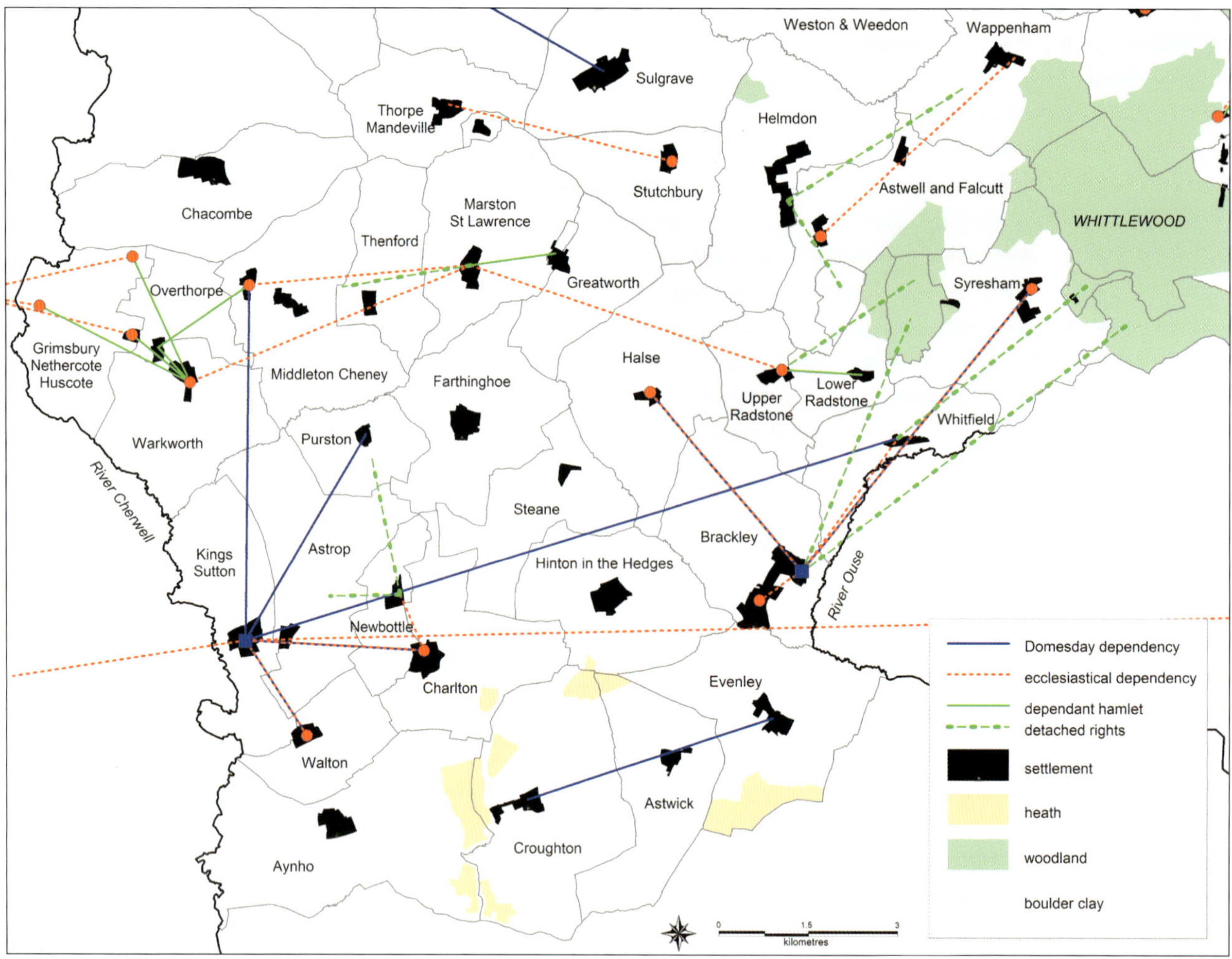

Figure 70. Map showing the secular and ecclesiastical links within the area of the Saxon royal estate of Kings Sutton, viewed in relation to medieval land use.

watershed, but with the best land lying centrally in the valley itself. Other examples span the Tove valley and the Cherwell-Ouse watershed. The possible boundaries of the estates can sometimes be refined through detailed mapping of the medieval landscape, as at Oundle.[64]

The patterns revealed can be demonstrated with the Saxon royal estate at Kings Sutton (Figure 70).[65] It seems to have comprised most of the Domesday hundreds of Sutton and Alboldstow (Figure 5), extending from the valley of the Cherwell on the west to the headwaters of the Ouse on the east, and on the north to the watershed with the Tove and Upper Cherwell. Subsidiary groupings of townships within the estate are suggested by tenurial and ecclesiastical links, with boundaries again tending to correlate with stream and watershed. Other linkages can be conjectured on comparable topographical and place name evidence. The dependencies of Marston extend from its marsh, perhaps once a pastoral area, to a *worth* or enclosure in the Cherwell valley at Warkworth. Brackley, a *leah* and thus also presumably pastoral, held Halse while beyond that at the head of the same valley lay Great*worth*, though there is no documentary record linking it to Brackley. The name *east wic* indicates that Astwick, despite its 1086 administrative link to Evenley, was originally dependent on a settlement to the west, perhaps Croughton or even Aynho in the Cherwell.

Around Kings Sutton there is a series of names suggesting communities with specific functions, being holdings of priests (Purston), ceorls (Charlton) and serfs (Walton). The principal central places (Kings Sutton, Brackley and Marston St Lawrence) also each have dependencies in townships on the boulder clay in Whittlewood. The latter have name elements which suggest they may have originated as detached pastures within the woodland zone: the *feld* of Whitfield, the *ham* of Syresham and the '*cleared ground*' of Radstone.[66] This is a reflection of the fact that major Saxon estates integrated varying resources, spread over a much longer distance than in the far more intensively arable landscapes of the medieval period. Similar links are hinted at in other Saxon estates that, before the hidation, may originally have straddled the Nene, such as Oundle or Earls Barton/Yardley Hastings.

The central place functions of the Saxon estates appear to have been dispersed in several different foci.

One appears to be the *burh* or residence, which may in many cases have been a re-occupied and refortified Iron Age hillfort. Fourteen settlements have *burh* name elements, though perhaps only 12 originate as Saxon defended residences.[67] Some early foci, like the hillfort at Irthlingborough and possibly one on Arbury Hill near Badby, lie over 1km from the estate centre.[68] Others lie within the village itself, as at Guilsborough were the rectilinear Iron Age hillfort, which may have been reoccupied in the Saxon period, has the medieval village appended to its side. A similar example may be Desborough, where the possible fort lay within ancient enclosures immediately east of village and church.[69] For most other *burh* settlements the hillfort or other defended focus, if it exists, has yet to be located.

The burhs seem typically to be paired with what is interpreted as a tribute centre.[70] Excavations, in what we have suggested as a single royal estate focussed on Irthlingborough, have shown early Saxon refortification of the Iron Age hillfort near Irthlingborough – presumably the *burh* – and high status activity, interpreted as the tribute centre, on the periphery of Higham Ferrers – the *ham*.[71] The burh is not always located in the core zone. This may in some cases, such as Whittlebury, have been determined simply by the location of Iron Age hillforts.[72] However, the presumed tribute centres are also sometimes found in peripheral areas. Examples are the estate centres at Yardley Hastings and Fawsley, which both lie in woodland zones. In some cases it is possible that this represents a late transfer – for example from Earls Barton to Yardley and from Daventry to Fawsley – so that the new estate centre could serve as a base for recreational hunting.

The possible influence of central place functions on the plan form of settlements can be seen at Higham Ferrers (Figure 71). An oval enclosure was discovered at the northern end of the town, immediately north of the 'Bond End'. Excavation has shown that it was of middle Saxon date but, as it was empty, it is presumed to have been for stock management. The entrance to the enclosure was controlled by a group of high status buildings set within a rectilinear enclosure. The whole complex was in existence in the 8th century, though it has early Saxon origins.[73] The plan form of the town, first mapped in the late 16th century, suggests it may represent infilling of a wide drove leading south from this Saxon site to a large tract of boulder clay in Rushden township. 'Drove' is used here to describe a wide route used for moving stock, examples of which survived into the early-modern period, when they were mapped, leading through arable to heath and fen, or through woodland. By that date they were typically bounded by a hedge, ditch or wall.[74] The settlement at Higham seems to have been transformed at some time before 1086 when the manor/castle and church were constructed beside and a market place dropped into the putative drove. The infill has begun

Figure 71. Map of the medieval small town of Higham Ferrers (1839) indicating church, castle and market place (M) with, at the north end, the major excavated features of what may be a middle Saxon administrative centre. The evidence is viewed against a background of the furlong pattern and simplified geology.

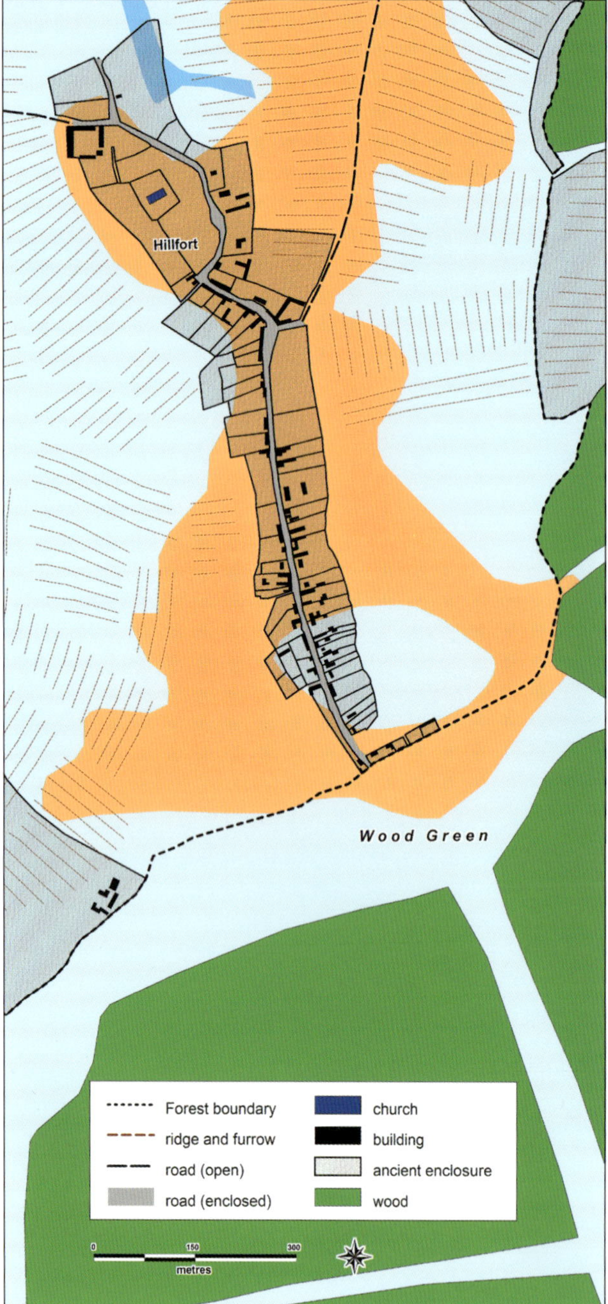

Figure 72. Map showing the plan form of Whittlebury (1797) in relation to the site of the Iron Age hillfort, viewed against the distribution of medieval woodland, the furlong pattern and simplified geology (geology legend p.99).

to be charted archaeologically. Half way between the Bond End and the market place the occupation seems to have 12th century origins, but far more extensive work is required throughout the town to test our hypothesis of settlement development.[75]

The site north of Bond End also provides an 11th century date for the encroachment of furlongs inwards onto former settlement and possibly also over adjacent pasture. Here a furlong was laid out over the oval enclosure and the high status occupation, following the site's desertion at some time in the 10th century. This is a good example of the way in which, in the late Saxon Period, occupation seems to contract within what become the medieval 'ancient enclosure' boundaries.[76] A similar process is seen at Langham Road and Furnells in Raunds.[77] At Higham this resulted, even on the earliest maps, in the loss from the settlement plan of all obvious traces of this key element of the Saxon settlement. Only with hindsight can that the small green in Bond End be seen as a possible remnant of a drove. Also there is the way the roads swing out from the green, skirting around either side of the high status occupation and oval enclosure. Higham thus demonstrates how ephemeral may be the evidence, even of the most important elements of Saxon occupation, in settlement plans derived from the earliest historic maps.

An almost identical form to that at Higham is seen in the plan of Whittlebury village (Figure 72). This was a 1086 dependency of the Saxon royal estate centre of Greens Norton but presumably had a royal residence in the 10th century, when a royal charter was signed in Whittlebury. Here the village occupied a putative drove that leads south from an oval enclosure, which has been proved to have originated as a hillfort,[78] into a wide tract of boulder clay. The latter area remained under woodland when the first map was drawn in the 17th century, when a drove of equal width to the eastern row of the village continued south-eastward from the settlement. In the Saxon estate centre at Brackley there were two adjacent oval enclosures – one occupied by the church – which sit on sand and limestone, avoiding the mudstone. They lie adjacent to virgate tenements in rectilinear plots set within the curving road network.[79] Another example is at Daventry. Here excavations have revealed extensive early-middle Saxon activity lying outside what appears, from the plan form of the town, to be a large curving enclosure containing the church.[80] Brixworth is another Saxon royal estate centre where there is an oval form in the village plan – perhaps the *worth* of the place name – which lies immediately down slope from the site of the middle Saxon monastery.[81]

Oval forms, which may represent stock enclosures, are hinted at in the plans of several villages in peripheral zones. At Denton the village green leads up to a possible large oval which, like some others, is defined by the road network and straddles a stream (Figure 73). At Cold Higham the road through Astcote and furlong boundaries on either side of Watling Street hint at the existence of a far larger oval enclosure. It is similar to that seen in cropmarks at Croughton, though this appears to be Iron Age in origin.[82] Another possible example is in Gretton, though here the evidence is more tenuous.[83] That some of these oval forms were indeed once defined by ditched boundaries is seen on the periphery of Brackley township, though here not associated with

Figure 73. A map of Denton in 1760 showing the oval form, defined by close boundaries and roads, at the southern end of the village. The roads and green lead up to but then skirt the oval area, which straddles a stream and had, by the medieval period, been partly covered by open field furlongs. (Courtesy of © The Marquess of Northampton).

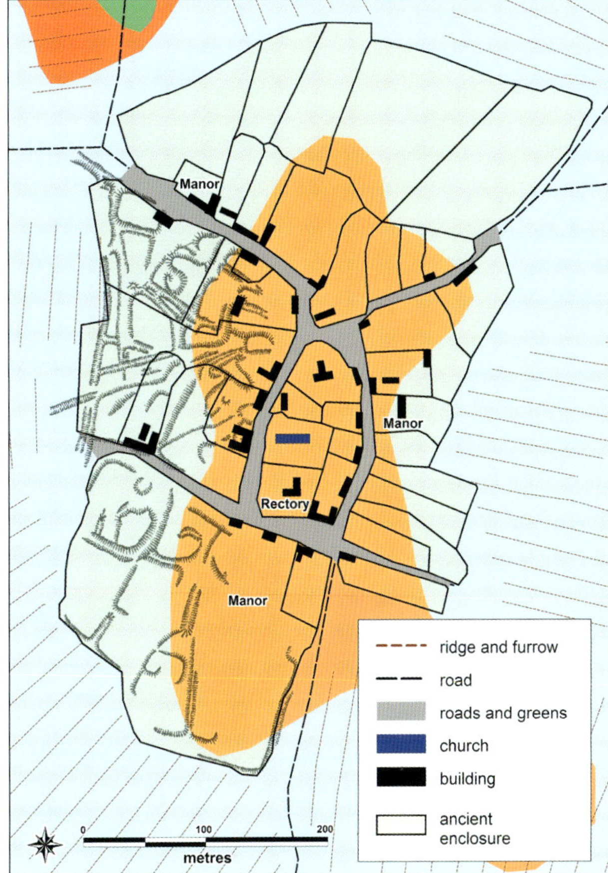

Figure 74. The plan form of Haselbech from the map of 1598 and earthwork evidence recorded by RCHM, viewed against a background of the furlong pattern and simplified geology (geology legend p.99).

medieval occupation. *Hwerveldic,* meaning a curving dyke, is recorded in *c.*1185. It can be identified straddling the boundary between Brackley and Halse, where the oval form is fossilised in part by a curving road and in part by the township boundary.[84] That large stock enclosures were still in use during the late Saxon period is suggested by the presence, in the Badby charter of pre 944, of the name 'stotfald' for an enclosure on Borough Hill in Daventry.[85]

There are certain trends in the distribution of village plan forms across the county. Rectilinear types are particularly common in the north and east of the county. In the south and west there is a tendency towards curvilinear forms, complex road networks and a greater prevalence of greens, though rectilinear forms do still occur here. Occasional they are highly regular, as at Eydon and Canons Ashby, which look similar to the highly rectilinear 'new' settlements in the east, particularly Woodnewton and Newton Bromswold. The origin of these variations in distribution can be sought through the analysis of the geology, relief and drainage of the sites, as well as medieval land use and the furlong and road pattern.

Haselbech, where the element *bech* reflects its hilltop location, provides a simple example (Figure 74). The church, rectory, principal manor and most of the tenements lie on a small 'island' of sand and gravel, on a hilltop otherwise dominated by boulder clay. The peripheral parts of the village, especially on the west which includes the areas deserted before 1598, lie on the boulder clay and probably represent the latest stages of medieval expansion.[86]

Such correlation of church and manor with per-

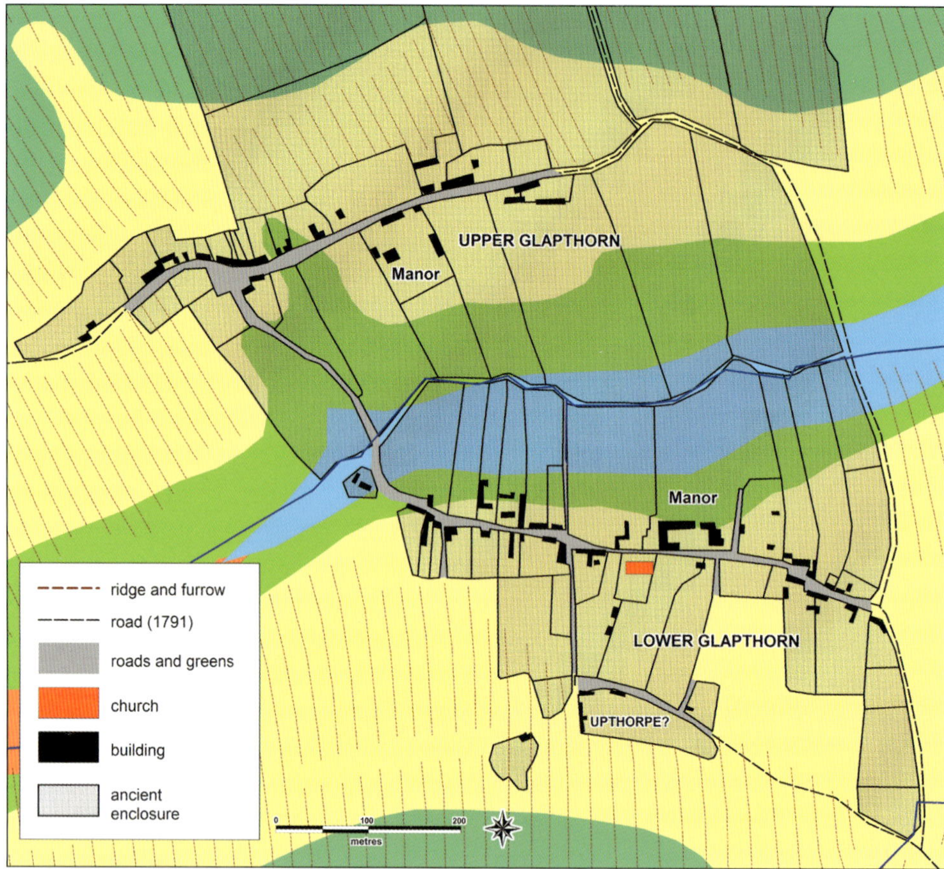

Figure 75. The plan form of Glapthorn from the map of 1814, viewed against a background of the furlong pattern and simplified geology (geology legend p.99).

meable geology is seen in villages across the county. Given the close association already noted between Saxon settlement and permeable geology, this suggests that, in the absence of archaeological data, geological type may provide an indicator of the primary foci within many villages. If so, then villages seem often to have expanded onto clay land from preferred settlement locations. In some cases the area of permeable geology was very small, suggesting some large villages saw extensive growth across clays, as perhaps at Marston St Lawrence. Other examples of major expansion onto boulder clay are at Woodend Green and Welford. Sometimes such expansion seems to have resulted in settlements that have a polyfocal form, with several ends, but which actually had a single original focus. Paulerspury provides a complex example where some ends are on clay and may result from expansion while others are on permeable geology and are more likely to represent early foci (Figure 90).

This is not to say that permeable geology is always a firm indicator of the early focus. At Kettering detailed documentary evidence from the late 13th to 15th centuries suggests phases of growth. Newlands was a peripheral development known to have been laid out in late 13th century, yet it sits on permeable geology, as do the manor and church at the other end of the town. However, what appear to be the primary virgate tenements lie on mudstone in an area adjacent to a possible small green.[87]

During the centuries of greatest pressure for settlement expansion, up to the early 14th century, it may have been the open field system that restricted village growth from the late Saxon core, field land was typically shared by many tenants and restrictions reinforced with strong manorial controls. This may be why, even where greens did exist at a distance from a village core, as at Great Brington and Boughton Green, settlement did not normally gravitate there in the haphazard fashion seen in parts of Norfolk.[88] In most situations in Northamptonshire, even where there was expansion onto greens or across open field, this seems to have occurred in a far more constrained fashion, resulting in highly nucleated villages.

There are many villages where complex plan form appears to have been determined, in part, by the underlying geology. One common form continues an early-middle Saxon pattern.[89] This is the paired settlement set on either side of a stream, exemplified by Glapthorn. Here a band of permeable geology creates a preferred settlement zone along either side of a small valley (Figure 75). The degree of separation of the two elements was dependent upon the spacing of these

Figure 76. The plan form of Alderton from the map of 1819 and earthwork evidence recorded by RCHM, viewed against a background of the furlong pattern and simplified geology (geology legend p.99).

opposing geological exposures. Where these strata merge as they progress upstream then two double rows of occupation may merge into one, as at Grafton Underwood. If the preferred strata lay wholly along the valley bottom then that is where the settlement is found, as at Southwick.[90] Thus as one moves upstream along the valley of the Wootton brook the villages are at first paired, as with Hackleton on the north and Piddington on the south, whereas at the valley head a single settlement, Horton, is set along the valley floor. Other examples point up the dangers inherent in plan form analysis. For example at Pytchley and Ecton, as a result of the pattern of geology and relief, there are paired rows of tenements that create a funnel shaped pattern which, in other contexts, might be interpreted as originatiing in a funnel shaped drove.

Paired settlements are common in Rockingham Forest and on the south-east side of the Nene downstream from Northampton. This is because here the boulder clay capped plateau is cut through by streams that have created many such preferred locations on opposing sides of narrow tributary valleys (Figure 64). In contrast, paired settlements are rare in the north-west of the county, which is dominated by mudstone vales with far more fragmented high ground of mainly permeable geology. This shows how the frequency of some plan forms across the county can be determined principally by physical geography.

A different type of paired settlement appears where discrete foci have developed on preferred locations at different heights on a valley side, where two different permeable geologies are separated by an impermeable band. At Alderton two discrete settlement foci seem to result from such a pattern, with little evidence of infilling between the two (Figure 76). On the higher level, on limestone, is the main area of settlement around the church and castle, with a small detached area to the south-west on the opposite side of a small slade. On the lower level, descending into the valley of the Tove, is an end which is set partly on a small permeable outcrop but expands out from that around a small green, which lies on mudstone. In many cases the geological influence on plan form is just one of a number of factors influencing plan form. Thus at Alderton it is possible that some of the tenements to the south-east of the castle represent infilling within a drove running north-east along the scarp. This is suggested by the fact that the wide routeway outside the village steps inward to become a narrow road when entering the village, while on the south side the back boundaries of the tenements continue the wider line of the drove (Figure 77).

Figure 77. The map of Alderton in c.1725 showing the way in which the tenements to the south-east of the castle appear to have been dropped into a wide road or drove, which at that date still continued at its full width to the east as a Cow Common. Other tenements immediately south of the church are also dropped into this wide routeway, for adjacent to them tiny greens still survived. (NRO MAP 4224)

In seeking a correlation between plan form and land use history, the most straightforward link might be expected where settlements record land use in their names. For most name elements our sample is probably too small to find consistent correlation of plan form. The commonest element is *leah*. Surviving leys, found on historic mapping in the wider landscape of the woodland zone, may provide a guide to the forms which originally underlay some settlements with *leah* names.[91] Leys appear in several different forms: some are linear and funnel up into woodland pastures on the plateau, while others funnel down into low pastures. There are also long leys, such as that to the west of the lodge in Harringworth park.[92] Such variety may explain why it is so difficult to identify a distinct settlement plan form associated with *leah* names. In addition to *leah* there were other pastures within the woodland zones which may have had distinct meanings, including *green* and *feld*. The colonisation of all such open areas by settlement was probably a complex process that was influenced by their scale and function.

In the upper Ise valley a ley called Tickley seems to be fossilised in the open field pattern. This provides a comparator for the plan form of the village of Weekley, which lies a kilometre to the south in a similar topographical and geological context (Figure 78). A series of Tickley names are recorded on the 1717 open field map of Geddington, which together form a funnel shaped area of pasture leading down the end of a slight spur. This is quite different to the typical open field pasture strips, which normally lay in wet slade bottoms. Upslope Tickley leads onto the limestone plateau, where it is aligned with and leads into a group of rectilinear enclosures of an Iron Age settlement and Roman villa.[93] As it descended into the Ise valley Tickley turned slightly northward towards Geddington village. Though distorted by medieval and later changes, the core of ancient enclosures of the village of Weekley, where not containing ridge and furrow, may occupy an area of similar form, leading down into the valley but turning southward towards the Saxon estate centre of Warkton.

Some topographical features recorded in settlement names do not influence plan form because the village lay a short distance away from it. This is inevitable where the feature could not be occupied, as with the marshes at Kelmarsh and Titchmarsh which lie to one side of the settlements (Figure 79). Others may not be accompanied by a distinctive plan form because the land use name related to a much wider zone. Thus at Great and Little Oakley the ley may have run along the whole of the narrow permeable zone between the two villages, where the upper Ise cuts through the boulder clay plateau. This will certainly be true of the villages of Old and Walgrave because, judging by other wolds in Northamptonshire, this wold will have been a very extensive area.

Some settlements appear to lie at the interface between the named feature and the wider landscape. This is most easily discerned with an island (*eg*), where physical geography indicates the original feature. Thus the river and a former marsh, approximately defined by an area of alluvium, identify the 'island' of Fotheringhay on the Nene. Both this and Eye, both technically peninsulas rather than islands, have their villages set along a narrow neck of land leading into and thus controlling access to, the island. The plans of both villages could be interpreted as occupation set within a wide drove (Figure 83).[94]

Settlements with *feld* names may also lie on such an interface. They almost always lie on boulder clay within the woodland zone or, as in the case of Luffield, on a small permeable area within extensive

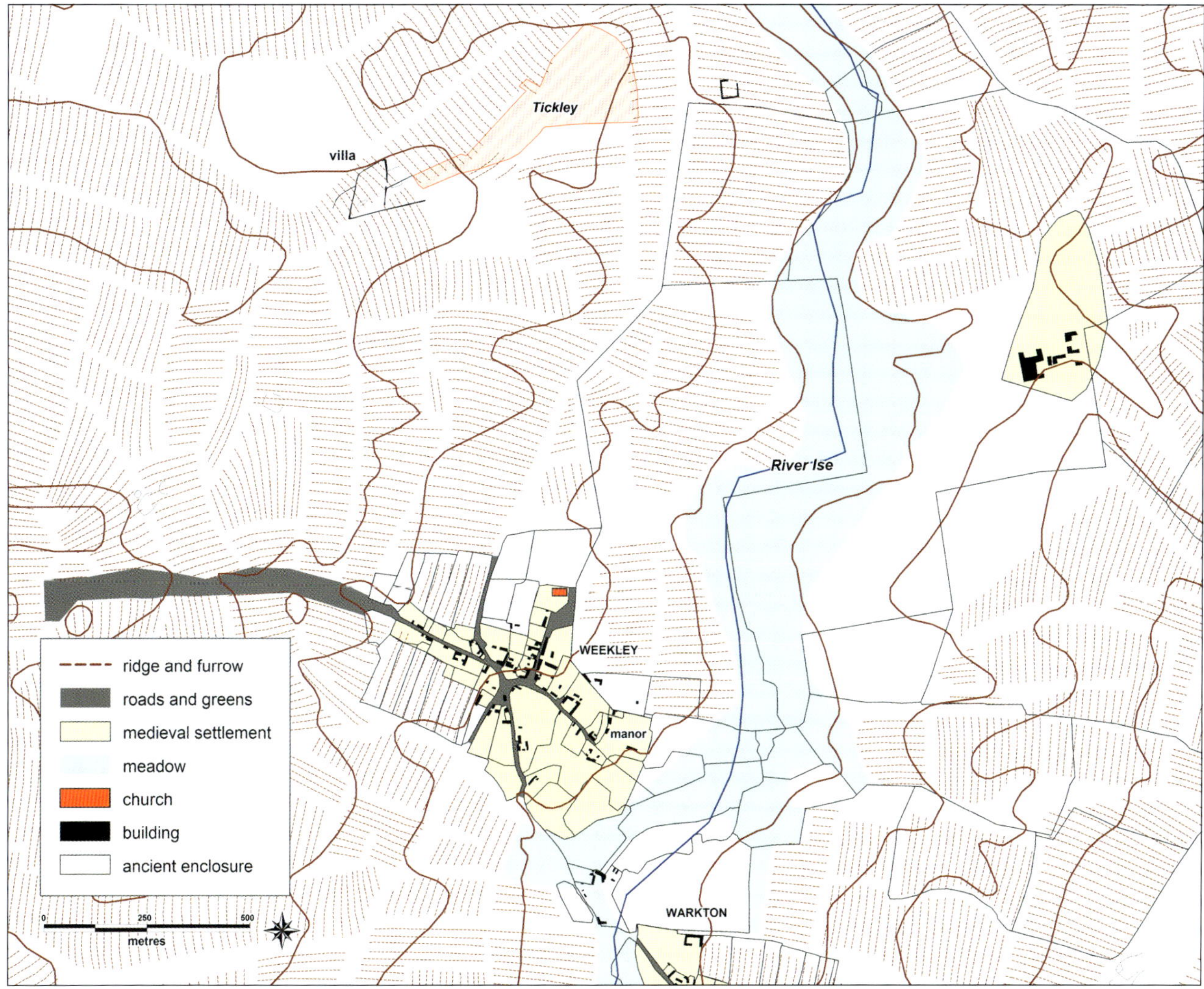

Figure 78. The plan form of Weekley village (1808) compared to the form of Tickley, an unoccupied leah, and contours at 10m intervals. Tickley was identified from place names and the furlong pattern recorded on the Geddington map of 1707 and in our medieval atlas. Mapping of the furlongs in part of this area proved problematic due to destruction caused by extensive modern quarrying, explaining the two large rectilinear areas near the villa which lack strips. Also shown are cropmarks enclosures of a defended Iron Age settlement and a Roman villa, into which Tickley may once have led.

woodland which lies on clay. The original character and scale of the *felds* is suggested by Benefield Lawn and Dryfield. Both on boulder clay in woodland next to Cottingham and are first recorded in the mid 12th century but were apparently never occupied.[95] When mapped in the late 16th century Benefield Lawn covered 455 acres (184ha.) while the area called then called Dryfield covered 106 acres (43ha). Churchfield township, which comprises 311 acres (126ha.), may provide a further indication as to the scale of these *felds,* for the Oundle charter of the late 10th century seems to indicate that the township corresponds to the feld – at that time wholly surrounded by woods.[96]

Benefield Lawn acquired a second name element (lawn) with a similar meaning to *feld*. A comparable link is the association of green names with *felds*, with examples including Tanfield Green in Corby and Sutfield Green in Wicken. Such linking of *feld* with green and lawn may indicate a pastoral function continuing over a long period. Such early land use for woodland greens has archaeological support in the case of Bulwick Green. Here a small stock enclosure, dated in excavation to the late Saxon period, lies adjacent to a larger undated oval enclosure which is respected by the road and revealed in aerial photographs (Figure 80).[97]

Wakefield Lawn in the heart of Whittlewood Forest, recorded on historic maps as covering 282 acres (114ha), is similar in scale and shape to Benefield Lawn. The lawn is thus likely to be the location of the *feld* of Wakefield. The deserted 1086 hamlet called Wakefield, which is set on permeable geology along a narrow valley to the east of the lawn, seems to lie in the corridor of open ground leading from the Tove valley up into the *feld*. Benefield near Oundle may be another case of a *feld*

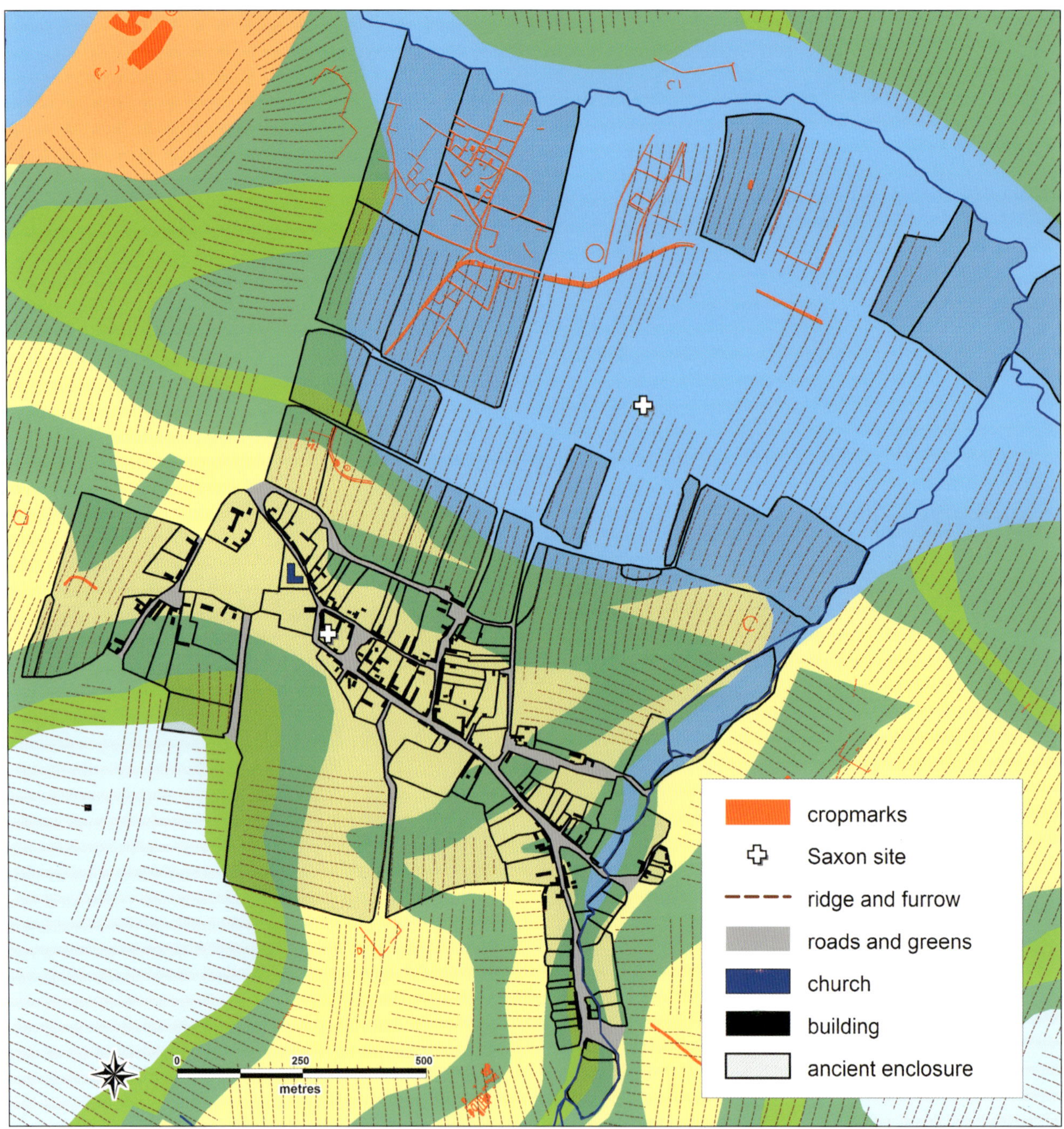

Figure 79. The plan form of Titchmarsh (1779) viewed in relation to the furlong pattern, cropmarks (NMP) of the Iron Age and Roman enclosures and roads, and simplified geology (geology legend see p.99). The probable location of the Saxon marsh of the village name may be identified by the large area of alluvium particularly where furlongs are absent, though the cropmarks might suggest the low lying area had been drained in the Roman period.

named settlement lying on the entrance to a feld. The late 10th century charter, granting the estate at Oundle to the Abbot of Peterborough records a ley leading into *Beringafeld*. This ley runs through the woodland along the permeable geology of a small tributary valley of the Nene. Unfortunately, in this case the surrounding boulder clay saw extensive assarting in the 12th century and so the former extent of the *feld* and its relationship to the settlement is not clear.[98]

At just 40 acres (16ha) the green recorded at Brafield on the Green may be just the northern remnant of a much larger *feld*, most of which was converted to arable furlongs in the late Saxon or earlier medieval (Figure 81). Brafield is one of the few Northamptonshire villages which lay wholly on boulder clay and the only one where the plan form seems to show a direct association with the *feld* itself. Part of the settlement was set along a road, perhaps originally a drove,

Figure 80. Aerial photograph showing the soilmarks and remnant earthwork of the late Saxon oval enclosure on the former Bulwick Green within Rockingham Forest. Beyond this the medieval Potter's Way runs up to then skirts around a second, much larger oval enclosure which is not visible on this image. The scatter of charcoal patches shows that much of the open area was at some time, probably in the medieval period, covered with woodland. (NMR NHC 2008/25 © Northamptonshire County Council).

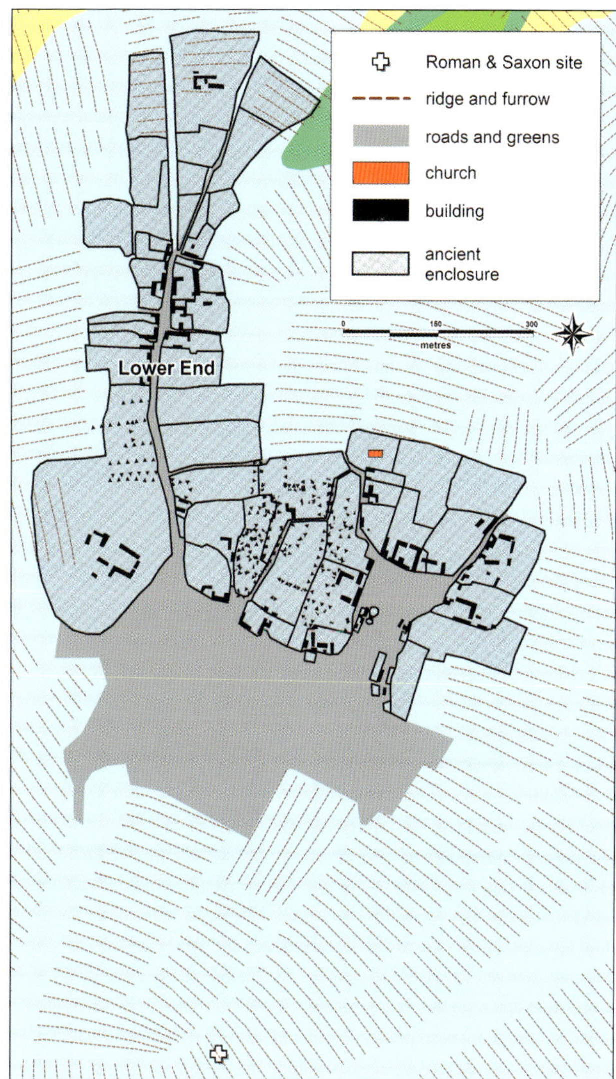

Figure 81. The plan form of Brafield on the Green from the map of 1829, supplemented with earthworks mapped in the NMP, viewed against a background of the furlong pattern and simplified geology (geology legend p.99).

leading up to the *feld* from Cogenhoe – which appears to be its associated settlement in the Nene valley. Such pairing of villages in the valley with adjacent ones on the clayland is repeated with other settlements along this stretch of the Nene.[99] Brafield appears to have expanded along the putative drove, up to and around the northern edge of the green. Where this and other routes from the valley seem to issue into the pasture. The origins of the village may however prove more complex, because a little to the south of the green, as recorded in the early 19th century, is a Roman settlement which continued in occupation in the early-middle Saxon period.

Where settlements lay on the periphery of woodland then, when the trees were cleared, the extensive ridings and greens could become a framework for settlement, leading to irregular and disjointed plan forms. This is seen at Silverstone, where in 1600 there was a scatter of settlement in various ends. Archaeological investigation has shown this is the result of piecemeal infill of droves and expansion along roads between the 11th to 14th centuries. Indeed the process continued into the 19th century, as comparison between the various historic maps demonstrates.[100] Another example with even more dispersed settlement is seen at Hartwell (Figure 91).

In some woodland and fen edge locations such droves survived into the medieval and beyond, because the pastures themselves survived. At Paston the drove was never wholly encroached upon or fully enclosed and remains a Registered Green today. At Dogsthorpe there may have been a drove of similar form to that at Paston but is only hinted at by the strip of closes lining the road, running north-eastward to the thwaite – a clearing of enclosed pasture or meadow (Figure 83).[101] Comparable forms are seen nearby at Gunthorpe and possibly Werrington. All have droves or drove-like settlement forms leading through the open field towards the crossing to the fen 'island' of Eye or to the adjacent fen edge.

This interaction of settlements with nearby areas of shared fen, which they typically accessed by wide droves, is most clearly demonstrated by a map of the North Fen compiled in 1543–4 (Figure 82).[102] The map was produced in connection with a dispute between the villages of Maxey and Glinton over shared rights in the North Fen. In the 16th century the fen here was clearly distinguished from the meadows, where

Figure 82. Map of the North Fen, shown in green, together with the villages which shared common rights there: Maxey (including Castle End and, adjacent to the river, Deeping Gate, Northborough, Glinton, and Peakirk (with Walderham Hall to its north-east). North is to the left. (© National Archive, reproduced by permission, MPI 1/251).

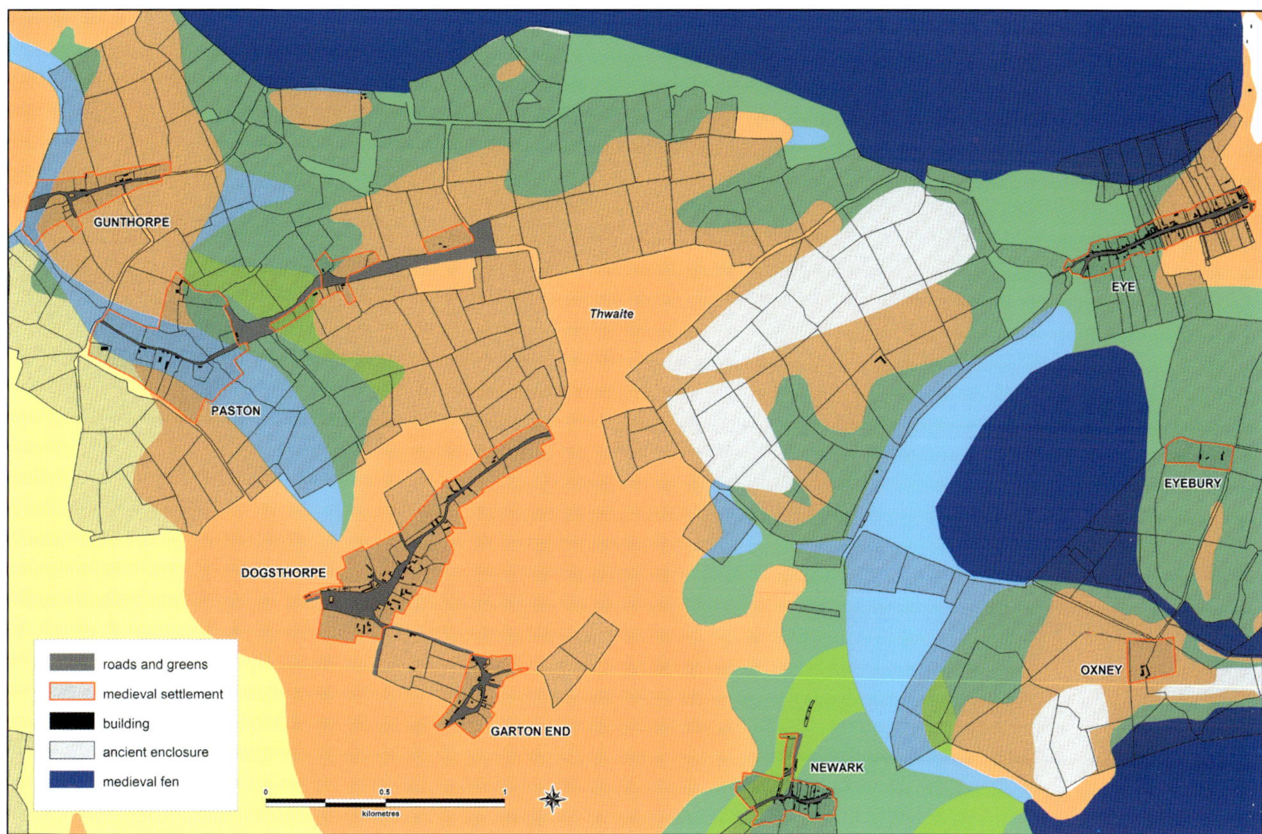

Figure 83. The plan form of settlements on the periphery of the fen in the Soke of Peterborough, viewed against a background of simplified geology (geology legend p.99). The linear form of several settlements seems to relate to the existence of droves leading from the higher ground and out towards the fen. At Paston much of the drove survives to its original extent, with only limited areas of encroachment.

the adjacent settlements also shared common rights. Another map, of *c.*1580, shows the meadow running along the low lying strip of ground from the Car Dyke, where it abuts the fen immediately south of Northborough, westward to Lolham Bridges.[103] On the 1543–4 map the fen is shown as a broad tract of land encompassed on the north and east by the river Welland and extending west and south to the Car Dyke (depicted in white). At its north-west corner a small block of fen extended west of the dyke towards Maxey and north to Deeping Gate beside the Welland. On the south-west a small tongue of fen also extended towards Glinton. Several small encroachments of arable, pasture and settlement lay within the fen: abutting Northborough were the North Fryth and South Fryth, the latter containing a tenement; then to the north-east of Peakirk was Parson's Close and, beyond that, the isolated medieval manorial site of Walderam Hall. The majority of the area was however common pasture shared between Maxey, Northborough, Glinton and Peakirk. While Peakirk abutted directly upon the south side of the fen, which it accessed via a bridge over the Dyke, the other settlements accessed the pasture via droves, which are shown on the map. That from Northborough, discussed below, funnelled out into a very wide strip of pasture which crossed the Car Dyke and ran between the two Fryths. At Glinton two roads seem to have definined a drove similar to that at Northborough, extending out of the fen and running to the village, though the village end of this feature was excised from the map. The drove from Maxey is far more like those seen at Paston and adjacent villages. It extends in a wide swathe west from the fen to enter a small green, which is visible in the south-eastern part of the village plan. Exactly how wide this drove was is difficult to determine as, in the absence of ridge and furrow surviving on the ground or on air photographs, our mapping of the furlongs lacks such resolution.

Where droves appear to have been infilled by settlement, as at Gunthorpe and Werrington, the chronology for such colonisation has yet to be determined. Unlike encroachment on a wide pasture, such as a *feld*, placing tenements within a drove may only have become practicable when its primary function, of large scale stock transfer, had been lost. The case of Eye village, first record in 1115, may provide some indication as to when this happened (Figure 83). The detailed survey of 1393–4 sequentially describes each tenement along first one and then the other side of the village street. It seems to represent

Figure 84. The plan form of Northborough (1819), viewed against a background of the furlong pattern and simplified geology (geology legend p.99). The large funnel shaped green appears to be an exceptionally wide drove, extending eastward towards the fen.

a plan form similar to that mapped in the early 19th century, when the village occupied the narrow neck of land connecting the island to the mainland. It is possible that the two parallel tenement rows, with their backside road, were set within a drove. If so, then this perhaps took place after the island was converted from pasture to arable, possibly sometime before 1115 when the settlement is first recorded.[104]

A similar pattern of droves leading to pastures may have existed around the great heath centred on Wittering. Here most villages, which have plan forms suggestive of infilled droves, are orientated along routes radiating from the heath towards the river meadows or other adjacent pastures. The clearest example is Thornhaugh.

The commonest settlement form seems to be where putative droves open downwards into a low pasture, although there are a few examples where settlement lies in a drove where it opens into high pastures, as at Hale in Apethorpe.[105] Dagnall has a similar linear form and the other two *healh* or 'nook' places (Hale in Preston Deanery and Hale in Courteenhall) also seem to be woodland edge settlements. Partial infill of a drove is seen at Quinton Green, where a major drove still functioned in 1723, leading into the wood pastures of Salcey Forest. Indeed, Quinton village itself may have similar but earlier origins on the same drove.[106] Many unoccupied droves are seen both in the woodland and, more rarely, fossilised in the open field. One example leads north-east from Warkton through the open field along a narrow tongue of the township into an area called the wold, beside Grafton Green.[107]

Major roads could also have a similar wide form and appear to have seen similar infill. Pilton is a good example, together with Harringworth and Deenethorpe which also lie on the same route. The best example, where the wide corridor remained partially open on the earliest maps, is at Wansford, where the Great North Road crossed the Nene.[108] These droves and wide major roads shade imperceptibly into what might otherwise be considered greens, as at Northborough where the route to the nearby meadow and fen widened into a large funnel shaped green (Figures 82 and 84). Similar funnels are perhaps hinted at in village plans such as Braunston. At its eastern end the village street opens out into a small green as it enters an 'island' of boulder clay which, by the early 14th century, was wholly under open field furlongs.

Compared to other regions, *green* settlement names are rare in the Midland Central Province and today Northamptonshire has only 25 Registered villages greens – amongst the smallest number of any county in England. Of the latter most are under 2 acres and the largest, Paston Ridings, is just 12 acres.[109] Our analysis of historic mapping has enabled the identification of 163 greens in the county. Of these 23 lie in towns and market villages. Although most were market places, they have been included in our analysis as some almost certainly originated as greens.

Many greens were removed at enclosure but,

because of limitations in the documentary record, we have rarely found them in anciently enclosed townships, or indeed in parliamentary enclosure townships where no enclosure or pre-enclosure map survives (Figure 86). Where an enclosure map exists and the green was largely or wholly encompassed by the settlement then it can normally be identified. In contrast, greens lying peripheral to or detached from settlements will be significantly under-represented in our data. Usually they can only be identified where an open field furlong or strip map survives.[110] Thus at Warmington the former existence of a large peripheral green could be seen from the enclosure map, from which it can be estimated at 9.75 ha because it was partly encompassed by occupation. However its full extent was 31 ha, when recorded on the strip map of 1621 (Figure 89).[111] Other places where the existence of a strip maps has enabled the accurate definition of the extent of peripheral greens include Newnham, Hanging Houghton and Brafield on the Green.[112] Where there is just an enclosure map, as at Ashton (Soke of Peterborough), the extent of large peripheral greens remains uncertain. At Kislingbury the remnant of the green was only recognised on the enclosure map as a result of local knowledge (Figure 51).[113]

Where earthwork ridge and furrow survives then open field extent can assist in defining the limits of greens, but open field reconstruction based on headlands rarely provides sufficient detail. For example, the majority of Brafield Green was originally shown as 'interpolated' open field on our mapping and this was only corrected as a result of careful analysis of the draft enclosure map. In the absence of such mapping the extent of the green at Woodend Green remains unknown, because in our medieval mapping it is subsumed into the wider 'woodland' zone. The extent of uncultivated pasture on Woodcroft Long Green was established in our mapping of the open field system, but its identification as a green required evidence from the historic maps, which also show the scattered occupation on its periphery (Figure 85).[114] It is likely that various other greens missed in our mapping will only be recognised, if at all, as a result of further documentary research. Based on our analysis of all furlong and strip maps for the county, which revealed greens of over 0.5 acres (0.2ha.) associated with 23% of depicted settlements, we might expect that at least a quarter of villages in the county once had greens.

The distribution map of greens within settlements only identifies open areas where they are larger than 0.5 acres (0.2ha.) or, for linear greens or droves, more than 40m wide (Figure 86). This is because it was impossible, from mapping alone, to distinguish greens from simple widening of roads at junctions. As a result some tiny named greens, such as that at the southern end of Little Ecton, have generally been excluded.[115] Where not directly abutting a settlement the many woodland greens and the three large named greens identified in the open fields (Great Brington, Warmington West Green and Boughton Green) have also been excluded from the analysis.

In some regions of England settlement dispersed around common edges during the medieval period, as in parts of Norfolk where many broad commons of hundreds of hectares survived into the early-modern.[116] In contrast, Hall argues that the majority of the extensive pastures in Northamptonshire were ploughed up before the Conquest or soon after. The pastures appear normally to have escaped conversion to arable only when they lay within woodland, where agriculture was restrained by forest law; in the fen, where land was too wet; or in the heaths, where parts were too dry and infertile.

We have not recognised any specific impact of heath land use on the plan form of associated settlements. In part this is because heathland pastures had become highly fragmented during the medieval, except for one or two areas, such as Bayard's Green on the Oxfordshire border. In the Saxon period they were probably far more extensive, as suggested by the wider distribution of heath names attached to medieval furlongs. There are just two settlements with heath names, East and West Haddon. They probably lay at a distance from the heath which gave them their names. This seems to have been on the hill which lies between them, where a small area of heath survived in the medieval, which heath furlong names show had been more extensive (Figure 6).

The largest area of pasture to survive was the fen, which had an important influence on the form of settlements, via the droves discussed above. The most common surviving pastures were however in the woodland. The largest include Rockinghamshire, at 650 acres (263 ha.), and the plain of Benefield, Weldon and Deenethorpe, at more than 390 acres (158 ha.), although charcoal hearths show medieval woodland originally covered large parts of the latter.[117] Most woodland greens were on a smaller scale, with Salcey Green at *c.*125 acres (50ha.) and Sudborough Great Green at 77 acres (31ha.) amongst the largest. A number of settlements interacted directly with these woodland pastures and the droves that led into them.

By *c.*1300 the champion landscapes of the county lacked large commons to provide the context for the expansion of medieval settlement and even where large detached greens are known, such as Boughton Green and Great Brington Green, settlement did not drift to them. As we have seen, only in a handful of villages, including Brafield, Kilsby and Barby, does occupation seem to have expanded onto substantial greens and yet even then the settlement retained a nucleated form.

Substantial amounts of pasture did survive within the open field landscape, in areas too wet for cultivation. Meadows, which were sometimes very extensive, did not normally provide a context for settlement, because

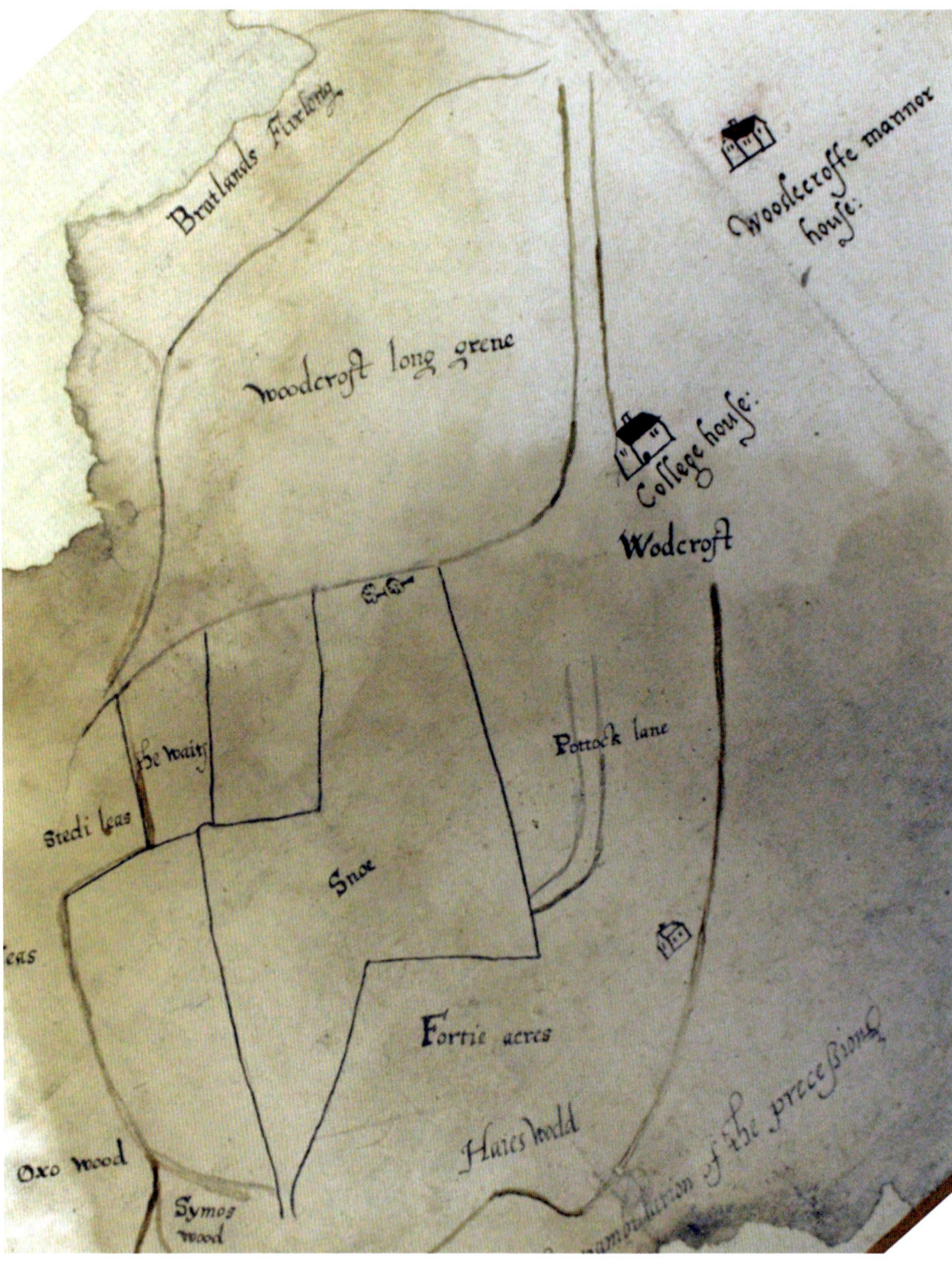

Figure 85. A late 16th century[118] map showing Woodcroft Long Green and, adjacent to it, the scattered occupation of Woodcroft, which lies in the southern tip of Etton township. To the south is woodland which lies on the highest ground. (NRO Map 1251).

they lay on floodplains, and so they are excluded from the following analysis. In all townships, though more frequent in some parts of the county due to factors of physical geography, there were narrow wet linear pastures in the bottom of small valleys and slades. These formed a significant context for the expansion of adjacent settlements. Far less common are pastures on valley sides, where water from overlying permeable geology issued out across clayland, creating small areas of gently or sometimes steeply sloping moor. This land use type has not been adequately considered in the present study because, without detailed documentary research, it is difficult to identify moors from other open field pasture. The little evidence that is available suggests that these wet moors were, in most cases, quite restricted in extent. Furlong and field names suggest some were lost to arable expansion in the medieval, as with Nether and Over Moor to the east of Braybrooke village.[119] They tended to survive on steeper slopes, particularly in parts of the west of the county where such topographical contexts are most common. One such example, at Creaton, is discussed below.

Comparison of the distribution of greens to the extent of open field pasture in each township does not show a significant association. This suggests that such pastures did not provide a major focus for the growth of green based settlement (Table 12). Neither do greens show a significant difference in their association with geology compared to that seen for medieval villages as a whole (Table 13). The one

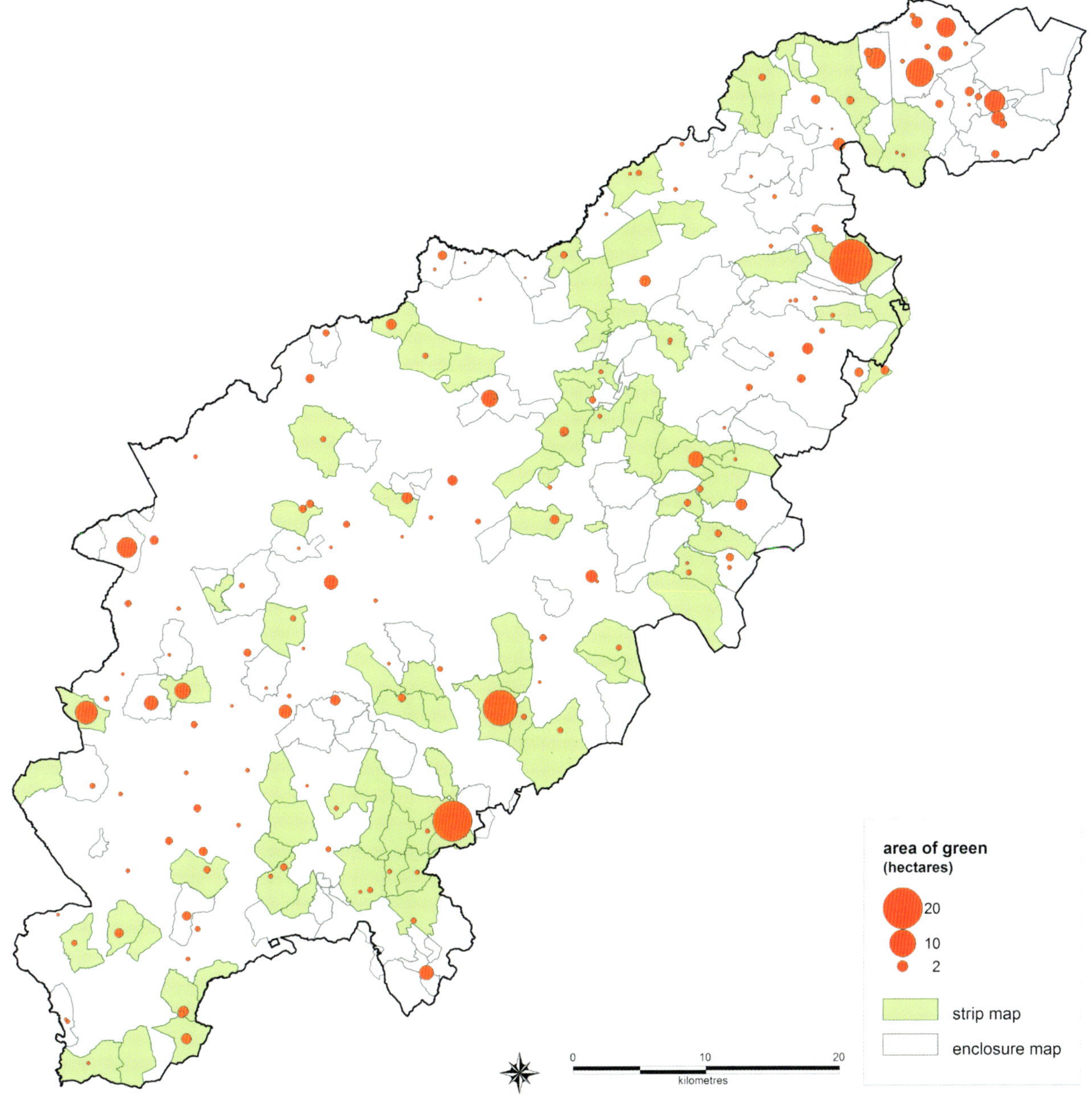

Figure 86. Map of Northamptonshire showing the distribution and extent of greens in relation to the survival of strip and enclosure maps.

major exception is sand and gravel, where greens are far more likely to exist. In part this reflects the concentration in the lower Welland valley, discussed below, where there are large greens on the low lying, often wet area of sands and gravels.

Although many large greens, plains and lawns have been recorded in the woodland zone, village greens do not show a strong woodland association. Only occasionally do woodland greens seem to have attracted occupation. The exceptions include small, probably late settlements such as Elm Green in Wicken, Quinton Green and – the largest example – Hartwell Green. There does appear to be a slight focus, particularly of larger greens, in the champion landscape of the west of the county (Figure 86). Unfortunately this area has the poorest survival of historic maps and so it is an aspect which it will be difficult to explore. Another group lie along the Nene valley, but it is the concentration in the northern part of the Soke which is most remarkable. This reflects two characteristics of the area: the series of long droves which lead to the fen; and the association of settlements with the edges of large wet linear pastures, on low lying alluvium and gravel, where the Welland valley approaches the fen.

Plan form analysis can be used to suggest many more greens, which were lost through encroachment prior to mapping. There are various examples of roads encompassing islands of settlement, some associated with very minor greens, which might represent

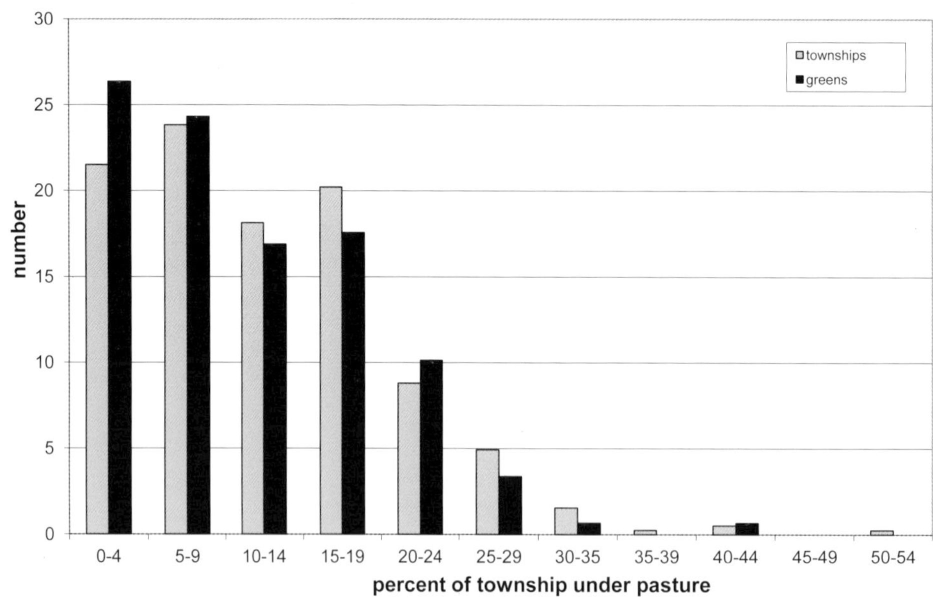

Table 12. The frequency of greens relative to the amount of open field pasture in a township.

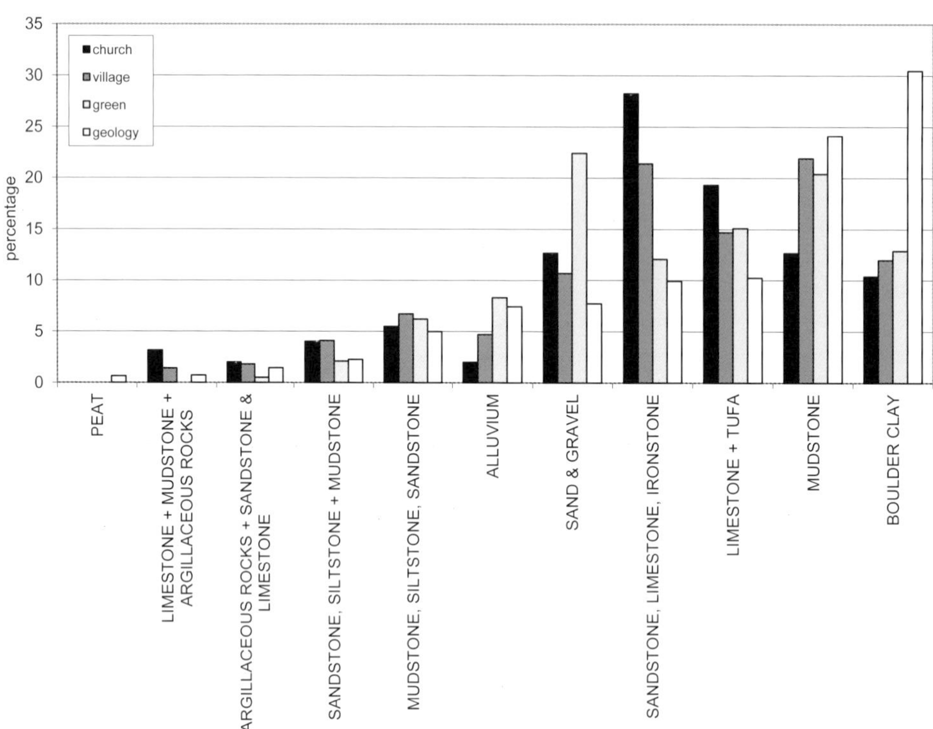

Table 13. The geological context of greens compared to the remainder of village areas and of churches, as a proxy for late Saxon village cores.

encroachment on larger lost greens. Examples are at Aynho, Duddington and Gretton.[120] However, detailed analysis of the greens recorded on historic maps, relating plan form to underlying and adjacent geology and topography, cautions against over-enthusiastic map regression. In many cases the boundaries of greens, including the curving boundaries of apparent islands of encroachment, actually correlate closely with the transition from permeable to impermeable geology. A good example is Hellidon, where the two greens on the northern periphery of the settlement lie on Lower Lias Clay, with the curving boundaries of occupation abutting the greens marking the edge of the more permeable Middle Lias geology. Thus, to take the curving roads of the interior of a settlement like Hellidon, or of others such as Newnham or

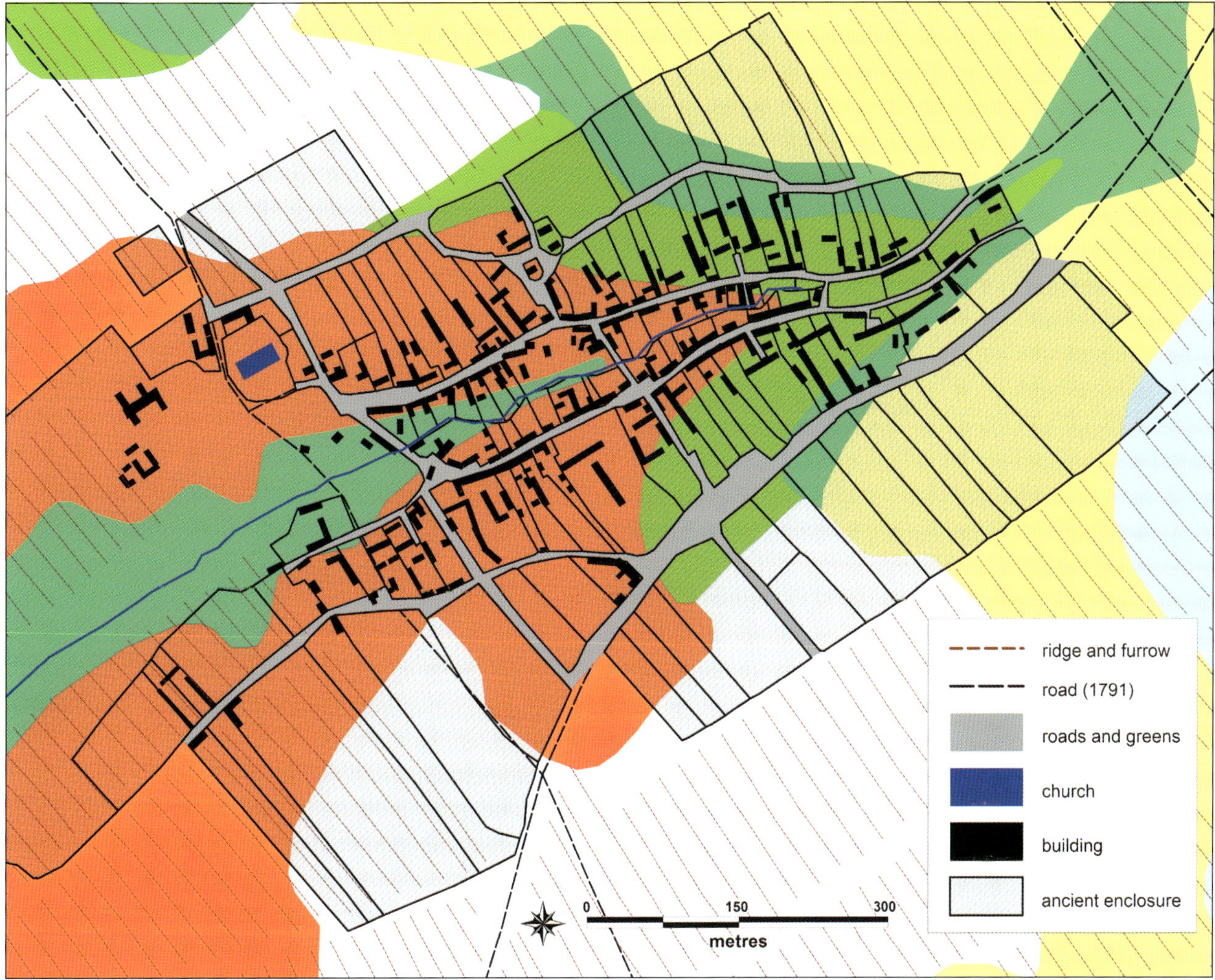

Figure 87. The plan form of Finedon (1807), viewed against a background of the furlong pattern and simplified geology (geology legend p.99).

Badby, as demonstrating encroachment over a once massive green may prove to be mistaken.

Seeking a relationship of settlement to other open field pasture is also difficult. This is because, at the scale of our mapped reconstruction, open field pasture extents are rarely accurate enough for plan form analysis. Only where ridge and furrow has been subject to earthwork survey or digital rectification of aerial data will the evidence be sufficiently exact.

Most problematic are the smaller pastures in the bottoms of slades and narrow valleys. In paired settlements, set on either side of such features, tenements could either turn their back upon the grass or face onto it. When there was large scale growth in such settlements, part of that expansion could be down into the low lying pasture. Where the primary settlement areas were close together the result could be coalescing of the two ends into a single village. This could result in an irregular plan form reflecting the winding course of the stream, as seen at Little Bowden, Luddington and Raunds. At Finedon the result was more regular, possibly because of the small scale and straightness of the stream on a very narrow valley floor (Figure 87). Here the inner rows perhaps represent encroachment on pasture which, earlier, the outer rows had originally faced. If the separation between the occupation on either side of the valley was great then merging might be just in the form of a linking road. At Helmdon this seems to have resulted in an irregular intermediate area, which is presumably the location of Middlebury (Figure 29).[121] This was set across the intervening clay between the more regular plan forms on permeable geology to the south (Overbury, the principal manor with the church) and to the north. The patterns could be even more complex, as at Byfield. Here two adjacent parallel streams provided preferred settlement locations from which occupation may have merged by expansion across a wide central zone, which appears to have contained a green.[122]

As noted above, this type of paired settlement is common in Rockingham Forest, where streams have dissected the plateau. Comparable but less regular examples are seen in the west. Here the geological formations produce a less consistent framework and greens are more in evidence within the settlement cores. At Morton Pinkney the opposing foci lie on permeable geology, with greens opening into a central slade, which may originally have been an area of intermediate wet pasture – the *mor* of the place name. Walgrave is another paired settlement where approaching roads funnel out into a strip of clay, between what were probably the two primary foci on permeable geology.

Such correlations between greens and certain geological boundaries are repeated again and again. While village greens can lie mainly on permeable geology, they typically open out into areas of impermeable geology, the greater part of which, by 1300, were occupied by open field furlongs. It is possible that these greens represent surviving remnants of grass at the edges of the extensive Saxon pastures conjectured by Hall. For example, one possible interpretation of the plan form of Creaton is that the two islands of development in the centre of the village, surrounded by roads, represent encroachment. If so then the present green may originally have extended from permeable geology, in the village core, down onto impermeable geology to the north-east. This was an area that, at enclosure in 1783, was called the moor. It is an example of a moor on sloping ground, where water issues from the boundary between overlying permeable and underlying impermeable geology.[123]

At Adstone the plan form is suggestive of a drove leading upslope with the green forming the beginning of a funnel opening out onto a wide area of boulder clay. Other examples include Guilsborough and Braunston. Greens issuing onto more extensive low wet pastures are exemplified by Ashton (Soke of Peterborough), where a large village green opens out onto a wider pasture known as Bainton green.[124] Such examples in the Soke need further study to establish if the greens could be the ends of droves linking low pastures to woodland and heath on the higher ground. Settlement may later have gravitated to one or other of the ends of these droves, as has already been suggested for Brafield and Weekley. At Etton there is, perhaps, a hint in the furlong pattern that a drove originally connected the wet pastures in the north to the wood pastures of Woodcroft in the south. Ailsworth may have had a similar origin.

Other villages, like Brafield, might have grown along such routes and out onto a distant green, but identifying examples has proved difficult. At Lilbourne it is 500m from the preferred location, occupied by the castle, church and rectory, to the clayland of the green on the hilltop, where most of the settlement now lies. This distance is comparable to the full length of the village of Brafield (Figure 81). Other settlements seem to show a similar spread. At Wellingborough one intact green (Broad Green), one partially infilled (Buckwell End Green) and one probable wholly infilled green (in West End), lie where lanes leading from the settlement core open out onto the higher boulder clay (Figure 88).[125] This settlement extends for more than a kilometre along a series of lanes and roads running between mudstones in the valley to the south-east up across permeable geology to the boulder clay in the north-west. However, in analysing the evolution of Wellingborough, we must take into account the influence on the plan form of the settlement's promotion to urban status in the 13th century. Also to be considered is the presence of the major national road from London to Oakham, which traverses the settlement from St Mary's End to Broad Green. There are comparable landscapes which were never occupied, which may provide a model for the precursor to Wellingborough. The clearest example is Little Oakley, where two lanes lead for nearly 1km from the village, on permeable geology beside the stream, up onto Broad Green and How Green, where they open out onto the boulder clay in the woodland zone beside Oakley Purlieu.[126]

Complex plan forms of the type seen at Wellingborough are repeated across the county. They may occur because two former pastoral zones lay in close proximity, separated by a preferred settlement zone on a narrow strip of permeable geology. At Newnham the settlement opens out at either end onto greens. One is set on the upper, the other on the lower strata of mudstone, while the majority of the village lies on mixed geology between the two. Nether Heyford may occupy what was a network of green and droves which ran across gravels, linking floodplain meadows beside the Nene with adjacent clayland pastures on slightly higher ground to the south. Similarly at Kislingbury a series of village roads extend from a green, where the village meets the edge of a tract of boulder clay, back in vaguely parallel form to the meadow on the north (Figures 27 and 51). At Kilsby major routes running through the village funnel out onto the boulder clay in southern part of village, while at Barby two minor roads join a green which lies on a small patch of boulder clay.

Warmington is one of the most intensively studied of these complex villages (Figure 89). In 1086 the main manor was held by Peterborough Abbey, but there were also subsidiary fees held by knights of the Abbey. One holding lay in Willybrook Hundred but the majority lay in Polebrook Hundred. The plan form can be interpreted by combining late medieval written sources with maps of the 17th and 18th centuries. This shows that in Mill End lay the Abbey's Burystead Manor, and adjacent to it, the chapel of St Andrew (already decayed by the 16th century), together with a group of freehold virgate tenements set around a small green.[127] Another group of free virgates lay adjacent to Blofield's Manor at the west

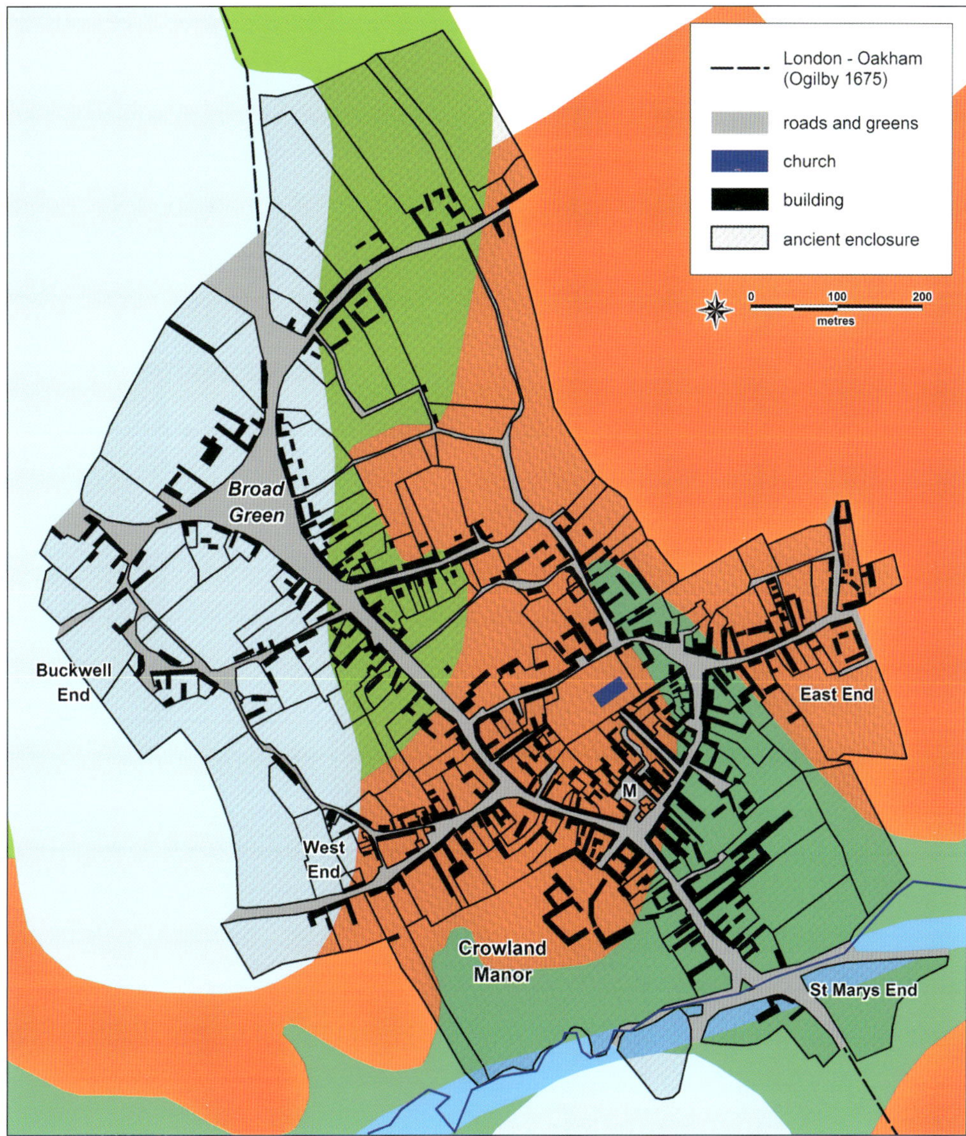

Figure 88. The plan form of the medieval small town of Wellingborough (1803), indicating the site of the manor and market place (M), viewed against a background of simplified geology (geology legend p.99).

end of Southorpe, while between these two ends lay Abbotsthorpe, which included the parish church.[128] The thorp name elements suggest separate Saxon hamlets which have coalesced to form a single village. Abbotsthorpe and Southorpe comprised rectilinear tenement rows set along either side of parallel roads leading from Croswell Hurst Green on the west to Great Green and Cranes Green in the east. Ridge and furrow in the backs of some tenements suggest that the row structure may represent expansion over open field strips. In 1621 another parallel road ran past Burystead manor and through Mill End into a pasture called Bolwell. Croswell Hurst Green on the west of the village connected to the riverside meadow, while on the east the greens opened onto an extensive area of mudstone, beyond which was a wide tract of boulder clay extending to the watershed.

There appears to have been some medieval encroachment on the west and particularly the north sides of Great Green, with Bolwell Closes perhaps subsequently added to the back of the tenements from a furlong to the north. Southorpe also saw limited encroachment onto Cranes Green. The central area of the settlement is divided up into blocks by the lanes but it is set on permeable geology and so these are unlikely to represent infill on more extensive greens.

Intensive fieldwalking has shown the origins of the settlement are even more complex. It has revealed an unusual number of early-middle Saxon sites, mainly on permeable geology bordering the western greens. The two sites identified within the village are likely to be part of a yet more extensive scatter of early settlement, inaccessible beneath modern occupation. Excavation, between Great Green and Mill End,

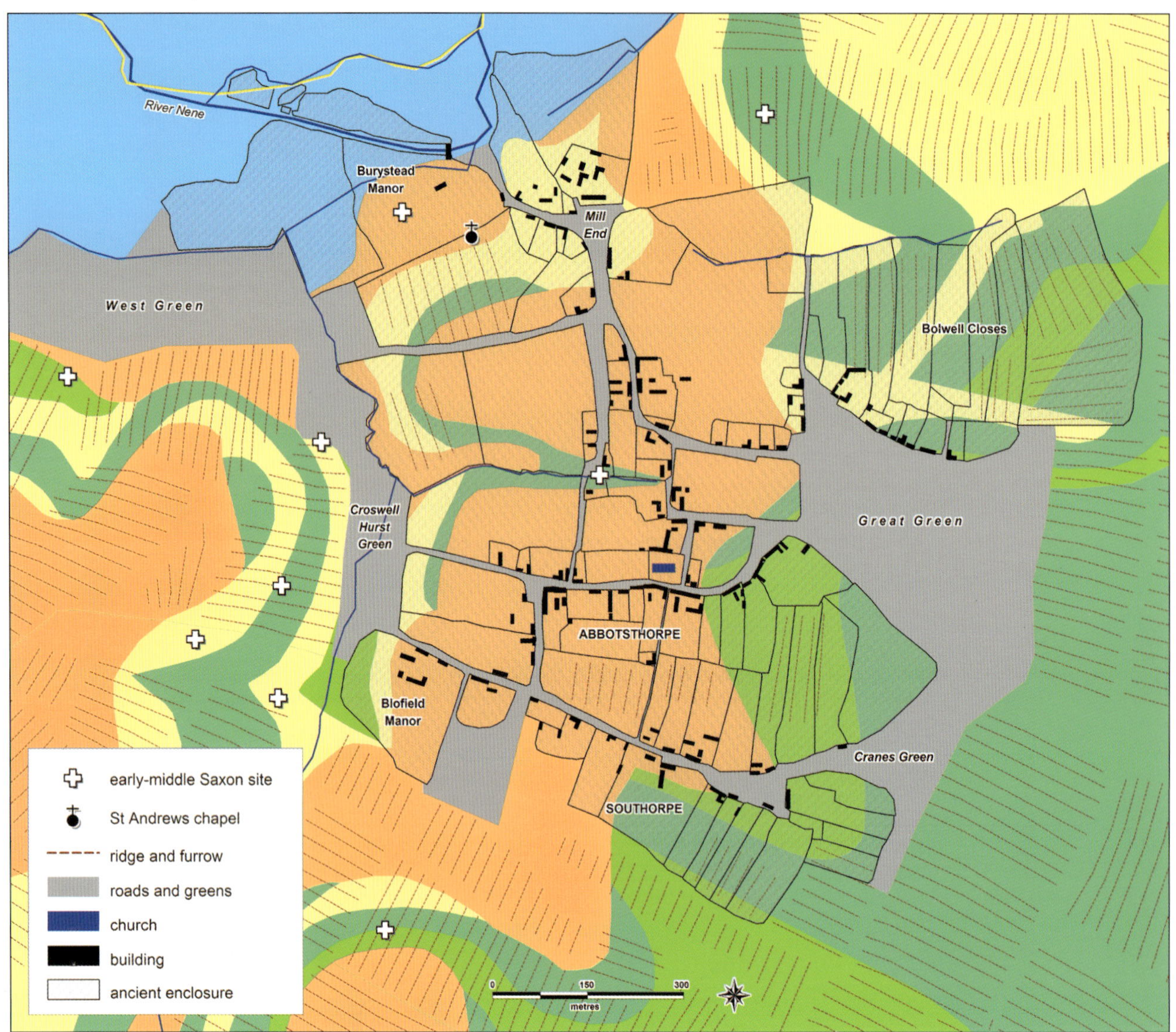

Figure 89. The plan form of Warmington (1775), indicating the site of the medieval manors and chapel, and the location of early-middle Saxon sites, viewed against a background of the furlong pattern and simplified geology (geology legend p.99). The full extent of the greens are defined from the map of 1621.

has also revealed part of a complex late Saxon and early medieval plan which is not represented in the surviving plan form. This reinforces the lesson, already demonstrated at Higham Ferrers, that early-modern plans can conceal as much as they reveal of a settlement's Saxon origins.[129]

Another polyfocal type, often incorporating small greens, is where two early foci on permeable geology have coalesced by expanding across intermediate clay land. For example, Long Buckby stretches between two small permeable foci at Salem and Coton. The two elements of Maidwell, which also had two parishes, lie on permeable geology but appear to have coalesced by spreading across a partly clay ridge, which is traversed by a major road.

Paulerspury is the most extensive and complex example (Figure 90). Its irregular, loosely agglomerated plan may have resulted from the expansion of two or possibly three foci – ends lying on small areas of permeable geology – into wood or wood pasture on the boulder clay. Medieval assarting was certainly happening in the western edge of the township at Monksbarn (see below), while the village's road network mirrors the pattern of woodland boundaries and ridings seen in the south of the township. The principal factor leading the ends to coalesce may have been the insertion of a manor and church between them. If so this had presumably occurred before 1086, by which time a church and manor already existed in the village.[130] Other Tove Valley townships in Whittlewood may show incompletely developed elements of this form. Thus Yardley Gobion and Moor End lie on either side of a boulder clay ridge but did not coalesce. Neither did Furtho and Temple

Figure 90. The semi-dispersed plan form of Paulerspury (1819), viewed against a background of the furlong pattern and simplified geology (geology legend p.99).

End, or the hamlets and farms of Heathencote. In the absence of detailed evidence for the road network it is unclear whether Lyveden also had a comparable agglomerated form, though it seems more likely to have been a looser scatter comparable to that seen at Hartwell (Figure 91).[131]

Hartwell had a complex plan, but the place is almost unique in the county because it was a township with an open field system that lacked a nucleated village. When adjacent townships also on the periphery of woodland in Salcey Forest, like Ashton and Roade, expanded they still retained a nucleated form. In contrast, at Hartwell the present village only came into existence in the 19th century, when settlement completed its drift onto Hartwell Green. Chapel End, now Chapel Farm, set on a small area of permeable geology, represents a typical village core in the woodland zone but, unlike those others, it did not see expansion (Figures 91 and 92).[132] Instead growth was in the form of semi-dispersed settlement scattered across the boulder clay. This was not simply because the permeable core was so small, for at Horton it was even smaller and yet that developed into a nucleated village, as did Denton. Hartwell has more in common with the pattern of settlement seen at Hanslope, immediately across the border in Buckinghamshire. The majority of the occupation lies in the north-east part of the township on the woodland edge. Assart and grove names in some of the closes here, as well as the plan form, suggest expansion into assarts along a network of ridings and out onto a woodland green. An almost identical pattern to that underlying Hartwell is seen in the adjacent surviving woodland, where a network of ridings led into Salcey Green.

Interestingly, in the 17th century Paulerspury and Hartwell were two of only a handful of townships in the county which had a highly complex open field system with many great fields – 10 and 8 respectively. Lyveden, which had an equally dispersed pattern of settlement appears not to have had a common field system at all. It is possible that in such situations there was far less constraint on settlement mobility than is seen elsewhere in the county, where two and three field systems are the norm. However, there is not a simple association between settlement form and the complexity of the field system, because Glapthorn and Cotterstock ran a single field system with seven great fields, yet retained a largely nucleated settlement pattern. Indeed, the tightly nucleated village of Finedon had 11 great fields, although in both these examples the field systems were actually run on a three course tilth in the early-modern period.[133]

This brings us to the issue of fully dispersed settlement, which was rare in medieval Northamptonshire. The farms, granges, hamlets and ends probably had two very different origins: one resulting from dispersal during the 12th and 13th centuries; the other, judging from place name and other evidence discussed above, probably a survival of elements of the early-middle Saxon pattern. The former are typically peripheral, being associated with woodland and fen where extensive pastures survived to a late

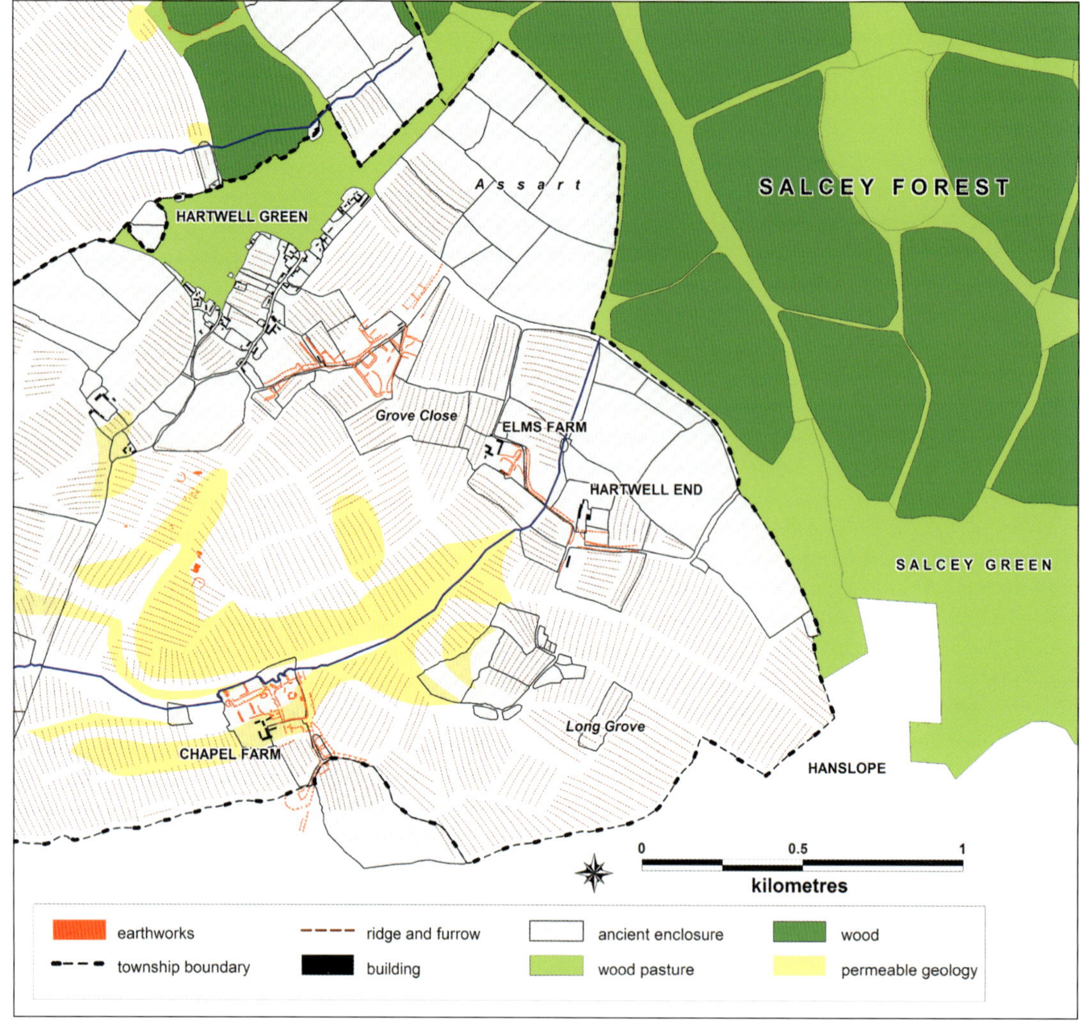

Figure 91. The semi-dispersed plan form of settlement in Hartwell township (1827), complemented by earthwork data mapped in the NMP, also indicating the pattern of woodland and greens and the extent of permeable geology.

date. The latter typically lie in core zones and are often dependencies within late Saxon estates.

Hall's analysis of the open field systems suggests that, in the late Saxon and earlier medieval, there was substantial clearance from woodland and conversion of peripheral pasture to arable. By the 13th century the scale of conversion from woodland seems to be far into decline with only Rushton, with some 300 acres of assart, seeing large scale clearance at that time.[134] In most cases the new arable was farmed from nucleated villages, rather than leading to settlement dispersal. Thus in most of Rockingham Forest, Salcey and the northern and western parts of Whittlewood, isolated sites are relatively rare.

Granges are the most common isolated settlements created in the medieval period. They are found in two main groups. On the fen 'islands' there are granges at Northolm, Singlesole, Eyebury, Oxney and Tanholt. The others lie mainly in woodland assarts. In Rockingham Forest and the woodlands of the Soke there were Biggin, Belsize, Provost Lodge and Pipewell Lower Grange (the Upper Grange may have been on the site of a 1086 hamlet). In Whittlewood there were Piddington Grange, Kingshill and Monksbarn. Even Calendar grange, on the periphery of Cottesbrooke township, in the sparsely wooded north-west, probably lay in a small area of former woodland because adjacent to it are Hockley field names.[135] While most granges were direct creations of the monastic houses, both Biggin and Monksbarn were created out of land assarted by others, before being acquired by the monasteries in the early 12th and 13th centuries respectively.[136] These assarts could be on very different scales: Biggin represented massive clearance, of nearly 1000 acres, by a major manorial lord; in contrast Monksbarn was created by piecemeal assarting undertaken by various lesser individuals. While the latter resulted in a single grange, because the land was brought together under a single monastic ownership, such piecemeal assarting

Figure 92. Aerial photograph of Hartwell End, when ridge and furrow still encompassed the site and showed how small the settlement had been. Traces of settlement earthworks extend to the left (south) of present farm, set on either side of a former road which runs along the hedgerow. Other former roads lead east and west from the settlement, running between the furlongs (NCCAP SP795496 © Northamptonshire County Council).

could result in a scatter of dispersed settlement. This may, in part, explain the pattern seen in the Lyveden valley in Rockingham Forest, Puxley in Whittlewood and Hartwell in Salcey.

Having examined the main forms of medieval settlement in the county it is necessary to return to the question of the origin of tenement rows, for these groups of contiguous house plots, which could be regular or irregular in form, dominated the plans of most of Northamptonshire's medieval villages.

Where these rows have rectilinear form the simplest interpretation is that the row derived its plan from being laid out over part of an open field furlong, with the boundaries of bundles of parallel strips being fossilised in the tenement boundaries. There are various situations where this explanation can be shown to be correct. However, it is rarely possible to determine, from plan form alone, whether a row created in this way was the result of a single planned event or a piecemeal process. Only where there is documentary evidence can the two normally be distinguished. Thus in Kettering, in the late 13th century, one of the two rectilinear tenement rows called Newlands was being laid out in a piecemeal, if highly regulated, process of expansion over open field at the edge of the settlement.[137] Another example of piecemeal enclosure resulting in a rectilinear row, only part of which came to be occupied, is seen taking place on the southern edge of Gretton between 1585 and 1832. Here most of a furlong, encompassed by a back lane, was enclosed to create mainly long narrow closes.[138]

Ridge and furrow is often seen in the closes at the rear of tenement rows, where it is usually seen as demonstrating expansion of occupation over a furlong. While this may often be correct, as always with plan form analysis an alternative sequence might produce the same result. The evidence might also result where there has been addition of closes to short tenements, by the enclosure of strips from the furlong immediately to the rear. This can be suggested at Weekley (Figure 78) and possibly also Bolwell Closes on the north side of Great Green at Warmington (Figure 89). At Plumpton there are strips in the back of both rows of tenements fronting the main street. Detailed examination of the plan suggests that, whereas the southern row may represent tofts and crofts taken directly from the furlong in one stage, the northern tofts are perhaps infill on a drove, with the crofts added to the back from an adjacent furlong at a later stage. In Brackley comparison of the draft enclosure and enclosure maps seems to show this very process taking place, with former open field strips being added to the back of short plots as late as 1829.[139] In some places, such as Upper

Glapthorn, the rows of short tenements never had long tofts added from the furlong to the rear (Figure 75).

While medieval expansion often took place over open field, leading to a rectilinear pattern of tenements, it should not be assumed that all tenement rows derive their plan form from underlying strips. It is very unlikely where the row is rotated by 90° relative to the adjacent strips, as for example on the west side of the green at Abthorpe. In other cases, such as the north-western row in Fotheringhay and other examples discussed above, the rows may represent infill on land, such as a drove, that was never part of an open field furlong. The shape of the underlying feature will then have determined whether the row had a regular or irregular form. Without excavation such a sequence cannot be proven, nor whether this occurred as a single planned event or was an incremental process, although plan form evidence for the latter exists in the north-eastern row at Thornhaugh.[140]

The plans of some 'new' or subsidiary settlements, such as Woodnewton, Newton Bromswold, Deenethorpe and Little Weldon, have a highly rectilinear form. It could be argued that this represents laying out of tenements over pre-existing furlongs.[141] However, in such situations the question then remains as to where the tenants lived who cultivated these putative pre-existing furlongs. For example, at Newton Bromswold the nearest other medieval settlement lay at least 1.5km away, at Buscotes, while the main settlement, at Higham, was over 4km distant.

A very different explanation for the origin of some tenement rows, particularly where they lie at the heart of a village, was demonstrated in the 1980s in extensive excavations in Raunds village and the hamlet of West Cotton. Here tenement rows were shown to have resulted from a phase of planning in the late Saxon period, possibly contemporary with the laying out of the strips in the open field.[142] Not all the plots appear to have been occupied at the outset and some were apparently never occupied. This may imply it was an allocation of land in severalty in proportion to each hide or virgate of land in the open field, rather than simply the laying out of house plots. The Rotten Row tenements in Raunds were laid out partly over an area of middle Saxon settlement, while at West Cotton the row lay on land which had never been cultivated. Thus, just as every irregular plan form should not be seen as the result of infill on a green, so every tenement row should not be interpreted as the result of laying out over a furlong. As the Raunds project has so clearly demonstrated, many important questions of village origins can only be answered through excavation. But not all such work need be on the scale seen in parts of Raunds. Some conclusions can be drawn from carefully targeted small scale investigation, as Parry demonstrated in his campaign of linear trenching in other parts of Raunds village, or through systematic test pitting which, together with fieldwalking, produced useful results at Silverstone and elsewhere in the Whittlewood project.[143]

Some of the tenements in Northamptonshire's medieval villages were of cottage or other tenures with little or no attached field land. Others were farms comprising virgate holdings, or parts thereof, with land distributed in strips through the open field. Where it has been possible to map tenement type onto village plans then often virgate tenements are seen to lie in the core of the settlement. Elsewhere in the settlement virgate and cottage may be intermixed, while consolidated areas of cottages tend to group on the periphery. The overall distribution of these different tenures may indicate significant phases of settlement evolution. This can be seen in the late medieval plans of the small towns of Oundle and Kettering and the village of Fotheringhay.[144] Neither the Raunds nor the Whittlewood projects were able to integrate documentary evidence at this level of detail, because the necessary documentary data is available for so few settlements in the county.

As an example we have taken here the villages of Church and Chapel Brampton, each of which had its own township but were grouped as a single parish. In 1086 there had been a single manor at Brampton, though the land was associated with two other nearby manors, usually, and there were more freemen than other tenants.[145] When mapped in 1584 there were 2 manors, 10 virgates and 13 cottages in Church Brampton, while in Chapel Brampton there were three manorial holdings, comprising 12 virgates and more than 18 cottage and other tenements.[146] At that time Chapel Brampton had a complex plan and it is difficult to disentangle the tenements of the various manorial holdings. In contrast, Church Brampton had a simple plan in which the status of almost every tenement can be established and the manors and rectory located. It is therefore Church Brampton that is discussed here (Figure 93).

The village had two medieval manor sites, identified with the Neville and Lisle fees, which had been formed by division of the parish's principal manor. This is presumably why the parish church lay here.[147] Interestingly, the plan form suggests the two manor sites might have been created from an original single manorial plot, separated by the extension south-westward of the main street. To the north-east of the manors the main street was lined on either side by virgate tenements, suggesting this may have been the original village core. At the south-western end of the settlement, along the road suggested as a late insertion, there are a few intermixed virgate and cottage tenements. These may be additions on the settlement periphery, perhaps over part of the demesne, for they abut the warren. It is equally possible that the pairing of virgate and cottage tenements here indicates subdivision of original virgate tenements to create new cottages,

Figure 93. The plan form of Church Brampton, based on the map of 1584, showing the types of tenement and the quantity of associated open field yardlands.

something that appears to have happened during the late medieval in Oundle. The church and parsonage have a peripheral location to the west. There they are associated with an area of purely cottage tenements, suggesting that this may represent the latest stage of the village's medieval growth. Whether this analysis of Church Brampton's evolution is correct can only be determined by archaeological investigation, but what it does show is how the analysis of plan form is much more effectively focussed when tenurial detail can be added.

Even when one can work from exceptional 16th century sources, many uncertainties remain. Of greatest concern is the enormous impact of population decline in the 14th and 15th centuries, which raises questions as to the degree to which the surviving pattern, even in the 16th century, really reflects that in the medieval. Ideally one needs to explore the pattern of tenure at an earlier date, to see the effects of change in the late medieval and to recognise, fossilised in the distribution of virgate, cottage and other tenures, the earlier processes of settlement growth. There are just a handful of rural settlements in the county where this is possible, particularly those largely or wholly owned by Peterborough Abbey that are included in the demesne surveys of circa 1400.[148]

Yet there is need for caution in interpreting such evidence. The documentary record is best where there was a strong manorial presence, while it is the settlements with the simplest plans that are the most easily reconstructed from written sources. In our analysis it tends to be places like Thornhaugh, Fotheringhay and Oundle, which are fairly regular and simple in form, that have proved amenable to analysis from early documentary sources. More complex places, such as Warmington, have proved far more difficult to reconstruct because of that very complexity, even where there is a relatively good documentary record.

In addition, settlements which had a single manorial lord tend to be those with complete surveys, whereas those with a complex manorial structure may have elements of the settlement excluded from the surveys. This is seen in villages with the best records, such as Irthlingborough in *c.*1400.[149] Two relatively small areas of the village, because they comprised tenements in subsidiary manors, were omitted from the survey and so cannot be reconstructed. In contrast, the tenements owned by Peterborough Abbey are described in great detail. It is not surprising that it is in the latter areas that the most regular, rectilinear tenement rows are found, for the laying out of tenements in a regular fashion is, perhaps, more likely to have been associated with a high level of manorial control. In contrast, the unrecorded areas appear more irregular when seen on later maps, something that is perhaps more likely where there were several lords and less rigid controls.

Thus the small sample of village where the documentary record enables detailed reconstruction of the late medieval pattern of tenure may not be fully representative of the range of Northamptonshire settlements. Yet, with such caveats in mind, these settlements still represent a key target for future research, for such analysis will add significantly to the more typical approach of plan form analysis that we have applied in the present study.

Appendix 1

List of map sources used for the township boundaries

Abington: NRO map 471
Abthorpe: NRO map 2942
Adstone: NRO map 855, T215, T213; Jesus Coll NH P1/1; OS 1st edition 1:10560
Ailsworth: NRO map 2674
Alderton: NRO maps 2906, 2926, 4211, 3127
Aldwincle: NRO maps 3761, 6331, 2885, Inclosure plan 60, T115; OS 1st edition 1:10560
Althorp: BL ADDMSS 78129 D
Apethorpe: NRO Inclosure plan 15
Appletree: NRO T208
Armston: Boughton House map Armston 1716
Arthingworth: adjacent township maps
Ashby Lodge: D Hall reconstruction
Ashby St Ledgers: NRO T41; D Hall reconstruction; OS 1st edition 1:10560
Ashley: NRO map 3002
Ashton (Oundle): NRO Inclosure plan 1
Ashton (Roade): NRO maps 2932, 4218, 454, 360, 440
Ashton (Ufford): see Ufford
Astcote: D Hall reconstruction
Aston Le Walls: NRO T208
Astrop: NRO Inclosure plan 20, map 5099, T48; OS 1:10560
Astwell and Falcutt: NRO map 2645, SC 234, Photostat 1026
Astwick: NRO T133, 118p/15
Aynho: NRO map 4612
Badby: NRO map 942
Bainton: see Ufford
Barby: NRO maps 4084, 4418
Barford: Glendon and Barford 1830 private collection
Barnack and Pilsgate: EX/M 275L
Barnwell All Saints: Boughton House map Barnwell *et al.* undated
Barnwell St Andrew: Boughton House map Barnwell *et al.* undated
Barton Seagrave: NRO T185
Benefield: NRO Inclosure Plan 4
Blakesley: NRO maps 461, 713, 4219, 2936; OS 1st edition 1:10560; modern parish boundary
Blatherwycke: TNA MR 1/314; NRO T189
Blisworth: NRO map 2931, Inc. 9
Boughton; Boughton House Maps Weekley Fields 1719, Geddington Fields 1717, Manors of Boughton, Warkton, Weekley and Geddington 1715
Boughton (Northampton): NRO FH 272, Inclosure Plan 43, Map 471; OS 1st edition 1:10560
Bozeat: NRO map 2839
Brackley: NRO map 841
Bradden: NRO maps 2936, 458
Brafield on the Green: NRO map 2828
Brampton Ash: NRO T166, T140; Kain and Oliver; OS 1st edition 1:10560
Braunston: NRO map 4084; OS 1st edition 1:10560
Braybrooke: NRO map 6393, Map X9947
Brigstock: NRO Inclosure Plan 60; TNA MPI 1/250
Brington Great and Little Brington: BL ADDMSS 78133 F, ADDMSS 78133 A
Brixworth: NRO map 1555, FH272
Brockhall: NRO map 5704, T31
Broughton: Boughton House Map Broughton 1728
Bugbrooke: NRO 53p/331
Bulwick: NRO maps 763a, 4527; TNA MR 1/314, MPE 1/459
Burghley: EX/M 275L, 276L
Burton Latimer: NRO Inclosure Plan 7
Buscot: NRO map 1663
Byfield: NRO map 3495
Caldecote: D Hall reconstruction; adjacent township maps
Canons Ashby: NRO map 855, T215; OS 1st edition 1:10560
Castle Ashby: Compton Muniments 1348
Castor: NRO maps 2674, 1202
Catesby: NRO map 6388
Chacombe: NRO T43
Chapel Brampton: NRO FH272
Charlton: P. Hayter, 2000; OS 1st edition 1:10560; adjacent township maps
Charwelton: NRO T45, Map 6388
Chelveston cum Caldecott: NRO maps 3007, 1004
Chipping Warden: NRO T20, T160, T16, 56p/501; OS 1st edition 1:10560
Church Brampton: NRO FH272
Church Stowe: NRO map 2837, T10; Northamptonshire Archaeology Vol. 16, pp. 136–141
Churchfield: NRO map 2858
Clay Coton: NRO T178
Clipston: D Hall reconstruction
Clopton: NRO T165
Cogenhoe: NRO maps 2841, 3659
Cold Ashby: NRO T212, Map 3125; SRO HB 56 2803; BL ADDMSS 78136 A; OS 1st edition 1:10560
Cold Higham and Grimscote: NRO maps 2913, 2868
Collingtree: NRO map 2846
Collyweston: NRO V2793
Corby: NRO Inclosure Plan 11, Map 2919
Cosgrove and Furtho: NRO maps 6325, 4214
Costow: NRO map 2677
Coton: NRO map 2176, LBY 1465
Cotterstock: NRO maps 4526, 2991, 2842
Cottesbrooke: NRO map 4427, T234

Cottingham: NRO Inclosure Plan 48, Maps 2329, 2919
Cotton: NRO maps 2328, 2329, FH272
Courteenhall: NRO maps 464, 2915, 1349, T28
Cranford St Andrew: NRO maps 1388, 3019
Cranford St John: NRO map 3019
Cransley: NRO maps 1430, 5505, T154, T228; Boughton House Broughton 1728; OS 1st edition 1:10560
Creaton: NRO T151, 184, Maps 4427, 1555; OS 1st edition 1:10560
Crick: NRO map 3215, T41; D Hall, 1989; OS 1st edition 1:10560
Croughton: NRO map 3513A+B
Culworth: NRO T230
Dallington: NRO map 2884
Dalscote: see Eastcote
Daventry: NRO Inclosure Plan 14, Map 942; A. E. Brown 1991
Deanshanger: NRO map 3635
Deene: NRO FH 272, BRU map 1
Deenethorpe: NRO FH 272
Denford: Boughton House Maps Denford c1730, Woodford 1731
Denton: Compton Muniments Map 1348
Desborough: NRO map 4642
Dingley: NRO T140
Dodford: NRO ZB 1837, Map 852
Draughton: NRO T5
Drayton: NRO map 942, Inclosure Plan 14; OS 1st edition 1:10560; A. E. Brown 1991
Duddington: NRO maps 2857, 3633
Duncote: NRO maps 4219, 2897
Duston: NRO map 6013
Earls Barton: NRO Inclosure Plan 56
East Carlton: NRO map 704
East Farndon: NRO map 2867; LRO MA\EN\A\199\1 DE1185; OS 1st edition 1:10560
East Haddon: NRO Inclosure Plan 28, T184, FH272, Map 1556; BL ADDMSS 78129 D; BL ADDMSS 78133 F
Eastcote and Dalscote: D Hall reconstruction
Easton Maudit: Compton Muniments Maps Easton Maudit 1812, Yardley Chase 1760
Easton Neston and Hulcote: NRO T188
Easton on the Hill: NRO Inclosure Plan 15; EX/M M399
Ecton: NRO map 2115
Edgcote: NRO T16
Elkington: NRO map 3125; BL ADDMSS 78136 A; OS 1st edition 1:10560
Elmington: NRO T108
Etton: NRO ML 860
Evenley: NRO 118p/15
Everdon Great and Little Everdon: NRO map 853, T205; OS 1st edition 1:10560
Eydon: NRO T215, T203, T160, 56p/501; OS 1st edition 1:10560
Eye: NRO 121p/10
Falcutt: see Astwell
Farthinghoe: NRO T139; BL ADDMSS 78146 A–D
Farthingstone: NRO T8, ZB 1837
Fawsley: NRO map 853; OS 1st edition 1:10560
Faxton: NRO map 702
Finedon: NRO map 625
Fineshade: TNA MR398, MR 1/314
Flore: NRO map 5259
Foscott: NRO maps 458, 2936
Fotheringhay: NRO map 467
Foxley: NRO map 713
Furtho: see Cosgrove
Gayton: NRO T15
Geddington: Boughton House Map Geddington Fields 1717; TNA MPI 1/250, MP BB 2; NRO Inclosure Plan 18
Glapthorn: NRO maps 4526, 2991, 2842
Glassthorpe: NRO ZB 1837
Glendon: Glendon 1830 private collection
Glinton: NRO ML 860
Grafton Regis: NRO maps 463, 4211, 457
Grafton Underwood: Boughton House Map Manor of Grafton 1748
Great Addington: NRO Inclosure Plan 2
Great Billing: NRO maps 470, 2828, 2115, 2841, 564
Great Doddington: NRO GD3, Inclosure Plans 34, 56, 47, Maps 2993, 2839
Great Harrowden: NRO map 1488
Great Houghton: NRO T153
Great Oakley: NRO map 895, FH272, Inclosure Plan 17; TNA MPE 1/457
Great Oxenden: LRO MA\EN\A\199\1 DE1185; OS 1st edition 1:10560; NRO T27; NRO map 6393
Great Weldon: NRO FH 272; OS 1st edition 1:10560
Greatworth: NRO T190
Greens Norton: NRO maps 4219, 2897
Grendon: NRO maps 2993, 2839, Inclosure Plan 56; Compton Muniments Maps; OS 1st edition 1:10560
Gretton: NRO Inclosure Plan 17, FH272
Grimsbury; Nethercote and Huscote: OS 1st edition 1:10560; NRO T43
Grimscote: see Cold Higham
Guilsborough: NRO LBY 1465, T30, Map 2176
Gunthorpe: NRO T65
Hackleton: adjacent township maps
Halse: NRO T214
Hanging Houghton: NRO maps 567, 568
Hannington: NRO Inclosure Plan 19
Hardingstone East End: D Hall reconstruction; NRO Inclosure Plans 46, 10b, Maps 69, 4524, T153
Hardingstone West End: D Hall reconstruction; NRO Inclosure Plans 46, 10b
Hardwick: TNA MPA 1/104
Hargrave: NRO 152p/512
Harlestone: NRO A95; BL ADDMSS 78133 F
Harpole: OS 1st edition 1:10560
Harrington: NRO T221, Map 4642
Harringworth: NRO map 4527
Hartwell: NRO maps 453, 360, 440, 2977, 2932, 4218
Haselbech: NRO map 561
Heathencote: NRO map 2926
Hellidon: NRO Inc Plan 54, Map 6388
Helmdon: NRO map 1702, T156
Helpston: NRO ML 860
Hemington: Boughton House Map Kingsthorpe and Hemington 1716
Hide: NRO maps 2932, 447
Higham Ferrers: NRO map 1004
Hinton: NRO maps 3495, T45, T9
Hinton in the Hedges: NRO C(A)3734/1
Holcot: NRO map 4044
Holdenby: NRO FH272
Hollowell: NRO T151, T184, Map 2176, Inclosure Plan 28
Horton: NRO maps 1351, 1350
Hothorpe: NRO map 2867, T206; OS 1st edition 1:10560

Hulcote: see Easton Neston
Huscote: see Grimsbury
Irchester: NRO maps 832, 3155, GD3, Inclosure Plans 41, 47
Irthlingborough: NRO Inclosure Plan 41, Map 1091
Isham: NRO Inclosure Plan 28
Islip: NRO map 2849
Kelmarsh: NRO T27
Kettering: NRO map 2648
Kilsby: NRO map 4084; OS 1st edition 1:10560
Kings Cliffe: NRO map 2860
Kings Sutton: NRO Inclosure Plan 20
Kingsthorpe: Boughton House Map Kingsthorpe and Hemington 1716
Kingsthorpe (Northampton): NRO Inclosure Plan 43, Map 471
Kirby (Gretton): NRO FH 272
Kirby (Woodend): see Woodend
Kislingbury: NRO map 2853
Knuston: NRO map 832, Inclosure Plan 41
Lamport: NRO maps 2683, 557, 568
Laxton: TNA MR398, MR 1/314; adjacent township maps
Lilbourne: NRO T178; OS 1st edition 1:10560
Lilford: NRO maps 3761, 3762
Litchborough: NRO T219, Map 713
Little Addington: NRO map 2927
Little Billing: NRO YZ 3714
Little Bowden: LRO MA\EN\A\199\1 DE1185
Little Harrowden: adjacent township maps
Little Houghton: NRO map 2828
Little Oakley: Boughton House Map Little Oakley 1727; NRO BRU Map 125
Little Oxenden: LRO MA\EN\A\199\1 DE1185; OS 1st edition 1:10560
Little Preston: NRO T213
Little Weldon: NRO FH 272; OS 1st edition 1:10560
Loddington: NRO T154
Long Buckby: NRO map 1556
Longthorpe: NRO maps 1026, 1202
Lower Boddington: NRO map 3133, T208; OS first edition 1:10560
Lower Radstone: NRO Photostat 1026, T156, Map 2645
Lowick: NRO maps 5154, 2849, 1409, 4323; OS 1st edition 1:10560
Luddington: NRO Inclosure Plan 22
Lutton: NRO map 1106B
Maidford: NRO map 461, T213, T219; OS 1st edition 1:10560
Maidwell: NRO map 1715
Marholm: NRO map 1072
Marston St Lawrence: NRO map 2677; OS 1st edition 1:10560
Marston Trussell: NRO map 2867
Mawsley: NRO T228, Map 702
Maxey: NRO ML 860
Mears Ashby: NRO T216, T229, Inclosure Plans 34, 36, Map 2115; OS 1st edition 1:10560
Middleton: NRO Inclosure Plan 48
Middleton Cheney: NRO Inclosure Plan 58
Milton: NRO maps 1202, 1072, T236
Milton Malsor: NRO map 2846
Moreton Pinkney: NRO T215
Moulton: NRO maps 1555, 4044, 564, 470, 471; OS 1st edition 1:10560
Murcott: BL ADDMSS 78141 A
Muscott: NRO T297, Map 5704; BL ADDMSS 78142; OS 1st edition 1:10560
Naseby: SRO HB 56 2803; NRO Inclosure Plan 53
Nassington: NRO Inclosure Plan 15
Nethercote: see Grimsbury
Nether Heyford: NRO T138, 53p/331, Maps 5259, 2837
Newbold: NRO ZB 1837
Newbottle: NRO map 5099
Newnham: NRO maps 3140, 942
Newton Bromswold: NRO maps 5441, 1663, 3007; OS 1st edition 1:10560
Newton Willows: Boughton House Map Newton Lordship 1717; TNA MP BB 2
Nobold: D Hall reconstruction
Nobottle: BL ADDMSS 78143
Northampton: NRO Inclosure Plans 43, 46, 10b, Maps 671, 2884, 6013, 5700
Northborough: NRO ML 860
Nortoft: NRO T30, LBY 1465
Norton: NRO ROP 2814, T297
Old: NRO maps 681, 702; OS 1st edition 1:10560
Onley: NRO maps 4084, 4418
Orlingbury: NRO Inclosure Plan 25, Map 1489
Orton: NRO maps 2878, 5505, 702, T221, T154, T5
Oundle: NRO map 2858
Overstone: NRO maps 564, 5264
Overthorpe: OS 1st edition 1:10560; NRO T43, Inclosure Plan 58
Papley: NRO map 2221
Passenham: NRO maps 4225, 4210, 3635, 4214, T204
Paston: NRO T65
Pattishall: D Hall reconstruction
Paulerspury: NRO maps 2926, 2906, 4211
Peakirk: NRO ML 860
Perio: NRO maps 5329, 2842
Peterborough: NRO ML 861
Piddington: NRO maps 1351, 1349, 2912, T11; OS 1st edition 1:10560
Pilsgate: see Barnack
Pilton: NRO T115
Pipewell: TNA MPE 1/457
Pitsford: NRO FH 272, Map 1555; OS 1st edition 1:10560
Plumpton: Jesus Coll NH P1/1, P1/2
Polebrook: Boughton House Map Polebrook 1733
Potcote: NRO maps 2913, 2868
Potterspury and Yardley Gobion: NRO map 4214
Preston Capes: NRO maps 855, 853
Preston Deanery: NRO T11, Maps 2915, 1349
Purston: NRO map 4205, T48; OS 1st edition 1:10560
Puxley: NRO map 4210
Pytchley: NRO T220
Quinton: NRO maps 2915, 1349, 464
Raunds: NRO map 4306
Raunds Cotton Fields: D Hall reconstruction; NRO map 4306
Ravensthorpe: NRO Inclosure Plan 28
Ringstead: NRO ML 1550
Roade: NRO maps 2932, 4218, 447
Rockingham: NRO maps 2328, 2329
Rothersthorpe: NRO Inclosure Plan 29
Rothwell: NRO map 2878
Rushden: NRO maps 5441, 1004
Rushton: Rushton 1732 private collection
Scaldwell: NRO map 681
Seawell: NRO map 461

Shutlanger: NRO V2796
Sibbertoft: NRO T206
Silsworth: D Hall, 1989; NRO map 3159; BL ADDMSS 78145 B
Silverstone: NRO maps 2996, 2948, 2898, 4210
Slapton: NRO maps 2936, 2942; OS 1st edition 1:10560
Slipton: NRO maps 1372, 1409, 4323; TNA MPI 1/250; OS 1st edition 1:10560
Snorscombe: NRO T205
Southorpe: NRO map 4431
Southwick: NRO map 5329; TNA MR 1/314
Spratton: NRO FH 272, T184, Map 1555; OS 1st edition 1:10560
Stamford St Martin: EX/M 276L
Stanford on Avon: NRO T178; BL ADDMSS 78136 A; OS 1st edition 1:10560
Stanion: Boughton House Map Stanion 1730
Stanwick: NRO map 3020
Staverton: NRO map 6388, ZB 1837; OS 1st edition 1:10560
Steane: BL ADDMSS 78146 A–D
Stoke Albany: OS 1st edition 1:10560; adjacent township maps
Stoke Bruerne: NRO V2796
Stoke Doyle: Shropshire County Library H/1444
Strixton: NRO map 2993
Stutchbury: NRO maps 2677, 1702, T190, T214; OS 1st edition 1:10560
Sudborough: NRO map 5154
Sulby: NRO T206; SRO HB 56 2803; OS 1st edition 1:10560
Sulgrave: adjacent township maps
Sutton: NRO map 4433
Sutton Bassett: NRO map 2999
Syresham: Magdalen Coll. -54; NRO Photostat 1026, T164, Map 2645
Sywell: NRO map 566, T216
Tansor: NRO map 4608
Teeton: NRO T184
Thenford: NRO T139, T43, Map 3518, Inclosure Plan 58; OS 1st edition 1:10560
Thornby: NRO T212
Thornhaugh and Wansford: NRO T198; BRO R1/162
Thorpe Achurch: NRO map 3773
Thorpe Lubbenham: NRO map 2867; OS 1st edition 1:10560
Thorpe Malsor: NRO map 5505
Thorpe Mandeville: NRO maps 3518, 2677
Thorpe Underwood: NRO maps 4642, 2878, T221
Thrapston: NRO map 5085
Thrupp: NRO T297
Thurning: NRO ML 1396
Tiffield: NRO map 2875
Titchmarsh: NRO Inclosure Plan 52
Towcester: D Hall reconstruction; adjacent township maps
Trafford: NRO 56p/501
Twywell: Boughton House Map Twywell 1736
Ufford, Ashton and Bainton: NRO 331p/502
Upper Boddington: NRO map 3133
Upper Heyford: NRO T21, T138, Map 5259
Upper Radstone: NRO Photostat 1026
Upper Stowe: NRO map 2837, T10; Northamptonshire Archaeology Vol. 16, pp. 136–141
Upton (Northampton): NRO T42
Upton (Soke): NRO map 997
Wadenhoe: NRO map 2847
Wakerley: EX/M 89
Walgrave: adjacent township maps
Walton: NRO Inclosure Plan 20, T48; OS 1st edition 1:10560; Charlton reconstruction
Walton (Soke): NRO map 4432
Wansford: see Thornhaugh
Wappenham: NRO map 2410; adjacent township maps
Warkton: NRO maps 1411, 1372, T185; Boughton House Map Warkton Fields 1716
Warkworth: OS 1st edition 1:10560; 1851 parish boundary; adjacent township maps
Warmington: NRO maps 6433, 2864
Watford: D Hall, 1989; NRO T41; BL ADDMSS 78141 A
Weedon Bec: NRO maps 2837, 852, ZB 1837, T8, T205; OS 1st edition 1:10560
Weekley: Boughton House Maps Weekley Fields 1719, Geddington Fields 1717, Manors of Boughton, Warkton, Weekley and Geddington 1715
Welford: NRO T298; BL ADDMSS 78136 A; OS 1st edition 1:10560
Wellingborough: NRO maps 3155, 625, 1091, Inclosure Plan 34, GD3; TNA MPA 1/104
Welton: NRO T41, T297, Map 1556, Inclosure Plan 14; BL ADDMSS 78141 A; OS 1st edition 1:10560
Werrington: NRO map 4432
West Farndon: NRO maps 3495, 3590, T160, T208, T9; OS 1st edition 1:10560
West Haddon: NRO maps 3125, 2176, 1556, T30, Inclosure Plan 28, LBY 1465; D Hall, 1989
Westhorp: NRO maps 2677, 2876
Weston and Weedon: NRO map 4341
Weston by Welland: NRO map 2999
Weston Favell: NRO map 470; OS 1st edition 1:10560
Whilton: NRO maps 1556, 5704, T297; BL ADDMSS 78142, ADDMSS 78133 F; OS 1st edition 1:10560
Whiston: NRO T150
Whitfield: NRO map 844
Whittlebury: NRO maps 6100, 4210, 4225
Wicken: NRO map 5692
Wigstorpe: NRO map 3782
Wilbarston: TNA MPE 1/457, MPE 1/459; NRO map 704; OS 1st edition 1:10560
Wilby: NRO Inclosure Plan 34
Winwick: NRO map 4448
Wittering: EX/M 70, 390
Wollaston: NRO Inclosure Plan 47, Map 4447
Woodend and Kirby: NRO maps 2936, 4341; OS 1st edition 1:10560; modern parish boundary
Woodford: Boughton House Map Woodford 1731
Woodford Halse: NRO maps 855, T45, T9; OS 1st edition 1:10560
Woodnewton: NRO Inclosure Plan 15
Wootton: NRO T28; adjacent township maps
Wothorpe: EX/M manor of Wothorpe 1615
Yardley Gobion: see Potterspury
Yardley Hastings: Compton Muniments maps 1348 Yardley Hastings 1760, draft enclosure, Yardley Chase 1760
Yarwell: NRO Inclosure Plan 15
Yelvertoft: NRO map 3125, T178; BL ADDMSS 78136 A; OS 1st edition 1:10560

Appendix 2

List of map sources used for the data in the EM pages and for all the GIS generated figures unless otherwise stated

Abington: 1742: NRO map 471
Abthorpe: 1824: NRO map 2942
Adstone: 1880: Ordnance Survey 1st edition 1:10560
Ailsworth: 1898: NRO 60p/504
Alderton: 1819: NRO map 2906
Aldwincle: 1817: Ordnance Survey 2in Surveyors' Drawings
Aldwincle: 1796: NRO map 3761
Aldwincle: 1816: NRO map 6331
Althorp: 1778: BL ADDMSS 78129 D
Apethorpe: 1778: NRO Inclosure Plan 15
Appletree: 1840: NRO T208
Armston: 1716: Boughton House Lordship of Armston
Arthingworth: 1768: D Hall reconstruction
Arthingworth: 1880: Ordnance Survey 1st edition 1:10560
Ashby St Ledgers: 1764: D Hall reconstruction
Ashby St Ledgers: 1880: Ordnance Survey 1st edition 1:10560
Ashley: 1807: NRO map 3002
Ashton (Oundle): 1810: NRO Inclosure Plan 1
Ashton (Roade): 1817: NRO map 2932
Ashton (Ufford): 1799: NRO 331p/502
Astcote: 1771: D Hall reconstruction
Astcote: 1880: Ordnance Survey 1st edition 1:10560
Aston le Walls: 1840: NRO T208
Astrop: 1880: Ordnance Survey 1st edition 1:10560
Astwell: 1765: NRO SC 234
Astwick: 1840: NRO T133
Aynho: 1793: NRO map 2816
Badby: 1779: NRO map 942
Bainton: 1799: NRO 331p/502
Barford: 1830: Glendon and Barford estate map private collection
Barby: 1778: NRO maps 4084
Barnack: 1800: EX/M 275L
Barnwell All saints: 1716: Boughton House Lordship of Barnwell
Barnwell St Andrew: 1716 Lordship of Barnwell
Barton Seagrave: 1842: NRO T185
Benefield: 1824: NRO Inclosure Plan 4
Biggin: 1919: NRO Box X5394 Smith of Oundle 511/1 sale catalogue
Blakesley: 1880: Ordnance Survey 1st edition 1:10560
Blatherwycke: 1847: NRO T189
Blisworth: 1808: NRO map 2931
Borough Fen: 1822: NRO ML 859
Boughton: 1715: Boughton House Manors of Boughton, Warkton Weekley and part of Geddington
Boughton (Northampton): 1880: Ordnance Survey 1st edition 1:10560
Bozeat: 1799: NRO map 2839
Brackley: 1814: Ordnance Survey 2in Surveyors' Drawings
Brackley: 1829: NRO map 841
Brackley: 1839: NRO T214
Brackley: 1590: NRO Photostat 1026
Brackley: 1763: Magdalen College Maps 54
Bradden: 1803: NRO map 2936
Brafield on the Green: 1829: NRO map 2838
Brampton Ash: 1839: NRO T166
Braunston: 1880: Ordnance Survey 1st edition 1:10560
Braybrooke: 1767: NRO map 6393
Brigstock: 1805: NRO Inclosure plan 60
Brigstock Parks: 1750: TNA MPI 1/250
Brixworth: 1848: NRO map 3014
Brockhall: 1672: NRO map 5704
Broughton: 1728: Boughton House Lordship of Broughton
Bugbrooke: 1779: NRO 53p/331
Bulwick: 1728: NRO map 763a
Burghley: 1814: EX/M 101
Burton Latimer: 1803: NRO Inclosure Plan 7
Buscot: 1793: NRO map 1663
Byfield: 1779: NRO map 3495
Caldecote: 1763: D Hall reconstruction
Caldecote: 1844: NRO T7
Castle Ashby: 1760: Compton Muniments
Castle Ashby: 1841: Compton Muniments Tithe map
Castor: 1898: NRO 60p/504
Catesby: 1638: NRO map 6388
Chacombe: 1840: NRO T43
Chapel Brampton: 1793: BL ADDMSS 78131 F
Charlton: 1773: P. Hayter, 2000 (reconstruction)
Charwelton: 1847: NRO T45
Chelveston cum Caldecott: 1801: NRO map 3007
Chipping Warden: 1880: Ordnance Survey 1st edition 1:10560
Church Brampton: 1793: BL ADDMSS 78131 H
Church Stowe: 1773: NRO map 2837
Churchfield: 1845: T114
Clay Coton: 1839: NRO T178
Clipston: 1776: D Hall reconstruction
Clipston: 1880: Ordnance Survey 1st edition 1:10560
Clopton: 1840: NRO T165
Cogenhoe: 1829: NRO Inclosure Plan 9
Cold Ashby: 1880: Ordnance Survey 1st edition 1:10560
Cold Higham: 1812: NRO maps 2913

Collingtree: 1780: NRO map 2846
Collyweston: 1841: NRO V2793
Corby: 1829: NRO Inclosure Plan 11
Cosgrove: 1880: Ordnance Survey 1st edition 1:10560
Costow: 1765: NRO map 2677
Coton: 1839: NRO map 2176
Cotterstock: 1814: NRO map 2842
Cottesbrooke: 1628: NRO map 4427
Cottingham cum Middleton: 1825: NRO Inclosure Plan 48
Cotton: 1615: NRO map 2328
Courteenhall: 1794: NRO map 4346
Cranford St Andrew: 1748: NRO map 1388
Cranford St John: 1805: NRO map 3019
Cransley: 1598: NRO map 1430
Creaton: 1880: Ordnance Survey 1st edition 1:10560
Crick: 1880: Ordnance Survey 1st edition 1:10560
Croughton: 1807: NRO map 3513
Culworth: 1839: NRO T230
Dallington: 1763: NRO map 2884
Dalscote: 1880: Ordnance Survey 1st edition 1:10560
Dalscote: D Hall reconstruction
Daventry: 1803: NRO Inclosure Plan 14
Deanshanger: 1772: NRO map 3635
Deene: 1612: NRO BRU map 1
Deene: 1738: NRO BRU map 8
Deenethorpe: 1585: NRO FH272
Deenethorpe: 1738: NRO BRU map 8
Denford: 1730: Boughton House Manor of Denford
Denton: 1760: Compton Muniments
Desborough: 1750: NRO map 4642
Dingley: 1837: NRO T140
Dodford: 1742: NRO map 852
Dodford: 1758: NRO ZB 1837
Draughton: 1838: NRO T5
Drayton: 1880: Ordnance Survey 1st edition 1:10560
Duddington: 1775: NRO map 2857
Duddington: 1798: NRO map 3633
Duncote: 1767: NRO map 4219
Duston: 1880: Ordnance Survey 1st edition 1:10560
Earls Barton: 1838: NRO Inclosure Plan 56
East Carlton: 1723: NRO map 704
East Farndon: 1781: NRO map 5499
East Farndon: 1880: Ordnance Survey 1st edition 1:10560
East Haddon: 1880: Ordnance Survey 1st edition 1:10560
East Warden: 1770: NRO map 3509a
Eastcote: 1880: Ordnance Survey 1st edition 1:10560
Eastcote: 1771: D Hall reconstruction
Easton Maudit: 1812: Compton Muniments
Easton Neston: 1849: NRO T188
Easton on the Hill: 1820: NRO Inclosure Plan 15
Ecton: 1759: NRO map 2121
Edgcote: 1880: Ordnance Survey 1st edition 1:10560
Elkington: 1775: BL ADDMSS 78136 A
Elmington: 1838: NRO T108
Etton: 1819: NRO ML 860
Evenley: 1779: NRO 118p/15
Eydon: 1880: Ordnance Survey 1st edition 1:10560
Eye: 1821: NRO map 4426
Falcutt: 1765: NRO SC 234
Farthinghoe: 1841: NRO T139
Farthingstone: 1880: Ordnance Survey 1st edition 1:10560
Farthingstone: 1812: Ordnance Survey 2in Surveyors Drawings
Fawsley: 1741: NRO map 853
Faxton: 1746: NRO map 702
Finedon: 1807: NRO map 625
Fineshade: 1588: TNA MR398
Flore: 1779: NRO map 5259
Foscott: 1725: NRO map 458
Fotheringhay: 1716: NRO map 467
Foxley: 1819: NRO map 713
Furtho: 1850: D Hall reconstruction
Furtho: 1850: NRO T2
Gayton: 1840: NRO T15
Great Billing: 1880: Ordnance Survey 1st edition 1:10560
Geddington: 1808: NRO Inclosure plan 18
Glapthorn: 1814: NRO map 2842
Glassthorpe: 1758: NRO ZB 1837
Glendon: 1830: Glendon and Barford Estate map private collection
Glinton: 1819: NRO ML 860
Grafton Regis: 1725: NRO map 463
Grafton Regis: 1721: NRO map 4211
Grafton Underwood: 1758: NRO map 1372
Great Addington: 1803: NRO Inclosure Plan 2
Great Brington: 1743: BL ADDMSS 78133 F
Great Doddington: 1840: Compton Muniments
Great Everdon: 1880: Ordnance Survey 1st edition 1:10560
Great Harrowden: 1754: NRO map 1488
Great Houghton: 1612: D Hall reconstruction
Great Houghton: 1839: NRO T153
Great Oakley: 1820: NRO map 898
Great Oxenden: 1880: Ordnance Survey 1st edition 1:10560
Great Weldon: 1585: NRO FH 272
Greatworth: 1845: NRO T190
Greens Norton: 1767: NRO map 4219
Grendon: 1880: Ordnance Survey 1st edition 1:10560
Gretton: 1832: NRO Inclosure Plan 17
Guilsborough: 1880: Ordnance Survey 1st edition 1:10560
Gunthorpe: 1791: NRO 253p/58
Hackleton: 1880: Ordnance Survey 1st edition 1:10560
Halse: 1839: NRO T214
Handley: 1849: NRO T134
Hanging Houghton: 1655: NRO maps 557, 568
Hannington: 1802: NRO Inclosure Plan 19
Hardingstone East End: 1765: D Hall reconstruction
Hardingstone East End: 1765: NRO Inclosure Plan 46
Hardingstone West End: 1766: D Hall reconstruction
Hardingstone West End: 1766: NRO Inclosure Plan 46
Hardwick: 1839: NRO T229
Hargrave: 1802: NRO 152p/512
Hargrave: 1802: D Hall reconstruction
Harlestone: 1829: NRO A95
Harpole: 1880: Ordnance Survey 1st edition 1:10560
Harrington: 1839: NRO T221
Harringworth: 1619: NRO map 4527
Harringworth: 1732: NRO map 763b
Hartwell: 1727: NRO map 360
Hartwell: 1827: NRO map 2977
Haselbech: 1840: NRO T231
Heathencote: 1819: NRO maps 2926
Hellidon: 1744: NRO Inc Plan 54
Helmdon: 1758: NRO map 1702
Helmdon: 1846: NRO T156
Helpston: 1819: NRO ML 860
Hemington: 1716: Boughton House Lordship of Hemington and Kingsthorpe
Hide: 1817: NRO map 2932

Higham Ferrers: 1839: NRO V2793
Higham Park: 1794: NRO T130
Hinton: 1880: Ordnance Survey 1st edition 1:10560
Hinton in the Hedges: 1880: Ordnance Survey 1st edition 1:10560
Holcot: 1839: NRO map 4044
Holdenby: 1842: NRO T224
Hollowell: 1755: NRO Inclosure Vol. D, p. 361
Hollowell: 1848: NRO T151
Horton: 1622: NRO map 1351
Hulcote: NRO T188
Irchester: 1880: Ordnance Survey 1st edition 1:10560
Irthlingborough: 1808: NRO Inclosure Plan 41
Isham: 1880: Ordnance Survey 1st edition 1:10560
Islip: 1800: NRO map 2849
Kelmarsh: 1838: NRO T27
Kettering: 1727: NRO map 1411
Kilsby: 1880: Ordnance Survey 1st edition 1:10560
Kings Cliffe: 1813: NRO map 2860
Kings Sutton: 1804: NRO Inclosure Plan 20
Kingsthorpe: 1716: Boughton House Lordship of Hemington and Kingsthorpe
Kingsthorpe (Northampton): 1767: NRO Inclosure Plan 43
Kingsthorpe (Northampton): 1880: Ordnance Survey 1st edition 1:10560
Kirby (Gretton): 1700: NRO FH 272
Kirby (Gretton): 1738: NRO BRU Map 8
Kirby (Gretton): 1832: NRO Inclosure Plan 17
Kirby (Woodend): 1880: Ordnance Survey 1st edition 1:10560
Kislingbury: 1779: NRO map 2853
Knuston: 1769: NRO map 832
Lamport: 1800: NRO map 689
Lamport: 1848: NRO map 2683
Laxton: 1880: Ordnance Survey 1st edition 1:10560
Lilbourne: 1880: Ordnance Survey 1st edition 1:10560
Lilford: 1794: NRO map 3761
Litchborough: 1843: NRO T219
Little Addington: 1831: NRO map 2840
Little Billing: 1742: NRO YZ 3714
Little Bowden: 1780: LRO MA\EN\A\199\1 DE1185
Little Brington: 1743: BL ADDMSS 78133 F
Little Everdon: 1880: Ordnance Survey 1st edition 1:10560
Little Harrowden: 1880: Ordnance Survey 1st edition 1:10560
Little Houghton: 1829: NRO map 2838
Little Oakley: 1727: NRO map 1386
Little Oakley: 1807: NRO Inclosure Plan 24
Little Preston: 1838: NRO T213
Little Weldon: 1585: NRO FH 272
Loddington: 1842: NRO T154
Long Buckby: 1765: NRO map 1556
Long Buckby: 1880: Ordnance Survey 1st edition 1:10560
Longthorpe: 1809: NRO map 1026
Lower Boddington: 1880: Ordnance Survey 1st edition 1:10560
Lower Radstone: 1590: NRO Photostat 1026
Lowick: 1817: Ordnance Survey 2in Surveyors' Drawings
Lowick: 1880: Ordnance Survey 1st edition 1:10560
Luddington: 1808: NRO Inclosure Plan 22
Lutton: 1802: NRO map 1106B
Maidford: 1880: Ordnance Survey 1st edition 1:10560
Maidford: 1812: Ordnance Survey 2in Surveyors' Drawings
Maidwell: 1850: NRO map 1715
Marholm: 1772: NRO map 1072
Marston St Lawrence: 1760: NRO map 2876
Marston Trussell: 1815: NRO map 2867
Mawsley: 1839: NRO T228
Maxey: 1819: NRO ML 860
Mears Ashby: 1880: Ordnance Survey 1st edition 1:1056
Middleton Cheney: 1770: NRO Inclosure Plan 58
Milton: 1582: NRO map 1202
Milton Malsor: 1780: NRO map 2846
Moreton Pinkney: 1761: D Hall reconstruction
Moreton Pinkney: 1848: NRO T215
Moulton: 1880: Ordnance Survey 1st edition 1:10560
Moulton Park: 1742: NRO map 471
Murcott: 1771: BL ADDMSS 78141 A
Muscott: 1849: NRO T297
Naseby: 1822: NRO Inclosure Plan 53
Nassington: 1778: NRO Inclosure Plan 15
Nether Heyford: 1880: Ordnance Survey 1st edition 1:10560
Newbold: 1758: NRO ZB 1837
Newbottle: 1621: NRO map 5099
Newnham: 1764: NRO maps 3140
Newton Bromswold: 1880: Ordnance Survey 1st edition 1:10560
Newton Willows: 1717: NRO map 1374
Nobold: 1776: D Hall reconstruction
Nobottle: 1715: BL ADDMSS 78143
Northampton: 1779: NRO map 5700
Northborough: 1819: NRO ML 860
Nortoft: 1848: NRO T30
Norton: 1755: NRO ROP 2814
Norton: 1849: NRO T297
Old: 1880: Ordnance Survey 1st edition 1:10560
Onley: 1840: NRO map 4418
Orlingbury: 1808: NRO YO 532
Orton: 1880: Ordnance Survey 1st edition 1:10560
Oundle: 1810: NRO map 2858
Overstone: 1763: NRO map 5264
Overthorpe: 1880: Ordnance Survey 1st edition 1:10560
Papley: 1632: NRO map 2221
Passenham: 1772: NRO map 1180
Passenham: 1845: NRO T204
Paston: 1791: NRO 253p/58
Pattishall: 1771: D Hall reconstruction
Pattishall: 1880: Ordnance Survey 1st edition 1:10560
Paulerspury: 1819: NRO map 2926
Peakirk: 1819: NRO ML 860
Peterborough: 1821: NRO ML 861
Piddington: 1880: Ordnance Survey 1st edition 1:10560
Pilsgate: 1800: EX/M 275L
Pilton: 1769: NRO map 3768
Pilton: 1838: NRO T115
Pipewell: 1650: TNA MPE 1/457
Pipewell: 1880: Ordnance Survey 1st edition 1:10560
Pitsford: 1880: Ordnance Survey 1st edition 1:10560
Plumpton: 1604: Jesus Coll NH P1/1
Polebrook: 1733: Boughton House Manor of Polebrook
Potcote: 1812: NRO map 2913
Potterspury: 1776: NRO map 4214
Preston Capes: 1742: NRO map 855
Preston Deanery: 1840: NRO T11
Purston: 1847: NRO T47
Purston: 1768: NRO map 4205

Purston: 1844: NRO T48
Puxley: 1880: Ordnance Survey 1st edition 1:10560
Puxley: 1608: NRO map 4210
Puxley: 1845: NRO T204
Pytchley: 1843: NRO T220
Quinton: 1723: NRO map 1349
Raunds: 1798: NRO map 4306
Raunds Cotton Fields: 1798 NRO map 4306
Ravensthorpe: 1795: NRO Inclosure Plan 28
Ringstead: 1841: NRO ML 1550
Roade: 1817: NRO map 2932
Rockingham: 1806: NRO map 2329
Rockingham Forest (Fermyn woods): 1728: NRO map 3112
Rockingham Forest (Geddington Chase): 1735: Boughton House Geddington Chase
Rockingham Forest (Morehay): 1637: TNA MR 1/314
Rockingham Forest (Pipewell woods): 1814: Ordnance Survey 2in Surveyors' Drawings
Rockingham Forest (Rockingham Bailiwick): 1838: NRO map 2919
Rockingham Forest (Sulehay): 1797: NRO map 1499
Rockingham Forest (Westhay): 1800: EX/M 119
Rothersthorpe: 1810: NRO Inclosure Plan 29
Rothwell: 1819: NRO map 2878
Rushden: 1779: D Hall reconstruction
Rushden: 1880: Ordnance Survey 1st edition 1:10560
Rushton: 1732: Manor of Rushton private collection
Salcey Forest: 1826: NRO map 2912
Scaldwell: 1851: NRO map 681
Seawell: 1750: NRO map 461
Shutlanger: 1844: NRO V2796
Sibbertoft: 1650: G Foard reconstruction
Sibbertoft: 1841: NRO T206
Silsworth: 1760: NRO map 3159
Silsworth: 1778: BL ADDMSS 78145 B
Silverstone: 1826: NRO map 2996
Slapton: 1880: Ordnance Survey 1st edition 1:10560
Slipton: 1814: Ordnance Survey 2in Surveyors' Drawings
Slipton: 1880: Ordnance Survey 1st edition 1:10560
Snorscombe: 1851: NRO T205
Southorpe: 1843: NRO map 4431; EX/M 275L
Southwick: 1794: NRO map 5330
Southwick: 1834: G Johnston reconstruction
Southwick and Perio: 1600: NRO map 5329
Spratton: 1880: Ordnance Survey 1st edition 1:10560
Stamford St Martin: 1773: EX/M 9
Stanford on Avon: 1880: Ordnance Survey 1st edition 1:10560
Stanion: 1805: NRO map 2856
Stanwick: 1838: NRO map 3020
Staverton: 1880: Ordnance Survey 1st edition 1:10560
Steane: 1783: BL ADDMSS 78146 A-D
Stoke Albany: 1880: Ordnance Survey 1st edition 1:10560
Stoke Bruerne: 1844: NRO V2796
Stoke Doyle: 1606: Shropshire County Library H/1444
Stoke Doyle: 1848: T207
Strixton: 1843: NRO map 2993
Stutchbury: 1880: Ordnance Survey 1st edition 1:10560
Sudborough: 1839: NRO map 5154
Sulgrave: 1880: Ordnance Survey 1st edition 1:10560
Sutton: 1900: NRO map 4433
Sutton Bassett: 1802: NRO map 2999
Syresham: 1763: Magdalen College Maps 54
Syresham: 1765: D Hall reconstruction
Sywell: 1725: NRO map 566
Sywell: 1763: NRO map 5264
Tansor: 1788: NRO map 4608
Teeton: 1842: NRO T184
Thenford: 1851: NRO T103
Thornby: 1840: NRO T212
Thornhaugh: 1818: BRO R1/164
Thornhaugh: 1751: BRO R1/305
Thornhaugh: 1757: BRO R1/162
Thorpe Achurch: 1772: NRO map 3773
Thorpe Malsor: 1777: NRO map 5505
Thorpe Malsor: 1880: Ordnance Survey 1st edition 1:10560
Thorpe Mandeville: 1774: NRO map 3518
Thrapston: 1781: NRO map 5085
Thrupp: 1849: NRO T297
Thurning: 1839: NRO ML 1396
Tiffield: 1780: NRO map 2875
Titchmarsh: 1779: NRO Inclosure Plan 52
Towcester: 1763: D Hall reconstruction
Towcester: 1840: NRO map 4473
Trafford: 1779: NRO 56p/501
Twywell: 1736: NRO map1409
Ufford: 1799: NRO 331p/502
Upper Boddington: 1758: NRO map 3133
Upper Heyford: 1758: NRO map 4179
Upper Radstone: 1880: Ordnance Survey 1st edition 1:10560
Upper Stowe: 1773: NRO map 2837
Upton: 1686: NRO map 997
Upton: 1848: NRO T42
Wadenhoe: 1795: NRO map 2847
Wakerley: 1772: NRO map 4124
Walgrave: 1880: Ordnance Survey 1st edition 1:10560
Walton: 1805: NRO map 4432
Wansford: 1818: BRO R1/164
Wansford: 1751: BRO R1/305
Wansford: 1757: BRO R1/162
Wappenham: 1812: Ordnance Survey 2in Surveyors' Drawings
Wappenham: 1880: Ordnance Survey 1st edition 1:10560
Warkton: 1808: NRO Inclosure plan 32
Warkworth: 1880: Ordnance Survey 1st edition 1:10560
Warmington: 1775: NRO map 2864
Watford: 1847: NRO T41
Watford: 1771: NRO map 3158
Weedon Bec: 1777: NPandP p 368 reconstruction
Weedon Bec: 1880: Ordnance Survey 1st edition 1:10560
Weekley: 1808: NRO Inclosure plan 18
Welford: 1880: Ordnance Survey 1st edition 1:10560
Welford: 1778: G Pitcher reconstruction
Welford: 1844: NRO T298
Wellingborough: 1803: NRO map 3635
Welton: 1880: Ordnance Survey 1st edition 1:10560
Werrington: 1805: NRO map 4432
West Farndon: 1880: Ordnance Survey 1st edition 1:10560
West Haddon: 1880: Ordnance Survey 1st edition 1:10560
Weston and Weedon: 1593: NRO map 4341
Weston by Welland: 1802: NRO map 2999
Weston Favell: 1798: NRO map 470
Whilton: 1880: Ordnance Survey 1st edition 1:10560
Whiston: 1840: NRO T150
Whitfield: 1608: NRO map 4210
Whitfield: 1797: NRO map 844

Whittlebury: 1797: NRO map 6100
Whittlewood Forest: 1608: NRO map 4210
Wicken: 1717: NRO map 5692
Wigsthorpe: 1769: NRO map 3782
Wilbarston: 1880: Ordnance Survey 1st edition 1:10560
Wilby: 1801: NRO Inclosure Plan 34
Winwick: 1839: NRO map 3125
Wittering: 1750: EX/M 390
Wollaston: 1789: NRO uncatalogued enclosure map of Wollaston
Wood Burcote (Towcester): 1840: NRO map 2922
Woodend: 1880: Ordnance Survey 1st edition 1:10560
Woodford: 1731: Boughton House Manor of Woodford
Woodford Halse: 1880: Ordnance Survey 1st edition 1:10560
Woodnewton: 1778: NRO Inclosure Plan 15
Wootton: 1880: Ordnance Survey 1st edition 1:10560
Wothorpe: 1772: EX/M 92
Yardley Chase: 1760: Compton Muniments
Yardley Hastings: 1776: Compton Muniments
Yardley Gobion: 1776: NRO map 4214
Yarwell: 1778: NRO Inclosure Plan 15
Yelvertoft: 1880: Ordnance Survey 1st edition 1:10560

Notes

Chapter 1

1. G. Foard, D. Hall and T. Partida (2009) *Rockingham Forest: An Atlas of the Medieval and Early-Modern Landscape,* Northampton, Northamptonshire Record Society. Available from http://www.northamptonshirerecordsociety.org.uk/.
2. Ibid. 11–14.
3. T. Williamson, R. Liddiard and T. Partida (2012) *Champion: the making and unmaking of Midland landscapes,* Exeter, Exeter Universtity Press.
4. NRO Inclosure Plan 22.
5. NRO Maps 4210, 2912.
6. G. Foard (1991) The Saxon Bounds of Oundle, *Northamptonshire Past and Present* 8; G. Foard, J. Ballinger and J. Taylor (2002) *Northamptonshire Extensive Urban Survey.* Http://Ads.Ahds.Ac.Uk/Catalogue/Projarch/Eus/; A. E. Brown, T. R. Key and C. Orr (1977) Some Anglo-Saxon Estates and their Boundaries in South-West Northamptonshire, *Northamptonshire Archaeology* 12.
7. Ex. M70.
8. http://archaeologydataservice.ac.uk/archives/view/midlandgis_ahrc_2010/index_map.html.
9. E.g. D. Hall (1995) *The Open Fields of Northamptonshire,* Northampton, Northamptonshire Record Society 38; Foard, Ballinger and Taylor (2002); A. Deegan and G. Foard (2007) *Mapping Ancient Landscapes in Northamptonshire,* Swindon, English Heritage.
10. RCHM (1975) *An Inventory of Archaeological Sites in North-East Northamptonshire,* London, HMSO I; RCHM (1979) *An Inventory of Archaeological Sites in Central Northamptonshire,* London, HMSO II; RCHM (1981) *An Inventory of Archaeological Sites in North-West Northamptonshire,* London, HMSO III; RCHM (1982) *An Inventory of Archaeological Sites in South-West Northamptonshire,* London, HMSO IV; RCHM (1985) *An Inventory of Archaeological Sites and Churches in Northampton,* London, HMSO; Deegan and Foard (2007); air photos in SMR; NMP data, available online at http://ads.ahds.ac.uk/catalogue/projArch/NMP/nnmp_eh_2003/index.cfm.
11. M. Rumbold (1998) Making your own Enclosure Map, *Northamptonshire Past and Present* 9.
12. Brown, Key and Orr (1977); P. Goodfellow (1985) Medieval bridges in Northamptonshire, *Northamptonshire Past and Present* 7.
13. Particularly the National Mapping Project (NMP) data held at ADS, enclosure awards and air photographs.
14. A. E. Brown and G. Foard (1994) *The Making of a County History: John Bridges' Northamptonshire,* Leicester, University of Leicester.
15. For a full discussion of historic maps including sub-types within the main types given above see T. Partida (in preparation) *Drawing the Lines: Enclosure in Northamptonshire, a GIS Study,* PhD, University of Huddersfield.
16. NRO Map 4671.
17. TNA MPC 1/42. The 'map' of the meadow in Fineshade in the cartulary of the Abbey there, dating from before 1208, is technically the earliest map from the county (see 'meadow' in Chapter 3): C. Delano-Smith and R. J. P. Kain (1999) *English Maps: A History,* London, British Library II, 14. However that of Pipewell Plain is the first which is of a form which can clearly be recognised as map.
18. NRO Photostat 1026.
19. TNA MPBB 1/2.
20. For a discussion of the disputes over the Brand and Weldon Plain see the *Rockingham Forest Atlas,* 21–22, 184, 248.
21. They may have been made for all the other bailiwicks in Rockingham and for Salcey but none has been identified.
22. NRO Map 4210; TNA MR 1/314. Forest maps were made for the Crown and depict the land in which they held an interest but did not necessarily own. As such they might perhaps be better described as 'specialist' rather than 'estate' maps but have been included here for simplicity.
23. BL ADDMSS 78133 F.
24. See chapter 5 for a full discussion of this issue.
25. NRO Maps 2913, 2868.
26. NRO Maps 2897, 3133.
27. R. Kain and R. R. Oliver (1995) *The Tithe Maps of England and Wales: A Cartographic Analysis and County by County Catalogue,* Cambridge, Cambridge University Press, 1–2.
28. NRO T23.
29. NRO Maps 460, 4224, 2906.
30. See Appendices.
31. NRO T234, T206, T228, T11, T199, T103, T217.
32. NRO T199, T169.

Chapter 2

1. Mapped in G. Foard and R. Morris (2012) *The Archaeology of English Battlefields,* York, CBA, 92.

2. Plans in S. Wrathmell (ed.) (2012) *Wharram: a Study of Settlement on the Yorkshire Wolds, XIII. A History of Wharram and its Neighbours.* York, 285–7, 293.
3. D. Hall (forthcoming) *The Open Fields of England.* Surveyed in 2001.
4. Dorset County Record Office, D11/1.
5. East Sussex Record Office, Iford tithe, TD/E 61.
6. D. V. Fowkes and G. R. Potter (1988) *William Senior's Survey of the Estates of the First and Second Earls of Devonshire c.1600–28,* Derbyshire Record Society 13, 123–6.
7. The maps are not 'definitive' because many furlong and field name-lists have yet to be converted from manuscript to electronic format and have therefore not been 'searched'. Overall trends are clear from the random sample electronically available.
8. D. Hall (1984) Fieldwork and documentary evidence for the layout and organization of early medieval estates. In K Biddeck (ed.) *Archaeological approaches to Medieval Europe,* Michigan University Press, 49 and 58.
9. H. S. A. Fox (1989) The People of the Wolds in Settlement History. In M. Aston, D. Austin and C. Dyer (eds) *The Rural Settlements of Medieval England;* Oxford, Blackwell.
10. S. C. Ratcliff (1946) *Elton Manorial Records 1279–1351,* Roxburghe Club, 135–231.
11. D. Hall (1992) Fenland Project 6: The South-Western Cambridgeshire Fenlands, *East Anglian Archaeology* 56 32.
12. S. Raban (ed.) (2011) *The Accounts of Godfrey of Crowland, Abbot of Peterborough 1299–1321.* Northampton, Northamptonshire Record Society 45, 35.
13. G. J. Turner (1899) *Select Pleas of the Forest,* London, Selden Society 13.
14. M. L Bazeley (1921) The Extent of the English Forest in the Thirteenth Century, *Transactions of the Royal Historical Society* iv.
15. P. Pettit (1968) *The Royal Forest of Northamptonshire: A study in their Economy 1558–1714,* Northamptonshire Record Society 23, 18–33.
16. Third Woods Report (1788) *House of Commons Journal* 43 559–61; Seventh Woods Report: Salcey (1791) *House of Commons Journal* 46 125; Eighth Woods Report: Whittlewood (1792) *House of Commons Journal* 47 141–87; Ninth Woods Report: Rockingham (1792) *House of Commons Journal* 47 188–229.
17. NRO G4116/7 and 8.
18. Bazeley (1921), 161.
19. E. King (1975) *Peterborough Abbey 1066–1310,* Cambridge University Press , 172–9.
20. H. C. Darby and I. B. Terrett (eds) (1971) *The Domesday Geography of Midland England.* Second edn., London: Cambridge University Press, 404 and 438.
21. J. E. B. Gover, A. Mawer and F. M. Stenton (1933) *The Place Names of Northamptonshire,* Cambridge, Cambridge University Press, 137; *Calendar of the Patent Rolls: Edward I, 1272–1307.* (1893–1901) London, HMSO, 540.
22. *Domesday Book,* 219 d.
23. F. M. Stenton (1930) *Facsimiles of Early Charters from Northamptonshire Collections,* Northamptonshire Record Society 4, 8.
24. Gover, Mawer and Stenton (1933), 1.
25. Ibid., 1.
26. Ibid., 190.
27. D. Willis (1916) *The Estate Book of Henry de Bray* c.*1289–1340,* London, Camden Society, 18.
28. Printed in Eighth Woods Report: Whittlewood (1792), p.106.
29. NRO Bru.O.vii.8.
30. Gover, Mawer and Stenton (1933), 153–5.
31. G. R. Elvey (1968) *Luffield Priory Charters,* Northamptonshire Record Society 22, 16.
32. G. Baker (1841) *The History and Antiquities of the County of Northampton,* London, Nichols II, 74.
33. A copy of the Salcey *Report* is NRO XYZ 1939.
34. Foard, Hall and Partida (2009).
35. Baker (1841), 74–90.
36. For a modern part-identification see D. Hall (2001b) The Woodland Landscapes of Southern Northamptonshire, *Northamptonshire Past and Present* 54, 59.
37. M. Page (2003) The Extent of Whittlewood Forest and the Impact of Disafforestation in the Later Middle Ages, ibid., 56.
38. Wise (1891) *Rockingham and the Watsons,* London, Elliot Stock, 128–79.
39. From TNA E32/74.
40. *The Book of Fees AD 1198–1242* (1920) London, HMSO, 9.
41. TNA, C 47/11/3/5; J. E. E. S. Sharp (ed.) (1906) *Calendar of Inquisitions Post Mortem: Edward I.* London, HMSO 2, 484–5.
42. Exeter 57/5.
43. O. Rackham (1987) *The History of the Countryside,* London, J. M. Dent, 138.
44. Elvey (1968), 16.
45. Magd. Charters, Evenley and Astwell 48 and 51.
46. *The Book of Fees AD 1198–1242* (1920), 9.
47. Society of Antiquaries MS 60, f 258d.
48. Foard, Hall and Partida (2009), 24, from Gover, Mawer and Stenton (1933).
49. Gover, Mawer and Stenton (1933), 60.
50. Hall (2001b), 36–7.
51. Hall, *Woodland Reports* to Forest Enterprise, copies in Northamptonshire HER.
52. Foard, Hall and Partida (2009), 240.
53. Hall, FE *Report* 2001; nearby a Roman villa and industrial site was excavated (Wessex Archaeology, Report 71512, online).
54. D. Hall (1975) Hartwell, Northamptonshire: A Parish Survey, *Council for British Archaeology, Group 9 Newsletter* 5 7–9; Forest Enterprise Report: Salcey; C. T. P. Woodfield (1980) The Egg Rings: a defended enclosure in Salcey Forest, *Northamptonshire Archaeology* 15 156–8.
55. NRO ZA 438.
56. NRO FH 3471.
57. NRO Bru. ASR 134; 1705–1716.
58. NRO Bru O.v.229 and Bru. I.iv.11.
59. Worc. Helmdon Box 13.
60. Willis (1916), 16–17.
61. TNA E 315/429.
62. Pettit (1968), facing p.110.
63. TNA LR 4/1/49.
64. TNA LR 4/1/91.
65. TNA LR 4/4/16.

66. TNA LR 4/3/37.
67. Foard, Hall and Partida (2009), 25.
68. Magd. Charters Brackley D 219; Syresham 46.
69. Worc. Boxes 20 and 29.
70. TNA C99/101/2.
71. *Domesday*, 226 c, d.
72. British Library, Harl. 56 F 1.
73. NRO LB 61 m.4.
74. TNA DL 44/1060.
75. NRO YZ 7446.
76. L. F. Salzman (ed.) (1937) *The Victoria History of the County of Northampton.* London, Oxford University Press 4, 14a.
77. Archives of Jesus College, Oxford, NH.1/1/2.
78. Jesus Coll. NH.1/4/2.
79. Pettit (1968), 86–88.
80. Eton College Records (ECR) 27/3–4.
81. ECR 27/59.
82. Rumbold (1998), 368, piece no. 201, at the south.
83. King (1975), 173–9.
84. Raban (ed.) (2011), 55, 60.
85. For Northants, TNA E32/79, 82, 92–4 and E32/116.
86. Foard, Hall and Partida (2009), 211–12.
87. NRO XYZ 438.
88. NRO FH 3471.
89. Magd. Charter, Brackley 33.
90. NRO ZA 438.
91. R. M. Serjeantson and W. Adkins (eds) (1906) *The Victoria History of the County of Northampton.* London, Constable 2, 156–8; Salzman (ed.) (1937), 278–9.
92. *Calendar of the Patent Rolls: Edward I, 1272–1307* (1893–1901) 403.
93. TNA C143/29/10.
94. NRO ZA 438.
95. NRO GH 328.
96. NRO FH 3471.
97. Worc. deeds Box 18, Piddington Grange Farm.
98. NRO YZ 3631.
99. NRO T11, 1841.
100. NRO ZA 438.
101. G. Baker (1822) *The History and Antiquities of the County of Northampton,* London, Nichols I, 629–30.
102. Ibid. 628 and 563.
103. J. Bridges (1791) *The History and Antiquities of Northamptonshire,* I, 172.
104. Baker (1822), 629.
105. Worc. Box 23, Helmdon.
106. NRO T156.
107. Raban (ed.) (2011)38 and 254.
108. S. Raban (2001) *The White Book of Peterborough,* Northamptonshire Record Society 41, xxvi.
109. Ex. 57/2.
110. Ex. 57/5 and 57/8.
111. W. J. B. Kerr (1925) *Higham Ferrers and its Ducal and Royal Castle and Park,* Privately, 150–73.
112. D. Hall and R. Harding (1985) *Rushden, a Duchy of Lancaster Village,* Rushden, Buscott, 97–109.
113. *The Great Roll of the Pipe for the twelfth year of the reign of King Henry the Second, AD 1165–1166* (1888) Pipe Roll Society 9, 64.
114. D. M. Stenton (1933) *Great Roll of Pipe 1 John 1199,* Pipe Roll Society 48, 16.
115. Hall and Harding (1985), 98–108.
116. Ibid., 104–5 from TNA E317/Northants/34.
117. Pettit (1968), 14n.
118. TNA E 315/419 f. 3–8.
119. Hall (2001b), 44.
120. *Contra* R. Jones and M. Page (2006) *Medieval Villages in an English Landscape: Beginnings and Ends,* Macclesfield, Windgather, 131 and 151.
121. Hall (2001b), 44.
122. *Cal. Inq. Post Mortem* x (1921) no. 325; NRO F III 47.
123. Foard, Hall and Partida (2009), 161.
124. TNA DL 43 8/6a.

Chapter 3

1. The methodology is given in Hall 1995, 39–42.
2. Foard, Hall and Partida (2009), 293.
3. Magd. Aynho Charter 66.
4. NRO, Map 2861.
5. NRO YZ 1463.
6. Foard, Hall and Partida (2009), 30.
7. Delano-Smith and Kain (1999), 14.
8. Willis (1916), 15.
9. NRO Map 1964.
10. Hall (1995), 96–7.
11. NRO Map 5695.
12. NRO Map 3020.
13. NRO Uncat. Thornton Coll. in Box V952.
14. BL MS 7 f.79d; Cross 1980.
15. Magd. 77/6, item 2.
16. NRO Hinton Glebe.
17. NRO D1652.
18. NRO Th 1596, no. 6.
19. D. Hall (2006) Aynho Fields, Open and Enclosed, *Northamptonshire Past and Present* 59, 14.
20. M. E. Briston and T. M. Halliday (eds) (2009) *The Pilsgate Manor of the Sacrist of Peterborough Abbey.* Northampton, Northamptonshire Record Society 43, item 144.
21. NRO YZ 3387.
22. NRO ZB 142/20 /10.
23. NRO Aston le Walls glebe terrier.
24. NRO Twywell glebe terrier.
25. Foard *et al.* (2009), 256, 277.
26. Ibid. 30, 31.
27. Gover, Mawer and Stenton (1933), 71, 83.
28. J. Morton (1712) *The Natural History of Northamptonshire,* London, 9.
29. Hall (1995) 59–61; 266–8.
30. Ex. 13/122.
31. Ex. 13/44.
32. Ex. uncat. Easton Box (2011).
33. Ex. 18/83.
34. Stowe, glebe terrier 1684.
35. NRO Encl Award Vol. B p.46 et seq.
36. NRO Map 5255 from NRO A95.
37. Willis (1916), 7, 45.
38. Ibid. 130.
39. Ibid. 44.
40. NRO A12, mid 13th century.
41. NRO A17.
42. NRO Encl. Enrol. Vol, N p.36.
43. TNA SC2/196/6, m.1.
44. Laughton 2001, 10, 20,

45. NRO 55P/233.
46. NRO Crick 92P/141 p.23.
47. NRO Markham Collection, uncat.
48. NRO Y(O) 12/13.
49. D. Hall (1982) *Medieval Fields,* Aylesbury, Shire 28, 45–55.
50. Foard, Hall and Partida (2009) 31–2.
51. J. A. Shepherd (1973) Field Systems of Yorkshire. In A. R. H. Baker and R. A. Butlin (eds) *Studies of field systems in the British Isles*; Cambridge, Cambridge University Press, 148–152; M. Harvey (1981) The origin of planned field systems in Holderness, Yorkshire. In T. Rowley (ed.) *The Origins of Open Field Agriculture*; London, Croom Helm, 186–7.
52. Hall (1995); Foard, Hall and Partida (2009) 29–36.
53. D. Hall (1989) Field Systems and Township Structure. In M. Aston, D. Austin and C. Dyer (eds) *The Rural Settlements of Medieval England: Studies dedicated to Maurice Beresford and John Hurst*; Oxford, Blackwell, 191–205; Hall (2006).
54. H. L. Gray (1915) *English Field Systems,* Harvard University Press.
55. Hall (1995) 51–5.
56. T. Williamson (2003) *Shaping medieval landscapes: settlement, society, environment,* Oxford, Windgather; S. Rippon (2008) *Beyond the Medieval Village,* Oxford University Press.
57. Hall (forthcoming).
58. Hall (2006).
59. Respectively NRO F X/1, F X/19, F X/42.
60. NRO F IV 1–18; Tithe Map T2, 1850.
61. From the Cosgrove Enclosure Award description 1767, NRO Enclosure Enrolment Volume B.
62. NRO ZB 5/3.
63. See Hall 1995, 1–7 for a description of relevant documents.
64. A. C. Chibnall (1965) *Sherington: Fiefs and Fields of a Buckinghamshire Village,* Cambridge University Press 259–76; Hall (1995) 39–47.
65. Full abstracts of Helmdon charters at Magdalen College, made by the Rev W. D. Macray in 1867, are available on the Helmdon village website.
66. Bridges (1791) 172–3; Baker (1822), 627–30.
67. Magd. Charters Helmdon 80 and 68.
68. Worc. Box 29.
69. Magd. Charter Helmdon 26.
70. Magd. Charter Helmdon 3.
71. Baker (1822), 629–30.
72. Worc. Box 13 Helmdon.
73. Magd. CP8/30.
74. Magd. Charter Helmdon 68.
75. E. G. Parry (1987) Helmdon Stone, *Northamptonshire Past and Present* 7, 258–269.
76. R. Marks (1998) *The Medieval stained glass of Northamptonshire,* Oxford University Press, 104 and pl.9.
77. Worc. Box 29.
78. Bridges (1791), I, 289.
79. Worc. Box 13, Helmdon.
80. NRO Map 1712.
81. NRO Helmdon glebe terriers in Box X588.
82. Worc. Helmdon Boxes 5 and12.
83. *Domesday*, 228 b, c.
84. H. E. Salter (1930) *Boarstall Cartulary,* Oxford Historical Society 88, 157–9, 169, 177, 195.
85. Compton Muniments 770B.
86. Ibid. 1348.
87. W. H. Hart and P. A. Lyons (eds) (1893) *Cartulary of Ramsey Abbey.* London, HMSO, 3 167.
88. Hall (1995), 243–5.
89. Hall (forthcoming).
90. Terrier references in Hall 1995, 243–5; Quality Book 1776 and field-names 1839 Crick 92P/116 and 106.
91. NRO Crick 92P/141 pp.4 and 13.
92. Jones and Page (2006).
93. RCHM (1982), 110.
94. Bridges (1791), I, 296.
95. NRO charters Furtho IV 1–18 record exchanges of strips with freeholders.
96. NRO Furtho X 16.
97. Copies held by the NMR at Swindon and some at NRO, Box X80.
98. D. Hall (2001a) *Turning the plough: Midland open fields: landscape character and proposals for management.* Northamptonshire County Council and English Heritage, 36.
99. NRO G4276.
100. Pettit (1968), 67–8.
101. Bridges (1791), I, 279.
102. Field 29 of T134 then pasture.
103. Illustrated in Hall 1982, 11 and visible on satellite images.
104. NRO Map 844.
105. Baker (1822), 275.
106. M. W. Beresford and J. K. S. St. Joseph (1979) *Medieval England: An Aerial Survey,* 2nd edn. Cambridge, Cambridge University Press, 39.

Chapter 4

1 M. Turner (1980) *English Parliamentary Enclosure: Its Historical Geography and Economic History*, Folkstone, Dawson; J. A. Yelling (1977) *Common Field and Enclosure in England 1450–1850*, London, Macmillan Press; J. L. Hammond and B. Hammond (1987) *The Village Labourer 1760–1832: A Study of the Government of England Before the Reform Bill,* Stroud, Alan Sutton; J. M. Neeson (1993) *Commoners: Common Right, Enclosure and Social Change in England, 1700–1820,* Cambridge, Cambridge University Press; L. Shaw-Taylor (2001) Labourers, Cows, Common Rights and Parliamentary Enclosure: The Evidence of Contemporary Comment *c.*1760–1810, *Past and Present* 171.
2. Turner (1980) 15.
3. Hall (1995); Partida, *in preparation.*
4. J. Chapman and S. Seeliger (2001) *Enclosure, Environment and Landscape in Southern England,* Stroud, Tempus, 13–19.
5. Yelling (1977), 8.
6. G. E. Mingay (1997) *Parliamentary Enclosure in England: An Introduction to its Causes, Incidence and impact 1750–1850,* Harlow, Longman, 60; M. Overton (1996) *Agricultural Revolution in England: The transformation of the agrarian economy 1500–1850,* Cambridge, Cambridge University Press 23, 158.
7. Partida, *in preparation.*
8. The dates of enclosure for those anciently enclosed places where no agreement or other formal document

has been identified are taken from D. Hall (1997–8) Enclosure in Northamptonshire, *Northamptonshire Past and Present* 9, 350–367.

9. M. E. Finch (1956) *Five Northamptonshire Families 1540–1640,* Northampton, Northamptonshire Record Society 19, 157.
10. Peterborough contained, in addition to the city, the hamlets of Dogsthorpe, Newark, Garton End and Eastfield as well as the grange at Oxney. There are some caveats in the assessment of township size notably multiple townships assessed together as the boundaries between them are not known. See Chapter 1.
11. See Chapter 3 for a discussion of the forests.
12. Barnwell St Andrew, Barnwell All Saints, Hemington and Armston.
13. J. Bridges (1791) *The History and Antiquities of Northamptonshire,* Oxford, II, 213–4, 400, 420, 403, 263, 346.
14. Ibid. 349.
15. The Montagu family descent is complex and the title becomes extinct twice. The family continues at Boughton House as the Dukes of Buccleuch and are related to the Brudenells at Deene.
16. R. Kain and H. Prince (2000) *Tithe Surveys for Historians,* Stroud, Phillimore, 10.
17. Foard, Hall and Partida (2009), 40, 231–232, 286.
18. Hall (2006) 7–22.
19. NRO FH272.
20. NRO FH272; T. Partida (2007) Early Hunting Landscapes in Northamptonshire, *Northamptonshire Past and Present* 60.
21. These maps also show the exchange and consolidation of lands between Hatton and Brudenell of Deene.
22. RCHM (1975), 33.
23. NRO FH 272 This is a book of surveys and maps made in the 1580s for Hatton which gives very good detail of Hatton's own lands but also other freeholders, tenants and exchanges. At Holdenby there are no other freeholders and no exchanges made.
24. Finch (1956), 157.
25. NRO BRU Map 6.
26. Finch (1956), 154–6; NRO BRU E vii.1
27. NRO Map 561; R. Kain, J. Chapman and R. R. Oliver (2004) *The Enclosure Maps of England and Wales,* Cambridge, Cambridge University Press, 159.
28. Finch (1956), 83–87.
29. Ibid., 90.
30. For a discussion of the roads in Haselbech see below.
31. NRO FH 2601.
32. Church Brampton NRO FH 272, BL ADDMSS 78131 H; Chapel Brampton NRO FH 272, BL ADDMSS 78131 F.
33. M. W. Beresford (1998) *The Lost Villages of England,* Revised. Stroud, Sutton; K. J. Allison, M. W. Beresford and J. G. Hurst (1966) *The Deserted Villages of Northamptonshire,* Leicester, Leicester University Press; M. W. Beresford and J. G. Hurst (1971) *Deserted Medieval Villages,* Woking, Lutterworth Press; G. Foard (2001a) Medieval Northamptonshire. In N. Cooper (ed.) *East Midlands Archaeological Research Framework Seminar Series* http://www.le.ac.uk/archaeology/east_midlands_research_framework.htm.
34. The deserted settlements represented here are defined as 'village', 'hamlet' or 'end' (see Chapter 6). Other types of deserted settlement such as isolated churches, castles or farms are not included.
35. Allison, Beresford and Hurst (1966)
36. J. E. Martin (1988) Sheep and Enclosure in Sixteenth-Century Northamptonshire, *Agricultural History Review* 36.
37. NRO Maps 704, 1432, 5099, 6388.
38. NRO maps 567/8 and Boughton House private collection.
39. Jesus College NH P1/3; NRO map 2221.
40. See Bibliography for some of the numerous works available.
41. NRO Maps 440 and 360; NRO YZ 5762; NRO Map 4218.
42. Tate W. E. (1967) *The English Village Community and the Enclosure Movements,* London, Gollancz, 93.
43. Mingay (1997), 60.
44. NRO ZA9053.
45. Mingay (1997), 69.
46. NRO SOX 336.
47. For a discussion of issues relating to maps see Chapter 1.
48. NRO Misc. Photostats 1197.
49. See Chapter 3 for pre-enclosure forests. For a full discussion of the definition of 'waste' see Partida, *in preparation.*
50. See Chapter 3 and Figure 1 for land use in the medieval.
51. C. Viallis and K. Collins (2004) *A Georgian Country Parson: The Rev. John Mastin of Naseby,* Northampton, Northamptonshire Record Society, 97.
52. NRO Inclosure Volume D, p.589.
53. The maps at Boughton House are the finest and include Brigstock, Broughton, Cranford, Denford, Geddington, Grafton Underwood, Little and Great Oakley, Luddington, Stanion, Twywell, Warkton, Weekley and Woodford. Others at NRO include Upper Boddington, Map 3133; Wollaston, Map 4447; Lutton, Map 2111B; Ashton, Roade and Hartwell Map 440.
54. NRO X9239.
55. BL ADDMSS 78133 F; NRO 350p/90; 206p/103; Box X1657; Compton Muniments map of Denton 1760.
56. T. Williamson (2002) *The Transformation of Rural England: Farming and the Landscape, 1700–1870,* Exeter, University of Exeter Press; W. Pitt (1809) *General View of the Agriculture of the County of Northampton,* London, 22, 277.
57. From village to village as the crow flies.
58. The estate owned some 70% of Little Oakley and 80% of both Warkton and Luddington.
59. There are three townships for which there was no act and the date is taken from the agreement for Wicken and from map evidence for Rockingham and Thornhaugh.
60. NRO Inclosure Volume A; G. Foard (1993) Ecton: its lost village and landscape park, *Northamptonshire Past and Present* 83, 43.
61. J. W. Anscomb (n.d. *c*.1965), *Inclosure: Notes on the Parliamentary Acts and Awards for Northamptonshire 1727–1844,* unpublished. (Copy available at NRO).
62. Partida, *in preparation.*
63. NRO V2793.

64. Kain and Oliver (1995), 350
65. Kain R. and Prince H. (1985) *The Tithe Surveys of England and Wales,* Cambridge, Cambridge University Press pp.10–22.
66. Ibid. 23.
67. Database and Partida, *in preparation.*
68. Mingay (1997), 118.
69. Ibid. 108.
70. Anscomb (Unpublished), 38.
71. Turner (1980), 18.
72. NRO SOX 336.
73. Wellingborough (1765), Arthingworth (1767) and East Haddon (1773) were 60ft whilst Benefield (1820) and Naseby (1820) were 30ft.
74. NRO Inclosure Volume N, p.475–493; Inclosure Plan 53.
75. SRO HB 56 2803.
76. Inclosure Volume N, 480.
77. NRO Transcripts 20.
78. I have used imperial measurements in order to make a more direct comparison with the figures given in the awards.
79. NRO map 5429.
80. NRO T231.
81. NRO Map 4774.
82. NRO T45, T212.
83. NRO Map 1715 this map has been given a date of *c.*1850 by the Record Office.
84. NRO Map 2926; ML 1405.
85. NRO T182.
86. NRO 255p/301.
87. J. Burchardt (2002) *The Allotment Movement in England, 1793–1873,* Woodbridge, Boydell, 244–251.
88. NRO T190, T139, T2, T41, T186, T10, T140, T215.
89. R. J. Moore-Colyer (1974) A 19th century Welsh Cattle Dealer in Northamptonshire, *Northamptonshire Past and Present* 5121–126.
90. It is not always obvious from the OS maps whether a building complex is a farm or field barn/s. At Naseby most are labelled as 'farms'.
91. Land Tax assessment 1820.
92. For a further discussion of these greens see chapter 6 and Partida, *in preparation.*
93. Jesus Coll. NH P1/1; BL ADDMSS 78143.
94. Rose of the Shires Report: Abthorpe will be available form http://resource.rockingham-forest-trust.org.uk/SiteResources/Data/Templates/0SiteRoot.asp?DocID=2andv1ID=anddocidfile=.
95. Rockingham Forest: Brigstock Bailiwick Act 1795 (NRO BSL 65), Award 1805 (NRO Inc. Vol. L.); Cliffe Bailiwick Act 1796 (NRO J(D) 601), Award 1806 (NRO Inc. Vol. L p.432); Rockingham Bailiwick Act 1832 (NRO YZ 6685), Award 1837 (NRO stack P11). Salcey Forest: Act 1825 (NRO X1693 bundle 21), Award 1826 (NRO Misc Photostat 1105). Whittlewood Forest: Haselborough Walk Act 1824 (NRO G3909), Award 1826 (NRO YZ 4910); Sholbrook Walk, Hanger Walk, Shrob Walk and Wakefield Walk, Act 1853 (NRO G4167), Award 1856 (NRO G4168).
96. NRO Brooke of Oakley 313/21.
97. There was some confusion over exact rights to Benefield lawn the Earl acknowledging the Crown may still hold some ownership and offering to purchase it.
98. NRO X4593.
99. NRO Hunnybun and Sykes box 2; 53a1.
100. Ibid. p.12.
101. Ibid. p.17.
102. NRO Brooke of Oakley 319/2.
103. NRO G4167.
104. NRO Misc Photostat 1105. This plan shows the location of the various plots to the different townships.
105. NRO G4168.
106. NRO X1693 bundle 21.
107. NRO G4168 p.4.
108. NRO X1693 bundle 21; G3909.
109. NRO Inclosure Plan 60; Inc. Vol. L. p.316.
110. TNA MPE 1/459; NRO Map 4365; NRO Inc. Vol. L p.432.
111. NRO J(D) 601.
112. R. J. Moore-Colyer (1996–7) Woods and Woodland Management: The Bailiwick of Rockingham, Northamptonshire *c.*1700–1840, *Northamptonshire Past and Present* 9, 258.

Chapter 5

1. RCHM (1975); RCHM (1979); RCHM (1981); RCHM (1982); RCHM (1985); Deegan and Foard (2007); air photos in SMR; NMP data, available online at http://ads.ahds.ac.uk/catalogue/projArch/NMP/nnmp_eh_2003/index.cfm.
2. The methodology for reconstruction is given in Rumbold (1998), 368–72.
3. NRO FH 272.
4. RCHM (1982).
5. Foard, Ballinger and Taylor (2002).
6. G. Foard (1985) The Administrative Organisation of Northamptonshire in the Saxon Period. In S. C. Hawkes, J. Campbell and D. Brown (eds) *Anglo-Saxon Studies in Archaeology and History*, 4, Oxford University Committee for Archaeology. The taxation work was undertaken for us in the 1970s by Stephen Mitchell, while at NCC. It survives in unpublished typescript in the NRO and appears hereafter as 'Mitchell'. The data was tabulated in GIS in the AHRC project and is available from ADS as part of the digital archive of that project.
7. B. K. Roberts and S. Wrathmell (2000) *An Atlas of Rural Settlement in England,* London, English Heritage; C. Lewis, P. Mitchell-Fox and C. Dyer (1997) *Village, Hamlet and Field: Changing medieval settlements in central England,* Manchester, Manchester University Press.
8. Northamptonshire SMR; National Mapping Programme for Northamptonshire discussed in Deegan and Foard (2007) and available online at http://ads.ahds.ac.uk/catalogue/projArch/NMP/nnmp_eh_2003/index.cfm; Gover, Mawer and Stenton (1933); Bridges (1791) I; ibid., II; W. Adkins, D. Ryland and R. M. Serjeantson (eds) (1902) *The Victoria History of the County of Northampton.* London, Constable 1; W. Page (ed.) (1930) *The Victoria History of the County of Northampton.* London, University of London 3; Serjeantson and Adkins (eds) (1906); Salzman (ed.) (1937).
9. The most intensive projects were at Raunds and in Whittlewood Forest, but there are many other

fieldwalking surveys of varying intensity and reliability, ranging from the non-systematic work in the Upper Nene by Hollowell to the detailed study of the Brigstock and Geddington area by Foster, Bellamy and Johnston. S. J. Parry (2006) *Raunds Area Survey: An archaeological study of the landscape of Raunds, Northamptonshire 1985–94,* Oxford, Oxbow Books; Jones and Page (2006); P. Foster (1988) *Changes in the Landscape: An Archaeological Study of the Clay Uplands in the Brigstock Area of Northamptonshire,* BA dissertation, University of Sheffield; R. Hollowell (1971) *Aerial photography and field-work in the Upper Nene Valley: a record of fifteen years' work,* Leicester, Northamptonshire Archaeological Society 6.

10. NRO map 3140; NRO map 2915; Gover, Mawer and Stenton (1933), 151.
11. The medieval Westhorp is noted by Briston and Halliday (2009) in various medieval documents. Westhorpe Closes are located on the 1799 map of Bainton, NRO 331p/502. Google Earth imagery dated 1/1/2006 (accessed 1/05/2012) shows three enclosures at the end of a short hollow way leading from the northern end of the village. A field visit revealed other earthworks which suggest these enclosures contain stone structures. However the enclosures may cut across the ridge and furrow to the south causing some problems of interpretation.
12. Foard, Hall and Partida (2009), 113; Gover, Mawer and Stenton (1933), 25 and 160; NRO map 4418.
13. Gover, Mawer and Stenton (1933), 97.
14. Foard, Hall and Partida (2009), 238 and 225.
15. RCHM (1975), 89.
16. The churches dataset was compiled from SMR, county histories, RCHM volumes and historic map analysis. Saxon churches identified from the presence of a priest or churches in 1086, complemented by archaeological evidence or the presence of early fabric noted in the SMR.
17. Gover, Mawer and Stenton (1933); Foard, Hall and Partida (2009), gazetteer.
18. W. T. Mellows (1927) *Henry of Pytchley's book of fees,* Kettering, 97.
19. A. E. Brown (1998) The Medieval Landscape. In R. Duffey (ed.) *The Story of Wadenhoe.*
20. Foard, Hall and Partida (2009), 58–63.
21. Parry (2006).
22. Foard (1993); Hall and Harding (1985); unpublished fieldwalking survey by G. Cadman, in SMR.
23. *Domesday,* 222 b, 219 d, 226 a. The location though not exact extent of marsh is suggested by an extensive alluvial area on BGS mapping, something also seen at Titchmarsh (Figure 79).
24. Foard, Hall and Partida (2009), 299; Gover, Mawer and Stenton (1933).
25. Beresford and Hurst (1971), 66; Roberts and Wrathmell (2000), 49–50.
26. Mitchell, where taxation groupings of townships are listed.
27. Foard (1985).
28. Foard, Hall and Partida (2009), 55.
29. Foard, Ballinger and Taylor (2002).
30. Bridges (1791), II, 290–95.
31. Foard, Hall and Partida (2009), 18.
32. D. Hayter (2003) Kings' Sutton: An Early Anglo-Saxon Estate?, *Northamptonshire Past and Present* 56.
33. Foard (1985), 186.
34. Foard, Hall and Partida (2009), fig. 56.
35. Foard (1985).
36. Parry (2006).
37. RCHM (1982); Report on fieldwalking survey by G. Cadman, in SMR.
38. Foard (1991) 179–189.
39. Listed buildings data: http://www.imagesofengland.org.uk/.
40. All have the name element *eg,* meaning island, although by the medieval they were not true islands. As at Fotheringhay, which is discussed below, Eye and Oxney were connected to the mainland by a narrow ridge.
41. *Domesday,* 221 b–222 a.
42. Foard (1985).
43. Parry (2006); unpublished excavation reports in SMR.
44. Foard, Hall and Partida (2009), 62.
45. Jones and Page (2006); Parry (2006).
46. Foard, Hall and Partida (2009), 186–9.
47. Jones and Page (2006) 170–2.
48. These names include *wild, wylde, hold, weld.* The one case of *woad* is probably a corruption of a *wold* name in Kingsthorpe (Oundle area) recorded in the 15th century. Details are in the names attached to the enclosure, land use, wood and lawn digital data sets from the AHRC project. Unlocated within townships are other wold names from furlongs, discussed by Hall in Figure 15, and others are given in Gover, Mawer and Stenton (1933), 271 and xxxi. Interpretation is based on the analysis there and in M. Gelling (2000) *Place-Names in the Landscape,* London, Phoenix Press.
49. NRO Map 4426 and ML861.
50. Foard (1991).
51. Discussed in Gelling (2000), 41–50.
52. Foard (1985); Gover, Mawer and Stenton (1933); Brown, Key and Orr (1977).
53. Foard, Hall and Partida (2009), 241.
54. Parry (2006); Foard, Hall and Partida (2009), 225.
55. Allison, Beresford and Hurst (1966); RCHM (1979), 43.
56. Foard, Hall and Partida (2009), 225; 1393 Rental: BL, Cotton, Nero CVII fol.85; Gover, Mawer and Stenton (1933).
57. G. Foard (1976) *The Recovery of Archaeological Evidence by Fieldwalking,* MA, University of London.
58. Gover, Mawer and Stenton (1933), 141; G. Foard (1978) Systematic Fieldwalking and the investigation of Saxon Settlement in Northamptonshire, *World Archaeology* 9.
59. Foard (1985).
60. Ibid.
61. B. Bellamy (1994) Anglo-Saxon dispersed sites and woodland at Geddington in the Rockingham Forest, *Landscape History* 16; B. Bellamy (1997) Little Newton, A Central Northamptonshrie Deserted Village, *Northamptonshire Archaeology* 27.
62. A. E. Brown, T. R. Key and C. Orr (1977) Some Anglo-Saxon Estates and their Boundaries in South-West Northamptonshire, ibid., 12; TNA MR1/314; NRO T48 and Map 1662–4.
63. Foard (1985).
64. Foard (1991); Foard, Hall and Partida (2009), 17–19.
65. Hayter (2003); F. M. Brown and C. Taylor (1978)

Settlement and Land Use in Northamptonshire: A comparison between the Iron Age and the Middle Ages. In B. Cunliffe and T. Rowley (eds) *Lowland Iron-Age Communities in Europe* 68, BAR; Foard (1985).

66. Gover, Mawer and Stenton (1933).
67. Peterborough, formerly Medeshamstead, is a post conquest use of *burg* for fortified town. Northborough is Northburg in the first reference in the 12th century, so it is perhaps a late name relative to Peterborough and not relevant to the present discussion. Ibid., 224 and 239.
68. Parry (2006), 139–146; A. E. Brown and T. R. Key (1977) The Badby and Newnham (Northamptonshire) charters, AD 944 and 1021–3, *English Place-Name Society Journal* 10.
69. G. Cadman, unpublished report on excavations at Guilsborough hillfort, in SMR; Foard, Hall and Partida (2009), 207–8.
70. Foard (1985).
71. Parry (2006); A. Hardy, B. M. Charles and R. J. Williams (2007) *Death and Taxes: The archaeology of a Middle Saxon estate centre at Higham Ferrers, Northamptonshire*, Oxford, Oxford Archaeology.
72. Jones and Page (2006); R. Jones (2004) An Iron Age hillfort at Whittlebury, Northants, *Northamptonshire Archaeology* 32.
73. Hardy, Charles and Williams (2007).
74. Paston, Figure 83; Easton on the Hill and Brigstock, Foard, Hall and Partida (2009), 128 and 113; Whittlebury, Figure 72.
75. Limited excavation indicated 12th century infill between market place and Bond End; S. Morris (2006) Higham Ferrers: Saffron Road, an archaeological evaluation, *Northamptonshire Archaeology* 34; C. Jones and A. Chapman (2003) A medieval tenement at College Street, Higham Ferrers, Northamptonshire, *Northamptonshire Archaeology* 31.
76. Hardy, Charles and Williams (2007), esp. p.55.
77. M. Audouy and A. Chapman (2009) *Raunds: The Origin and Growth of a Midland Village AD 450–1500,* Oxford, Oxbow.
78. Jones (2004).
79. Foard, Ballinger and Taylor (2002) Brackley, 15.
80. I. Soden (1996–7) Saxon and Medieval Settlement Remains at St John's Square, Daventry, *Northamptonshire Archaeology* 27. A. E. Brown (1991) *Early Daventry.*
81. NRO map 1555.
82. Deegan and Foard (2007), 129.
83. Foard, Hall and Partida (2009), 61.
84. Gover, Mawer and Stenton (1933), 278; Foard, Ballinger and Taylor (2002); NRO map 841.
85. Brown, Key and Orr (1977).
86. NRO Map 561.
87. Foard, Ballinger and Taylor (2002).
88. P. Wade-Martins (1980) *Village sites in Launditch Hundred,* Dereham, Norfolk, Norfolk Archaeological Unit.
89. Parry (2006).
90. Foard, Hall and Partida (2009), 221 and 270.
91. Those quoted here from open field evidence are only those where 'ley' is an integral part of the name and thus more likely to be early. This avoids confusion with later use of ley for pasture created out of furlongs. Thus in Harringworth we have included Bosley but excluded Appelton Leys (NRO Map 763b).
92. NRO: Map 4527.
93. NMP; D. Jackson and B. Dix (1986–7) Late Iron Age and Roman Settlement at Weekley, Northamptonshire, *Northamptonshire Archaeology* 21.
94. Foard, Hall and Partida (2009), Figure 37.
95. Benefield Lawn has been known since the 19th century as Beanfield Lawn, presumably to avoid confusion with the village of Benefield near Oundle. Ibid., 111, 139 and 198–9.
96. Foard (1991).
97. Foard, Hall and Partida (2009), 228; D. Jackson (1980) An Earthwork at Harringworth, Northants, *Northamptonshire Archaeology* 15 158–60; RCHM (1975), 49; NCC AP SP9494 30.
98. Foard, Hall and Partida (2009), 18 and 170.
99. Foard (1985), 190.
100. Jones and Page (2006) 120 and 171; NRO maps 4210 and 2948; OS 6 inch mapping 1880s.
101. NRO 253p/58; Gelling (2000), 210.
102. TNA MPI 1/251.
103. NRO Map 1233, dated by T. Partida between *c.*1570 and 1592 based on the work of the surveyor, Partida (in preparation).
104. BL Cotton Nero C. Vii f.167v; NRO map 4426; Gover, Mawer and Stenton (1933), 234.
105. Foard, Hall and Partida (2009), 59 and 60.
106. NRO maps 1349 and 2915.
107. Foard, Hall and Partida (2009), 105.
108. Ibid. 63, 205, 227, 256 and 283.
109. Roberts and Wrathmell (2000); W. G. Hoskins and L. D. Stamp (1963) *The common lands of England and Wales,* London, Collins; additions on the current Register are largely not historic greens.
110. Occasionally other pre-enclosure maps do record greens, as with the Ordnance Surveyors Drawings of the 1810s for Thurning, which was not enclosed until 1836.
111. NRO Maps 2864, 6433.
112. NRO Maps 3140, 567, 567, 2928.
113. NRO 331p/502; Map 2853.
114. NRO Map 1251.
115. Foard (1993), 349.
116. Faden's map of Norfolk, 1797. A. Macnair and T. Williamson (2010) *William Faden and Norfolk's 18th-Century Landscape,* Oxford, Oxbow.
117. G. Foard (2001b) Medieval Land Use, Settlement and Industry in Rockingham Forest, Northants, *Medieval Archaeology* 47.
118. The map is undated but another document dated 1570 (NRO FM Charter 747 Vol. 1) suggests that the map was made at this time.
119. Field names from 1767, NRO map 6393.
120. NRO Aynho Map 4612; Foard, Hall and Partida (2009), 210–12 and 222–5.
121. RCHM (1982), 81.
122. NRO Map: 3495.
123. Creaton Inclosure Papers, NRO A178 et seq: claims; letters of 1782–3 re fencing Andrews' allotment on the Moor and the Cow Pasture; NRO Inclosure Volume 8, p. 534: Andrews' allotments 4–6 are on the Cowpasture. This is another context, like those already demonstrated for Northborough and Brafield

on the Green, where further documentary research may require limited retraction of the extent of furlongs shown in the Atlas mapping. However, it is equally possible that an early moor had been cultivated by 1300 but then, because it was marginal land, had reverted to cow pasture in the early-modern period.

124. Briston and Halliday (eds) (2009) map 2.
125. Foard, Ballinger and Taylor (2002).
126. Foard, Hall and Partida (2009), 85, 112 and 252.
127. Bridges (1791), II, 482; SC6 Hen VIII 2787; map and survey in Oundle School: Survey of Warmington 1621, copy is NRO Misc Photostat 1108.
128. A survey of 1393 which describes many but not all of the tenements has been interpreted with reference to later maps and surveys. BL Cotton Nero CVII fol.85.
129. Unpublished fieldwork reports in SMR.
130. *Domesday*, 226 b.
131. Foard, Hall and Partida (2009), 16.
132. NCC AP SP7848 12.
133. Hall (1995), 51–5. Hall (2001a), 16–17 and related archive of digital data in SMR. Study of the extensive documentary record for Hartwell may enable the reasons for its unusual plan form to be better understood, particularly if complemented by archaeological investigation. R. Lennard (1916) Rural Northamptonshire under the Commonwealth, in P. Vinogradoff (ed.), *Oxford Studies in Social and Legal History*, 5.
134. J. A. Raftis (1974) *Assart Data and Land Values: Two Studies in the East Midlands 1200–1350*, Toronto.
135. NRO T30.
136. R. Jones (2002) The Luffield Priory Grange at Monksbarn, Whittlebury, Northants, *Northamptonshire Archaeology* 30; Mellows (1927), 76; King (1975).
137. Foard, Ballinger and Taylor (2002).
138. Foard, Hall and Partida (2009), 222–5.
139. NRO map 845 and 841.
140. NRO map 2942; Foard, Hall and Partida (2009), 62 and 59.
141. Ibid., 301, 205 and 294.
142. Audouy and Chapman (2009); Parry (2006); A. Chapman (2010) *West Cotton, Raunds: a study of medieval settlement dynamics, AD 450–1450*. Oxford, Oxbow..
143. Jones and Page (2006).
144. Foard, Ballinger and Taylor (2002); Foard, Hall and Partida (2009), 62.
145. *Domesday*, 223a and 224b.
146. The 1584 map provides data on each tenement. NRO FH272.
147. Bridges (1791), I, 488–492.
148. J. E. Martin (1978) *Cartularies and Registers of Peterborough Abbey*, Northamptonshire Record Society, 26–7.
149. Survey of Irthlingborough in 1404–5, BL Cotton MS. Nero C vii f112 et seq.

Abbreviations

BGS	British Geological Survey
BL	British Library
BRO	Bedfordshire Record Office
ECR	Eton College Records
Ex.	Exeter Muniments, Burghley House, Stamford
LRO	Leicestershire Record Office
Magd.	Magdalen College Archives, Oxford, Northamptonshire Estates
NCC	Northamptonshire County Council
NMP	National Mapping Programme
NPP	Northamptonshire Past and Present, published annually by NRS
NRO	Northamptonshire Record Office, Northampton
NRS	Northamptonshire Record Society, Northampton
OS	Ordnance Survey
SMR	Sites and Monuments Record
SRO	Suffolk Record Office
TNA	The National Archive, Kew
Worc.	Worcester College Archives, Oxford, Northamptonshire Estates
VCH	Victoria County History, Northamptonshire

Bibliography

Adkins, W., Ryland, D. and Serjeantson, R. M. (eds) (1902) *The Victoria History of the County of Northampton*. 4 vols. London, Constable.

Allison, K. J., Beresford, M. W. and Hurst, J. G. (1966) *The Deserted Villages of Northamptonshire*, Leicester, Leicester University Press.

Anscomb, J. W. (n.d. *c*.1965) *Inclosure: Notes on the Parliamentary Acts and Awards for Northamptonshire 1727–1844*, Unpublished

Audouy, M. and Chapman, A. (2009) *Raunds: The Origin and Growth of a Midland Village AD 450–1500*, Oxford, Oxbow.

Baker, G. (1822) *The History and Antiquities of the County of Northampton*, 2 vols, (I), London, Nichols.

Baker, G. (1841) *The History and Antiquities of the County of Northampton*, 2 vols, (II), London, Nichols.

Bazeley, M. L. (1921) The Extent of the English Forest in the Thirteenth Century, *Transactions of the Royal Historical Society* iv, 140–72.

Bellamy, B. (1994) Anglo-Saxon dispersed sites and woodland at Geddington in the Rockingham Forest, *Landscape History* 16.

Bellamy, B. (1997) Little Newton, A Central Northamptonshrie Deserted Village, *Northamptonshire Archaeology* 27, 200–10.

Beresford, M. W. (1998) *The Lost Villages of England* (revised edn.), Stroud, Sutton.

Beresford, M. W. and Hurst, J. G. (1971) *Deserted Medieval Villages*, Woking, Lutterworth Press.

Beresford, M. W. and St. Joseph, J. K. S. (1979) *Medieval England: An Aerial Survey* (2nd edn.) Cambridge Air Surveys, 2, Cambridge, Cambridge University Press.

The Book of Fees AD 1198–1242 (1920) London, HMSO.

Bridges, J. (1791) *The History and Antiquities of Northamptonshire*, II vols, (I and II).

Briston, M. E. and Halliday, T. M. (eds) (2009) *The Pilsgate Manor of the Sacrist of Peterborough Abbey*. Northampton, Northamptonshire Record Society.

Brown, A. E. (1991) *Early Daventry*.

Brown, A. E. (1998) The Medieval Landscape. In R. Duffey (ed.) *The Story of Wadenhoe*.

Brown, A. E. and Key, T. R. (1977) The Badby and Newnham (Northamptonshire) charters, AD 944 and 1021–3, *English Place-Name Society Journal* 10, 1–6.

Brown, A. E. and Foard, G. (1994) *The Making of a County History: John Bridges' Northamptonshire*, Leicester, University of Leicester.

Brown, A. E., Key, T. R. and Orr, C. (1977) Some Anglo-Saxon Estates and their Boundaries in South-West Northamptonshire, *Northamptonshire Archaeology* 12, 155–76.

Brown, F. M. and Taylor, C. (1978) Settlement and Land Use in Northamptonshire: A comparison between the Iron Age and the Middle Ages. In B. Cunliffe and T. Rowley (eds) *Lowland Iron-Age Communities in Europe*, 68, 77–89. Oxford, BAR.

Burchardt, J. (2002) *The Allotment Movement in England, 1793–1873*, Woodbridge, Boydell.

Calendar of the Patent Rolls: Edward I, 1272–1307. (1893–1901) 4 vols. London, HMSO.

Chapman, A. (2010) *West Cotton, Raunds: a study of medieval settlement dynamics, AD 450–1450*, Oxford, Oxbow.

Chapman, J. and Seeliger, S. (2001) *Enclosure, Environment and Landscape in Southern England*, Stroud, Tempus.

Chibnall, A. C. (1965) *Sherington: Fiefs and Fields of a Buckinghamshire Village*, Cambridge University Press.

Darby, H. C. and Terrett, I. B. (eds) (1971) *The Domesday Geography of Midland England*. Second edn., London: Cambridge University Press.

Deegan, A. and Foard, G. (2007) *Mapping Ancient Landscapes in Northamptonshire*, Swindon, English Heritage.

Delano-Smith, C. and Kain, R. J. P. (1999) *English Maps: A History*, The British Library Studies in Map History Volume II, (II), London, British Library.

Eighth Woods Report: Whittlewood (1792) *House of Commons Journal* 47, 141–87.

Elvey, G. R. (1968) *Luffield Priory Charters* (22), Northamptonshire Record Society.

Finch, M. E. (1956) *Five Northamptonshire Families 1540–1640*, Publications of the Northamptonshire Record Society (19), Northampton, Northamptonshire Record Society.

Foard, G. (1976) The Recovery of Archaeological Evidence by Fieldwalking, MA (University of London).

Foard, G. (1978) Systematic Fieldwalking and the investigation of Saxon Settlement in Northamptonshire, *World Archaeology* 9, 356–274.

Foard, G. (1985) The Administrative Organisation of Northamptonshire in the Saxon Period. In S. C. Hawkes, J. Campbell and D. Brown (eds) *Anglo-Saxon Studies in Archaeology and History*, 4, 185–222. Oxford University Committee for Archaeology.

Foard, G. (1991) The Saxon Bounds of Oundle, *Northamptonshire Past and Present* 8, 179–89.

Foard, G. (1993) Ecton : its lost village and landscape park, *Northamptonshire Past and Present* 8, 335–53.

Foard, G. (2001a) *Medieval Northamptonshire*, East Midlands Archaeological Research Framework Seminar Series, http://www.le.ac.uk/archaeology/east_midlands_research_framework.htm

Foard, G. (2001b) Medieval Land Use, Settlement and Industry in Rockingham Forest, Northants, *Medieval Archaeology* 47, 41–95.

Foard, G. and Morris, R. (2012) *The Archaeology of English Battlefields*, York, CBA.

Foard, G., Ballinger, J. and Taylor, J. (2002) Nor-thamptonshire Extensive Urban Survey, (Northamptonshire County Council, http://ads.ahds.ac.uk/catalogue/projArch/EUS/).

Foard, G., Hall, D. and Partida, T. (2009) *Rockingham Forest: An Atlas of the Medieval and Early-Modern Landscape*, Northampton, Northamptonshire Record Society.

Foster, P. (1988) Changes in the Landscape: An Archaeological Study of the Clay Uplands in the Brigstock Area of Northamptonshire, BA dissertation (University of Sheffield).

Fowkes, D. V. and Potter, G. R. (1988) *William Senior's Survey of the Estates of the First and Second Earls of Devonshire c.1600–28* (13), Derbyshire Record Society.

Fox, H. S. A. (1989) The People of the Wolds in Settlement History. In M. Aston, D. Austin and C. Dyer (eds) *The Rural Settlements of Medieval England*, 77–101. Oxford, Blackwell.

Gelling, M. (2000) *Place-Names in the Landscape*, London, Phoenix Press.

Goodfellow, P. (1985) Medieval bridges in Nor-thamptonshire, *Northamptonshire Past and Present* 7, 143–58.

Gover, J. E. B., Mawer, A. and Stenton, F. M. (1933) *The Place Names of Northamptonshire*, Cambridge, Cambridge University Press.

Gray, H. L. (1915) *English Field Systems*, Harvard University Press.

The Great Roll of the Pipe for the twelfth year of the reign of King Henry the Second, AD 1165–1166 (1888), Pipe Roll Society Publications (9), Pipe Roll Society.

Hall, D. (1975) Hartwell, Northamptonshire: A Parish Survey, *Council for British Archaeology, Group 9 Newsletter* 5, 7–9.

Hall, D. (1982) *Medieval Fields*, Shire archaeology (28), Aylesbury, Shire.

Hall, D. (1984) Fieldwork and documentary evidence for the layout and organization of early medieval estates. In K Biddeck (ed.) *Archaeological approaches to Medieval Europe*, Michigan University Press.

Hall, D. (1989), Field Systems and Township Structure. In M. Aston, D. Austin and C. Dyer (eds) *The Rural Settlements of Medieval England: Studies dedicated to Maurice Beresford and John Hurst*, 191–205. Oxford, Blackwell.

Hall, D. (1992) Fenland Project 6: The South-Western Cambridgeshire Fenlands, *East Anglian Archaeology* 56.

Hall, D. (1995) *The Open Fields of Northamptonshire*, The Publications of the Northamptonshire Record Society (38), Northampton, Northamptonshire Record Society.

Hall, D. (1997–8) Enclosure in Northamptonshire, *Northamptonshire Past and Present* 9, 351–68.

Hall, D. (2001a) Turning the plough: Midland open fields: landscape character and proposals for management (Northampton: Northamptonshire County Council).

Hall, D. (2001b) The Woodland Landscapes of Southern Northamptonshire, *Northamptonshire Past and Present* 54, 33–46.

Hall, D. (2006) Aynho Fields, Open and Enclosed, *Northamptonshire Past and Present* 59, 7–22.

Hall, D. (forthcoming) *The Open Fields of England*.

Hall, D. and Harding, R. (1985) *Rushden, a Duchy of Lancaster Village*, Rushden, Buscott.

Hammond, J. L. and Hammond, B. (1987) *The Village Labourer 1760–1832: A Study of the Government of England Before the Reform Bill*, Stroud, Alan Sutton.

Hardy, A., Charles, B. M. and Williams, R. J. (2007) *Death and Taxes: The archaeology of a Middle Saxon estate centre at Higham Ferrers, Northamptonshire*, Oxford, Oxford Archaeology.

Hart, W. H. and Lyons, P. A. (eds) (1893) *Cartulary of Ramsey Abbey*. 3 vols. London, HMSO.

Harvey, M. (1981) The origin of planned field systems in Holderness, Yorkshire. In T. Rowley (ed.) *The Origins of Open Field Agriculture*, 184–201. London, Croom Helm.

Hayter, D. (2003) Kings' Sutton: An Early Anglo-Saxon Estate?, *Northamptonshire Past and Present* 56, 7–21.

Hayter, P. (2000) *Charlton and Newbottle, The History of Two Villages*, Charlton and Newbottle History Society.

Hollowell, R. (1971) *Aerial photography and field-work in the Upper Nene Valley: a record of fifteen years' work*, Bulletin of the Northamptonshire Federation of Archaeological Societies, (6), Leicester, Northamptonshire Archaeological Society.

Hoskins, W. G. and Stamp, L. D. (1963) *The common lands of England and Wales*, London, Collins.

Jackson, D. (1980) An Earthwork at Harringworth, Northants, *Northamptonshire Archaeology* 15, 158–60.

Jackson, D. and Dix, B. (1986–7) Late Iron Age and Roman Settlement at Weekley, Northamptonshire, *Northamptonshire Archaeology* 21, 41–93.

Jones, C. and Chapman, A. (2003) A medieval tenement at College Street, Higham Ferrers, Northamptonshire, *Northamptonshire Archaeology* 31, 125–36.

Jones, R. (2002) The Luffield Priory Grange at Monksbarn, Whittlebury, Northants, *Northampton-shire Archaeology* 30, 126–39.

Jones, R. (2004) An Iron Age hillfort at Whittlebury, Northants, *Northamptonshire Archaeology* 32, 107–9.

Jones, R. and Page, M. (2006) *Medieval Villages in an English Landscape: Beginnings and Ends*, Oxford, Windgather.

Kain, R., Chapman, J. and Oliver, R. R. (2004) *The Enclosure Maps of England and Wales*, Cambridge, Cambridge University Press.

Kain, R. and Oliver, R. R. (1995) *The Tithe Maps of England and Wales: A Cartographic Analysis and County by County Catalogue*, Cambridge, Cambridge University Press.

Kain R. and Prince H. (1985) *The Tithe Surveys of England and Wales*, Cambridge Studies in Historical Geography, Cambridge, Cambridge University Press.

Kain, R. and Prince, H. (2000) *Tithe Surveys for Historians*, Stroud, Phillimore.

Kerr, W. J. B. (1925) *Higham Ferrers and its Ducal and Royal Castle and Park*, Privately.

King, E. (1975) *Peterborough Abbey 1066–1310*, Cambridge University Press.

Laughton, J. (2001) Catesby in the Middle Ages: an interdisciplinary study. *Northamtonshire Past and Present* 54.

Lennard, R. (1916) Rural Northamptonshire under the Commonwealth. In P. Vinogradoff (ed.), *Oxford Studies in Social and Legal History*, 5.

Lewis, C., Mitchell-Fox, P. and Dyer, C. (1997) *Village, Hamlet and Field: changing medieval settlements in central England*, Manchester, Manchester University Press.

Macnair, A. and Williamson, T. (2010) *William Faden and Norfolk's 18th-Century Landscape*, Oxford, Oxbow.

Marks, R. (1998) *The Medieval stained glass of Northamptonshire*, Oxford University Press.

Martin, J. E. (1978) *Cartularies and Registers of Peterborough Abbey*, Northamptonshire Record Society.

Martin, J. E. (1988) Sheep and Enclosure in Sixteenth-Century Northamptonshire, *Agricultural History Review* 36, 39–54.

Mellows, W. T. (1927) *Henry of Pytchley's book of fees*, Northamptonshire Record Society, 2, Kettering.

Mingay, G. E. (1997) *Parliamentary Enclosure in England: An Introduction to its Causes, Incidence and impact 1750–1850*, Harlow, Longman.

Moore-Colyer, R. J. (1974) A 19th century Welsh Cattle Dealer in Northamptonshire, *Northamptonshire Past and Present* 5, 121–6.

Moore-Colyer, R. J. (1996–7) Woods and Woodland Management: The Bailiwick of Rockingham, Northamptonshire *c*.1700–1840, *Northamptonshire Past and Present* 9, 253–58.

Morris, S. (2006) Higham Ferrers: Saffron Road, an archaeological evaluation, *Northamptonshire Archaeology* 34, 97–102.

Morton, J. (1712) *The Natural History of Northamptonshire*, London.

Neeson, J. M. (1993) *Commoners: Common Right, Enclosure and Social Change in England, 1700–1820*, Past and Present Publications, Cambridge, Cambridge University Press.

Ninth Woods Report: Rockingham (1792) *House of Commons Journal* 47, 188–229.

Overton, M. (1996) *Agricultural Revolution in England: The transformation of the agrarian economy 1500–1850*, Cambridge Studies in Historical Geography (23), Cambridge, Cambridge University Press.

Page, M. (2003) The Extent of Whittlewood Forest and the Impact of Disafforestation in the Later Middle Ages, *Northamptonshire Past and Present* 56, 22–34.

Page, W. (ed.), (1930), *The Victoria History of the County of Northampton*. 4 vols. London, University of London.

Parry, E. G. (1987) Helmdon Stone, *Northamptonshire Past and Present* 7, 258–69.

Parry, S. J. (2006) *Raunds Area Survey: An archaeological study of the landscape of Raunds, Northamptonshire 1985–94*, Oxford, Oxbow Books.

Partida, T. (2007) Early Hunting Landscapes in Northamptonshire, *Northamptonshire Past and Present* 60, 44–60.

Partida, T. (in preparation), Drawing the Lines: Enclosure in Northamptonshire, a GIS Study, PhD (University of Huddersfield).

Pettit, P. (1968) *The Royal Forest of Northamptonshire: A study in their Economy 1558–1714* (23), Northamptonshire Record Society.

Pitt, W. (1809) *General View of the Agriculture of the County of Northampton*, London.

Raban, S. (2001) *The White Book of Peterborough* (41), Northamptonshire Record Society.

Raban, S. (ed.) (2011) *The Accounts of Godfrey of Crowland, Abbot of Peterborough 1299–1321*. Northampton, Northamptonshire Record Society.

Rackham, O. (1987) *The History of the Countryside*, London, J. M. Dent.

Raftis, J. A. (1974) *Assart Data and Land Values: Two Studies in the East Midlands 1200–1350*, Toronto.

Ratcliff, S. C. (1946) *Elton Manorial Records 1279–1351*, Roxburghe Club.

RCHM (1975) *An Inventory of Archaeological Sites in North-East Northamptonshire*, IV vols, Royal Commission on Historical Monuments (I), London, HMSO.

RCHM (1979) *An Inventory of Archaeological Sites in Central Northamptonshire*, IV vols, Royal Commission on Historical Monuments (II), London, HMSO.

RCHM (1981) *An Inventory of Archaeological Sites in North-*

West Northamptonshire, IV vols, Royal Commission on Historical Monuments (III), London, HMSO.

RCHM (1982) *An Inventory of Archaeological Sites in South-West Northamptonshire*, IV vols, Royal Commission on Historical Monuments (IV), London, HMSO.

RCHM (1985) *An Inventory of Archaeological Sites and Churches in Northampton*, Royal Commission on Historical Monuments, London, HMSO.

Rippon, S. (2008) *Beyond the Medieval Village*, Oxford University Press.

Roberts, B. K. and Wrathmell, S. (2000) *An Atlas of Rural Settlement in England*, London, English Heritage.

Rumbold, M. (1998) Making your own Enclosure Map, *Northamptonshire Past and Present* 9, 368–72.

Salter, H. E. (1930) *Boarstall Cartulary*, (88), Oxford Historical Society.

Salzman, L.F. (ed.) (1937) *The Victoria History of the County of Northampton*. 4 vols. London, Oxford University Press.

Serjeantson, R. M. and Adkins, W. (eds) (1906) *The Victoria History of the County of Northampton*. London, Constable.

Seventh Woods Report: Salcey (1791) *House of Commons Journal* 46.

Sharp, J. E. E. S. (ed.) (1906) *Calendar of Inqusitions Post Mortem: Edward I*. London, HMSO.

Shaw-Taylor, L. (2001) Labourers, Cows, Common Rights and Parliamentary Enclosure: The Evidence of Contemporary Comment *c*.1760–1810, *Past and Present* 171, 95–126.

Shepherd, J. A. (1973) Field Systems of Yorkshire. In A. R. H. Baker and R. A. Butlin (eds) *Studies of field systems in the British Isles*, 145–87. Cambridge, Cambridge University Press.

Soden, I. (1996–7) Saxon and Medieval Settlement Remains at St John's Square, Daventry, *Northamptonshire Archaeology* 27, 51–100.

Steane, J. M. (1975) The Medieval Parks of Northamptonshire. *Northamptonshire Past and Present* V, 211–233.

Stenton, D. M. (1933) *Great Roll of Pipe 1 John 1199* (48), Pipe Roll Society.

Stenton, F. M. (1930) *Facsimiles of Early Charters from Northamptonshire Collections*, (4), Northamptonshire Record Society.

Tate W. E. (1967) *The English Village Community and the Enclosure Movements*, London, Gollancz.

Third Woods Report (1788) *House of Commons Journal* 43, 559–61.

Turner, G. J. (1899) *Select Pleas of the Forest* (13), London, Selden Society.

Turner, M. (1980) *English Parliamentary Enclosure: Its Historical Geography and Economic History* Studies in Historical Geography, Folkstone, Dawson.

Viallis, C. and Collins, K. (2004) *A Georgian Country Parson: The Rev. John Mastin of Naseby*, Northampton, Northamptonshire Record Society.

Wade-Martins, P. (1980) *Village sites in Launditch Hundred*, East Anglian archaeology report; no. 10, Dereham, Norfolk, Norfolk Archaeological Unit.

Williamson, T. (2002) *The Transformation of Rural England: Farming and the Landscape, 1700–1870*, Exeter, University of Exeter Press.

Williamson, T. (2003) *Shaping medieval landscapes: settlement, society, environment*, Oxford, Windgather.

Williamson, T., Liddiard, R. and Partida, T. (2012) *Champion: the making and unmaking of Midland landscapes*, Exeter, Exeter Universtity Press.

Willis, D. (1916) *The Estate Book of Henry de Bray* c.*1289–1340*, London, Camden Society.

Wise (1891) *Rockingham and the Watsons*, London, Elliot Stock.

Woodfield, C. T. P. (1980) The Egg Rings: a defended enclosure in Salcey Forest, *Northamptonshire Archaeology* 15, 156–8.

Wrathmell, S. (ed.) (forthcoming) *Wharram: a Study of Settlement on the Yorkshire Wolds, XIII. A History of Wharram and its Neighbours*.

Yelling, J. A. (1977) *Common Field and Enclosure in England 1450–1850*, London, Macmillan Press.

Index

Page numbers in italic denote illustrations

The Atlas Maps

Key Maps

The key maps relate to the pages for both the medieval period *c.*1300 and the early-modern period *c.*1770.

The map below indicates the area covered by each of the following five keys. To locate a particular place of interest go to the key map that covers the area e.g. key map 1 for the Soke of Peterborough. These keys show the individual atlas pages with townships named, and page numbers which apply to both the medieval and early-modern periods.

The maps are presented at 1:25,000 scale to make them comparable to the modern Ordnance Survey *Explorer* series. Numeric National Grid References are given at five-kilometre intervals.The same fonts, colours and styles have been used for both data sets, for consistency and simplicity for the user. Overlaps are indicated on the key pages and a small overlap is included in the gutter to avoid loss of data. Arrows containing adjacent page numbers are also included.

Data within the previously published area of Rockingham Forest that overlaps with this Atlas has been included.

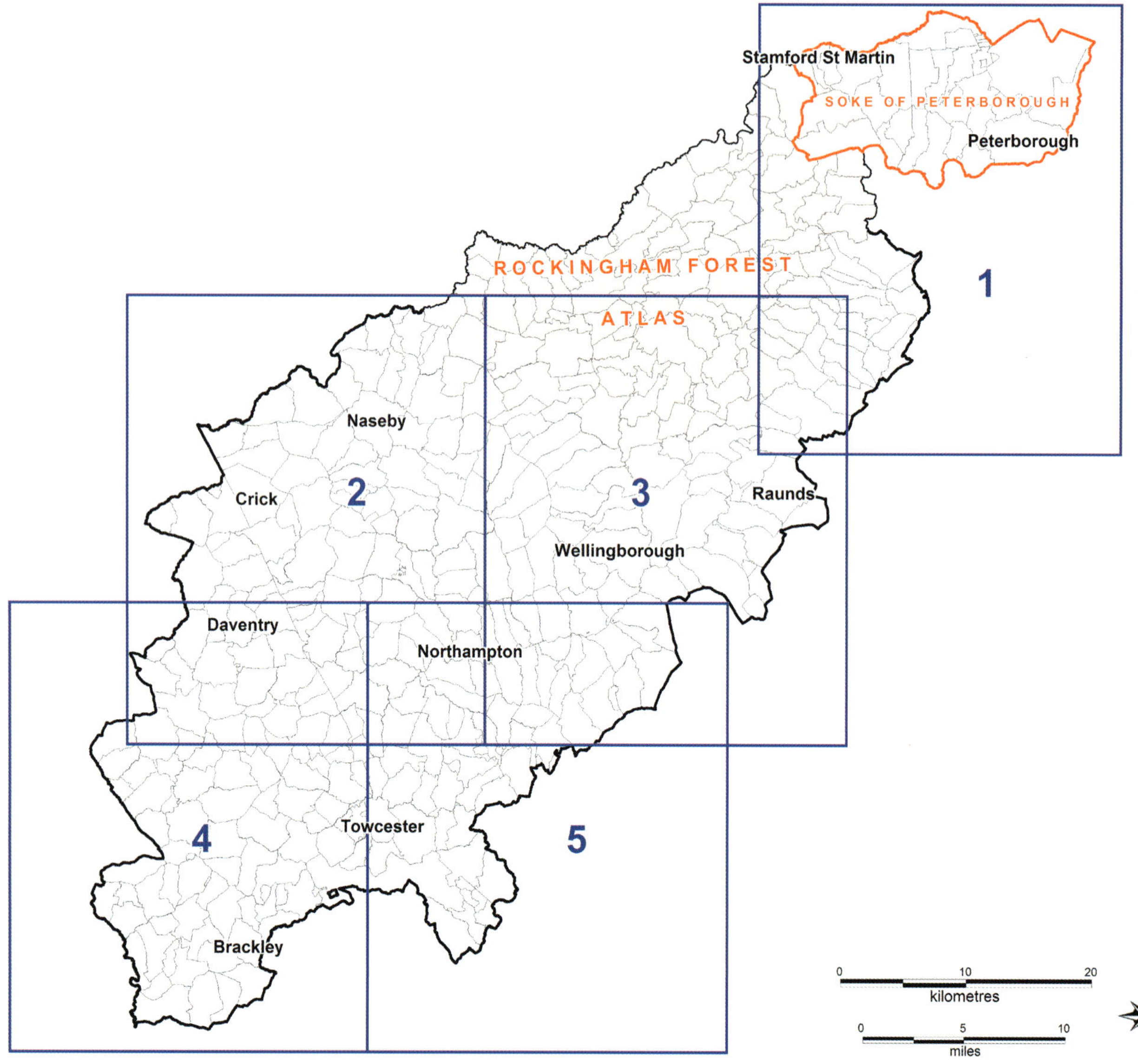

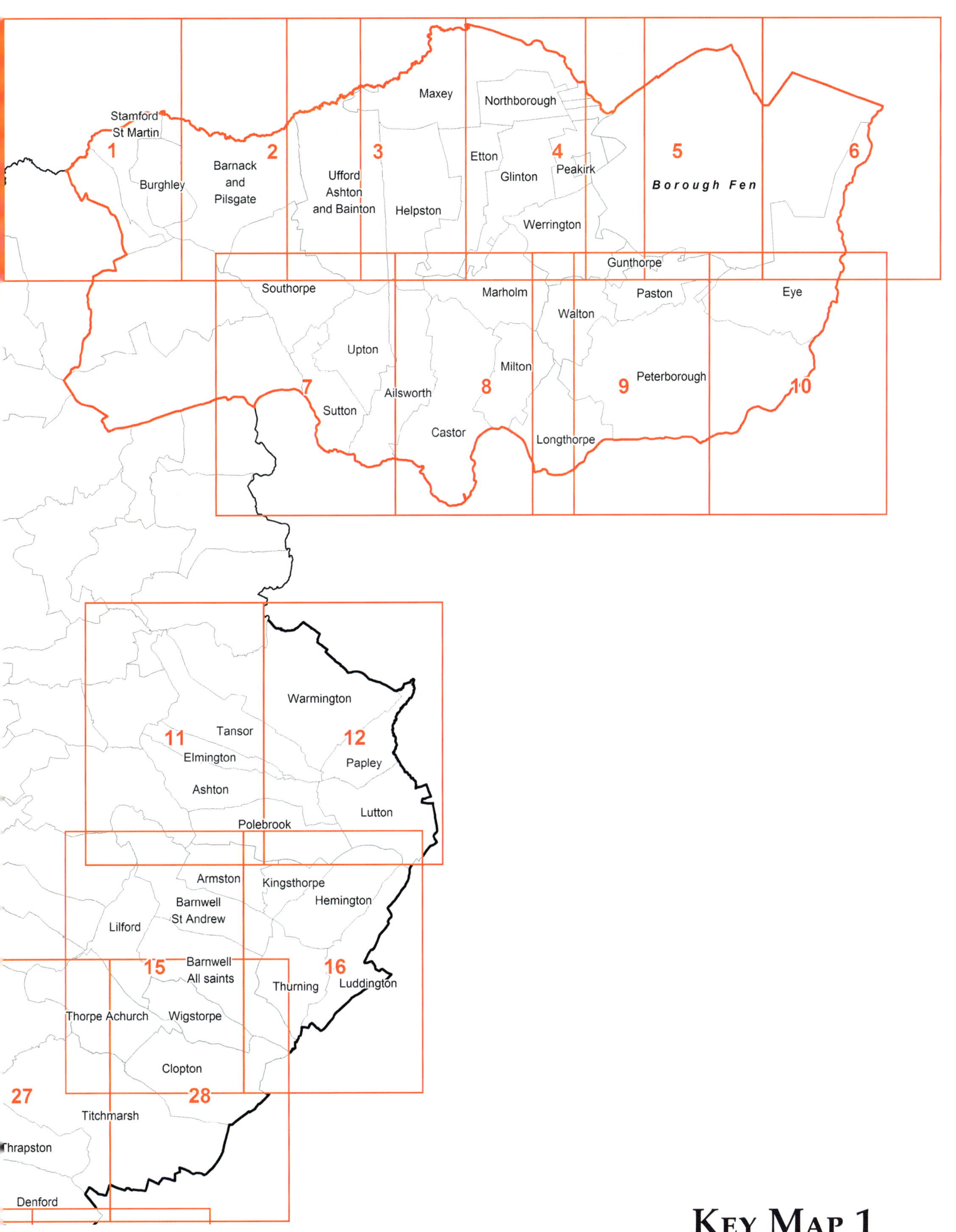
Stamford
St Martin
1
Burghley
Barnack
and
Pilsgate
2
Ufford
Ashton
and Bainton
3
Maxey
Helpston
Northborough
Etton
Glinton
4
Peakirk
Werrington
5
Borough Fen
6
Gunthorpe
Southorpe
Marholm
Paston
Eye
Walton
Upton
Milton
7
Ailsworth
8
9
Peterborough
10
Sutton
Castor
Longthorpe
Warmington
Tansor
11
12
Elmington
Papley
Ashton
Lutton
Polebrook
Armston
Kingsthorpe
Hemington
Barnwell
St Andrew
Lilford
15
Barnwell
All saints
16
Thurning
Luddington
Thorpe Achurch
Wigstorpe
Clopton
27
28
Titchmarsh
Thrapston
Denford

Key Map 1

KEY MAP 2

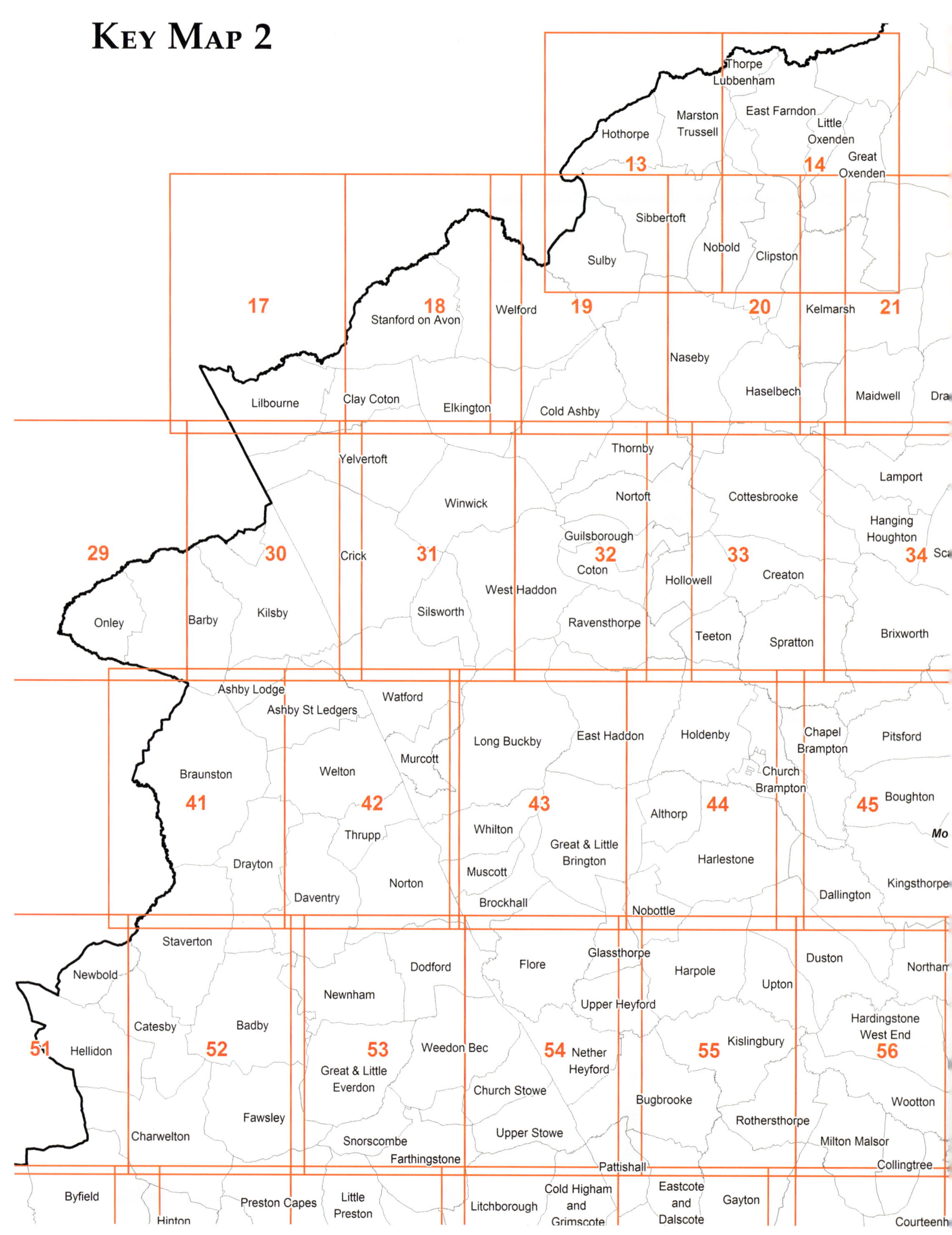

13
14
Thorpe Lubbenham
Hothorpe
Marston Trussell
East Farndon
Little Oxenden
Great Oxenden
17
18
Stanford on Avon
Welford
19
Sibbertoft
Sulby
Nobold
Clipston
20
Kelmarsh
21
Lilbourne
Clay Coton
Elkington
Cold Ashby
Naseby
Haselbech
Maidwell
Dra
Yelvertoft
Thornby
Lamport
Winwick
Nortoft
Cottesbrooke
Hanging Houghton
29
30
Crick
31
Guilsborough
32
Coton
33
34
Sc
Hollowell
Creaton
West Haddon
Onley
Barby
Kilsby
Silsworth
Ravensthorpe
Teeton
Spratton
Brixworth
Ashby Lodge
Ashby St Ledgers
Watford
Long Buckby
East Haddon
Holdenby
Chapel Brampton
Pitsford
Murcott
Braunston
Welton
Church Brampton
41
42
43
44
45
Boughton
Althorp
Thrupp
Whilton
Mo
Great & Little Brington
Harlestone
Drayton
Muscott
Kingsthorpe
Norton
Daventry
Dallington
Brockhall
Nobottle
Staverton
Glassthorpe
Duston
Dodford
Flore
Harpole
Northam
Newbold
Upton
Newnham
Upper Heyford
Catesby
Badby
Hardingstone West End
51
Hellidon
52
53
Weedon Bec
54
Nether Heyford
55
Kislingbury
56
Great & Little Everdon
Church Stowe
Bugbrooke
Wootton
Fawsley
Rothersthorpe
Upper Stowe
Charwelton
Snorscombe
Milton Malsor
Farthingstone
Pattishall
Collingtree
Byfield
Preston Capes
Little Preston
Cold Higham and Grimscote
Eastcote and Dalscote
Gayton
Litchborough
Hinton
Courteenh

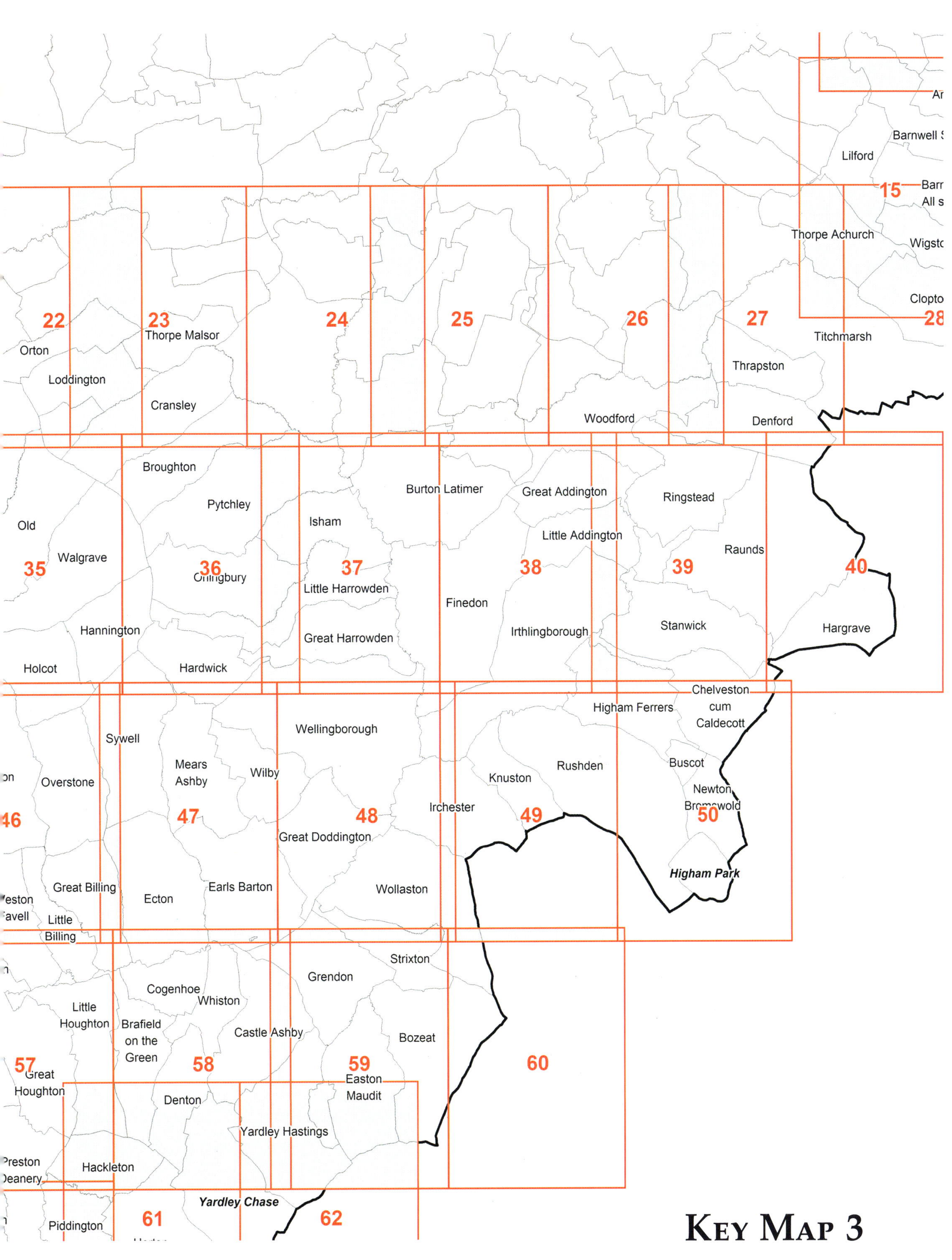

Lilford
15
Thorpe Achurch
28
Titchmarsh
22
Orton
Loddington
23
Thorpe Malsor
Cransley
24
25
26
Woodford
27
Thrapston
Denford
Broughton
Pytchley
Old
Walgrave
35
36
Hannington
Holcot
Hardwick
Isham
37
Little Harrowden
Great Harrowden
Burton Latimer
Finedon
Great Addington
Little Addington
38
Irthlingborough
Ringstead
Raunds
39
Stanwick
40
Hargrave
Chelveston
cum
Caldecott
Higham Ferrers
Rushden
Knuston
49
Buscot
Newton
50
Higham Park
Sywell
Overstone
46
Mears
Ashby
Wilby
47
Wellingborough
48
Great Doddington
Irchester
Great Billing
Ecton
Earls Barton
Wollaston
Little
Billing
Strixton
Grendon
Cogenhoe
Whiston
Little
Houghton
Brafield
on the
Green
Castle Ashby
Bozeat
57
Great
Houghton
58
59
Easton
Maudit
60
Denton
Yardley Hastings
Hackleton
Yardley Chase
Piddington
61
62

KEY MAP 3

KEY MAP 4

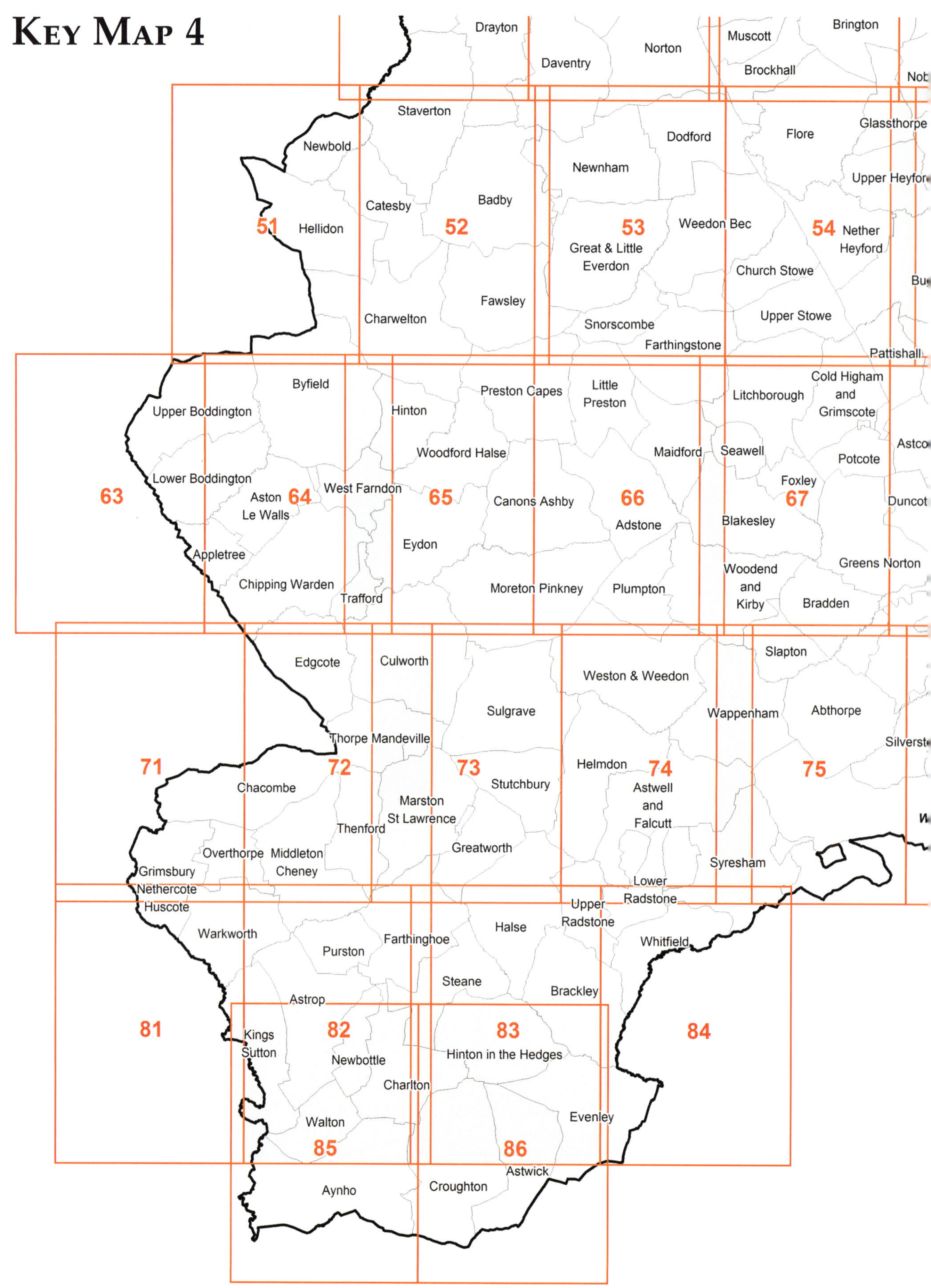
Drayton
Daventry
Norton
Muscott
Brington
Brockhall
Staverton
Newbold
Dodford
Flore
Glassthorpe
Newnham
Catesby
Badby
Upper Heyford
51
Hellidon
52
53
Weedon Bec
54
Nether Heyford
Great & Little Everdon
Church Stowe
Fawsley
Charwelton
Upper Stowe
Snorscombe
Farthingstone
Pattishall
Byfield
Preston Capes
Little Preston
Cold Higham and Grimscote
Litchborough
Upper Boddington
Hinton
Woodford Halse
Maidford
Seawell
Potcote
Lower Boddington
Foxley
63
Aston Le Walls
64
West Farndon
65
Canons Ashby
66
67
Duncote
Adstone
Blakesley
Eydon
Appletree
Greens Norton
Woodend and Kirby
Chipping Warden
Moreton Pinkney
Plumpton
Trafford
Bradden
Edgcote
Culworth
Slapton
Weston & Weedon
Sulgrave
Wappenham
Abthorpe
Thorpe Mandeville
71
72
73
Helmdon
74
75
Chacombe
Stutchbury
Astwell and Falcutt
Marston St Lawrence
Thenford
Greatworth
Overthorpe
Middleton Cheney
Syresham
Grimsbury
Nethercote
Huscote
Lower Radstone
Upper Radstone
Halse
Warkworth
Purston
Farthinghoe
Whitfield
Steane
Brackley
Astrop
81
Kings Sutton
82
83
84
Newbottle
Hinton in the Hedges
Charlton
Evenley
Walton
85
86
Astwick
Aynho
Croughton

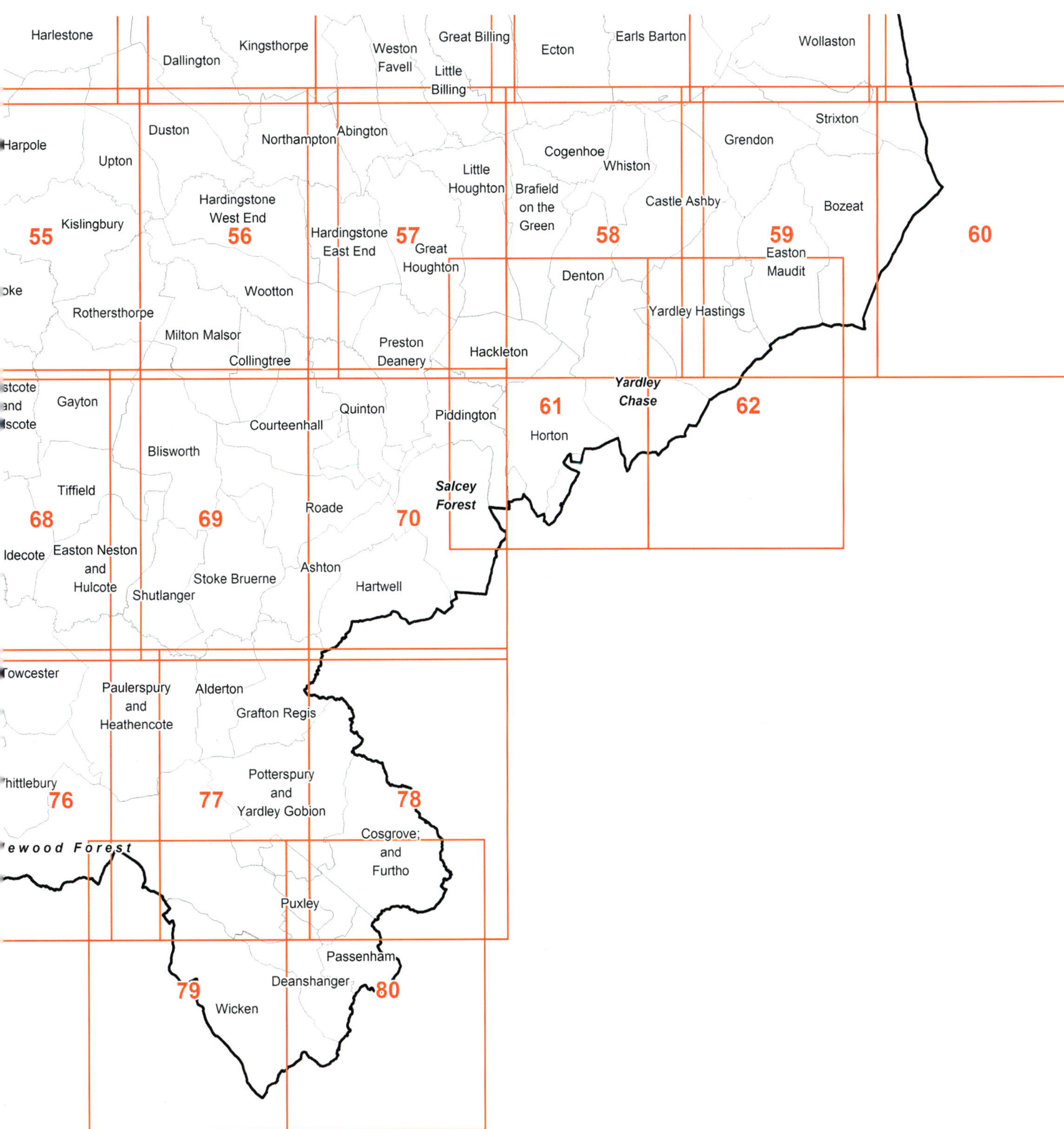

Harlestone
Dallington
Kingsthorpe
Weston Favell
Great Billing
Little Billing
Ecton
Earls Barton
Wollaston
Harpole
Duston
Northampton
Abington
Upton
Cogenhoe
Whiston
Grendon
Strixton
Little Houghton
Brafield on the Green
Castle Ashby
Bozeat
Hardingstone West End
Kislingbury
55
56
Hardingstone East End
57
Great Houghton
58
59
Easton Maudit
60
Denton
Wootton
Rothersthorpe
Yardley Hastings
Milton Malsor
Preston Deanery
Hackleton
Collingtree
Gayton
Yardley Chase
Quinton
Piddington
61
62
Courteenhall
Horton
Blisworth
Tiffield
Salcey Forest
Roade
68
69
70
Easton Neston and Hulcote
Ashton
Stoke Bruerne
Hartwell
Shutlanger
Paulerspury and Heathencote
Alderton
Grafton Regis
Potterspury and Yardley Gobion
76
77
78
Cosgrove; and Furtho
Puxley
Passenham
Deanshanger
79
80
Wicken

Key Map 5

Medieval Atlas

The medieval mapping shows the landscape as it was *c*.1300 at the height of medieval expansion. Woodland too was at this date fairly static being largely preserved within the royal forests. Most of the data was collected from field survey and complemented by aerial photography and historic maps.

A brief description of each of the data sets is given below but for a full discussion of methodology see Chapter 1.

Saxon site: The location of Saxon sites, most of which are likely to be settlements, is as presented in the *Rockingham Atlas* pp.46–54, based on analysis of data in the SMR, RCHME volumes, Hall's fieldwalking records, Parry 2006 and Jones and Page 2006.

Saxon burial: The location of Saxon burials from SMR.

Settlement (uncertain extent): A point location of places where there is known to have been a medieval settlement but where it is not possible to map an area. All are labelled with their name, and the three for which no name is known are labelled 'unnamed'.

Settlement (unlocated): A point location within an area where it is known there was a settlement but where the exact location is uncertain.

Church: The location of medieval churches derived from research by Glenn Foard.

Chapel: The location of medieval chapels derived from research by Glenn Foard

Rivers and streams: Water in this data set is derived primarily from the streams and slades mapped as part of the base data. This has been supplemented by water digitised from the OS 1:10,560 mapping of the 1880s. Care has been taken to exclude any obviously late water courses such as those associated with industry, canals, reservoirs and drainage. Water in Borough Fen is excluded as it is not possible to establish what the water courses were in the medieval. The rivers Nene and Welland are shown as a thicker line.

Ridge and furrow strip: Each of the drawn strips represents about four on the ground. The representation gives the correct orientation, relative length of strips and curvature. However, the nature of the vectorising process tends to flatten the curves given a less acute reverse-S curvature than would have existed on the ground.

Headland: Headlands are low narrow banks separating the furlongs. They have been mapped from field survey supplemented by documentary sources.

Open field: This data set shows the full extent of the arable open fields and is the background to the ridge and furrow strips. Where there are no strips shown it is because no archaeological or documentary evidence survives to map the furlongs, though it is known to have been open field.

Open field pasture: This represents land within the open fields that was never ploughed. Pasture often takes the form of ribbons of grass with the furlongs, frequently associated with streams and slades, but can also be substantial blocks of grass. The location of open field pasture is greatly influenced by soils and topography. Only the larger areas are mapped, very small strips are not represented.

Meadow: Meadow was grassland that was periodically waterlogged making it unsuitable for arable land but providing rich hay for fodder.

Fen: Fen was the wet peaty western edge of the Wash Fenland, drained in the mid-17th century. Most of the peat has now wasted away. Upstream, as at Northborough, there was much admixture of alluvium with the peat, but it was still called 'fen' and now differs only slightly from normal river alluvium.

Heath: Heaths are associated with particular geological types and are found on decalcified limestone and Northampton Sands and Ironstone.

Woodland: This data set shows the extent of woodland and includes woods, assarts and wood pasture. For the forests the coppice boundaries from the early modern period have been edited to remove any obviously late ones then superimposed on the medieval woodland to assist location.

Settlement area: This represents the full *probable* extent of medieval settlement. It was created using variety of sources including field survey of the pre-medieval archaeology and open field data, earthwork data from NMP and RCHME surveys, soils, aerial photographs, and historic maps. It has been further refined by the creation of polygons identifying roads and greens within the settlement core and on periphery by using early-modern sources, earthwork data, and medieval land use data. This has been overlain in white on the settlement area to give structure. The roads in Northampton have been edited from Speed.

Township boundary: The township boundaries are mapped from the earliest possible source and all maps that depict the boundaries are consulted. It is therefore usual for the data to come from more than one map source and not uncommon for there to be as many as six sources for any one township. Whilst the boundaries are largely from early-modern sources it is likely (on the basis of the open field survey data) that many, probably most, were in existence, and running along the course presented, in the Middle Ages. It is uncertain if detached blocks existed in the same form in this period and they are not labelled in these pages.

No data: The large blocks of 'no data' indicate areas where it has not been possible to establish the medieval land use due to urban development or large scale mineral extraction. In addition there are some small areas associated with settlements of uncertain extent where the land use on the periphery of the settlement is unidentified.

Legend

▲ Saxon site

▼ Saxon burial

● settlement (uncertain extent)

★ settlement (unlocated)

church

chapel

rivers and streams

ridge and furrow strip

headland

open field

open field pasture

meadow

fen

heath

woodland

settlement area

township boundary

no data

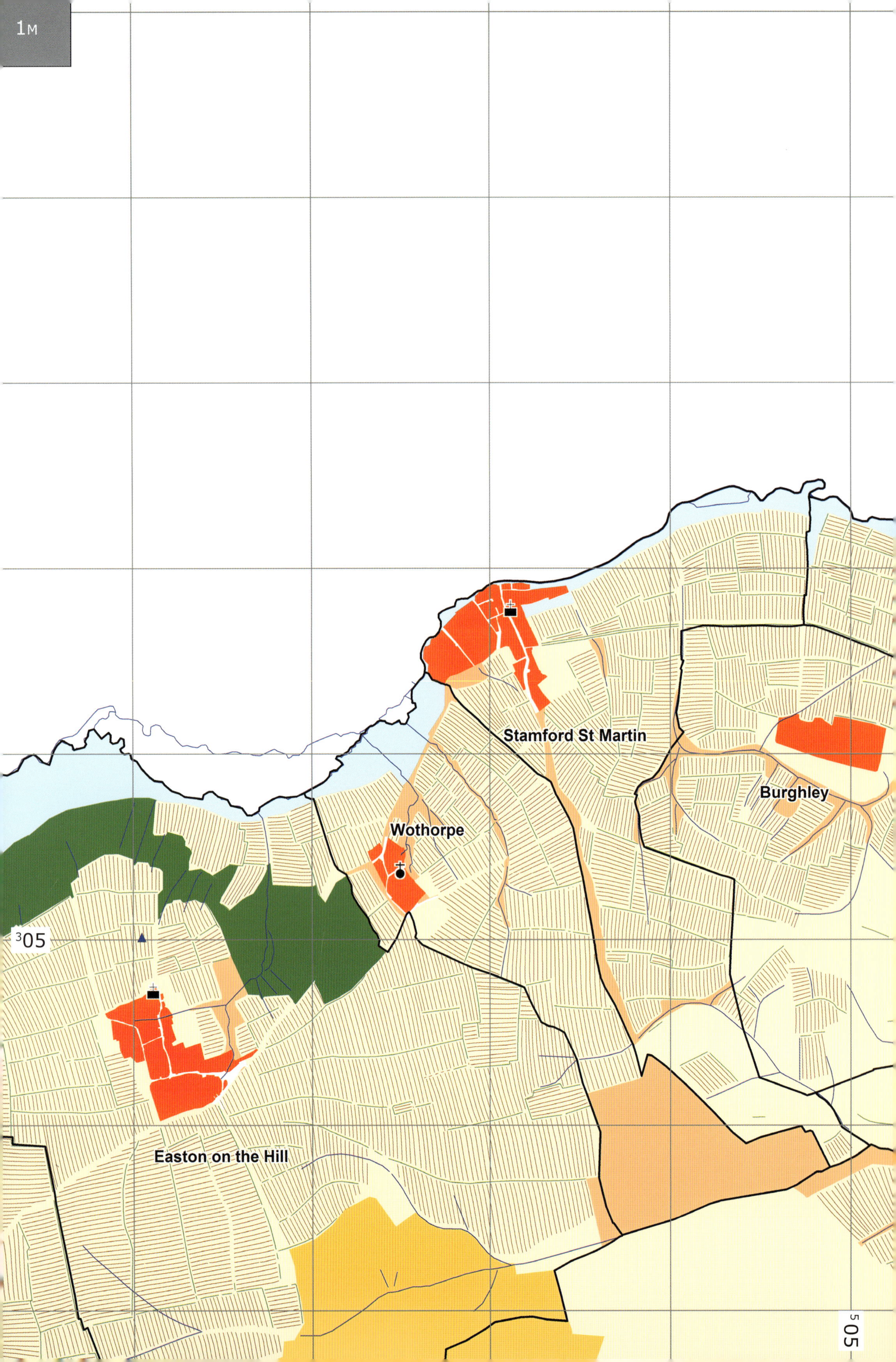
1M
Stamford St Martin
Burghley
Wothorpe
Easton on the Hill
305
505

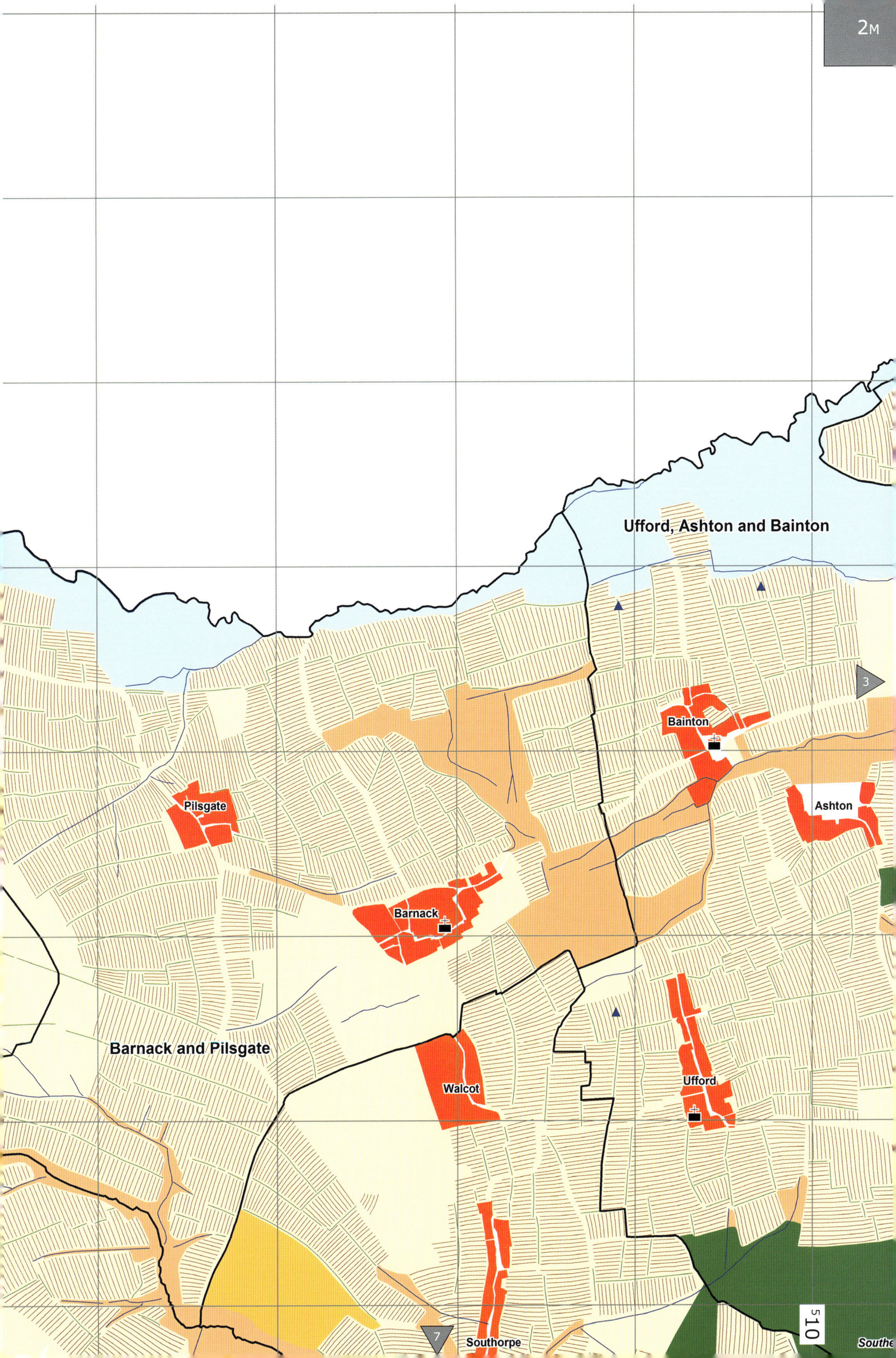
Ufford, Ashton and Bainton
3
Bainton
Pilsgate
Ashton
Barnack
Barnack and Pilsgate
Walcot
Ufford
7
Southorpe
510

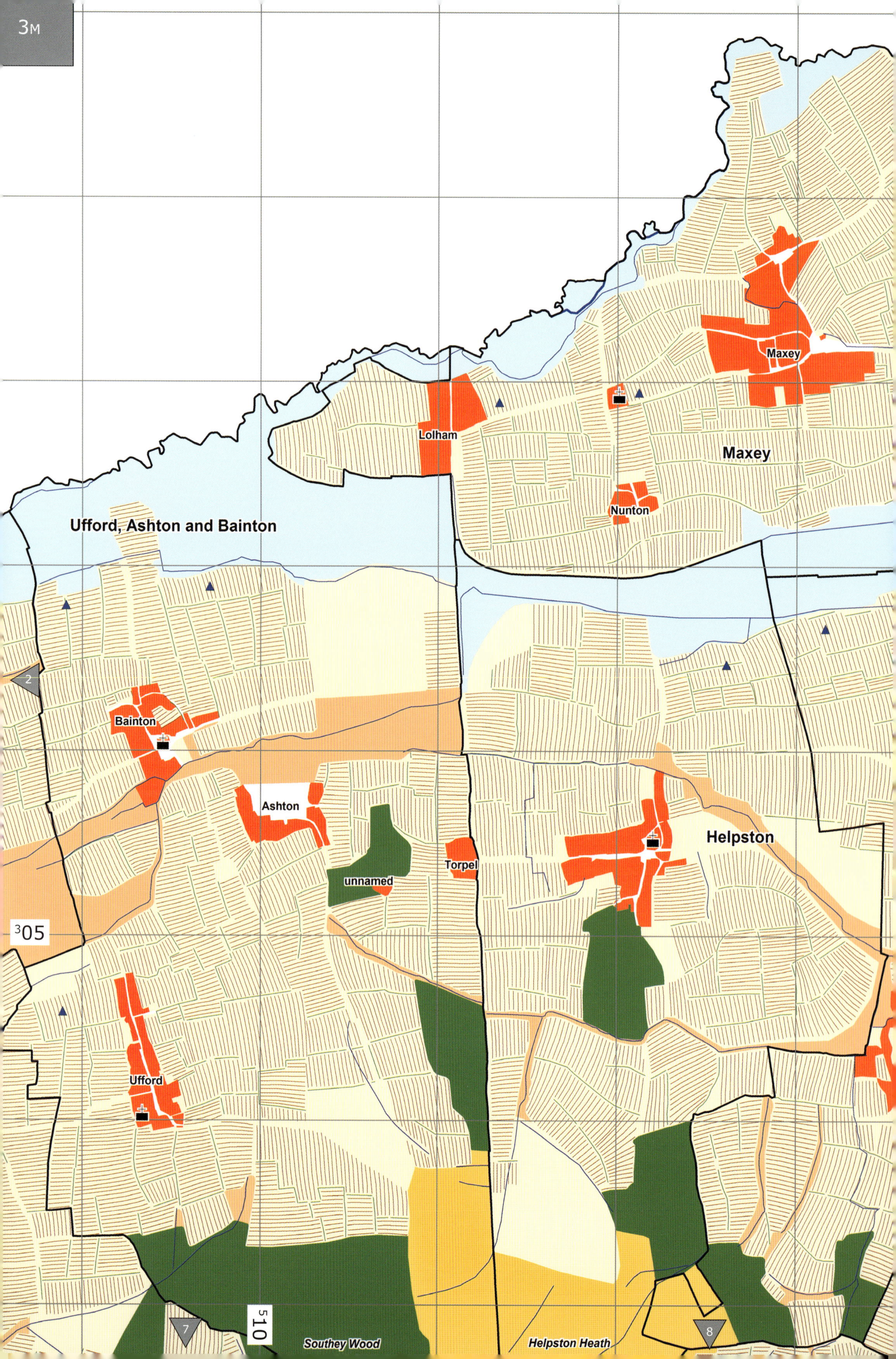
3M
Maxey
Lolham
Maxey
Nunton
Ufford, Ashton and Bainton
2
Bainton
Ashton
Torpel
unnamed
Helpston
305
Ufford
7
510
Southey Wood
Helpston Heath
8

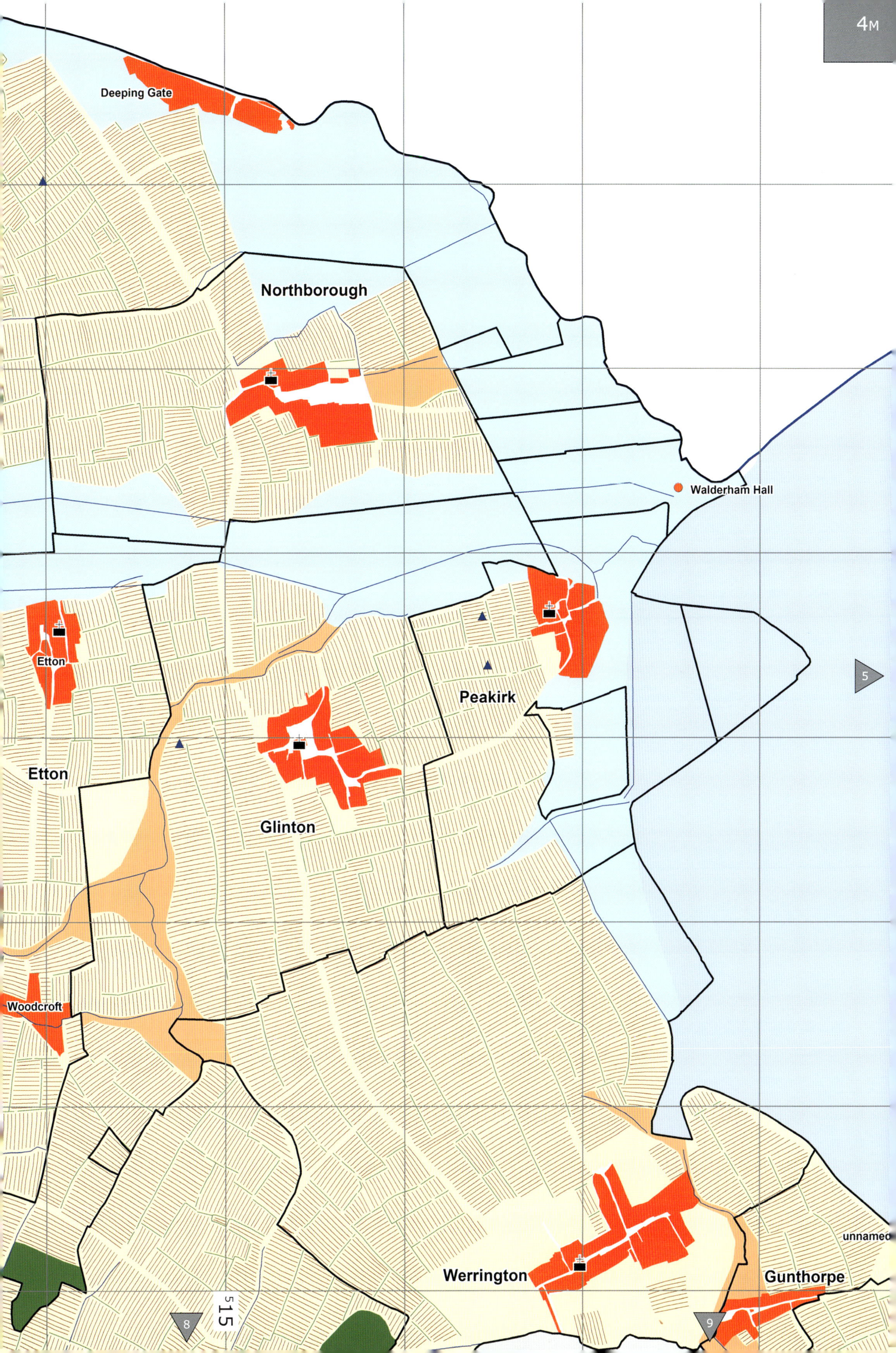

4M
Deeping Gate
Northborough
Walderham Hall
Etton
Etton
Peakirk
5
Glinton
Woodcroft
Werrington
Gunthorpe
unnamed
8
515
9

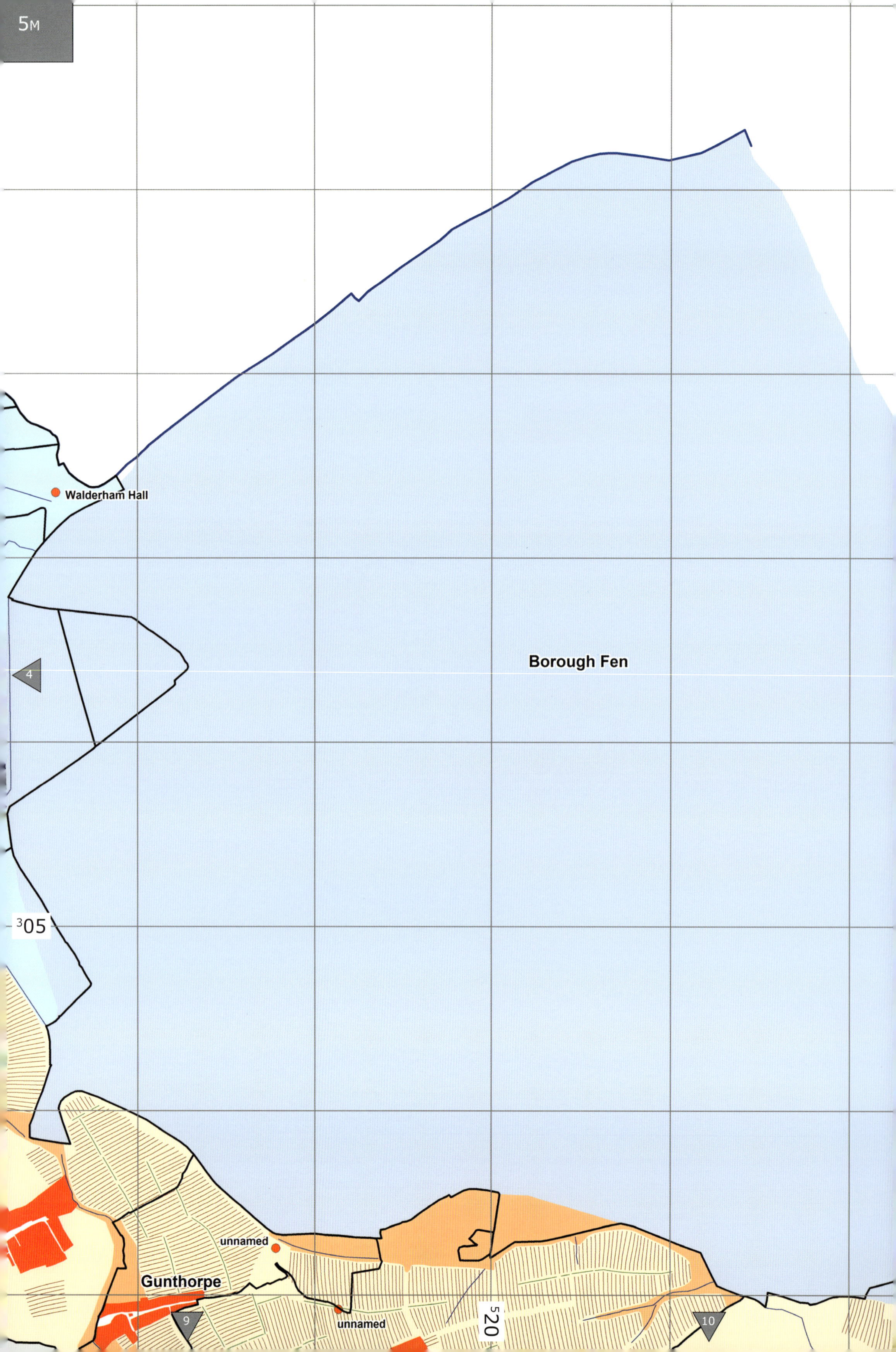
5M
Walderham Hall
4
Borough Fen
305
unnamed
Gunthorpe
9
unnamed
520
10

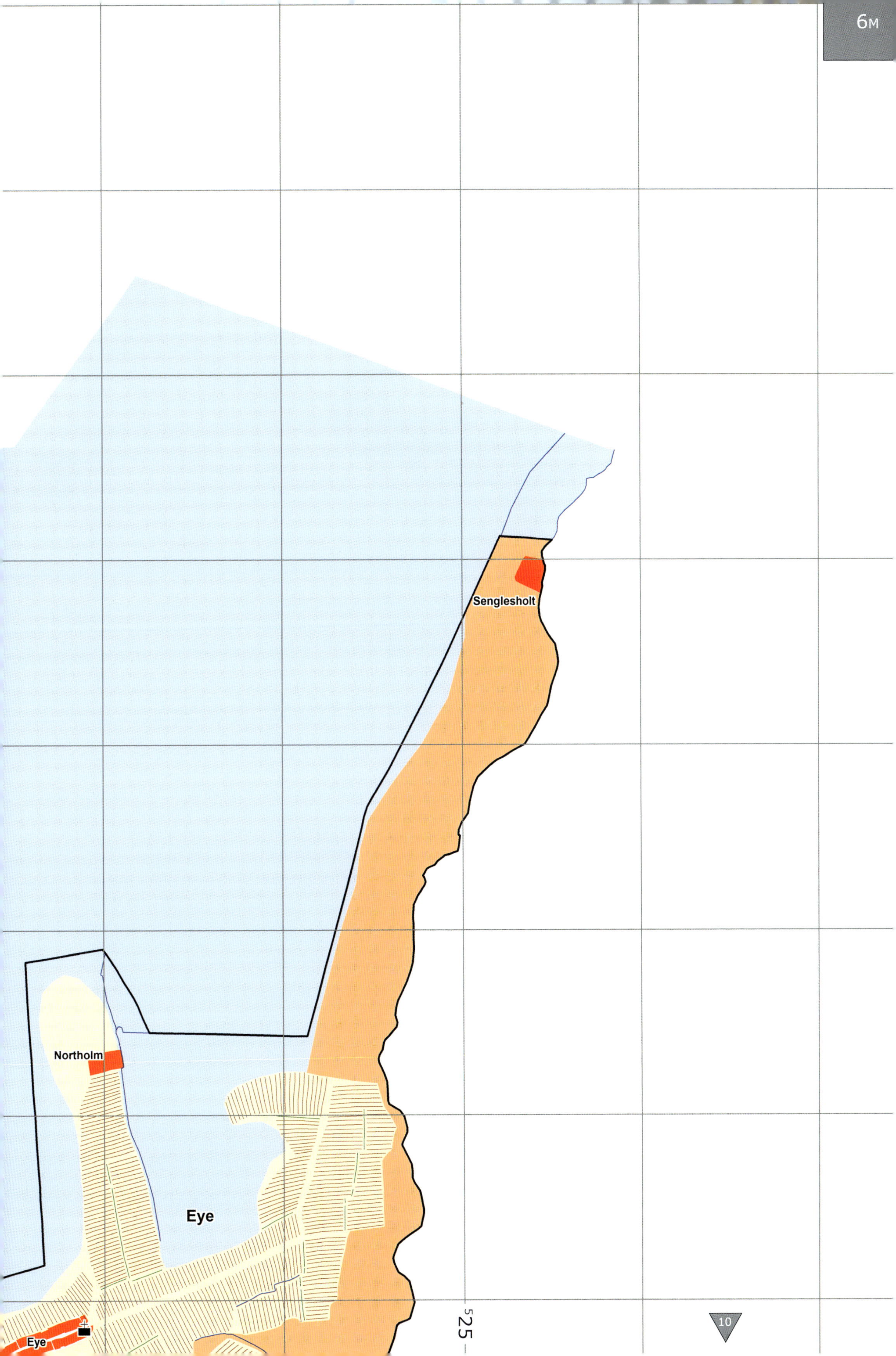
Sengleshott
Northolm
Eye
Eye
525
10

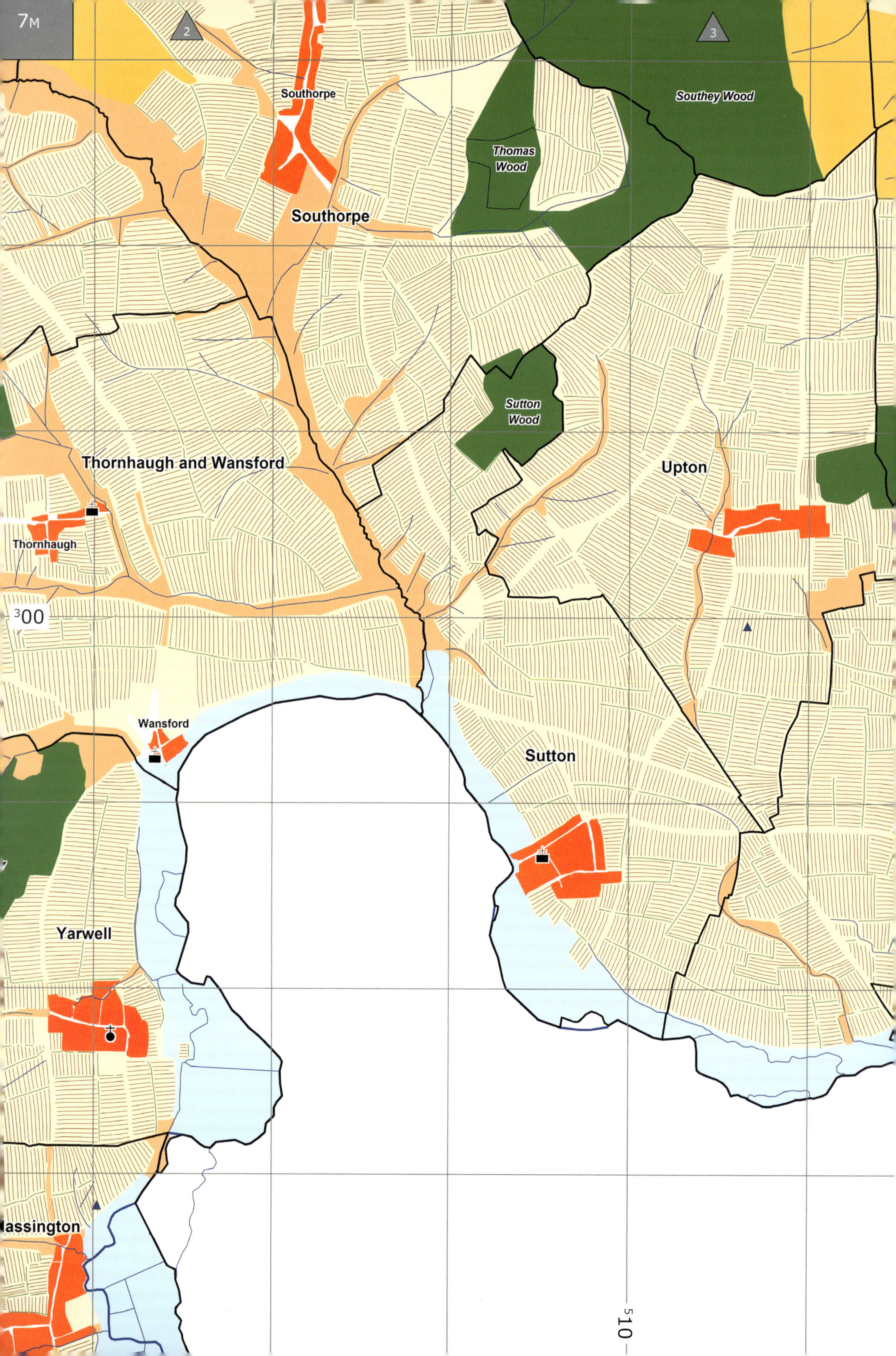
2
3
Southorpe
Southey Wood
Thomas Wood
Southorpe
Sutton Wood
Thornhaugh and Wansford
Upton
Thornhaugh
300
Wansford
Sutton
Yarwell
assington
510

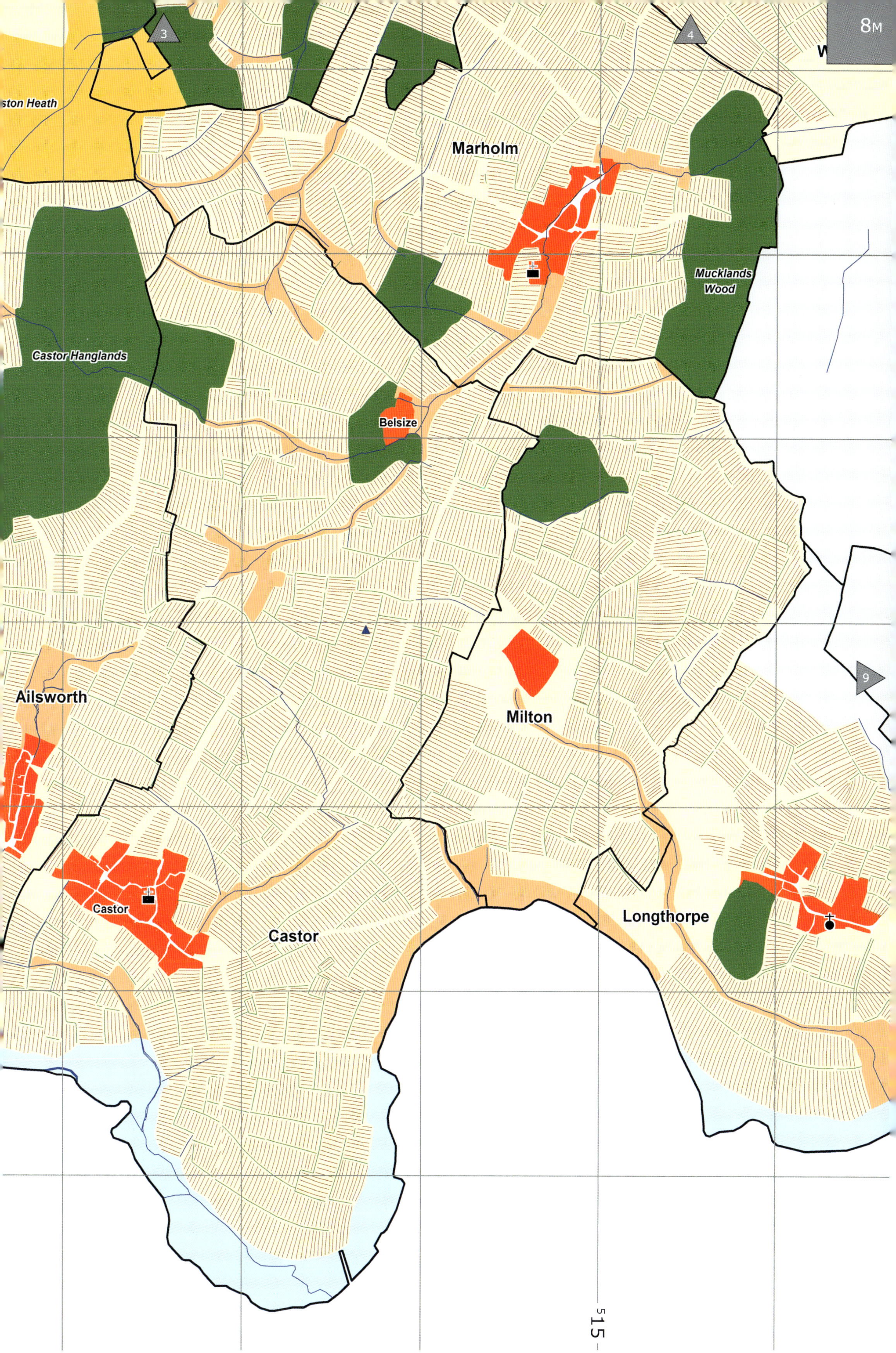

8M
3
4
ston Heath
Marholm
Mucklands Wood
Castor Hanglands
Belsize
Ailsworth
9
Milton
Castor
Castor
Longthorpe
515

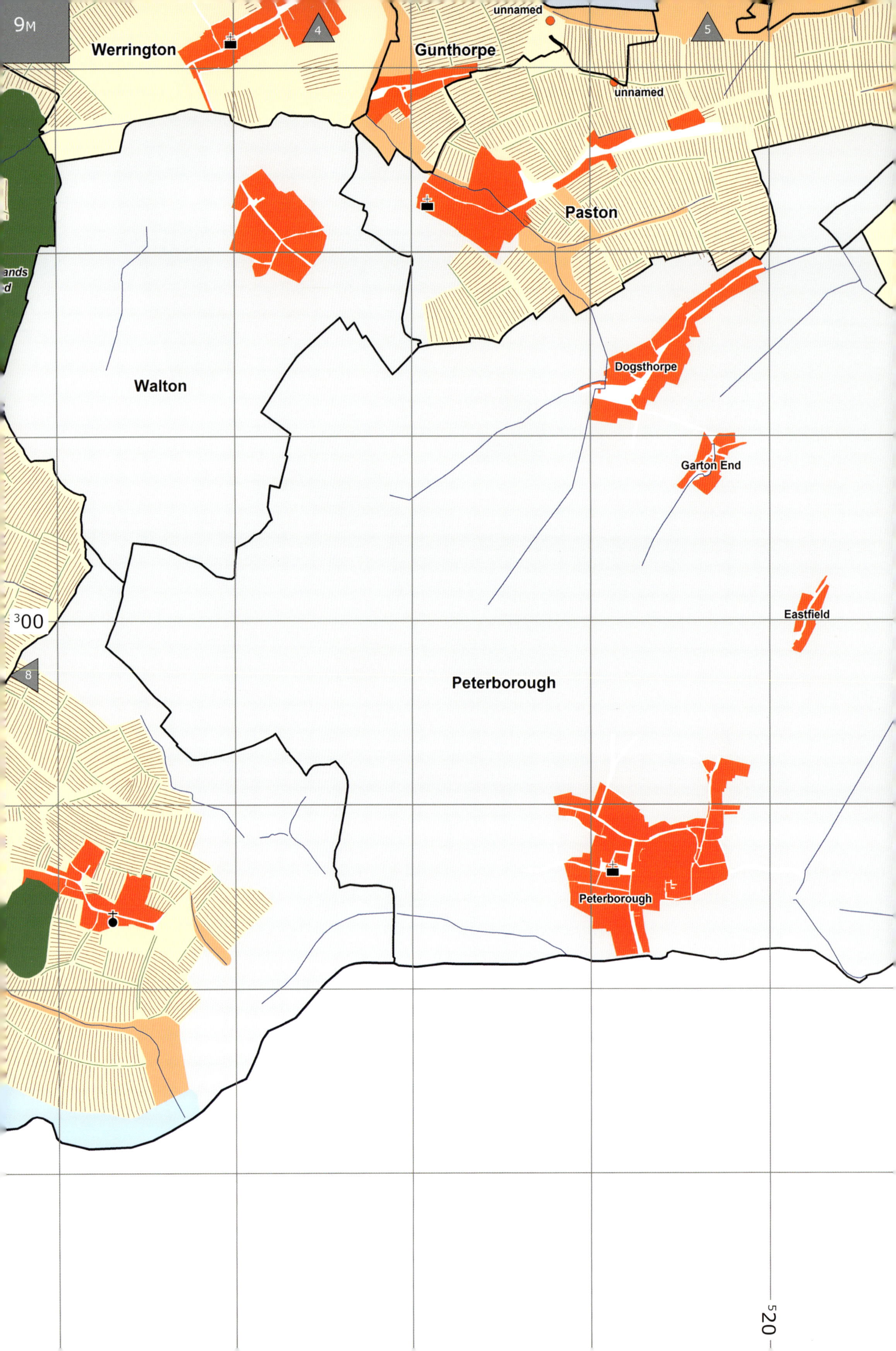
9M
Werrington
4
Gunthorpe
unnamed
5
unnamed
Paston
ands
d
Walton
Dogsthorpe
Garton End
300
Eastfield
8
Peterborough
Peterborough
520

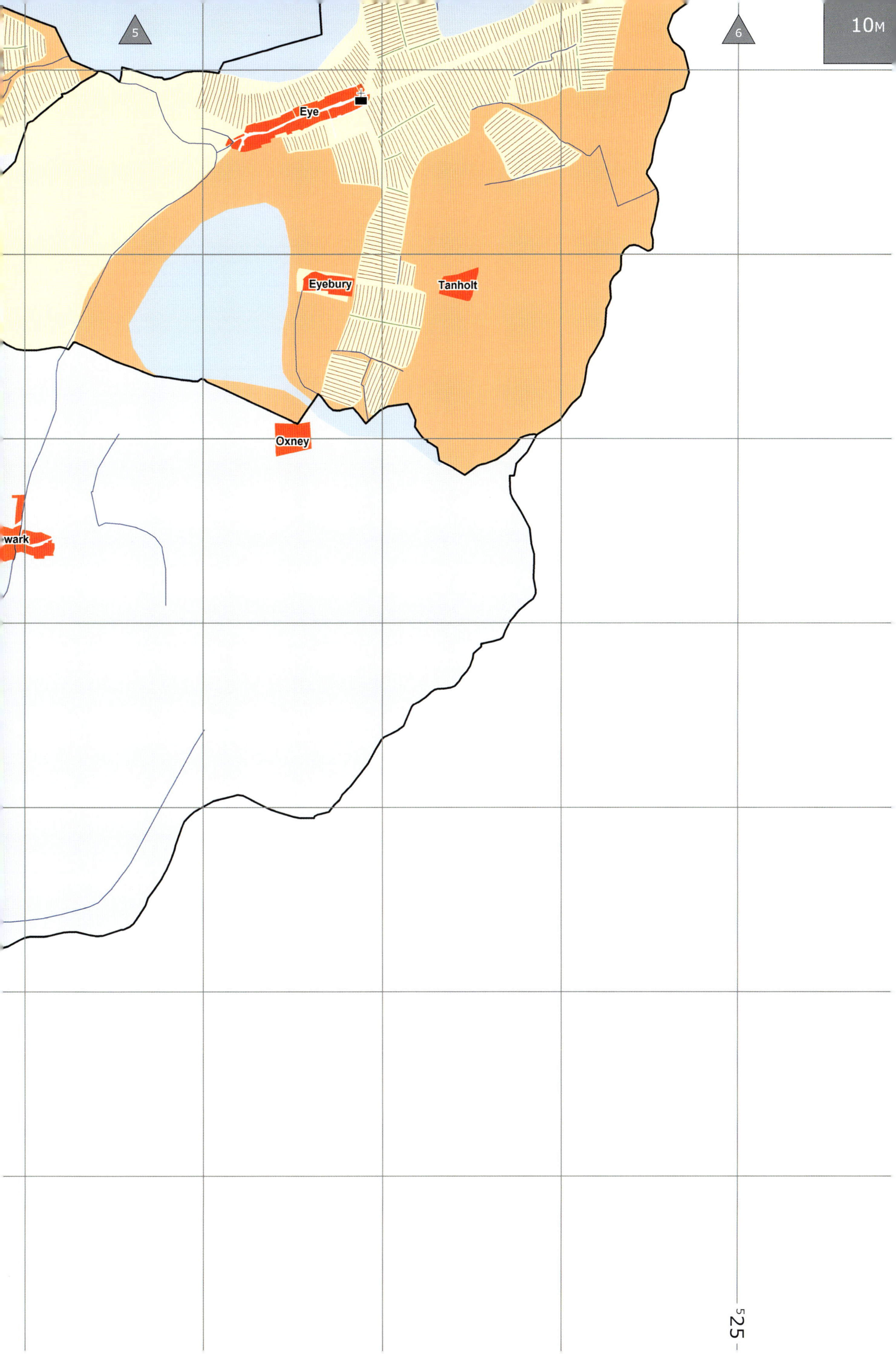
10M
5
6
Eye
Eyebury
Tanholt
Oxney
wark
525

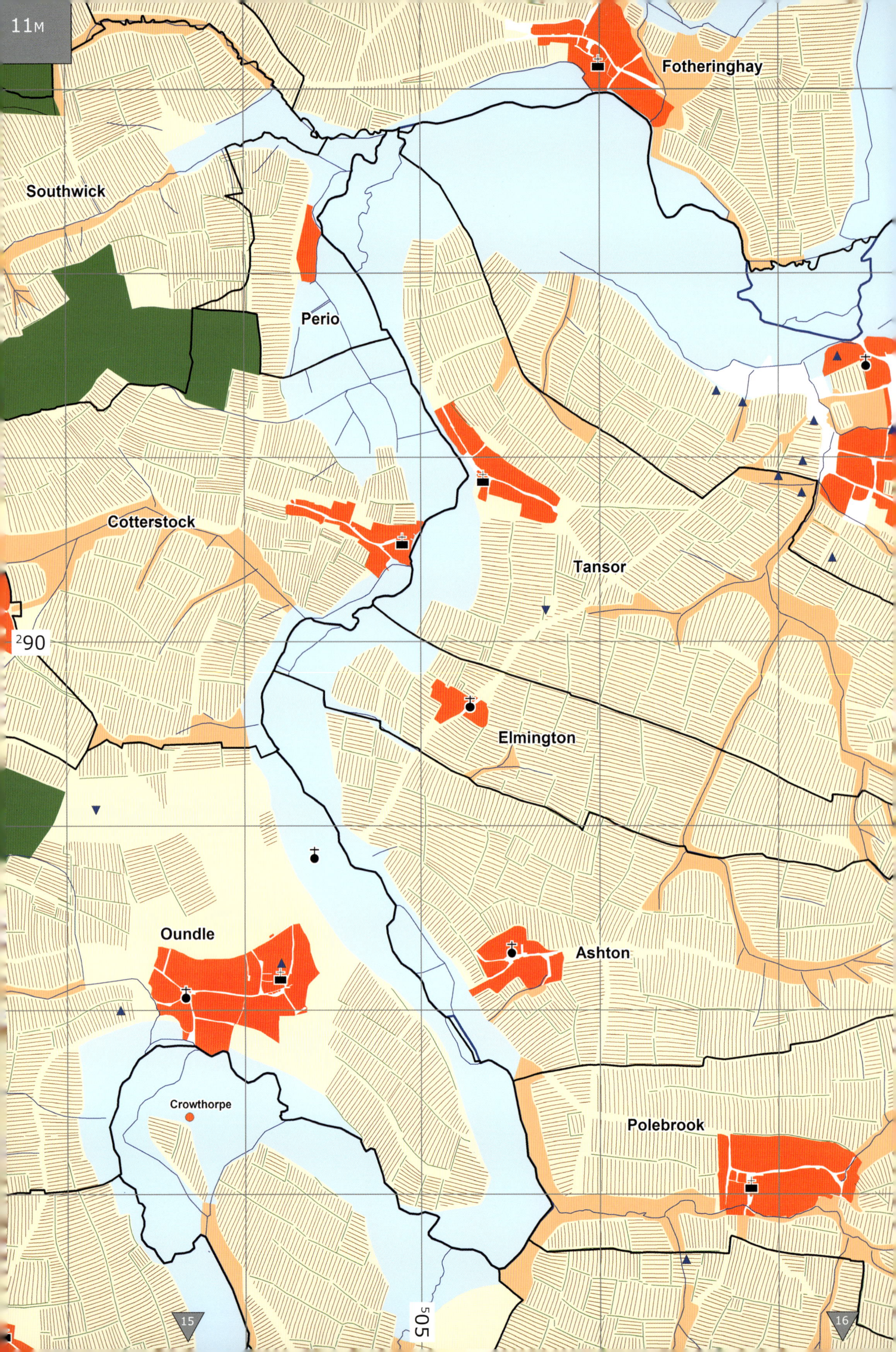

11M
Fotheringhay
Southwick
Perio
Cotterstock
Tansor
290
Elmington
Oundle
Ashton
Crowthorpe
Polebrook
15
505
16

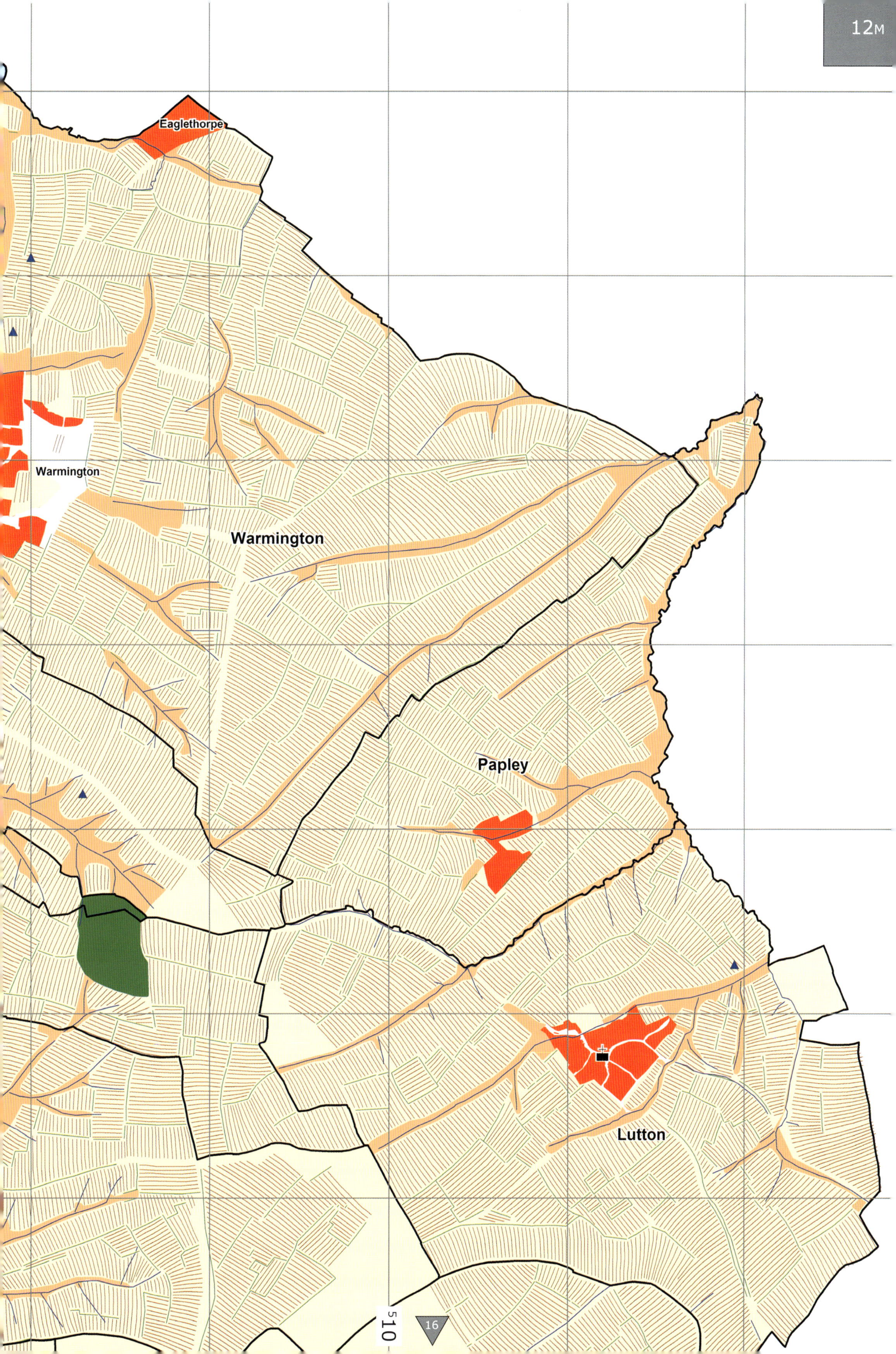
Eaglethorpe
Warmington
Warmington
Papley
Lutton
510
16

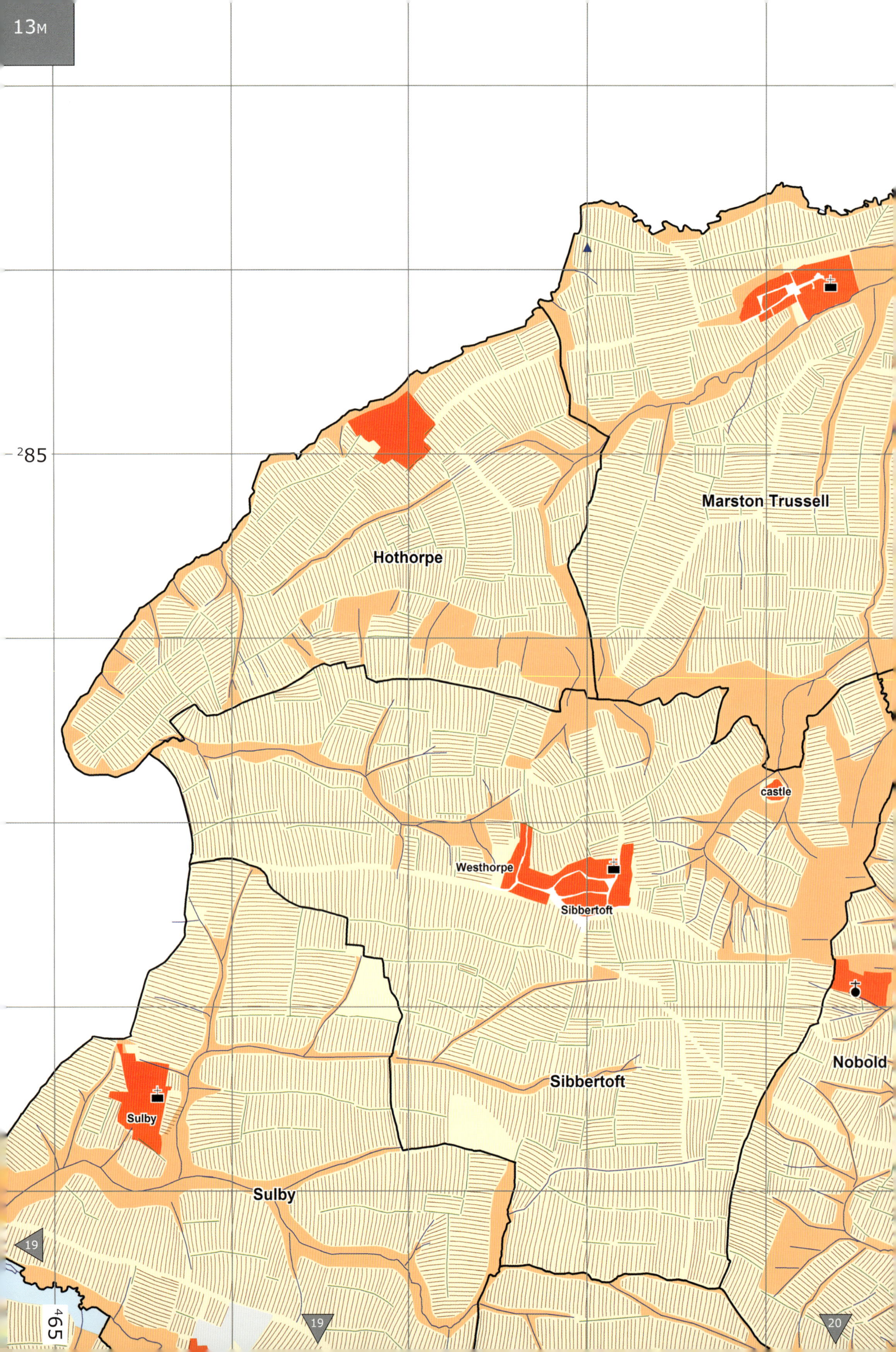

285
Marston Trussell
Hothorpe
castle
Westhorpe
Sibbertoft
Nobold
Sibbertoft
Sulby
Sulby
19
19
20
465

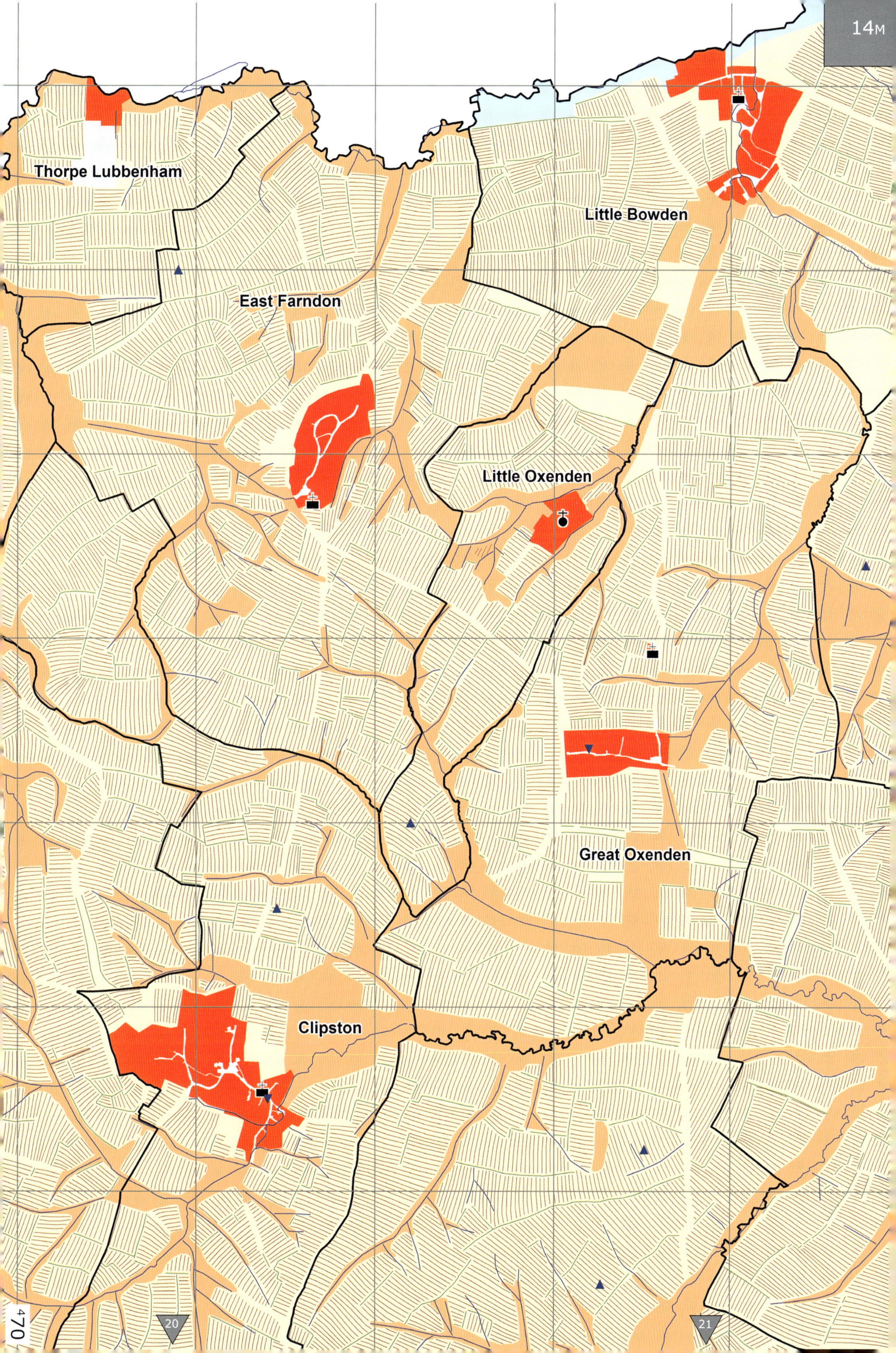
Thorpe Lubbenham
Little Bowden
East Farndon
Little Oxenden
Great Oxenden
Clipston
20
21

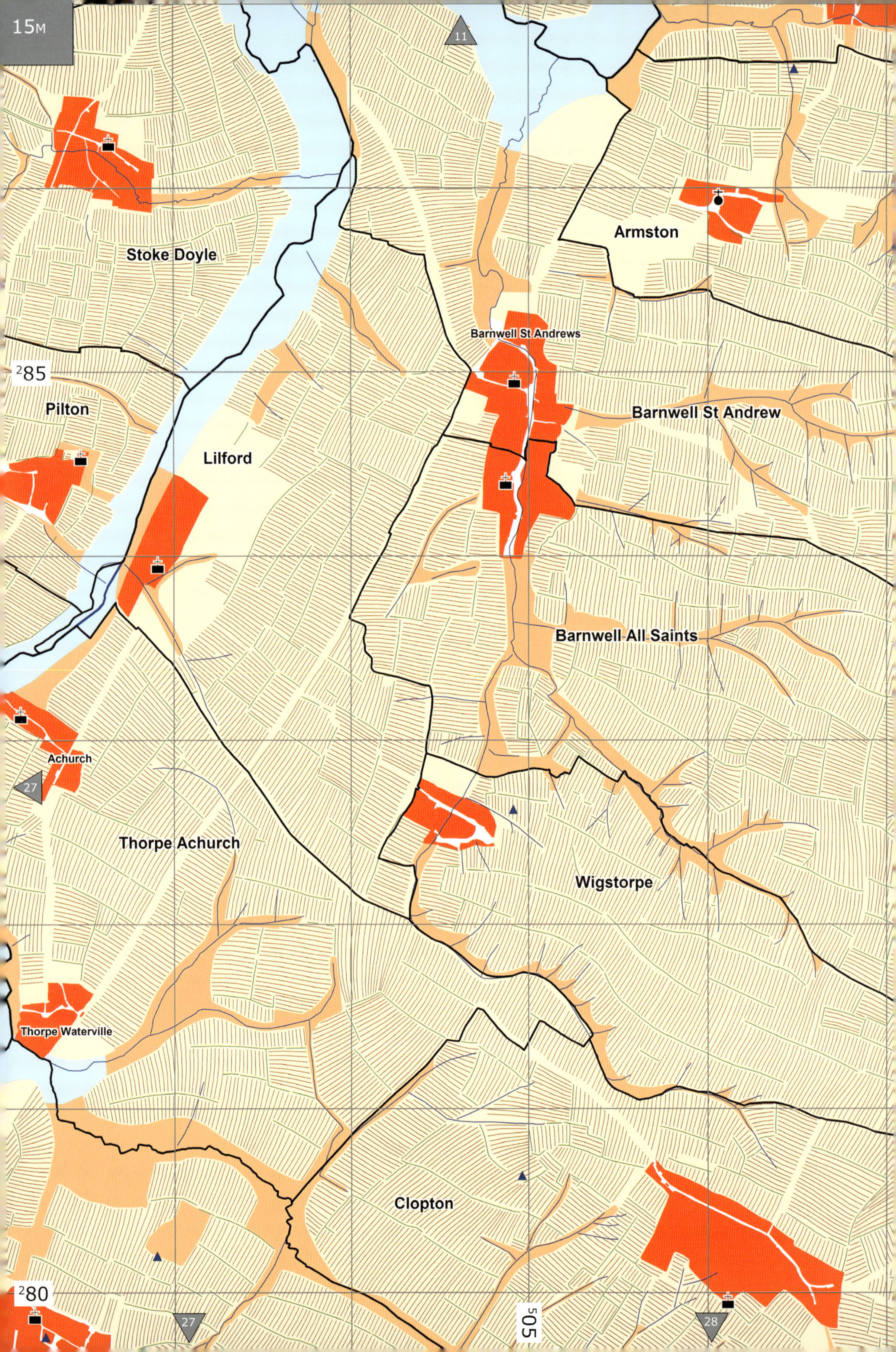
15M
11
Stoke Doyle
Armston
Barnwell St Andrews
285
Barnwell St Andrew
Pilton
Lilford
Barnwell All Saints
Achurch
27
Thorpe Achurch
Wigstorpe
Thorpe Waterville
Clopton
280
27
505
28

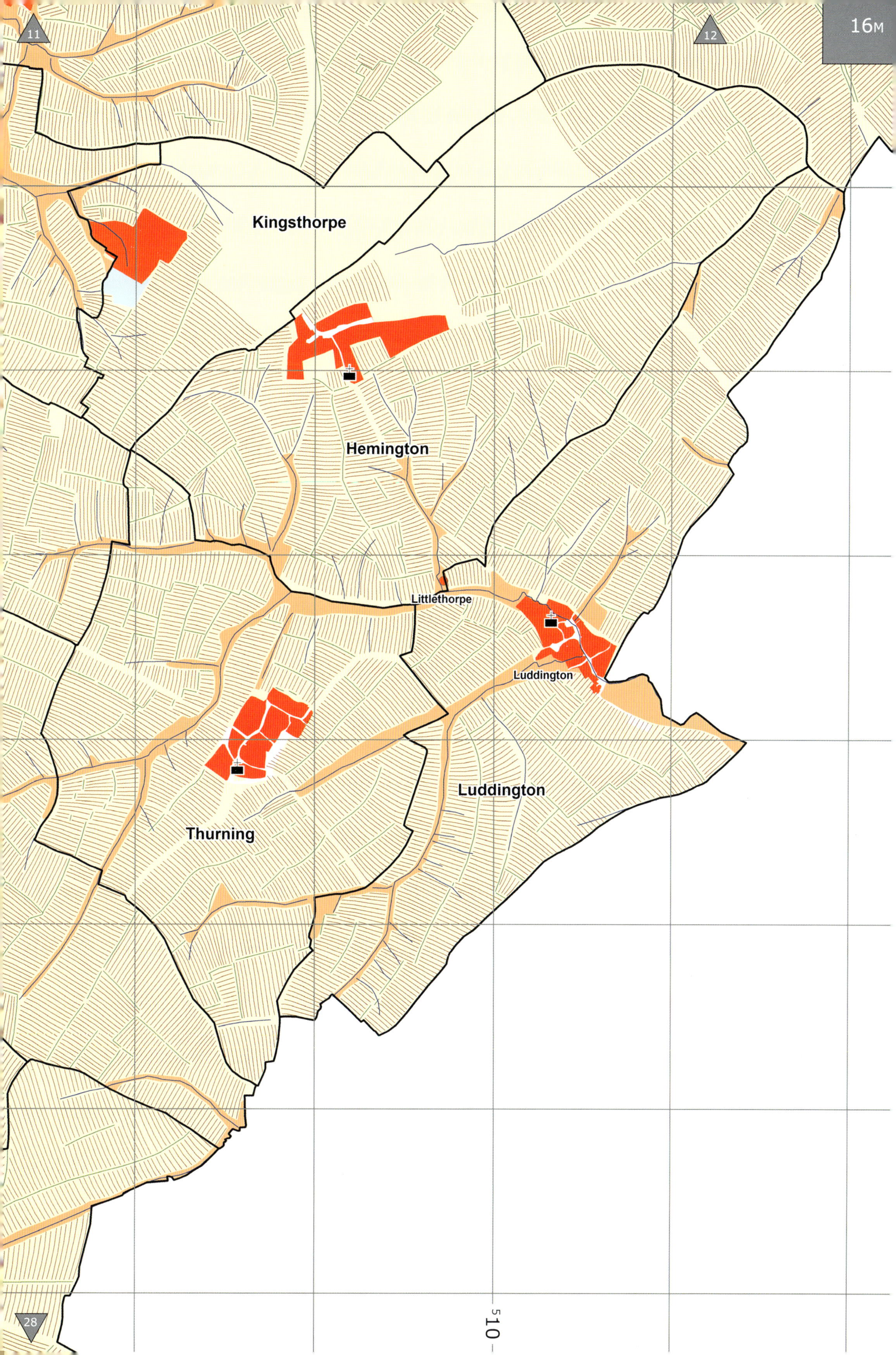
11
12
Kingsthorpe
Hemington
Littlethorpe
Luddington
Luddington
Thurning
28
510

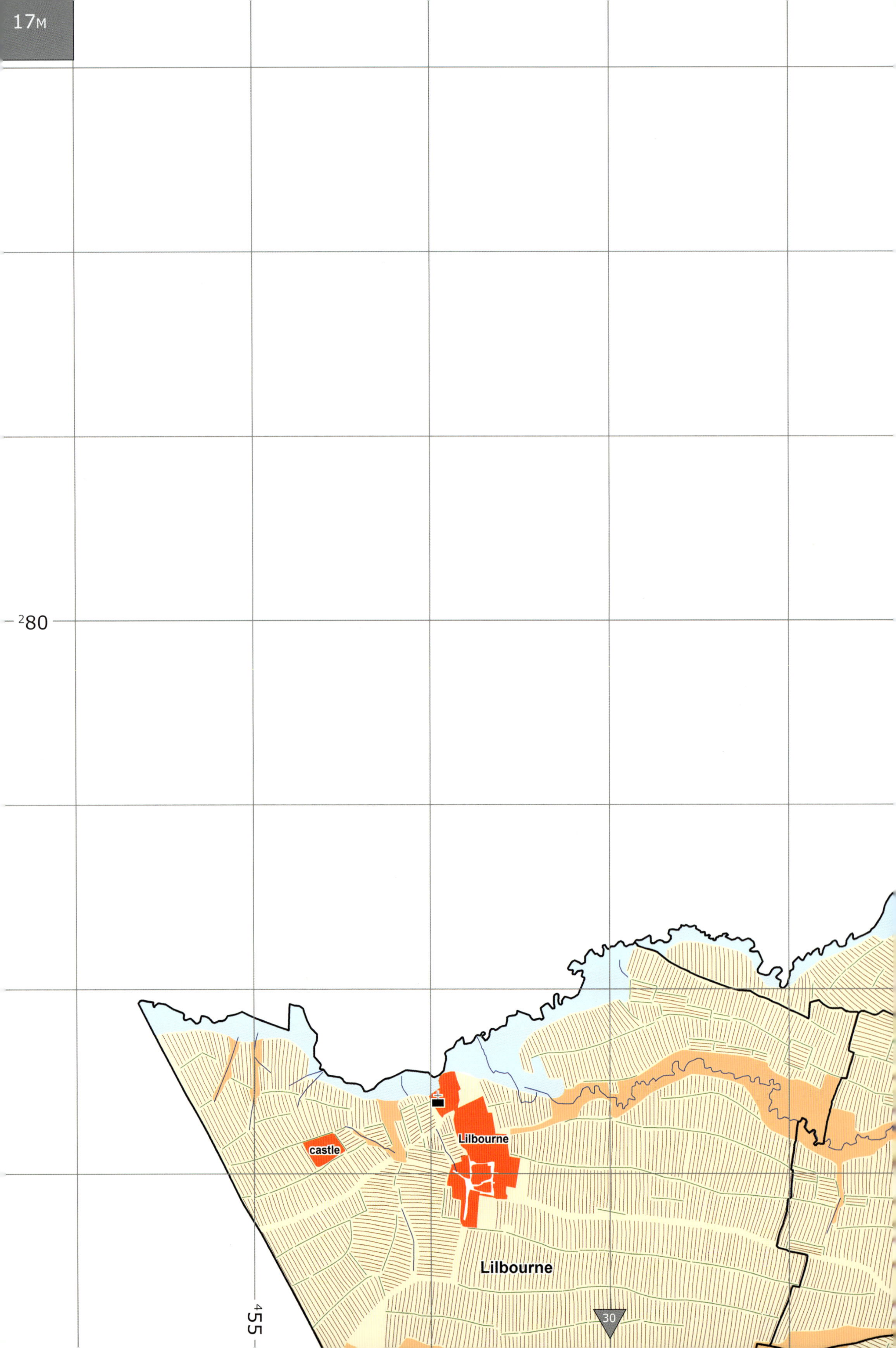

²80
castle
Lilbourne
Lilbourne
⁴55
30

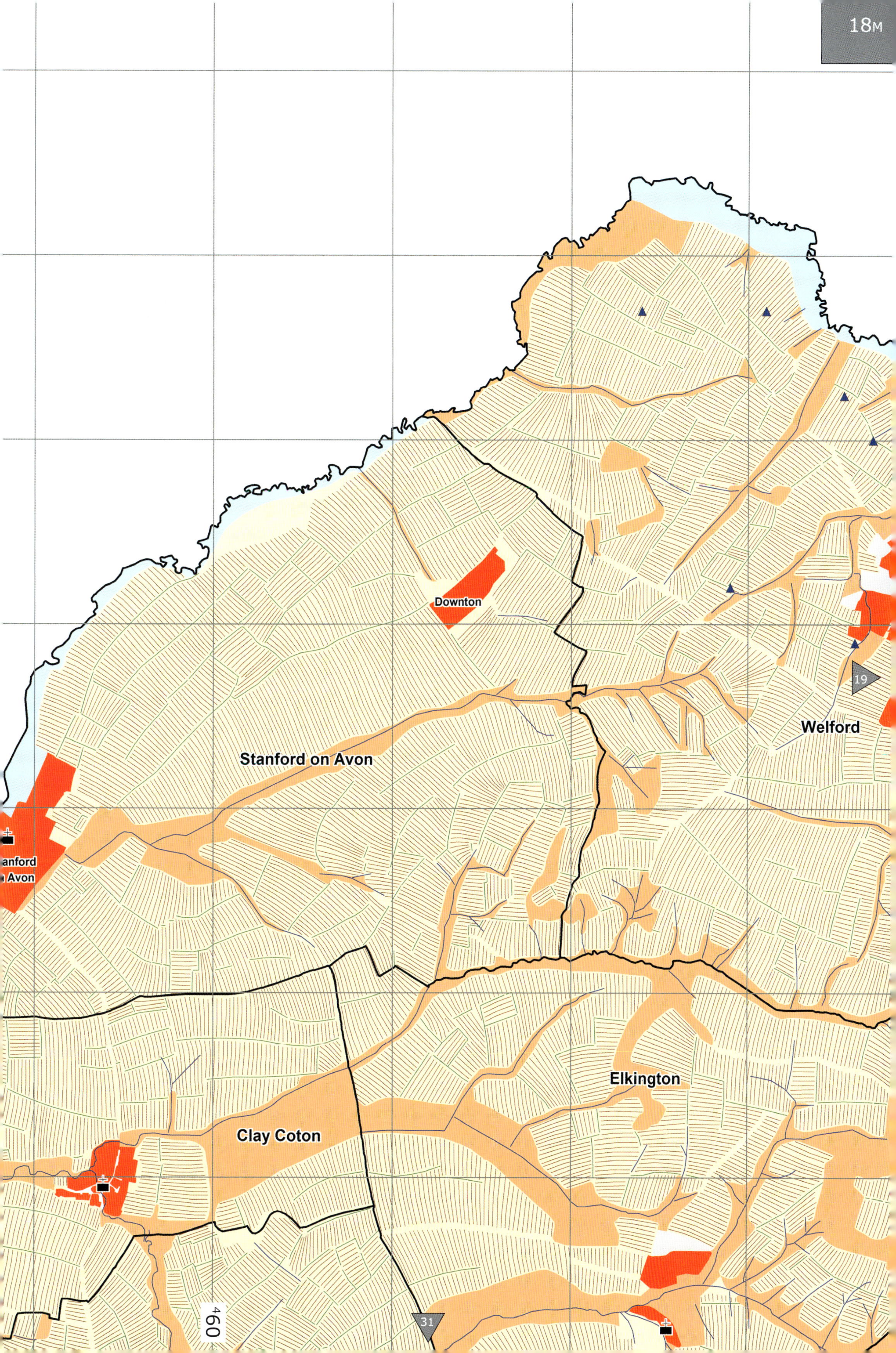
Downton
Stanford on Avon
anford
Avon
Welford
19
Elkington
Clay Coton
460
31

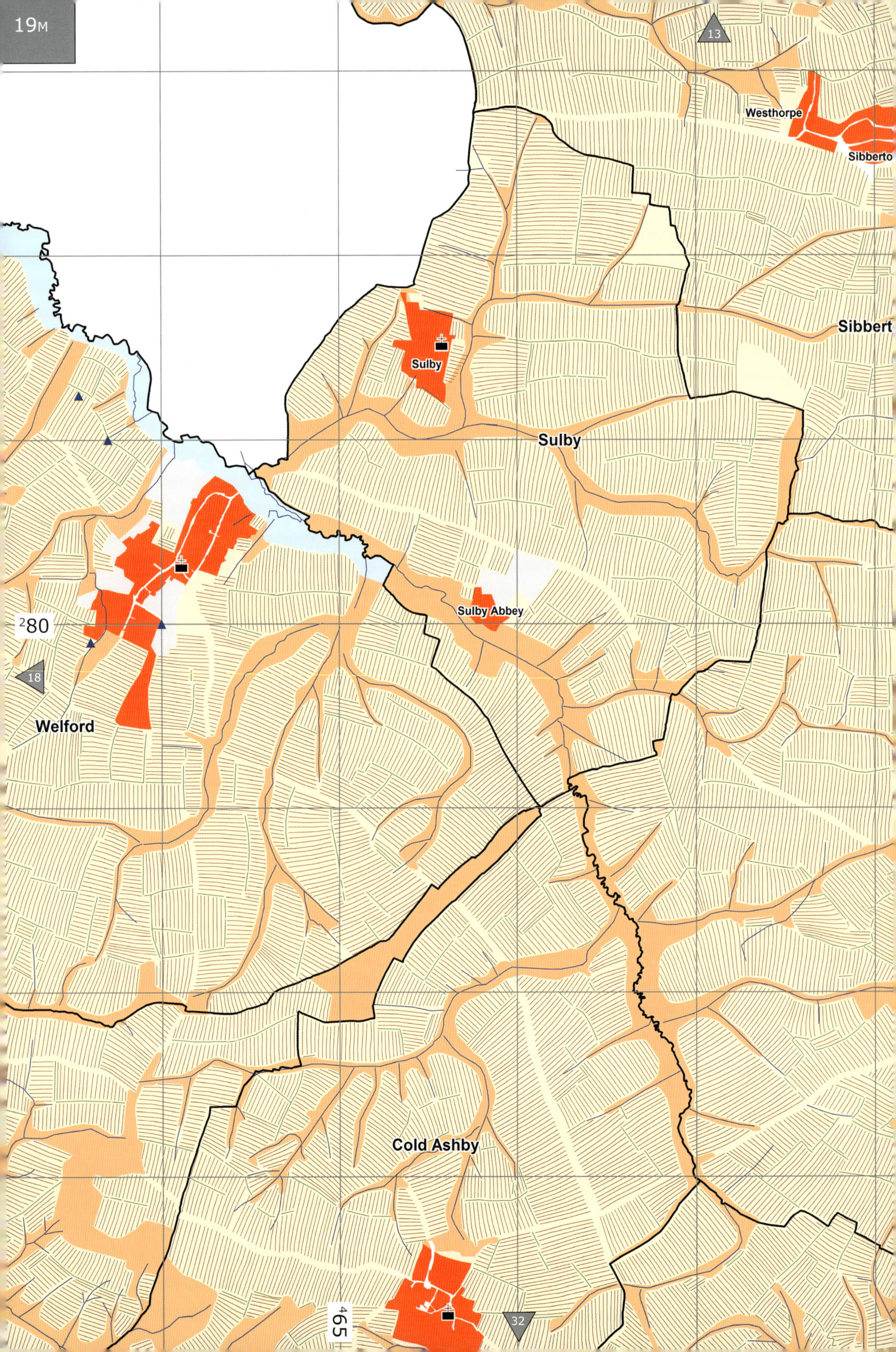
13
Westhorpe
Sibberto
Sibbert
Sulby
Sulby
Sulby Abbey
280
18
Welford
Cold Ashby
465
32

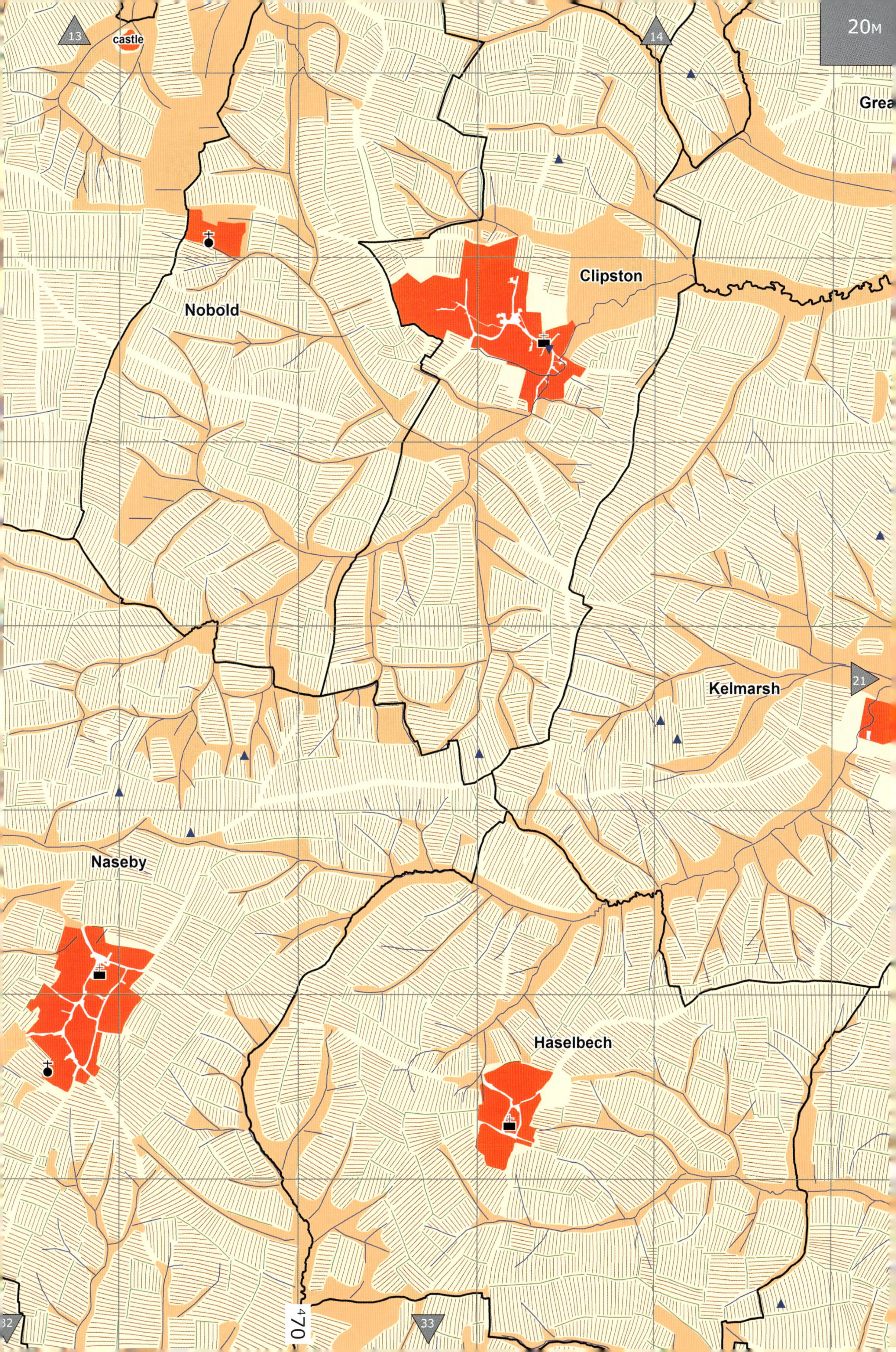

20M
13
castle
14
Grea
Nobold
Clipston
21
Kelmarsh
Naseby
Haselbech
32
470
33

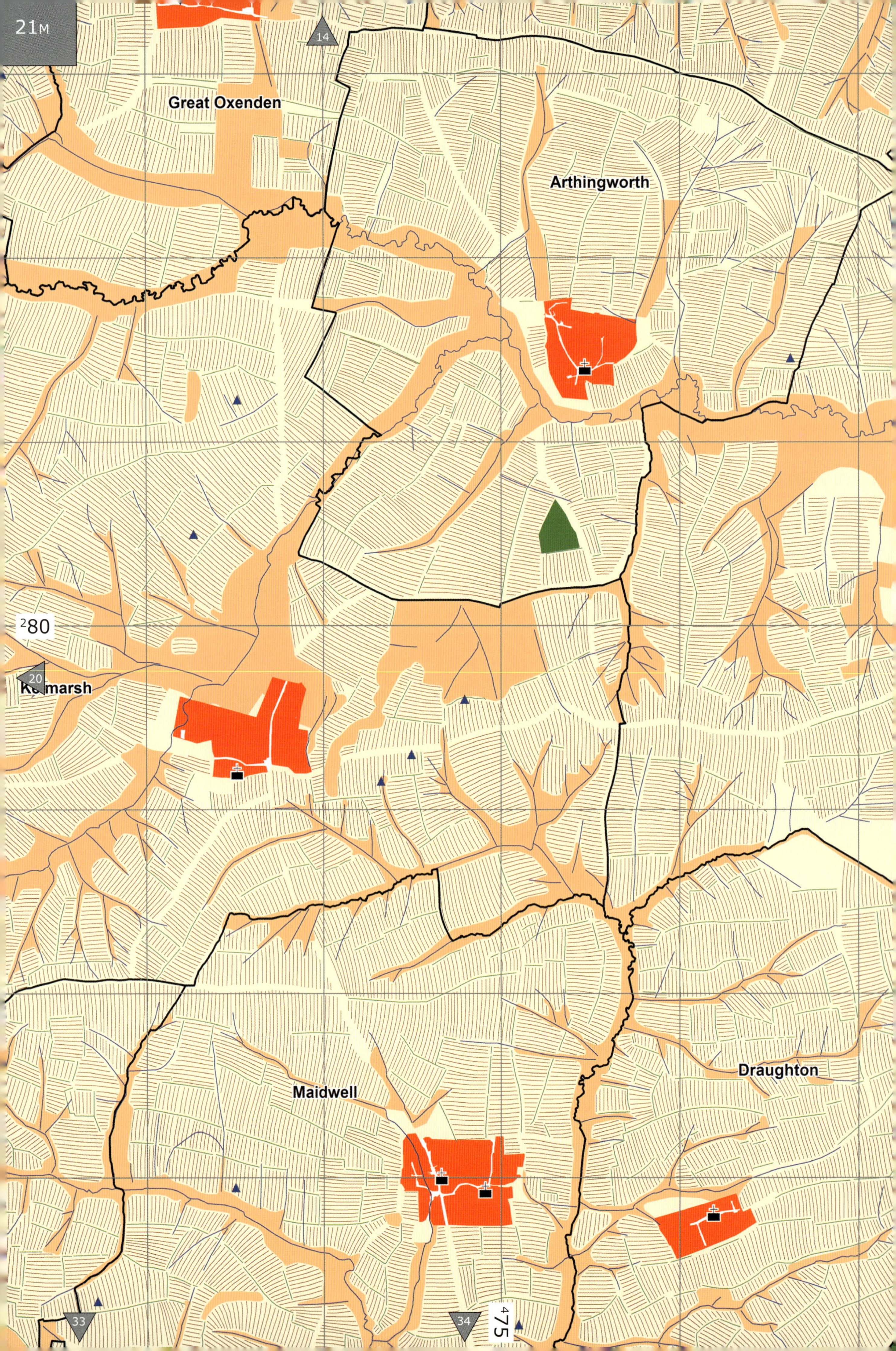
14
Great Oxenden
Arthingworth
280
20
Kelmarsh
Maidwell
Draughton
33
34
475

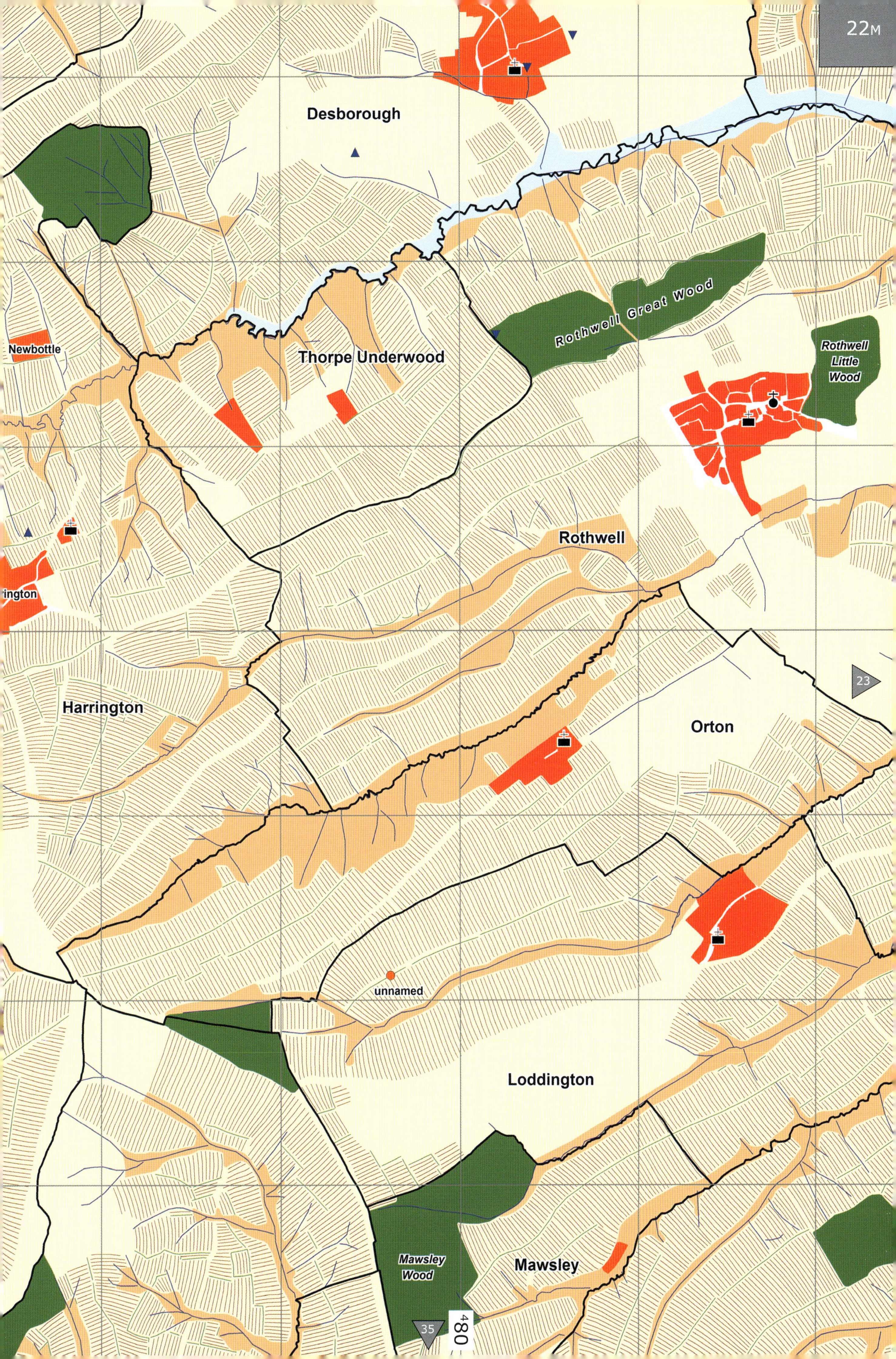

Desborough
Newbottle
Thorpe Underwood
Rothwell Great Wood
Rothwell Little Wood
Rothwell
ington
Harrington
Orton
23
unnamed
Loddington
Mawsley Wood
Mawsley
35
480

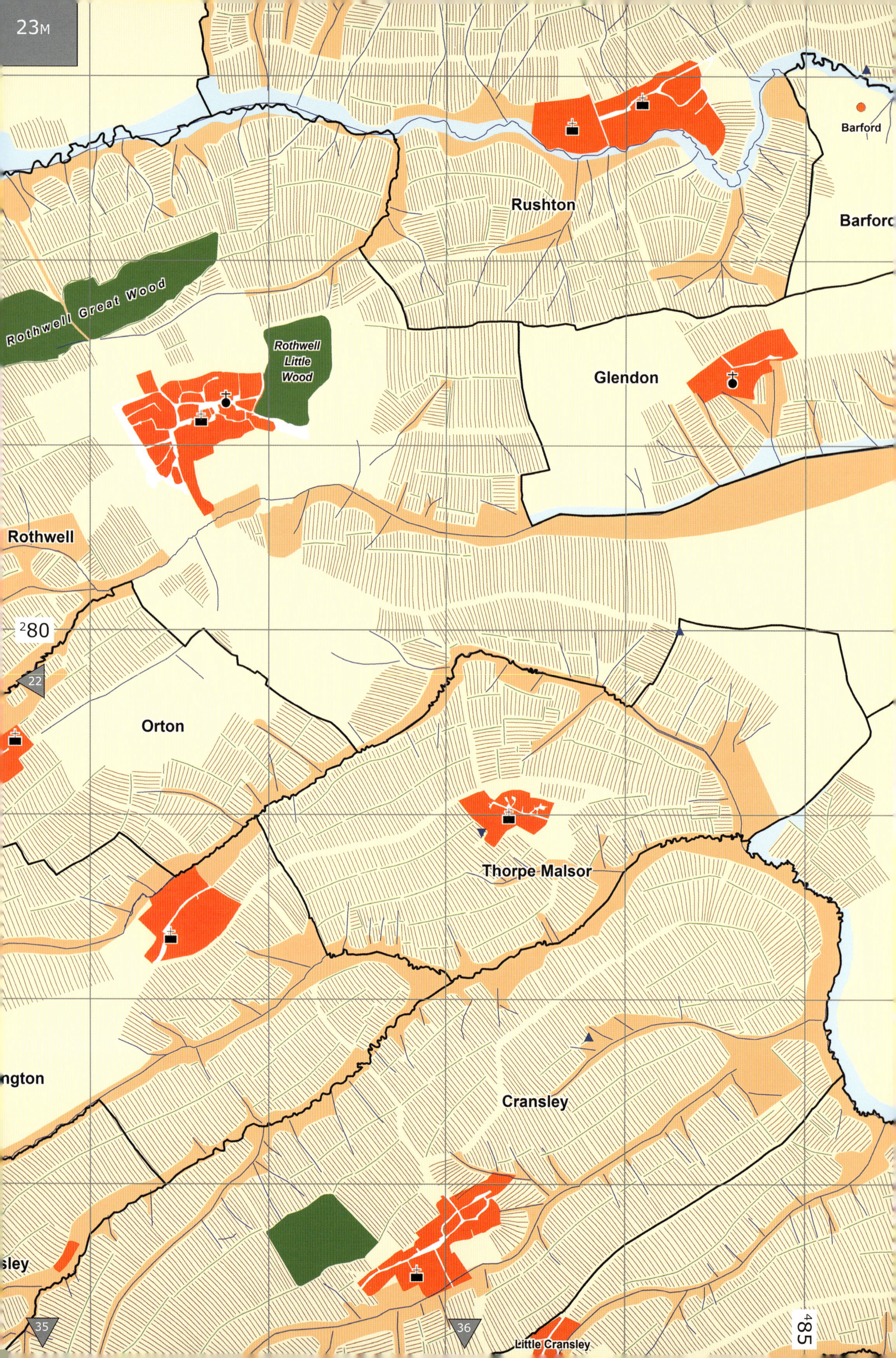
Barford
Rushton
Barford
Rothwell Great Wood
Rothwell Little Wood
Glendon
Rothwell
280
22
Orton
Thorpe Malsor
ngton
Cransley
sley
35
36
Little Cransley
485

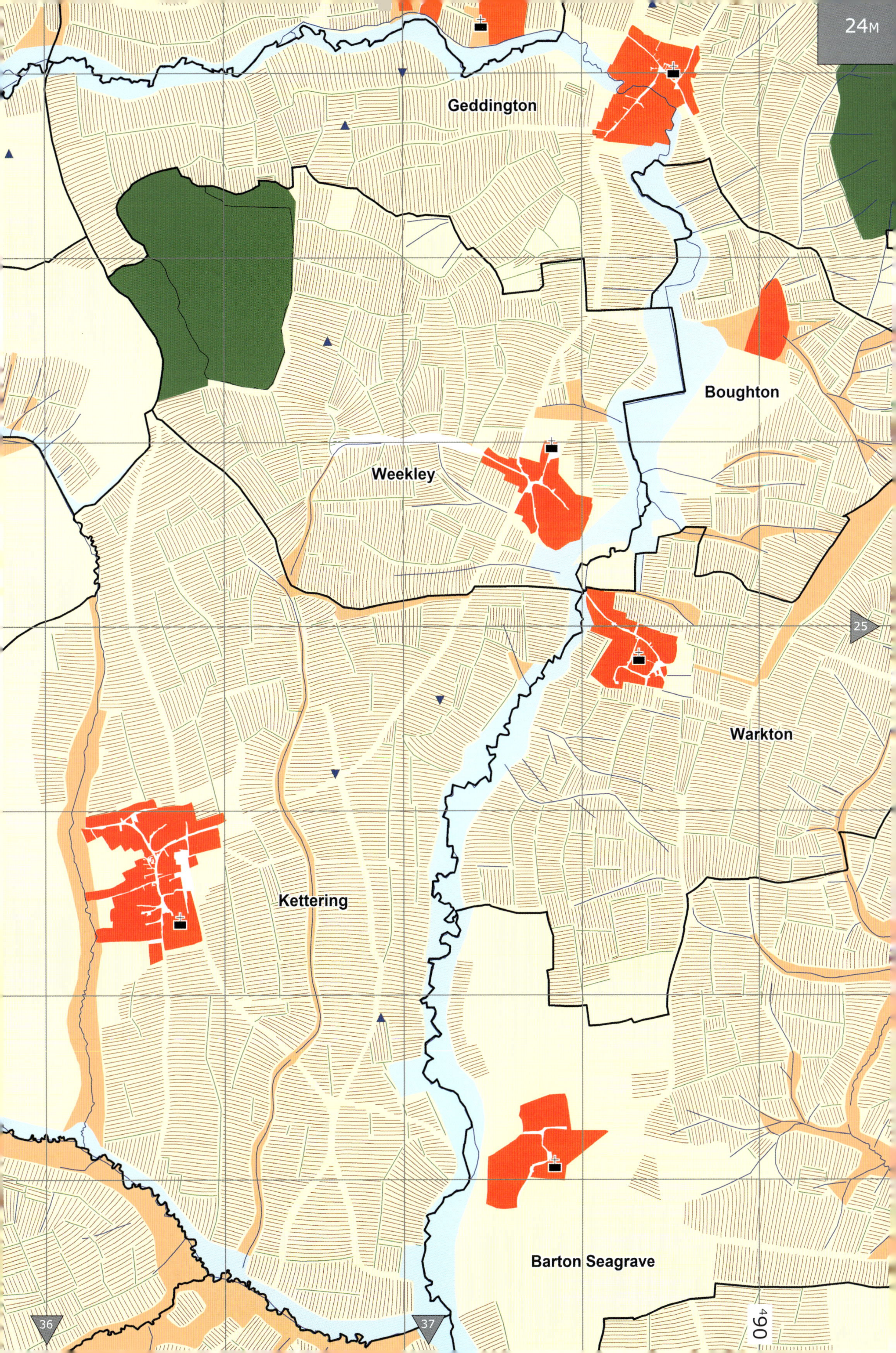
Geddington
Boughton
Weekley
Warkton
Kettering
Barton Seagrave
25
36
37
490

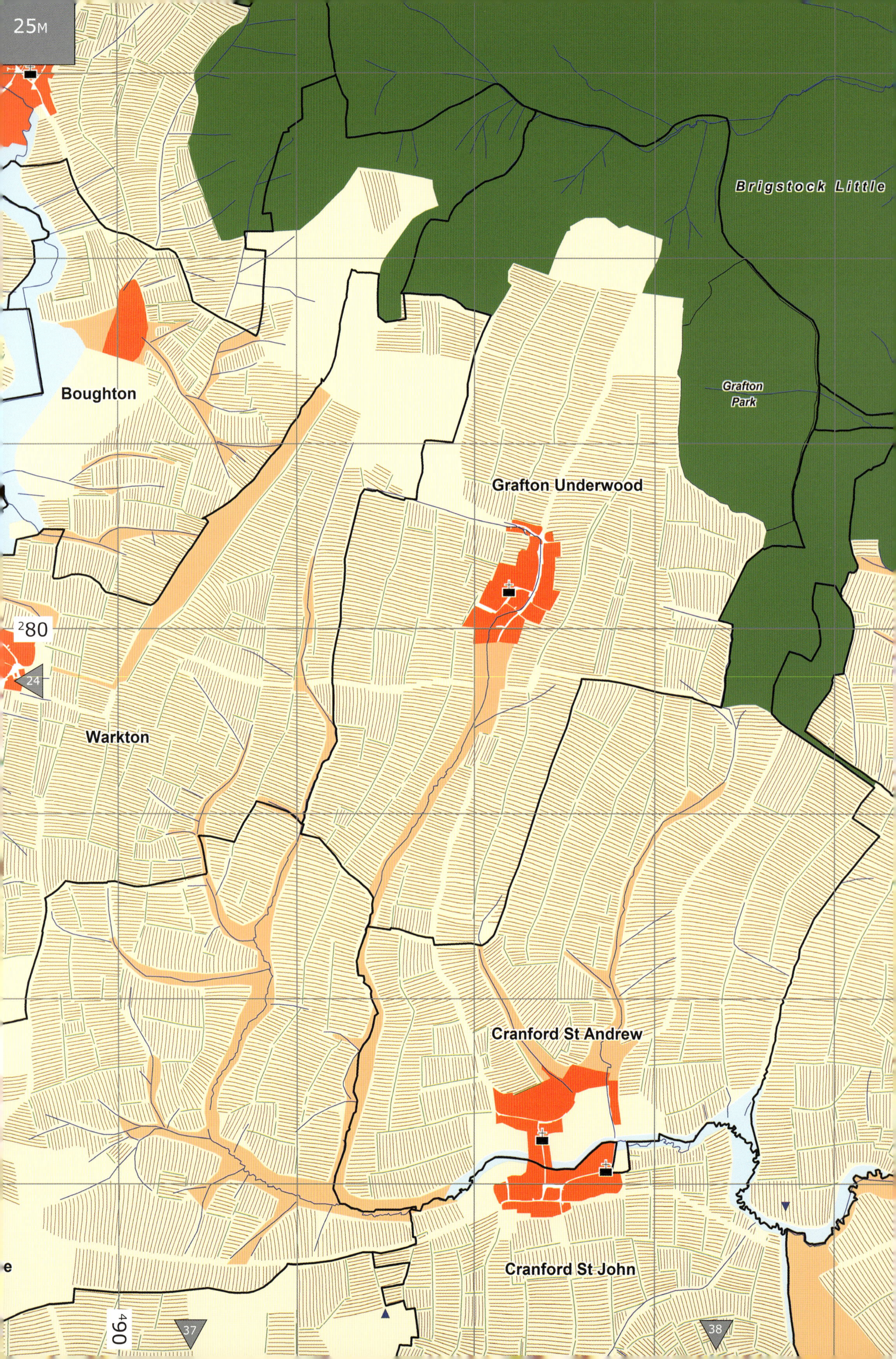

25M
Brigstock Little
Boughton
Grafton Park
Grafton Underwood
280
24
Warkton
Cranford St Andrew
Cranford St John
e
490
37
38

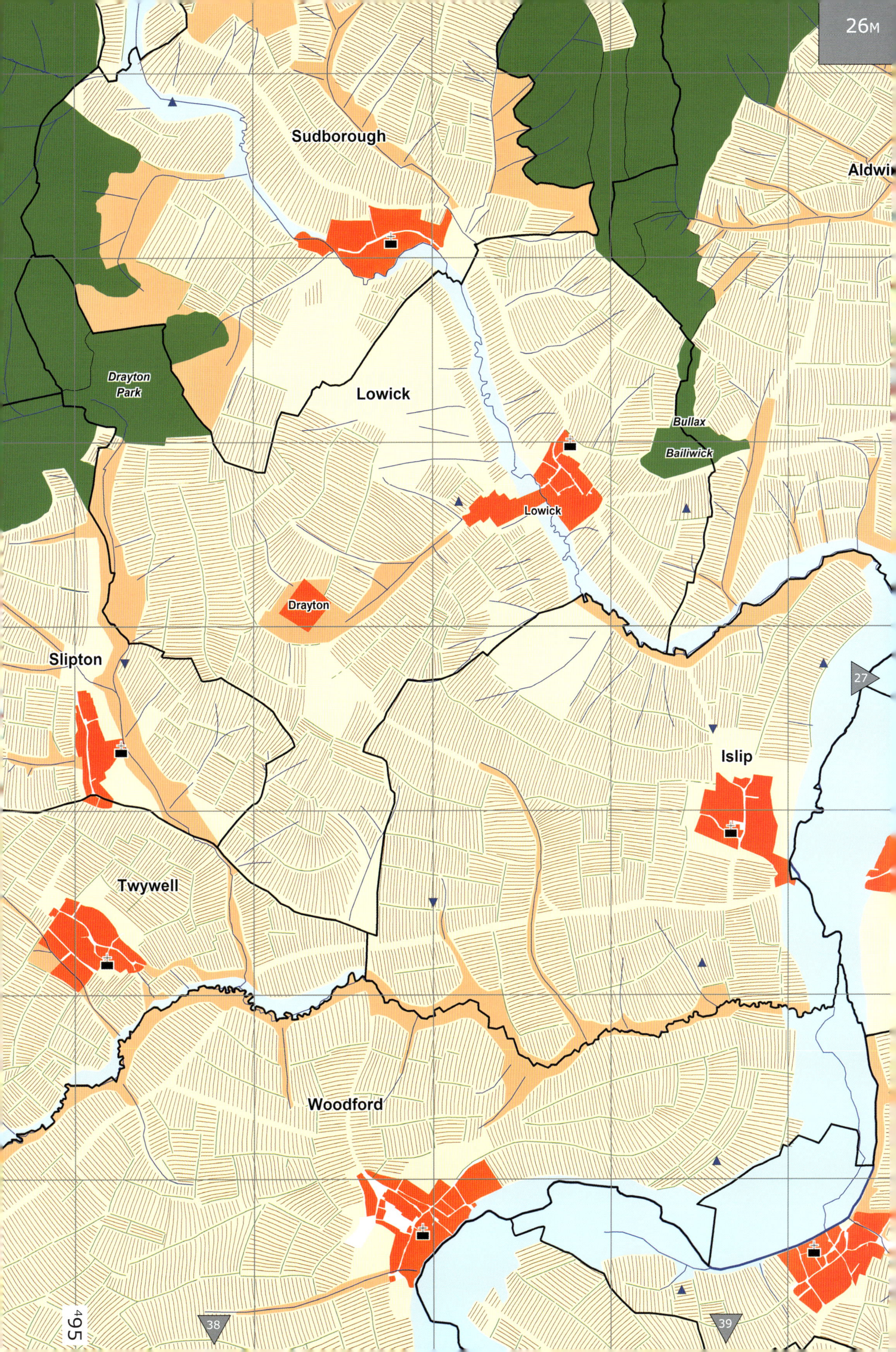
26M
Sudborough
Aldwi
Drayton
Park
Lowick
Bullax
Bailiwick
Lowick
Drayton
Slipton
27
Islip
Twywell
Woodford
38
39

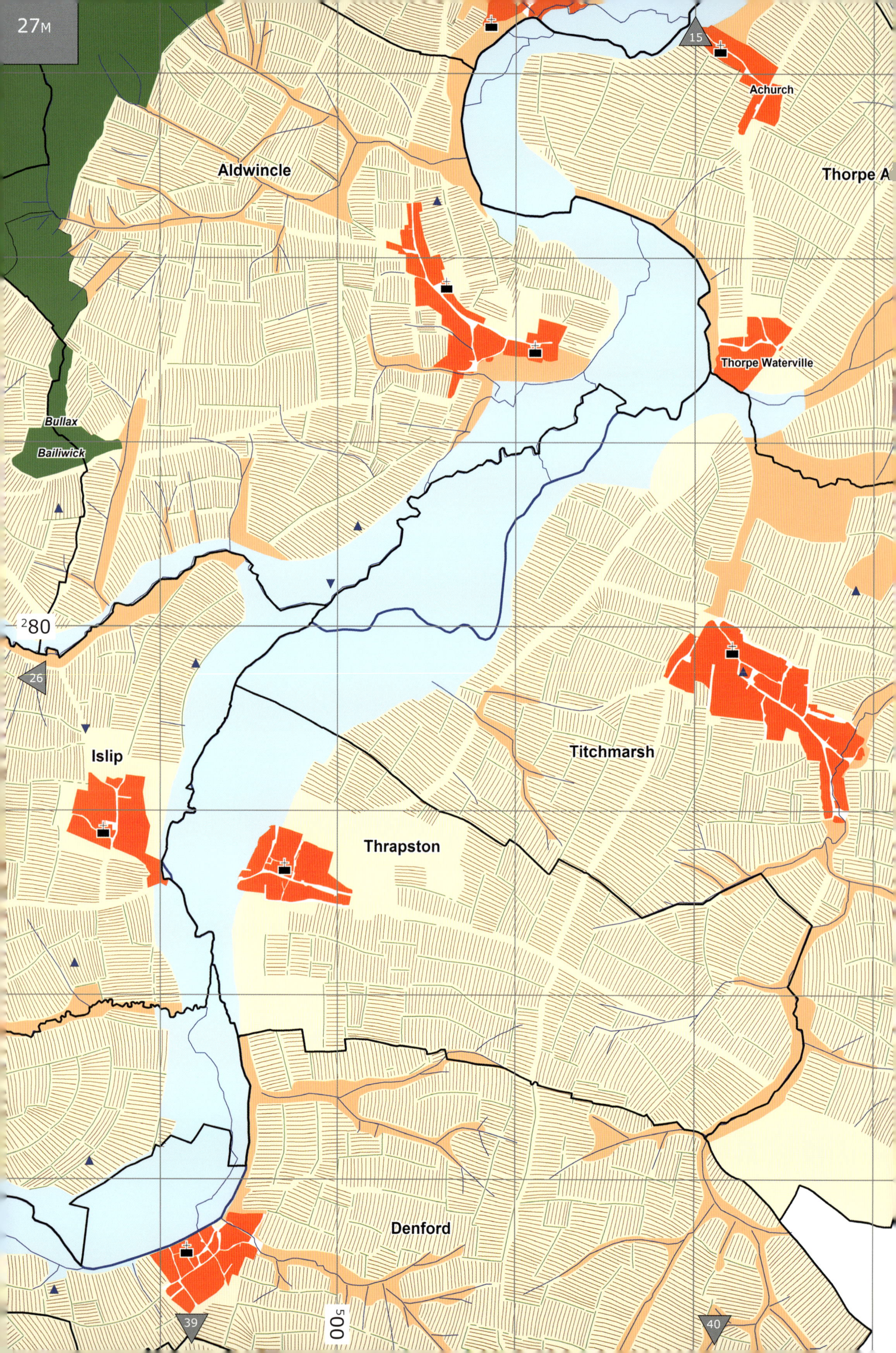

27M
Achurch
Aldwincle
Thorpe A
Thorpe Waterville
Bullax
Bailiwick
280
Islip
Titchmarsh
Thrapston
Denford
500
15
26
39
40

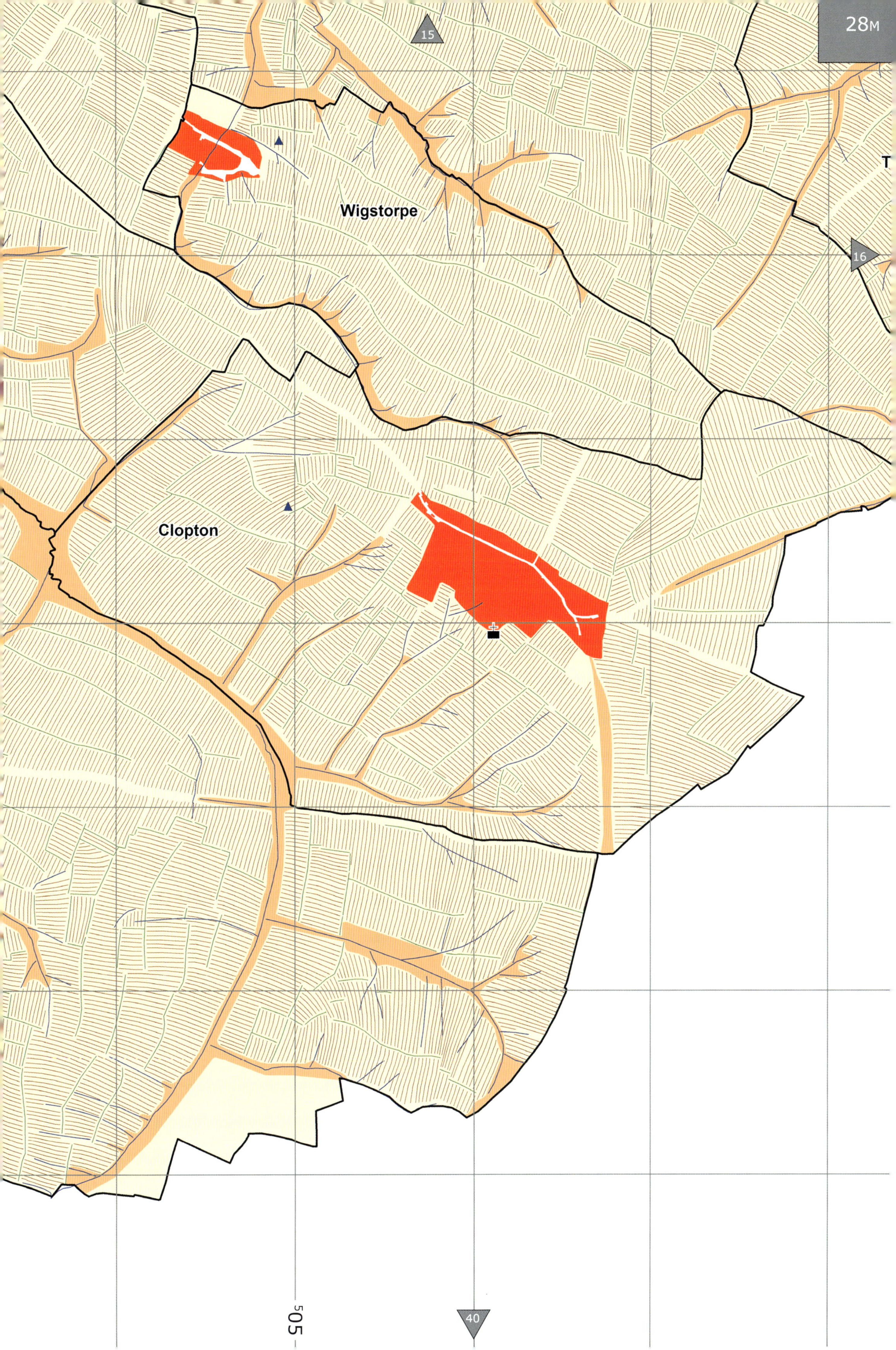
28M
15
Wigstorpe
T
16
Clopton
505
40

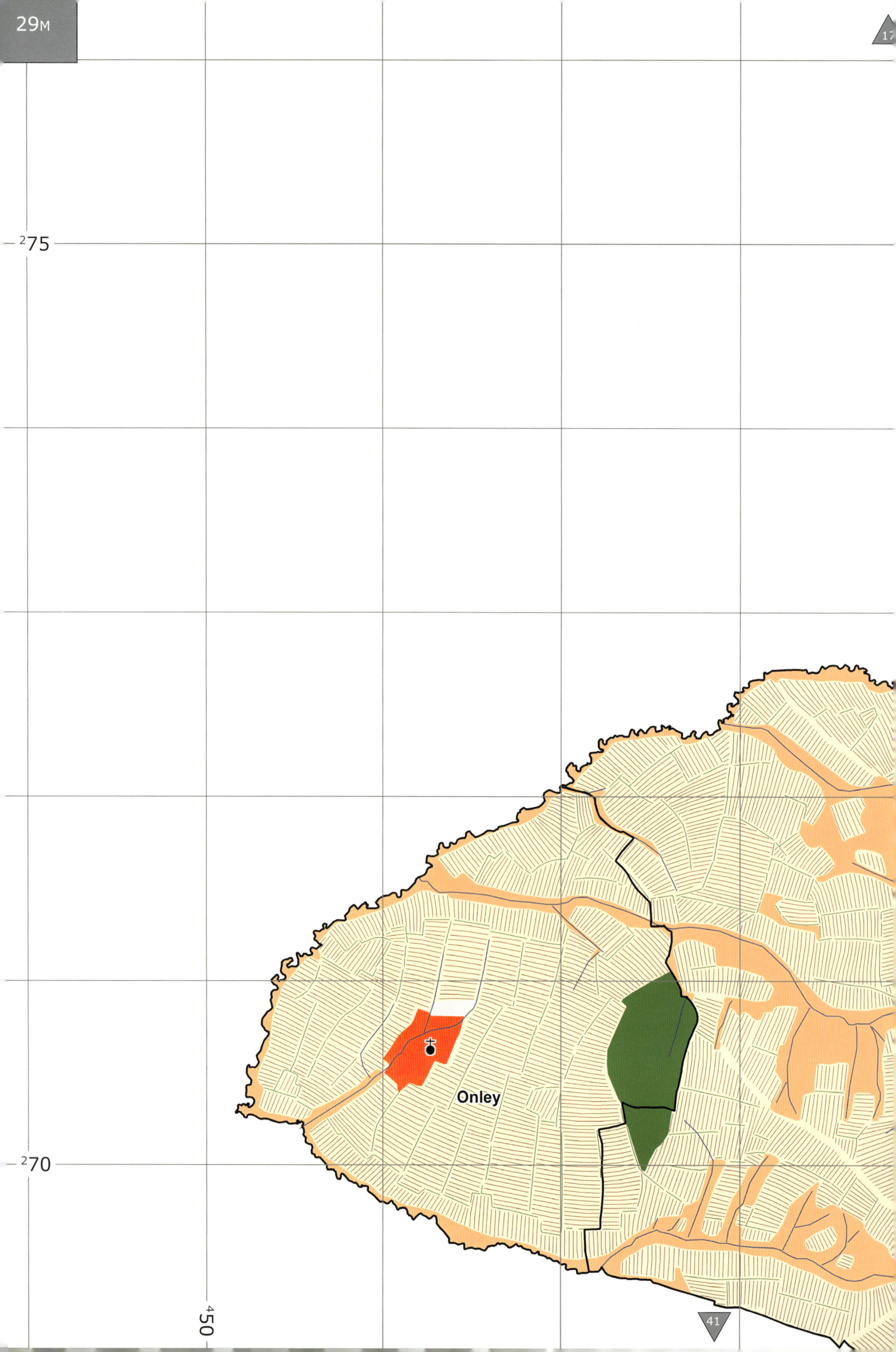
17
²75
²70
⁴50
Onley
41

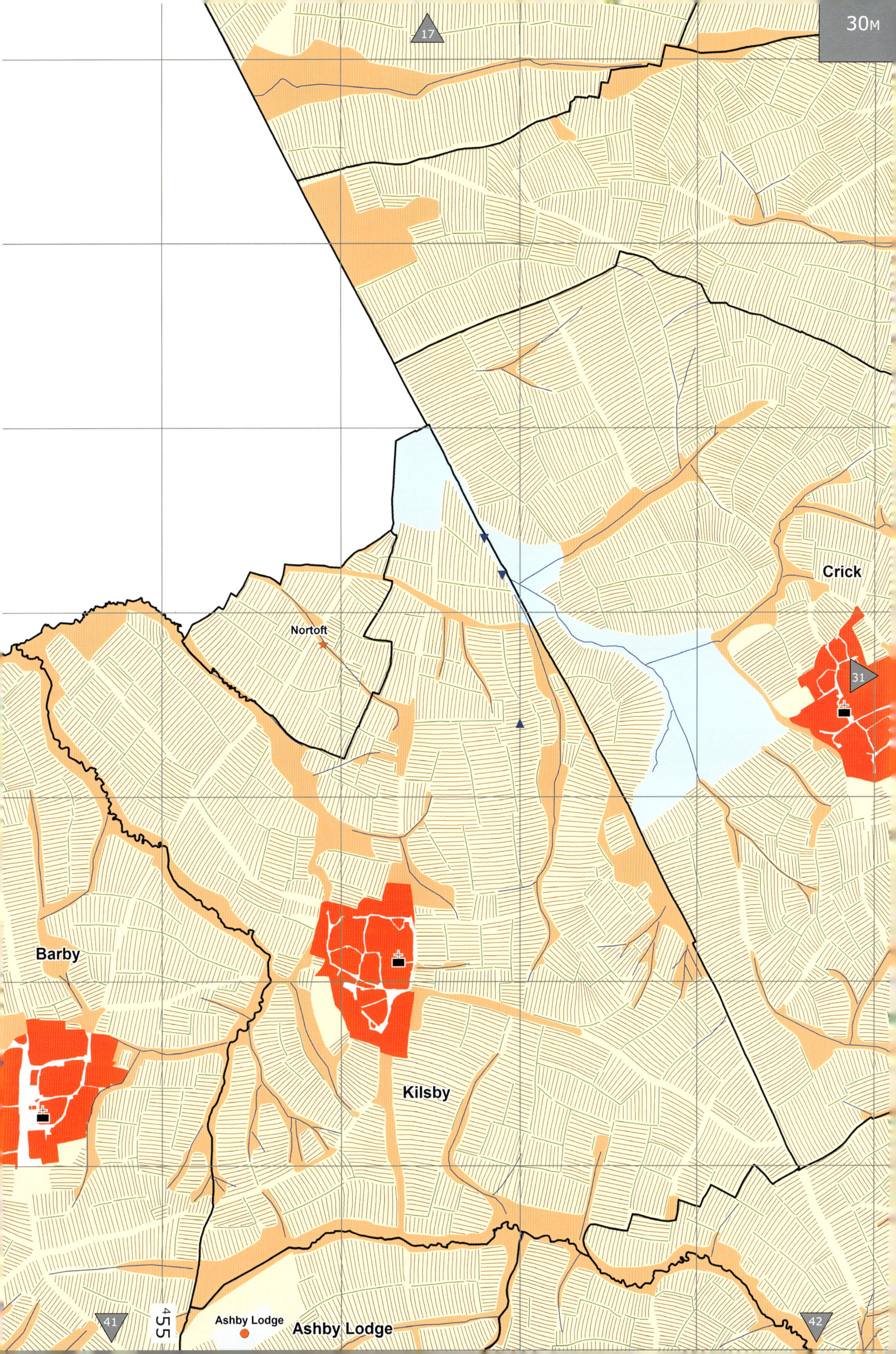
17
Crick
31
Nortoft
Barby
Kilsby
41
455
Ashby Lodge
Ashby Lodge
42

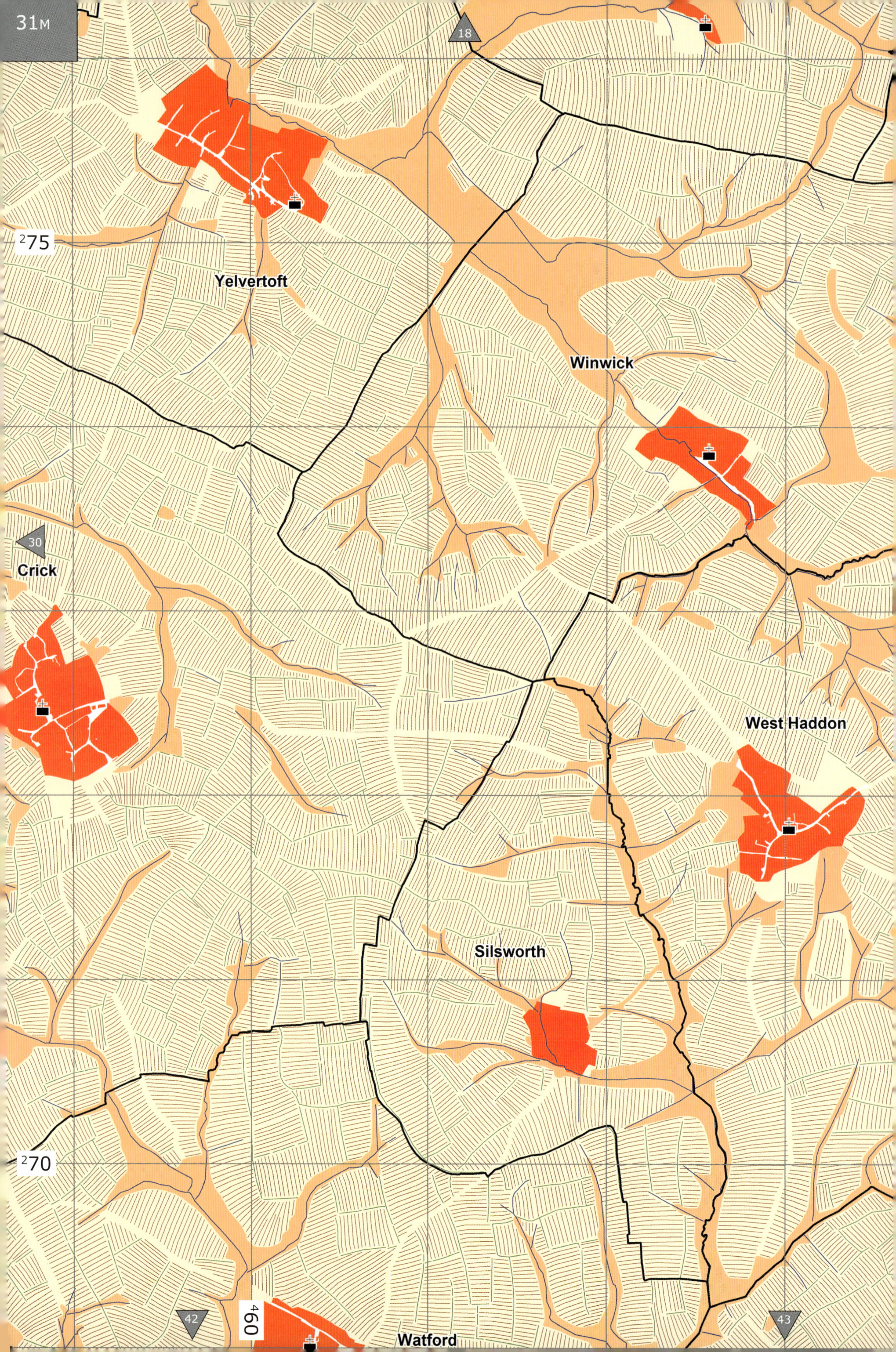

31M
18
275
Yelvertoft
Winwick
30
Crick
West Haddon
Silsworth
270
42
460
Watford
43

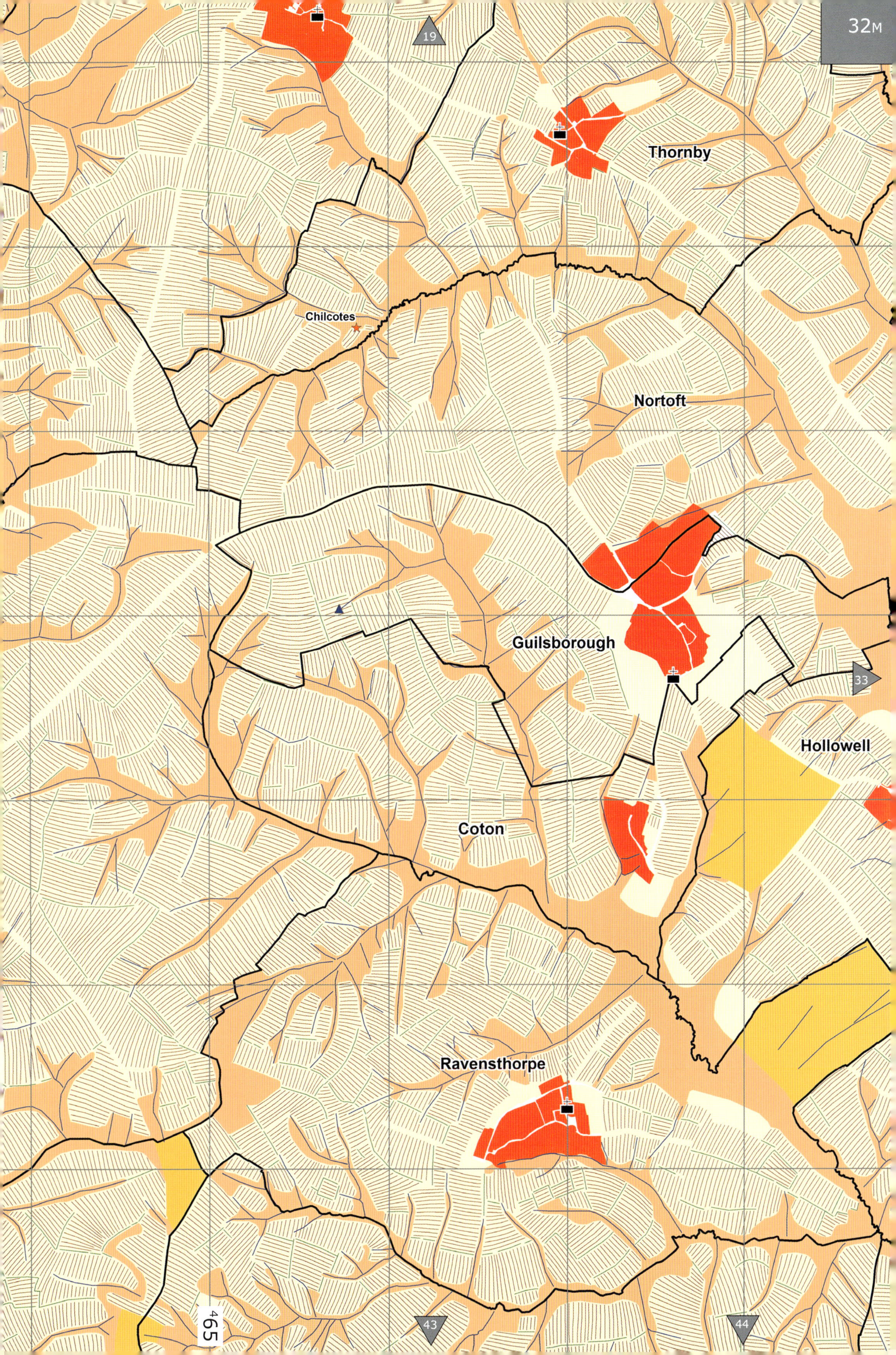
19
Thornby
Chilcotes
Nortoft
Guilsborough
33
Hollowell
Coton
Ravensthorpe
43
44

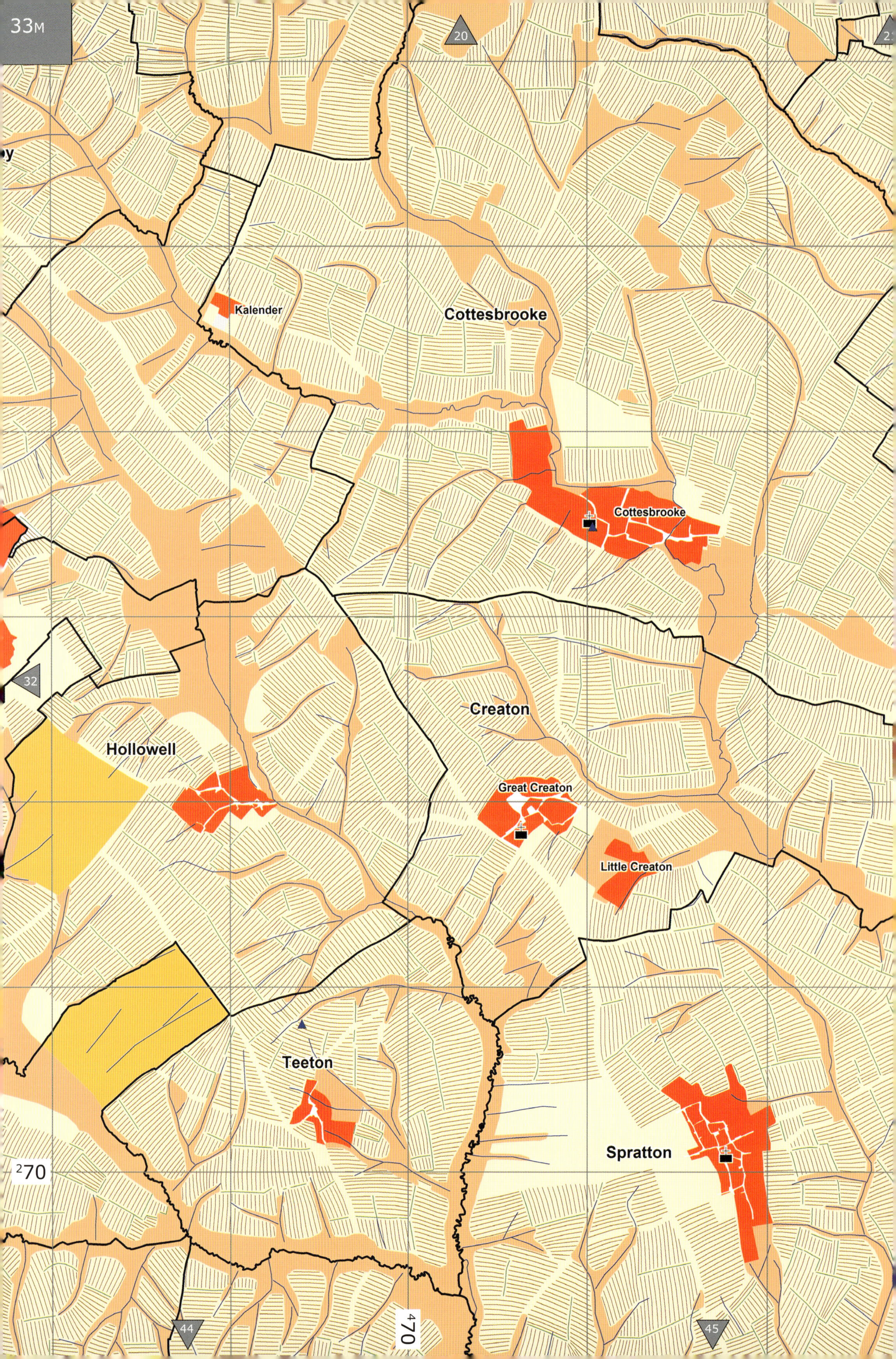
Kalender
Cottesbrooke
Cottesbrooke
Creaton
Great Creaton
Little Creaton
Hollowell
Teeton
Spratton
20
32
44
45
270
470

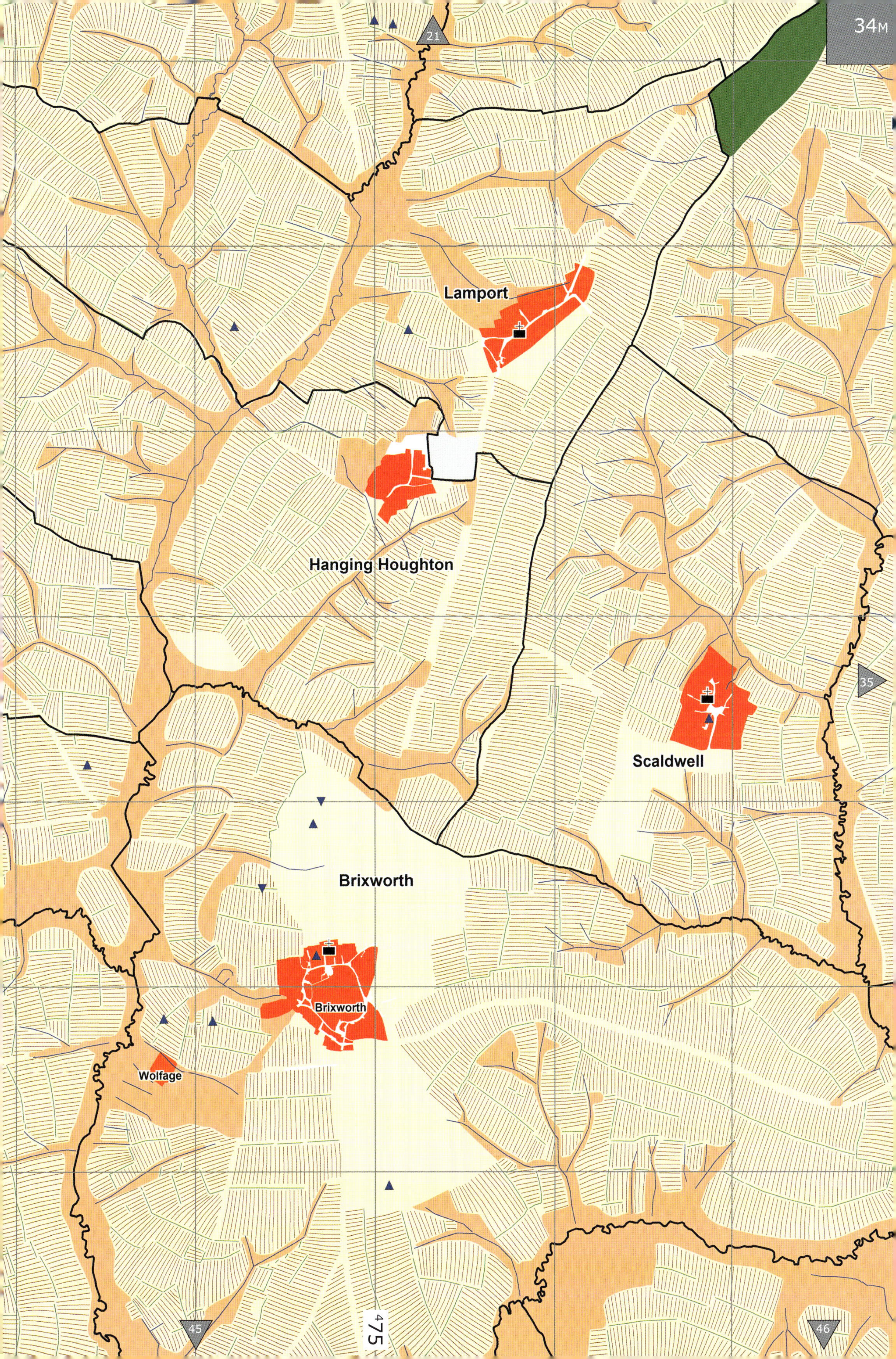
21
Lamport
Hanging Houghton
Scaldwell
35
Brixworth
Brixworth
Wolfage
45
475
46

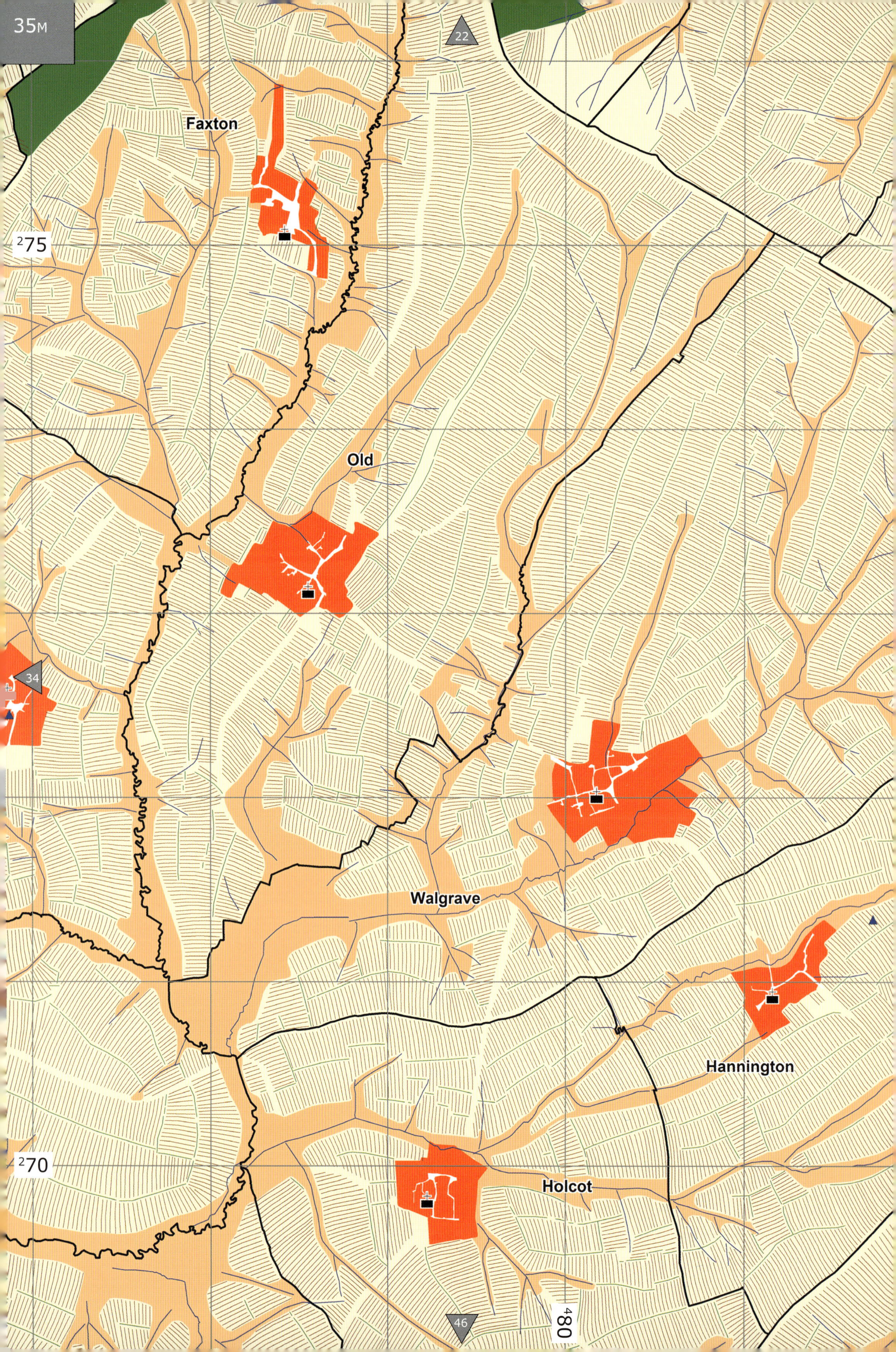
35M
22
Faxton
275
Old
34
Walgrave
Hannington
270
Holcot
46
480

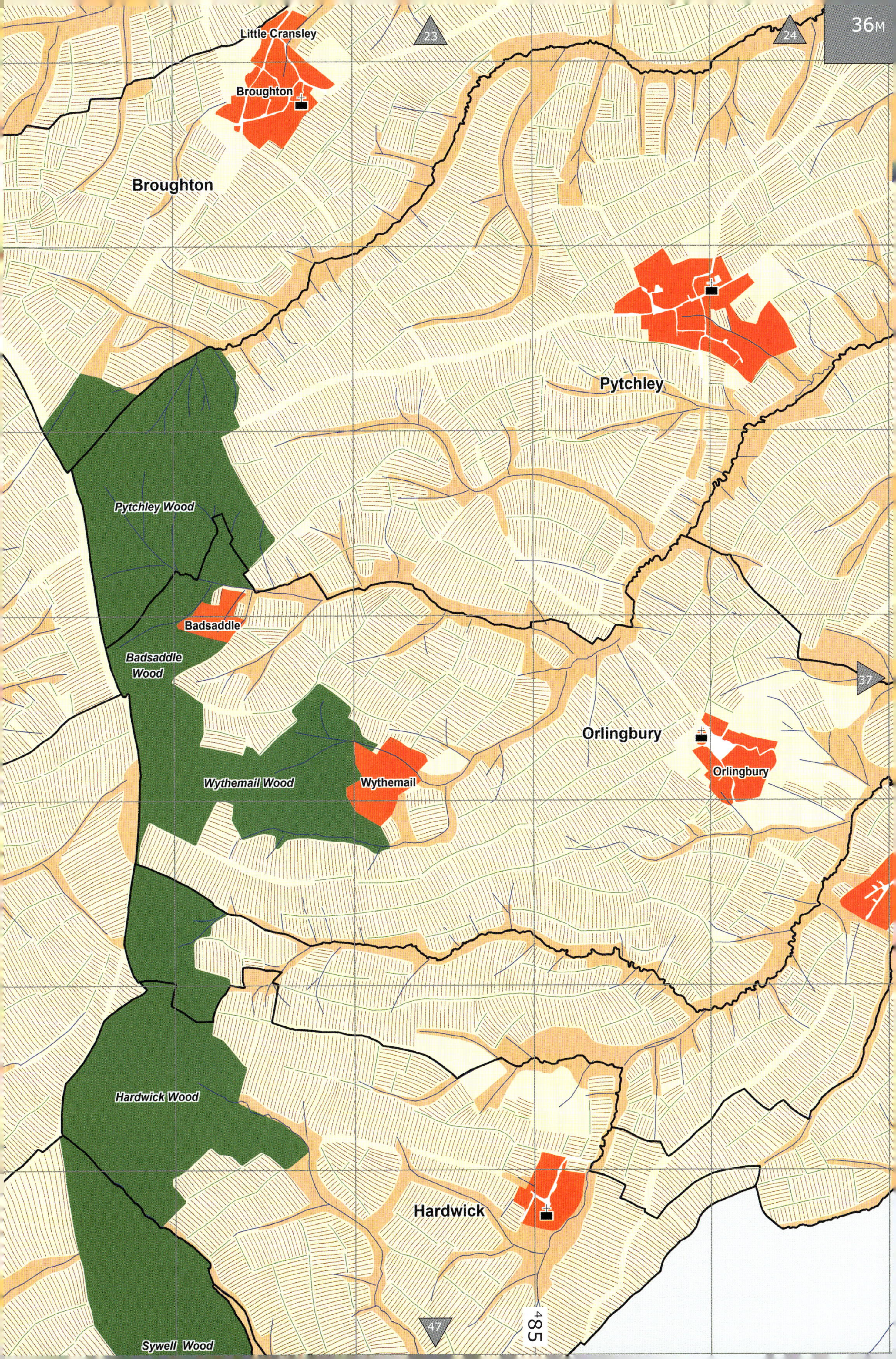

23
24
Little Cransley
Broughton
Broughton
Pytchley
Pytchley Wood
Badsaddle
Badsaddle Wood
37
Orlingbury
Orlingbury
Wythemail Wood
Wythemail
Hardwick Wood
Hardwick
Sywell Wood
47
485

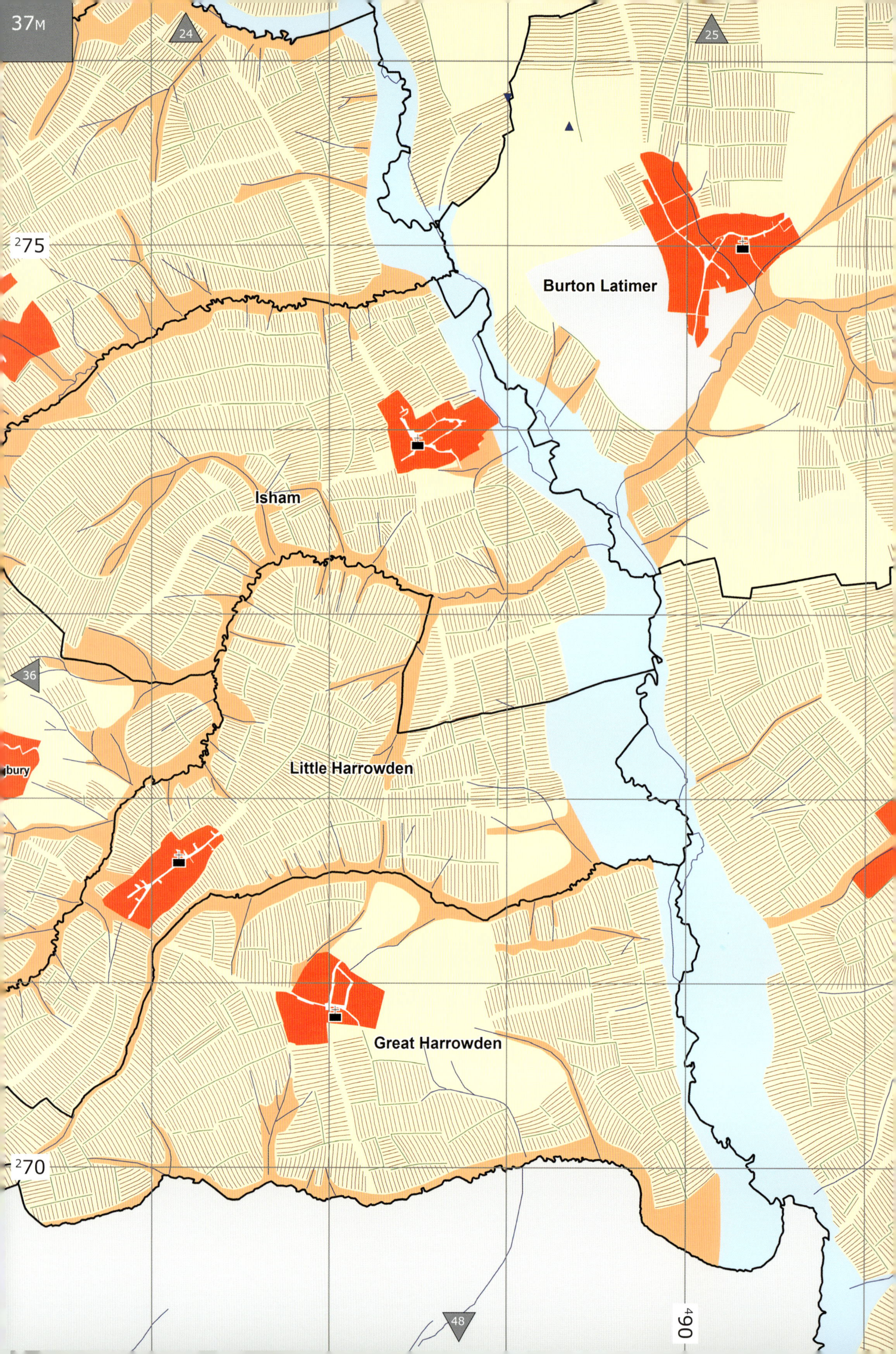
24
25
275
Burton Latimer
Isham
36
bury
Little Harrowden
Great Harrowden
270
48
490

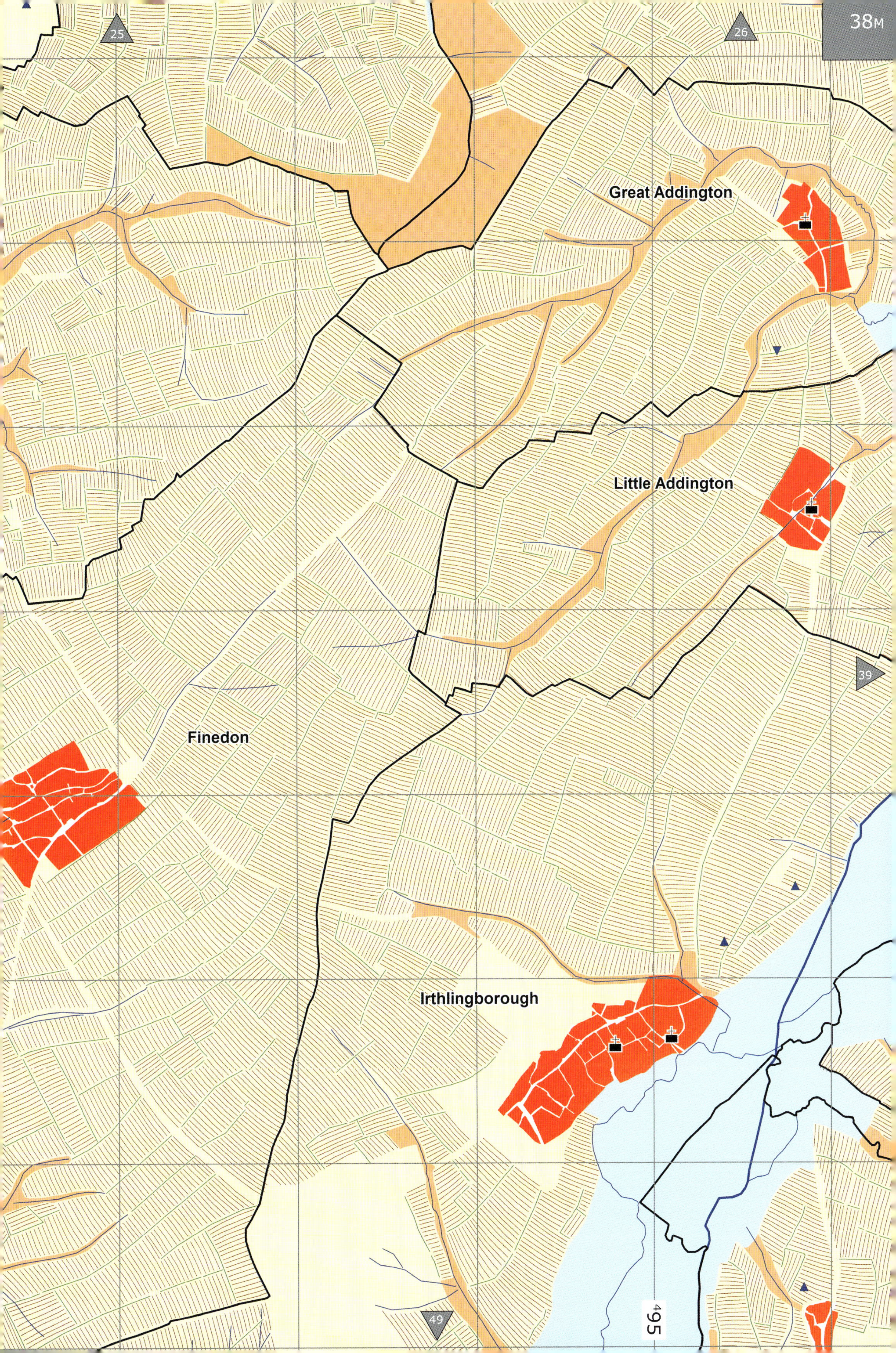
25
26
Great Addington
Little Addington
39
Finedon
Irthlingborough
49

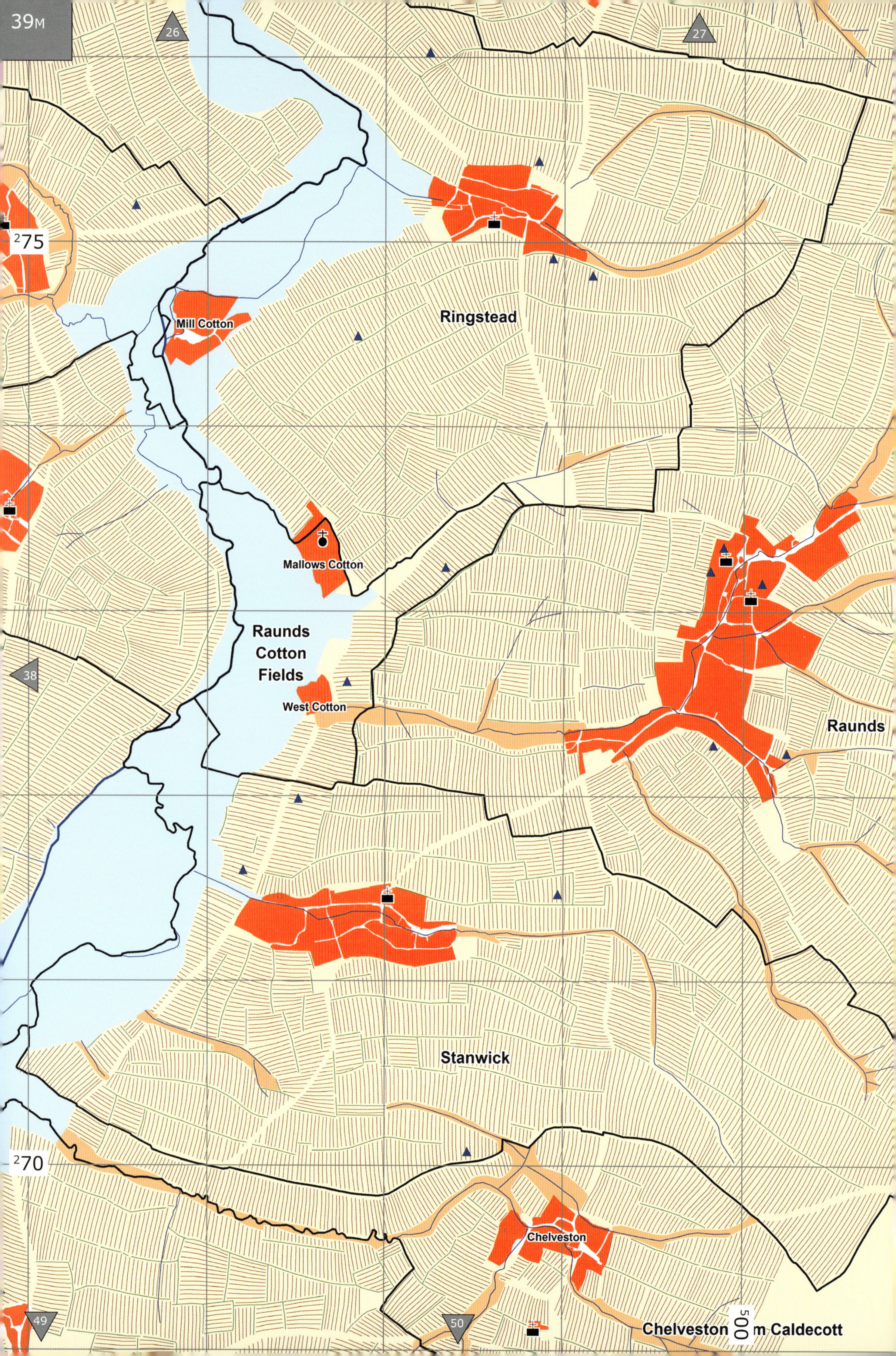
26
27
275
Mill Cotton
Ringstead
Mallows Cotton
Raunds
Cotton
Fields
38
West Cotton
Raunds
Stanwick
270
Chelveston
49
50
Chelveston
500
m Caldecott

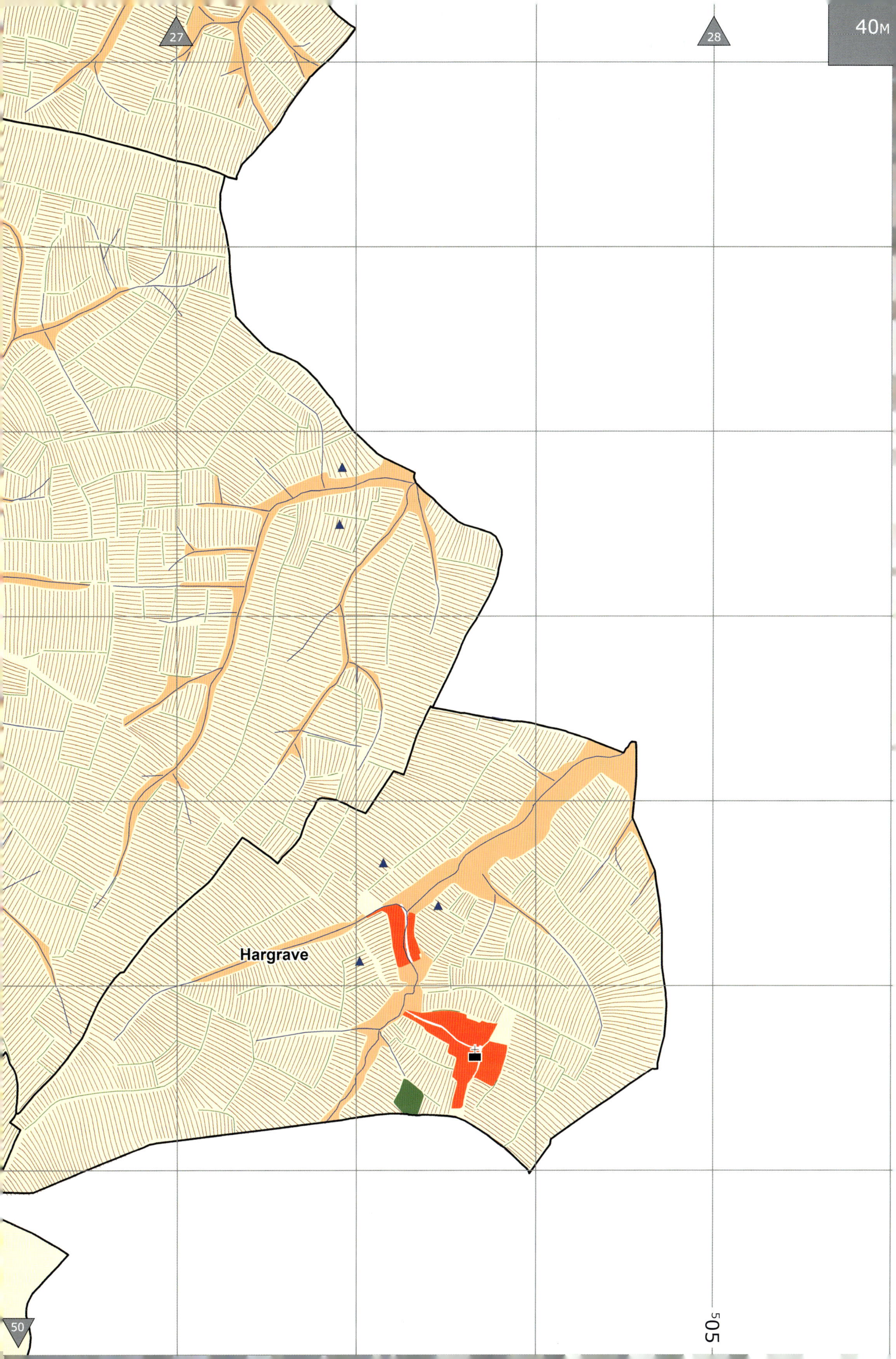
40M
27
28
Hargrave
50
505

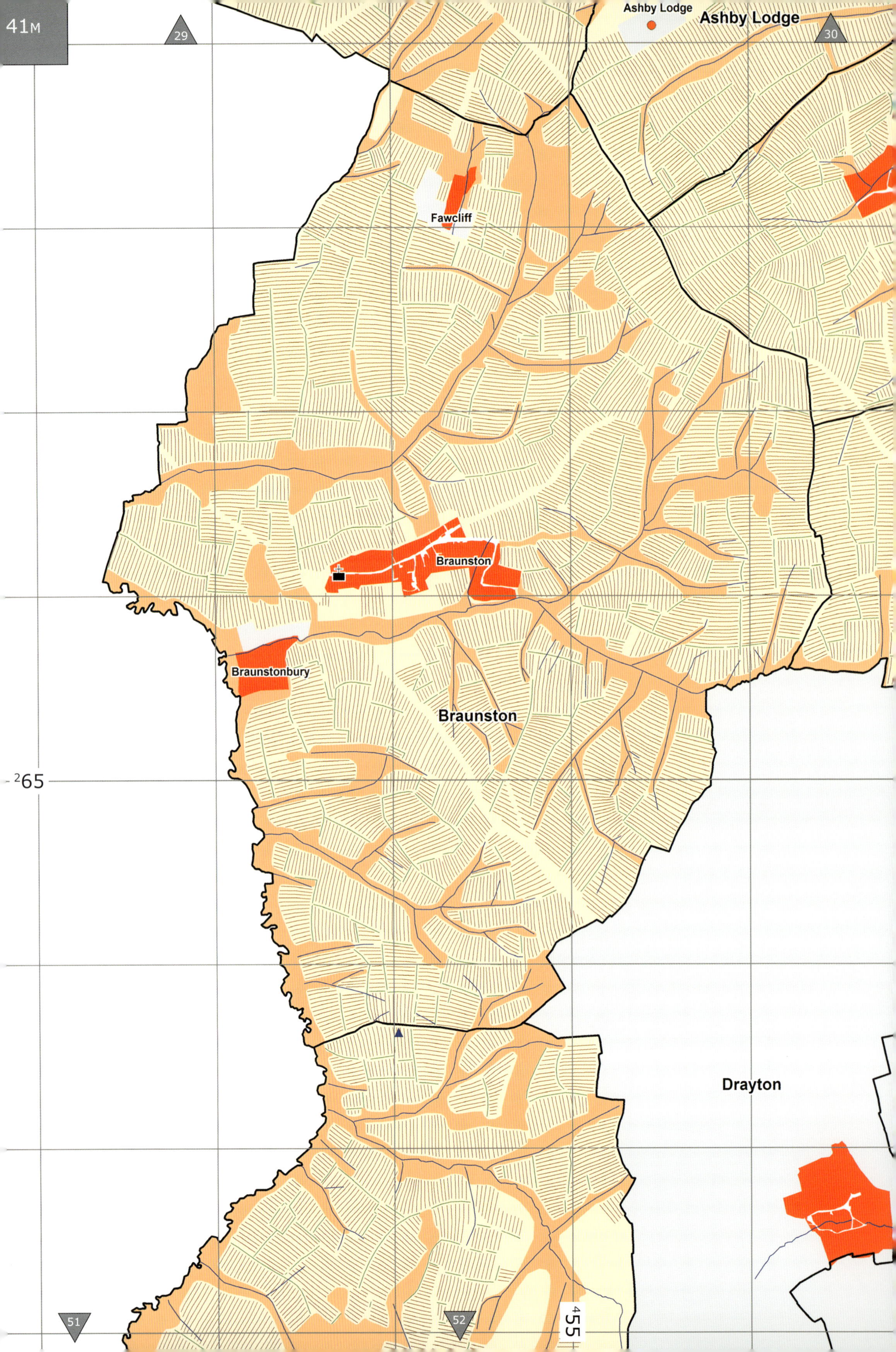

29
Ashby Lodge
Ashby Lodge
30
Fawcliff
Braunston
Braunstonbury
Braunston
265
Drayton
51
52
455

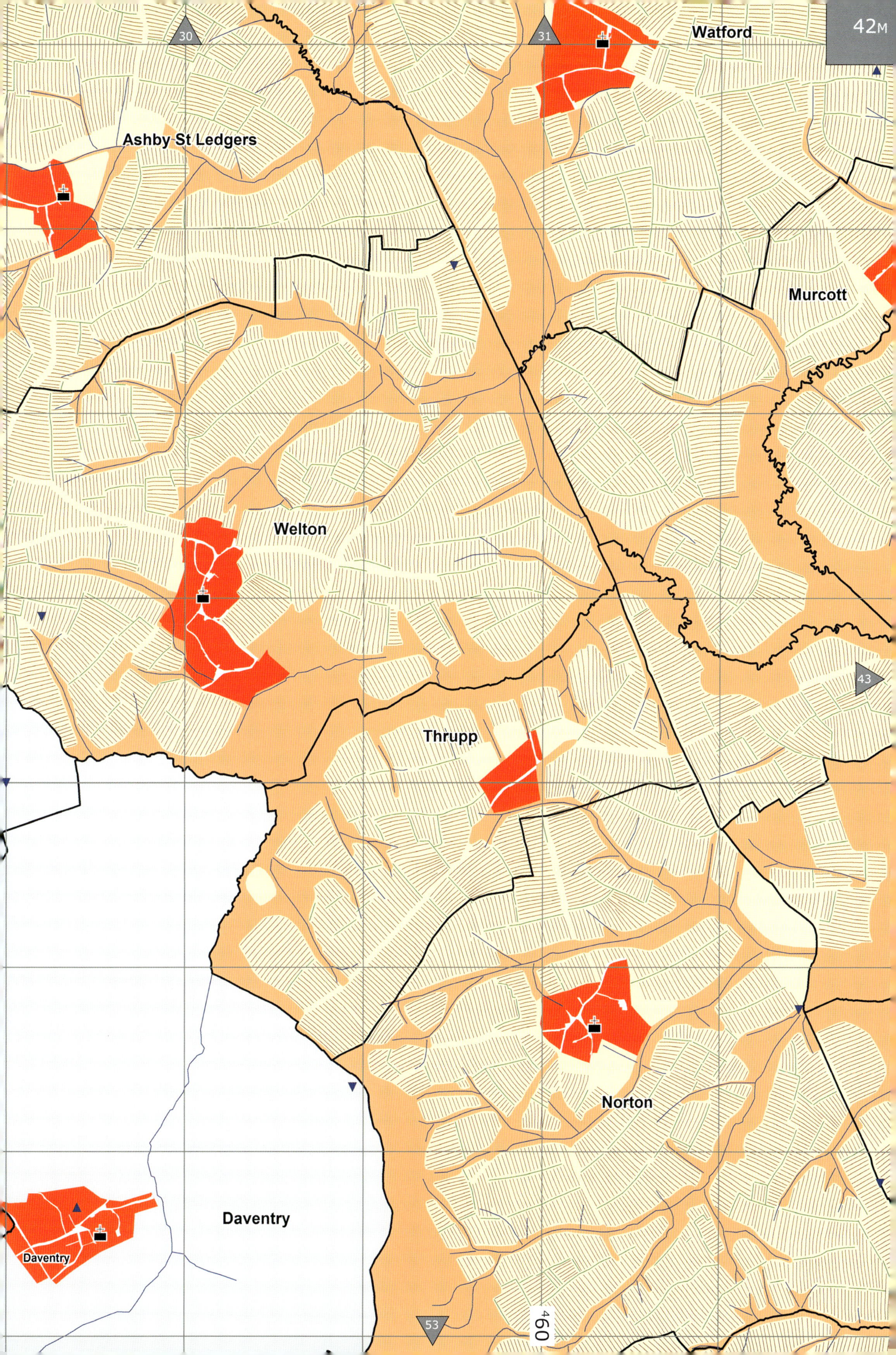
30
31
Watford
Ashby St Ledgers
Murcott
Welton
43
Thrupp
Norton
Daventry
Daventry
53
460

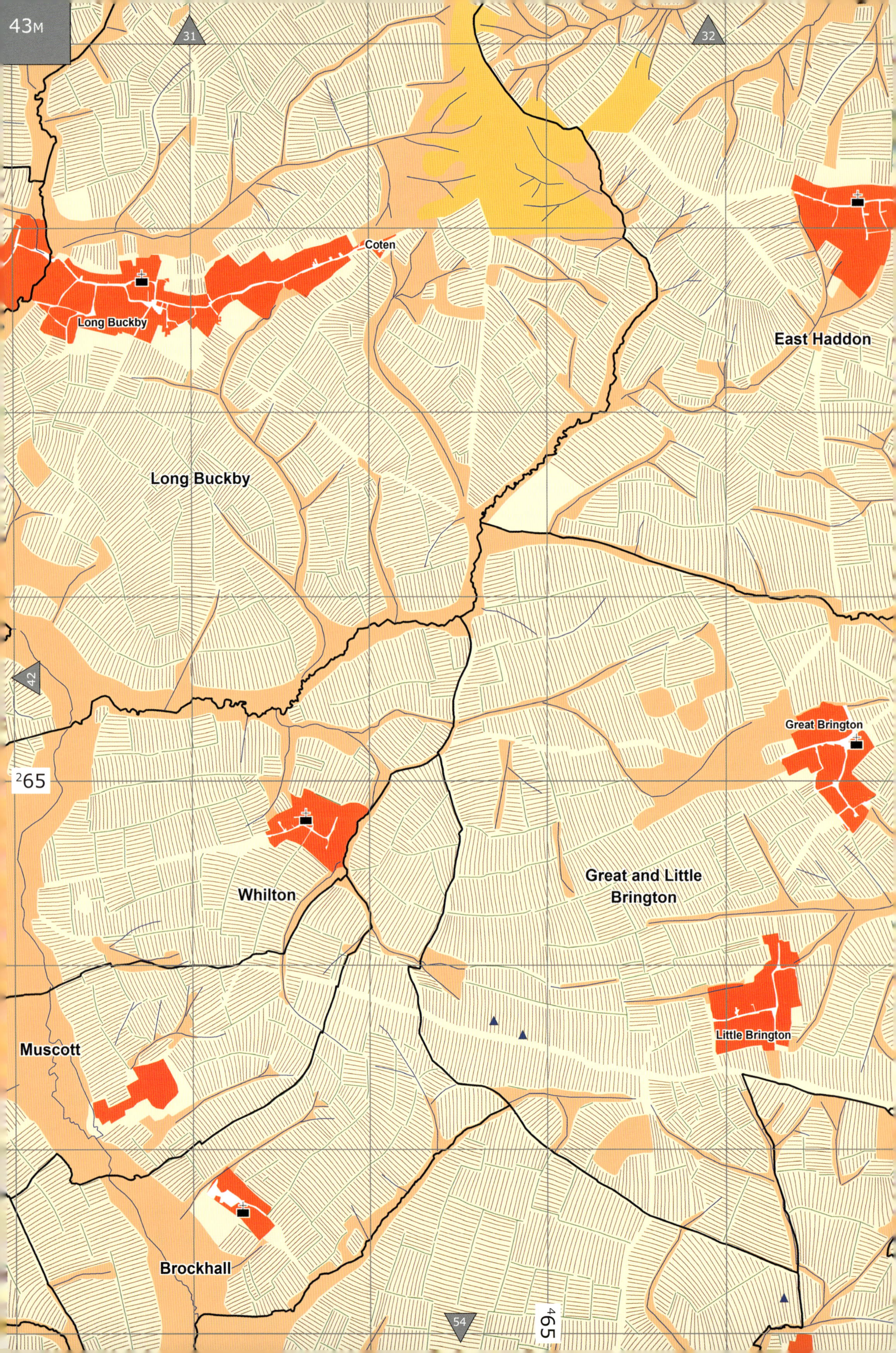

43M
31
32
Coten
Long Buckby
East Haddon
Long Buckby
42
Great Brington
265
Whilton
Great and Little
Brington
Muscott
Little Brington
Brockhall
54
465

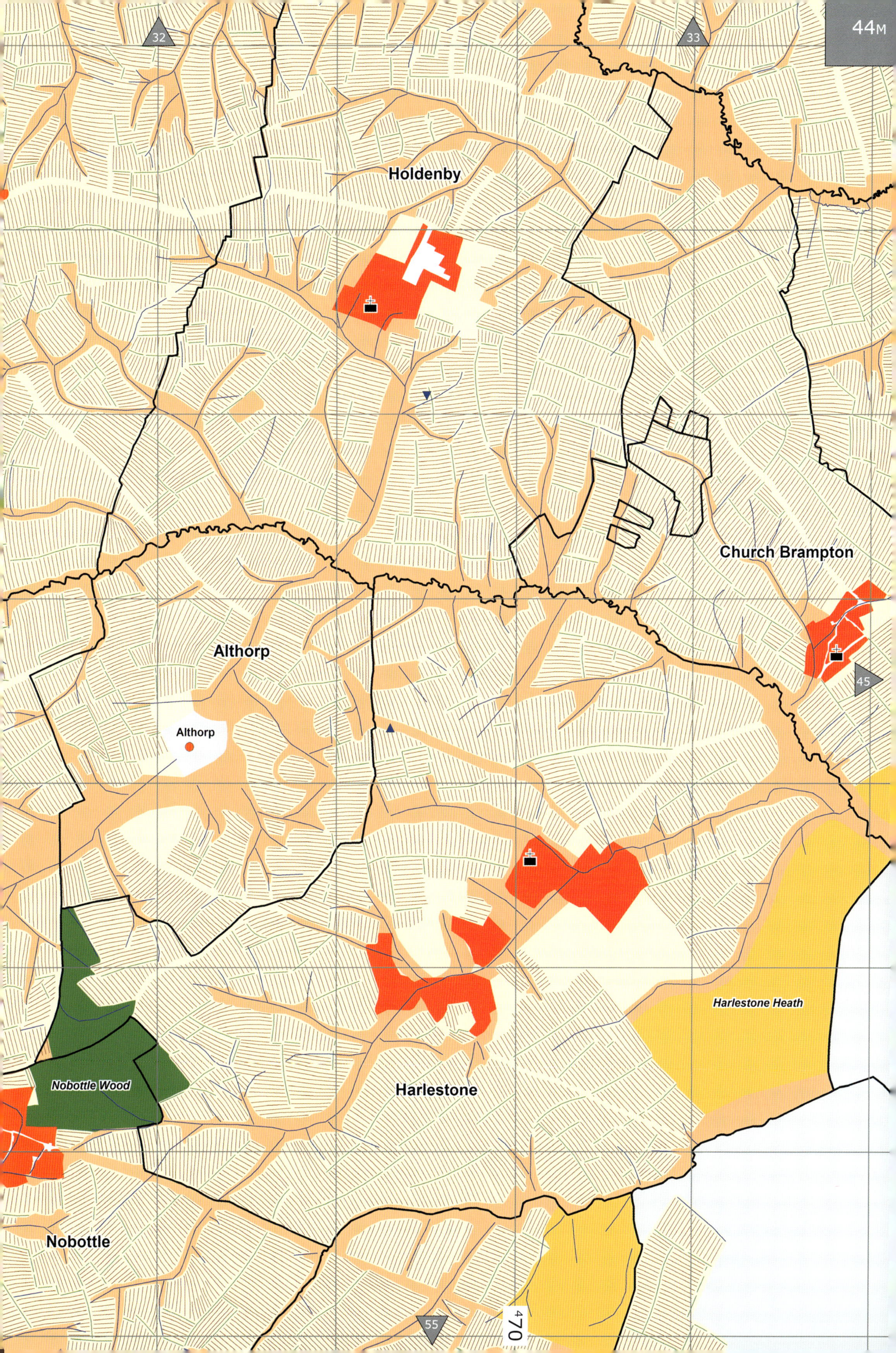
32
33
Holdenby
Church Brampton
Althorp
Althorp
45
Harlestone Heath
Nobottle Wood
Harlestone
Nobottle
55
470

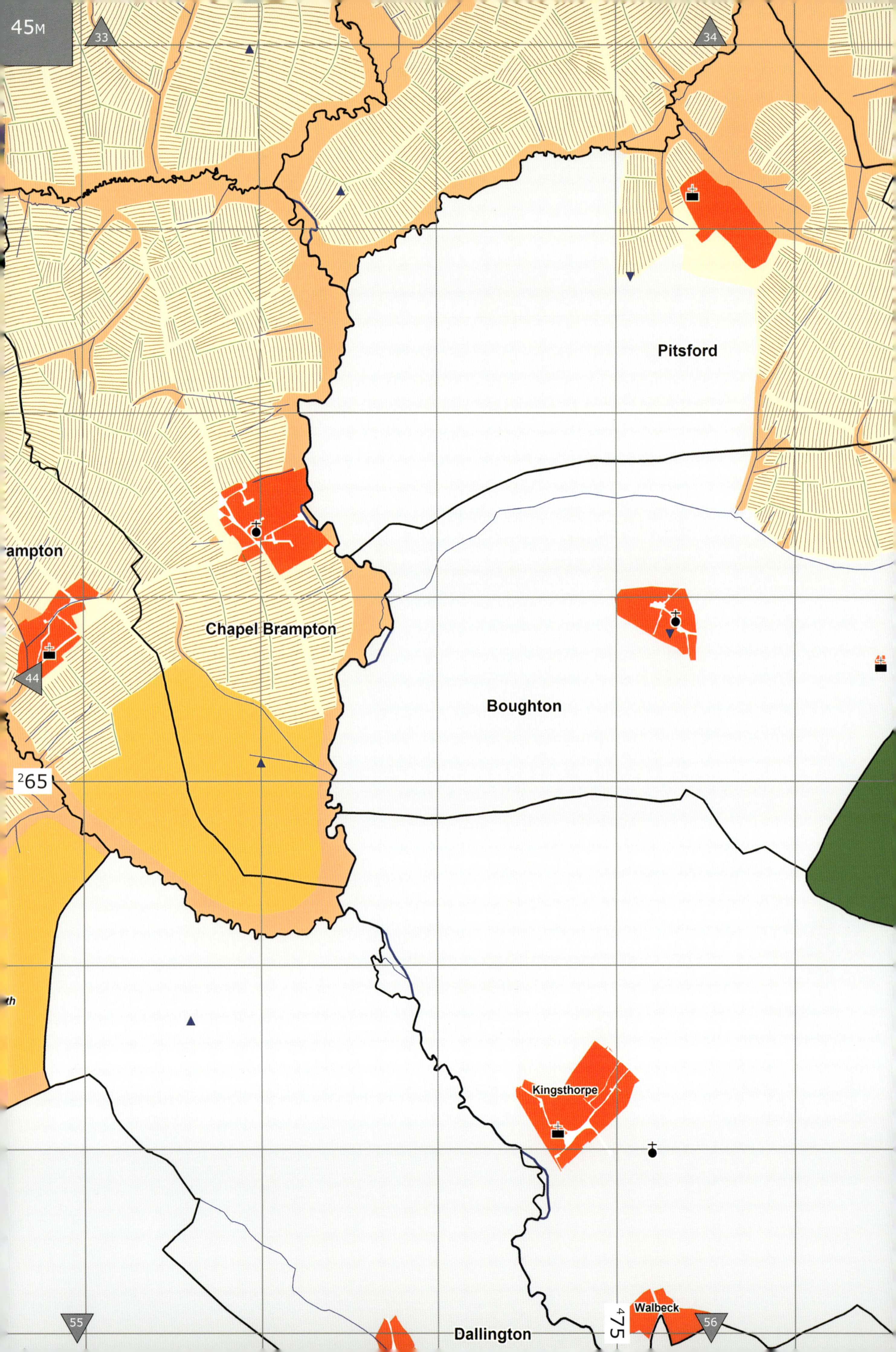
33
34
Pitsford
ampton
Chapel Brampton
44
Boughton
265
th
Kingsthorpe
Walbeck
55
Dallington
475
56

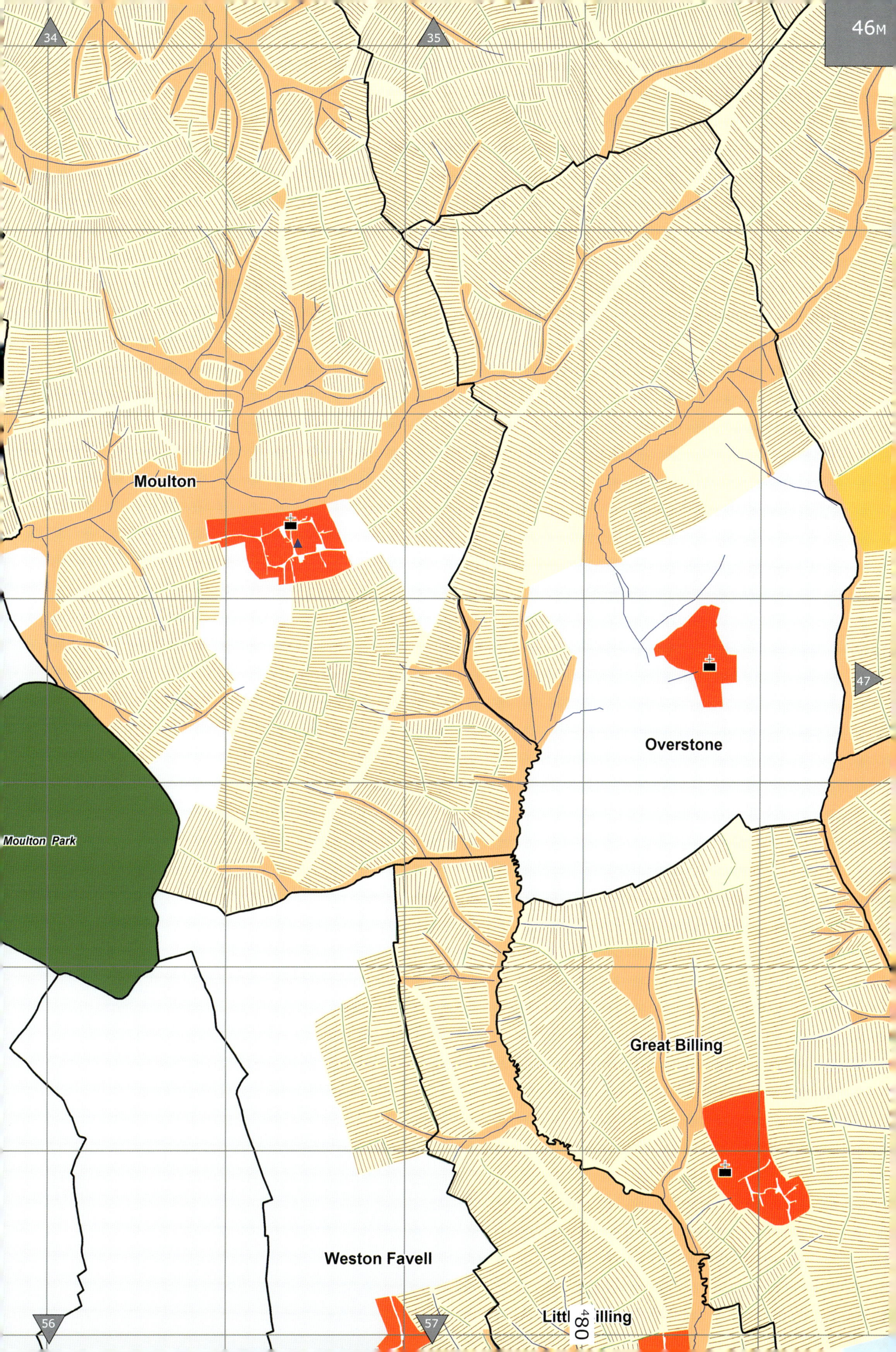
34
35
Moulton
Overstone
47
Moulton Park
Great Billing
Weston Favell
56
57

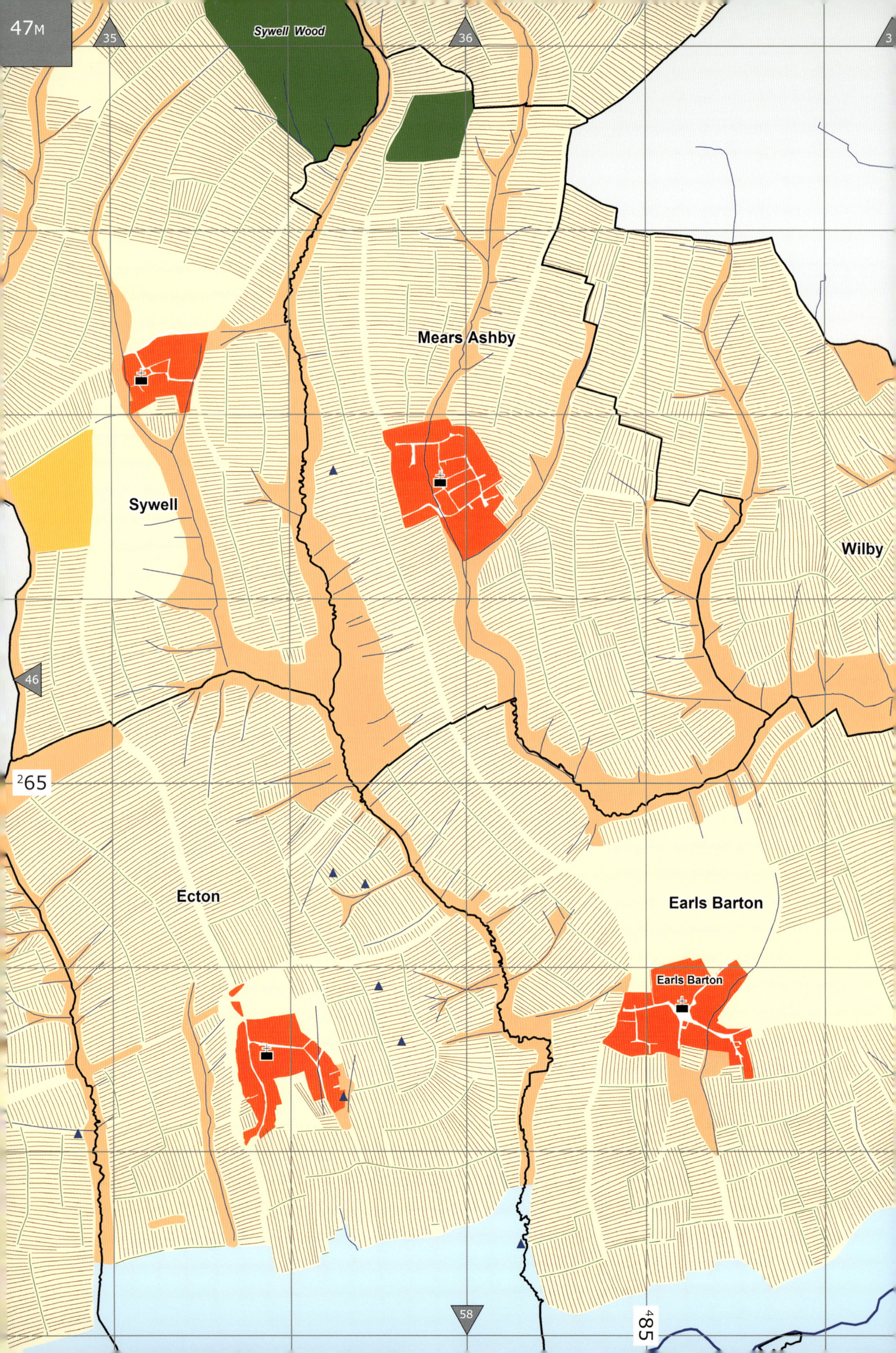
47M
35
36
3
Sywell Wood
Mears Ashby
Sywell
Wilby
46
²65
Ecton
Earls Barton
Earls Barton
58
⁴85

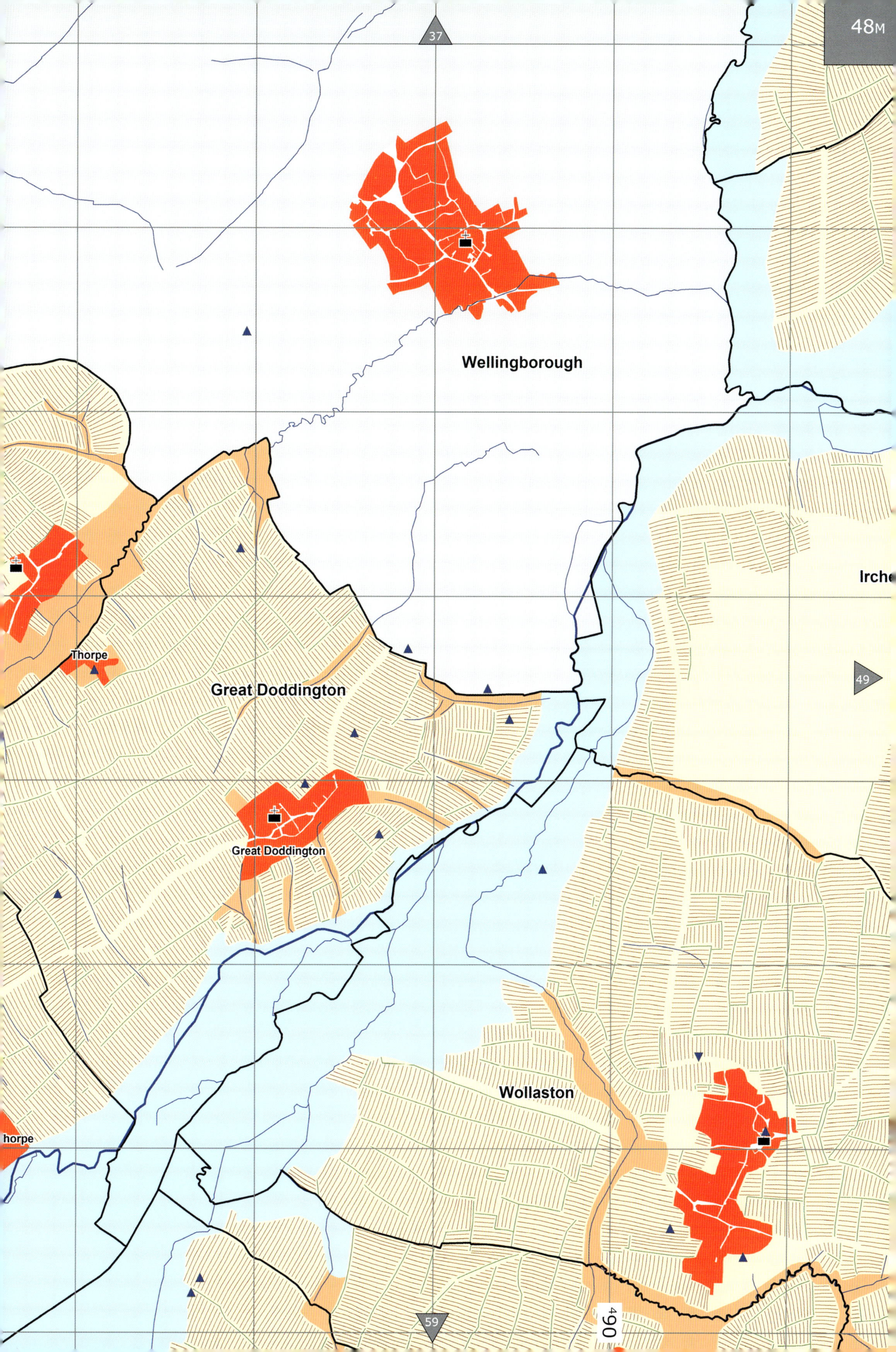

48M
37
Wellingborough
Irche
Thorpe
Great Doddington
49
Great Doddington
Wollaston
horpe
59
490

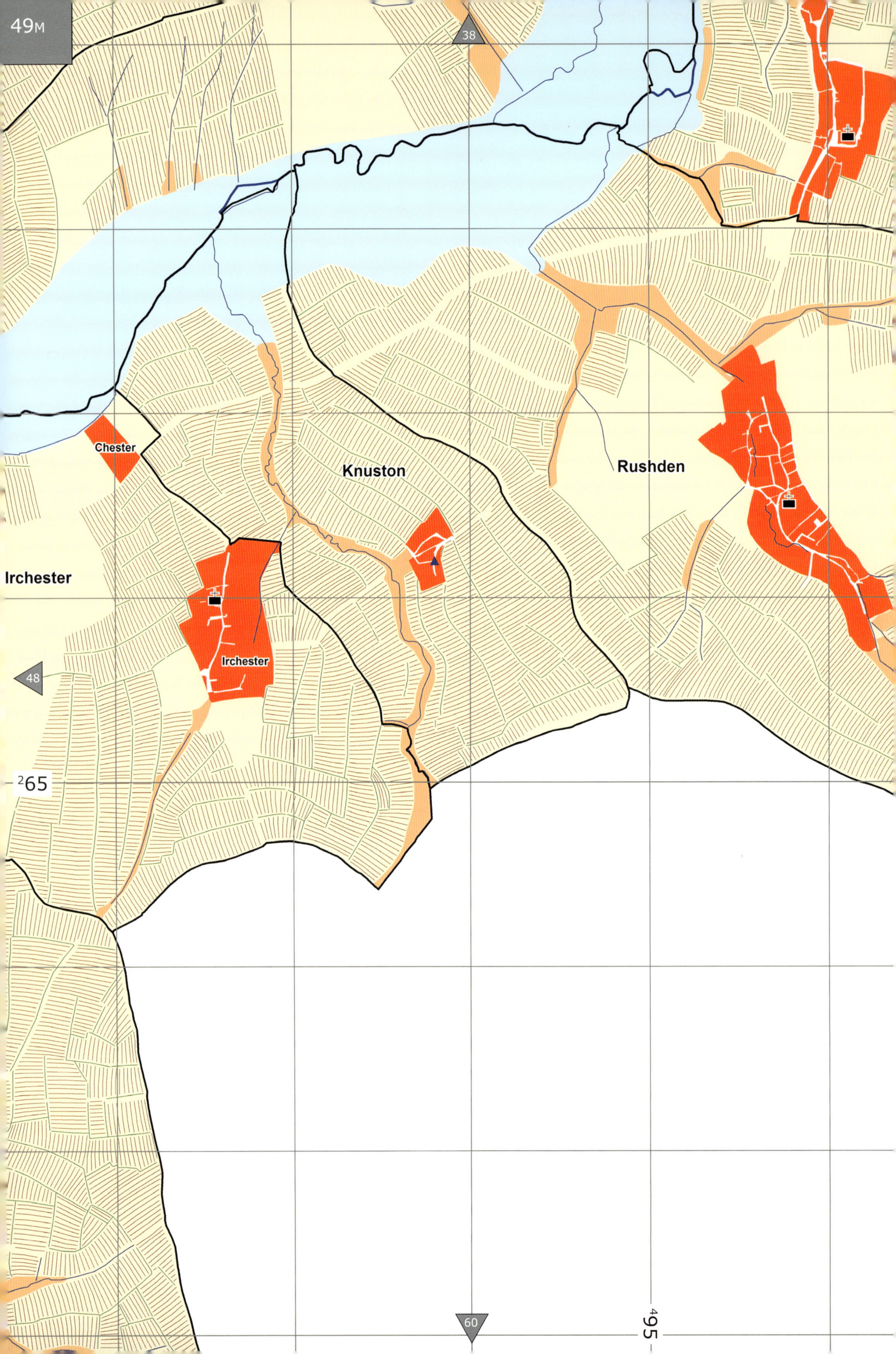
38
Chester
Knuston
Rushden
Irchester
Irchester
48
²65
60
⁴95

Chelveston cum Caldecott
39
Caldecott
Higham Ferrers
Buscot
Buscot
Newton Bromswold
Higham Park
500

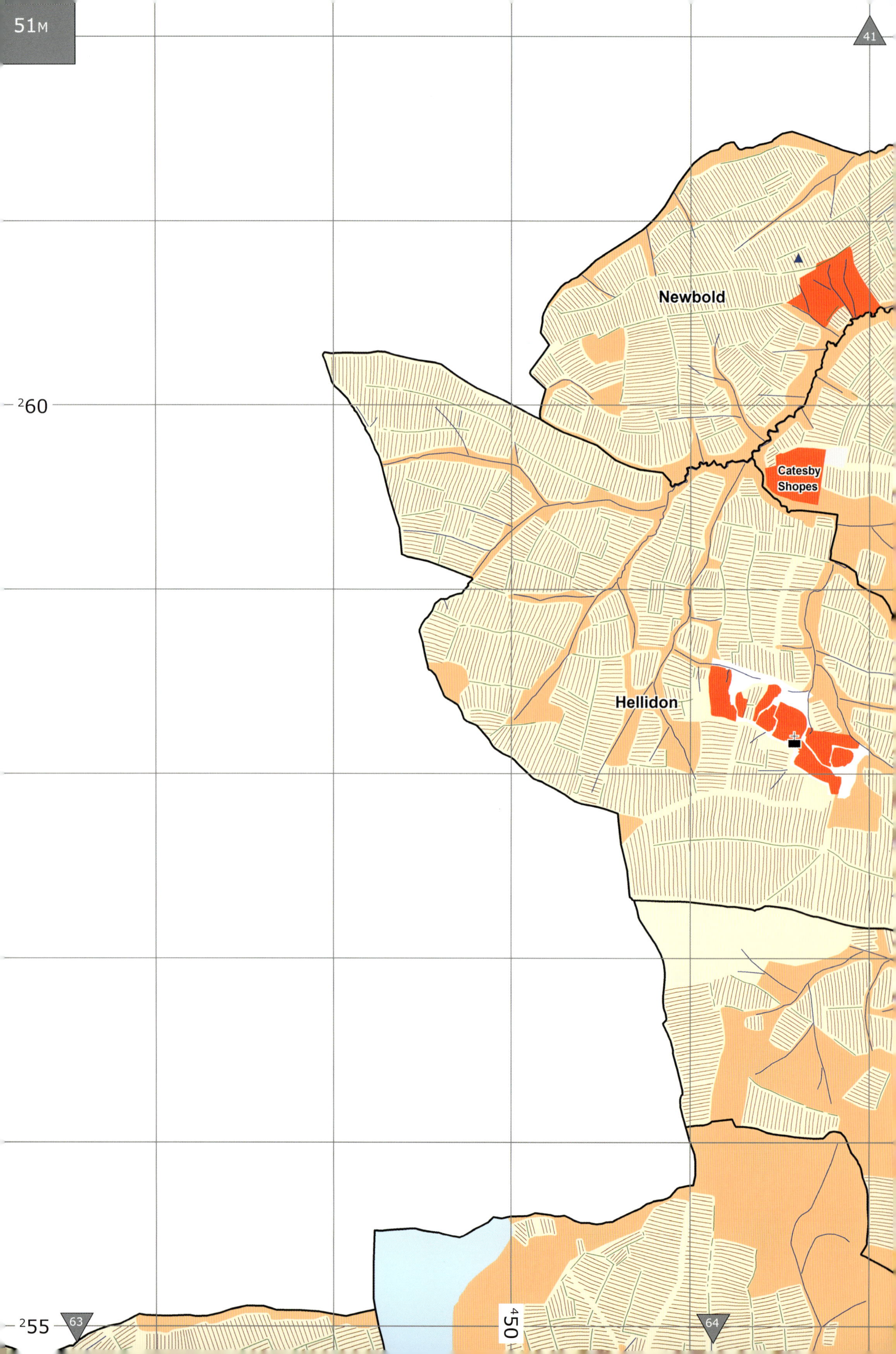
41
Newbold
²60
Catesby
Shopes
Hellidon
²55
63
⁴50
64

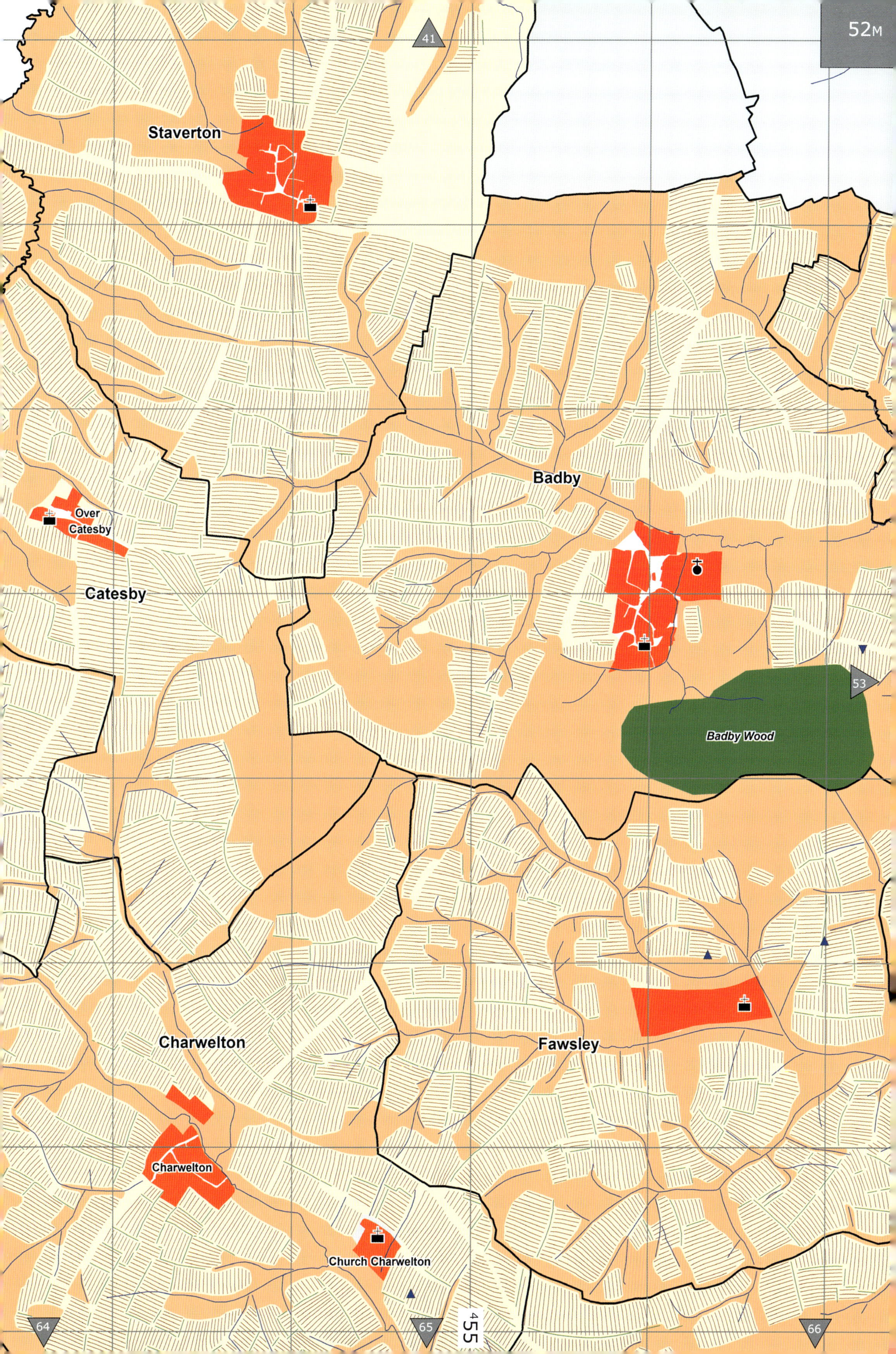
52M
41
Staverton
Badby
Over
Catesby
Catesby
53
Badby Wood
Charwelton
Fawsley
Charwelton
Church Charwelton
64
65
66

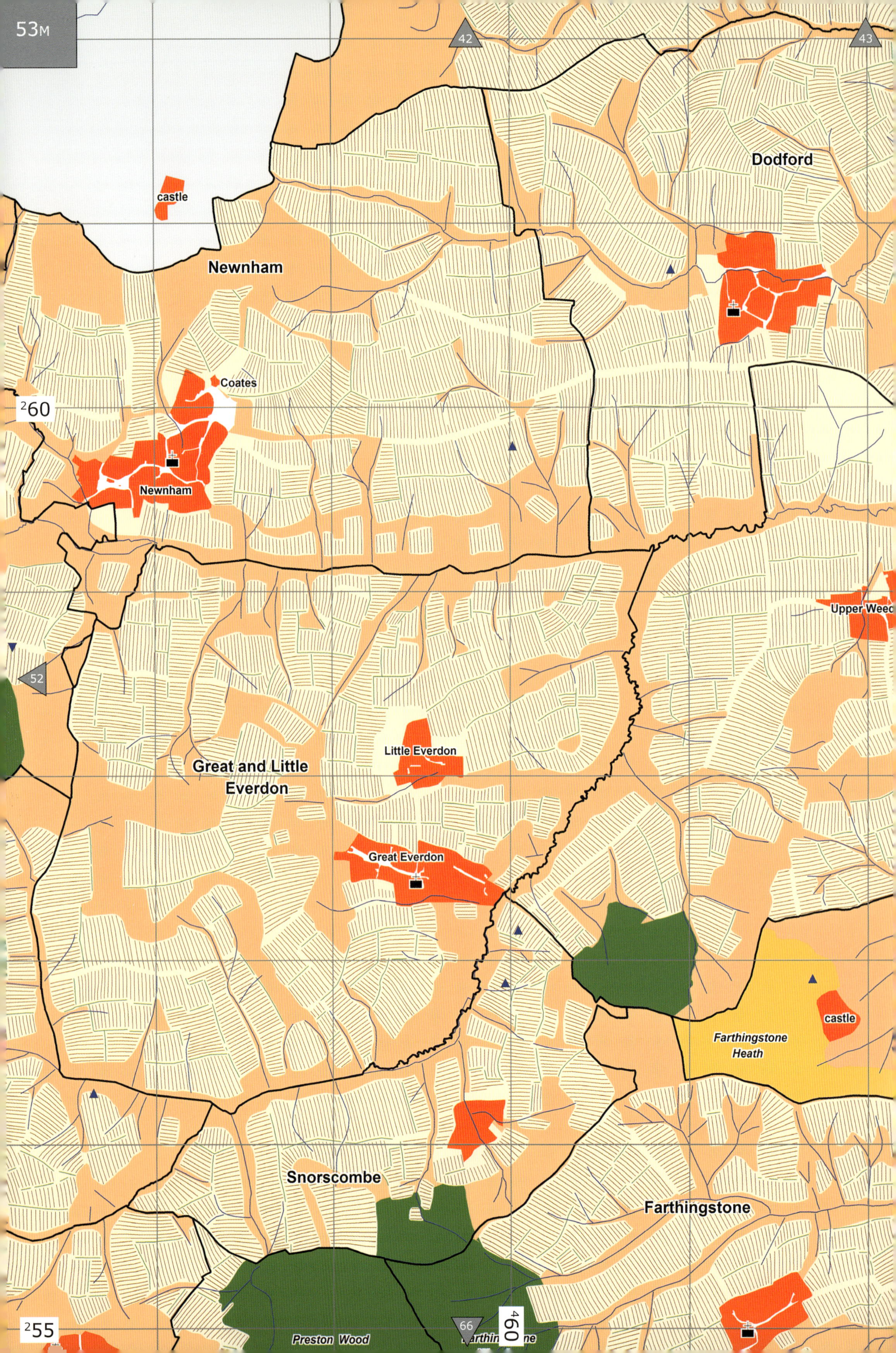
53M
42
43
castle
Newnham
Dodford
Coates
260
Newnham
Upper Weed
52
Little Everdon
Great and Little
Everdon
Great Everdon
castle
Farthingstone
Heath
Snorscombe
Farthingstone
255
66
460
Preston Wood

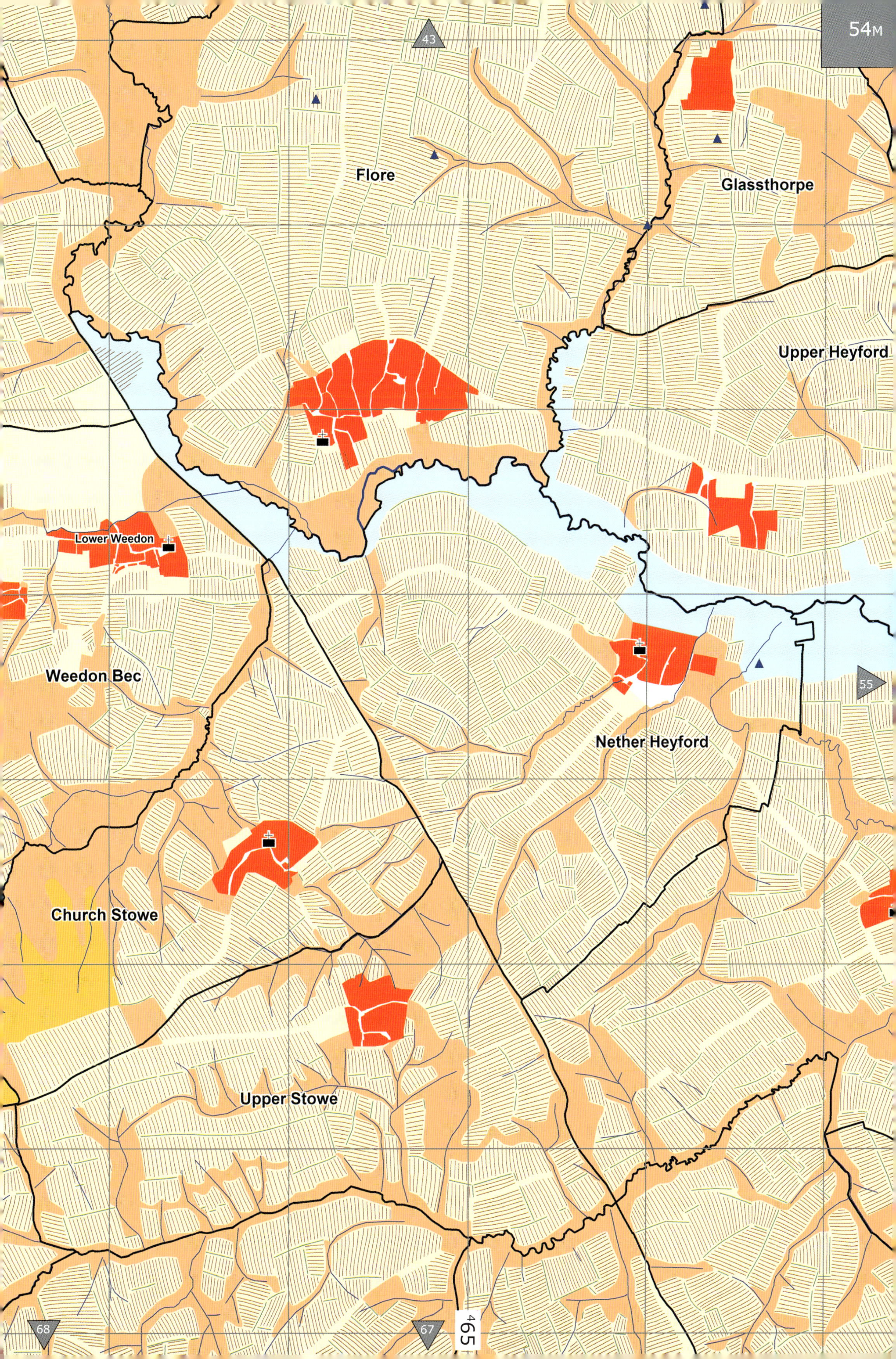
43
Flore
Glassthorpe
Upper Heyford
Lower Weedon
Weedon Bec
Nether Heyford
55
Church Stowe
Upper Stowe
68
67

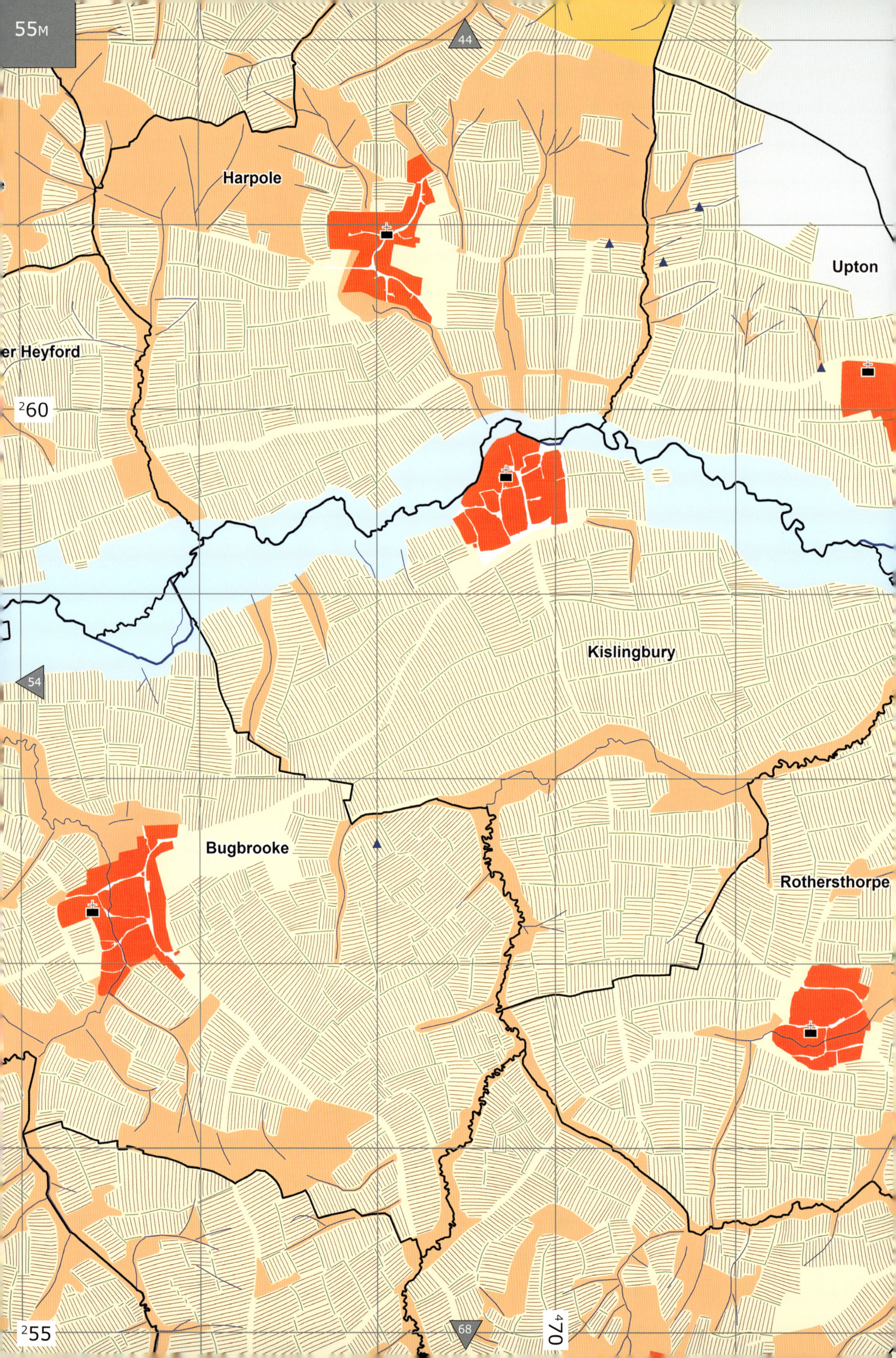
44
Harpole
Upton
er Heyford
260
Kislingbury
54
Bugbrooke
Rothersthorpe
255
68
470

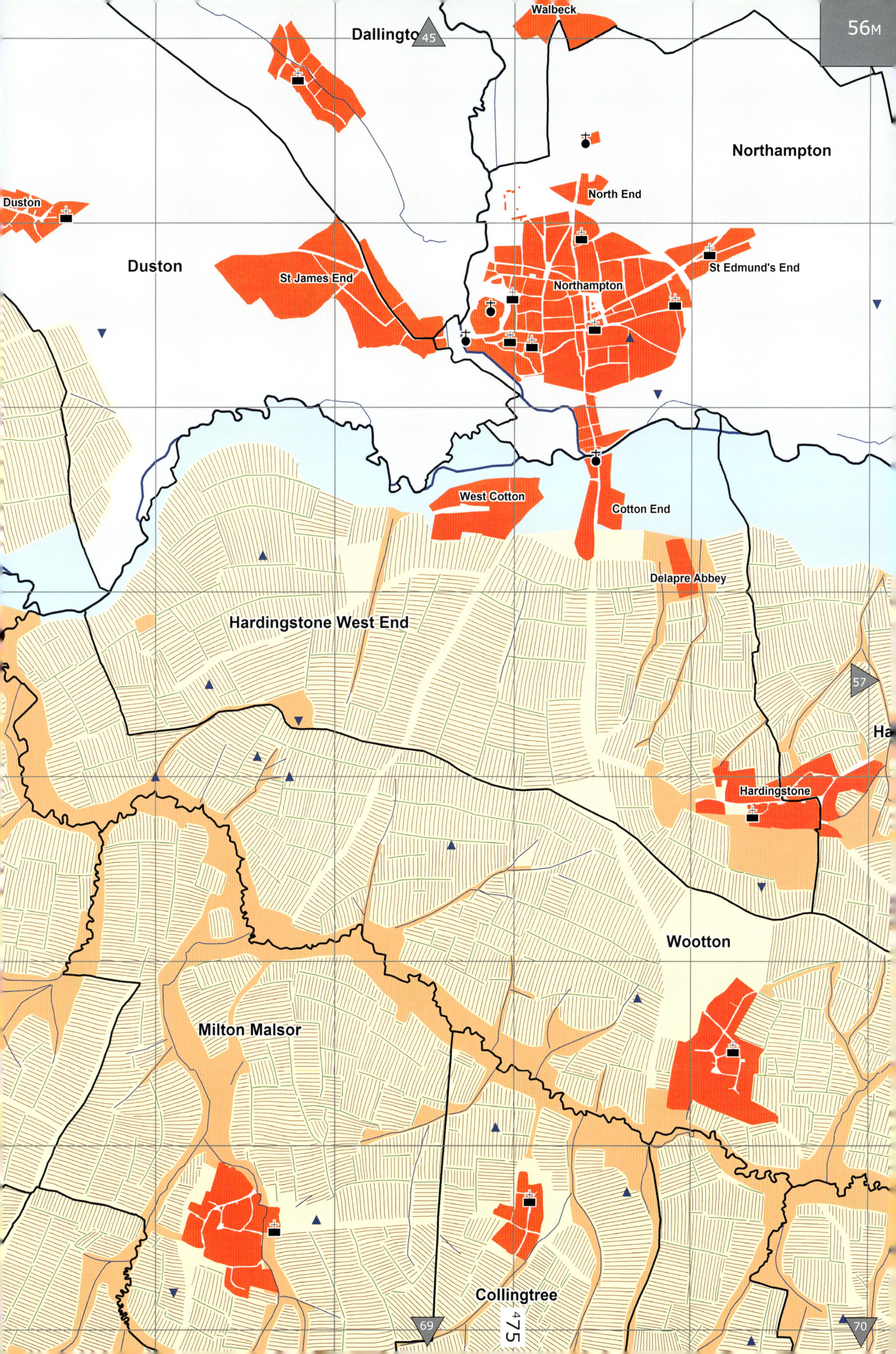

Walbeck
Dallingto
45
Northampton
North End
Duston
Duston
St James End
Northampton
St Edmund's End
West Cotton
Cotton End
Delapre Abbey
Hardingstone West End
57
Ha
Hardingstone
Wootton
Milton Malsor
Collingtree
69
70

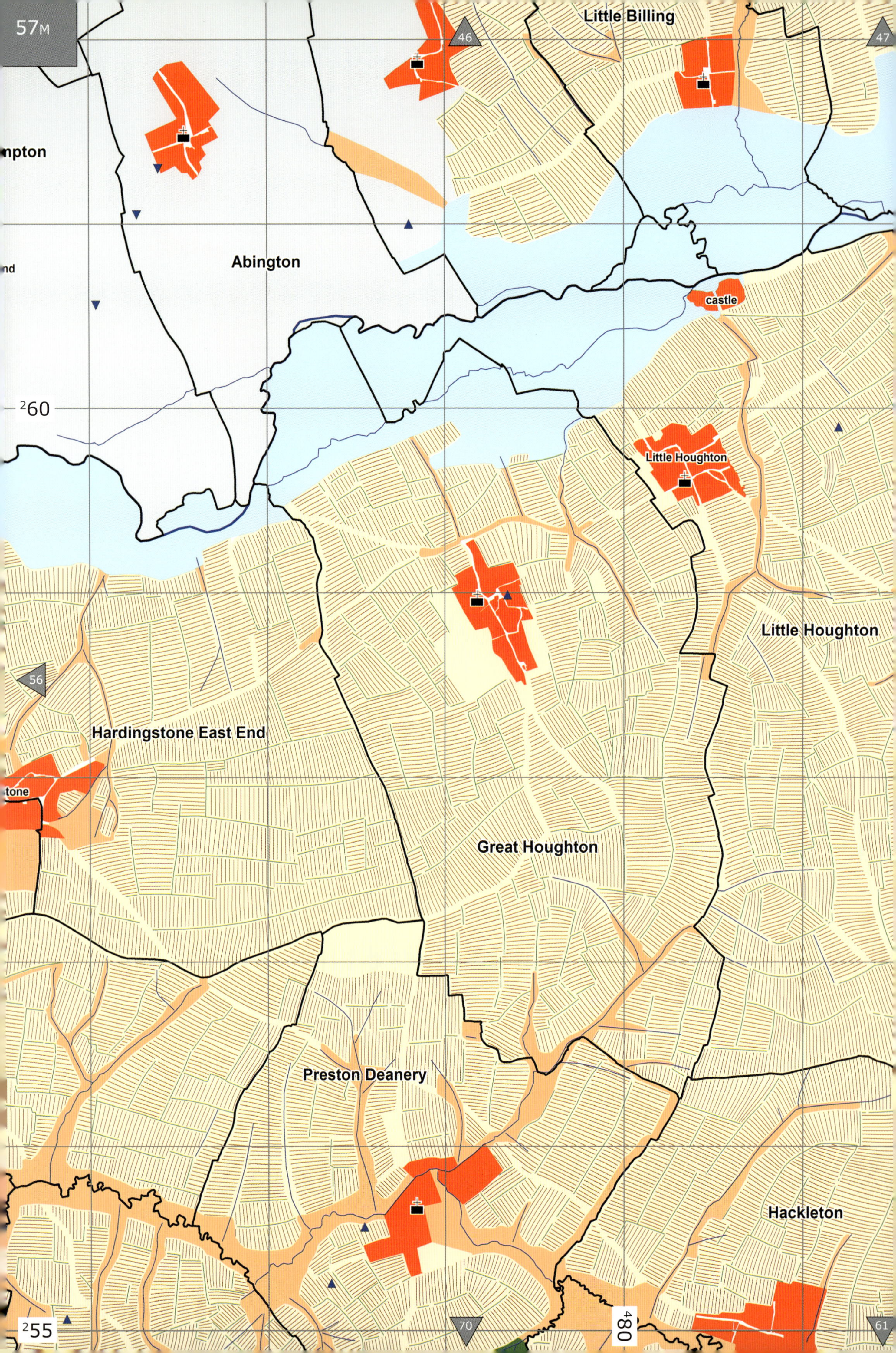

Little Billing
46
47
npton
Abington
nd
castle
²60
Little Houghton
Little Houghton
56
Hardingstone East End
stone
Great Houghton
Preston Deanery
Hackleton
²55
70
480
61

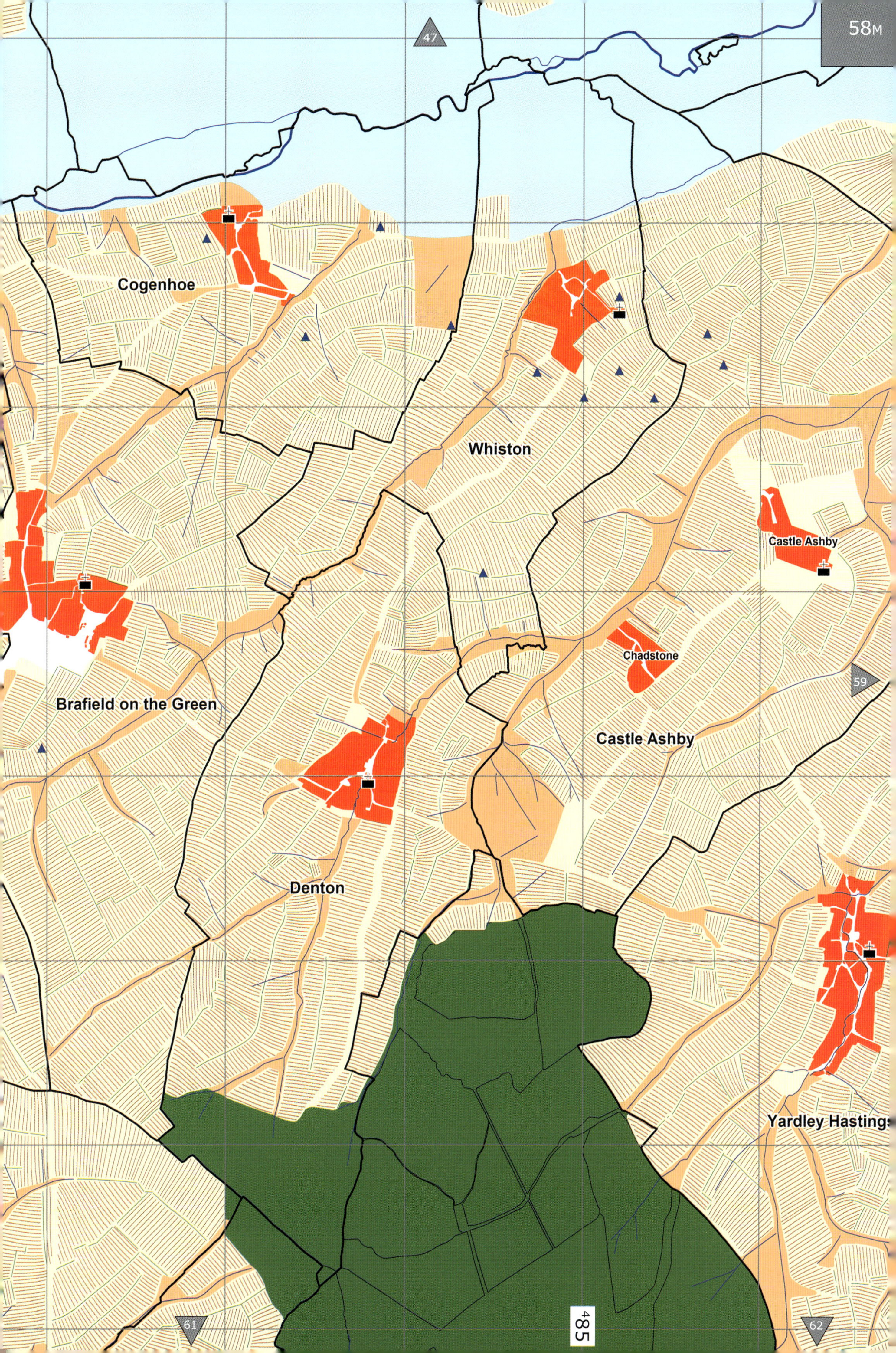
58M
47
Cogenhoe
Whiston
Castle Ashby
Chadstone
59
Brafield on the Green
Castle Ashby
Denton
Yardley Hasting
61
62

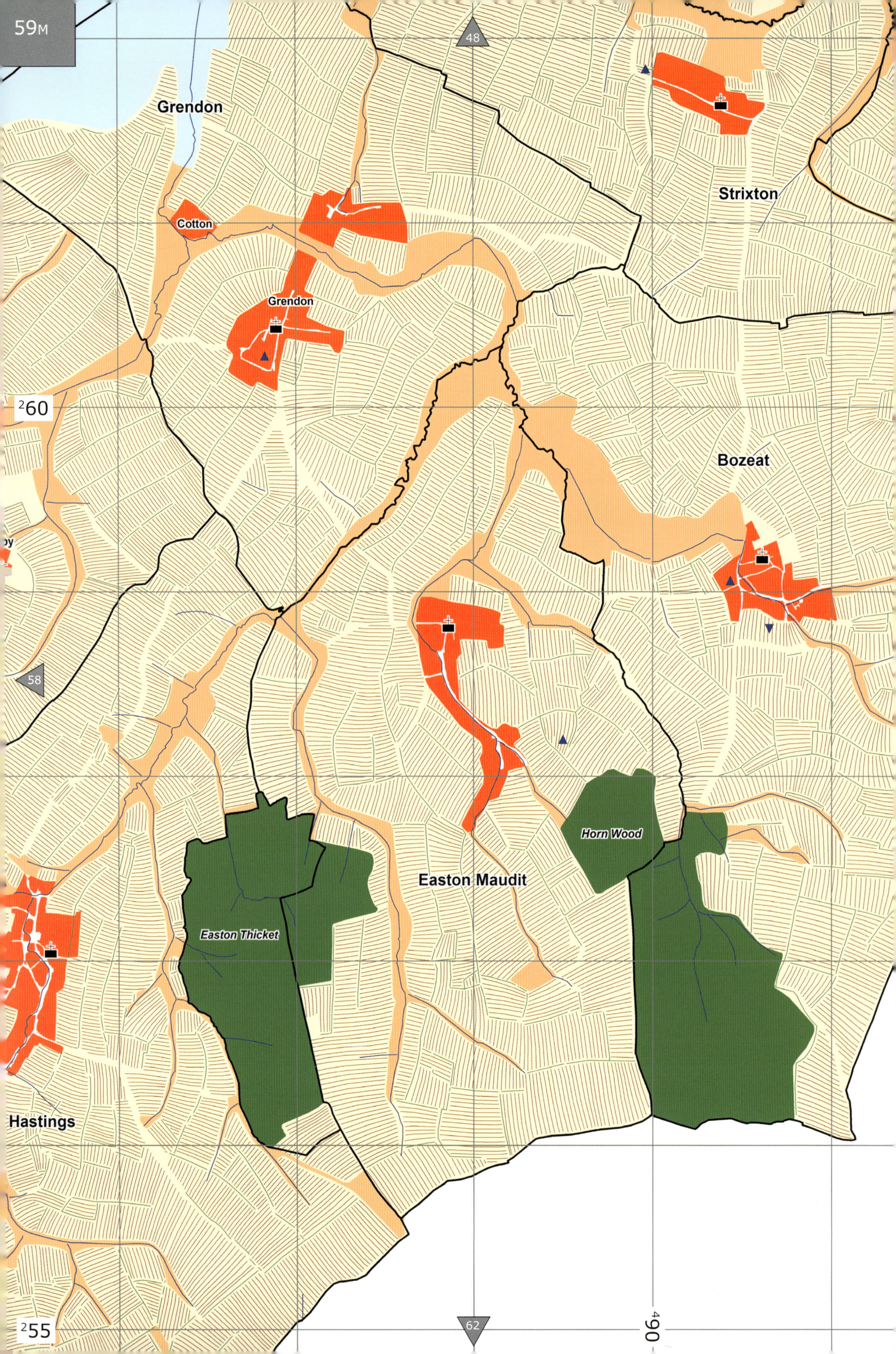

48
Grendon
Cotton
Grendon
Strixton
260
Bozeat
58
Horn Wood
Easton Thicket
Easton Maudit
Hastings
255
62
490

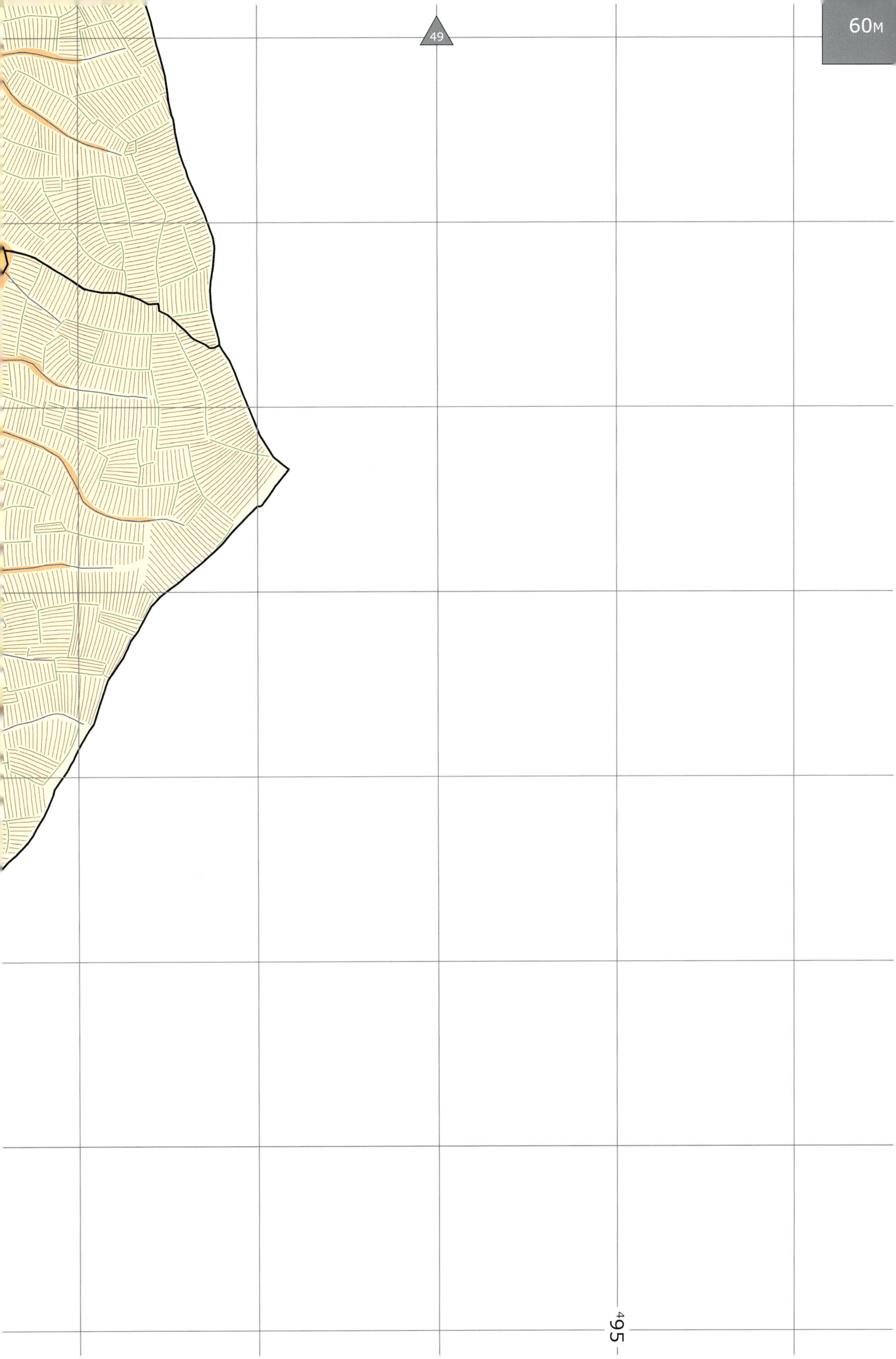
60м
49
495

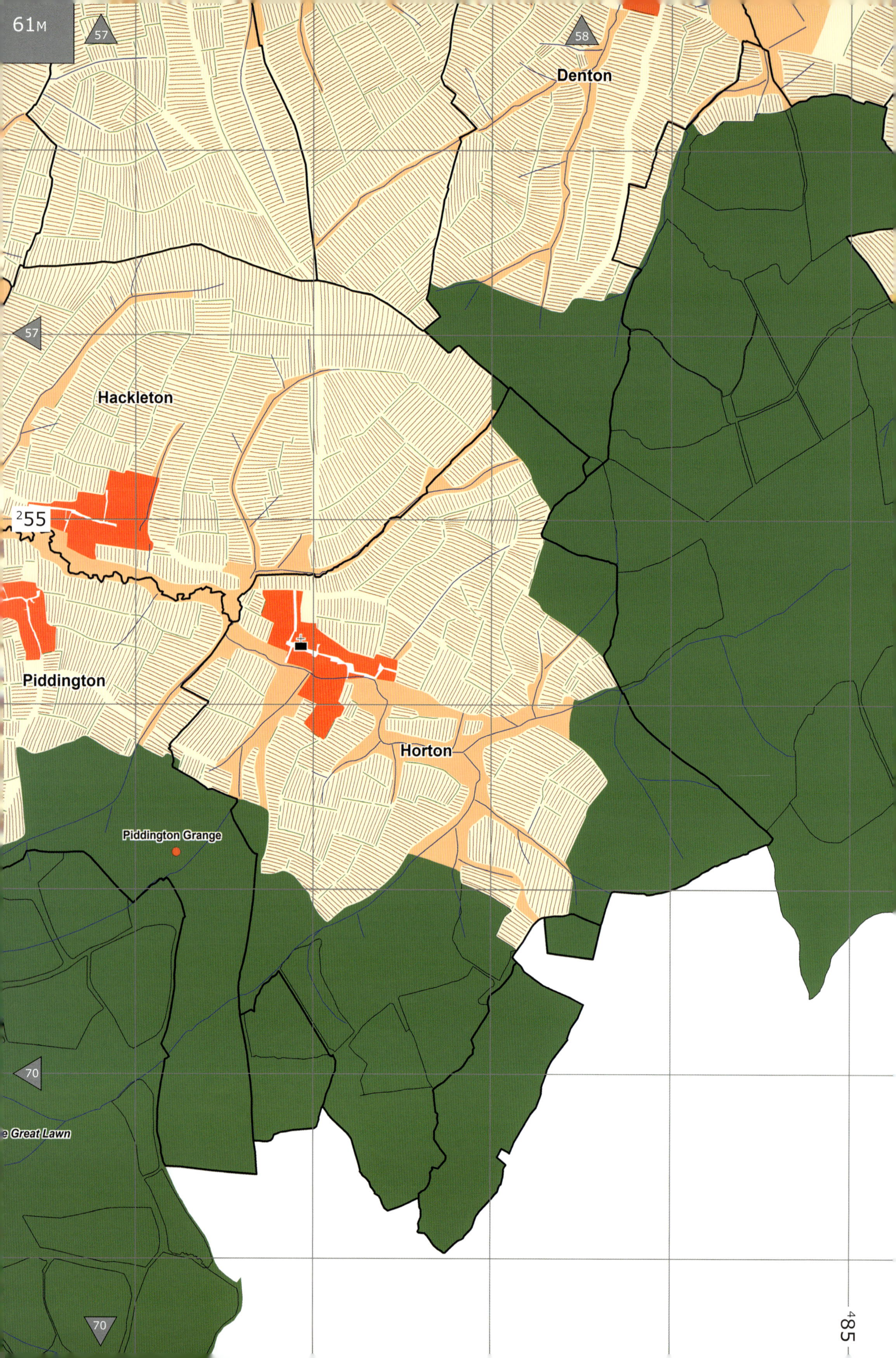

61M
57
58
Denton
57
Hackleton
²55
Piddington
Horton
Piddington Grange
70
e Great Lawn
70
⁴85

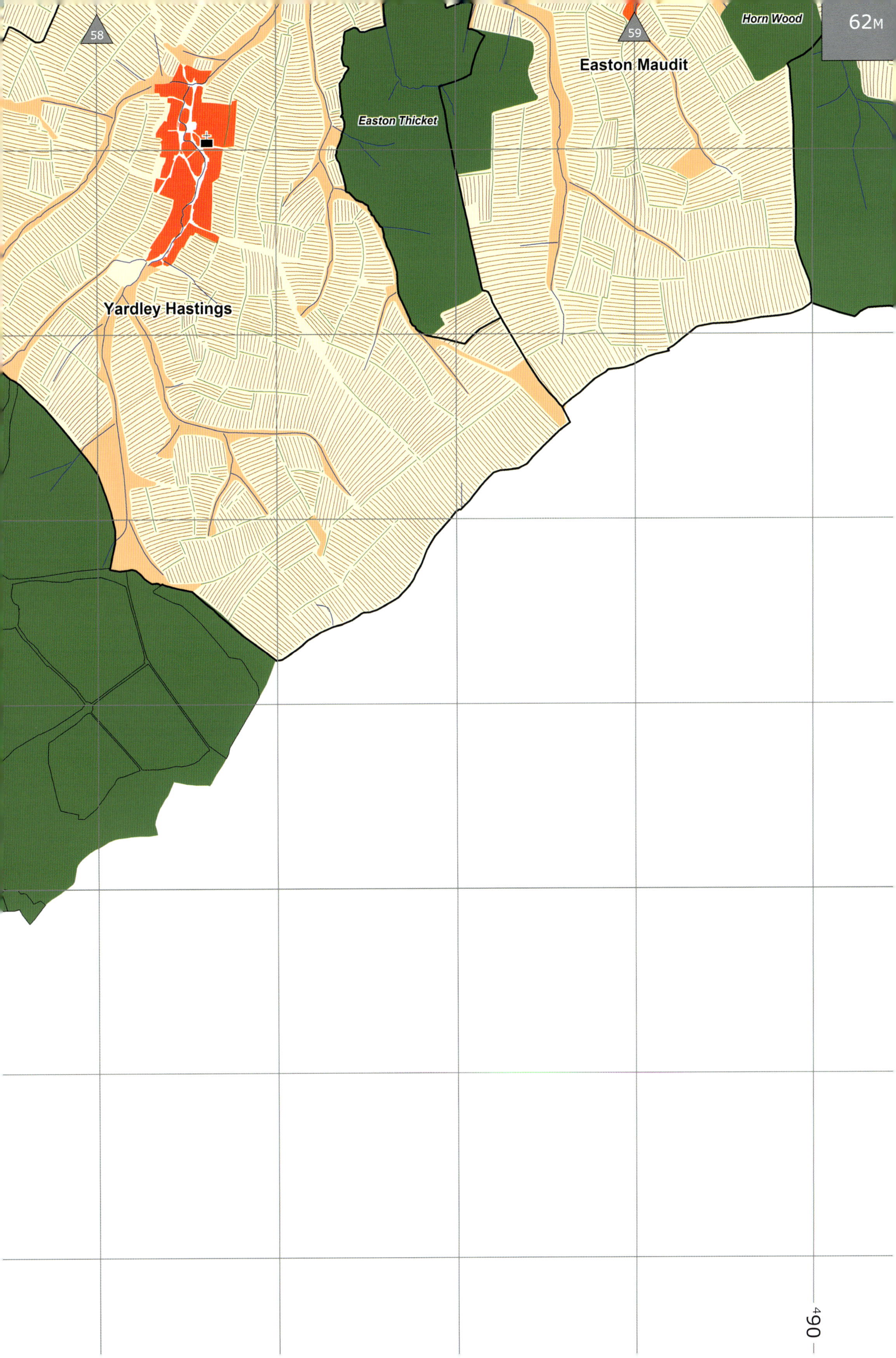

62M
58
59
Horn Wood
Easton Maudit
Easton Thicket
Yardley Hastings
490

51
Upper
Lower
250
445
71

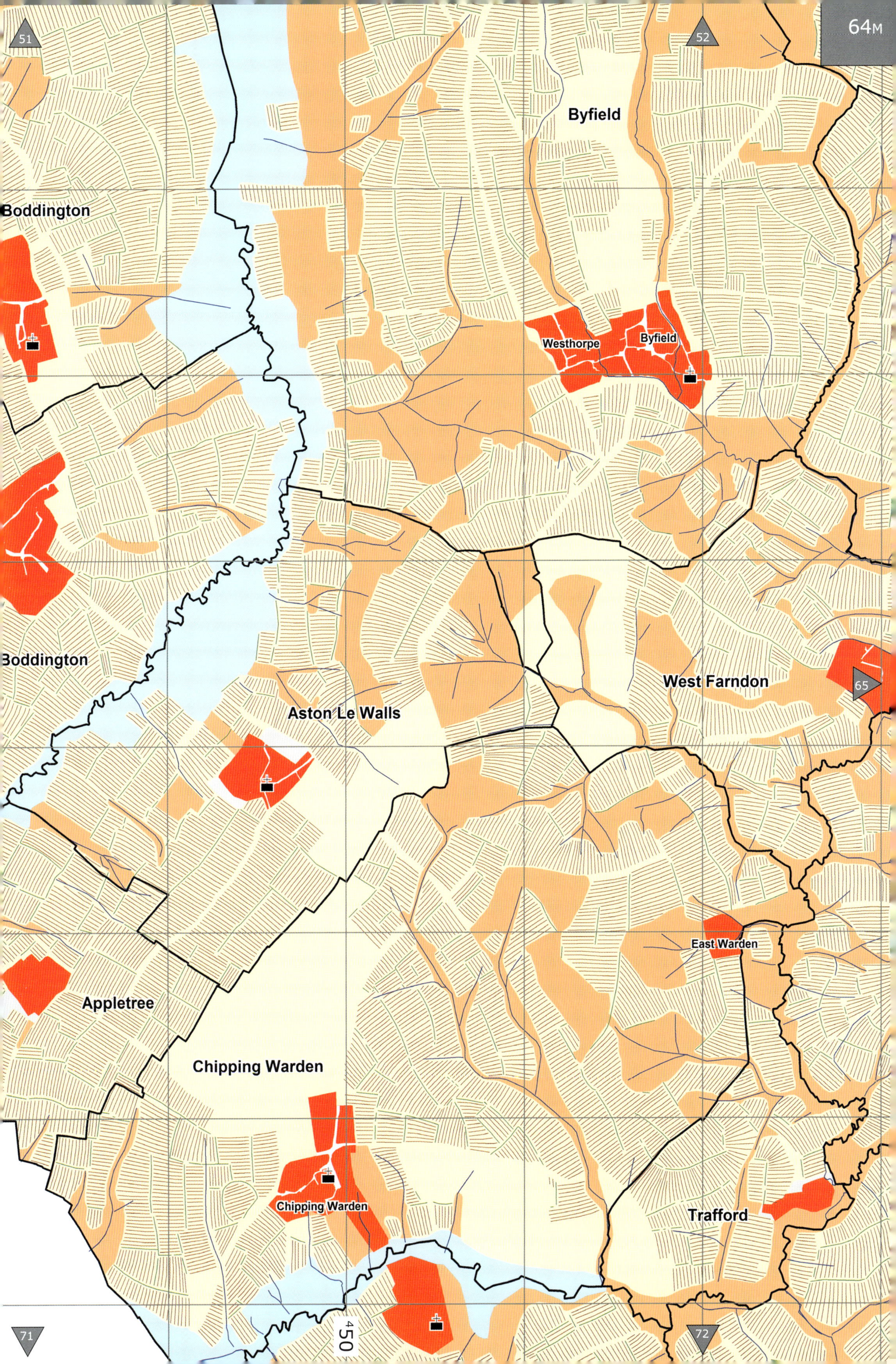
51
52
Byfield
Boddington
Westhorpe
Byfield
West Farndon
65
Boddington
Aston Le Walls
East Warden
Appletree
Chipping Warden
Chipping Warden
Trafford
450
71
72

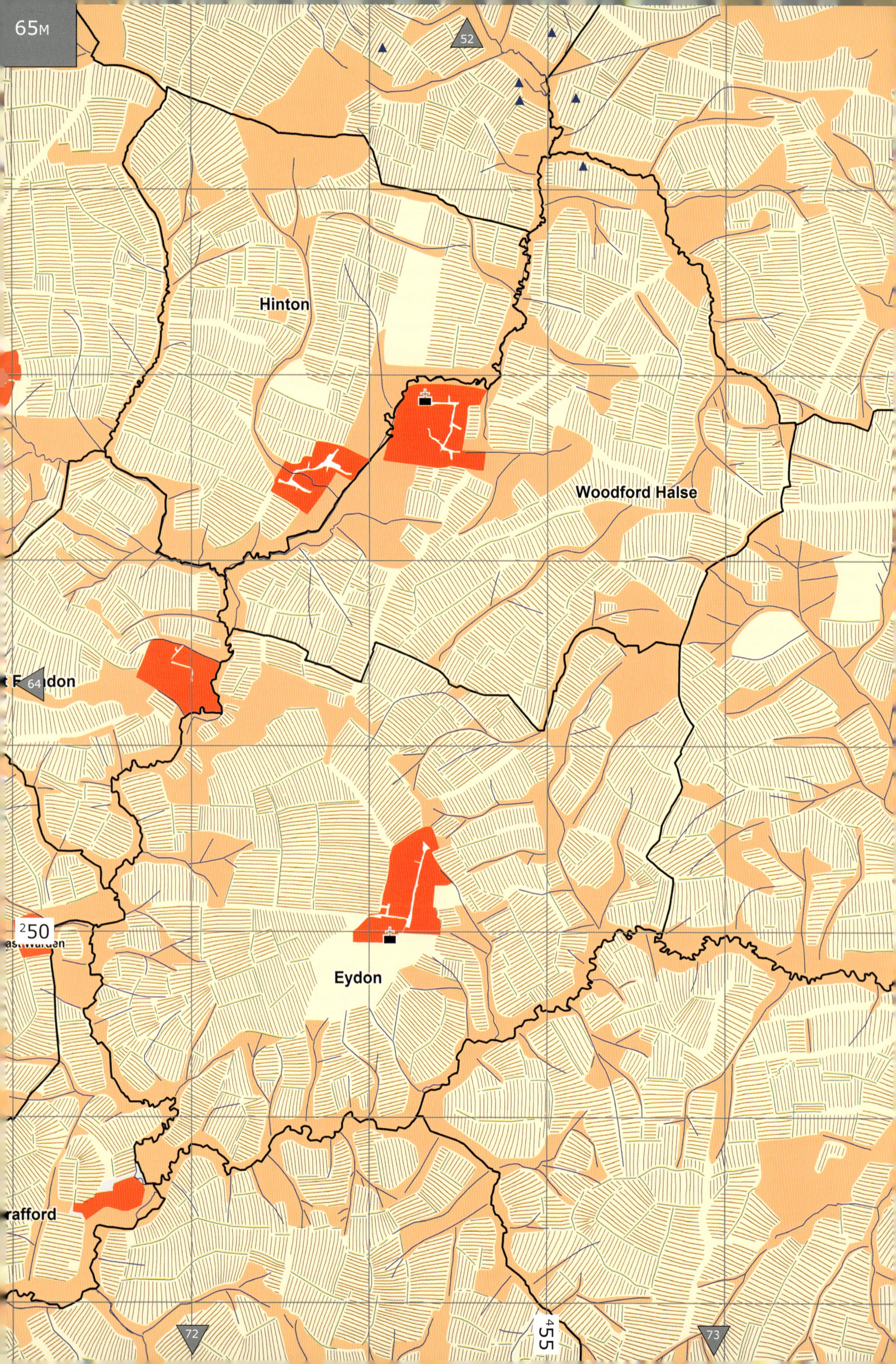

65M
52
Hinton
Woodford Halse
64
250
Eydon
rafford
72
455
73

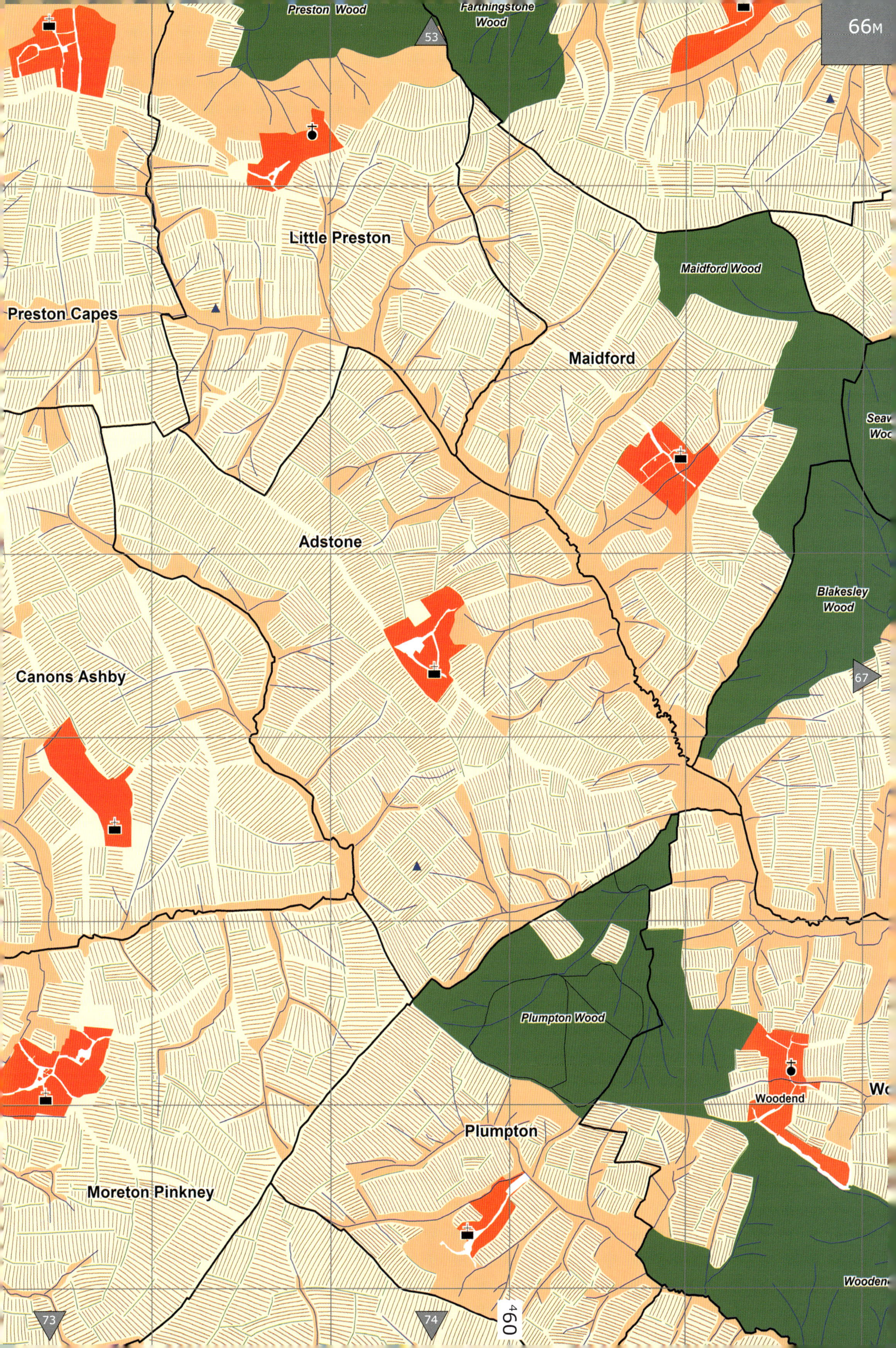
Preston Wood
Farthingstone Wood
53
Little Preston
Preston Capes
Maidford Wood
Maidford
Adstone
Blakesley Wood
67
Canons Ashby
Plumpton Wood
Woodend
Plumpton
Moreton Pinkney
73
74
460

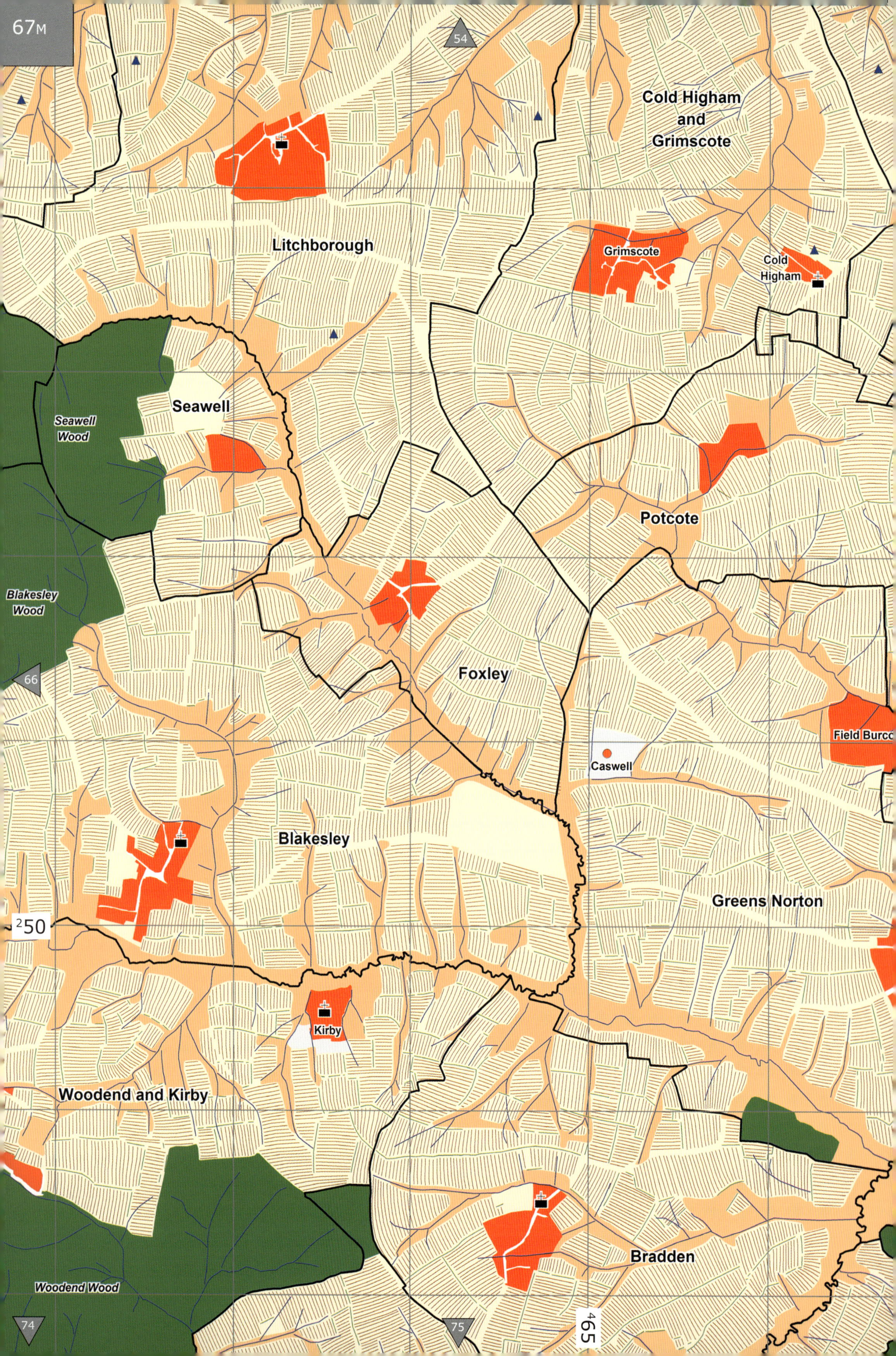
54
Cold Higham and Grimscote
Litchborough
Grimscote
Cold Higham
Seawell
Seawell Wood
Potcote
Blakesley Wood
66
Foxley
Field Burcote
Caswell
Blakesley
Greens Norton
250
Kirby
Woodend and Kirby
Bradden
Woodend Wood
74
75
465

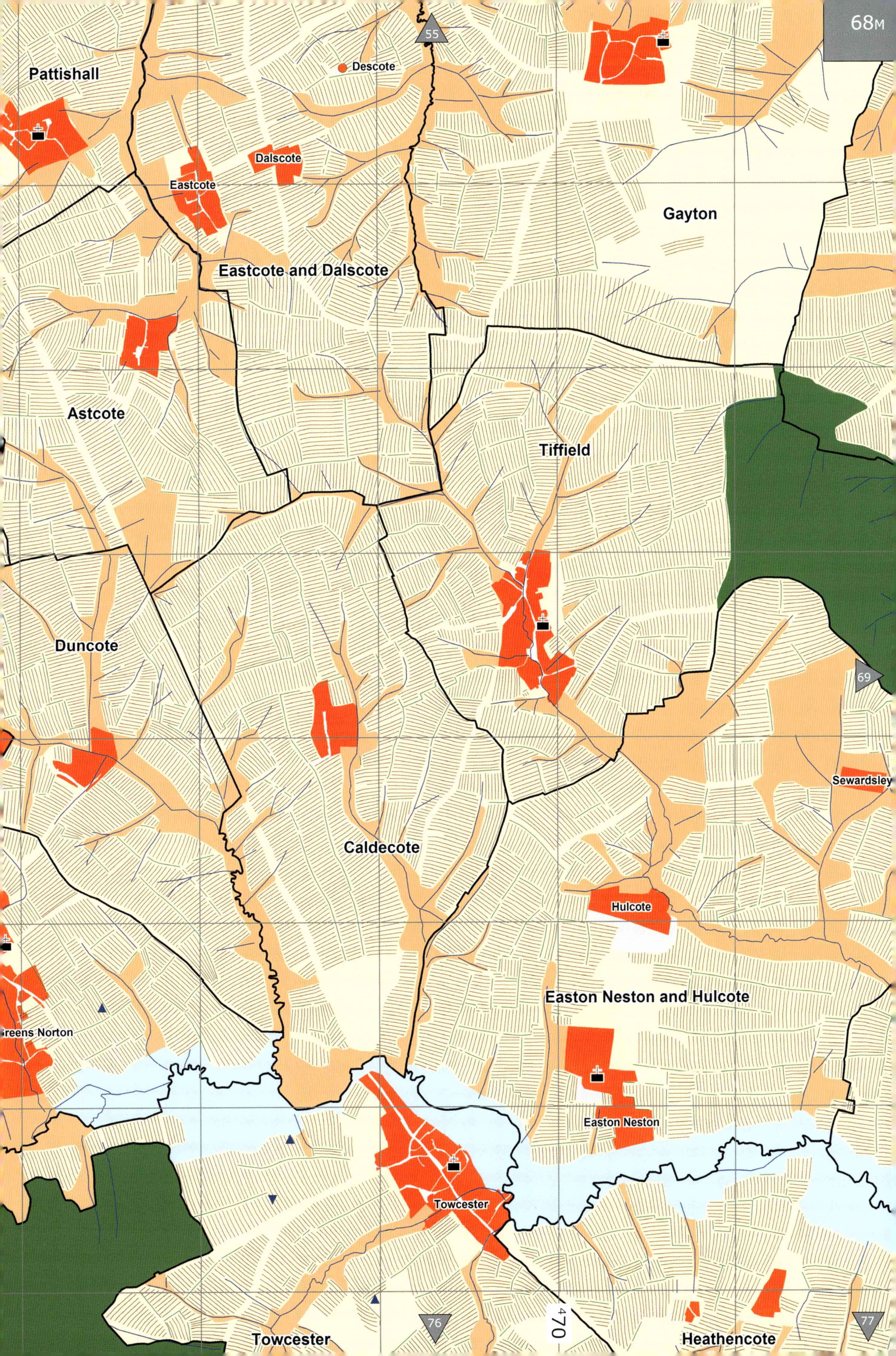
55
Pattishall
Descote
Dalscote
Eastcote
Gayton
Eastcote and Dalscote
Astcote
Tiffield
Duncote
69
Sewardsley
Caldecote
Hulcote
Easton Neston and Hulcote
Greens Norton
Easton Neston
Towcester
Towcester
76
470
Heathencote
77

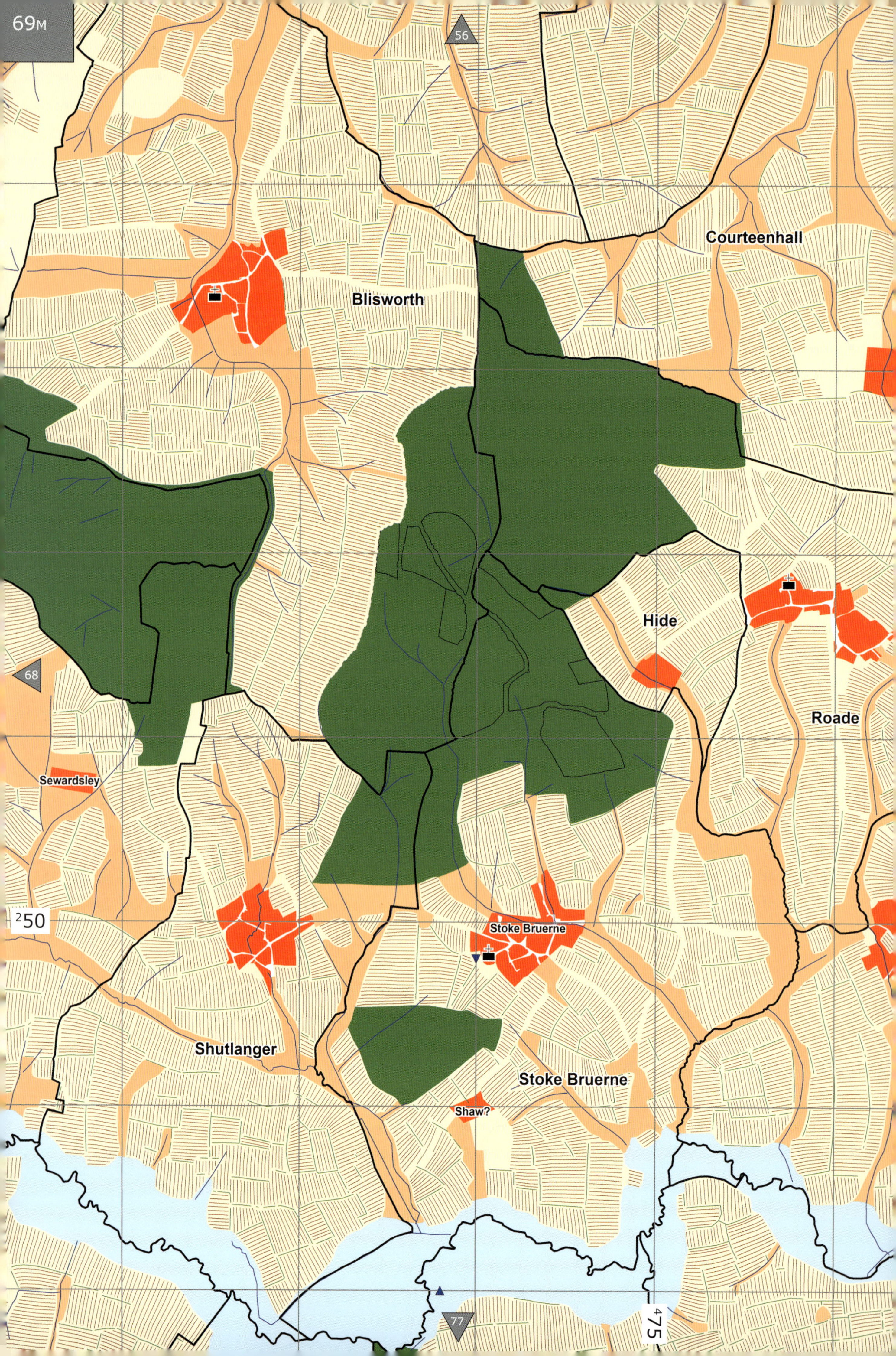

56
Courteenhall
Blisworth
Hide
68
Roade
Sewardsley
250
Stoke Bruerne
Shutlanger
Stoke Bruerne
Shaw?
77
475

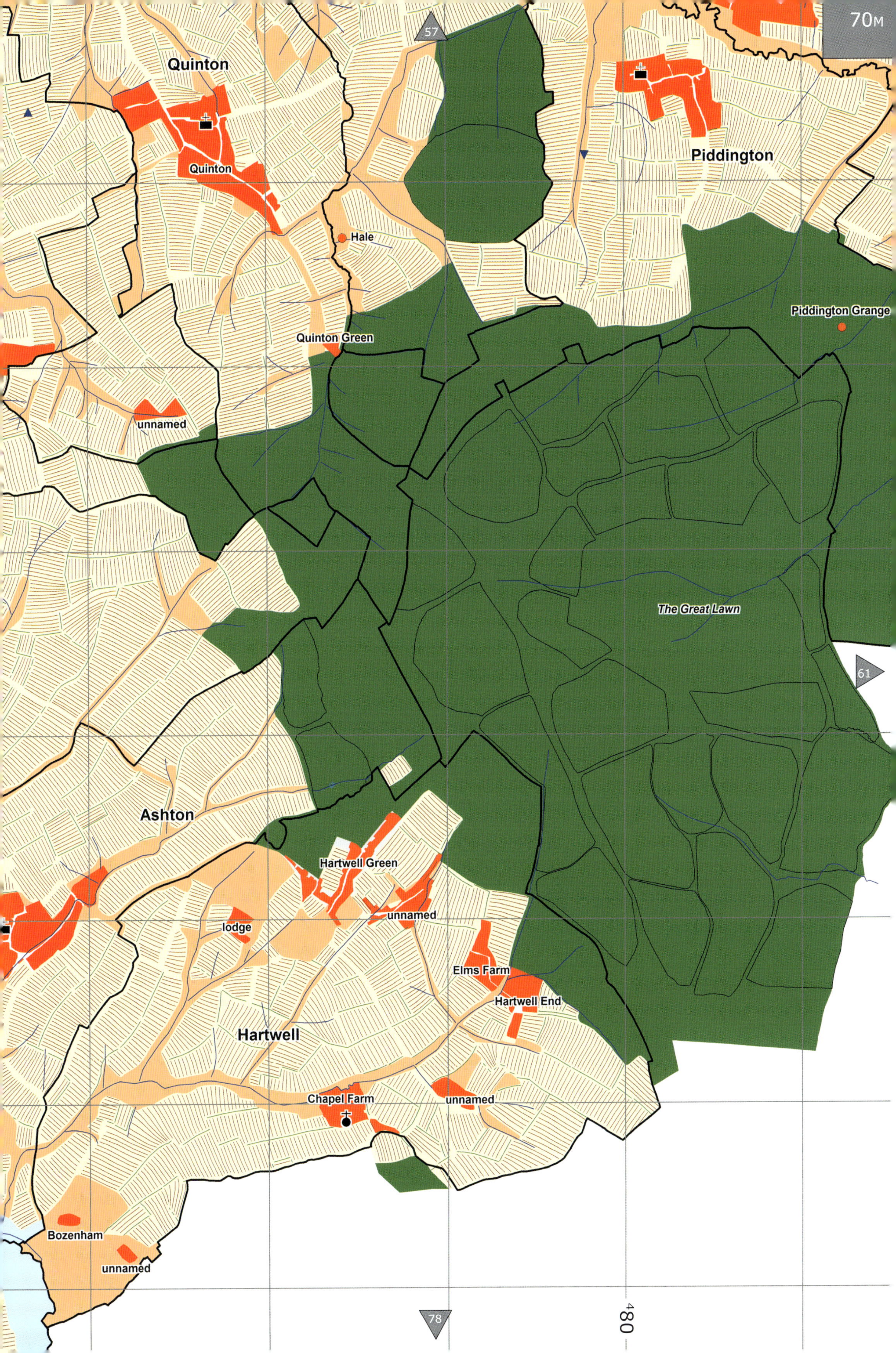

70M
57
Quinton
Quinton
Hale
Piddington
Piddington Grange
Quinton Green
unnamed
The Great Lawn
61
Ashton
Hartwell Green
unnamed
lodge
Elms Farm
Hartwell End
Hartwell
Chapel Farm
unnamed
Bozenham
unnamed
78
480

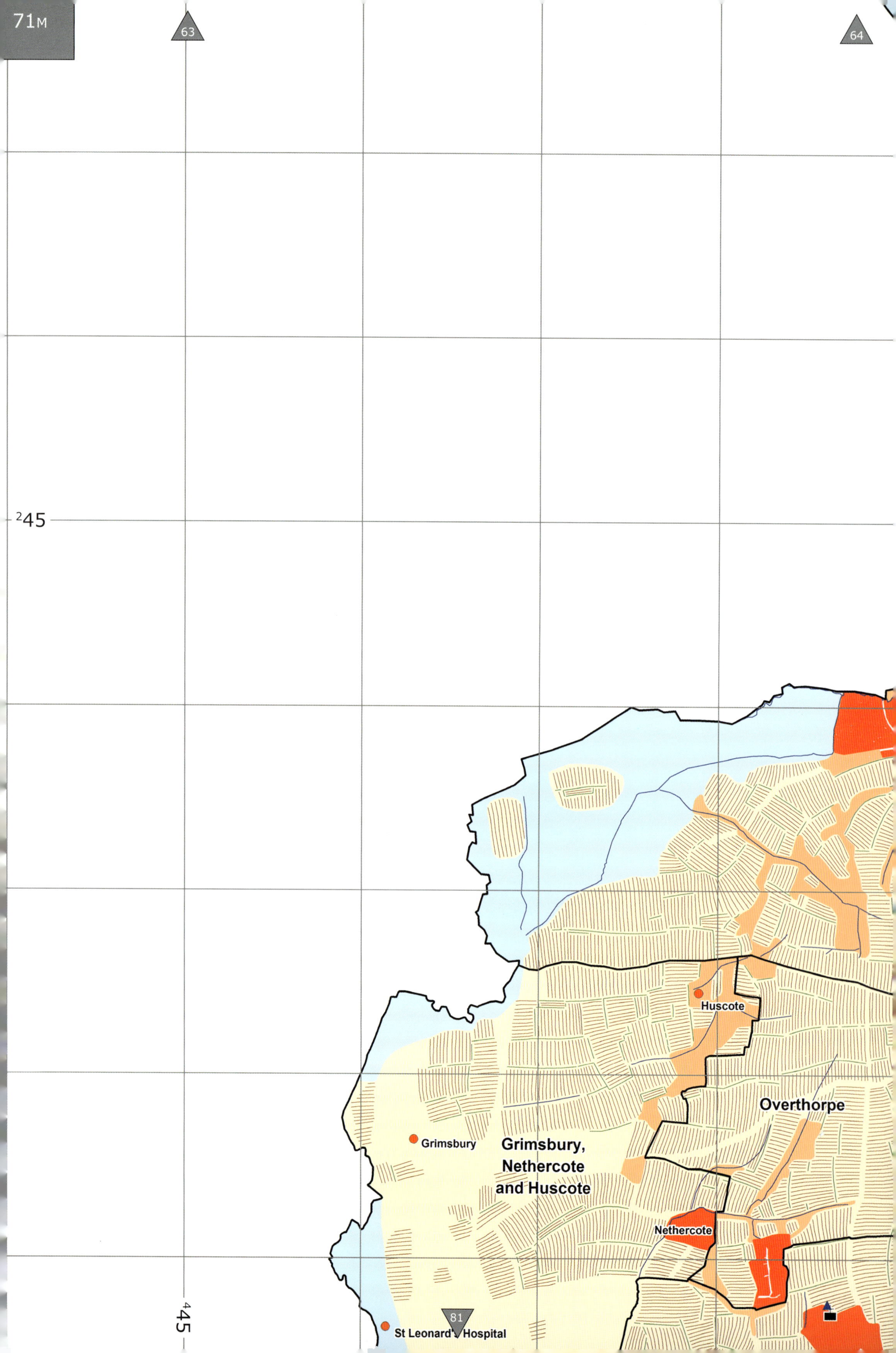
63
64
²45
⁴45
81
Huscote
Overthorpe
Grimsbury
Grimsbury,
Nethercote
and Huscote
Nethercote
St Leonard's Hospital

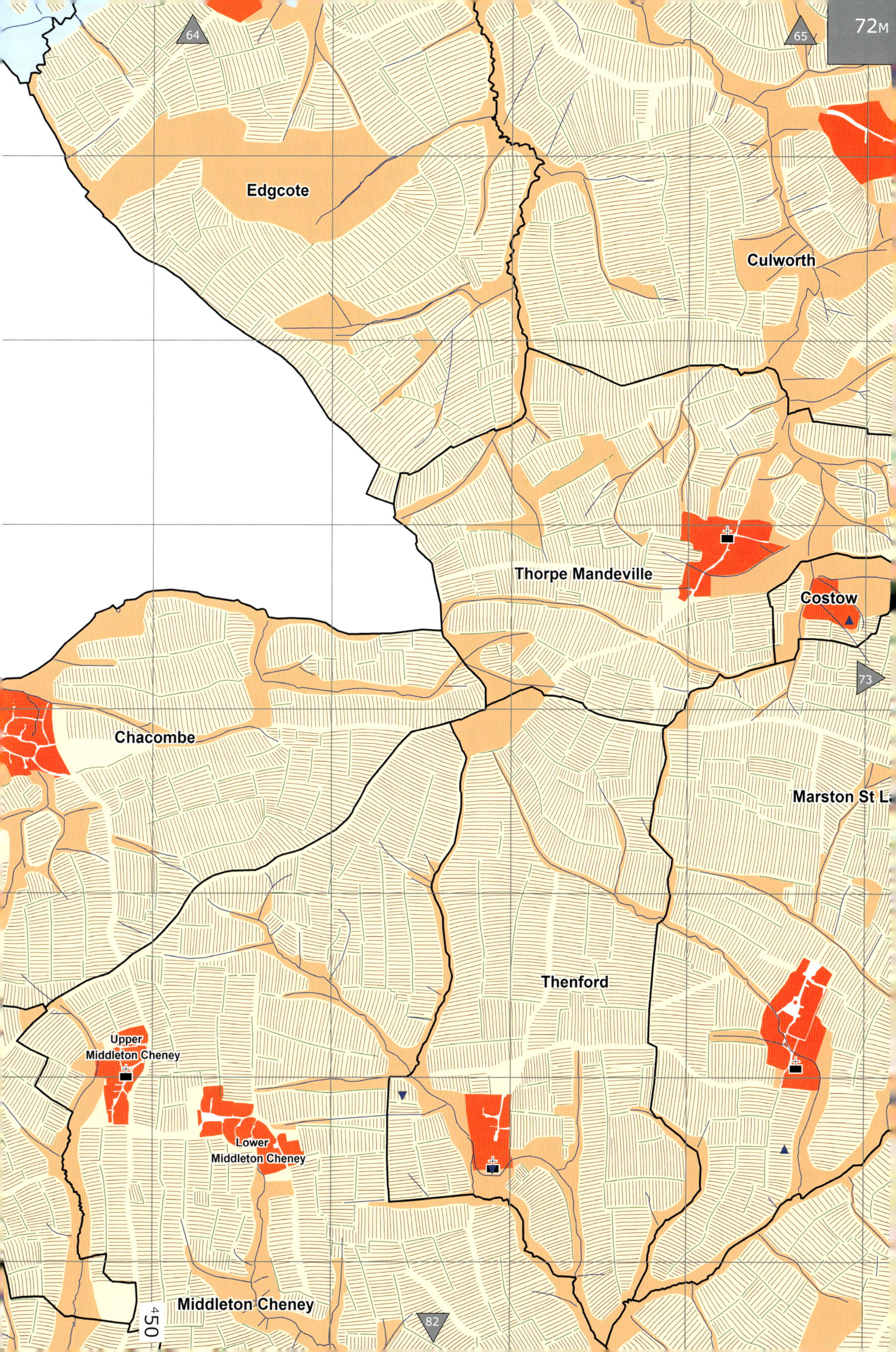
64
65
Edgcote
Culworth
Thorpe Mandeville
Costow
73
Chacombe
Marston St L
Thenford
Upper
Middleton Cheney
Lower
Middleton Cheney
Middleton Cheney
450
82

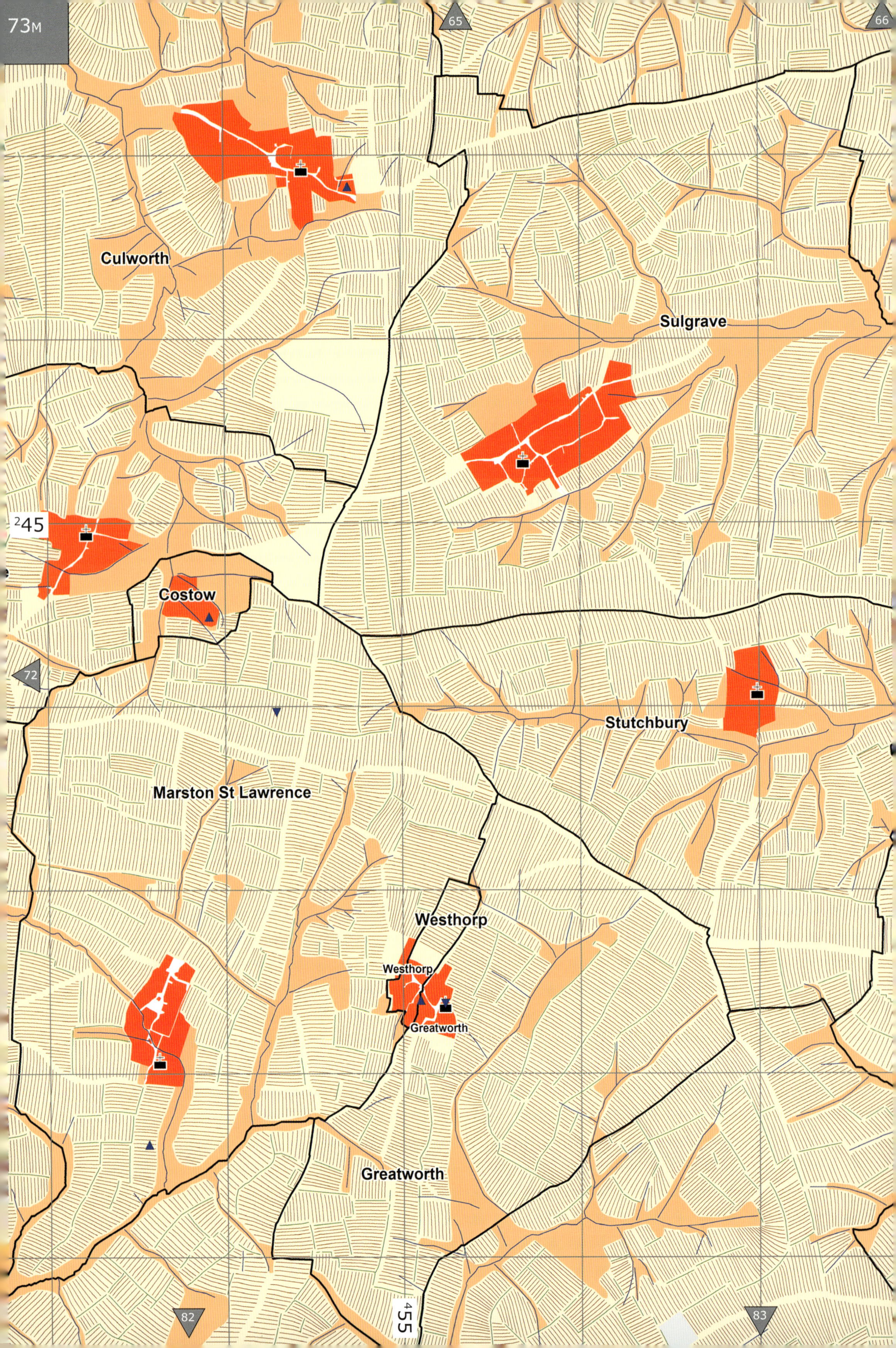

73M
65
66
Culworth
Sulgrave
245
Costow
72
Stutchbury
Marston St Lawrence
Westhorp
Westhorp
Greatworth
Greatworth
82
455
83

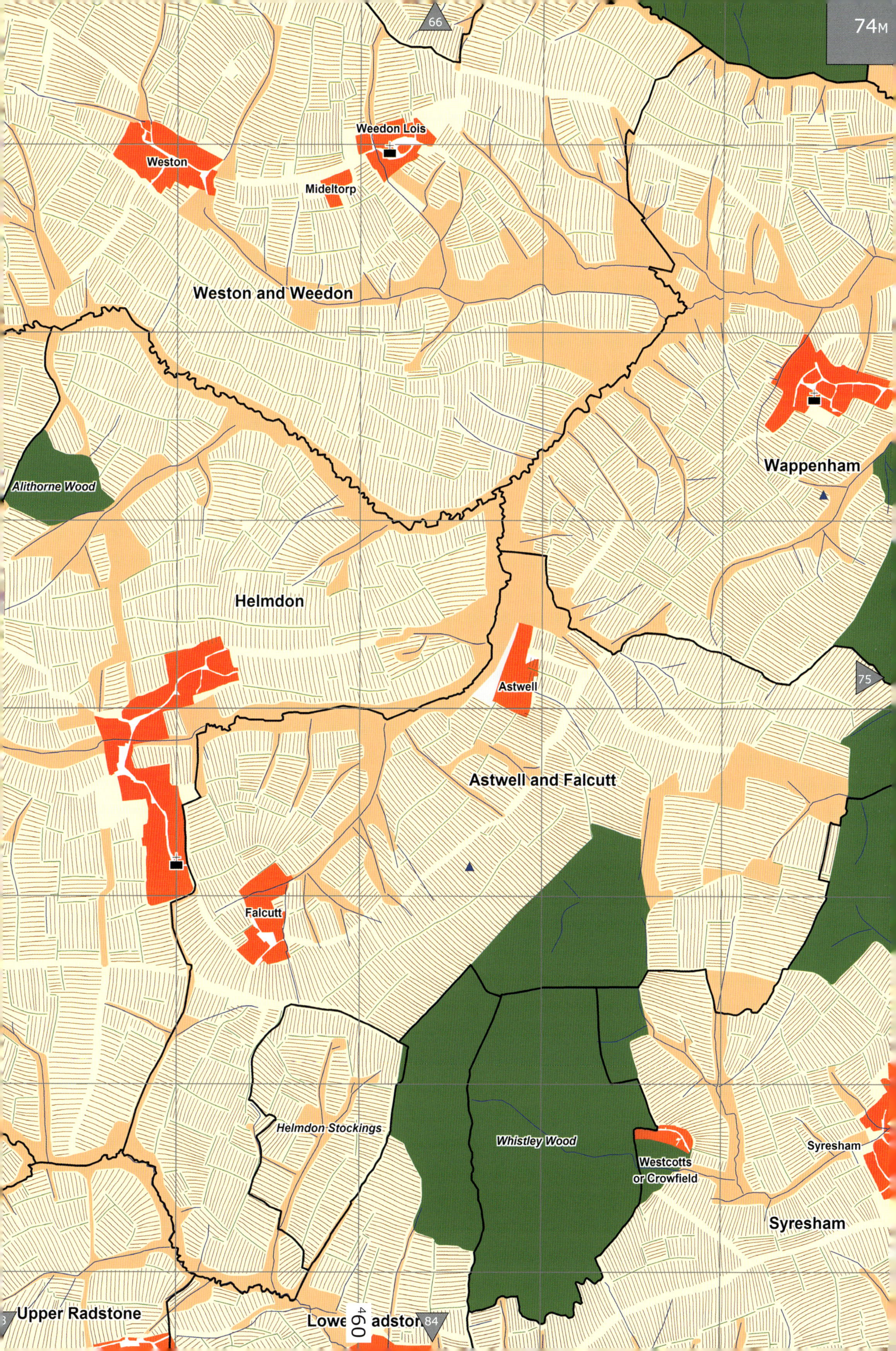

74M
66
Weedon Lois
Weston
Mideltorp
Weston and Weedon
Wappenham
Alithorne Wood
Helmdon
75
Astwell
Astwell and Falcutt
Falcutt
Helmdon Stockings
Whistley Wood
Westcotts
or Crowfield
Syresham
Syresham
Upper Radstone
Lowe
460
adston
84

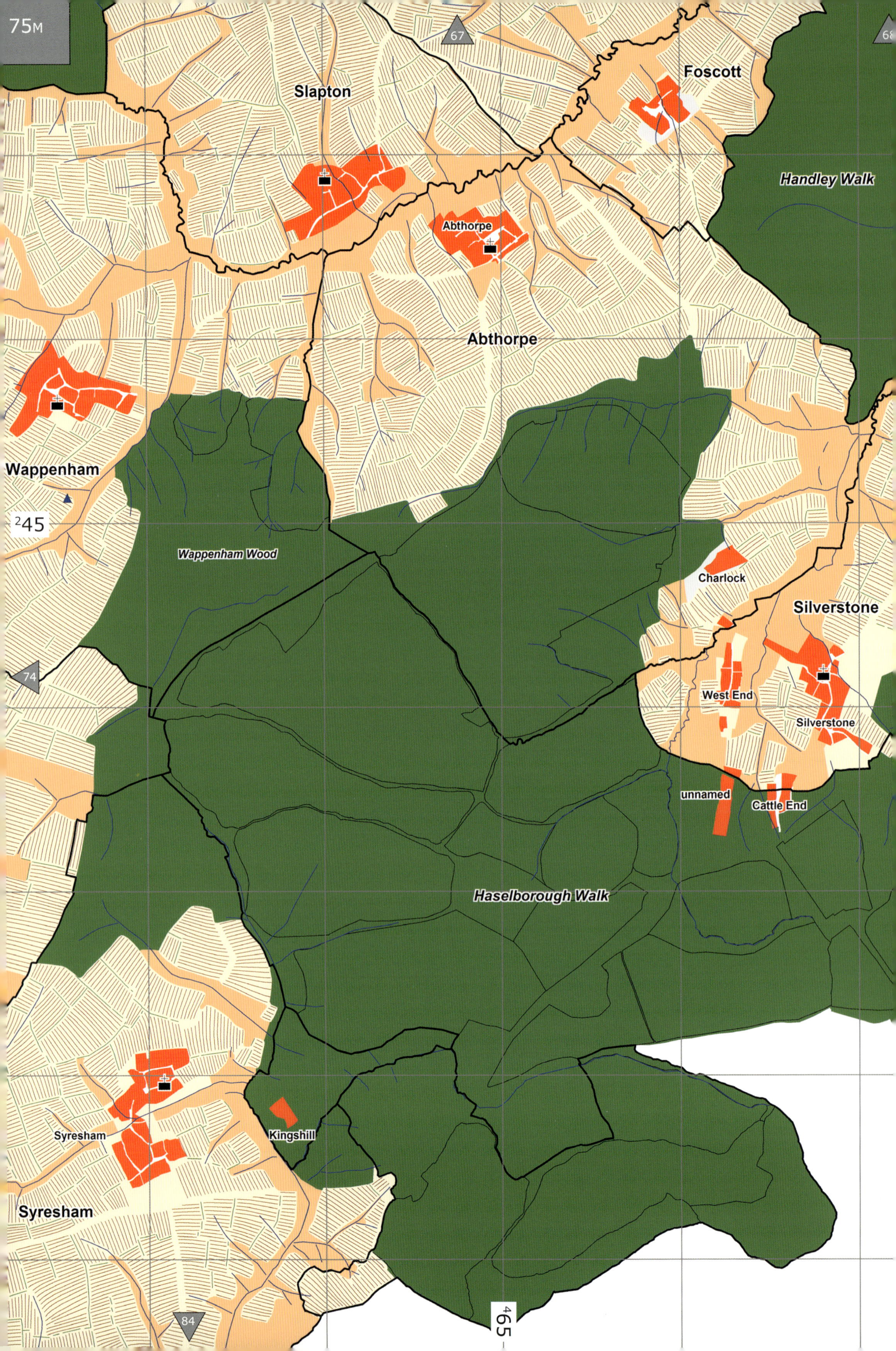
75M
67
68
Foscott
Slapton
Handley Walk
Abthorpe
Abthorpe
Wappenham
245
Wappenham Wood
Charlock
Silverstone
74
West End
Silverstone
unnamed
Cattle End
Haselborough Walk
Syresham
Kingshill
Syresham
84
465

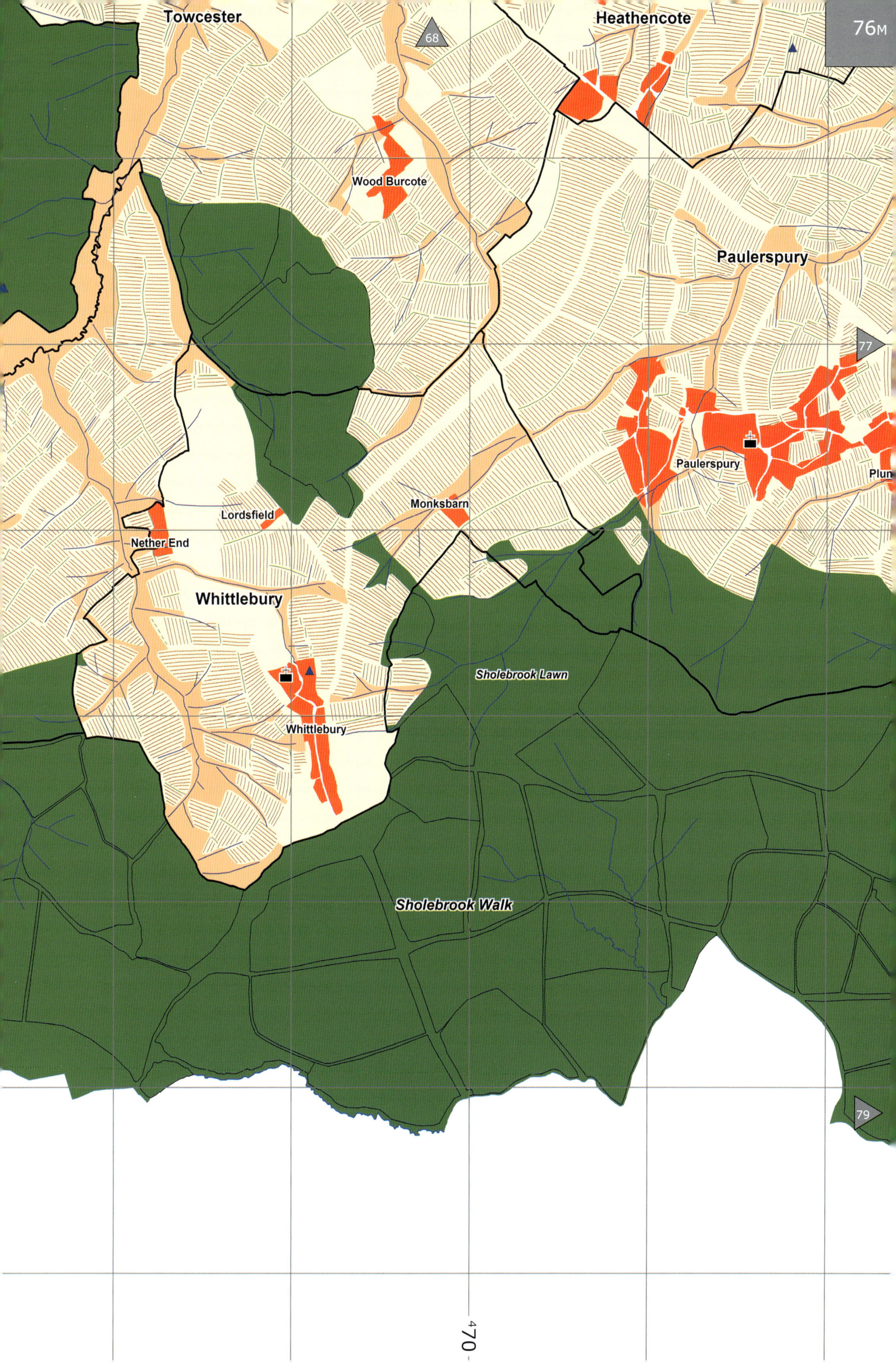

Towcester
68
Heathencote
76M
Wood Burcote
Paulerspury
77
Paulerspury
Plun
Lordsfield
Monksbarn
Nether End
Whittlebury
Sholebrook Lawn
Whittlebury
Sholebrook Walk
79
470

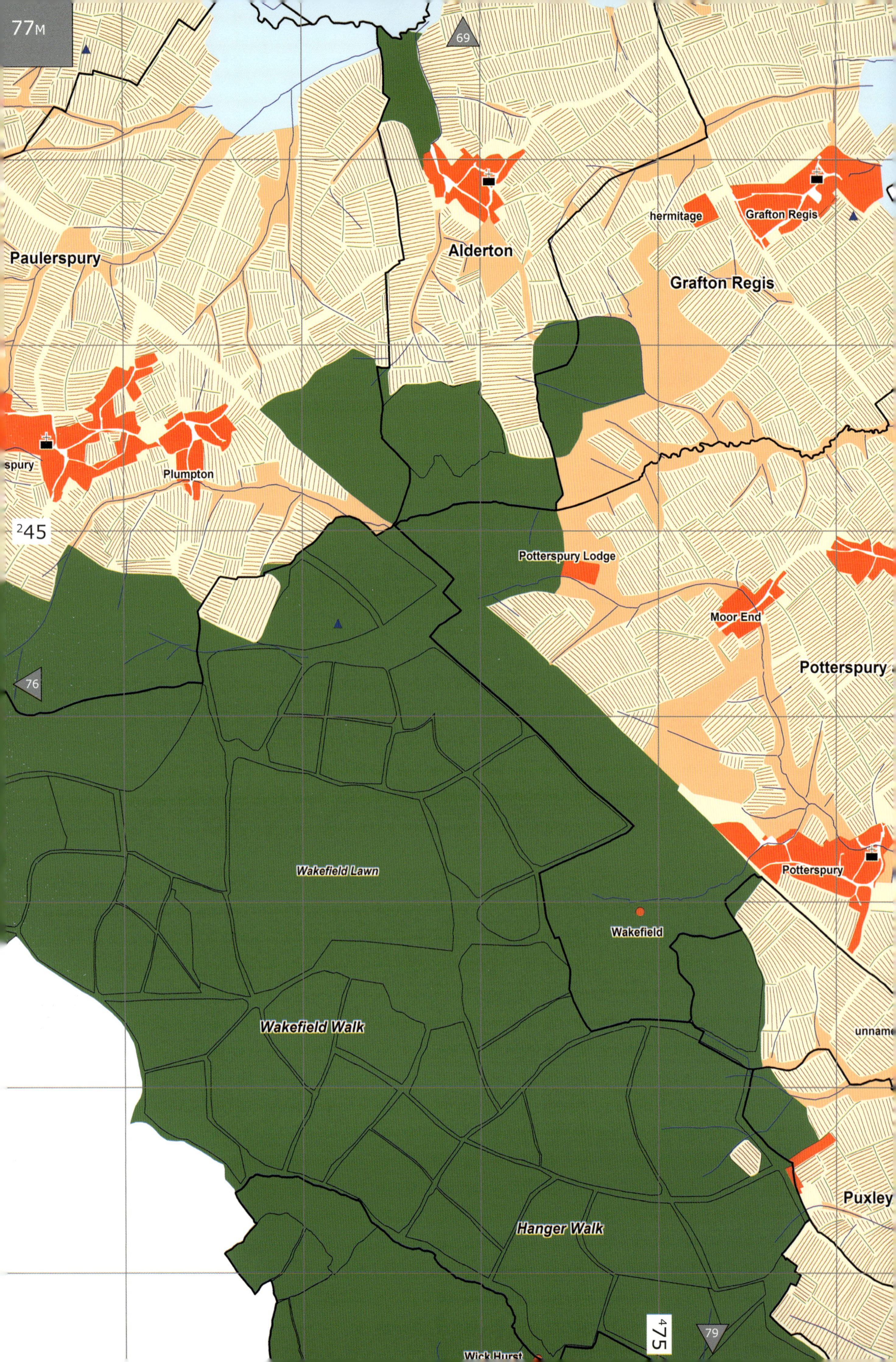

69
Paulerspury
Alderton
hermitage
Grafton Regis
Grafton Regis
spury
Plumpton
245
Potterspury Lodge
Moor End
Potterspury
76
Wakefield Lawn
Potterspury
Wakefield
Wakefield Walk
unname
Puxley
Hanger Walk
475
79
Wick Hurst

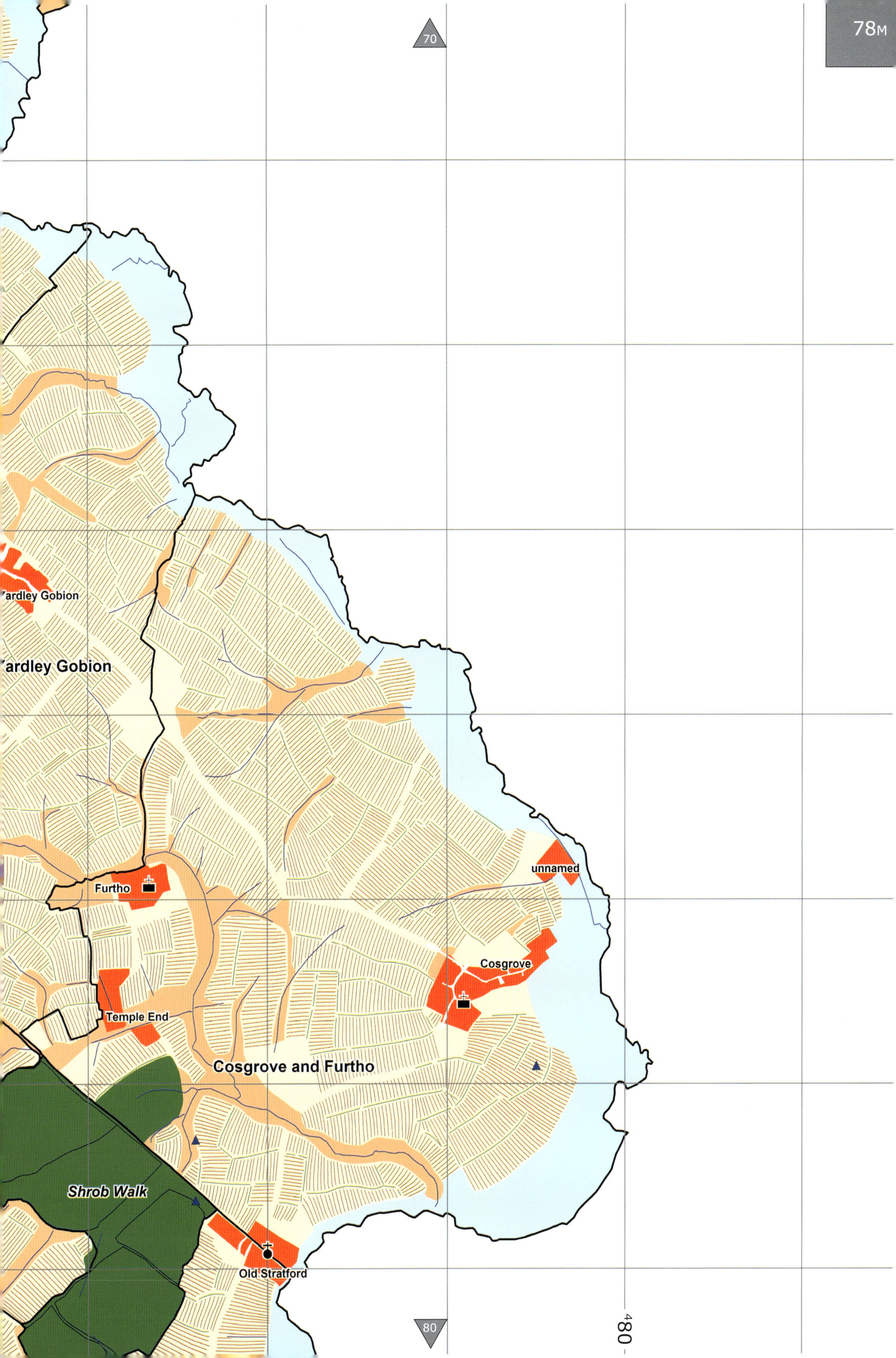
70
ardley Gobion
'ardley Gobion
Furtho
unnamed
Cosgrove
Temple End
Cosgrove and Furtho
Shrob Walk
Old Stratford
80
480

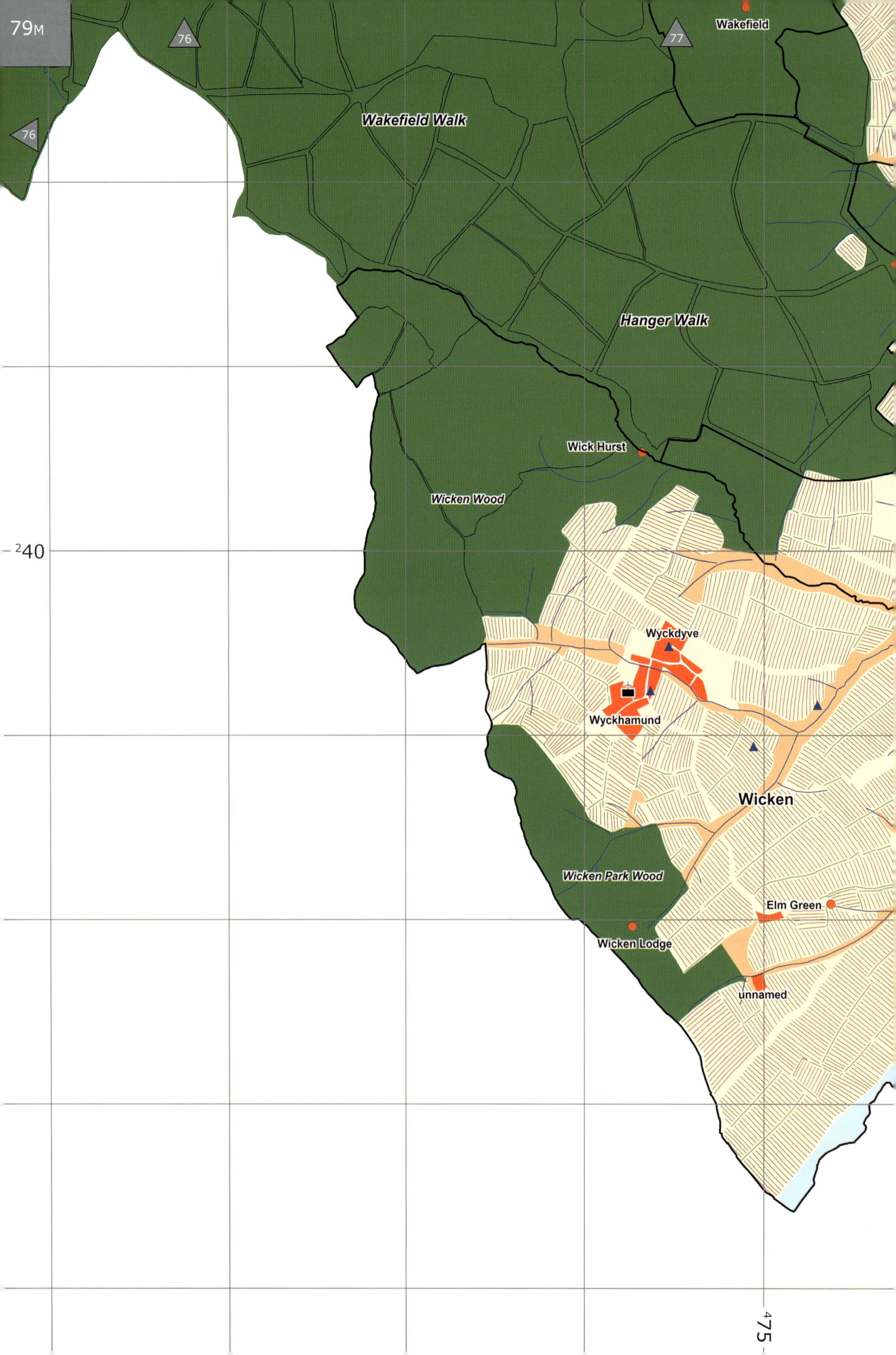
79M
76
77
Wakefield
76
Wakefield Walk
Hanger Walk
Wick Hurst
Wicken Wood
240
Wyckdyve
Wyckhamund
Wicken
Wicken Park Wood
Elm Green
Wicken Lodge
unnamed
475

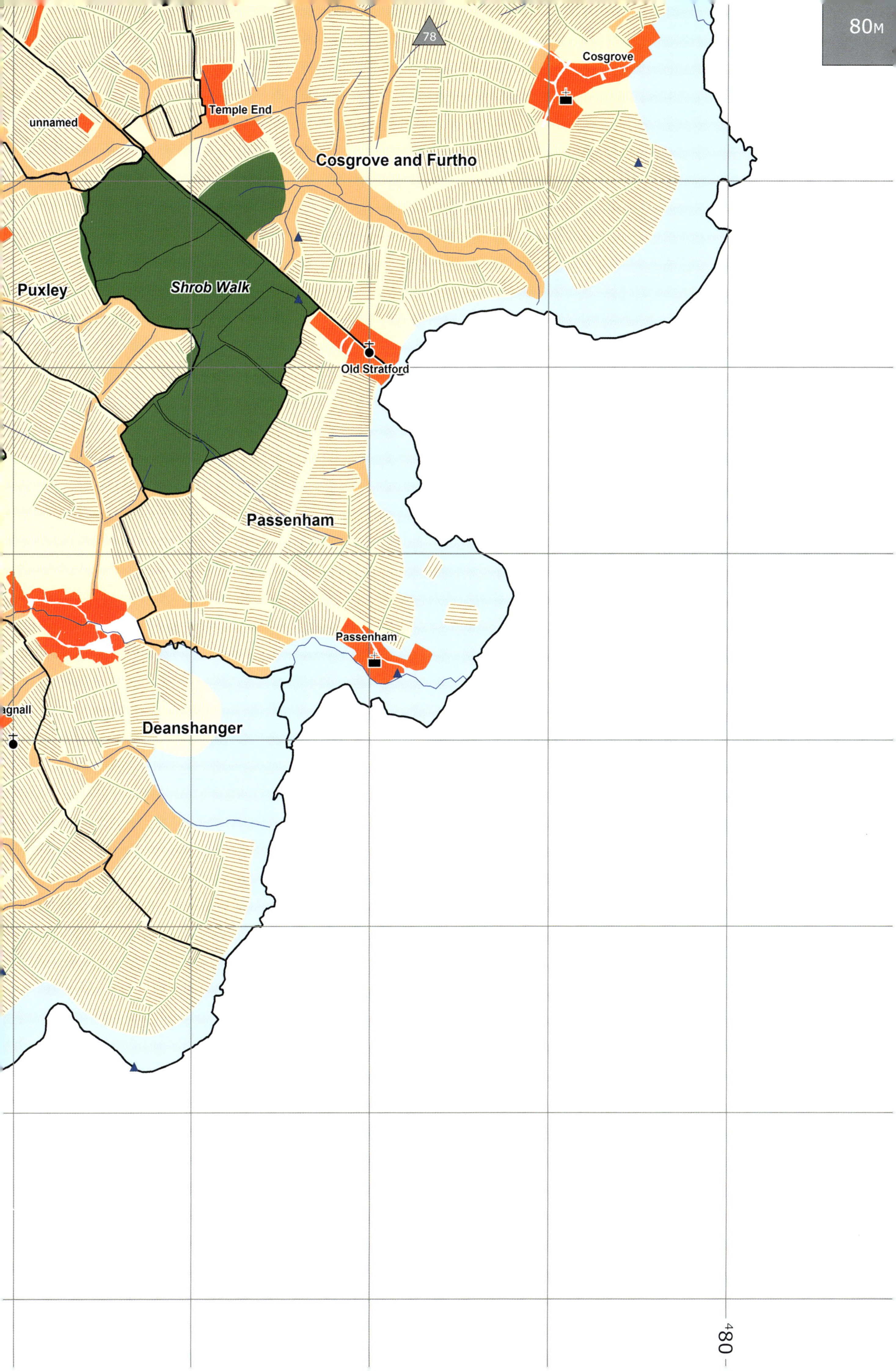
78
Cosgrove
Temple End
unnamed
Cosgrove and Furtho
Puxley
Shrob Walk
Old Stratford
Passenham
Passenham
Deanshanger
agnall
480

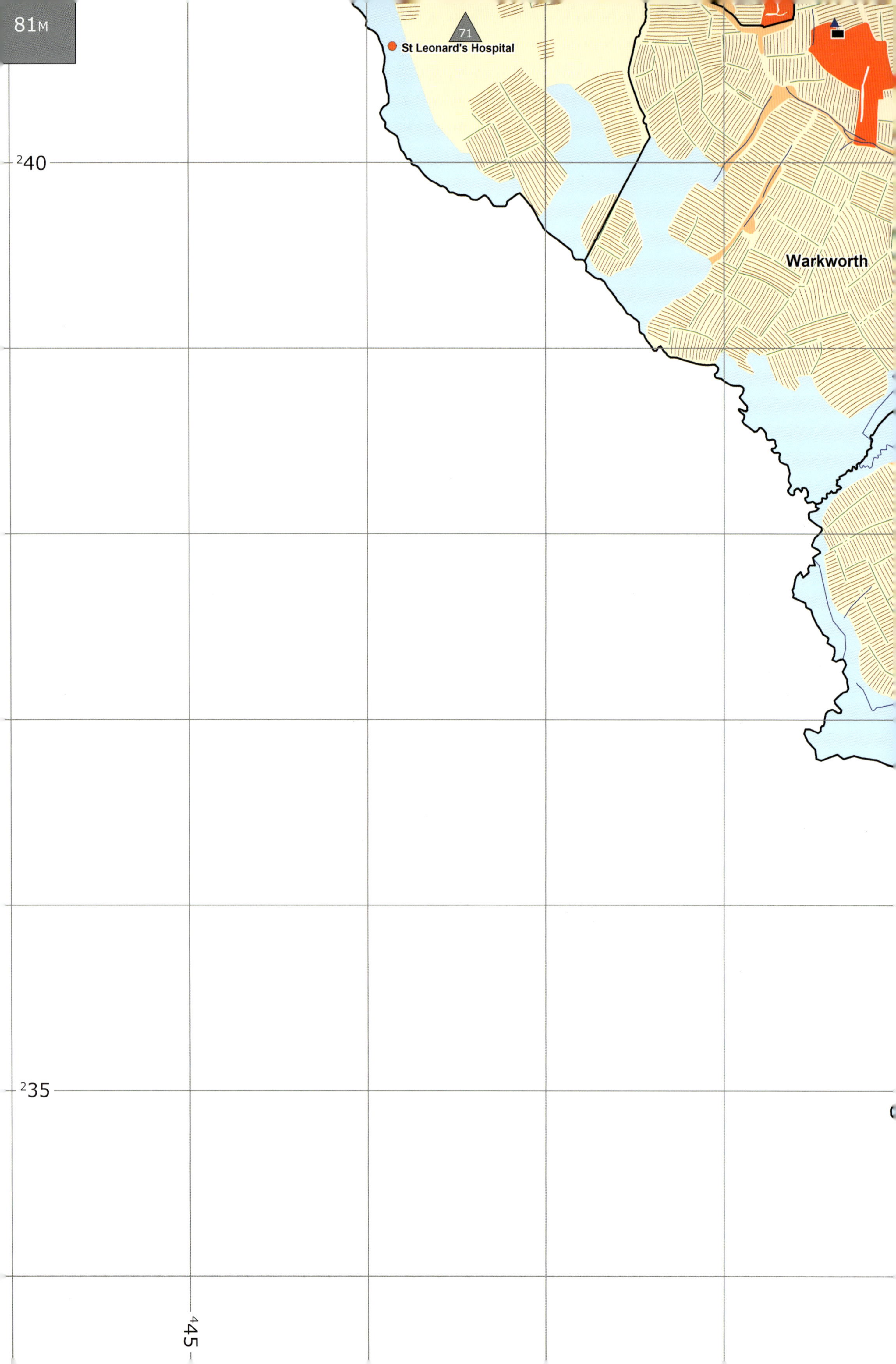
71
St Leonard's Hospital
Warkworth
240
235
445

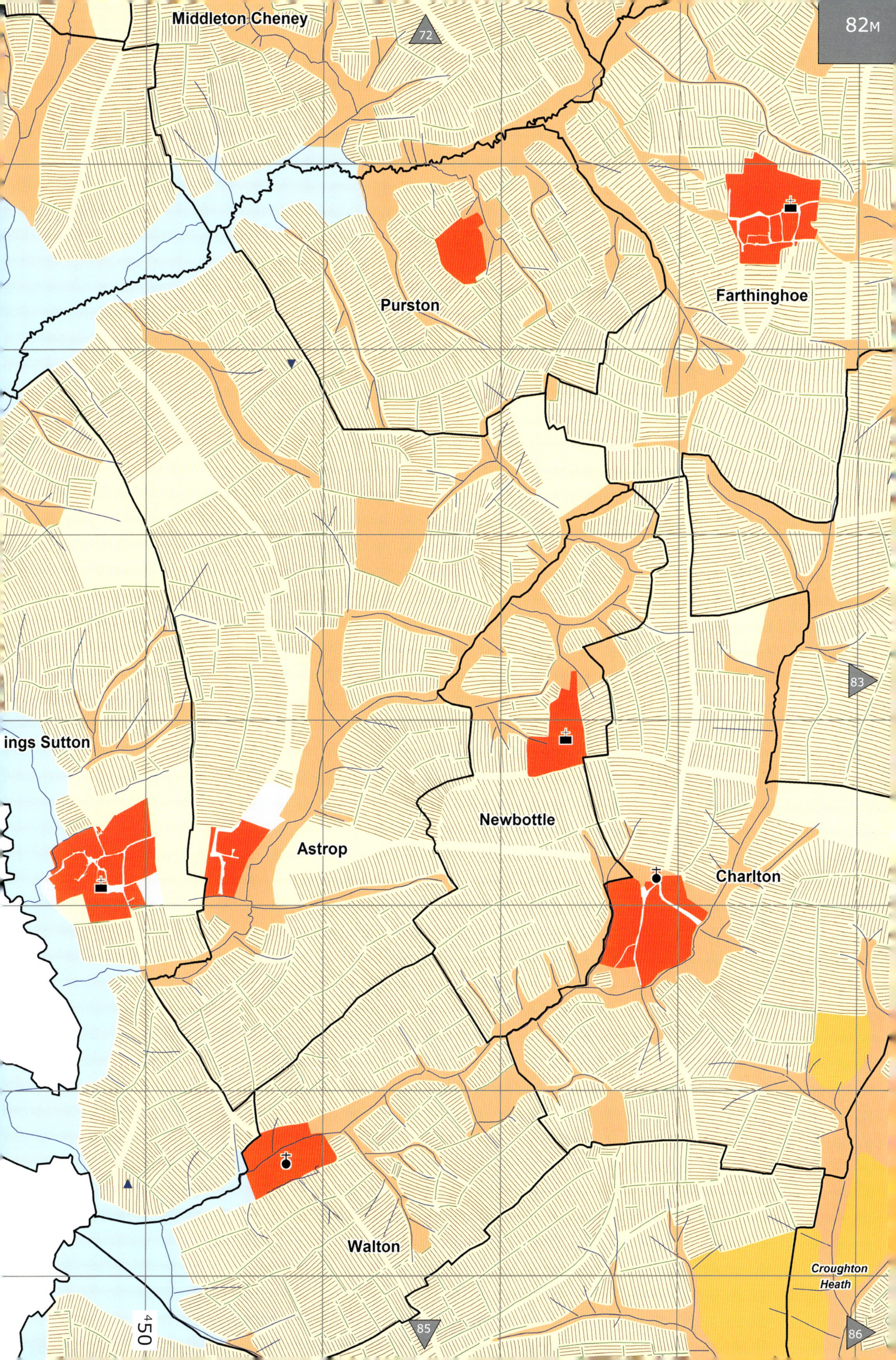
Middleton Cheney
72
Purston
Farthinghoe
83
ings Sutton
Newbottle
Astrop
Charlton
Walton
Croughton
Heath
450
85
86

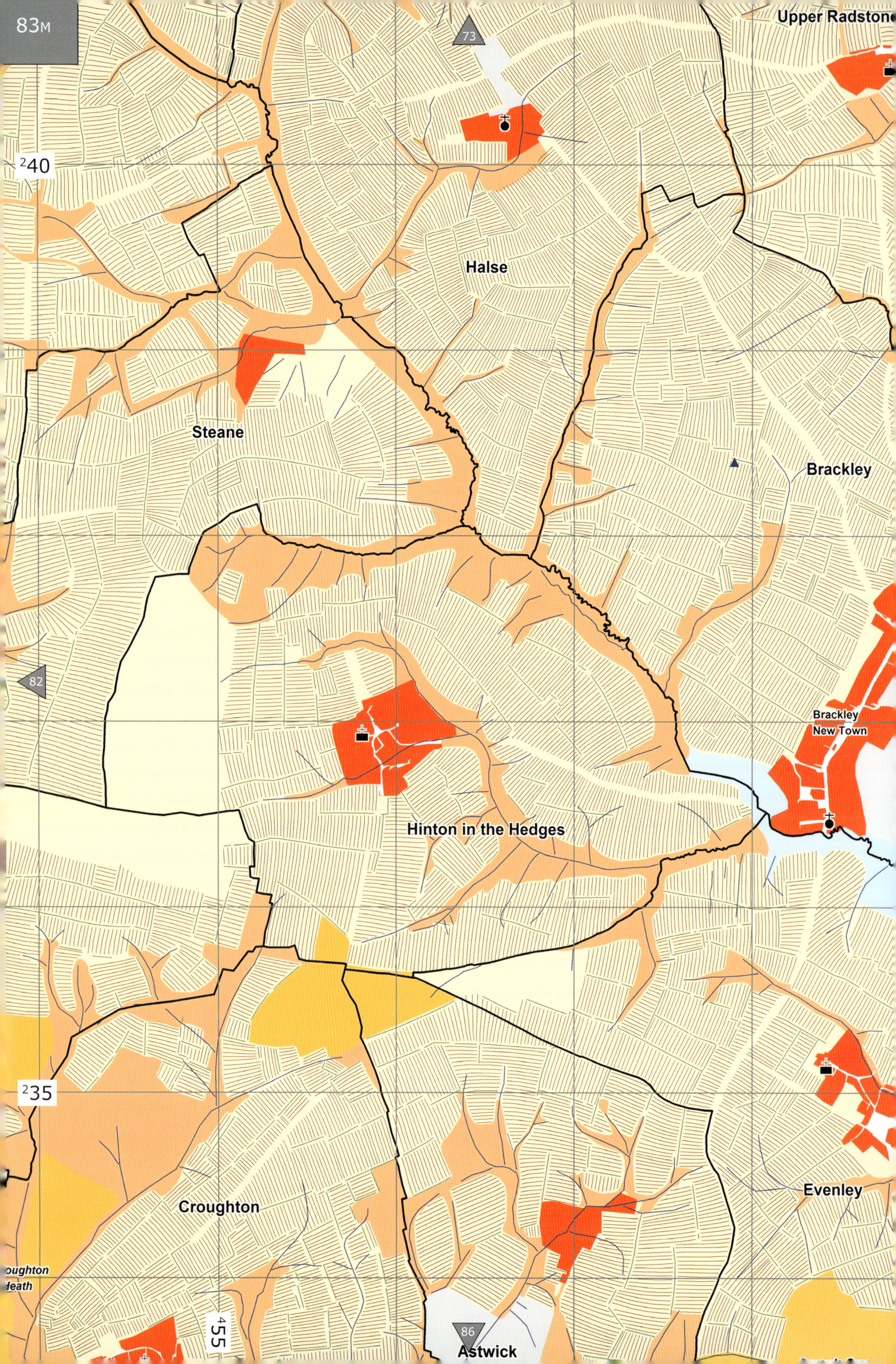

83M
73
Upper Radstone
240
Halse
Steane
Brackley
82
Brackley
New Town
Hinton in the Hedges
235
Croughton
oughton
leath
455
86
Astwick
Evenley

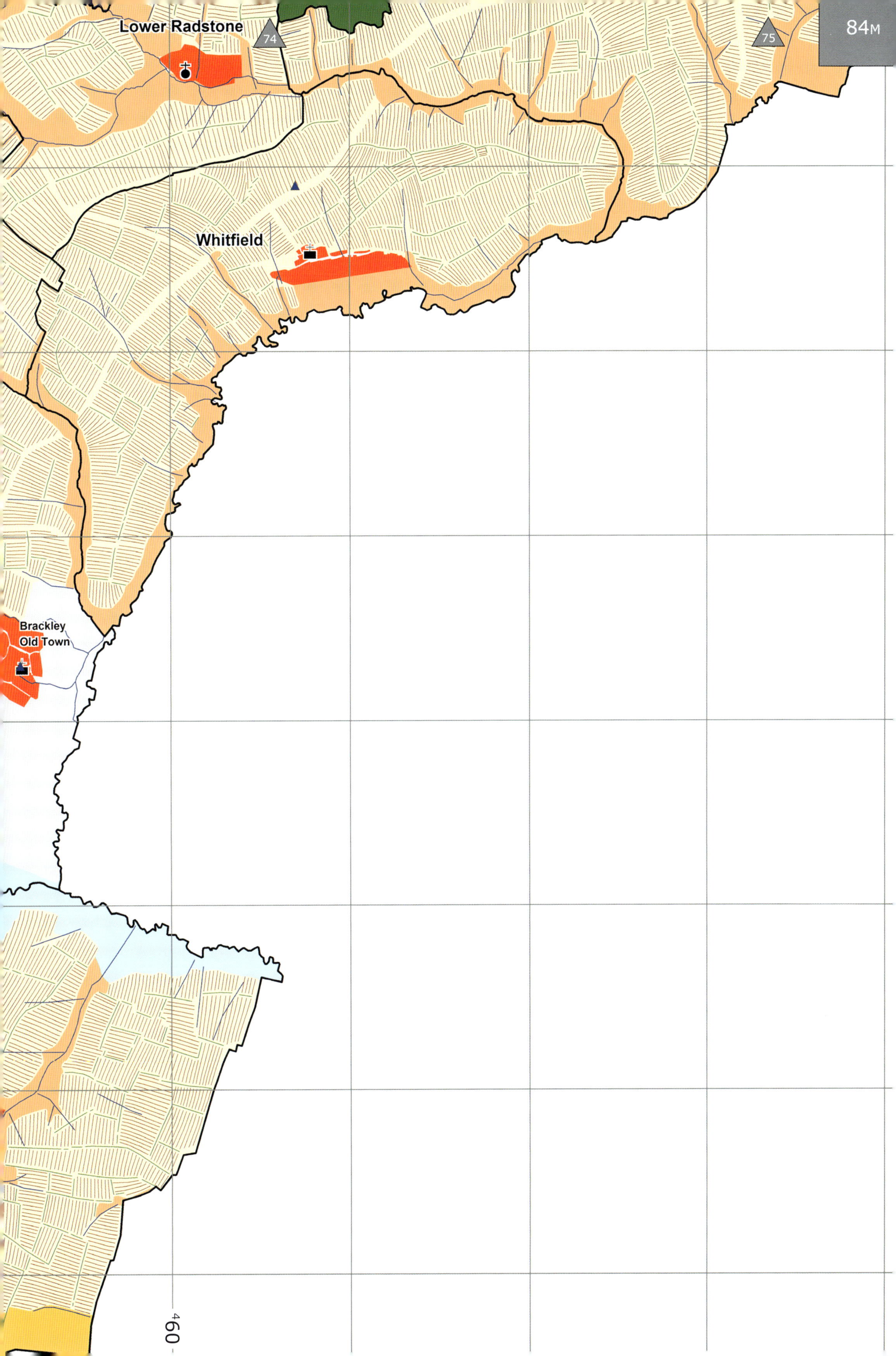
Lower Radstone
74
75
Whitfield
Brackley
Old Town
460

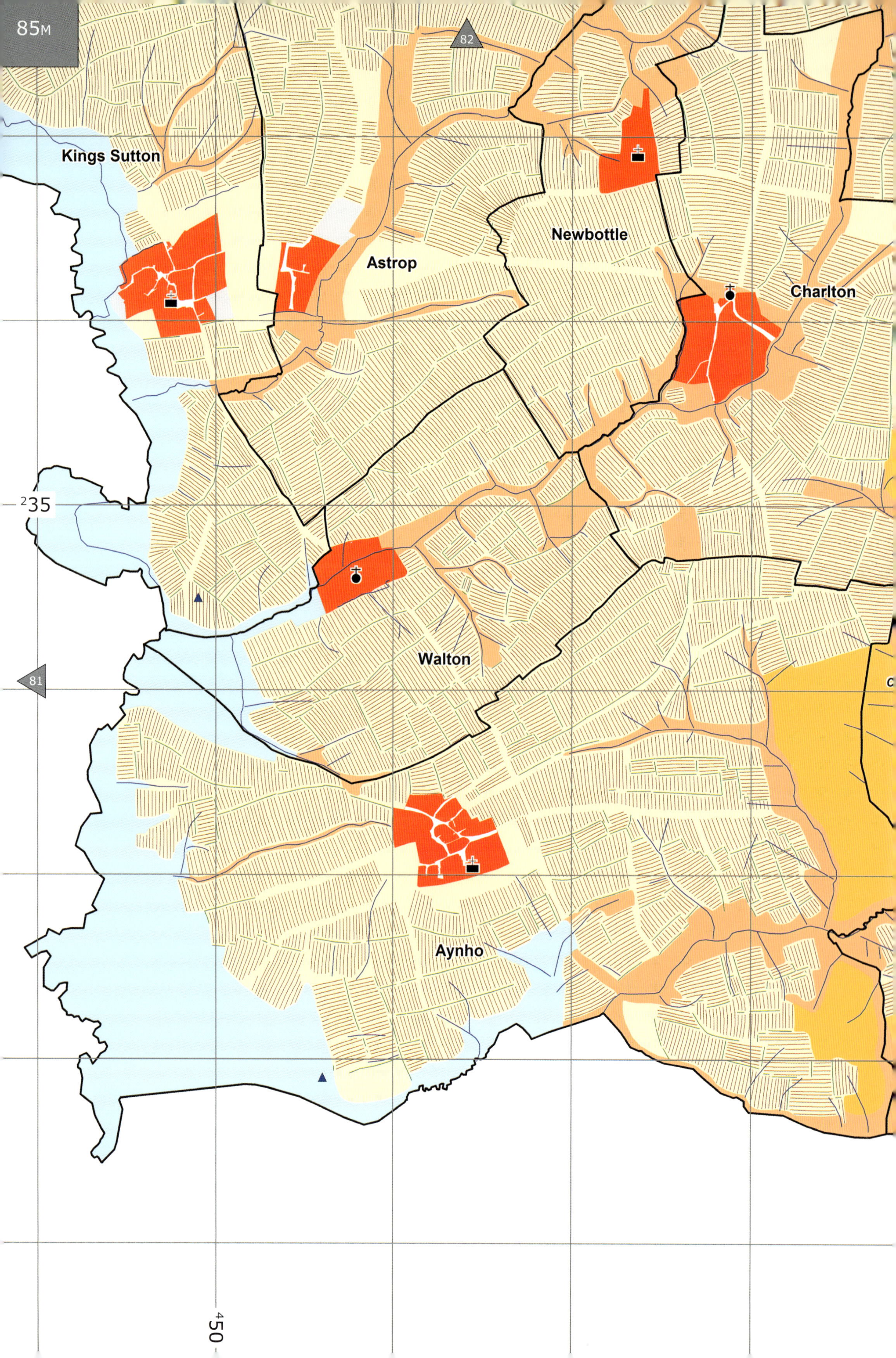

85M
82
Kings Sutton
Astrop
Newbottle
Charlton
²35
Walton
81
Aynho
⁴50

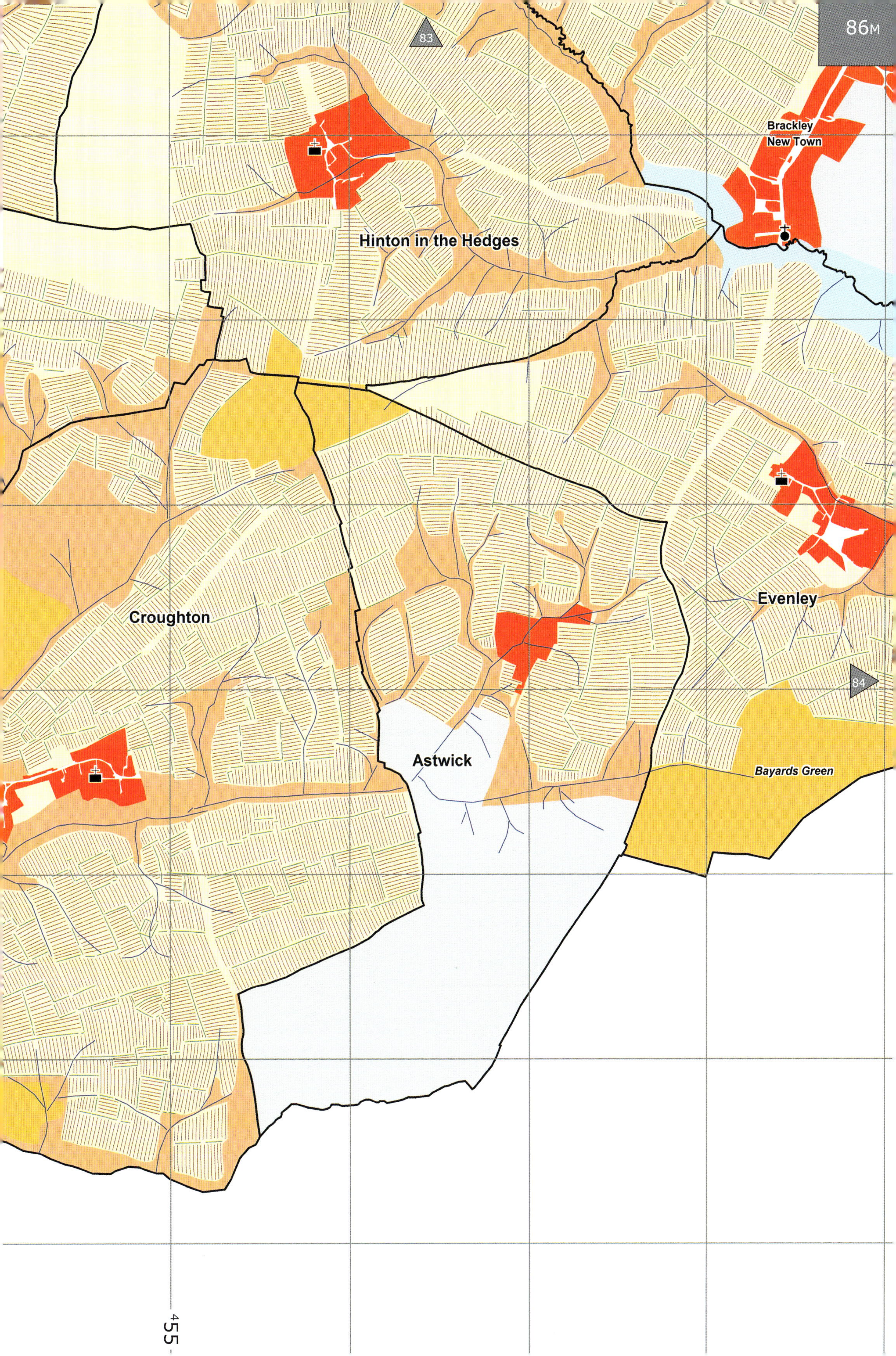
83
Brackley New Town
Hinton in the Hedges
Evenley
Croughton
84
Astwick
Bayards Green
455

Early-Modern Atlas

The early-modern mapping shows the landscape as it was *c.*1770 at the height of Parliamentary enclosure in the county. The 461 source maps are of widely different dates as indicated in the appendices. Some twenty-two of the source maps are reconstructions, usually of enclosure awards, and these are indicated in the appendices. It is possible that there had been some alteration to landscape features, particularly infilling of closes or removal of hedges, in the period between the date of the map and 1770.

Two of the data sets, ridge and furrow, and meadows, are taken from the medieval data. Though there may have been some modification of the open fields the research has shown that where they were still in operation in the early-modern period they were largely unchanged and so the use of this data is considered valid. A brief description of each of the data sets is given below but for a full discussion of methodology see Chapter 1.

Ridge and furrow strips: The furlong data depicted here for those areas still operating open fields is taken from the medieval data. Some of the arable may have been altered by conversion to pasture, but where it remains the furlongs are unlikely to have been reorganised. Most of the source maps do not show ridge and furrow and it has not been recorded as part of the early-modern data sets

Open field: The open field depicted on the maps is the full extent as shown on the source maps and includes arable and pasture. There will have been some pasture within the open fields in the form of baulks and along slades, and in some areas substantial pasture in cow commons. These are rarely shown on the source maps and so are not depicted here.

Meadow: The meadow from the medieval data has been utilised for the early-modern atlas pages. For those townships where there were still functioning open fields it is likely that the meadows were also still functioning. Source maps rarely show meadows.

Fen: Fen occurs only in the Soke of Peterborough. The extent of the fen is taken from enclosure maps and the particularly straight boundaries are therefore likely to be enclosure impositions rather than the true boundary of the fen pre-enclosure.

Heath: The heaths recorded are all those depicted on the source maps. It is known that there were others still functioning at the time of enclosure but either the source map does not shown them, as at Ravensthorpe and Long Buckby, or there is no contemporary map as at Harlestone and Hollowell. Each of the features is labelled with the name as given on the source map.

Greens, plains, lawns and ridings: This data set comprises features mostly associated with wood pasture such as lawns and ridings. However, it also includes greens within townships such as at Great Brington and Brafield, and large village greens such as at Nether Heyford. Some sources depict an open area within a settlement but do not label it as a 'green'. Further research was undertaken to see if these areas could be identified as greens from other sources. In particular the OS first edition 1:10,560 mapping from the 1880s was utilised to establish if such places were still open or labelled as greens at this date. If so they were added to the data set, as at Creaton, Deanshanger, Faxton, and Earls Barton. For some places substantial greens were recorded, such as at Warmington and Northborough, but it has not been possible to map them from the available sources. Each of the features is labelled with the name as given on the source map.

Wood: Individual coppices as well as plantations and spinneys are included in this data set. All features are labelled with the name given in the source map.

Building: All buildings depicted on the source maps are recorded. For those places with little or no enclosure outside of the settlement core the only buildings within the wider landscape were those associated with milling, or hunting such as lodges. Anciently enclosed places may have several farm complexes and isolated barns outside of the settlement core. Buildings can also be seen within some of the forests and these would also be associated with hunting.

Enclosure: Each individual enclosed plot or 'close' has been recorded. They are distinguished by colour from the enclosed areas for which there is no information to identify internal boundaries (see below). Therefore the very large closes seen in some places were that size at the time of the map and usual reflect the early date of the map showing large sheep closes, as at Brockhall, or indicate landscape parks as at Althorp.

Enclosure extent: This data set includes those areas that are known to have been anciently enclosed but for which no map has been identified, or a map shows only part of the township, or the data is reconstructed from other documentary sources. It also includes areas that are shown on a map as enclosed but for which no internal boundaries are given, such as glebe land on tithe maps. It can cover whole townships as at Lilbourne, or parts of a township as at Moreton Pinkney.

Rivers and streams: Water has been digitized primarily from the OS 1:10,560 mapping of the 1880s. For almost the entire county this is later than the date of enclosure. Some early streams would have been altered or disappeared altogether into underground drainage systems, whilst conversely new drains and channels might have been introduced. Tributaries of the Nene and channels around mills were particularly complicated, as were the post enclosure drains in the Soke. By utilising historic maps an attempt was made to identify and exclude later water courses as well as include those that were present at enclosure. Any post-enclosure 'industrial' water such as that associated with brick works, tramways and quarries, especially around the towns, was not recorded. Canals were not recorded to this data set although they may be visible in places as linear gaps between the closes, as at Stoke Bruerne. The rivers Nene and Welland are identified by a thicker line. Where this coincides with a township boundary it can be difficult to see though a 'wiggly' township boundary usually denotes a water course.

Lakes and ponds: Large bodies of water, lakes and ponds, were recorded if they over 500m in length. For smaller bodies of water the line of the stream is continued through the centre. Reservoirs were not recorded.

Township boundary: The township boundaries are mapped from the earliest possible source and all maps that depict the boundaries are consulted. It is therefore usual for the data to come from more than one map source and not uncommon for there to be as many as six sources for any one township. Detached blocks are identified and labelled e.g. Cogenhoe (Det.).

Roads from Eayre 1791: Major roads shown on Eayre's map have been recorded where possible.

No map data: The areas for which no contemporary map has been identified are shown as grey.

Legend

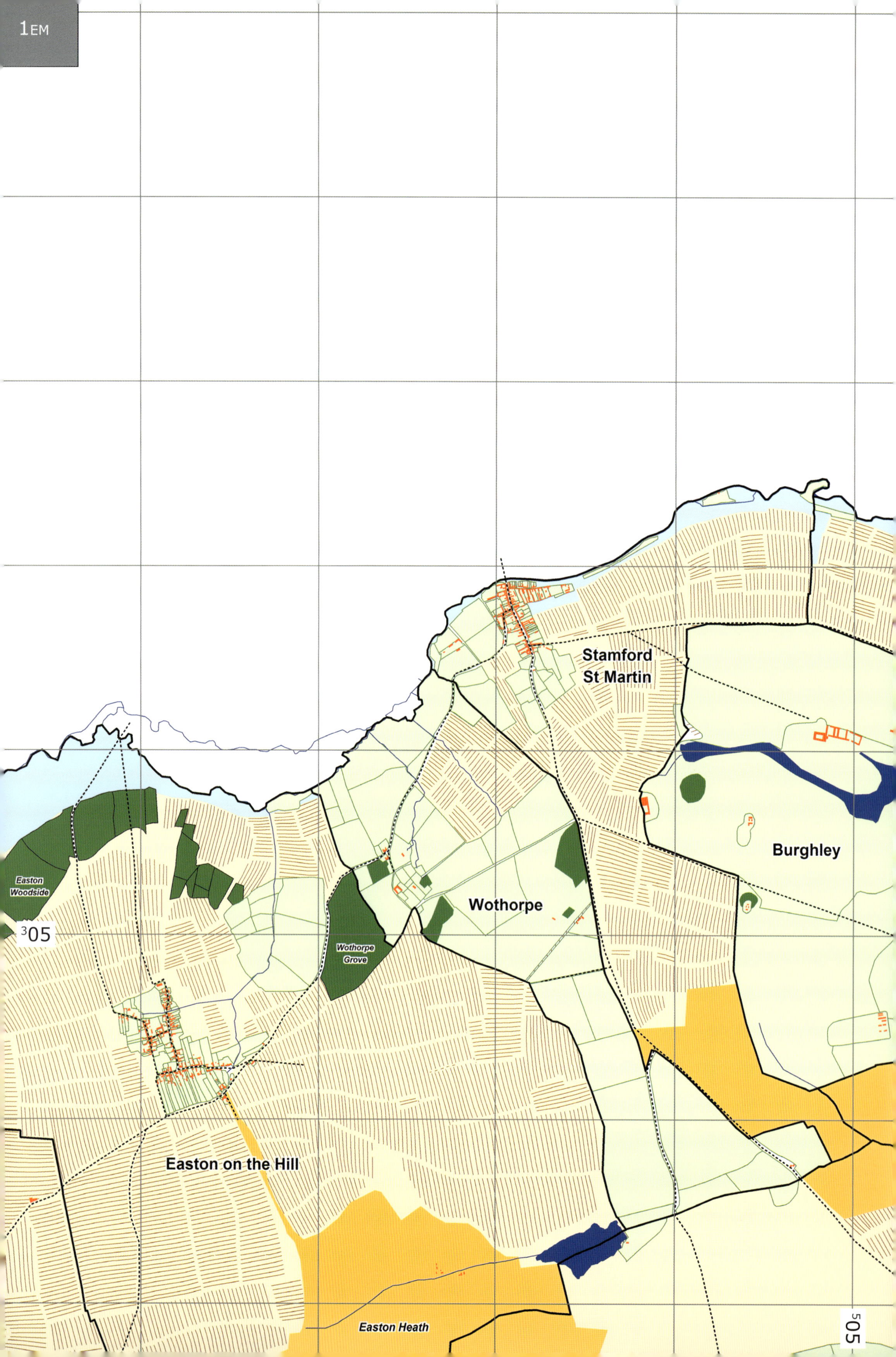
Stamford
St Martin
Burghley
Wothorpe
Easton
Woodside
305
Wothorpe
Grove
Easton on the Hill
Easton Heath
505

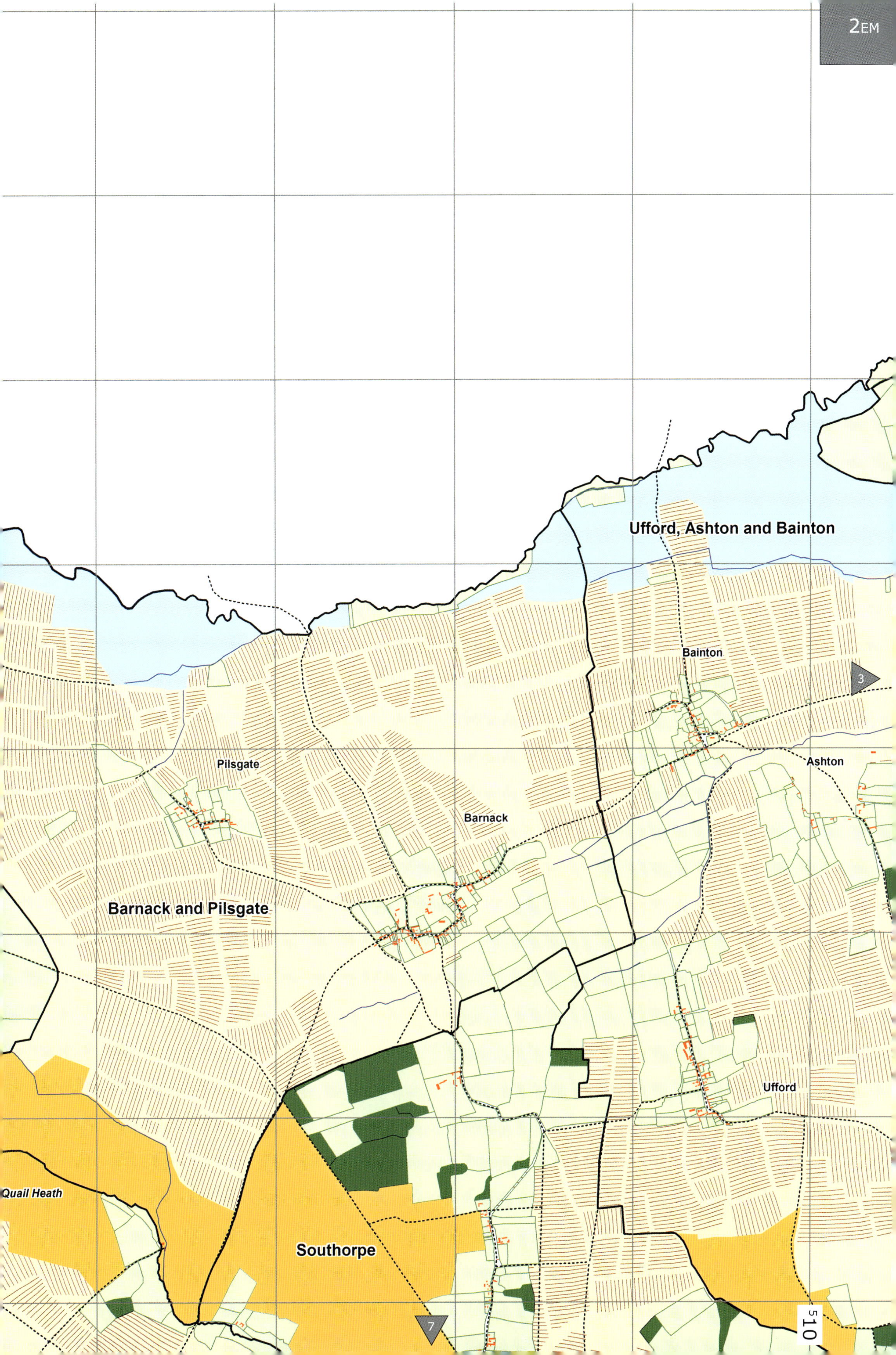

2EM
Ufford, Ashton and Bainton
Bainton
3
Ashton
Pilsgate
Barnack
Barnack and Pilsgate
Ufford
Quail Heath
Southorpe
7
510

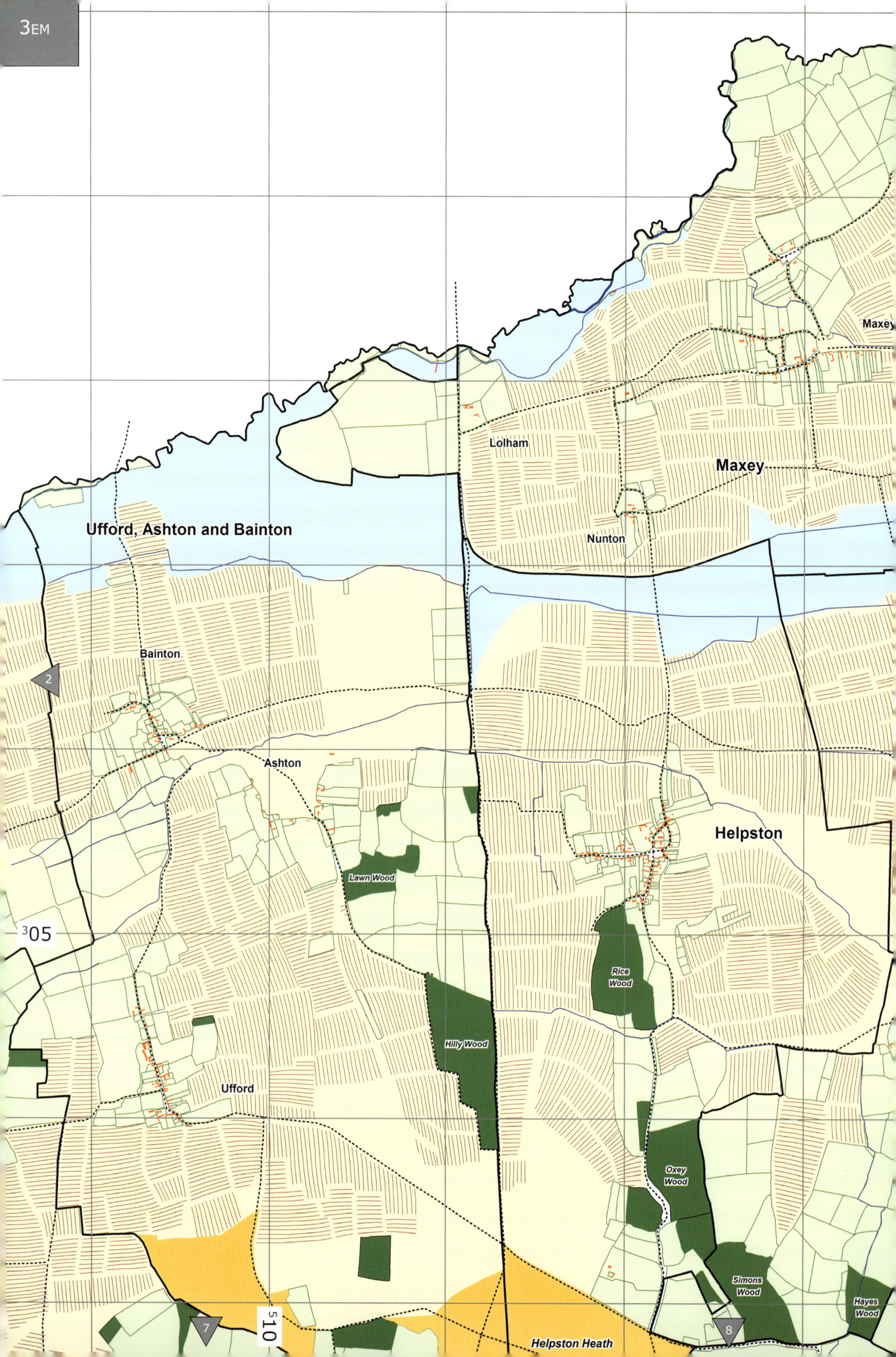

Ufford, Ashton and Bainton
Lolham
Maxey
Maxey
Nunton
Bainton
2
Ashton
Helpston
Lawn Wood
Rice Wood
Hilly Wood
Ufford
Oxey Wood
Simons Wood
Hayes Wood
Helpston Heath
7
8
305
510

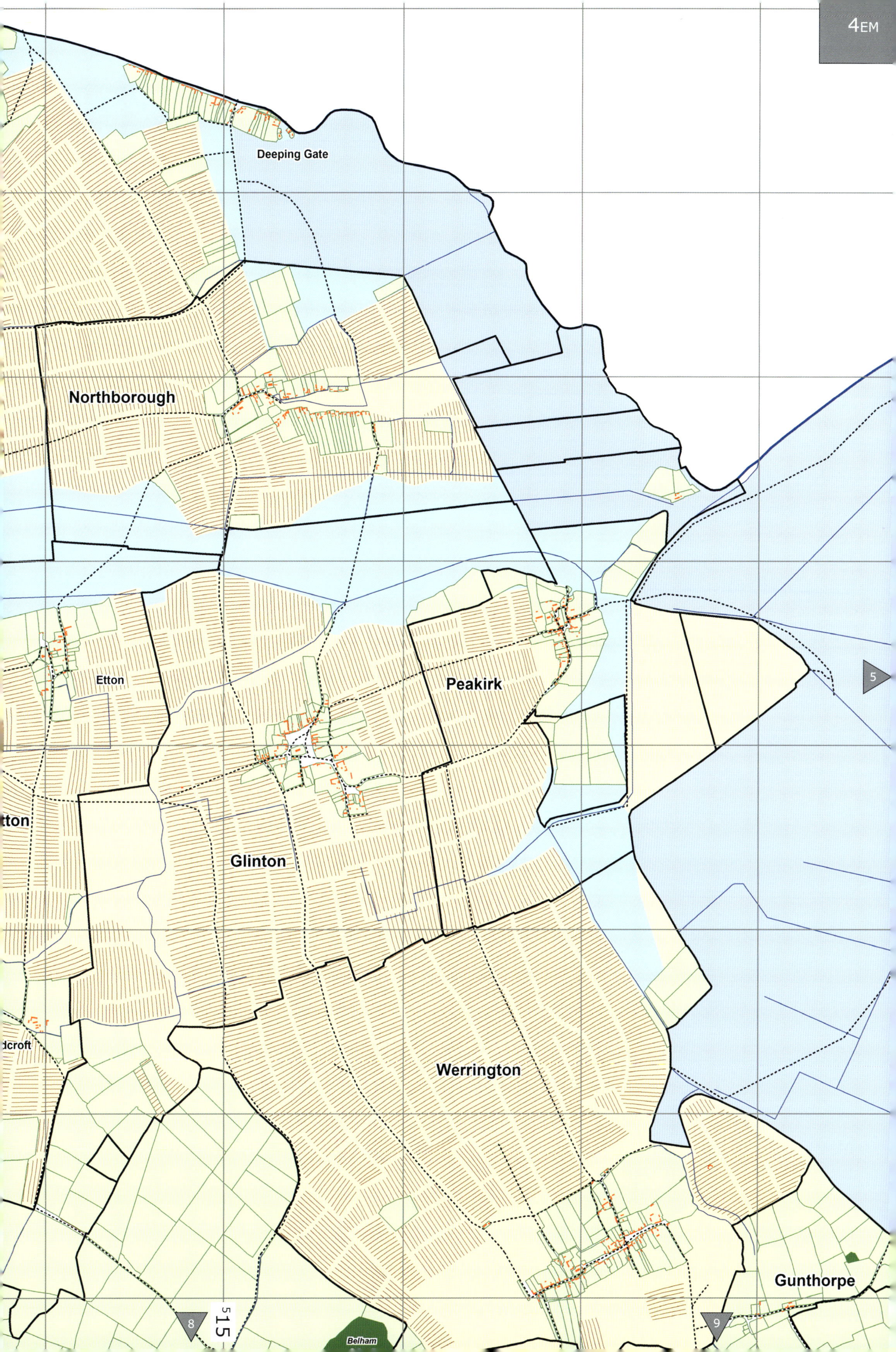

Deeping Gate
Northborough
Etton
Peakirk
tton
Glinton
dcroft
Werrington
Gunthorpe
Belham
5
8
9
515

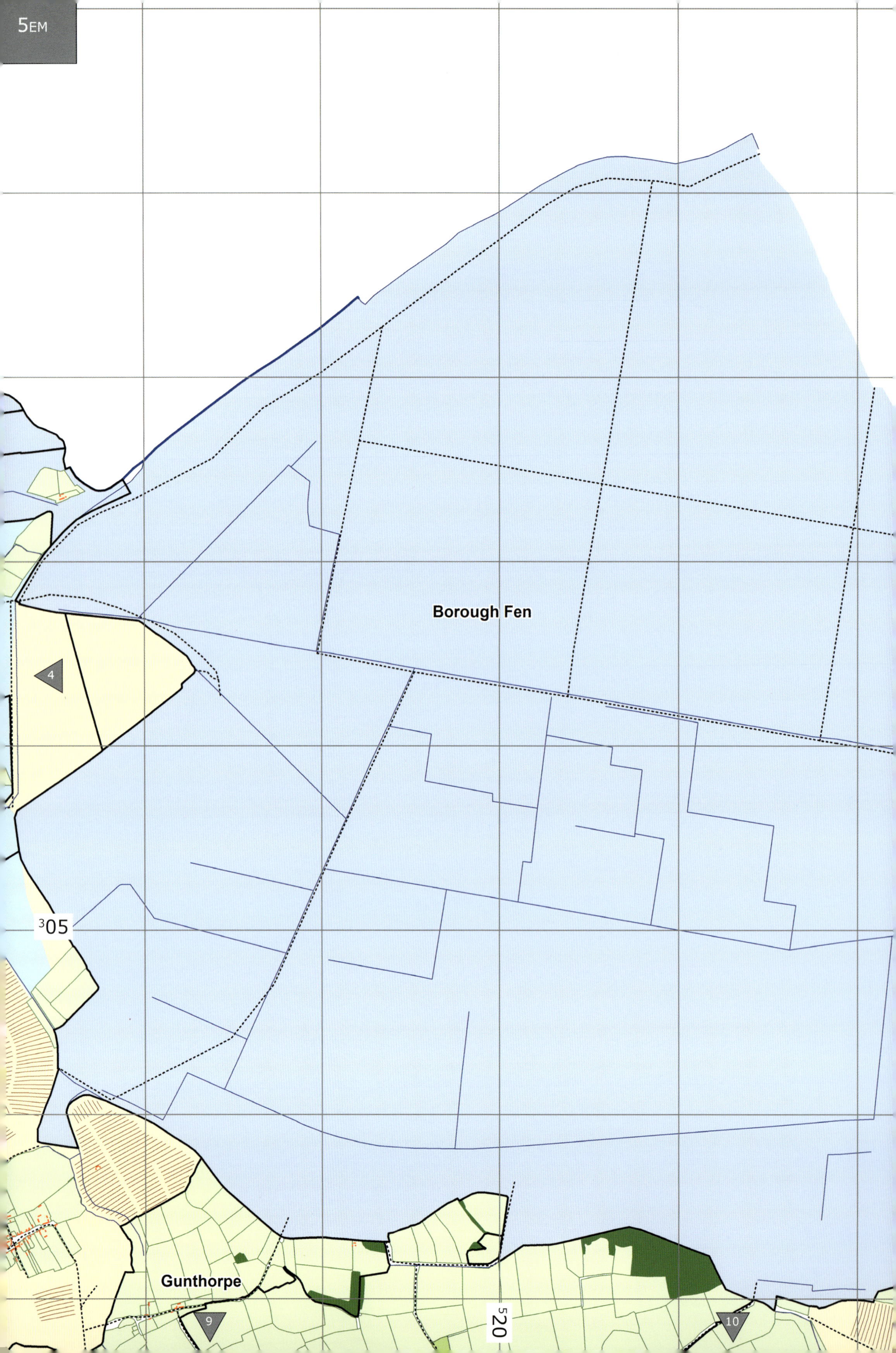

Borough Fen
Gunthorpe
4
9
10
305
520

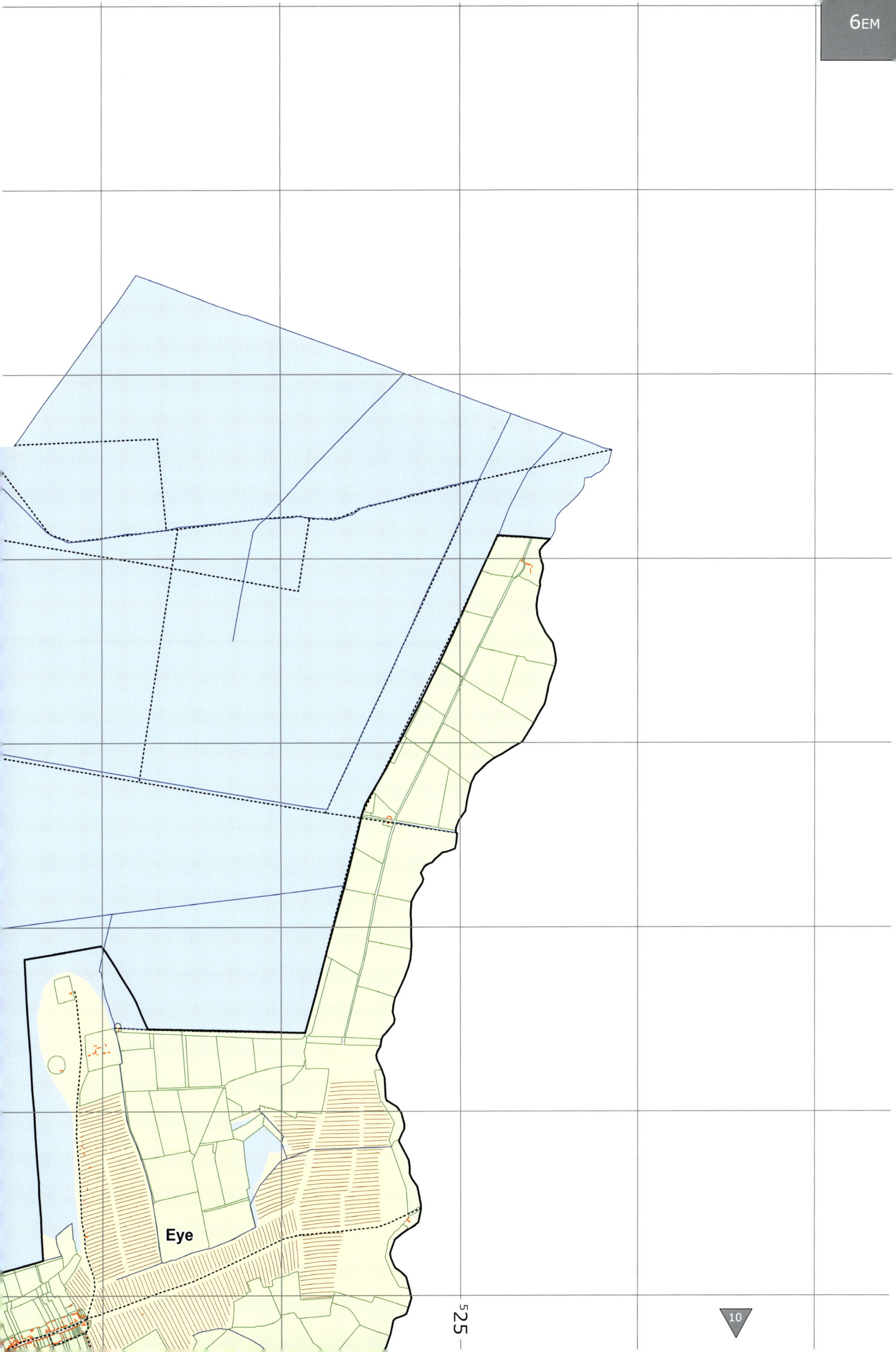

6EM
Eye
525
10

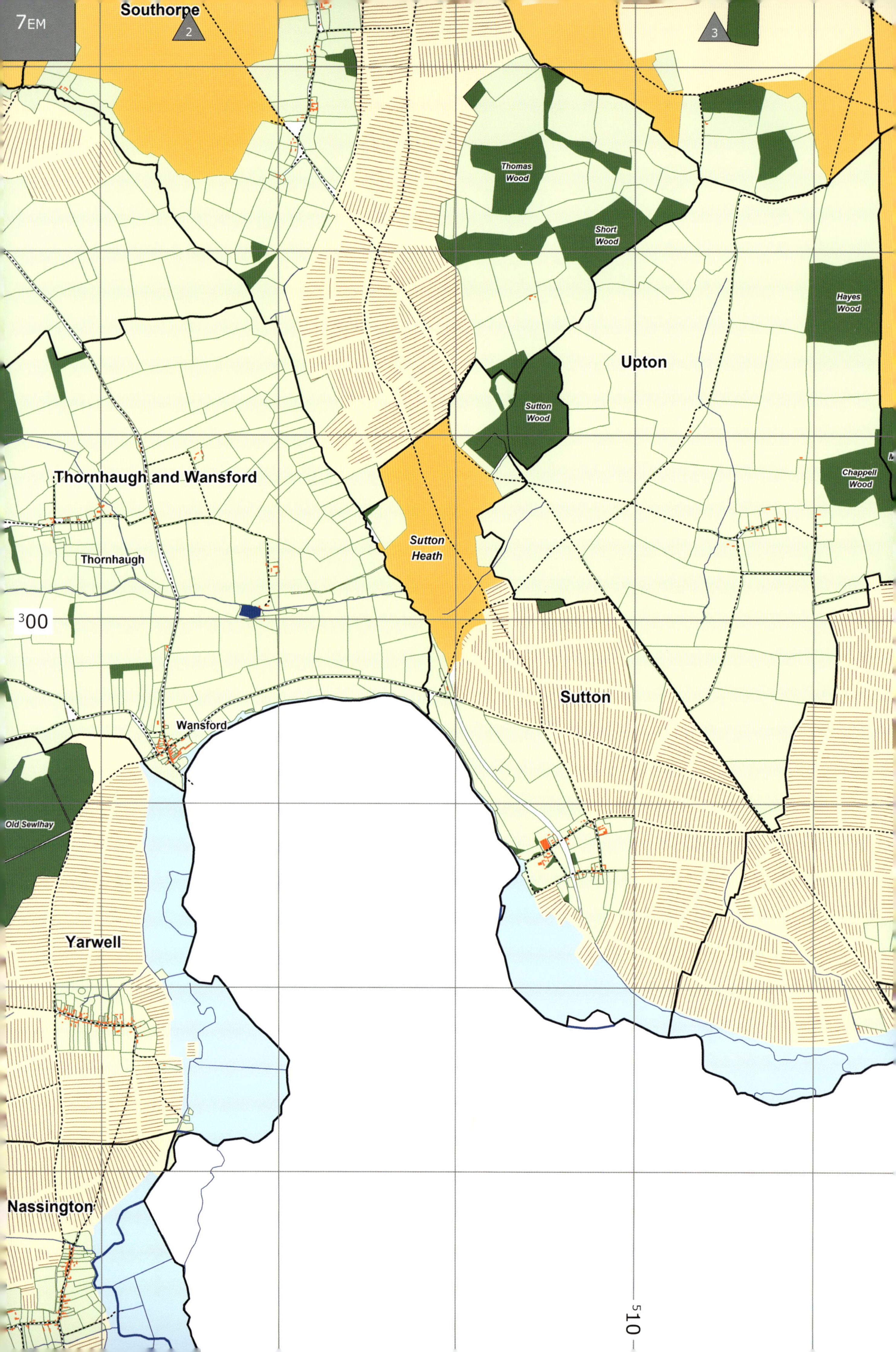
Southorpe
2
3
Thomas Wood
Short Wood
Hayes Wood
Upton
Sutton Wood
Chappell Wood
Thornhaugh and Wansford
Sutton Heath
Thornhaugh
300
Sutton
Wansford
Old Sewlhay
Yarwell
Nassington
510

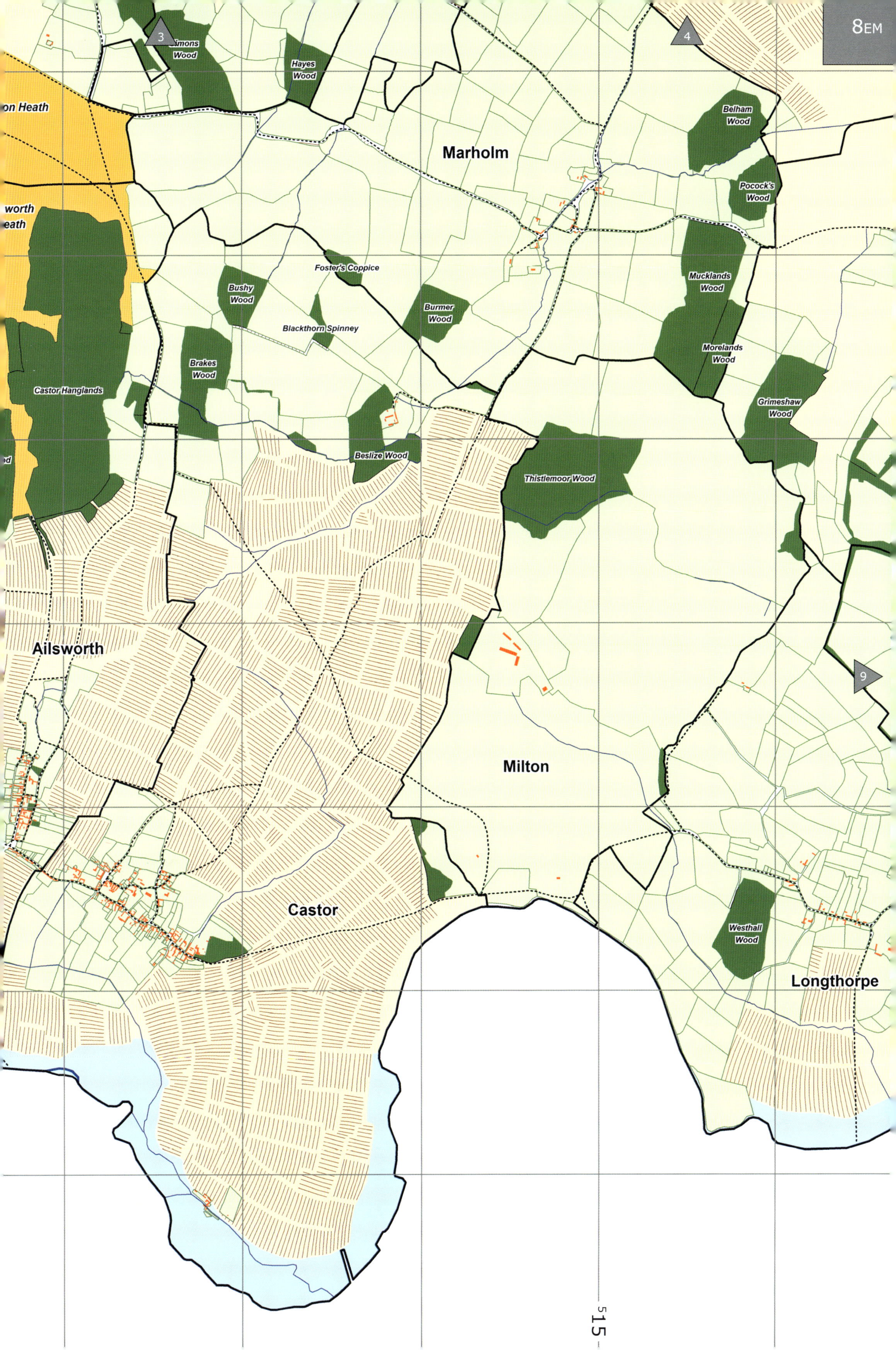
8EM
3
4
9
Hayes Wood
Marholm
Belham Wood
Pocock's Wood
Foster's Coppice
Bushy Wood
Blackthorn Spinney
Burmer Wood
Mucklands Wood
Morelands Wood
Brakes Wood
Castor Hanglands
Grimeshaw Wood
Beslize Wood
Thistlemoor Wood
Ailsworth
Milton
Castor
Westhall Wood
Longthorpe
515

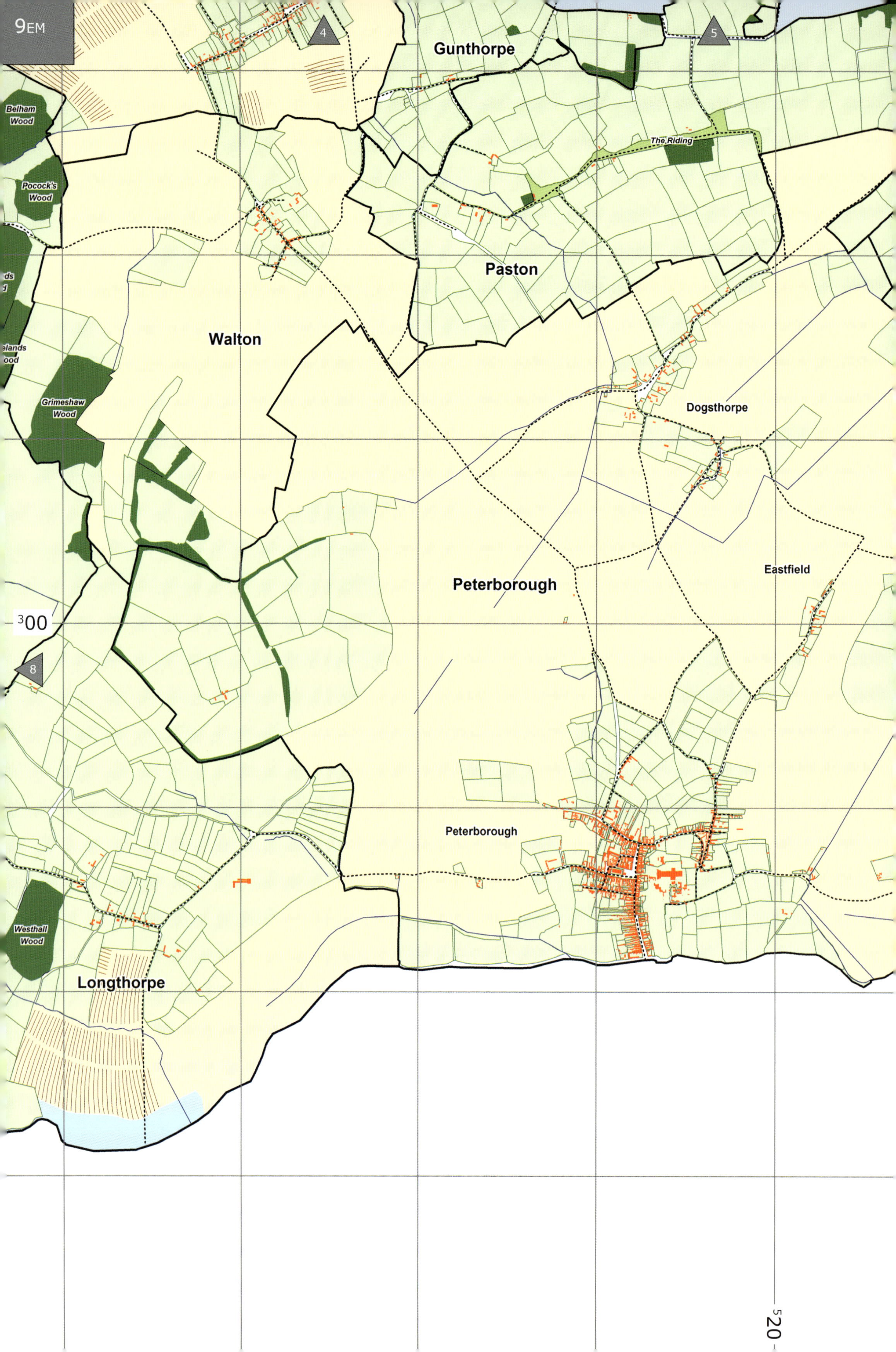

Gunthorpe
Belham Wood
Pocock's Wood
The Riding
Paston
Walton
Dogsthorpe
Grimeshaw Wood
Peterborough
Eastfield
300
Peterborough
Westhall Wood
Longthorpe
520

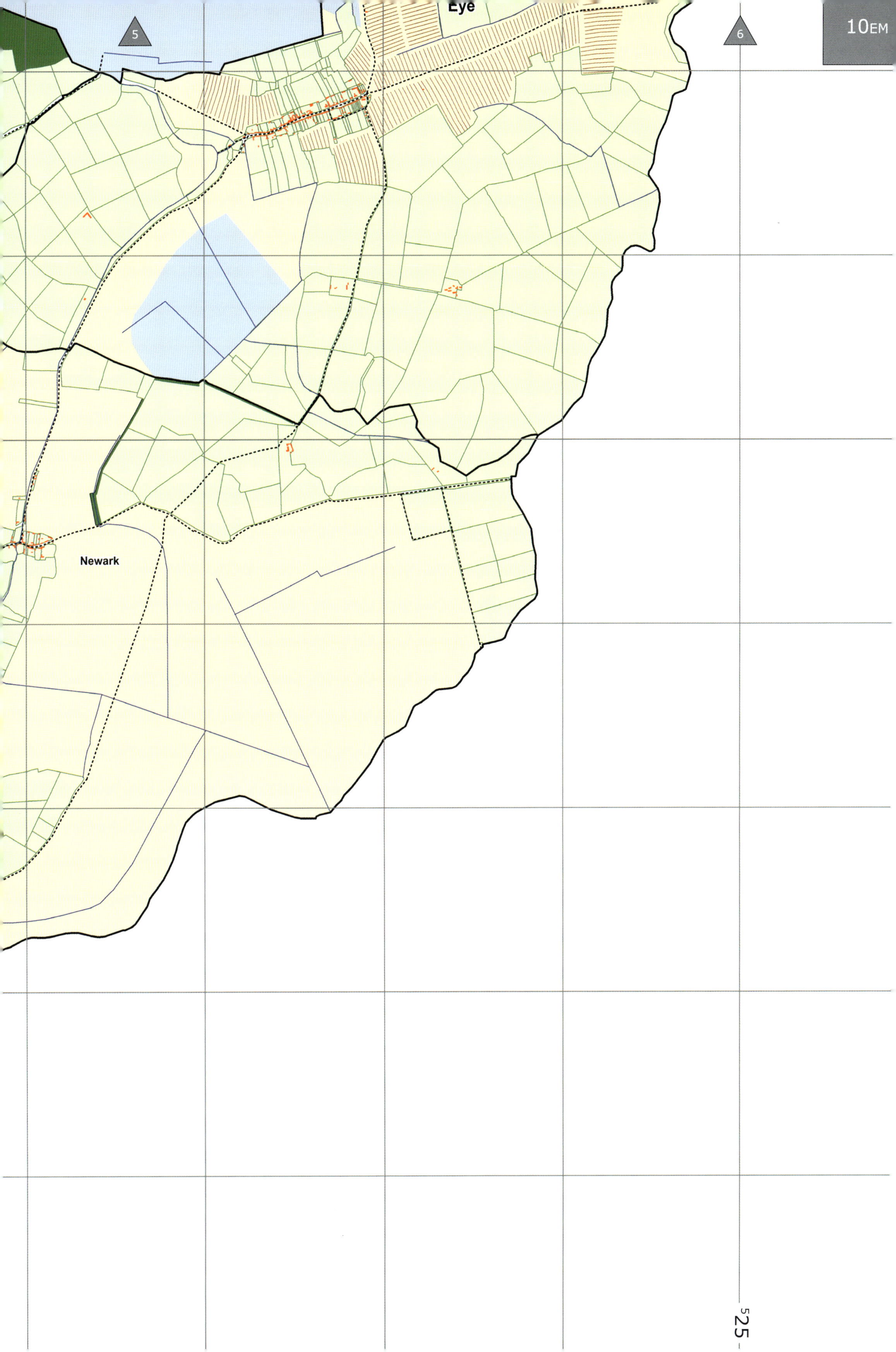
10EM
Eye
5
6
Newark
525

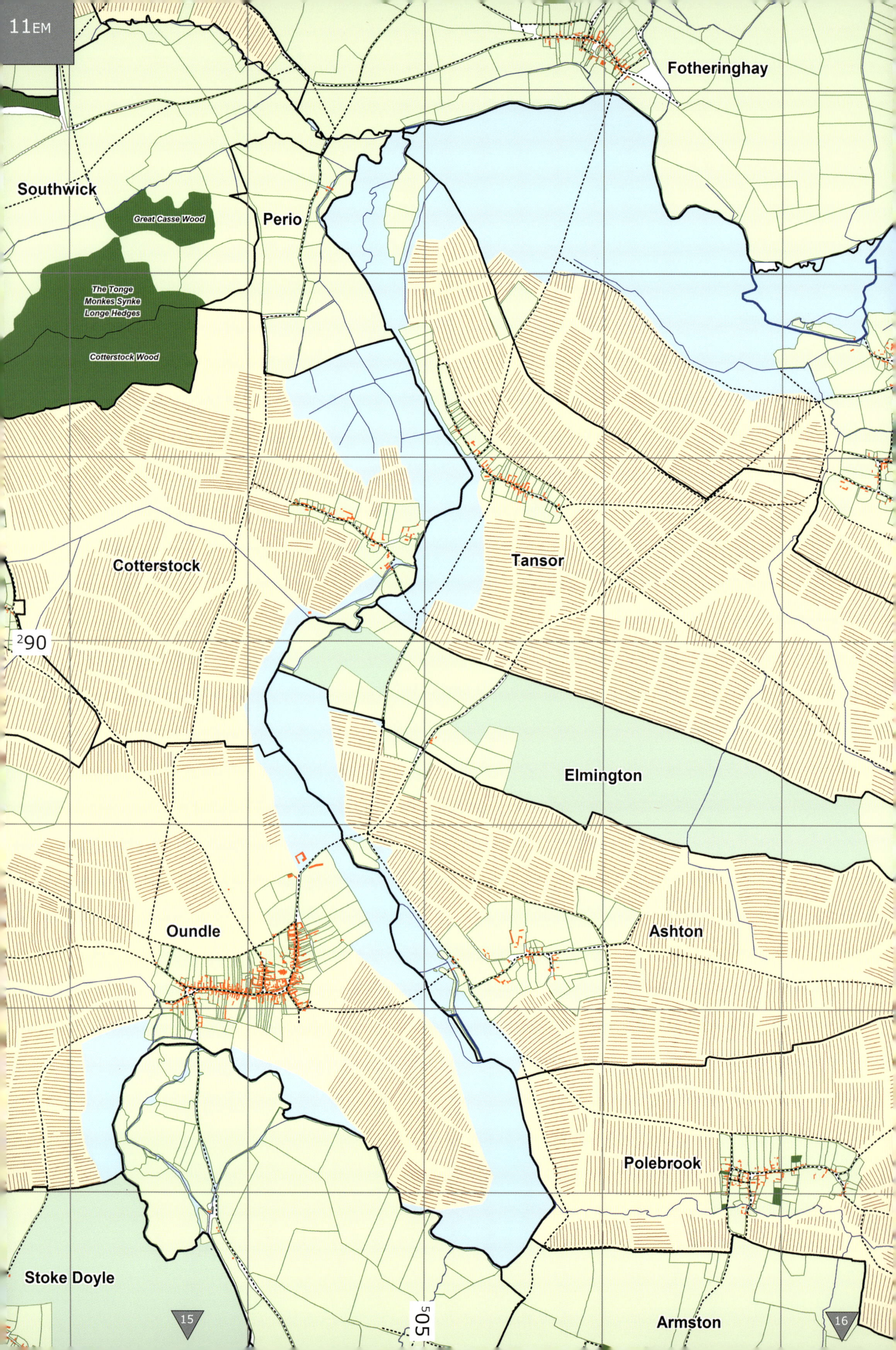
11EM
Fotheringhay
Southwick
Great Casse Wood
Perio
The Tonge
Monkes Synke
Longe Hedges
Cotterstock Wood
Cotterstock
Tansor
290
Elmington
Oundle
Ashton
Polebrook
Stoke Doyle
15
505
Armston
16

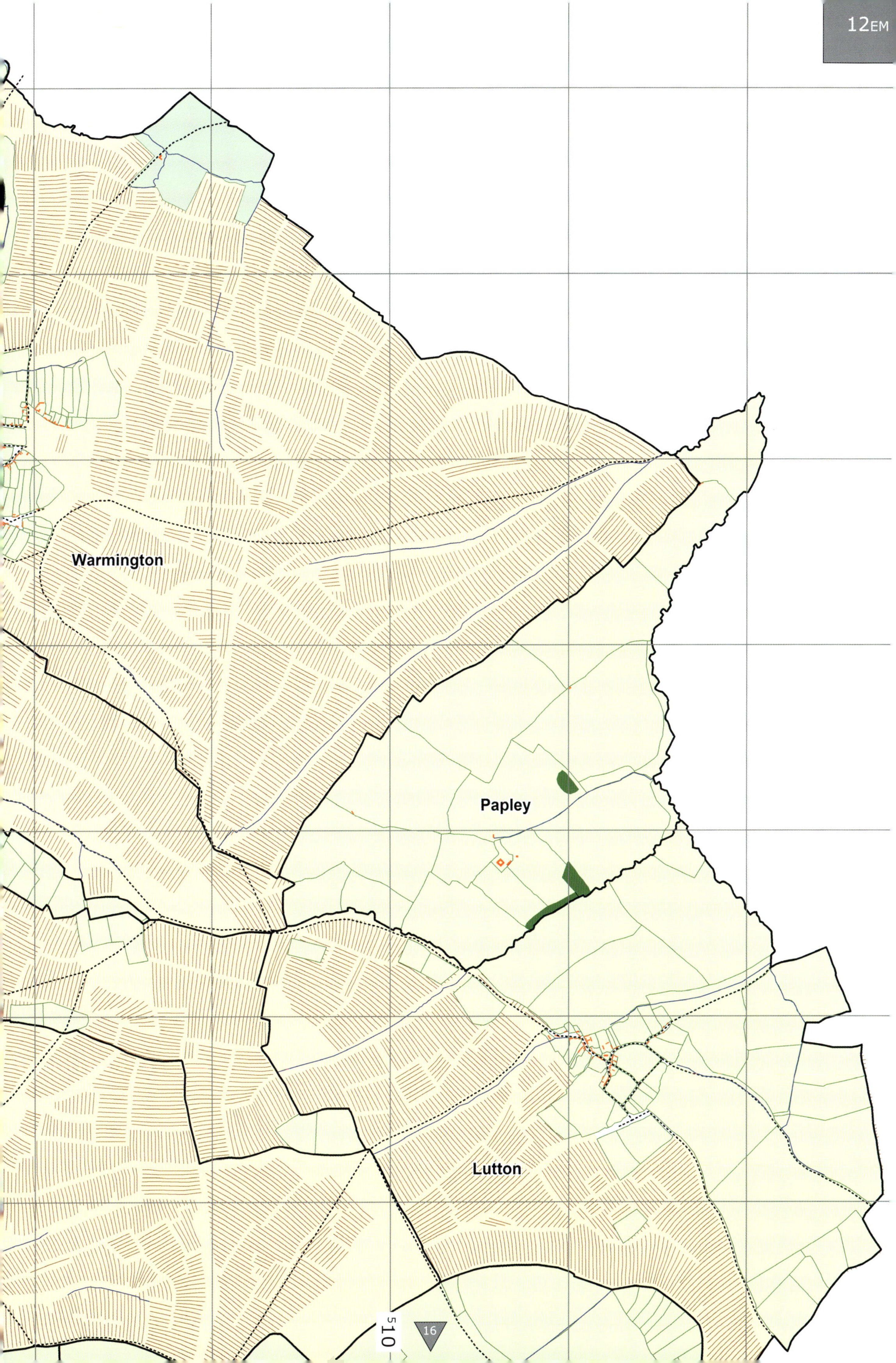
Warmington
Papley
Lutton
510
16

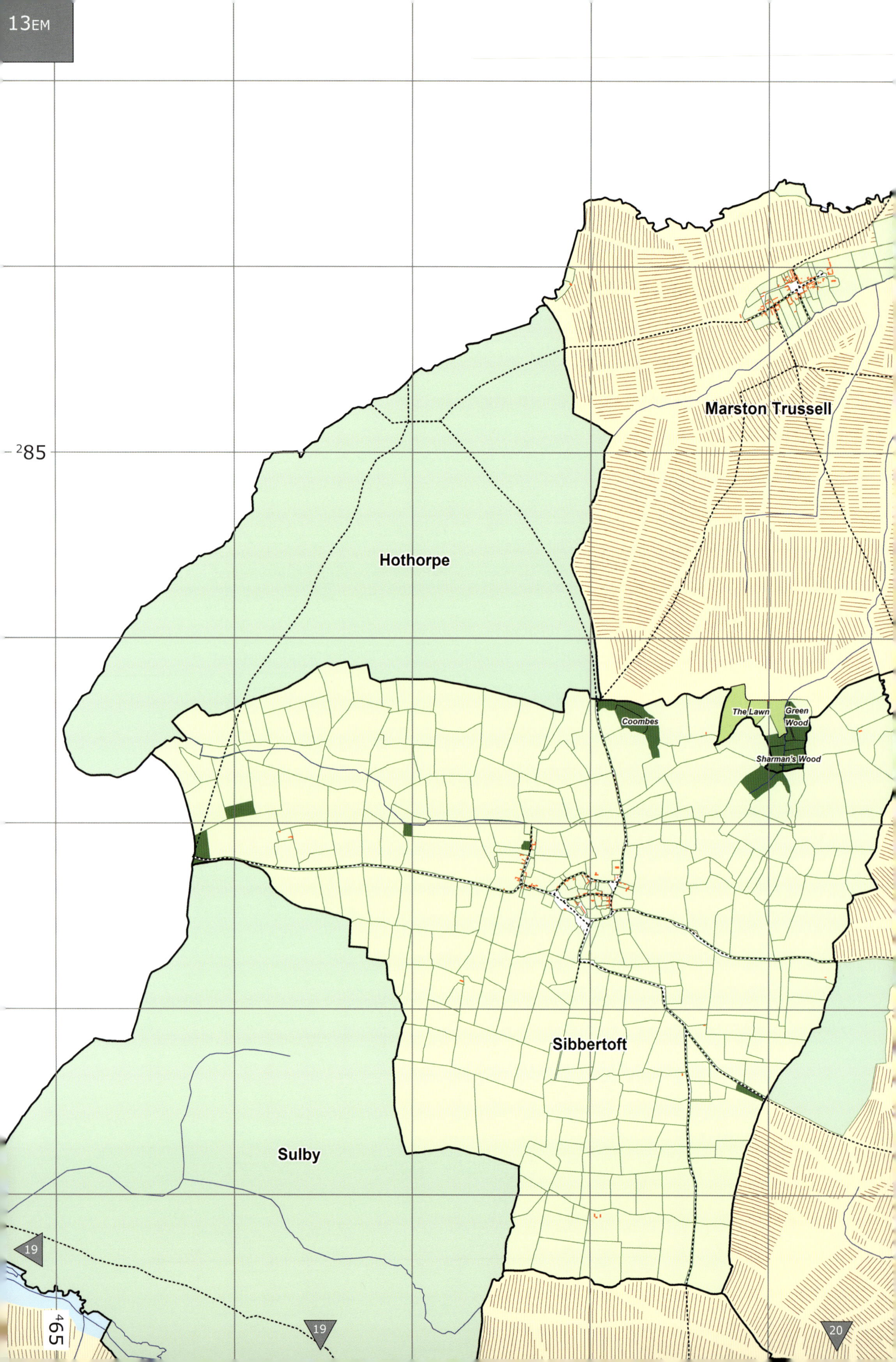
285
Marston Trussell
Hothorpe
Coombes
The Lawn
Green Wood
Sharman's Wood
Sibbertoft
Sulby
19
19
20
465

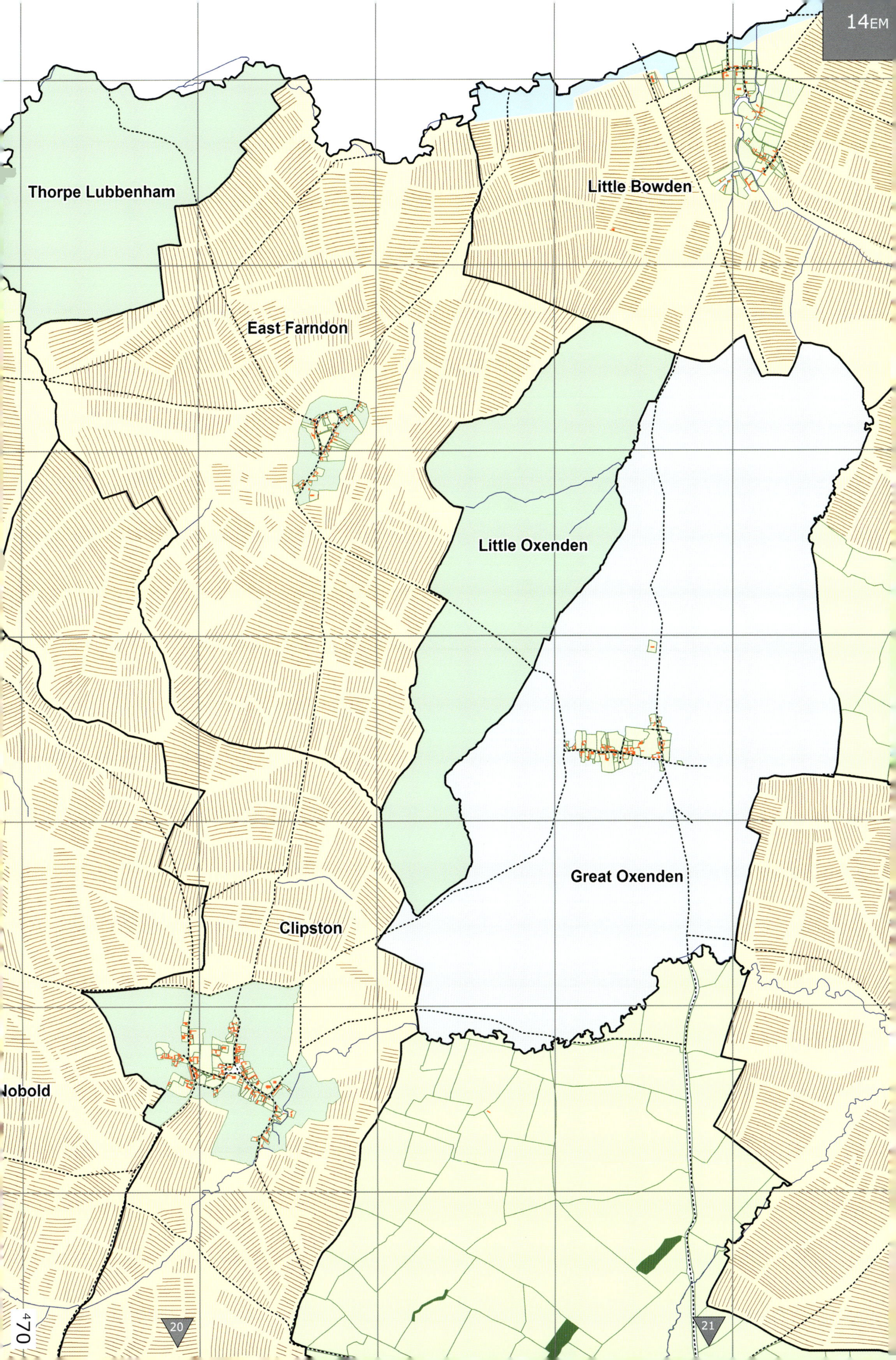
Thorpe Lubbenham
Little Bowden
East Farndon
Little Oxenden
Great Oxenden
Clipston
lobold
20
21

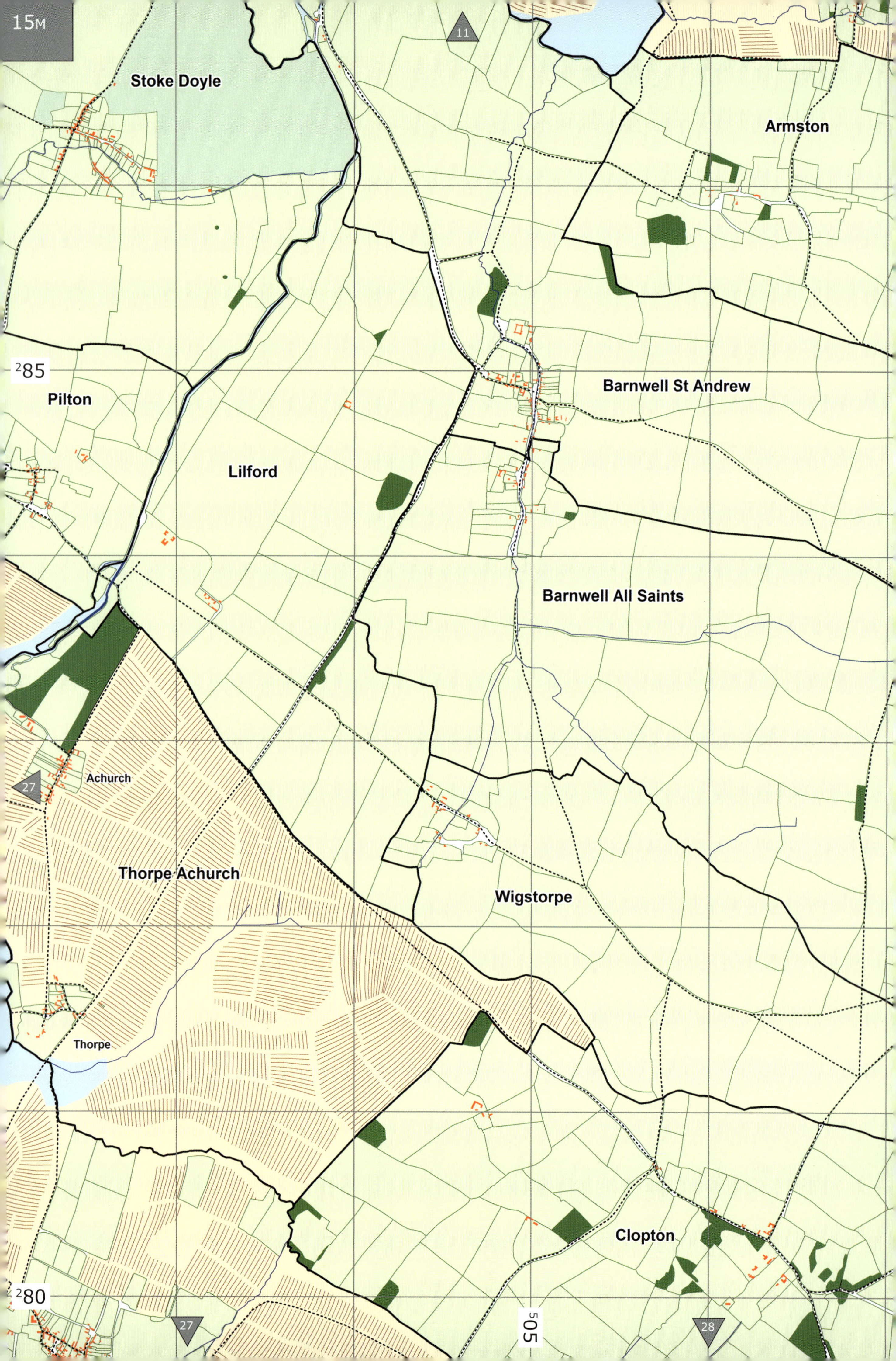

15M
11
Stoke Doyle
Armston
285
Pilton
Barnwell St Andrew
Lilford
Barnwell All Saints
27
Achurch
Thorpe Achurch
Wigstorpe
Thorpe
Clopton
280
27
505
28

11
12
Kingsthorpe
Hemington
Thurning
Luddington
28
510

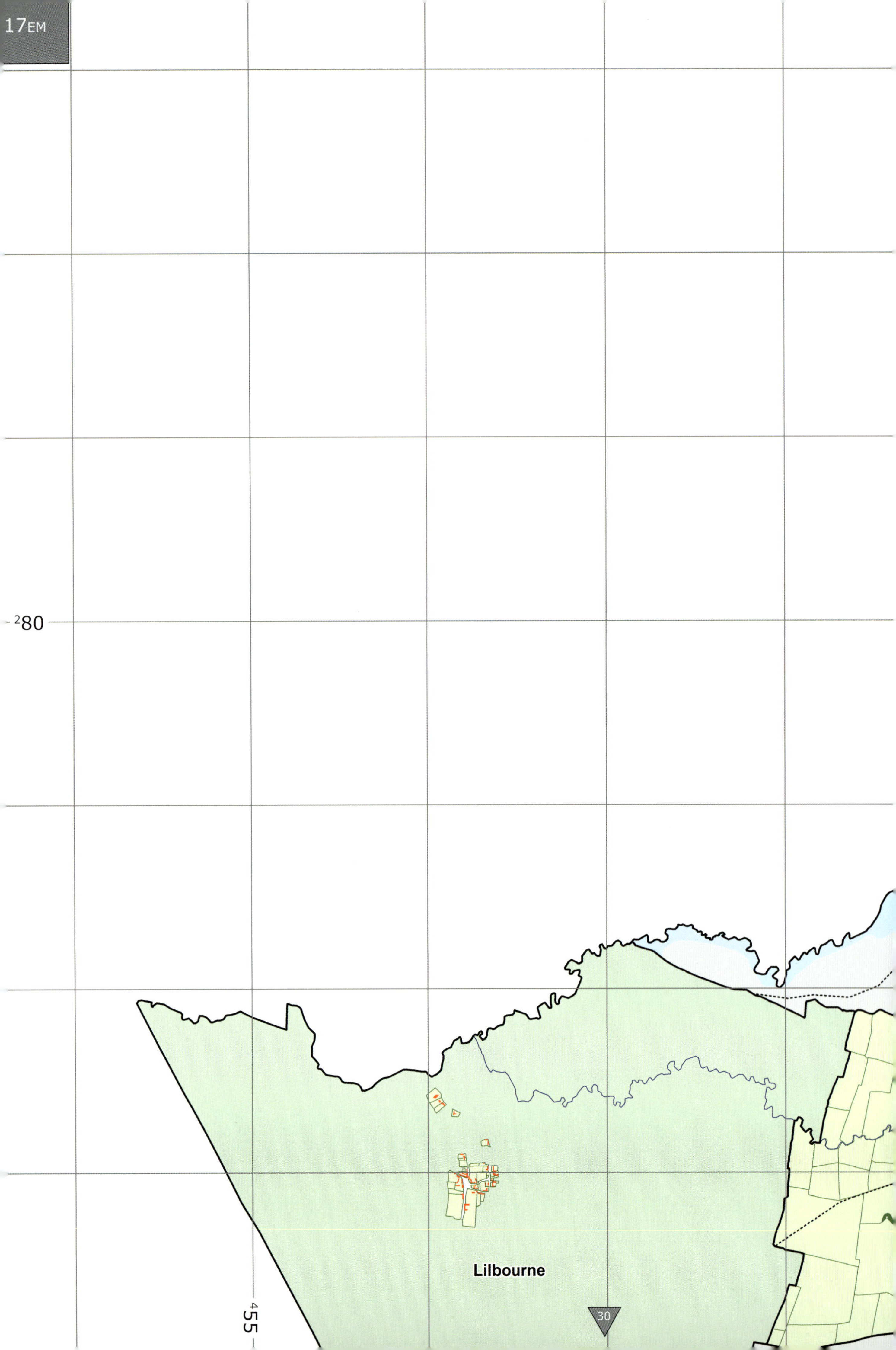

²80
Lilbourne
⁴55
30

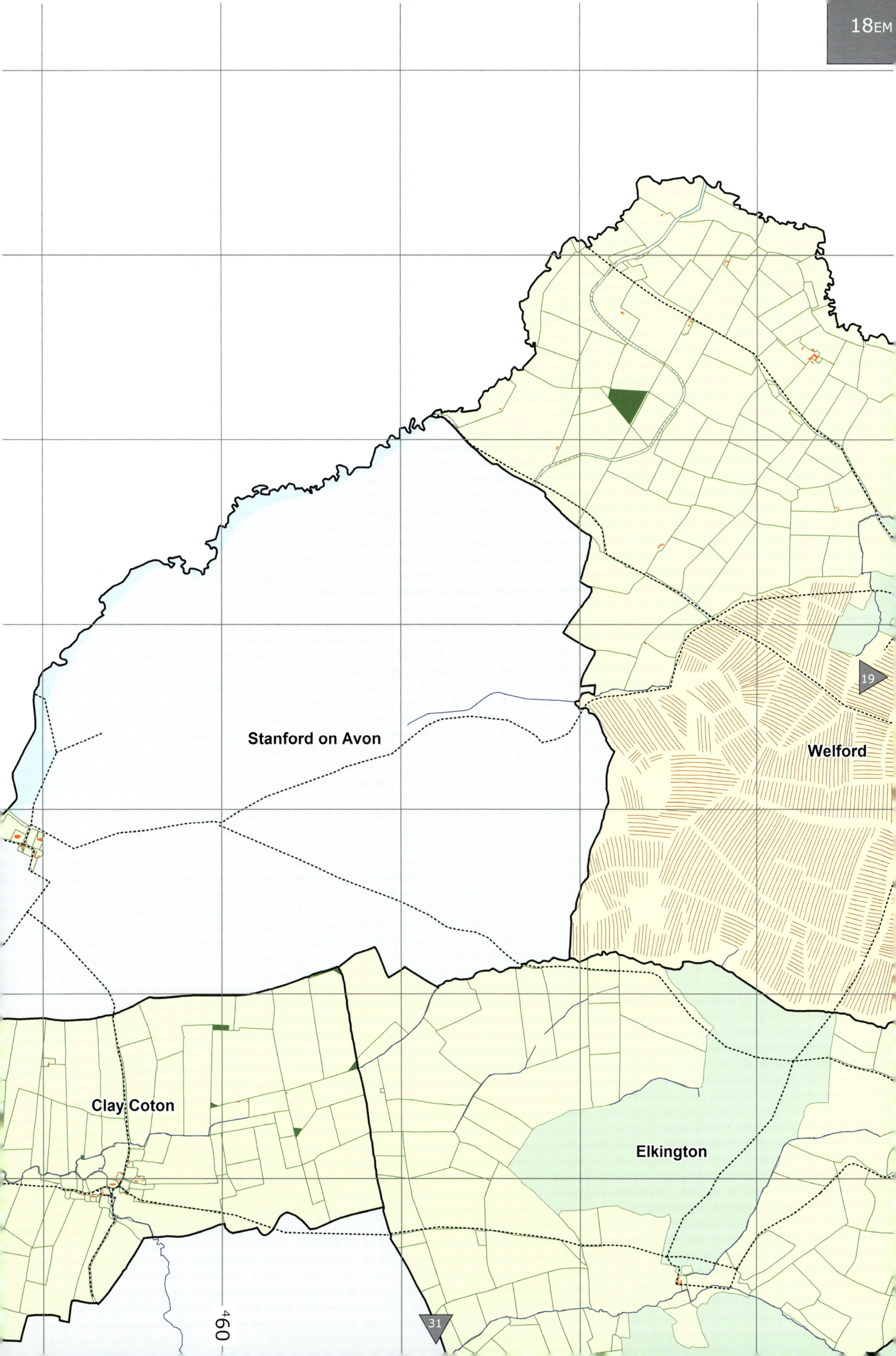
Stanford on Avon
Welford
19
Clay Coton
Elkington
460
31

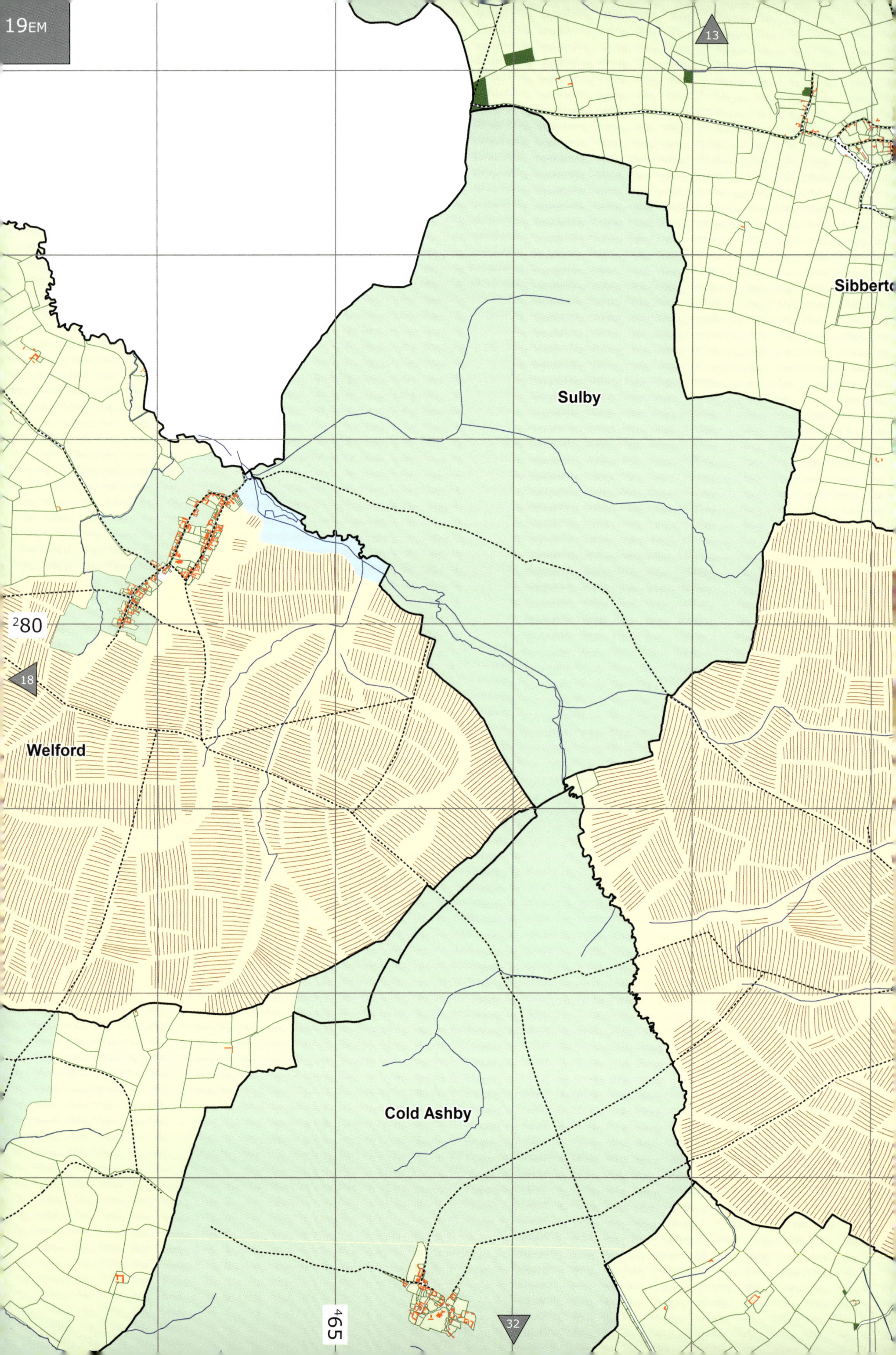

19EM
13
Sibberto
Sulby
280
18
Welford
Cold Ashby
465
32

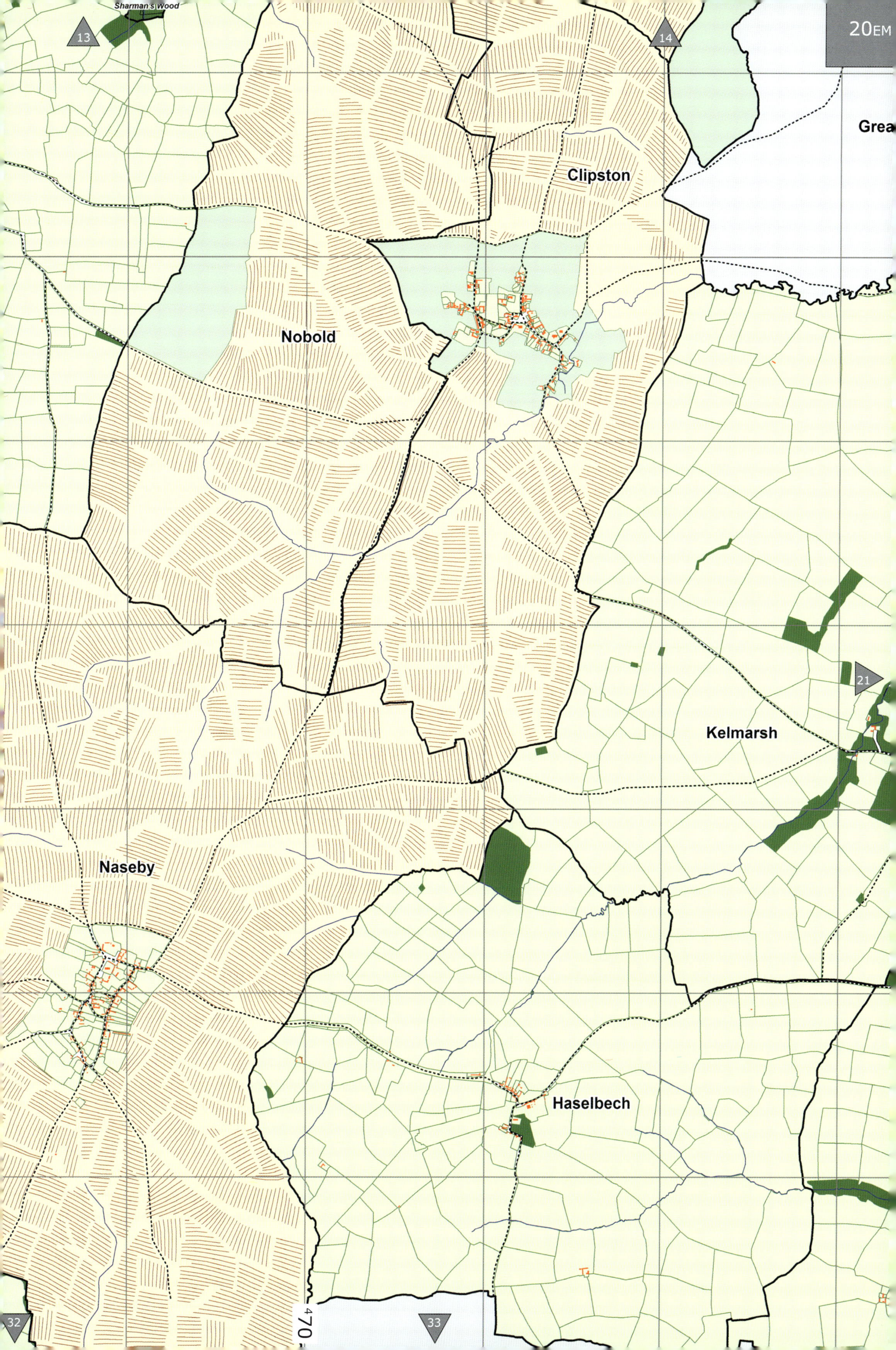

Sharman's wood
13
14
20EM
Grea
Clipston
Nobold
21
Kelmarsh
Naseby
Haselbech
32
470
33

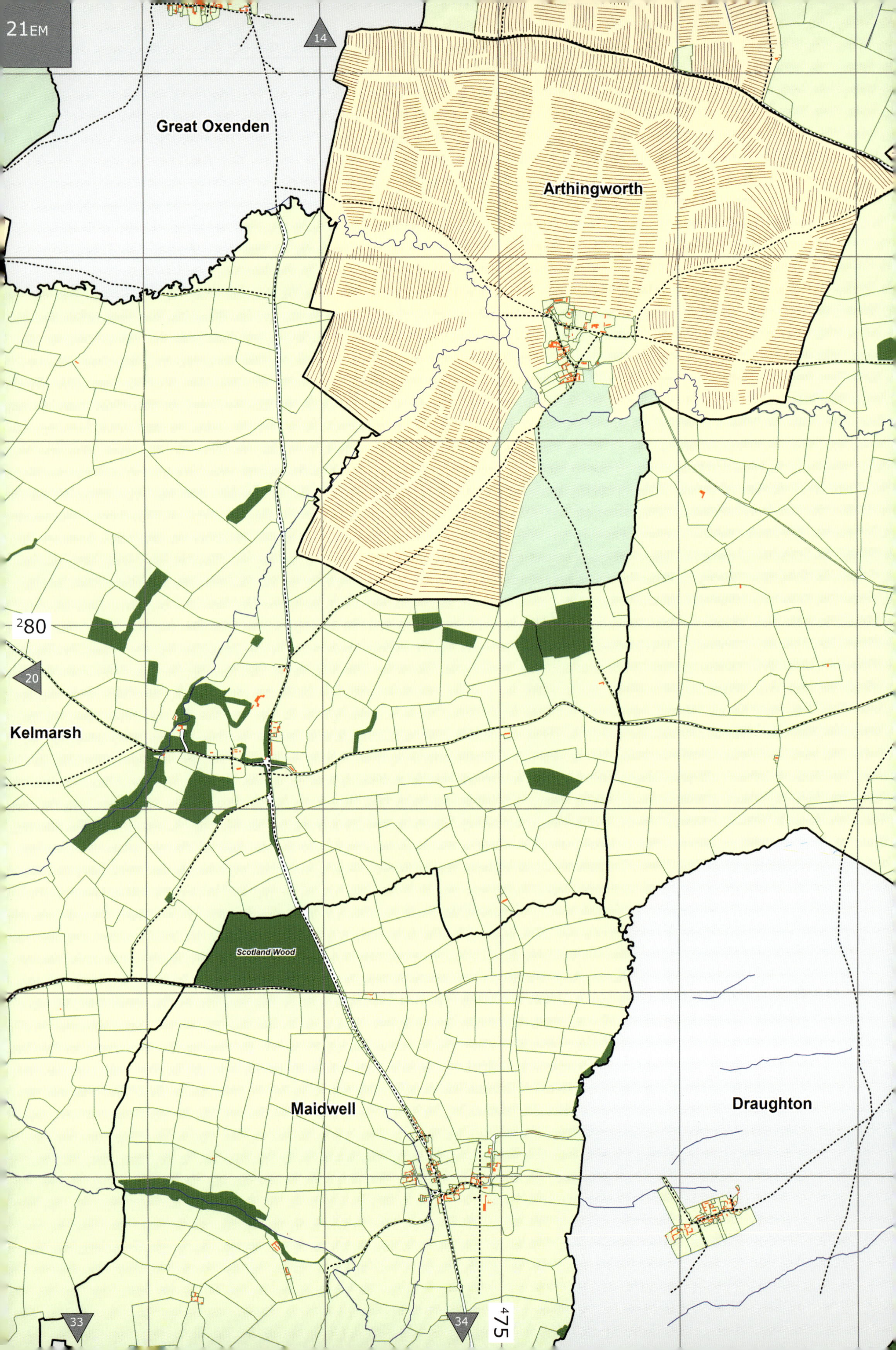

14
Great Oxenden
Arthingworth
280
20
Kelmarsh
Scotland Wood
Maidwell
Draughton
33
34
475

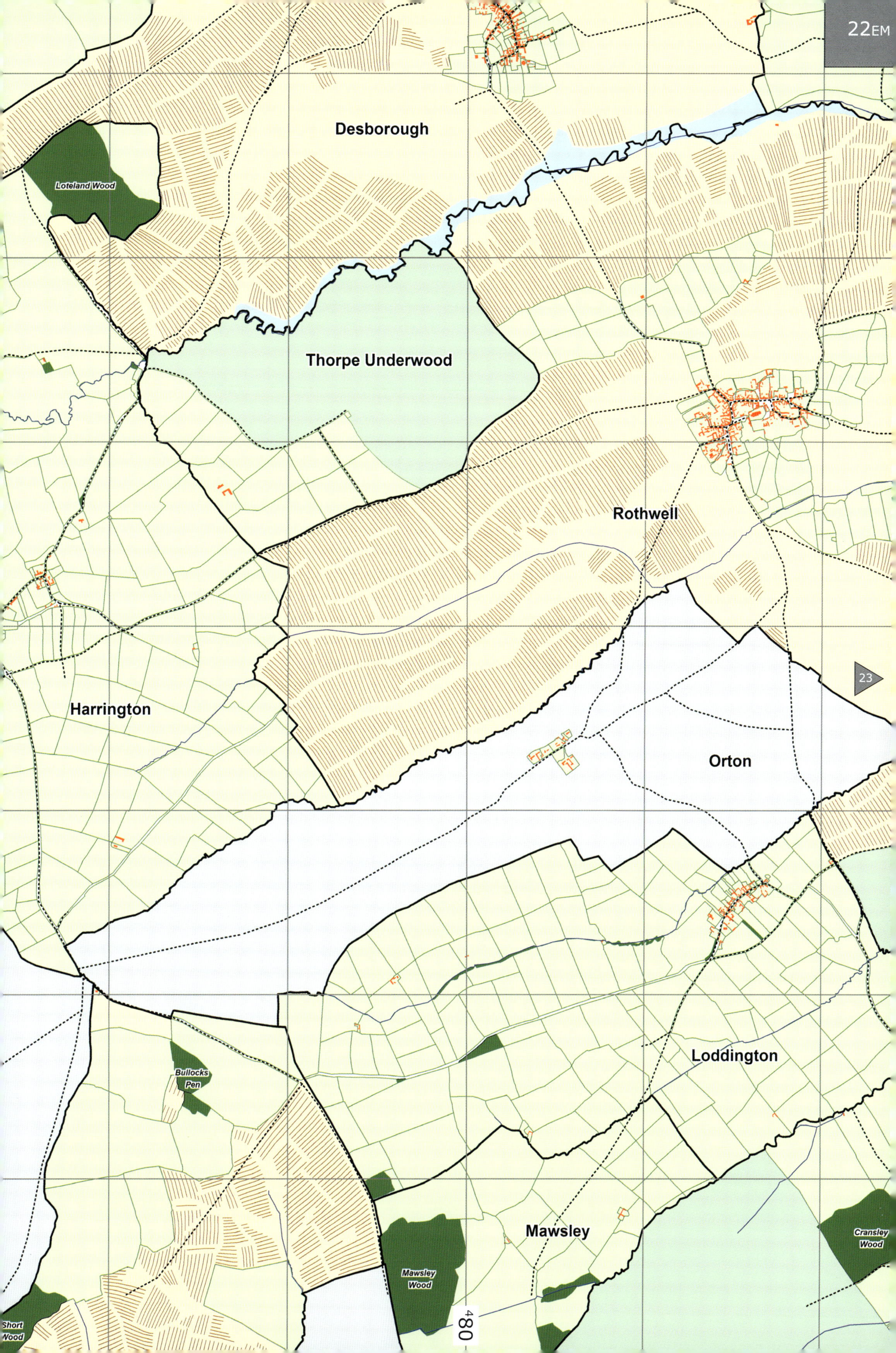
Desborough
Loteland Wood
Thorpe Underwood
Rothwell
Harrington
Orton
Loddington
Bullocks Pen
Mawsley
Mawsley Wood
Cransley Wood
Short Wood
23
480

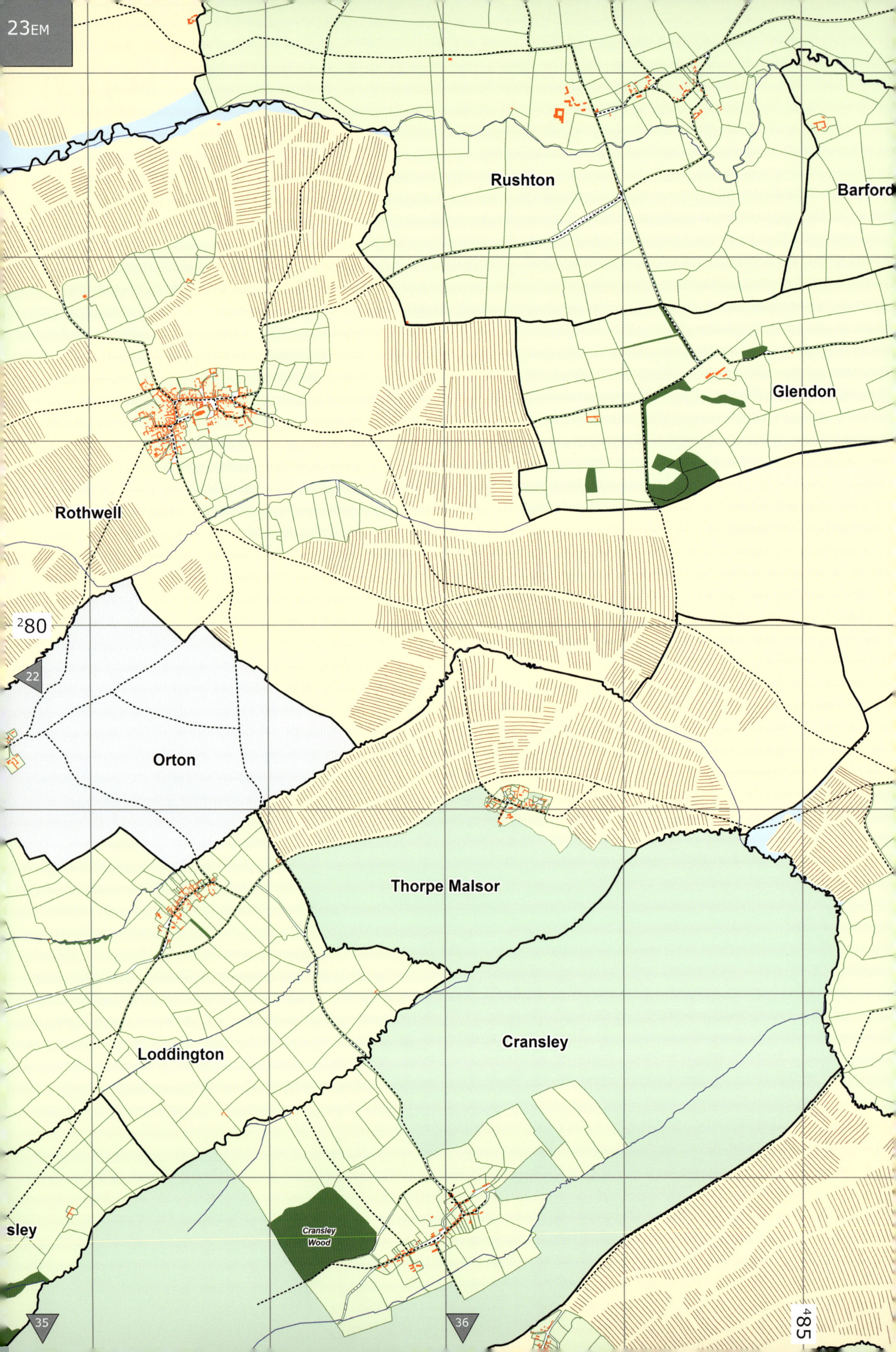
23EM
Rushton
Barford
Glendon
Rothwell
280
22
Orton
Thorpe Malsor
Cransley
Loddington
sley
Cransley Wood
35
36
485

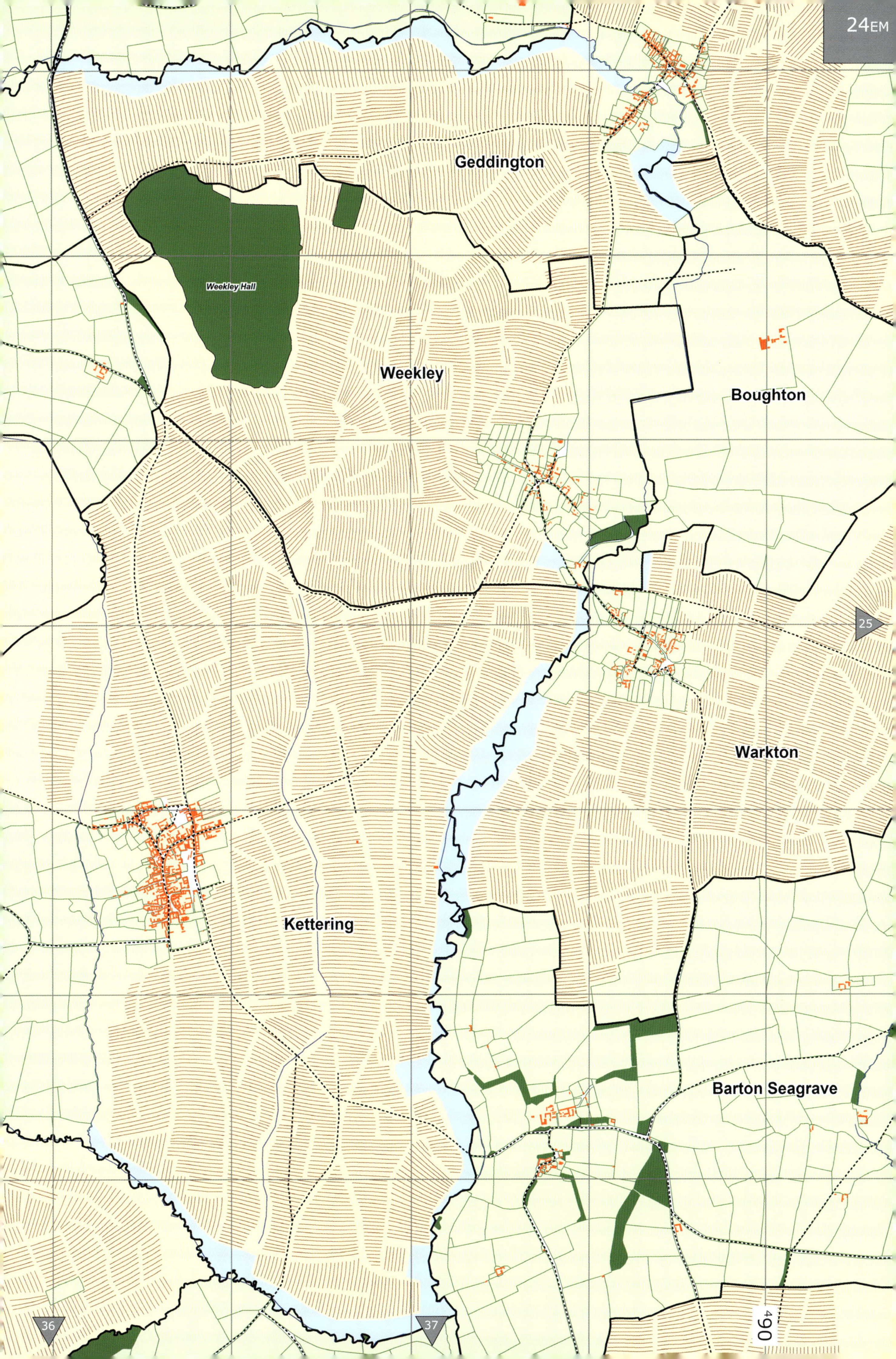
Geddington
Weekley Hall
Weekley
Boughton
25
Warkton
Kettering
Barton Seagrave
36
37

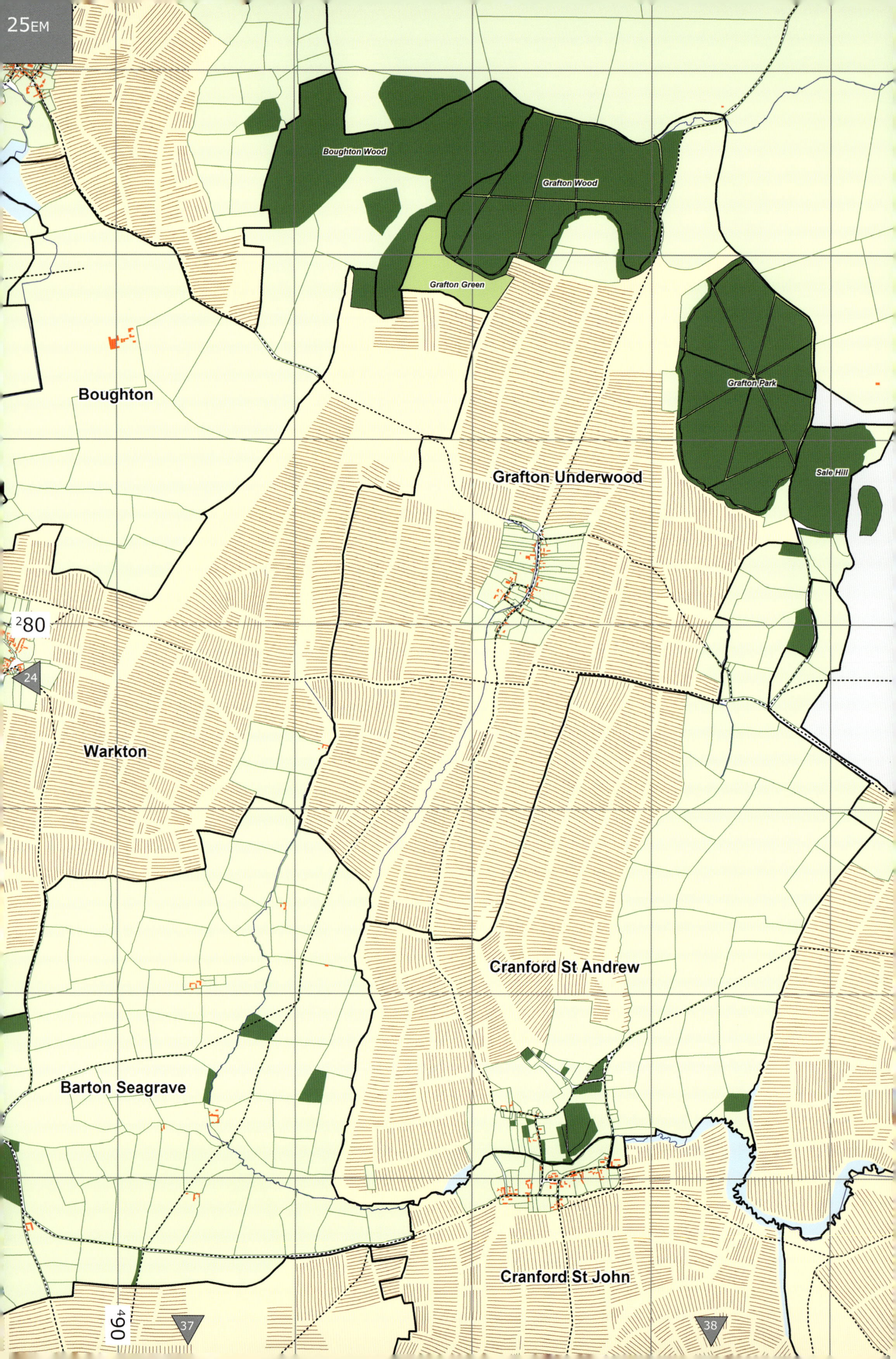
25EM
Boughton Wood
Grafton Wood
Grafton Green
Grafton Park
Sale Hill
Boughton
Grafton Underwood
280
24
Warkton
Cranford St Andrew
Barton Seagrave
Cranford St John
490
37
38

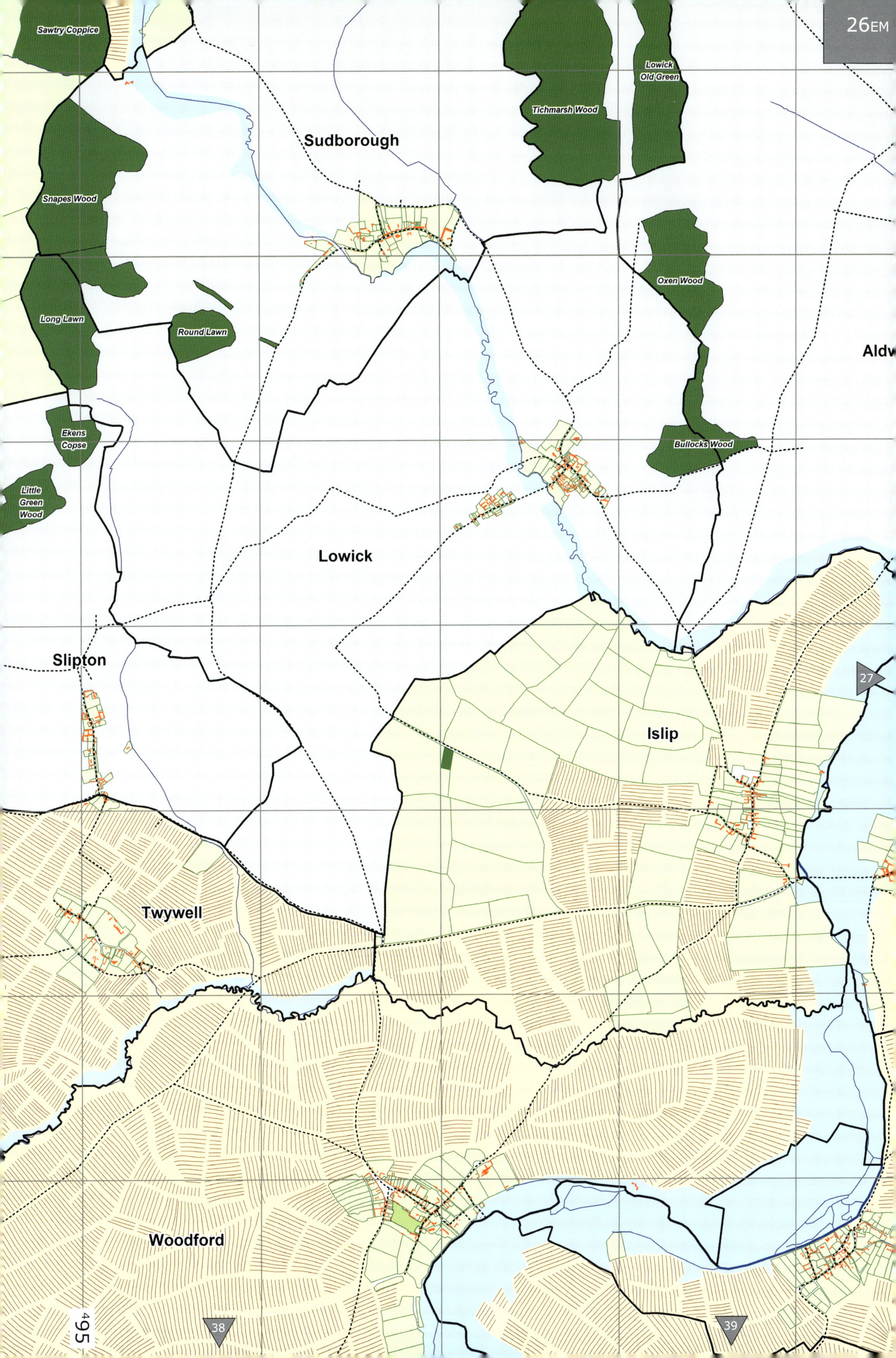

Sawtry Coppice
Lowick Old Green
Tichmarsh Wood
Sudborough
Snapes Wood
Oxen Wood
Long Lawn
Round Lawn
Aldw
Ekens Copse
Bullocks Wood
Little Green Wood
Lowick
Slipton
27
Islip
Twywell
Woodford
38
39

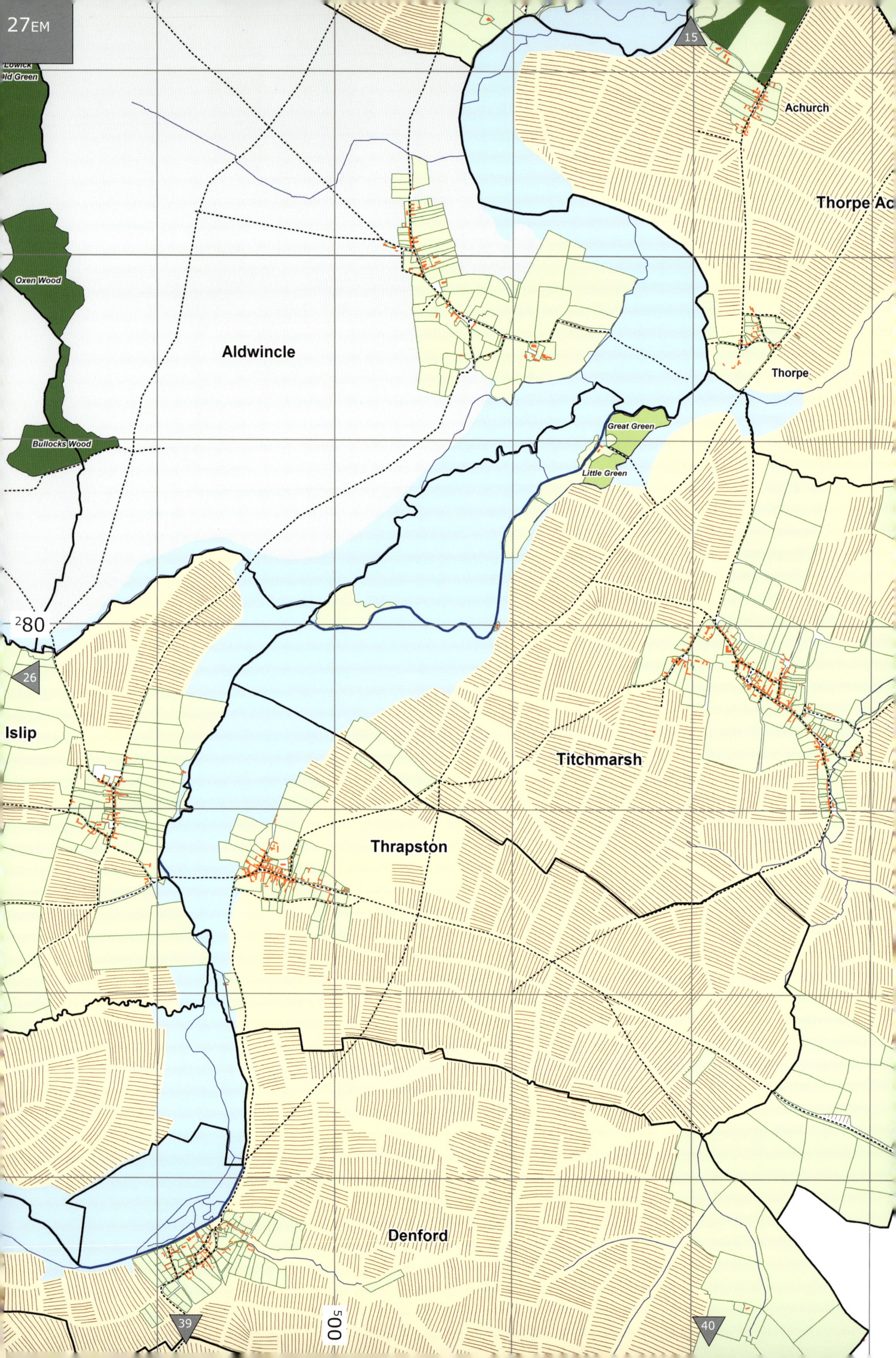

15
Lowick
old Green
Achurch
Thorpe Ac
Oxen Wood
Aldwincle
Thorpe
Great Green
Bullocks Wood
Little Green
280
26
Islip
Titchmarsh
Thrapston
Denford
39
500
40

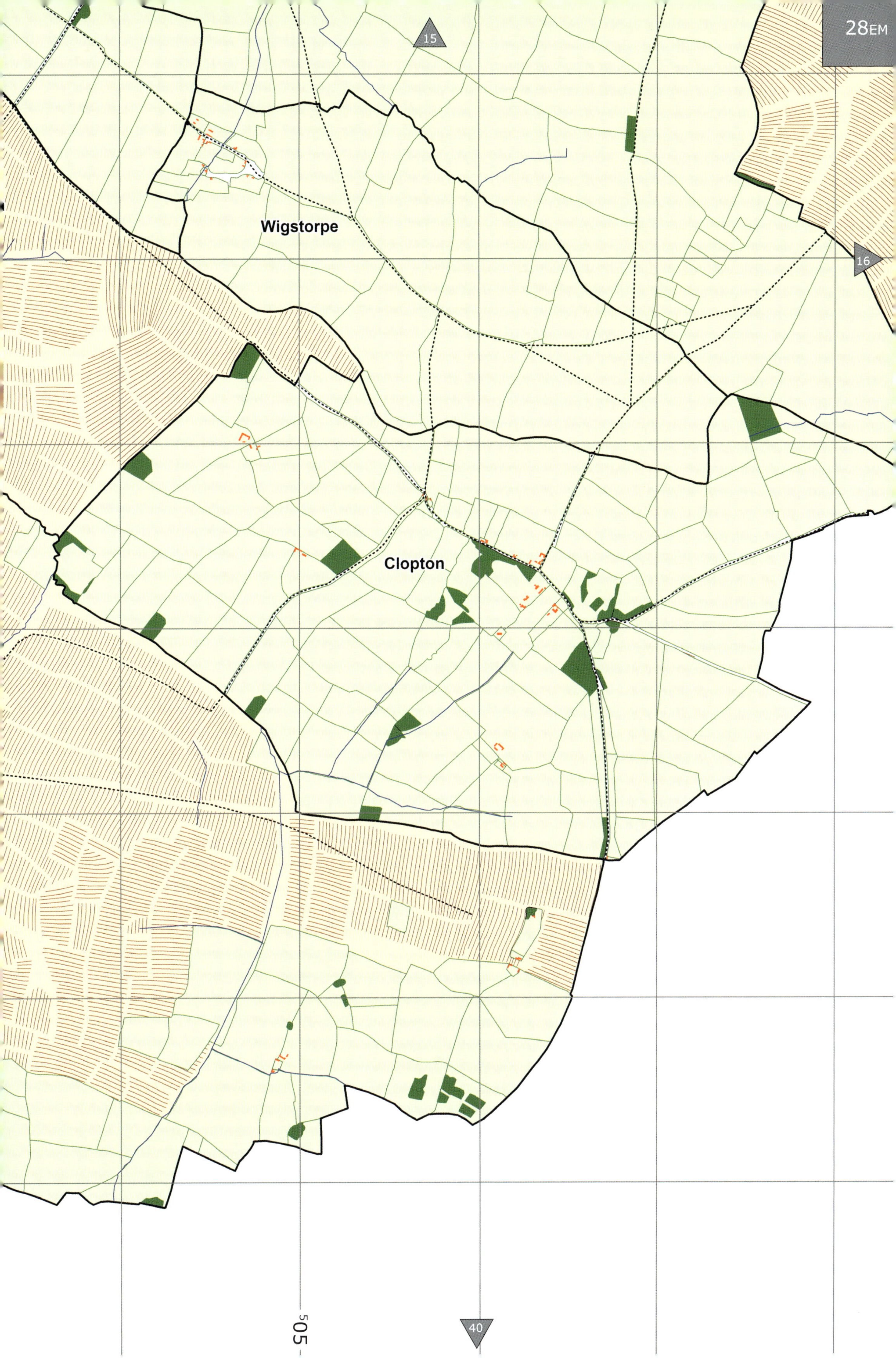
15
Wigstorpe
16
Clopton
505
40

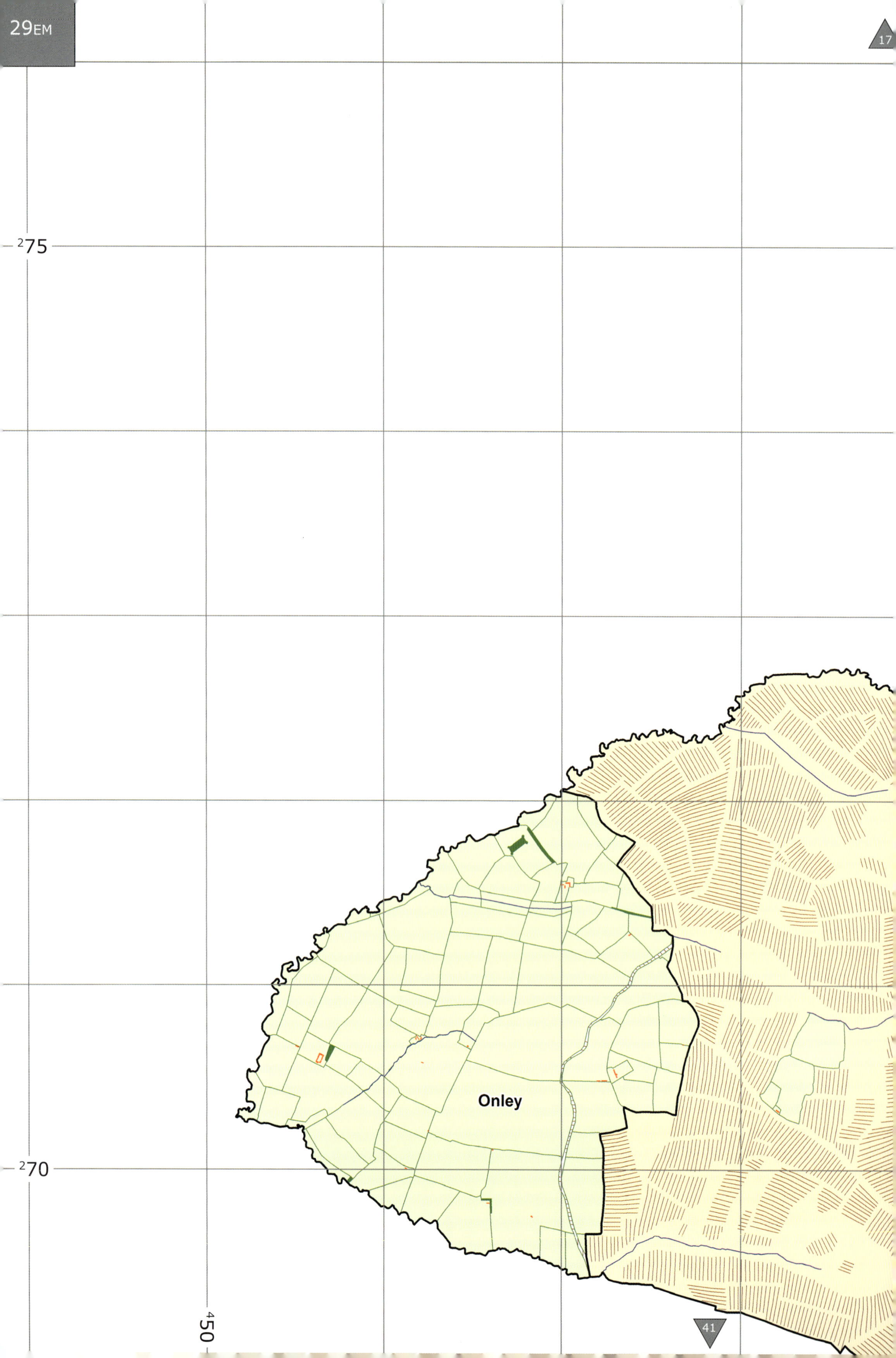
17
275
Onley
270
450
41

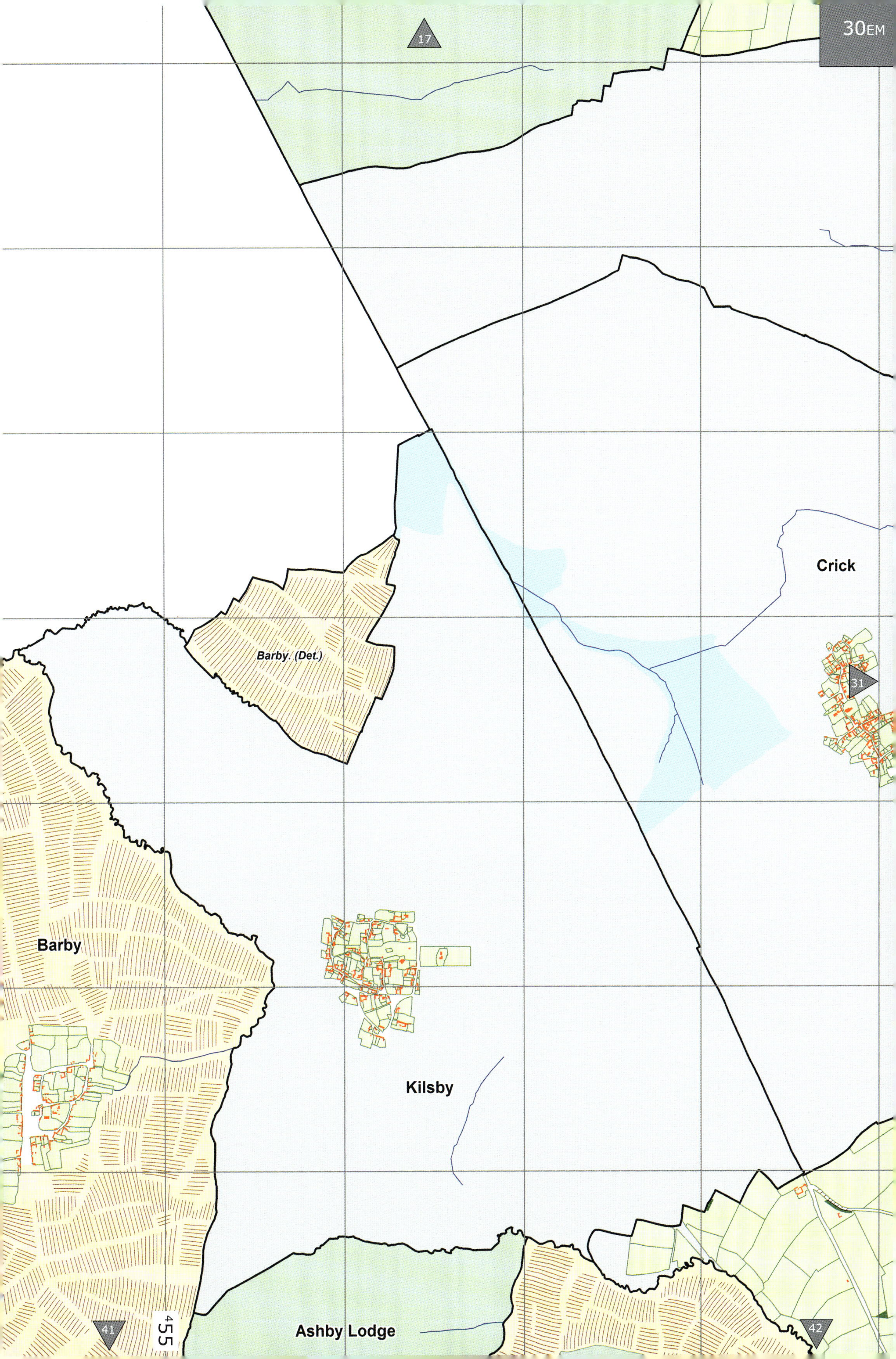

17
Crick
31
Barby. (Det.)
Barby
Kilsby
Ashby Lodge
41
455
42

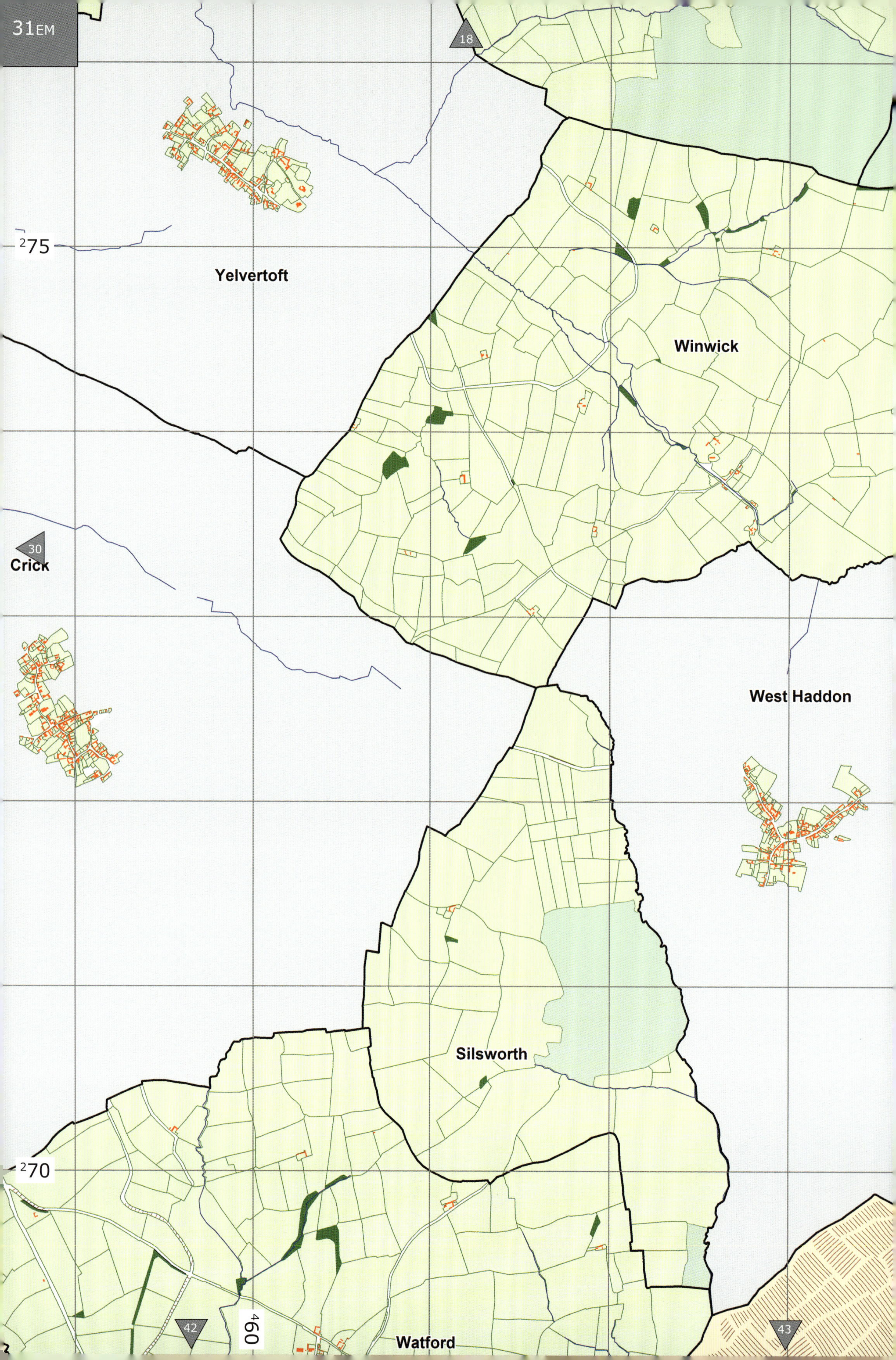
18
275
Yelvertoft
Winwick
30
Crick
West Haddon
Silsworth
270
42
460
Watford
43

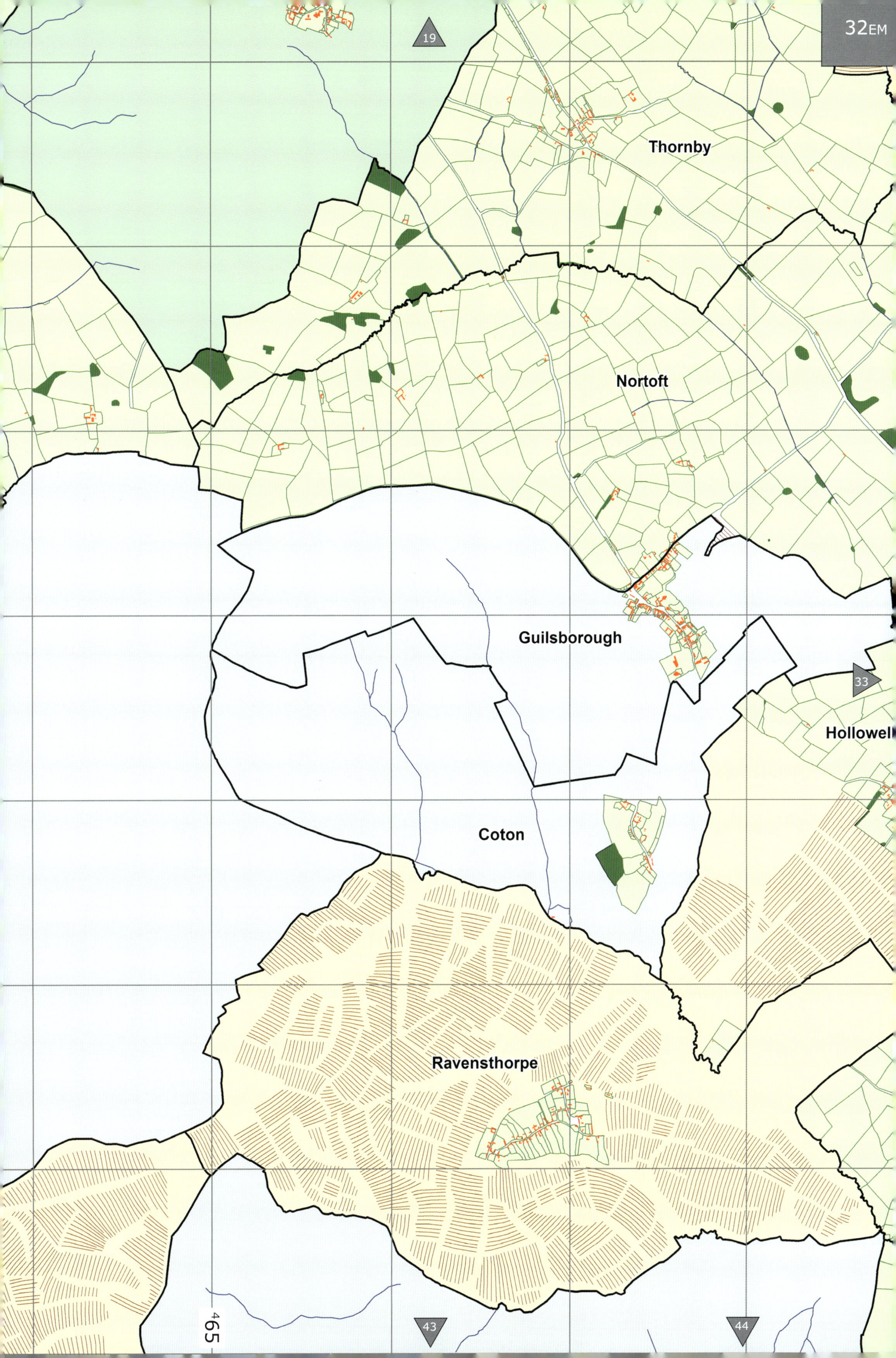
19
Thornby
Nortoft
Guilsborough
33
Hollowel
Coton
Ravensthorpe
43
44

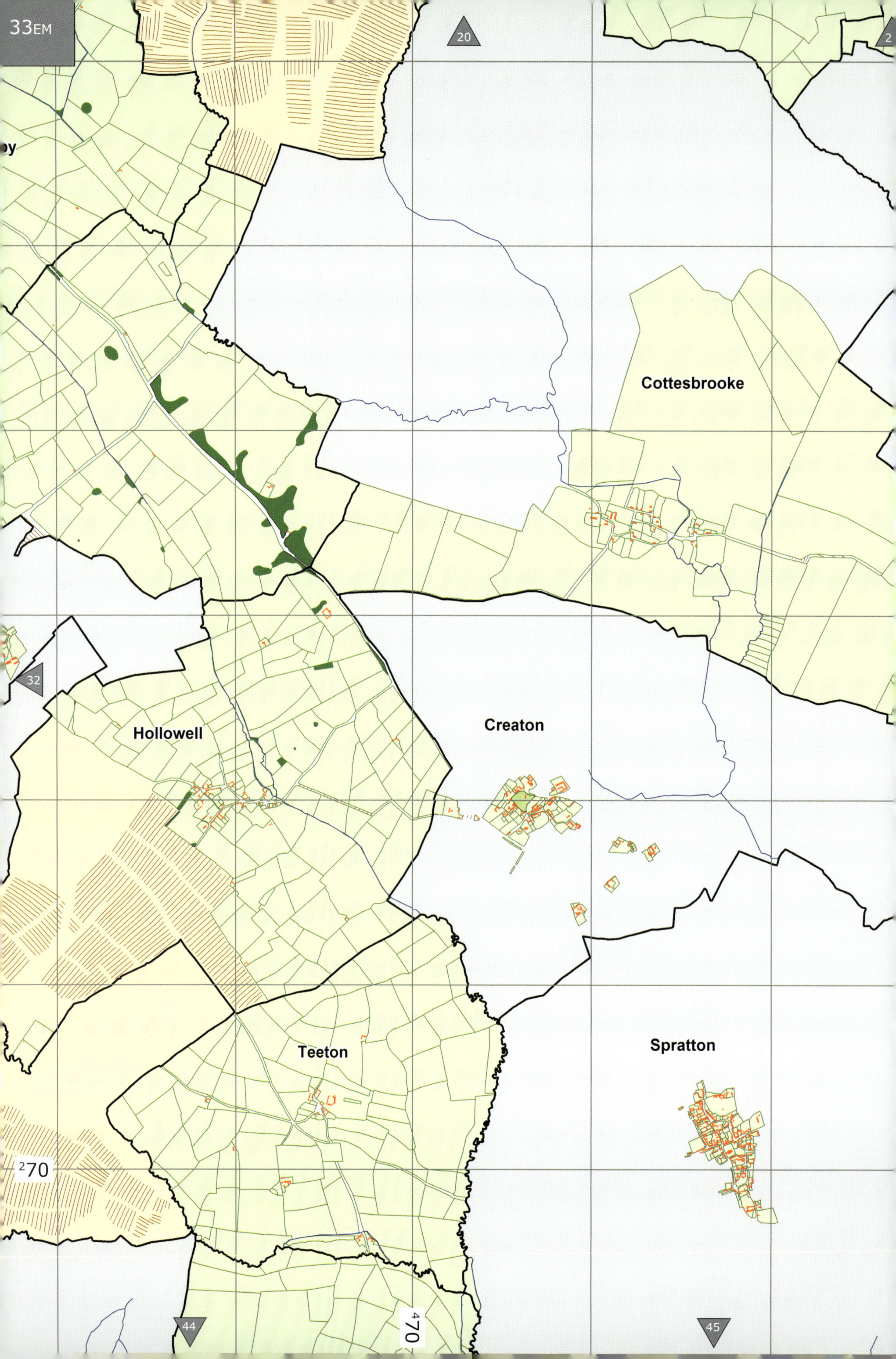
20
2
ey
Cottesbrooke
32
Creaton
Hollowell
Teeton
Spratton
270
470
44
45

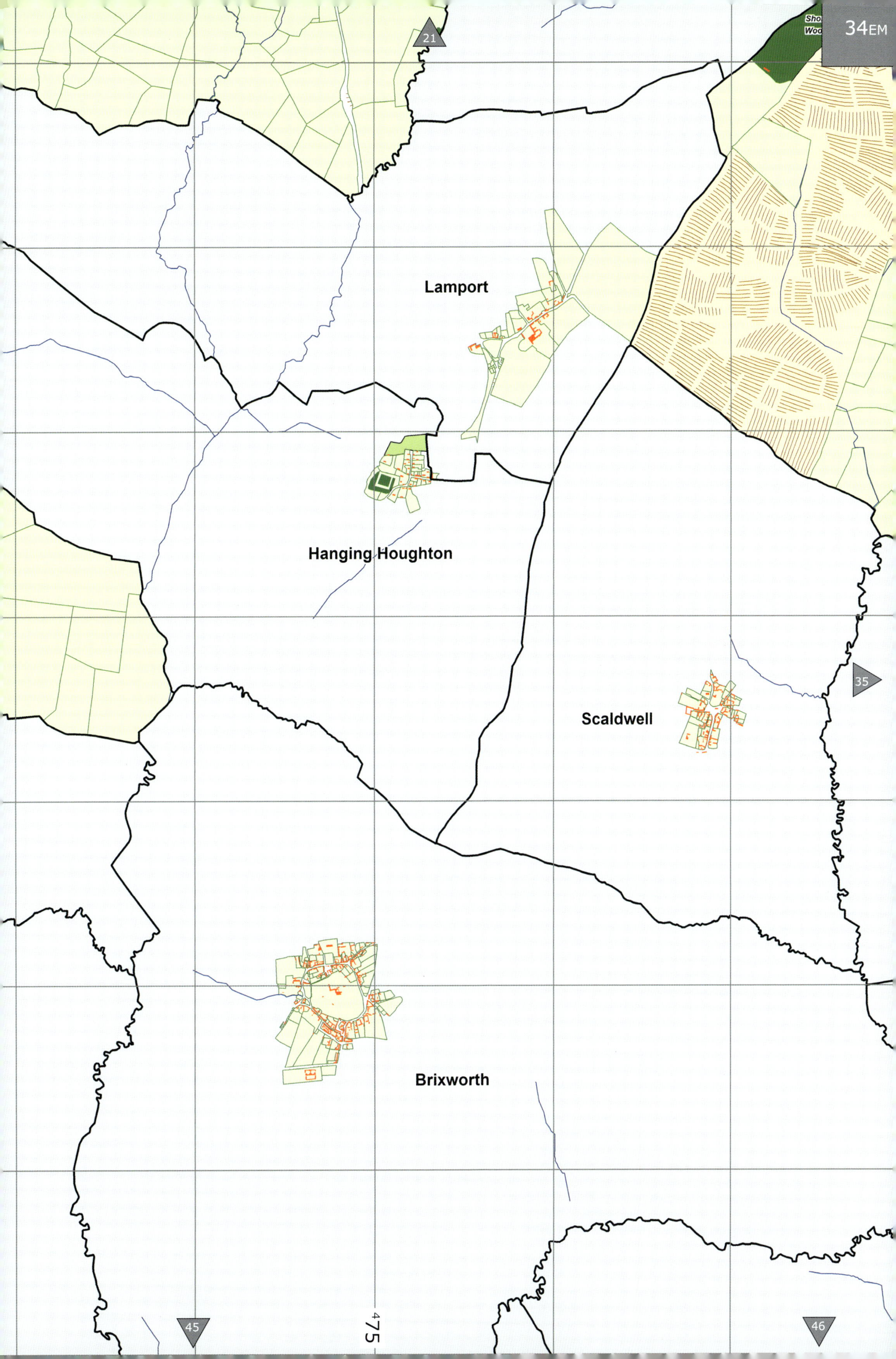
21
Sho
Woo
Lamport
Hanging Houghton
35
Scaldwell
Brixworth
45
46

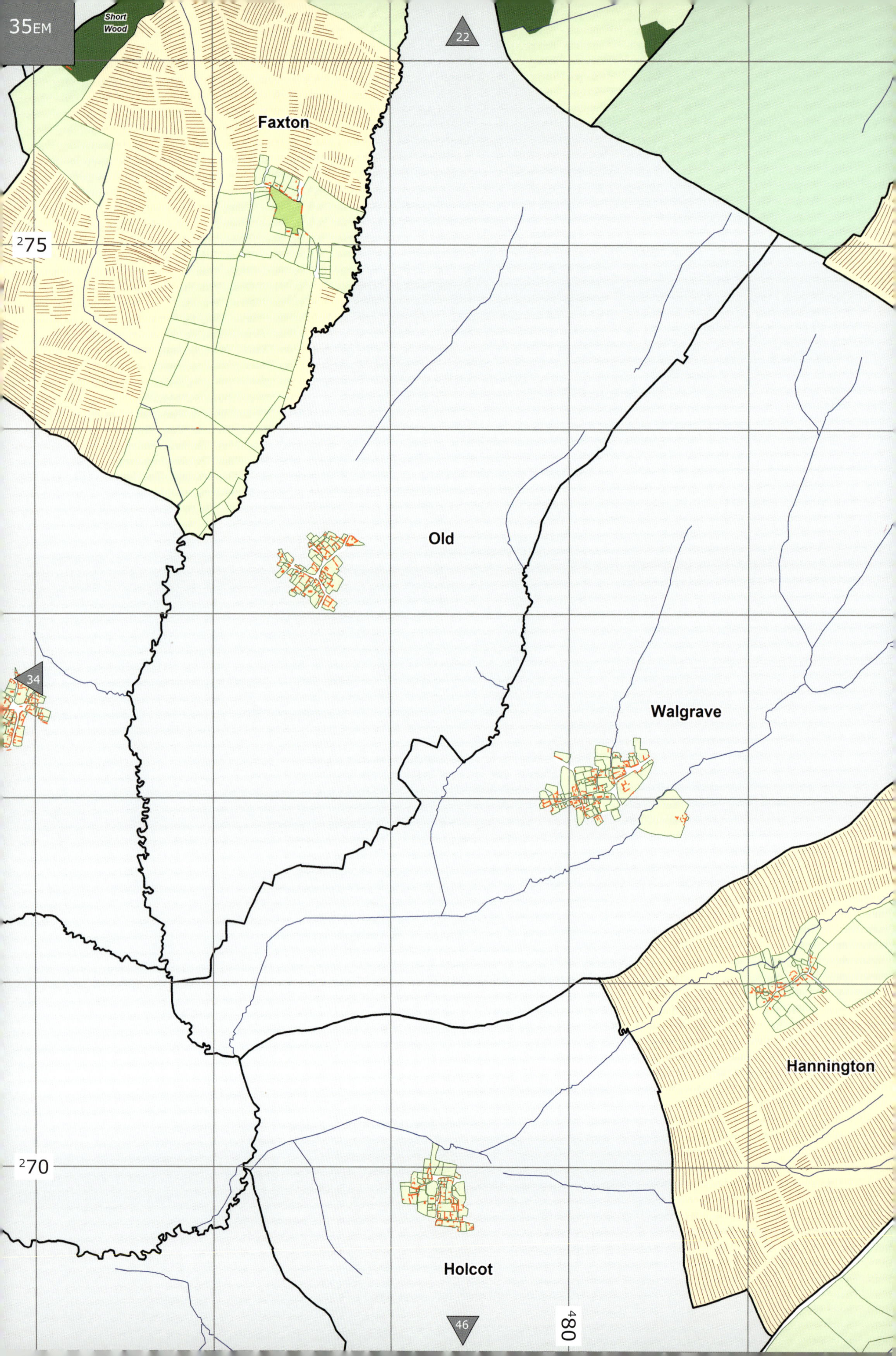
Short Wood
22
Faxton
275
Old
34
Walgrave
Hannington
270
Holcot
46
480

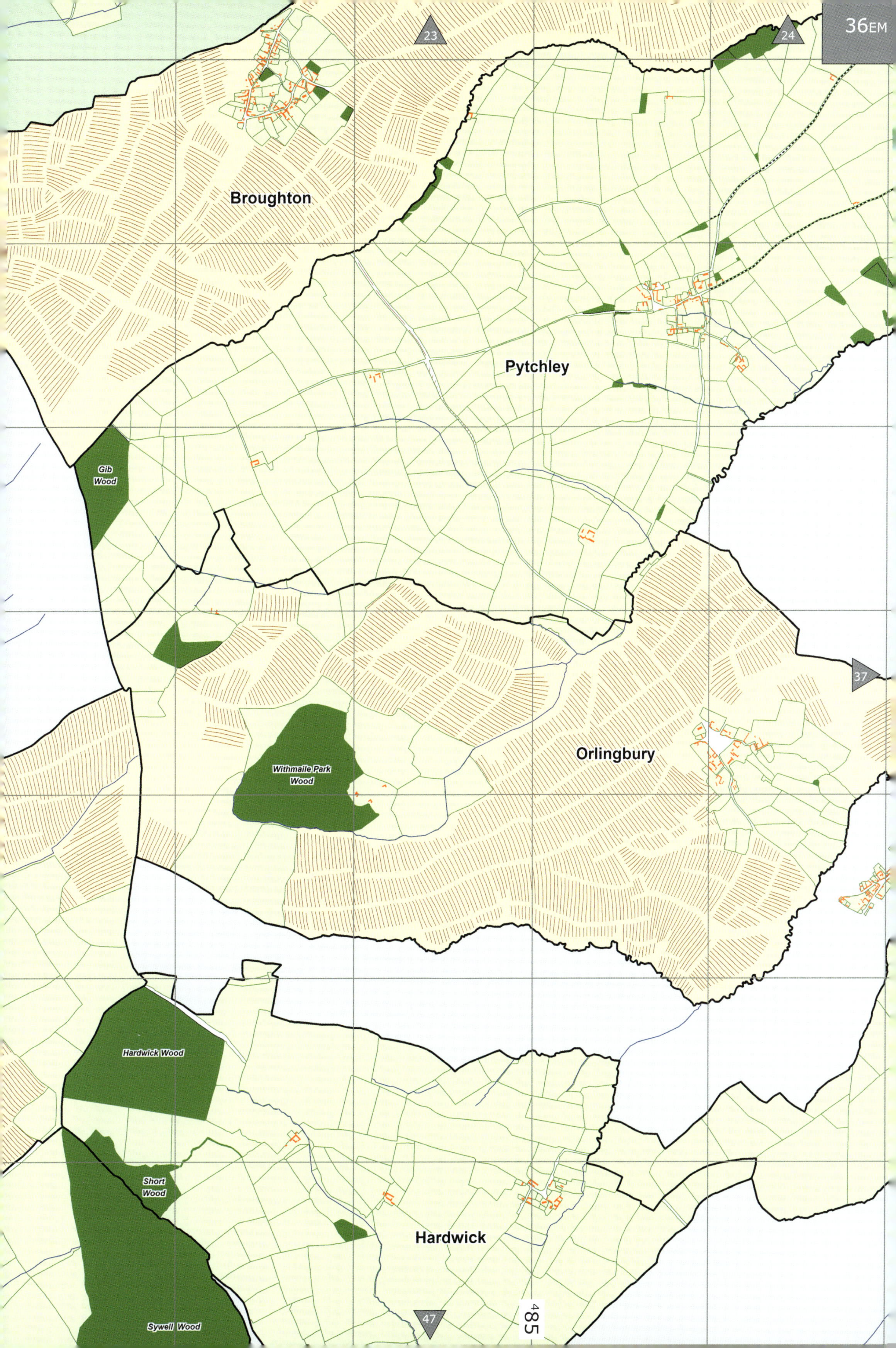

23
24
Broughton
Pytchley
Gib Wood
37
Orlingbury
Withmaile Park Wood
Hardwick Wood
Short Wood
Hardwick
Sywell Wood
47
485

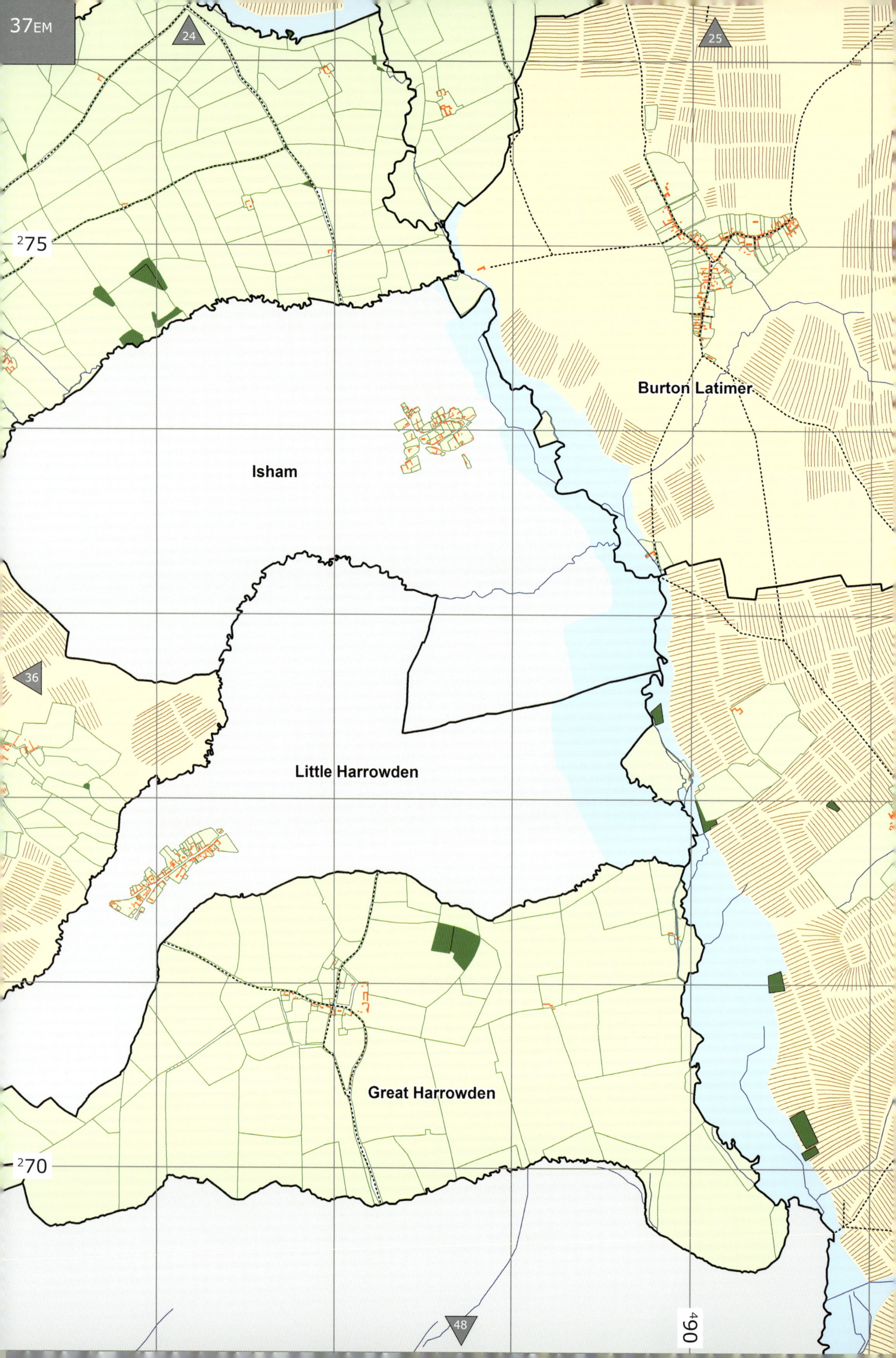

24
25
²75
Burton Latimer
Isham
36
Little Harrowden
Great Harrowden
²70
48
⁴90

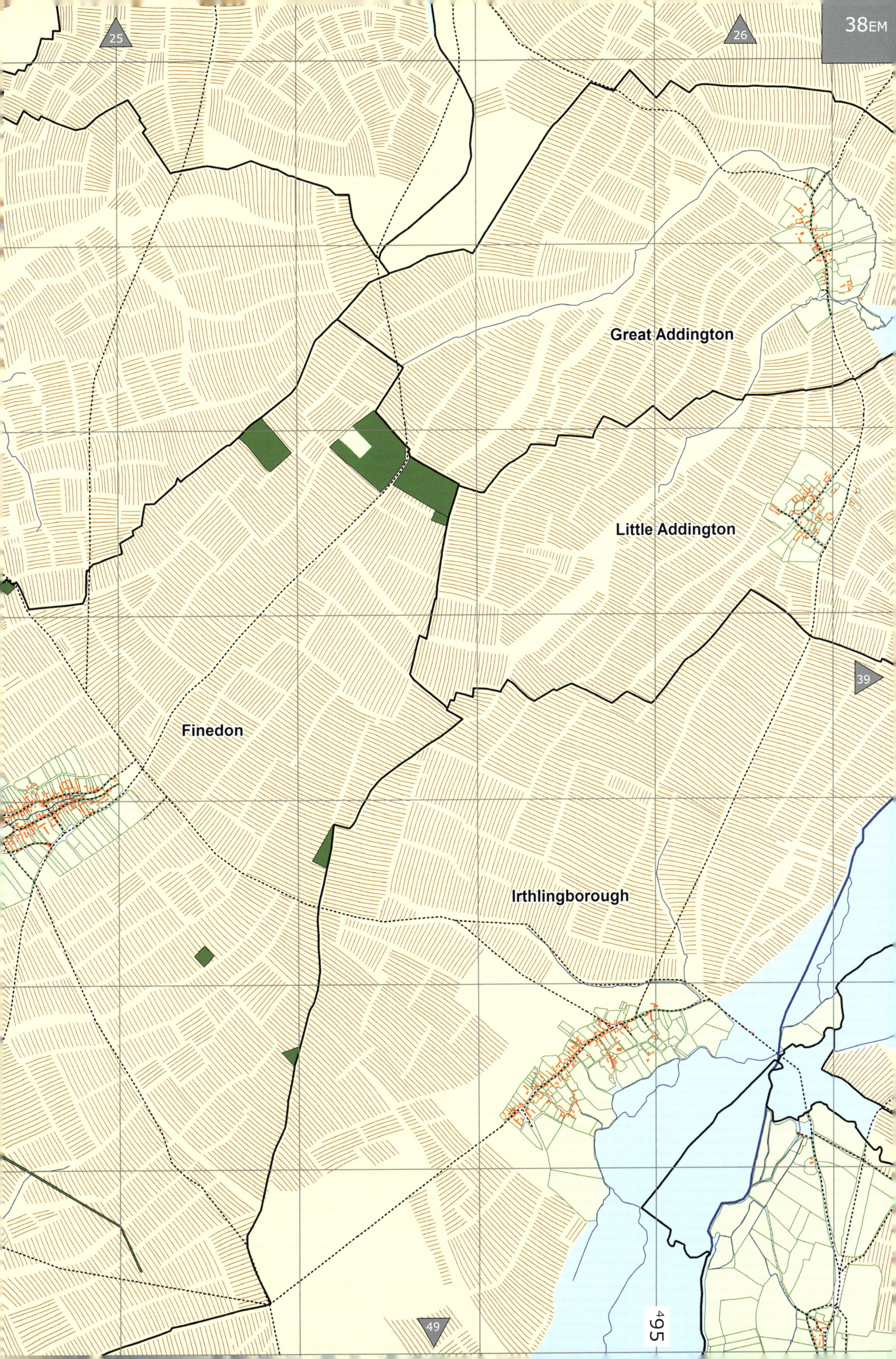

25
26
Great Addington
Little Addington
Finedon
Irthlingborough
39
49
495

26
27
275
Ringstead
38
Raunds
Cotton
Fields
Raunds
Stanwick
270
Chelveston
49
50
500
Chelveston cum Caldecott

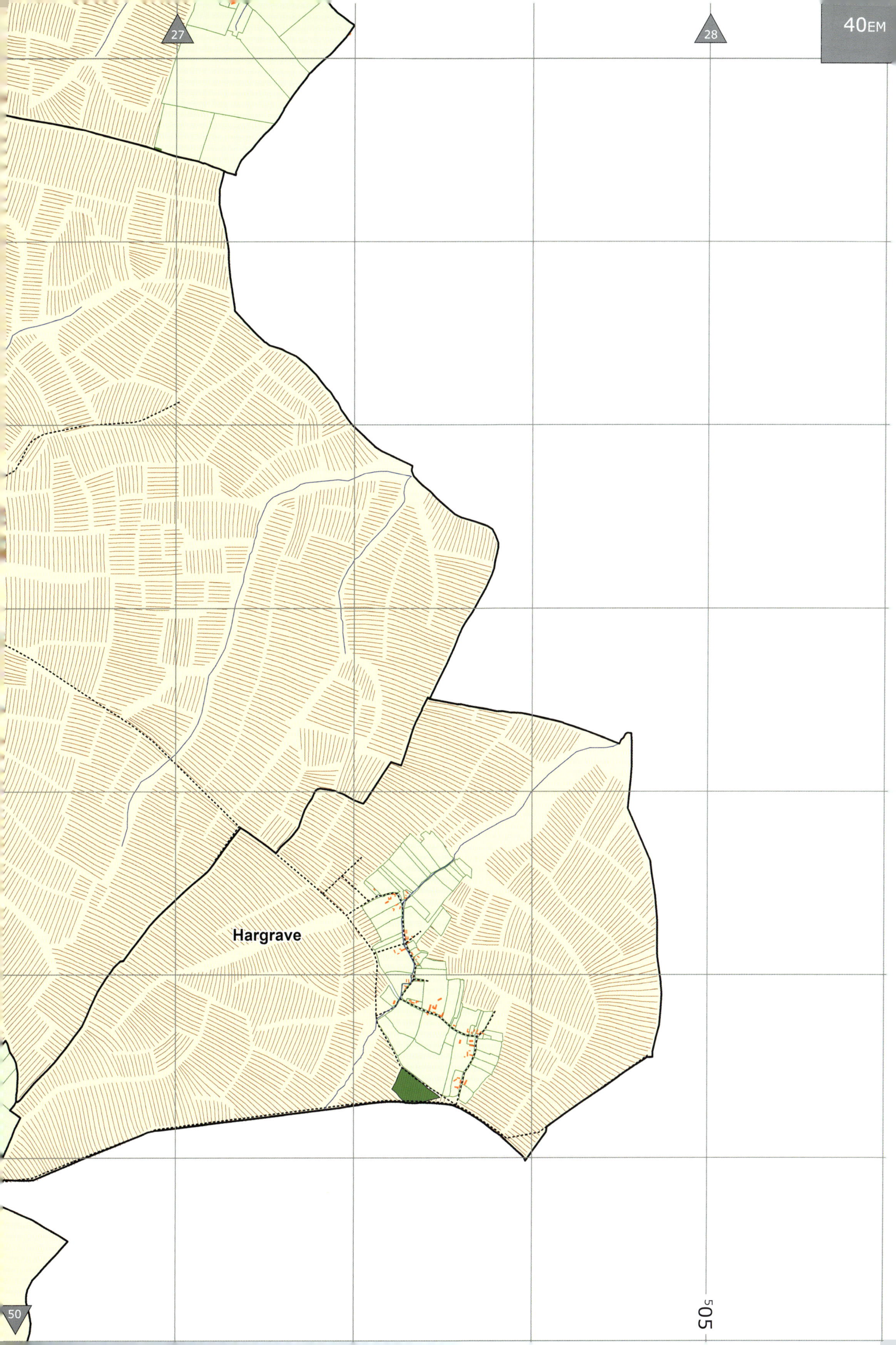
27
28
Hargrave
50
505

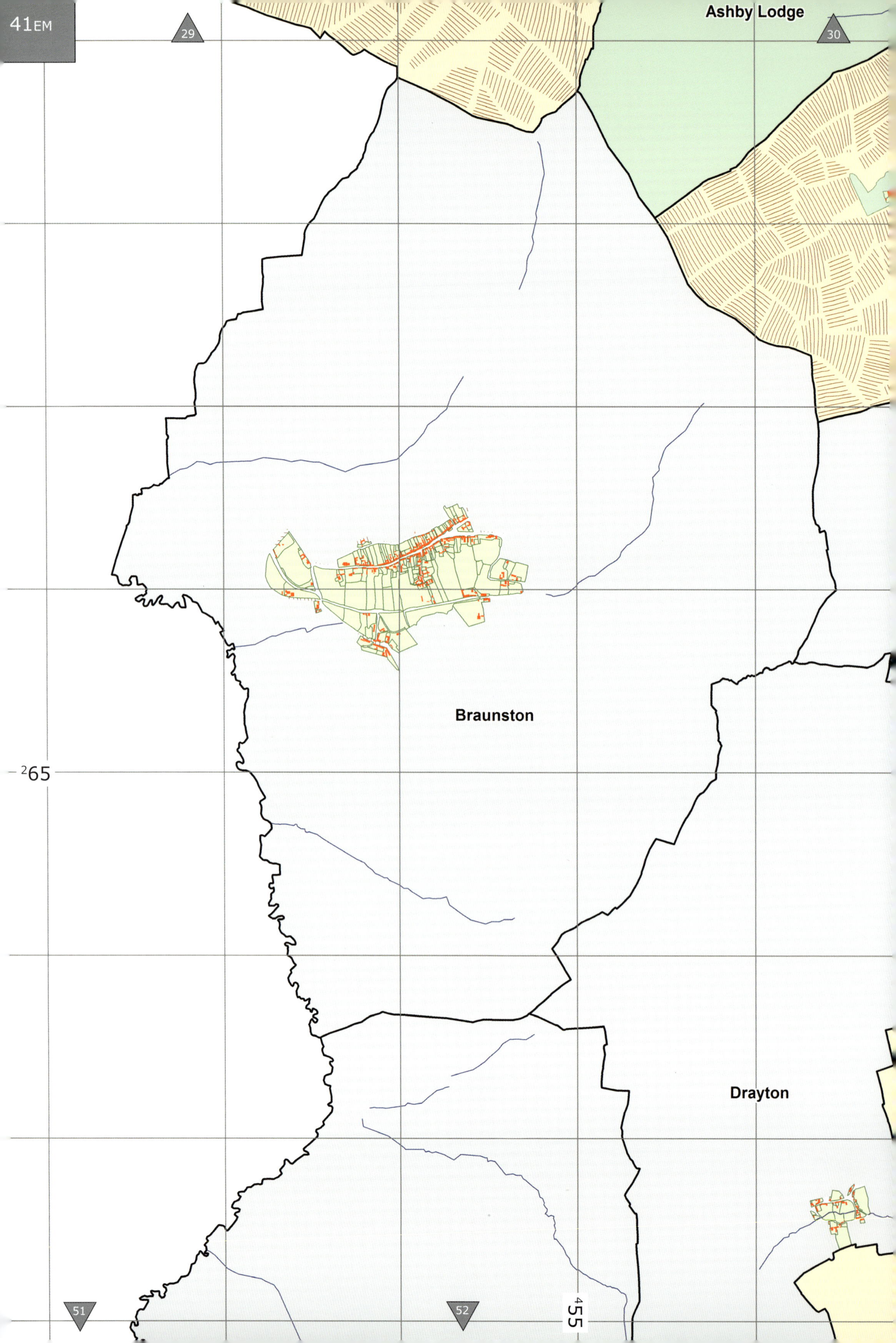

29
Ashby Lodge
30
Braunston
²65
Drayton
51
52
⁴55

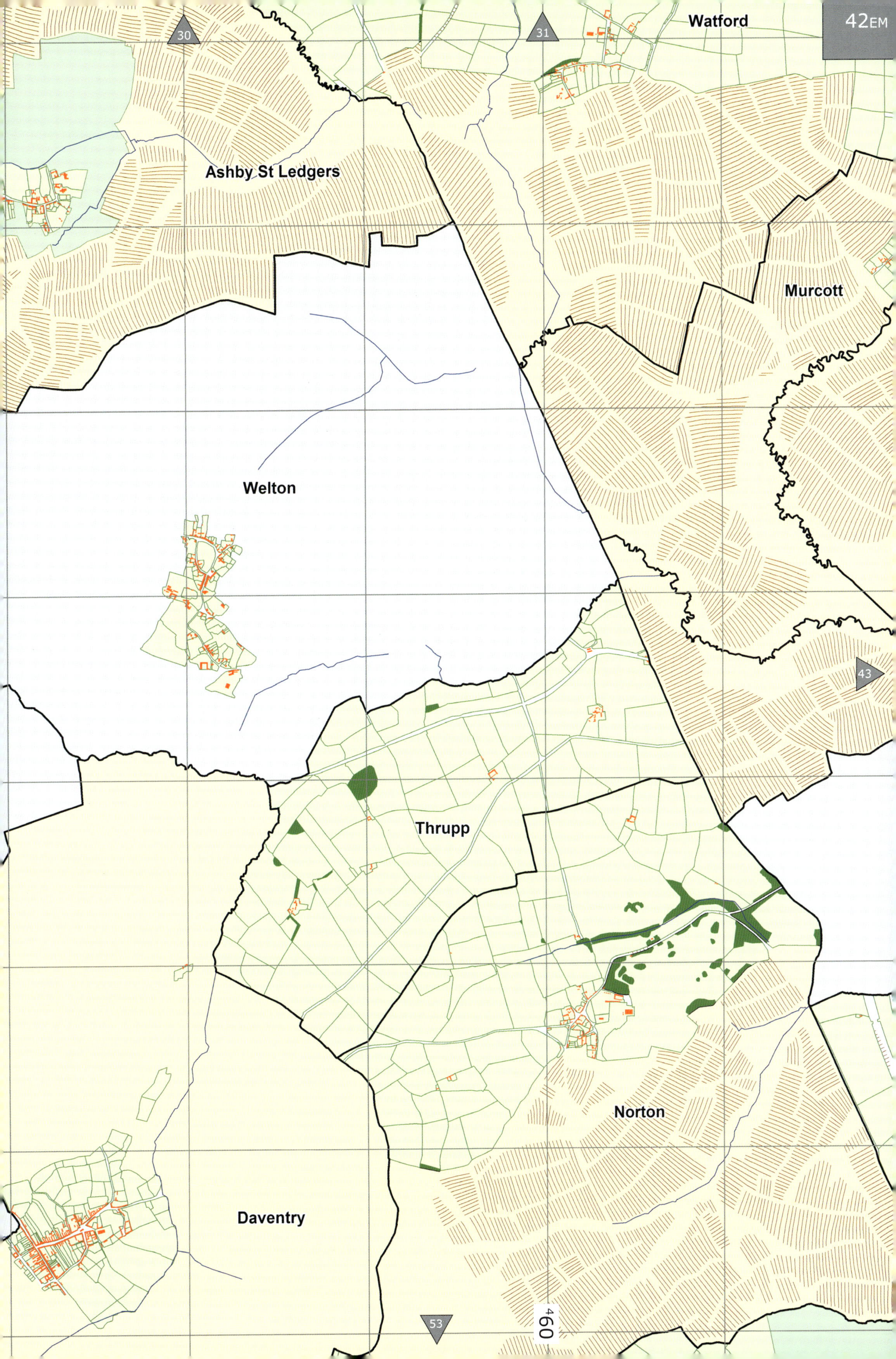
30
31
Watford
Ashby St Ledgers
Murcott
Welton
43
Thrupp
Norton
Daventry
53

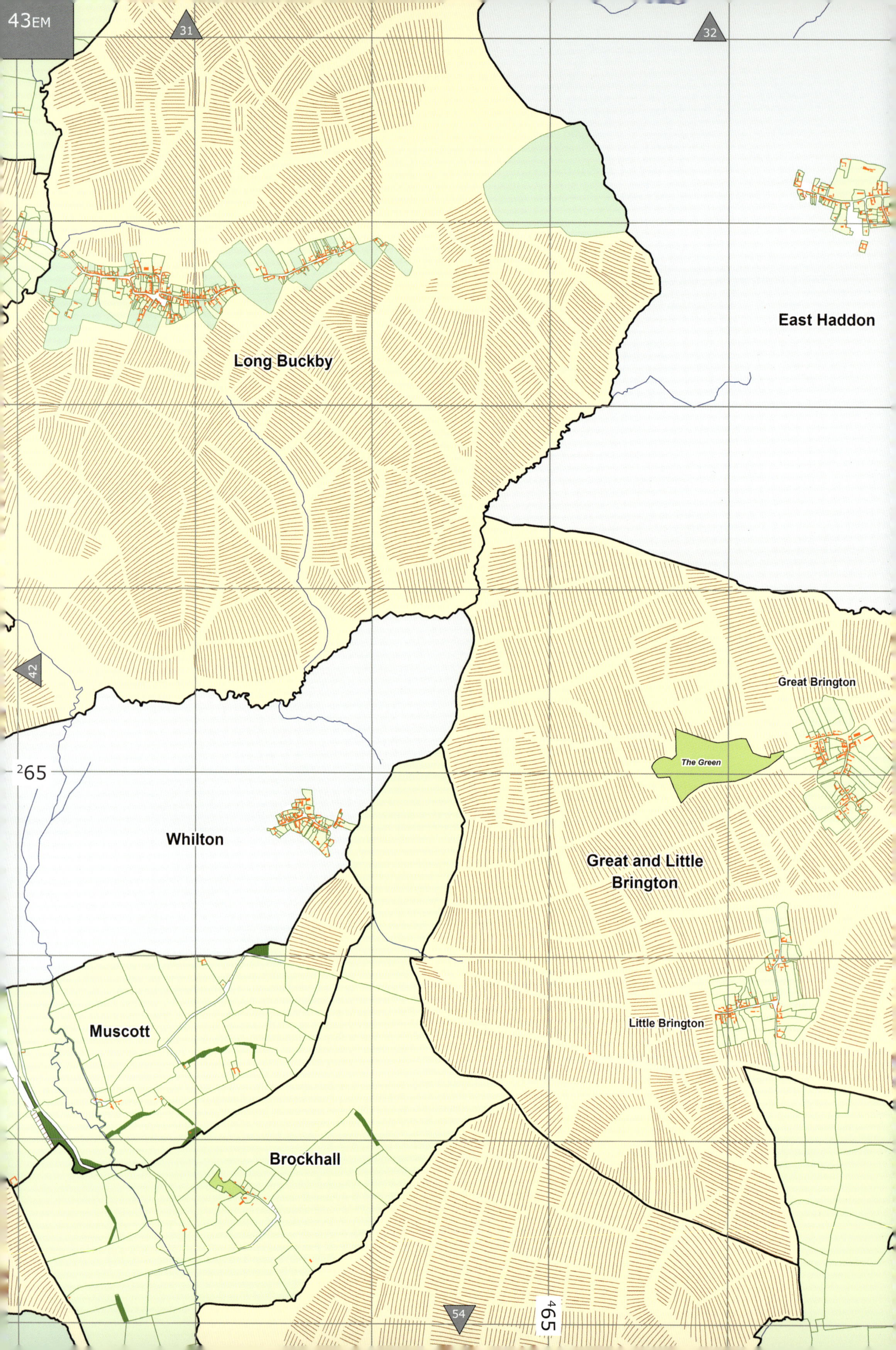
31
32
Long Buckby
East Haddon
42
Great Brington
The Green
²65
Whilton
Great and Little
Brington
Muscott
Little Brington
Brockhall
54
⁴65

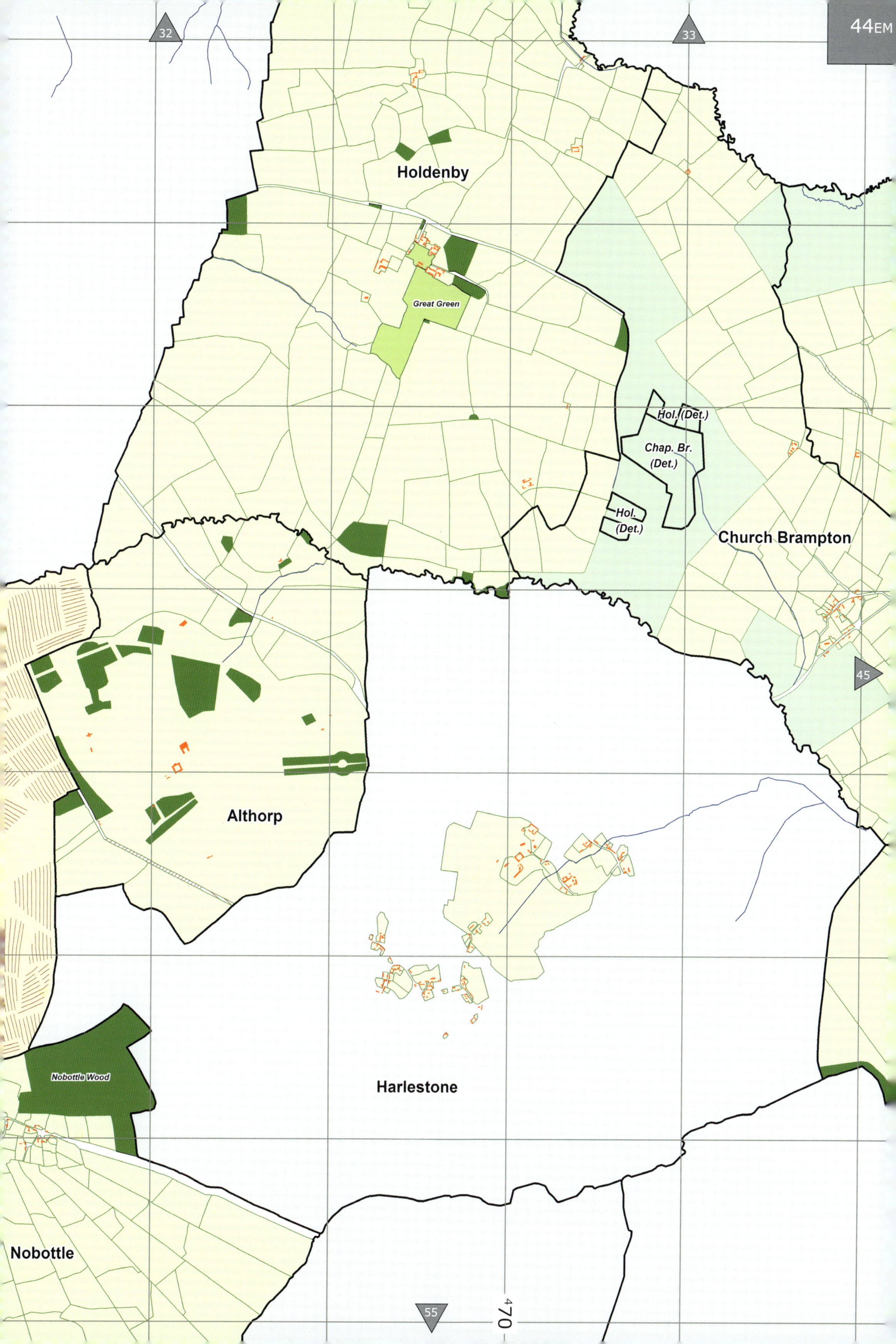

32
33
Holdenby
Great Green
Hol. (Det.)
Chap. Br. (Det.)
Hol. (Det.)
Church Brampton
45
Althorp
Harlestone
Nobottle Wood
Nobottle
55
470

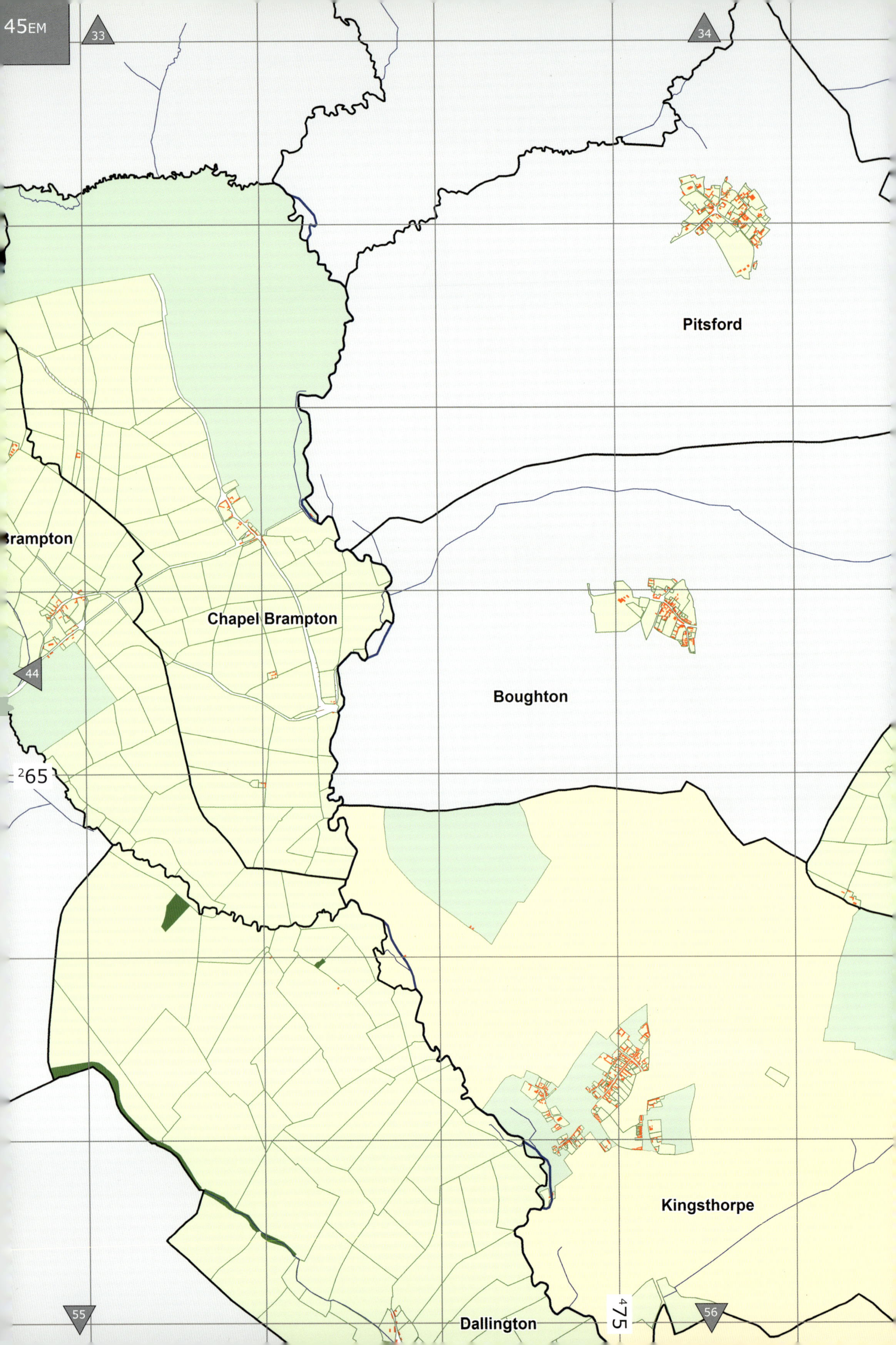
33
34
Pitsford
Brampton
Chapel Brampton
44
Boughton
265
Kingsthorpe
55
Dallington
475
56

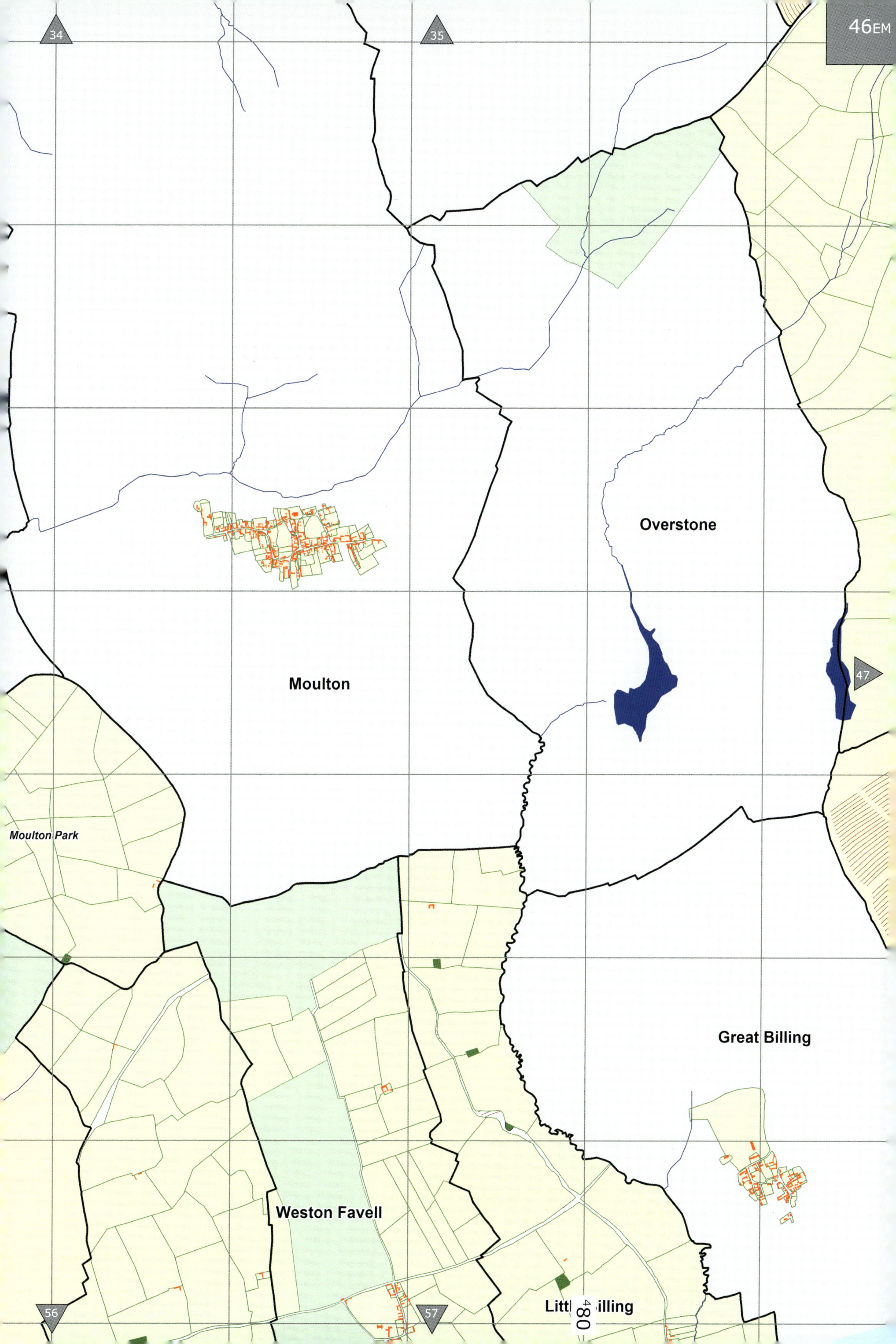
46EM
34
35
47
56
57
Overstone
Moulton
Moulton Park
Great Billing
Weston Favell
Littl illing

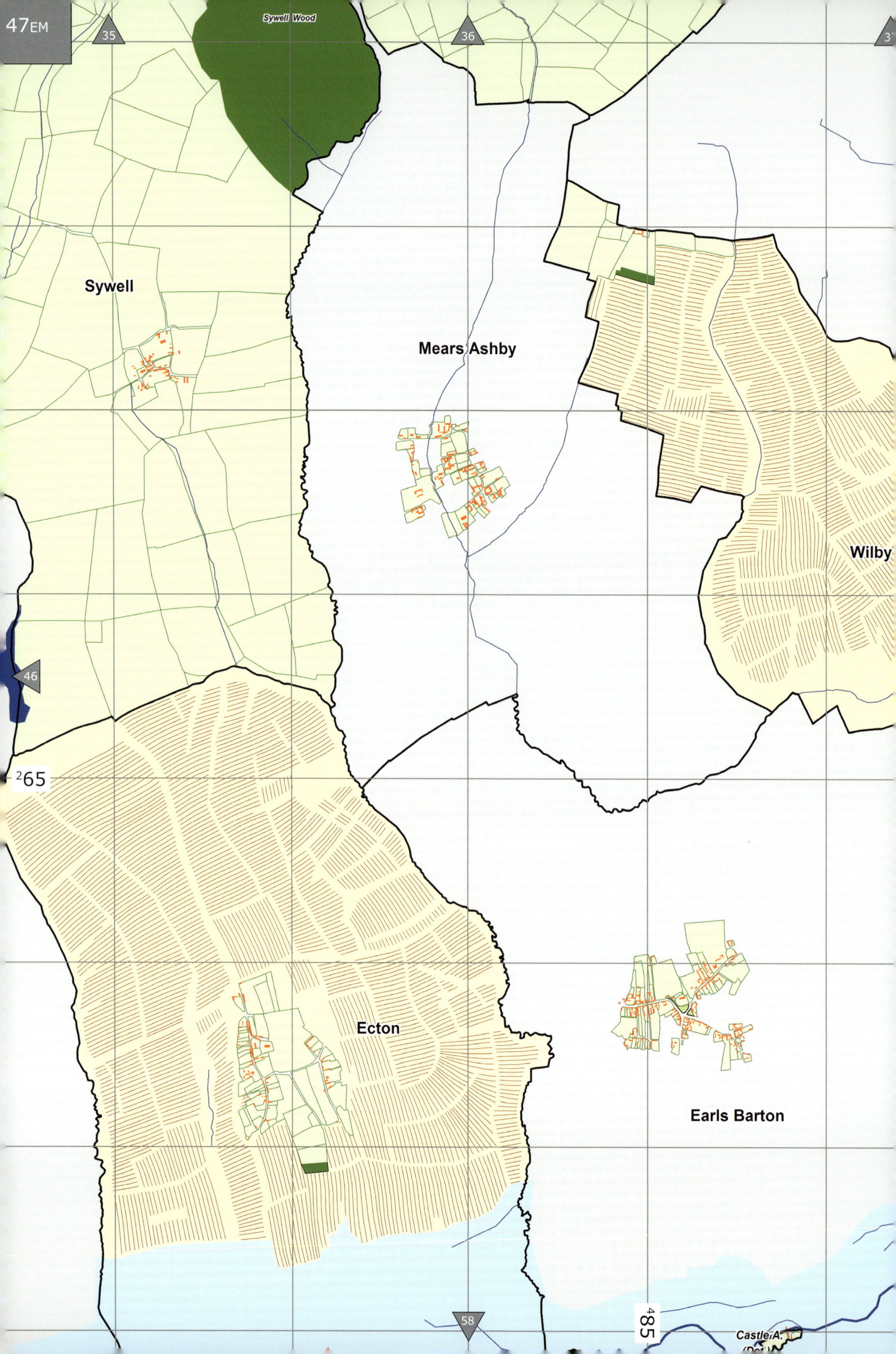
Sywell Wood
35
36
Sywell
Mears Ashby
Wilby
46
265
Ecton
Earls Barton
58
485
Castle A.

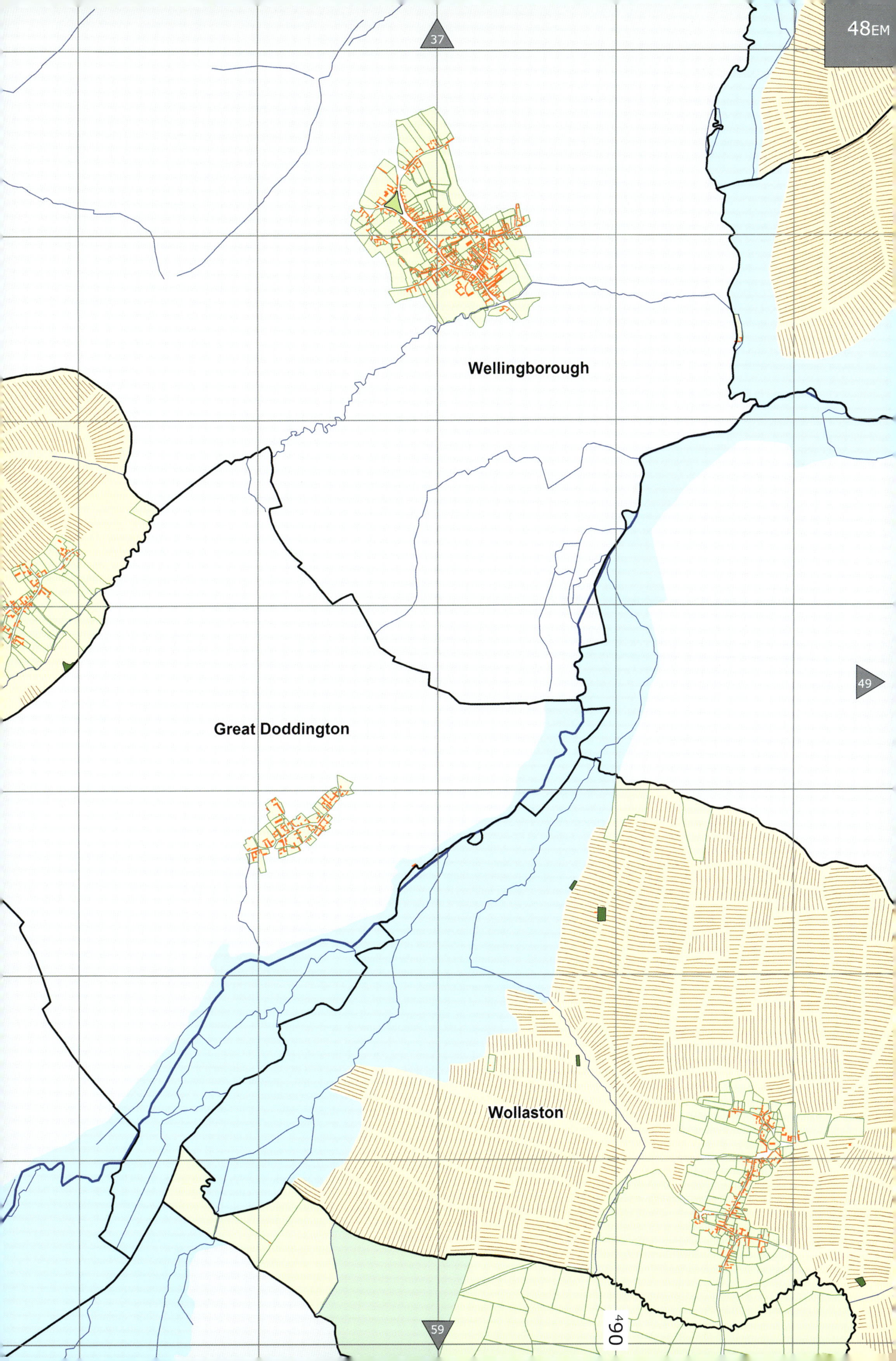

37
Wellingborough
Great Doddington
49
Wollaston
59
490

38
Rushden
Knuston
Irchester
48
265
60
495

Chelveston cum Caldecott
39
Caldecott
Higham Ferrers
Buscot
Newton Bromswold
Higham Park
500

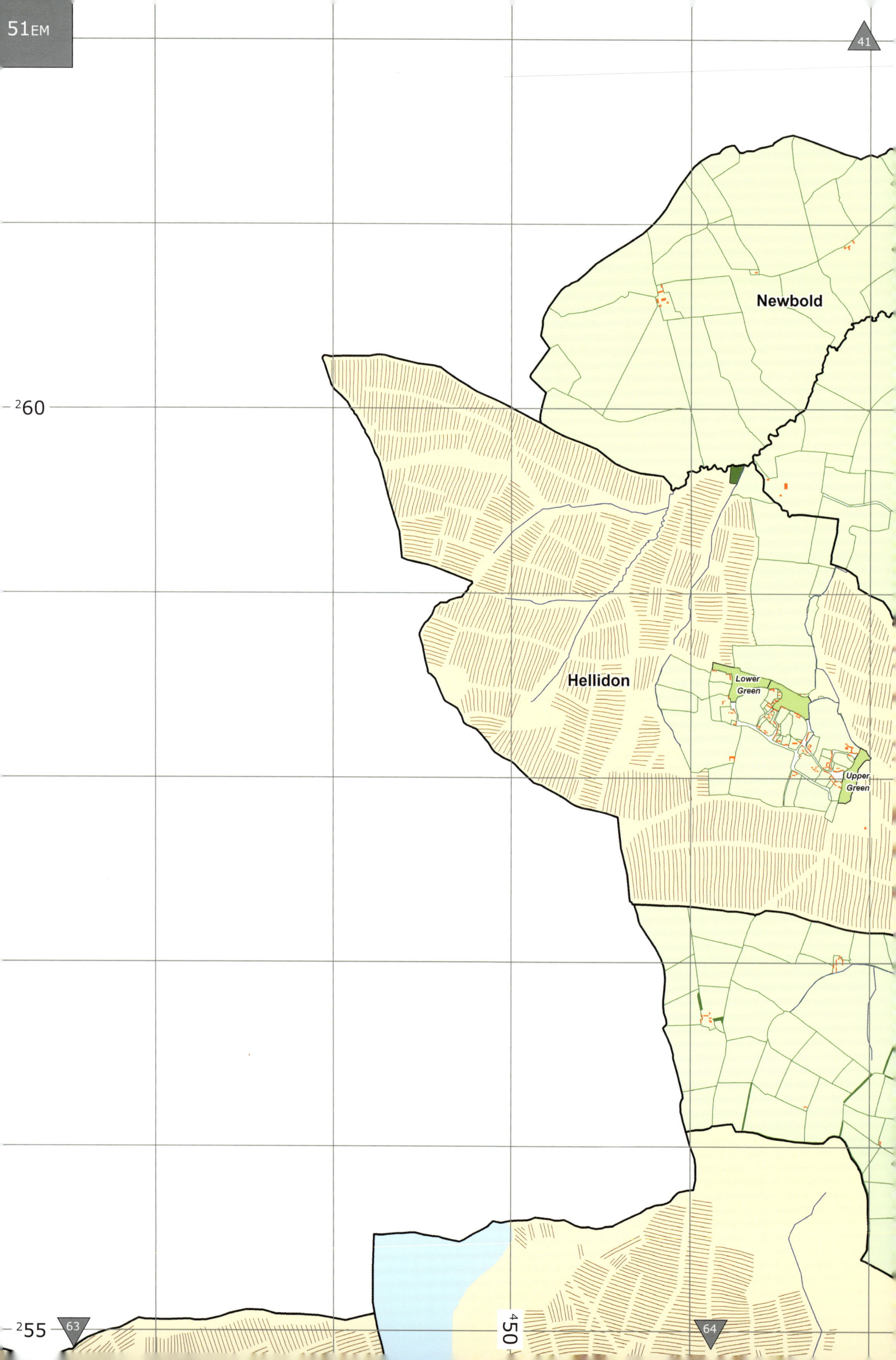
41
Newbold
260
Hellidon
Lower Green
Upper Green
255
63
450
64

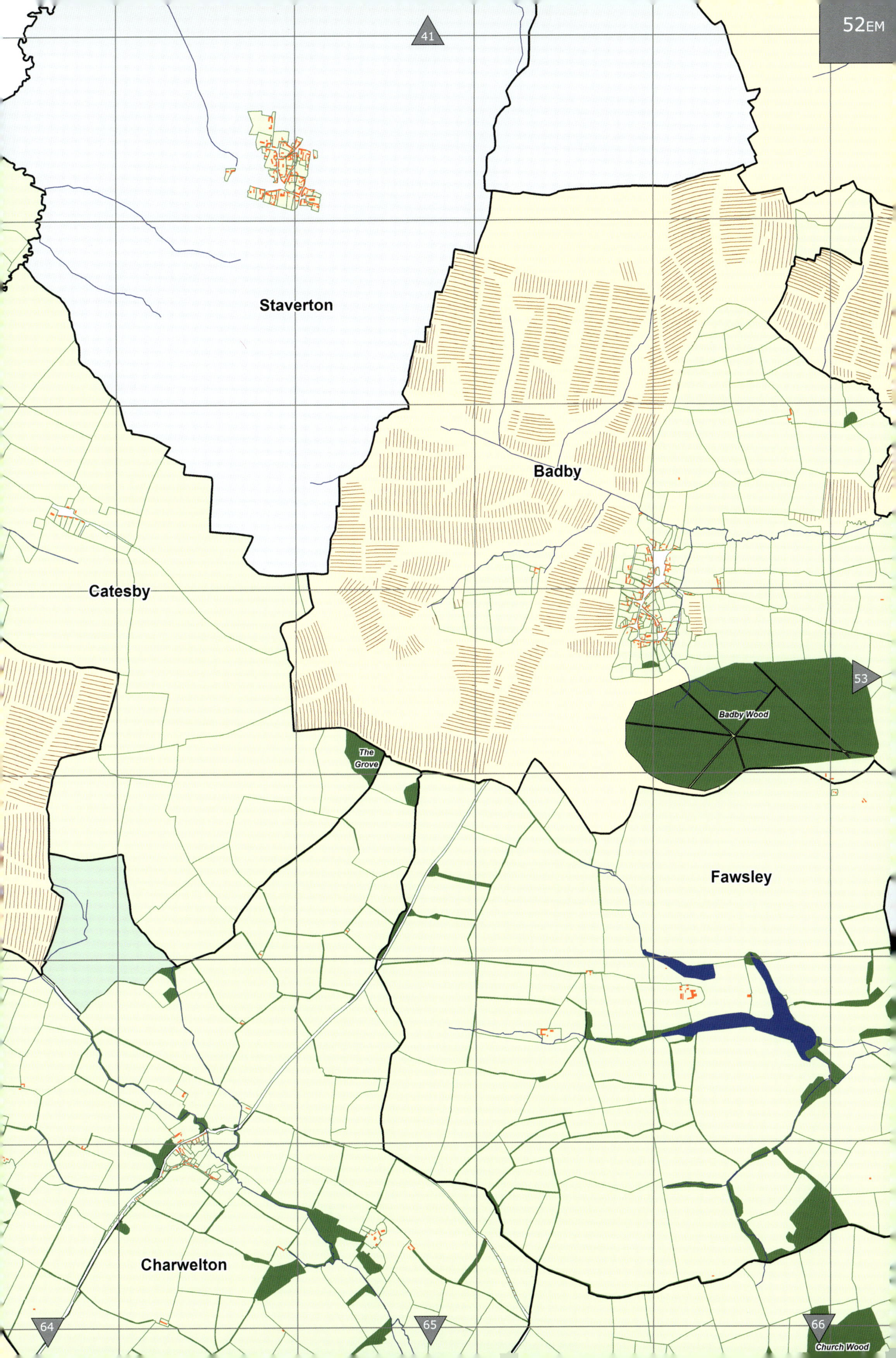
41
Staverton
Badby
Catesby
53
Badby Wood
The Grove
Fawsley
Charwelton
64
65
66
Church Wood

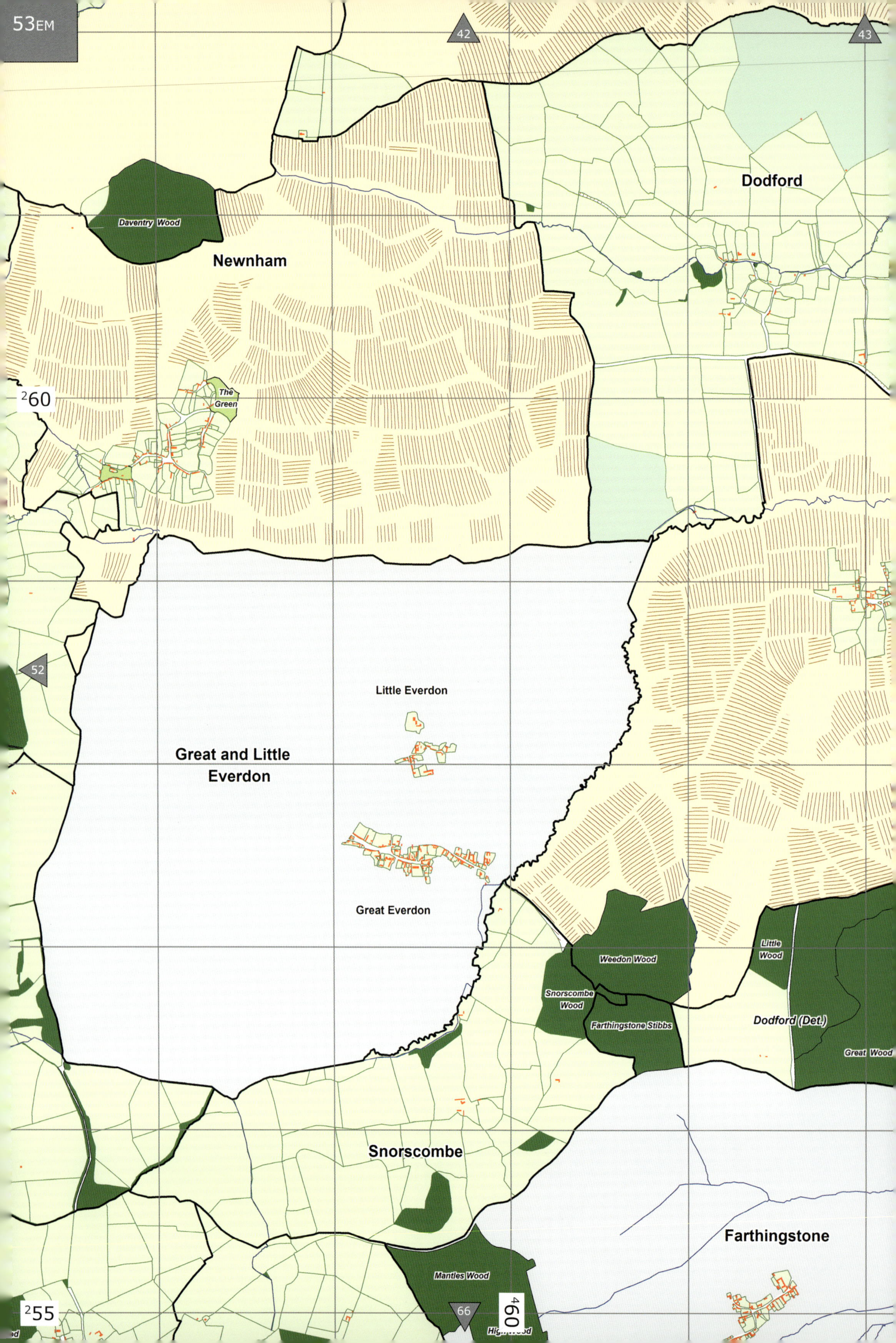
42
43
Dodford
Daventry Wood
Newnham
The Green
260
52
Little Everdon
Great and Little Everdon
Great Everdon
Weedon Wood
Little Wood
Snorscombe Wood
Farthingstone Stibbs
Dodford (Det.)
Great Wood
Snorscombe
Farthingstone
Mantles Wood
255
66
460

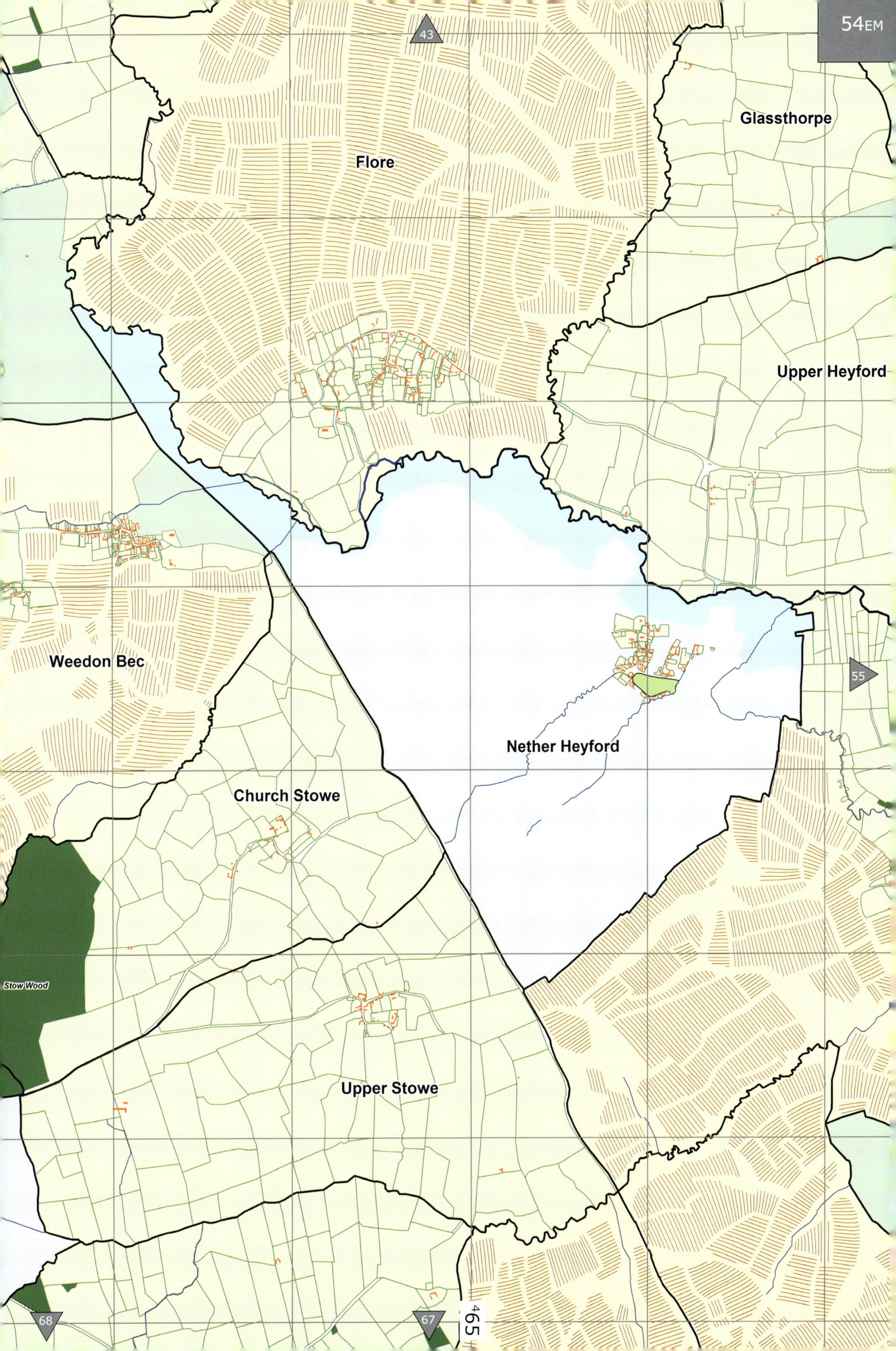
43
Glassthorpe
Flore
Upper Heyford
Weedon Bec
55
Nether Heyford
Church Stowe
Stow Wood
Upper Stowe
68
67

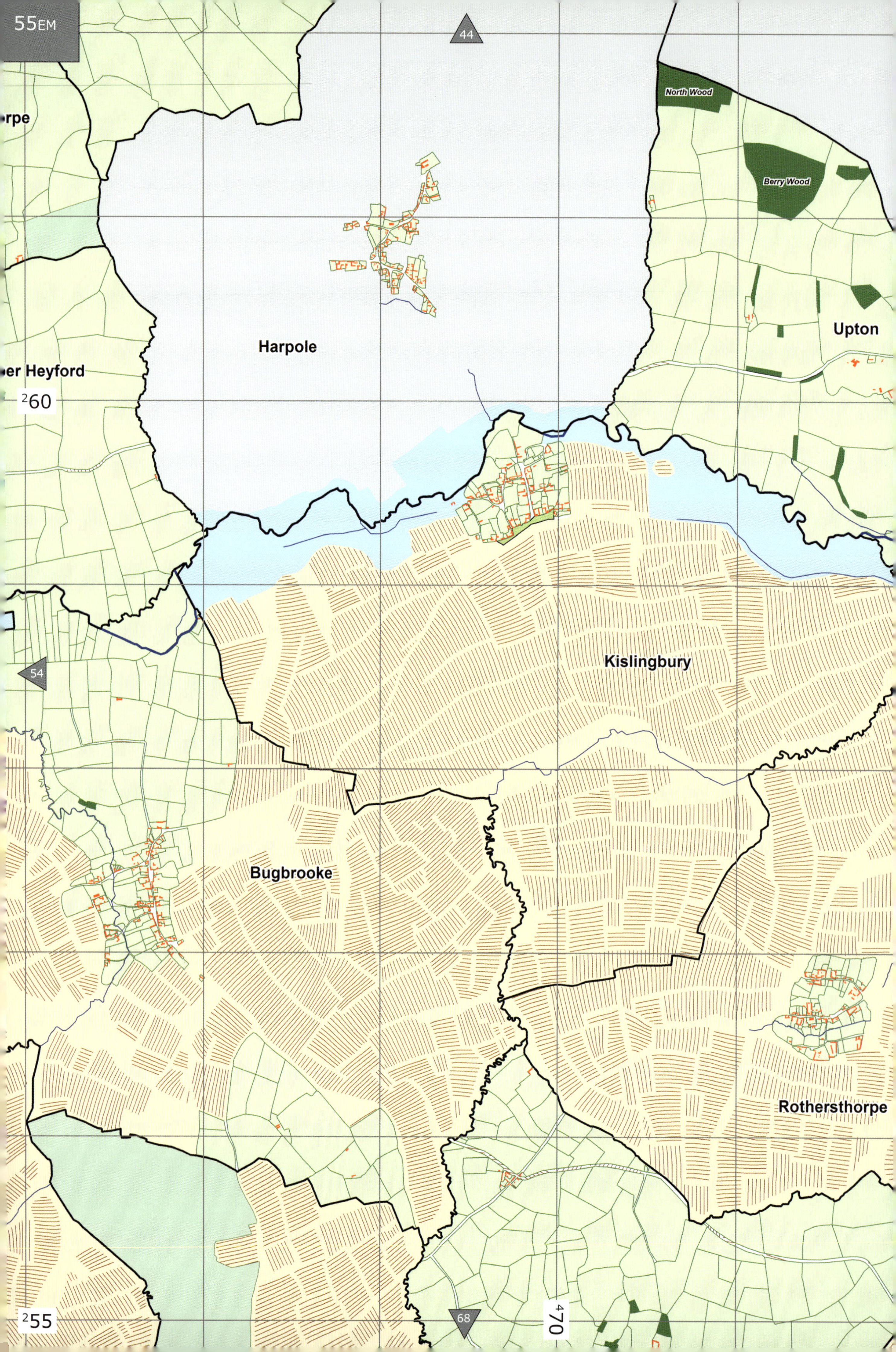
44
North Wood
Berry Wood
rpe
Harpole
Upton
er Heyford
260
54
Kislingbury
Bugbrooke
Rothersthorpe
255
68
470

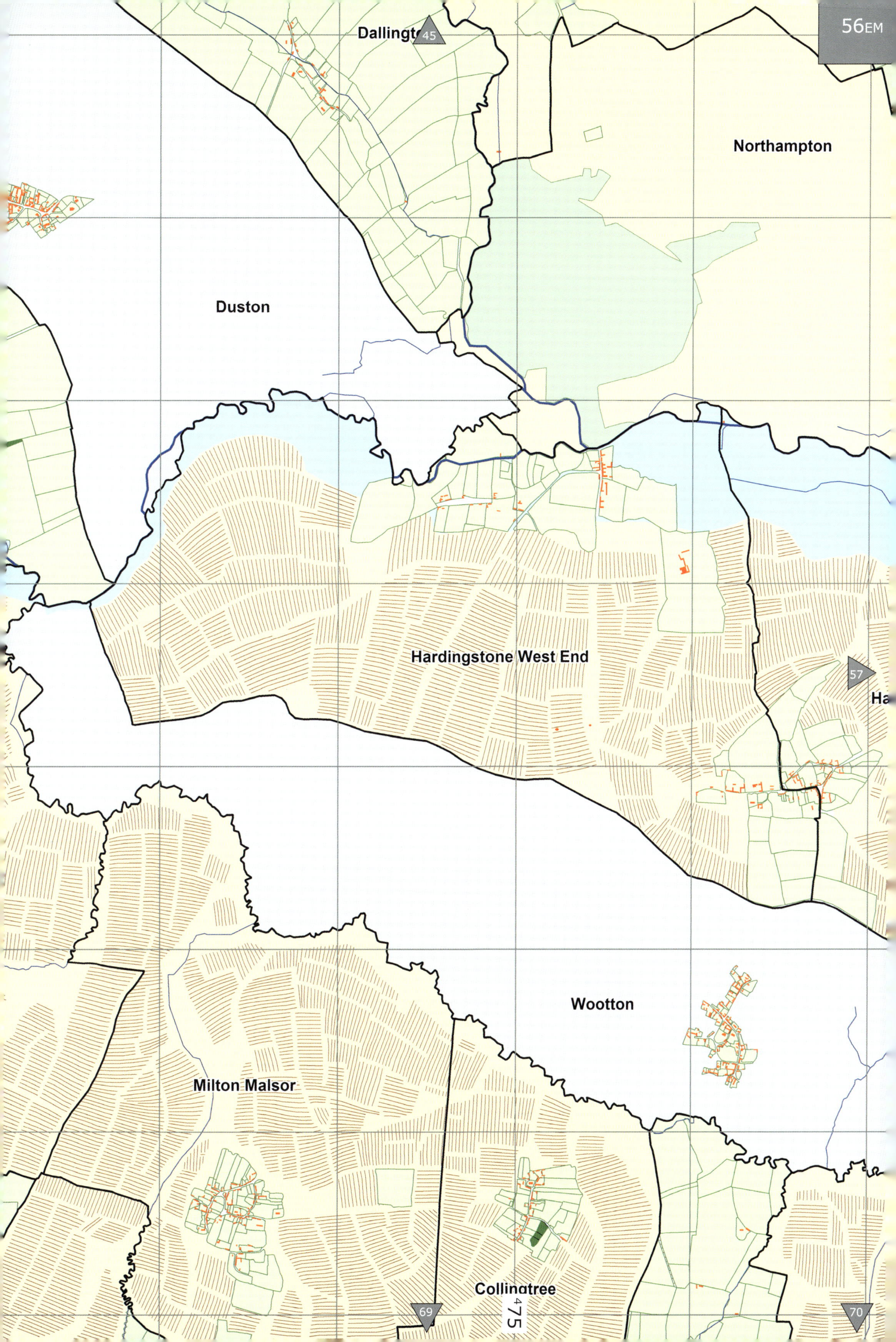
Dallingt
45
Northampton
Duston
Hardingstone West End
57
Ha
Wootton
Milton Malsor
Collingtree
69
4
75
70

46
Little Billing
47
mpton
Abington
Brafield
(Det.)
260
56
Hardingstone East End
Little Houghton
Great Houghton
Hackleton
Preston Deanery
255
70
480
61

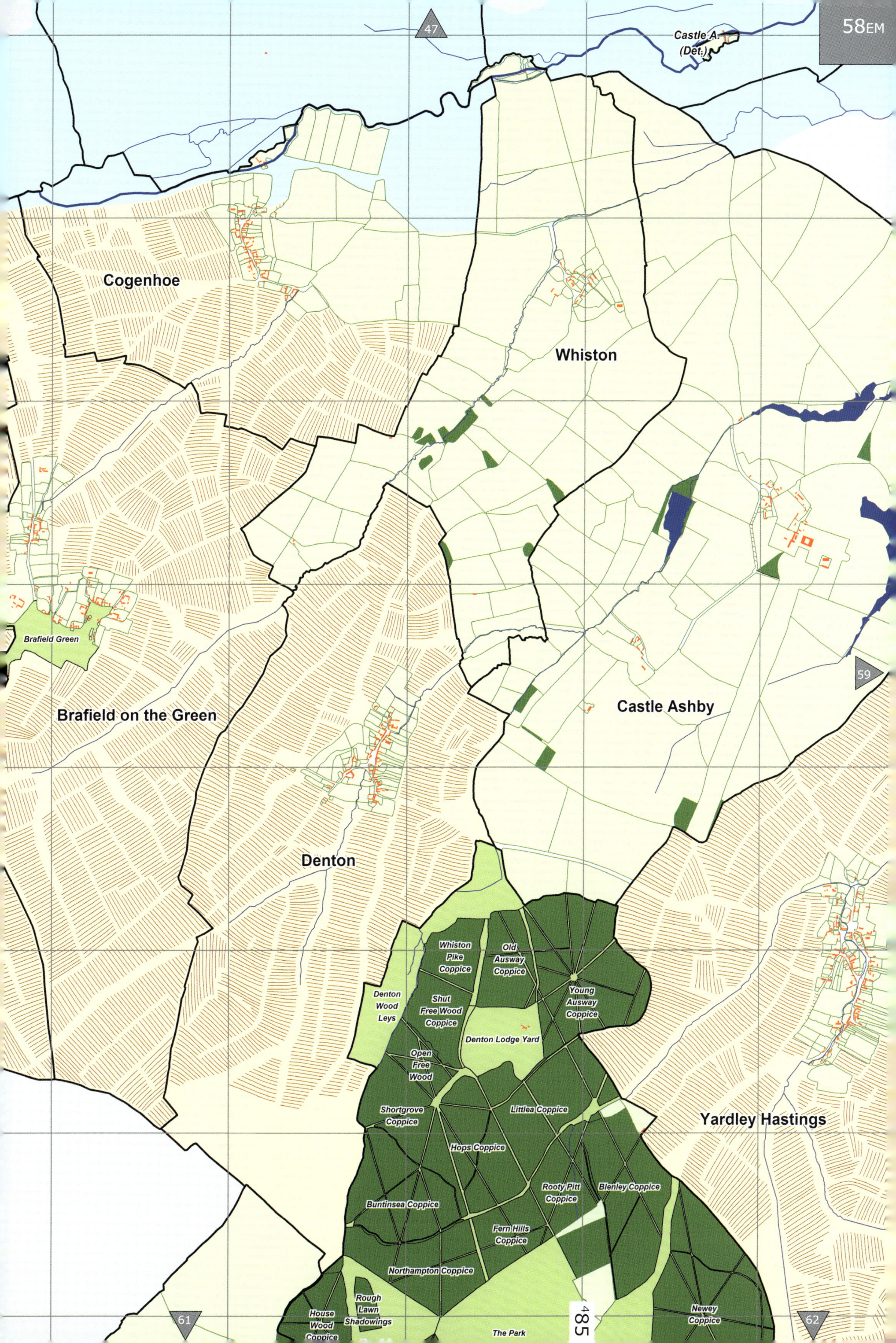
47
Castle A. (Det.)
Cogenhoe
Whiston
Brafield Green
Brafield on the Green
Castle Ashby
59
Denton
Whiston Pike Coppice
Old Ausway Coppice
Young Ausway Coppice
Denton Wood Leys
Shut Free Wood Coppice
Denton Lodge Yard
Open Free Wood
Shortgrove Coppice
Littlea Coppice
Yardley Hastings
Hops Coppice
Rooty Pitt Coppice
Blenley Coppice
Buntinsea Coppice
Fern Hills Coppice
Northampton Coppice
Rough Lawn Shadowings
House Wood Coppice
The Park
Newey Coppice
61
62
485

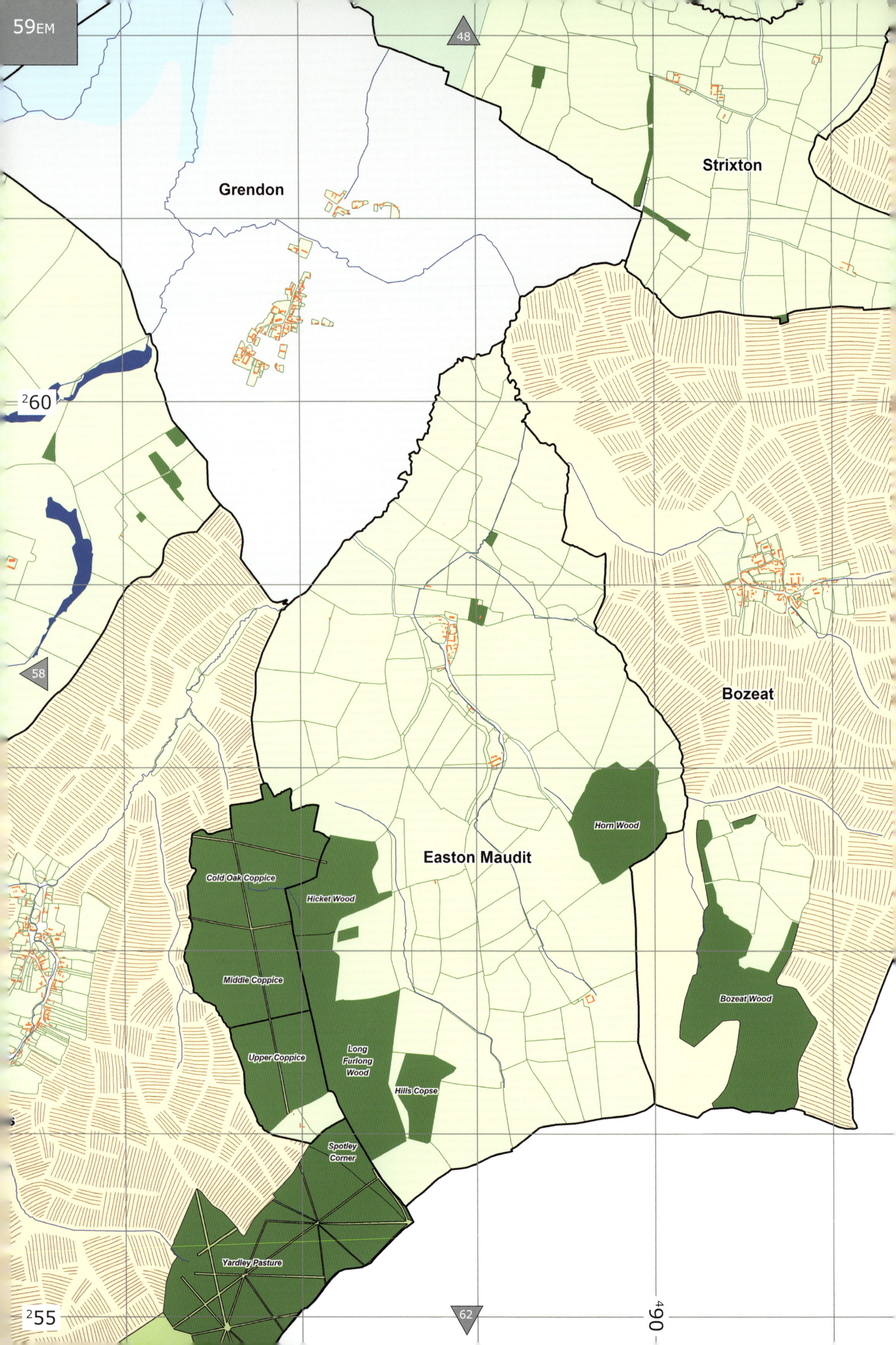
48
Grendon
Strixton
²60
Bozeat
58
Easton Maudit
Horn Wood
Cold Oak Coppice
Hicket Wood
Middle Coppice
Bozeat Wood
Upper Coppice
Long
Furlong
Wood
Hills Copse
Spotley
Corner
Yardley Pasture
²55
62
490

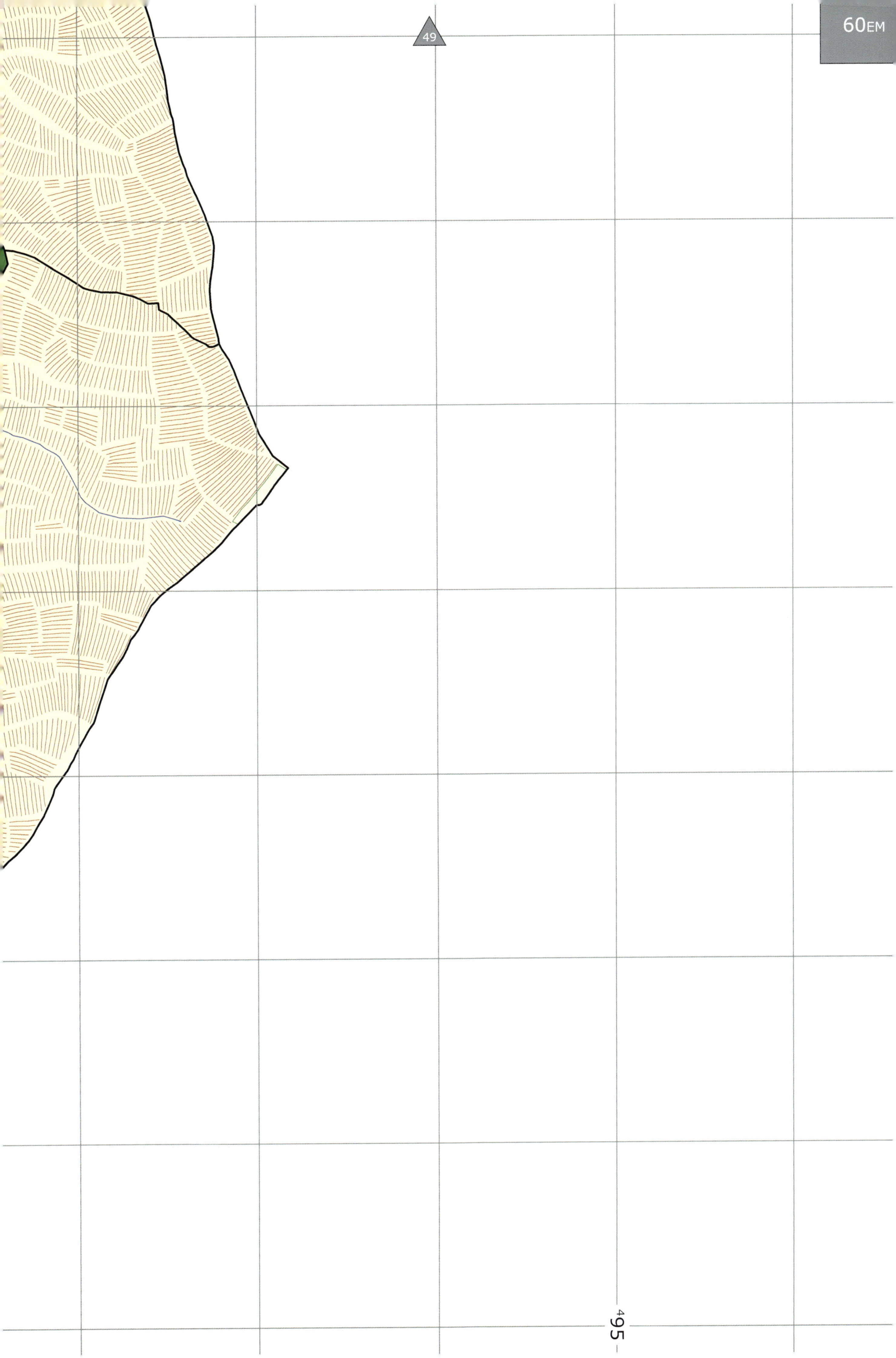
60EM
49
495

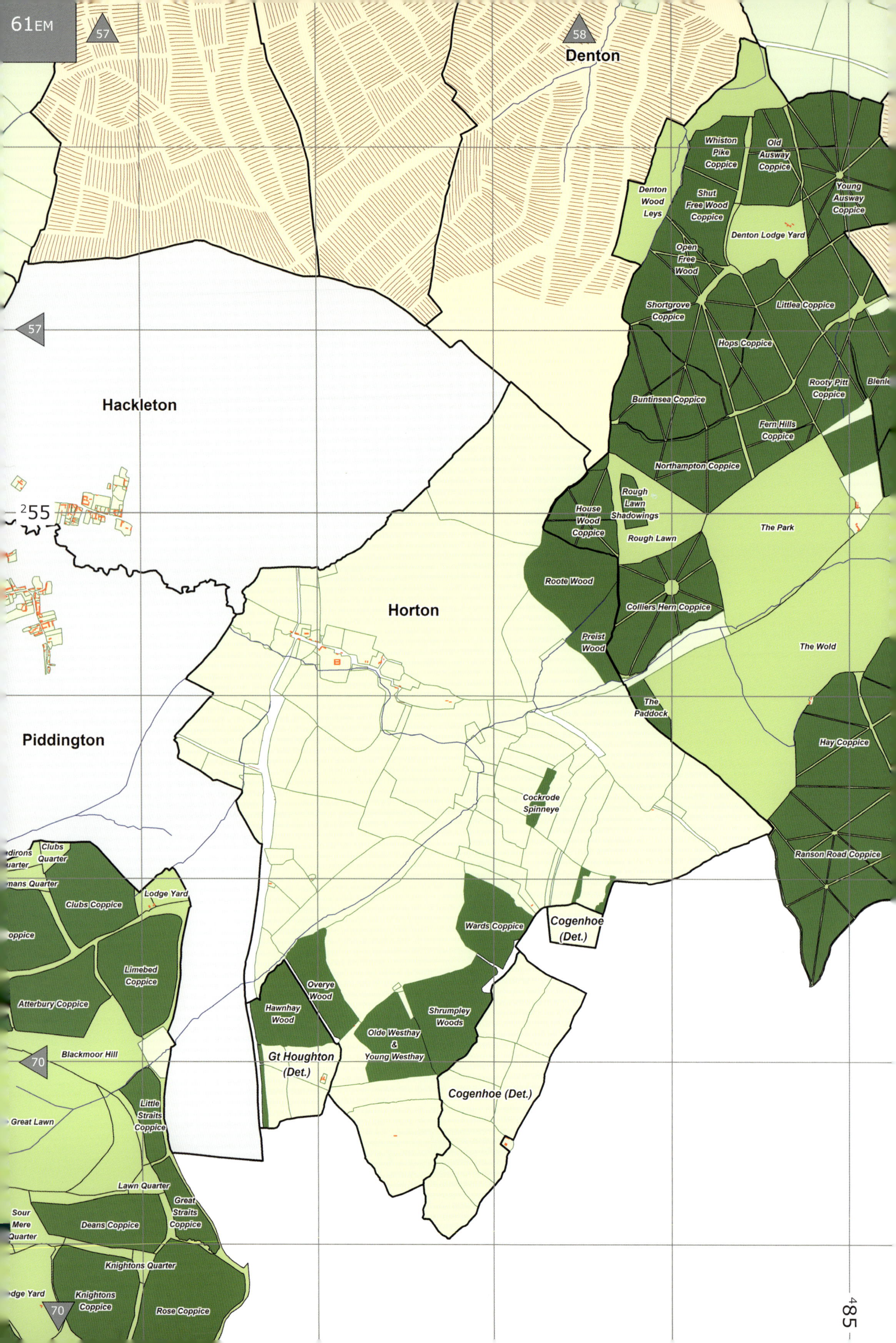
57
58
Denton
Whiston Pike Coppice
Old Ausway Coppice
Young Ausway Coppice
Denton Wood Leys
Shut Free Wood Coppice
Denton Lodge Yard
Open Free Wood
Shortgrove Coppice
Littlea Coppice
Hops Coppice
57
Rooty Pitt Coppice
Hackleton
Buntinsea Coppice
Fern Hills Coppice
Northampton Coppice
Rough Lawn Shadowings
House Wood Coppice
The Park
255
Rough Lawn
Roote Wood
Horton
Colliers Hern Coppice
Preist Wood
The Wold
The Paddock
Piddington
Hay Coppice
Cockrode Spinneye
Clubs Quarter
Ranson Road Coppice
Lodge Yard
Clubs Coppice
Cogenhoe (Det.)
Wards Coppice
Limebed Coppice
Overye Wood
Atterbury Coppice
Hawnhay Wood
Shrumpley Woods
Olde Westhay & Young Westhay
Gt Houghton (Det.)
Blackmoor Hill
70
Cogenhoe (Det.)
Little Straits Coppice
Great Lawn
Lawn Quarter
Great Straits Coppice
Sour Mere Quarter
Deans Coppice
Knightons Quarter
Knightons Coppice
70
Rose Coppice

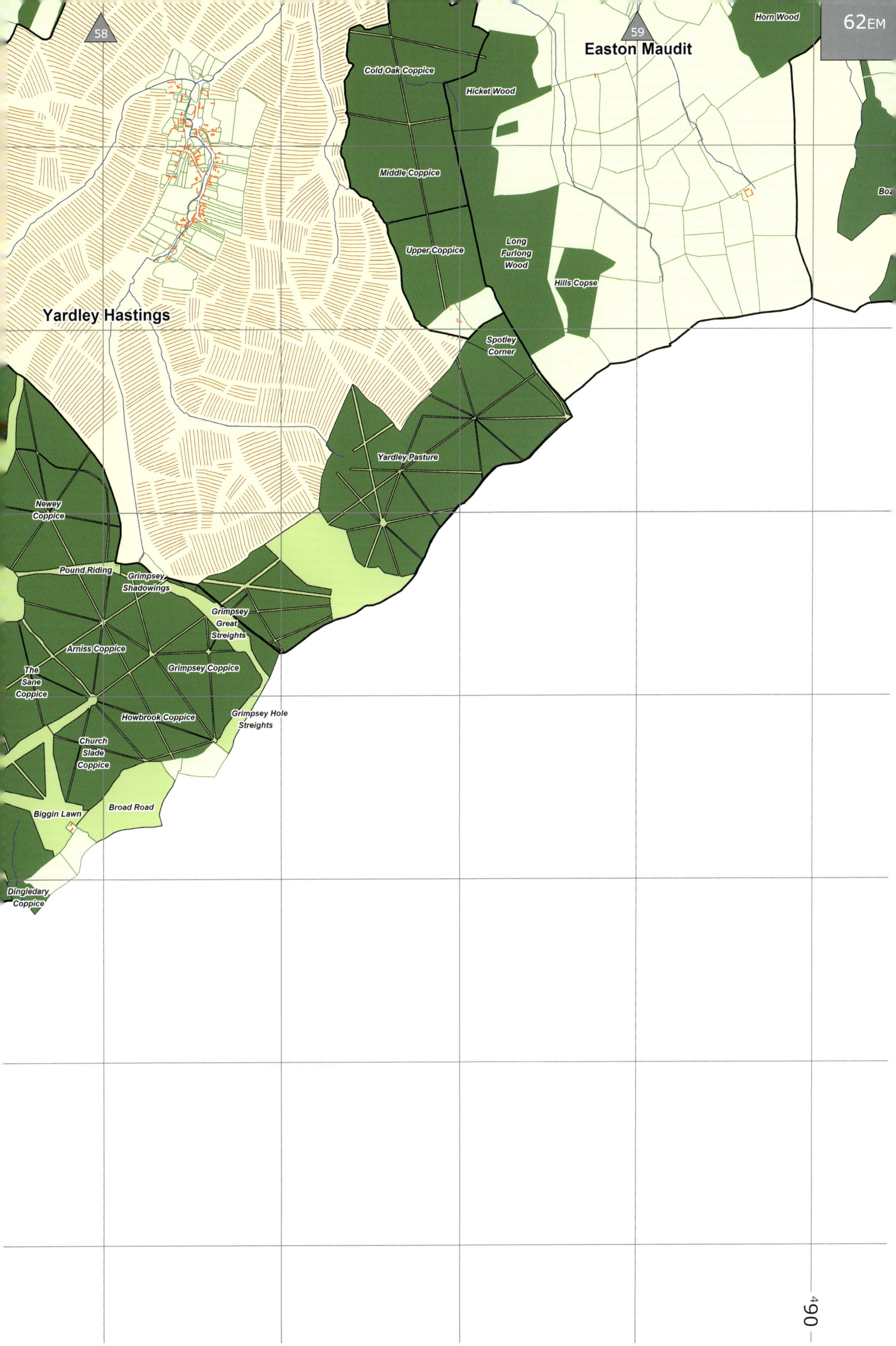
58
59
Easton Maudit
Horn Wood
Cold Oak Coppice
Hicket Wood
Middle Coppice
Upper Coppice
Long Furlong Wood
Hills Copse
Yardley Hastings
Spotley Corner
Yardley Pasture
Newey Coppice
Pound Riding
Grimpsey Shadowings
Grimpsey Great Streights
Arniss Coppice
Grimpsey Coppice
The Sane Coppice
Howbrook Coppice
Grimpsey Hole Streights
Church Slade Coppice
Broad Road
Biggin Lawn
Dingledary Coppice
490

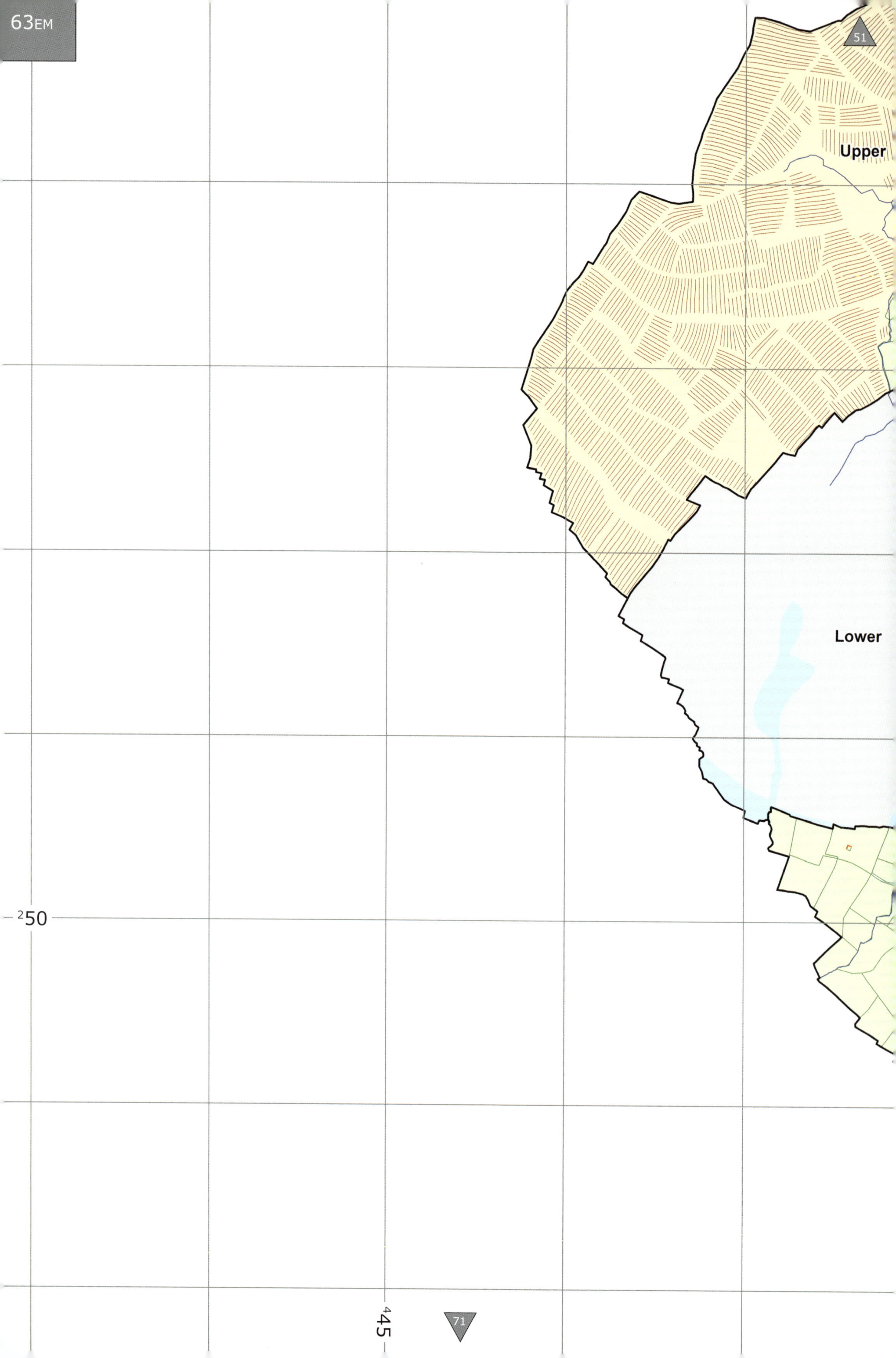
51
Upper
Lower
250
445
71

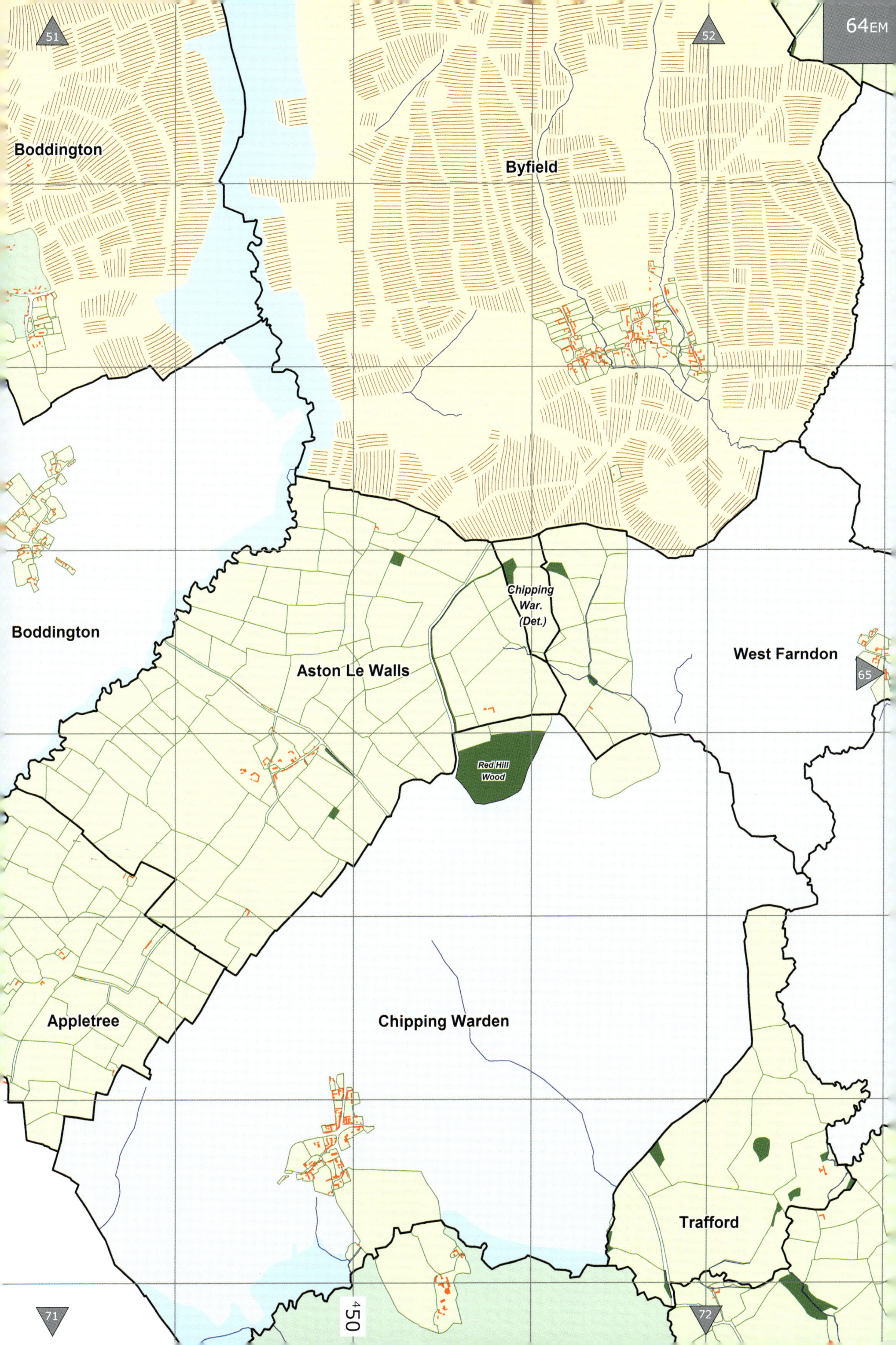
51
52
Boddington
Byfield
Chipping
War.
(Det.)
Boddington
West Farndon
65
Aston Le Walls
Red Hill
Wood
Appletree
Chipping Warden
Trafford
71
450
72

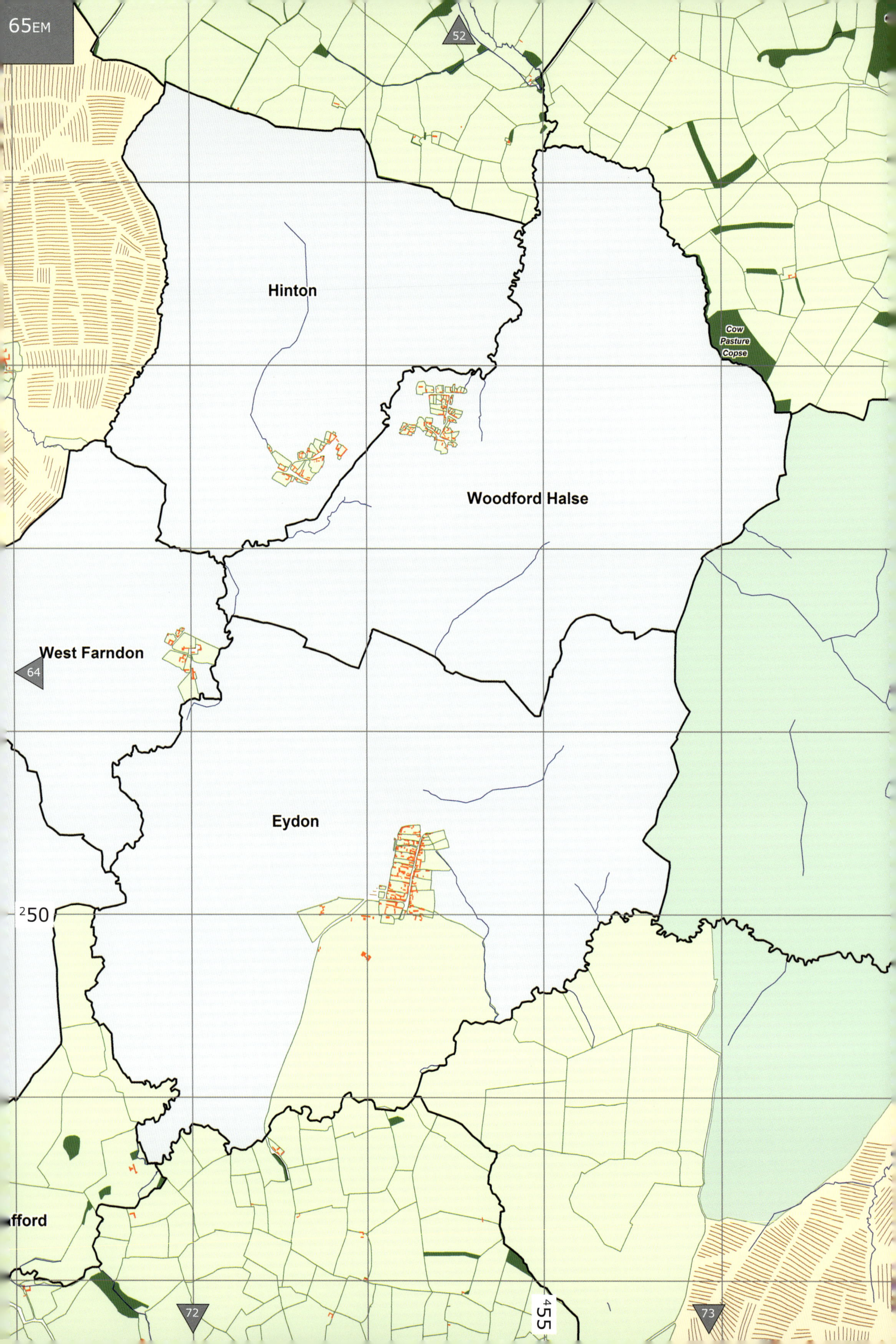
52
Hinton
Cow
Pasture
Copse
Woodford Halse
West Farndon
64
Eydon
250
fford
72
455
73

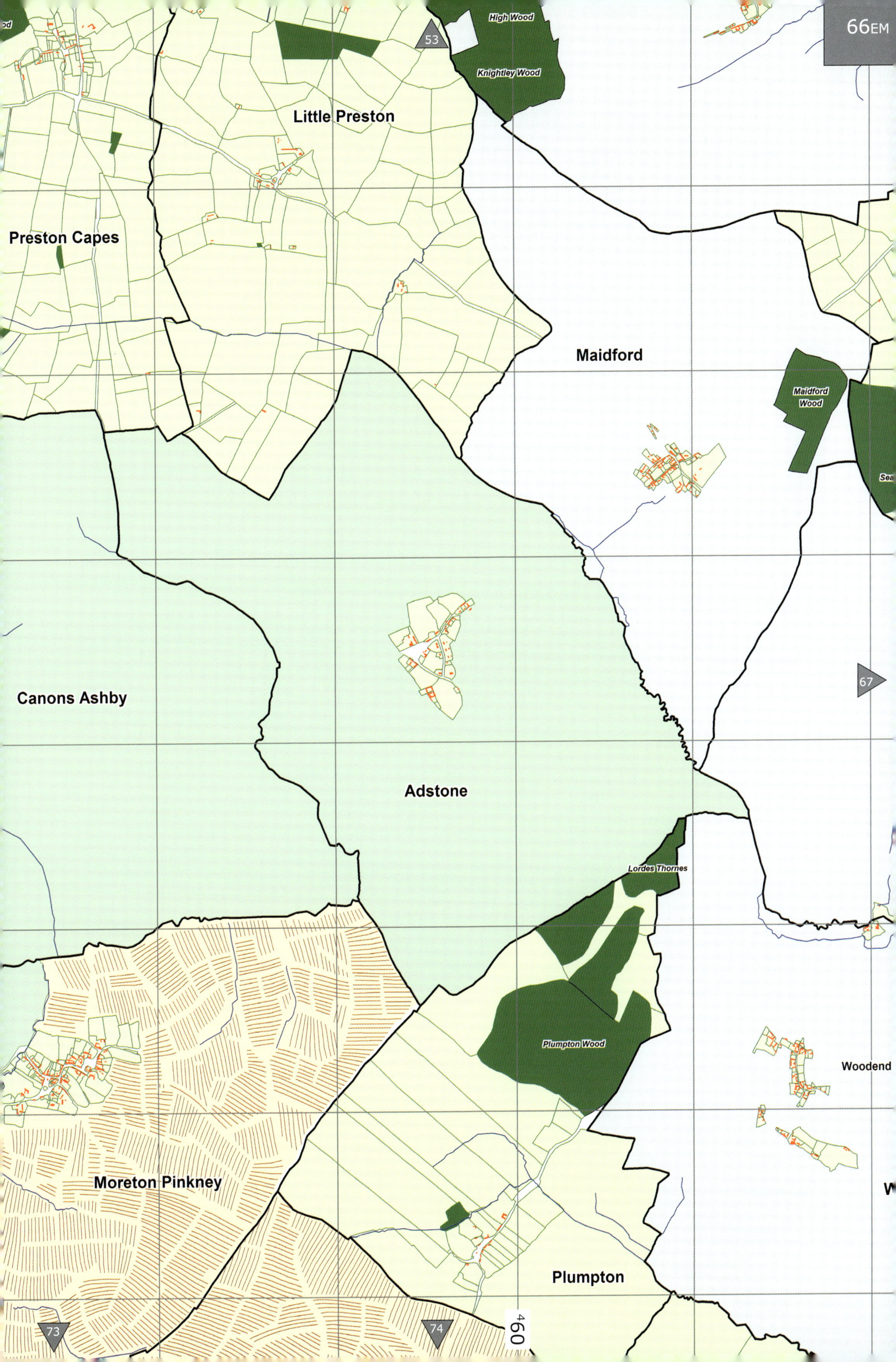
High Wood
Knightley Wood
53
Little Preston
Preston Capes
Maidford
Maidford Wood
Canons Ashby
67
Adstone
Lordes Thornes
Plumpton Wood
Woodend
Moreton Pinkney
Plumpton
73
74
460

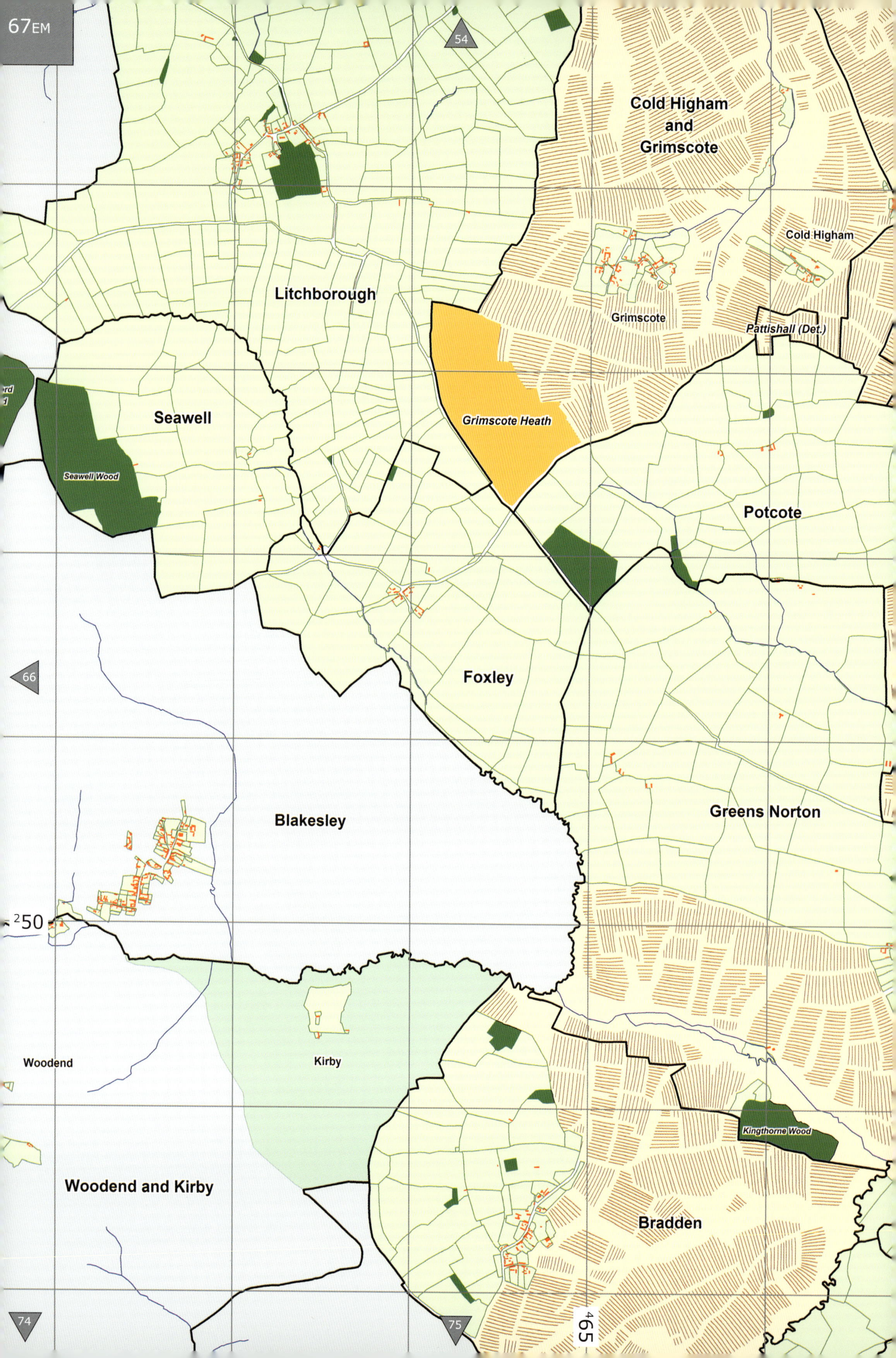
54
Cold Higham
and
Grimscote
Cold Higham
Grimscote
Pattishall (Det.)
Litchborough
Seawell
Seawell Wood
Grimscote Heath
Potcote
Foxley
66
Greens Norton
Blakesley
250
Woodend
Kirby
Kingthorne Wood
Woodend and Kirby
Bradden
74
75
465

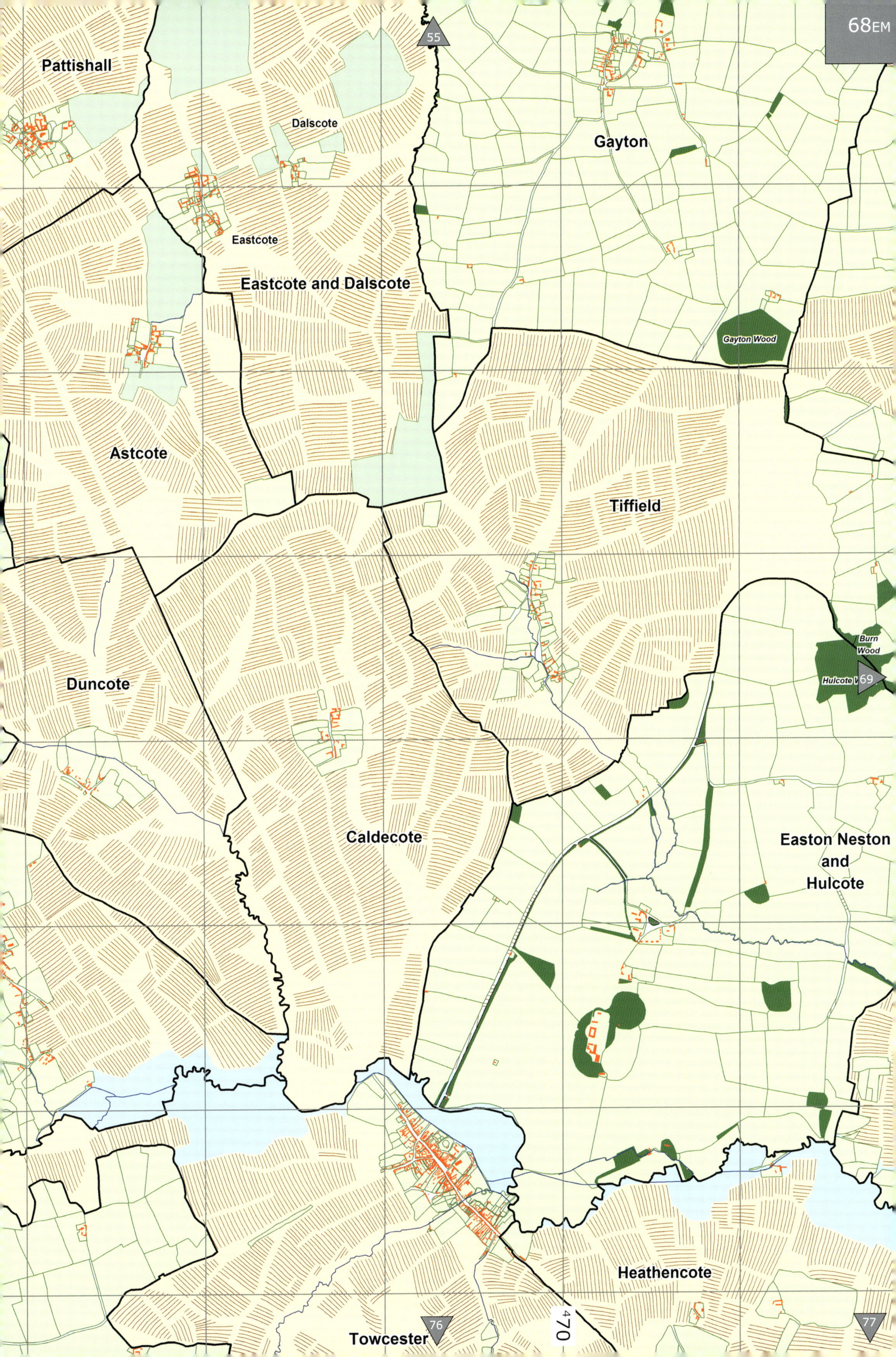
55
Pattishall
Dalscote
Gayton
Eastcote
Eastcote and Dalscote
Gayton Wood
Astcote
Tiffield
Burn Wood
Hulcote
69
Duncote
Caldecote
Easton Neston and Hulcote
Heathencote
76
470
77
Towcester

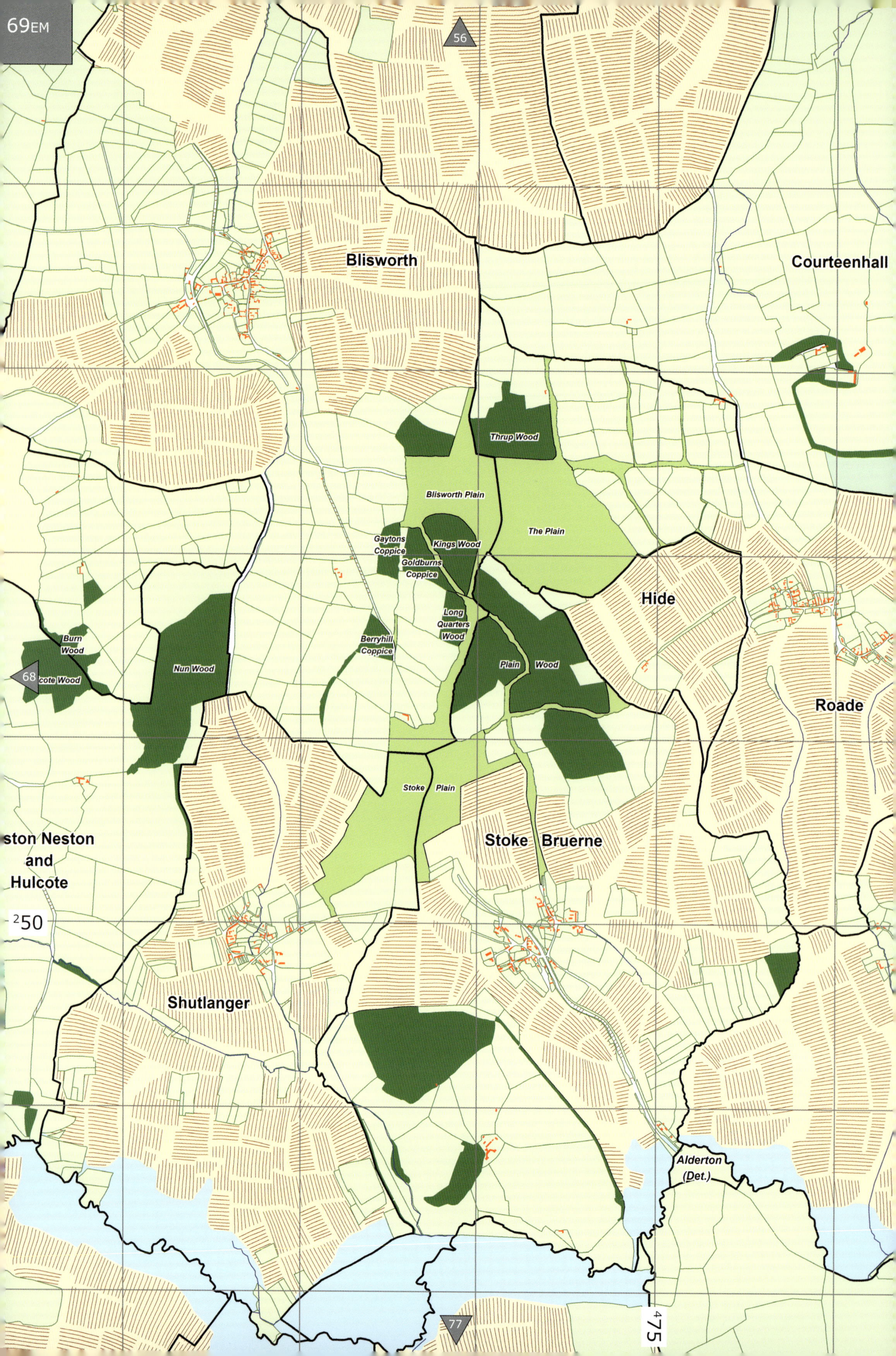
56
Blisworth
Courteenhall
Thrup Wood
Blisworth Plain
The Plain
Gaytons Coppice
Kings Wood
Goldburns Coppice
Hide
Long Quarters Wood
Burn Wood
Berryhill Coppice
68
cote Wood
Nun Wood
Plain
Wood
Roade
Stoke
Plain
ston Neston and Hulcote
Stoke Bruerne
250
Shutlanger
Alderton (Det.)
475
77

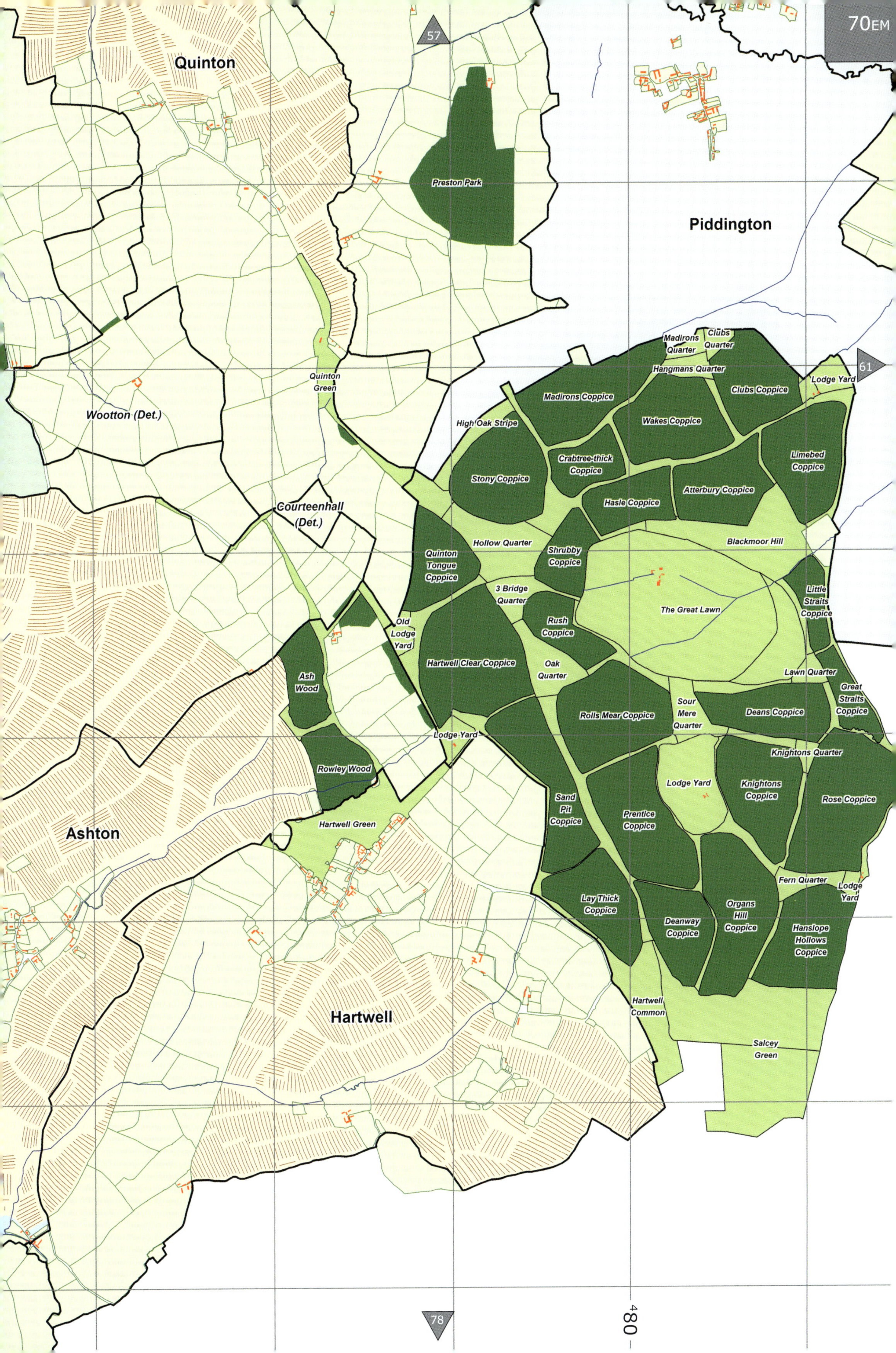

57
Quinton
Preston Park
Piddington
Madirons Quarter
Clubs Quarter
Hangmans Quarter
Clubs Coppice
Lodge Yard
61
Madirons Coppice
Wakes Coppice
Quinton Green
Wootton (Det.)
High Oak Stripe
Stony Coppice
Crabtree-thick Coppice
Limebed Coppice
Atterbury Coppice
Hasle Coppice
Courteenhall (Det.)
Hollow Quarter
Shrubby Coppice
Blackmoor Hill
Quinton Tongue Cpppice
3 Bridge Quarter
Little Straits Coppice
The Great Lawn
Rush Coppice
Old Lodge Yard
Ash Wood
Hartwell Clear Coppice
Oak Quarter
Lawn Quarter
Great Straits Coppice
Sour Mere Quarter
Rolls Mear Coppice
Deans Coppice
Lodge Yard
Knightons Quarter
Rowley Wood
Lodge Yard
Knightons Coppice
Sand Pit Coppice
Rose Coppice
Prentice Coppice
Hartwell Green
Ashton
Fern Quarter
Lodge Yard
Lay Thick Coppice
Organs Hill Coppice
Deanway Coppice
Hanslope Hollows Coppice
Hartwell Common
Hartwell
Salcey Green
78
480

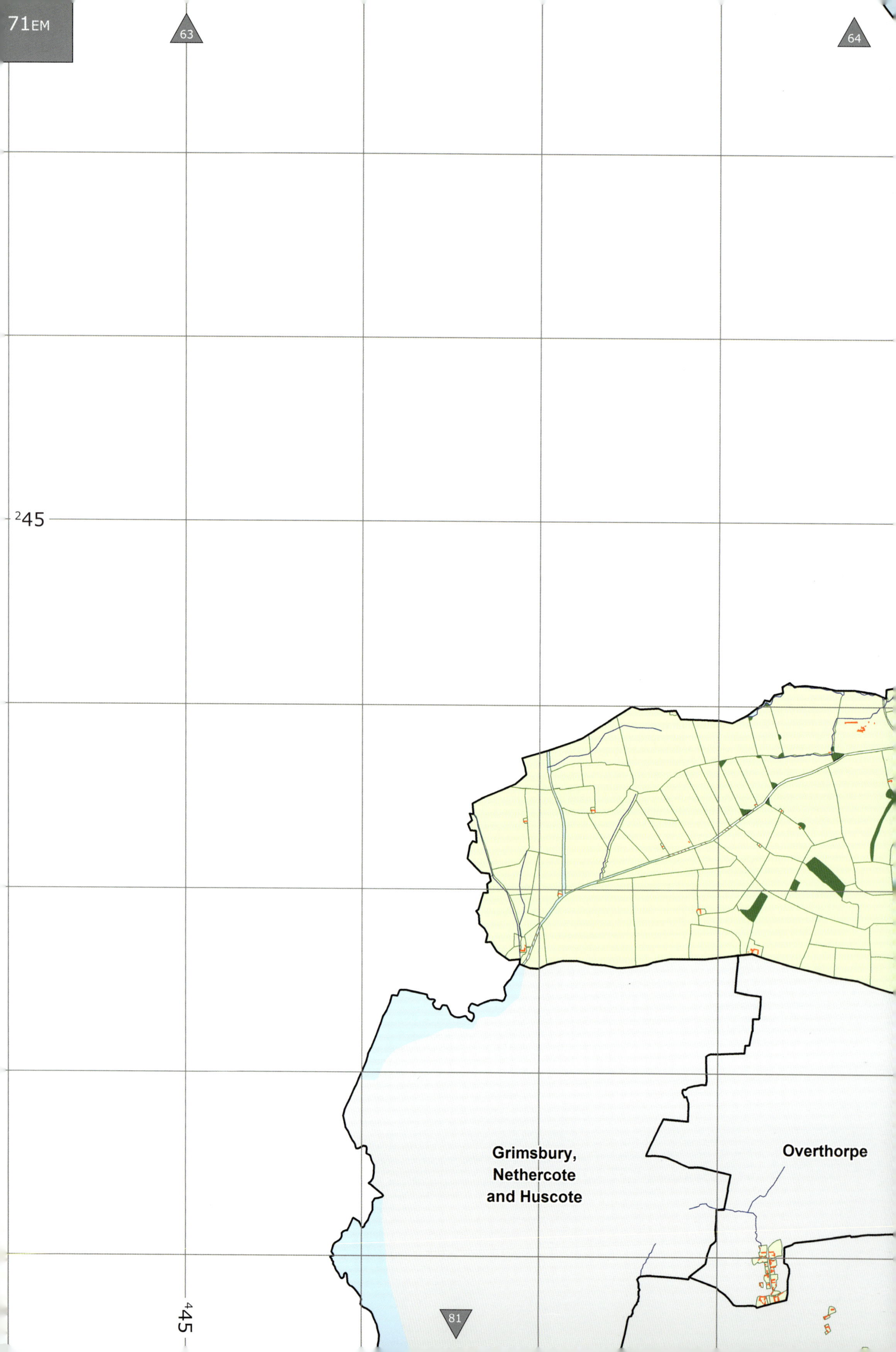
63
64
²45
Grimsbury,
Nethercote
and Huscote
Overthorpe
⁴45
81

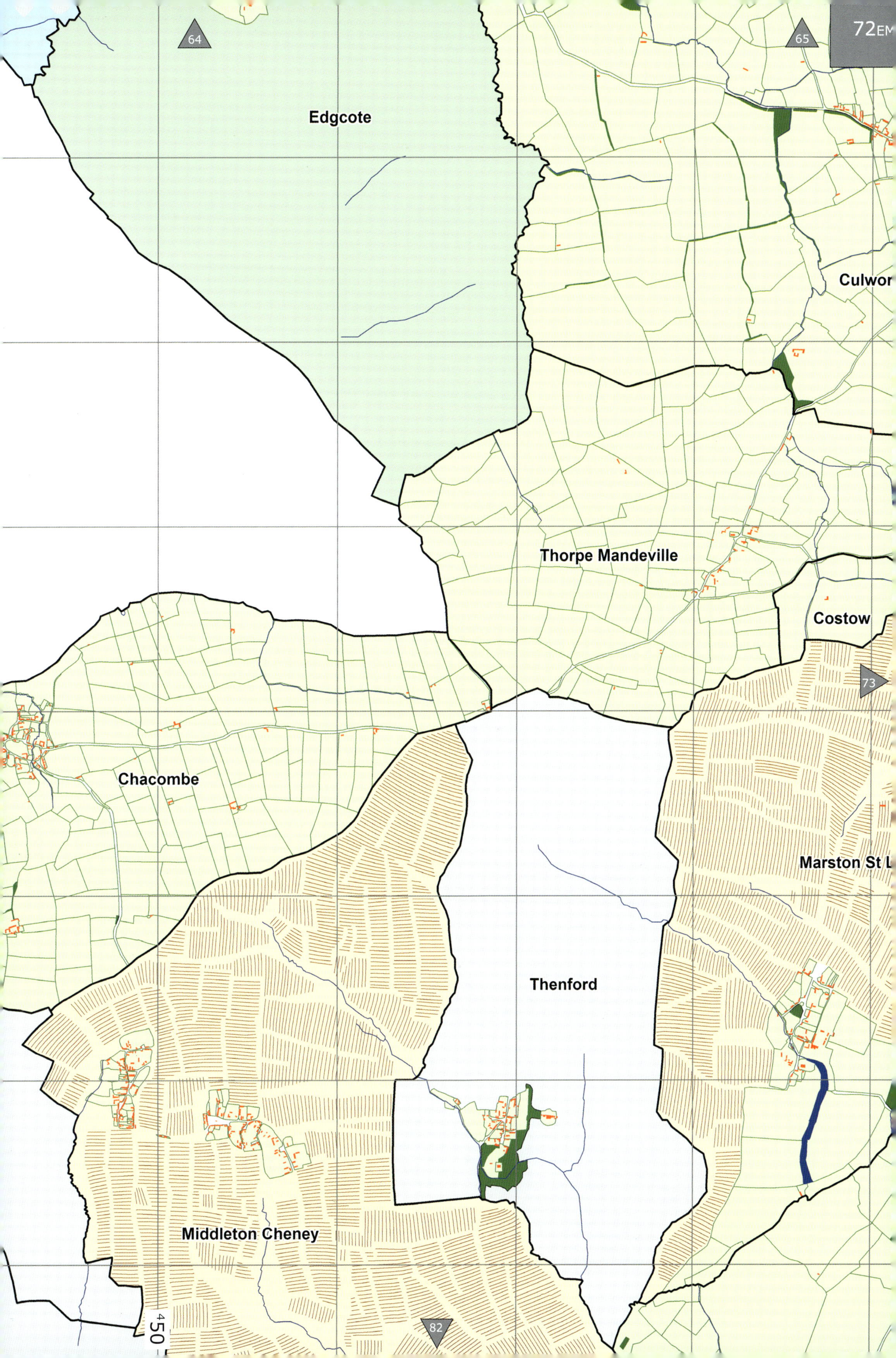
64
65
Edgcote
Culwor
Thorpe Mandeville
Costow
73
Chacombe
Marston St L
Thenford
Middleton Cheney
450
82

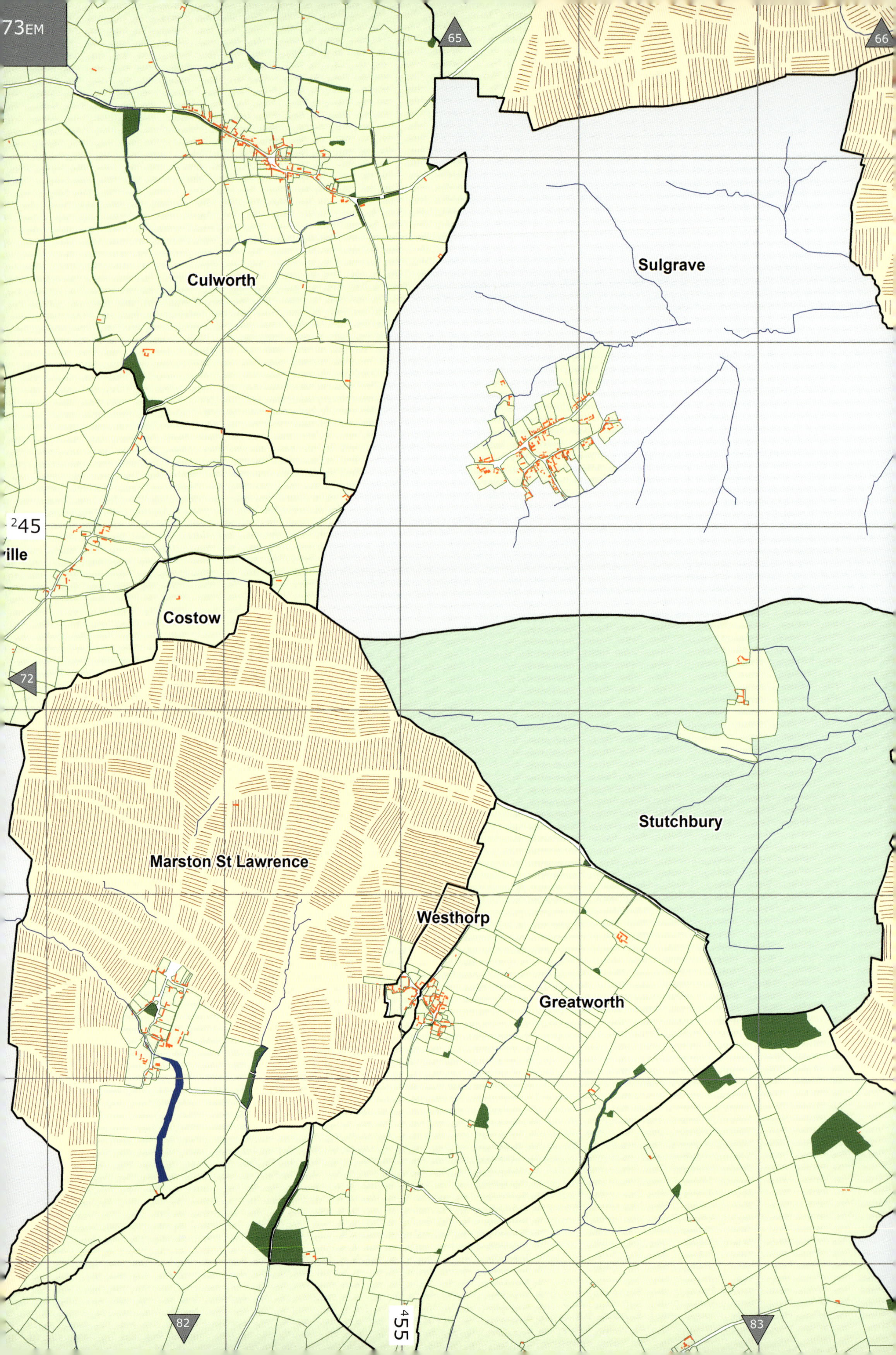
65
66
Culworth
Sulgrave
245
ille
Costow
72
Marston St Lawrence
Stutchbury
Westhorp
Greatworth
82
455
83

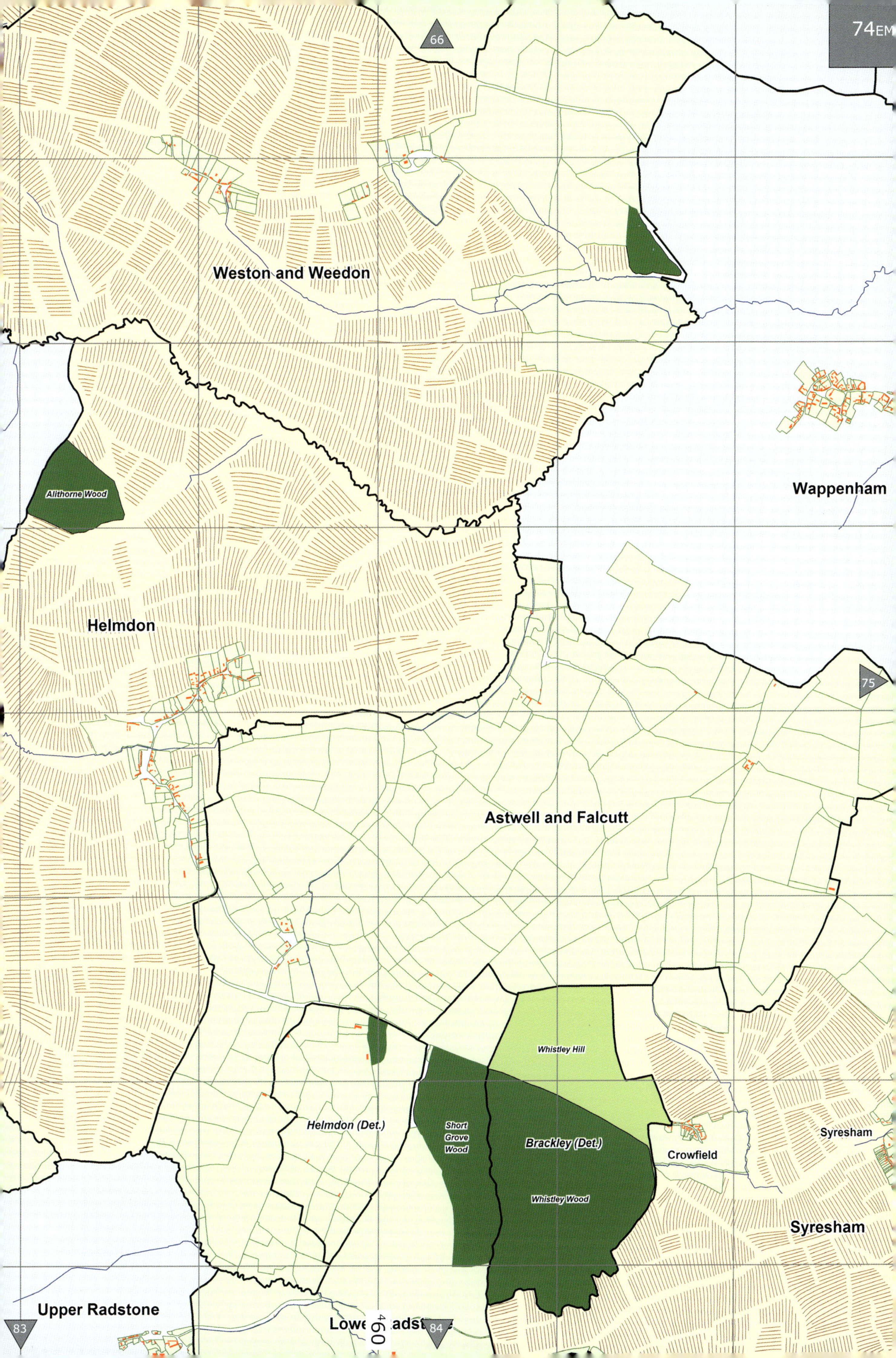
66
Weston and Weedon
Alithorne Wood
Helmdon
Wappenham
75
Astwell and Falcutt
Whistley Hill
Helmdon (Det.)
Short
Grove
Wood
Brackley (Det.)
Crowfield
Syresham
Whistley Wood
Syresham
Upper Radstone
83
84
460

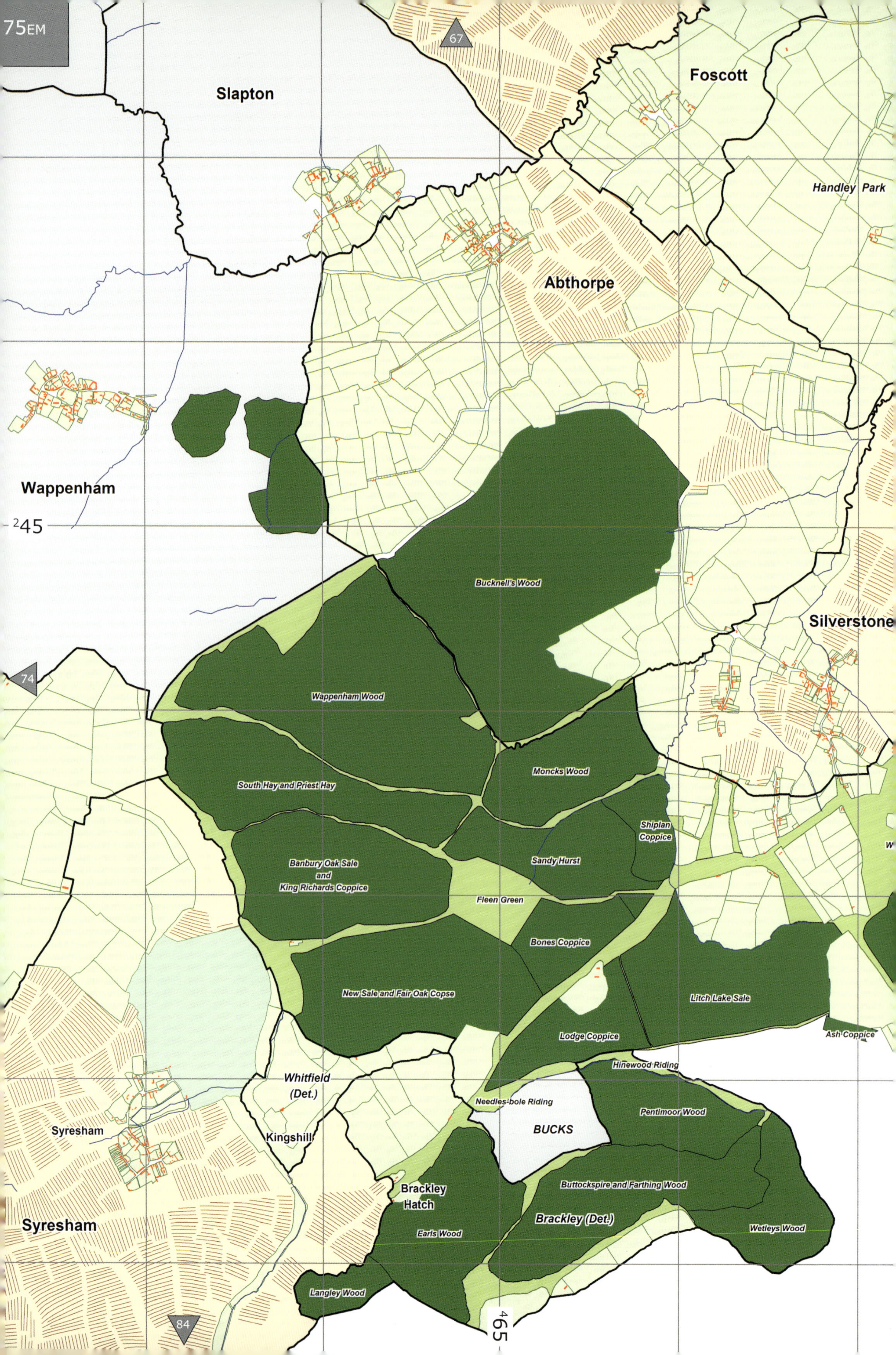
67
Slapton
Foscott
Handley Park
Abthorpe
Wappenham
245
Bucknell's Wood
Silverstone
74
Wappenham Wood
Moncks Wood
South Hay and Priest Hay
Shiplan Coppice
Sandy Hurst
Banbury Oak Sale and King Richards Coppice
Fleen Green
Bones Coppice
New Sale and Fair Oak Copse
Litch Lake Sale
Lodge Coppice
Ash Coppice
Hinewood Riding
Whitfield (Det.)
Needles-bole Riding
Pentimoor Wood
BUCKS
Syresham
Kingshill
Buttockspire and Farthing Wood
Brackley Hatch
Brackley (Det.)
Syresham
Earls Wood
Wetleys Wood
Langley Wood
84
465

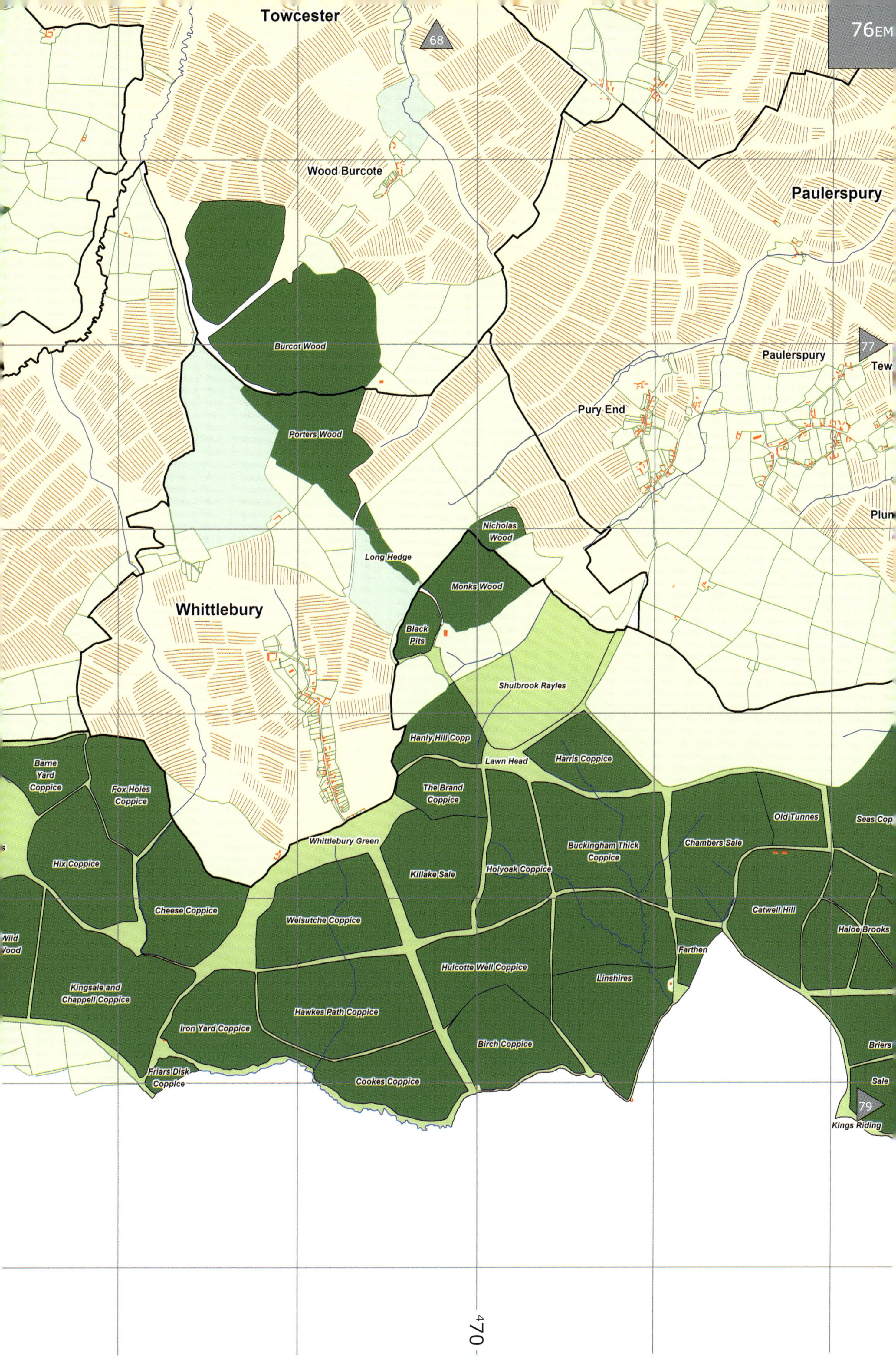
Towcester
68
Wood Burcote
Paulerspury
Burcot Wood
Paulerspury
77
Tew
Pury End
Porters Wood
Plun
Nicholas Wood
Long Hedge
Monks Wood
Whittlebury
Black Pits
Shulbrook Rayles
Hanly Hill Copp
Lawn Head
Harris Coppice
Barne Yard Coppice
Fox Holes Coppice
The Brand Coppice
Old Tunnes
Seas Cop
Whittlebury Green
Buckingham Thick Coppice
Chambers Sale
Hix Coppice
Killake Sale
Holyoak Coppice
Cheese Coppice
Catwell Hill
Welsutche Coppice
Haloe Brooks
Wild Wood
Farthen
Hulcotte Well Coppice
Linshires
Kingsale and Chappell Coppice
Hawkes Path Coppice
Iron Yard Coppice
Birch Coppice
Briers
Friars Disk Coppice
Cookes Coppice
Sale
79
Kings Riding
470

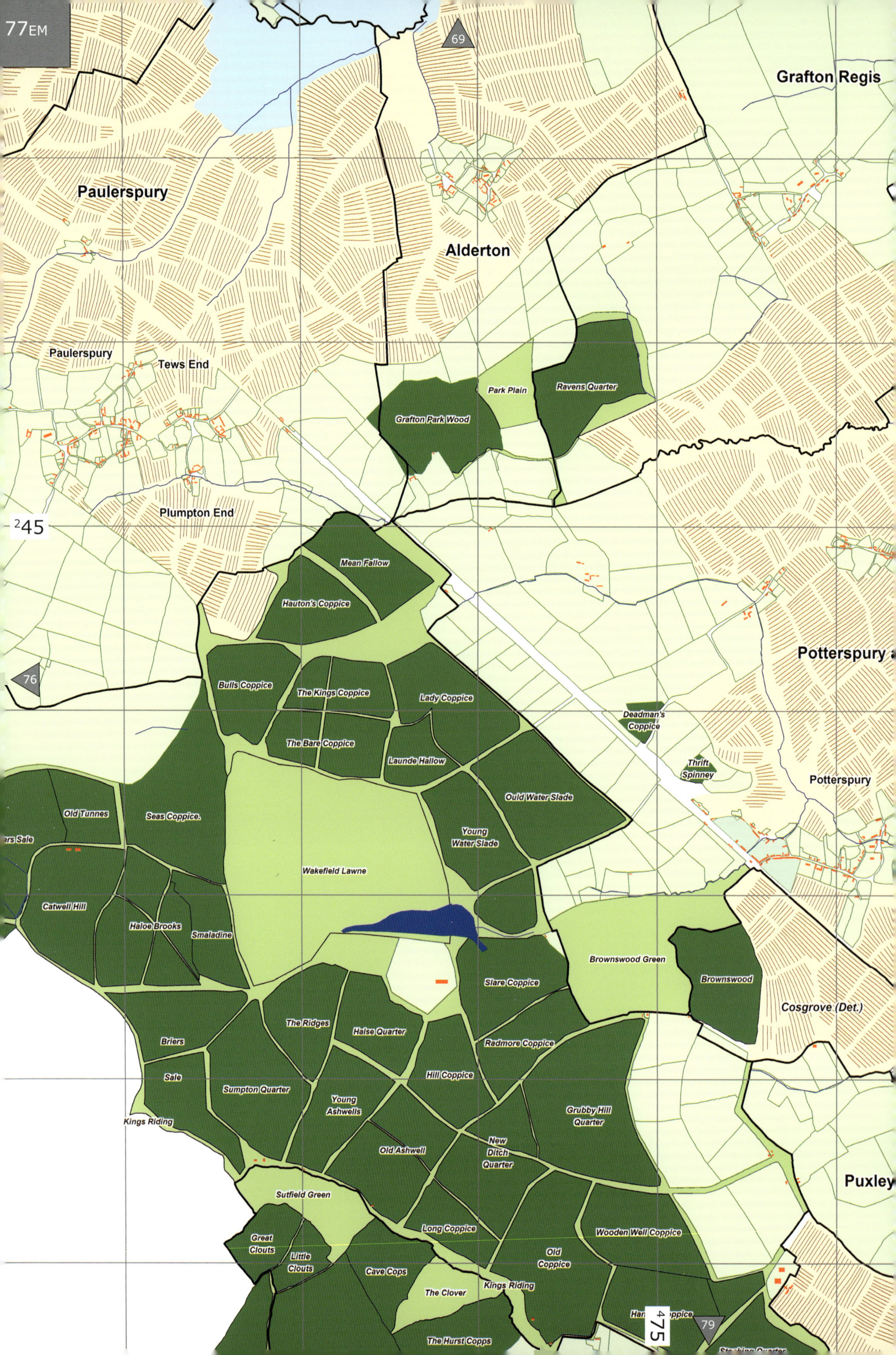

69
Grafton Regis
Paulerspury
Alderton
Paulerspury
Tews End
Park Plain
Ravens Quarter
Grafton Park Wood
Plumpton End
245
Mean Fallow
Hauton's Coppice
76
Potterspury
Bulls Coppice
The Kings Coppice
Lady Coppice
Deadman's Coppice
The Bare Coppice
Launde Hallow
Thrift Spinney
Potterspury
Old Tunnes
Seas Coppice.
Ould Water Slade
Young Water Slade
Wakefield Lawne
Catwell Hill
Haloe Brooks
Smaladine
Brownswood Green
Brownswood
Slare Coppice
Cosgrove (Det.)
The Ridges
Halse Quarter
Radmore Coppice
Briers
Sale
Hill Coppice
Sumpton Quarter
Young Ashwells
Grubby Hill Quarter
Kings Riding
New Ditch Quarter
Old Ashwell
Sutfield Green
Puxley
Long Coppice
Wooden Well Coppice
Great Clouts
Little Clouts
Old Coppice
Cave Cops
Kings Riding
The Clover
475
79
The Hurst Copps

70
Yardley Gobion
Yardley Gobion
Furtho
Cosgrove
and
Furtho
Cosgrove
Old Castle Coppice
Young Castle Coppice
Shrob
Meadow
Armitage
Coppice
Pond Ryding coppice
80
480

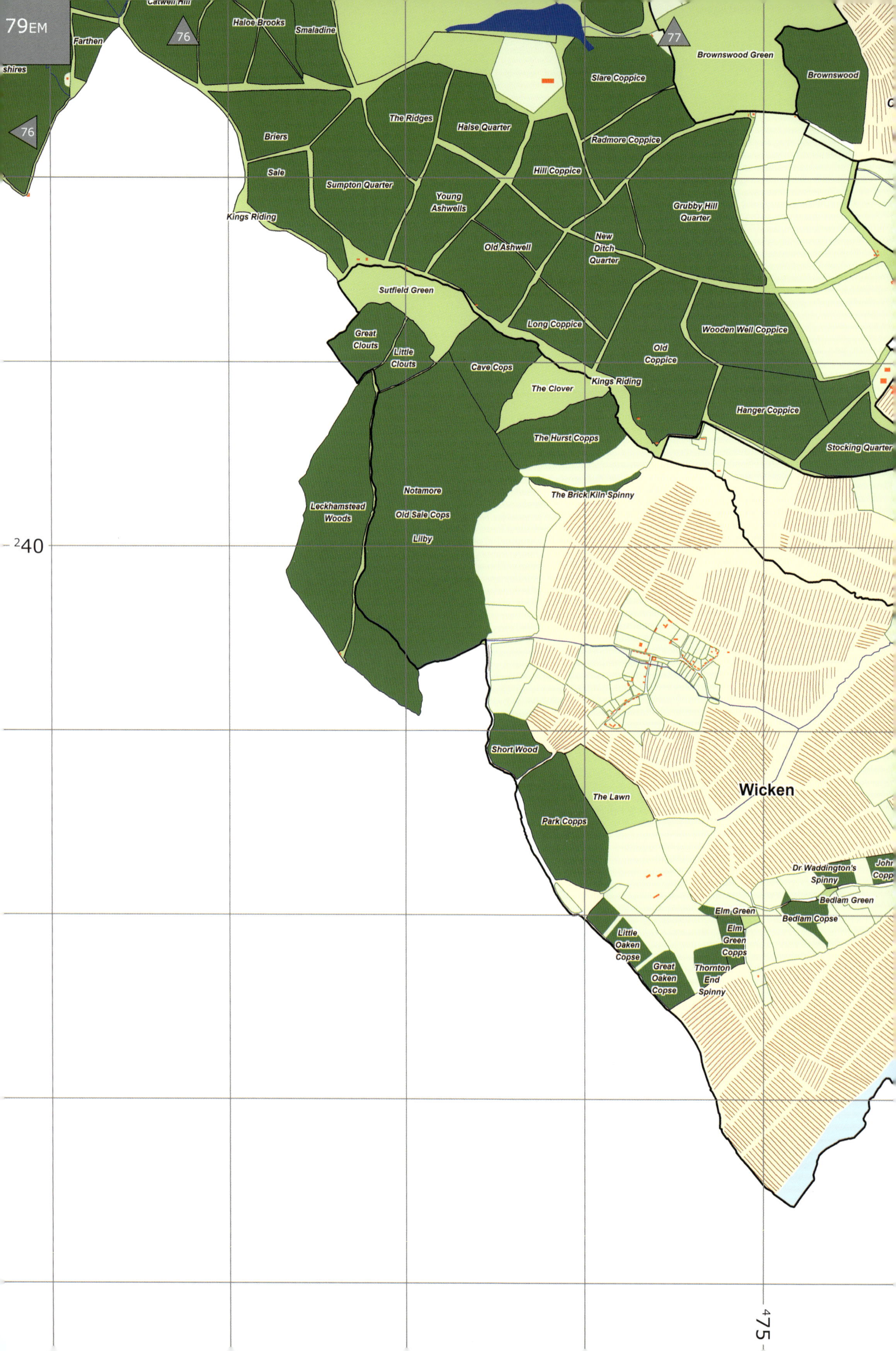
Catwell Hill
Haloe Brooks
Smaladine
Farthen
76
77
shires
Brownswood Green
Brownswood
Slare Coppice
The Ridges
Halse Quarter
Briers
Radmore Coppice
Hill Coppice
Sale
Sumpton Quarter
Young Ashwells
Grubby Hill Quarter
Kings Riding
New Ditch Quarter
Old Ashwell
Sutfield Green
Long Coppice
Wooden Well Coppice
Great Clouts
Little Clouts
Old Coppice
Cave Cops
Kings Riding
The Clover
Hanger Coppice
The Hurst Copps
Stocking Quarter
The Brick Kiln Spinny
Notamore
Leckhamstead Woods
Old Sale Cops
Lilby
240
Short Wood
The Lawn
Wicken
Park Copps
Dr Waddington's Spinny
Bedlam Green
Elm Green
Bedlam Copse
Little Oaken Copse
Elm Green Copps
Great Oaken Copse
Thornton End Spinny
475

78
Furtho
Cosgrove
and
Furtho
Cosgrove
ve (Det.)
Old Castle Coppice
Young Castle Coppice
Puxley
Shrob
Meadow
Armitage
Coppice
Pond Ryding coppice
Cole Coppice
Passenham
The Green
Deanshanger
Middle
Wood
480

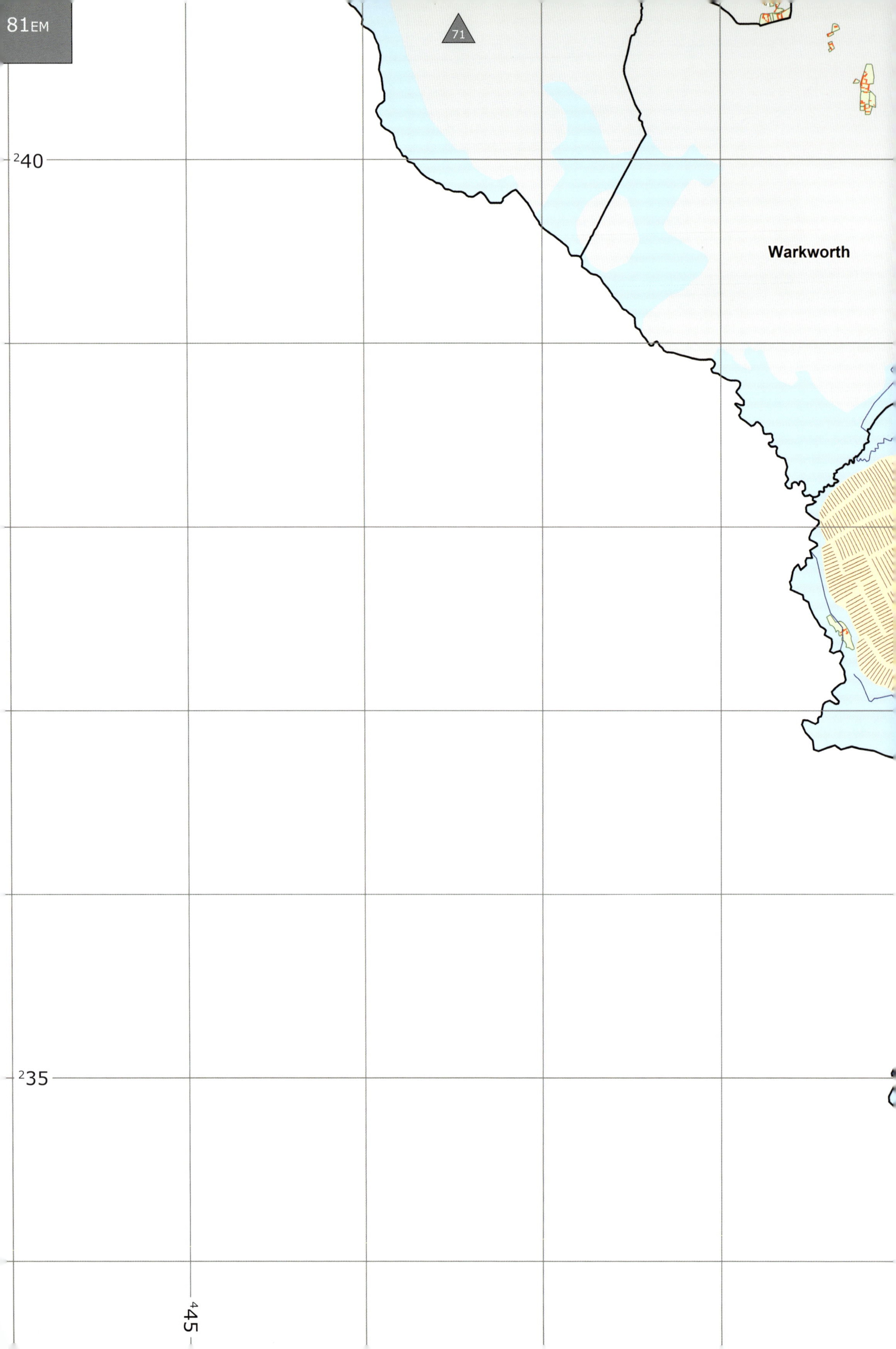

71
240
Warkworth
235
445

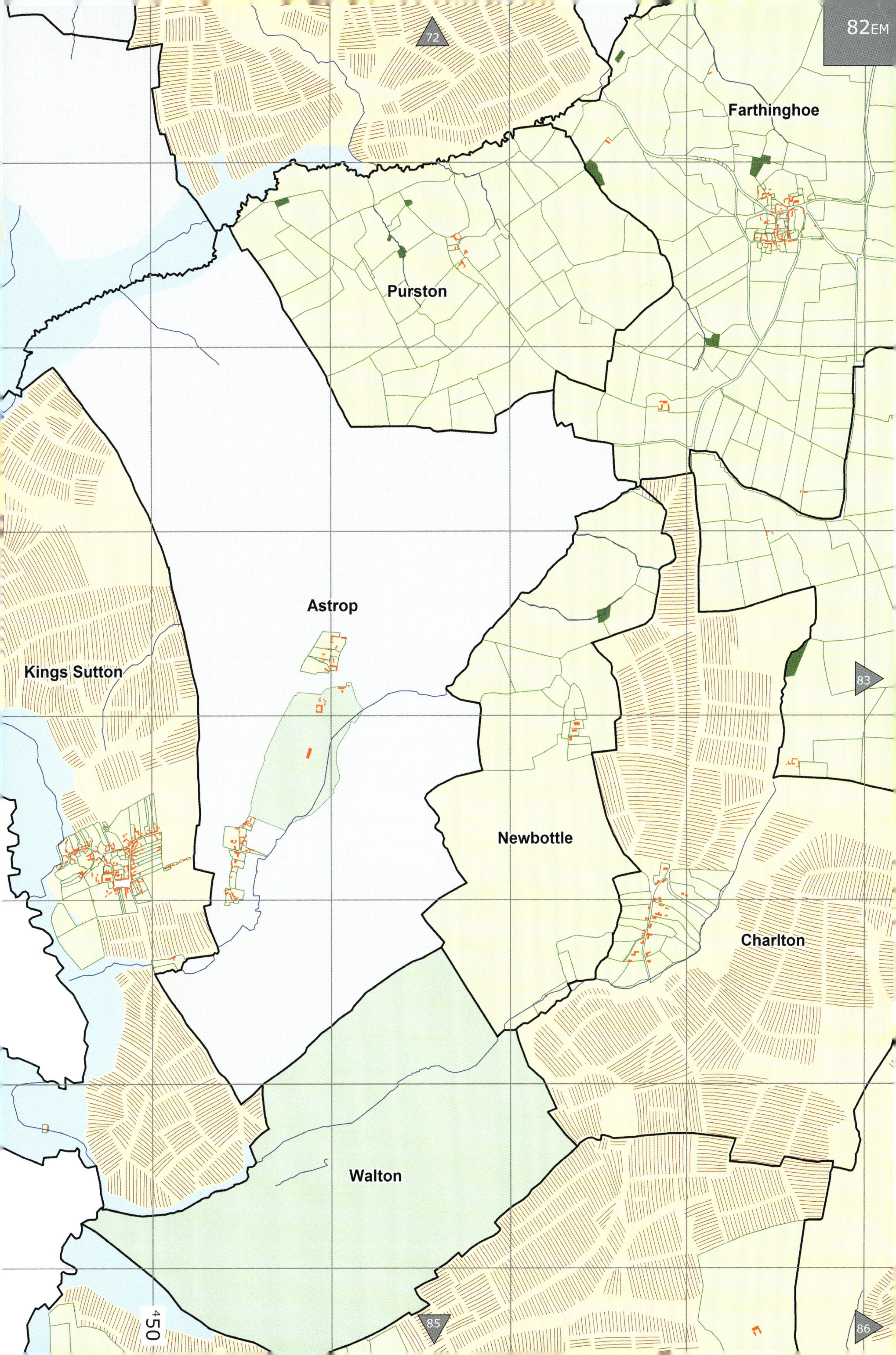
72
Farthinghoe
Purston
Astrop
Kings Sutton
83
Newbottle
Charlton
Walton
450
85
86

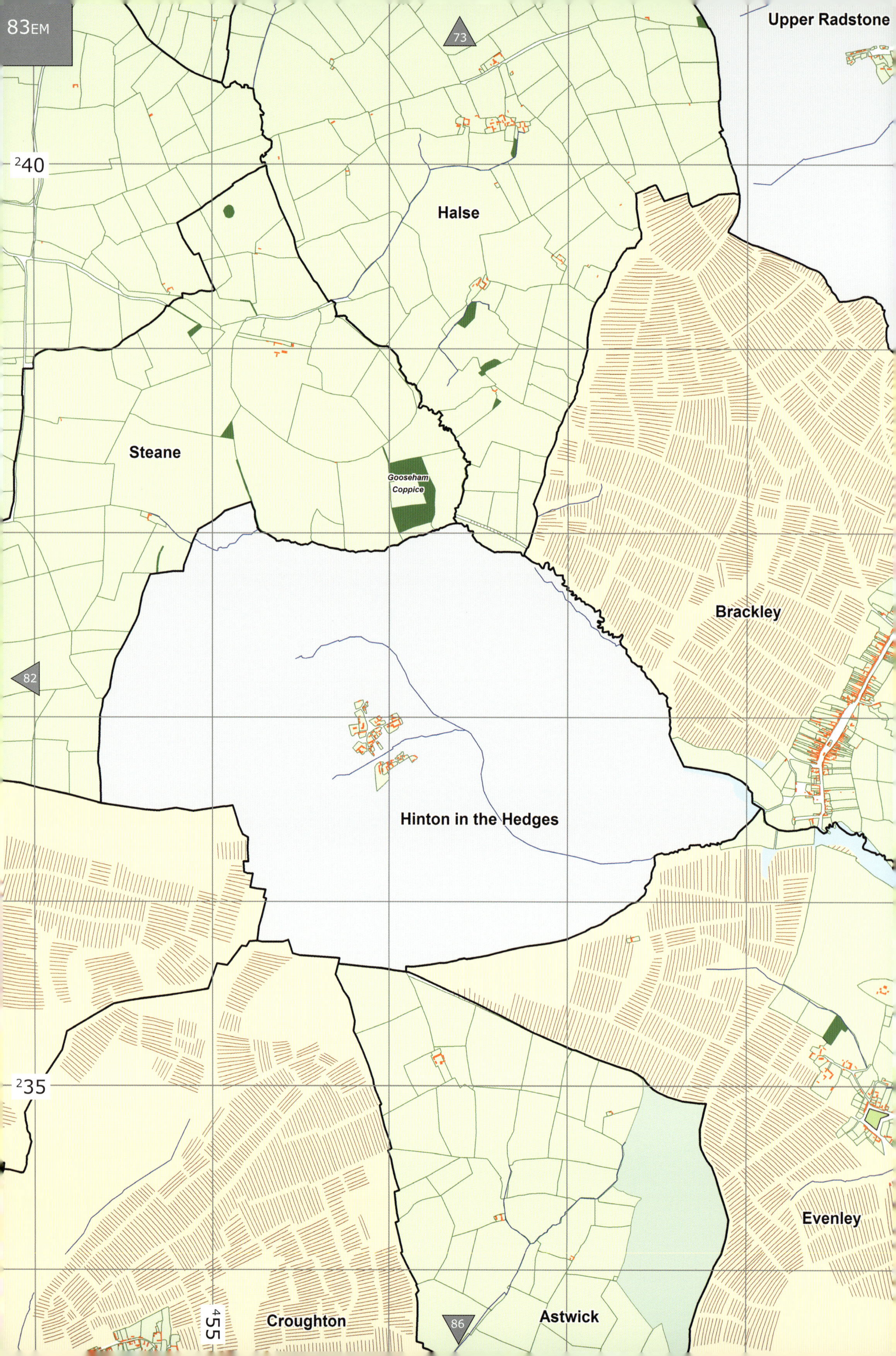

Upper Radstone
73
²40
Halse
Brackley
Steane
Gooseham Coppice
82
Hinton in the Hedges
²35
Evenley
⁴55
Croughton
86
Astwick

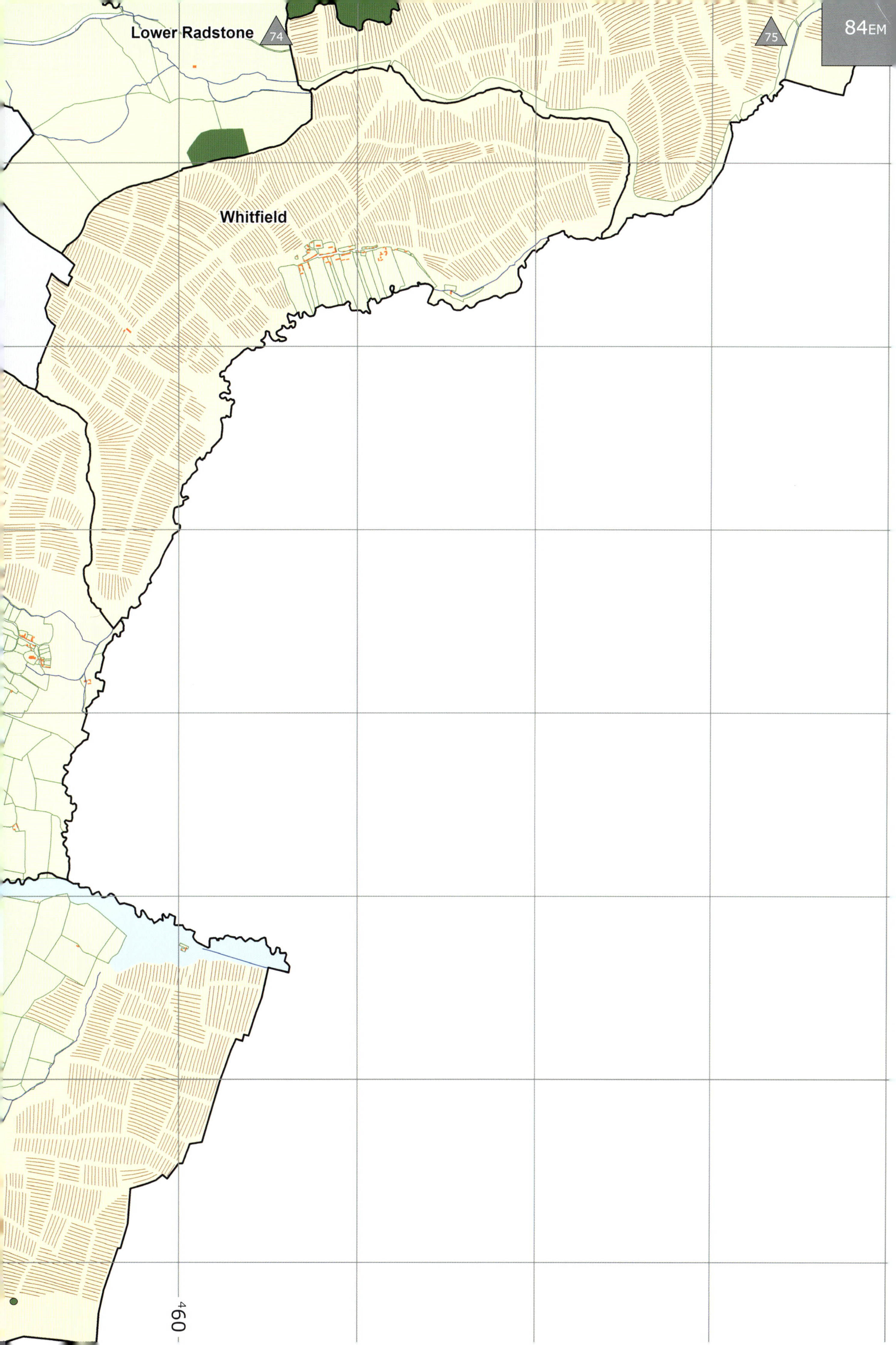
Lower Radstone
74
75
Whitfield
460

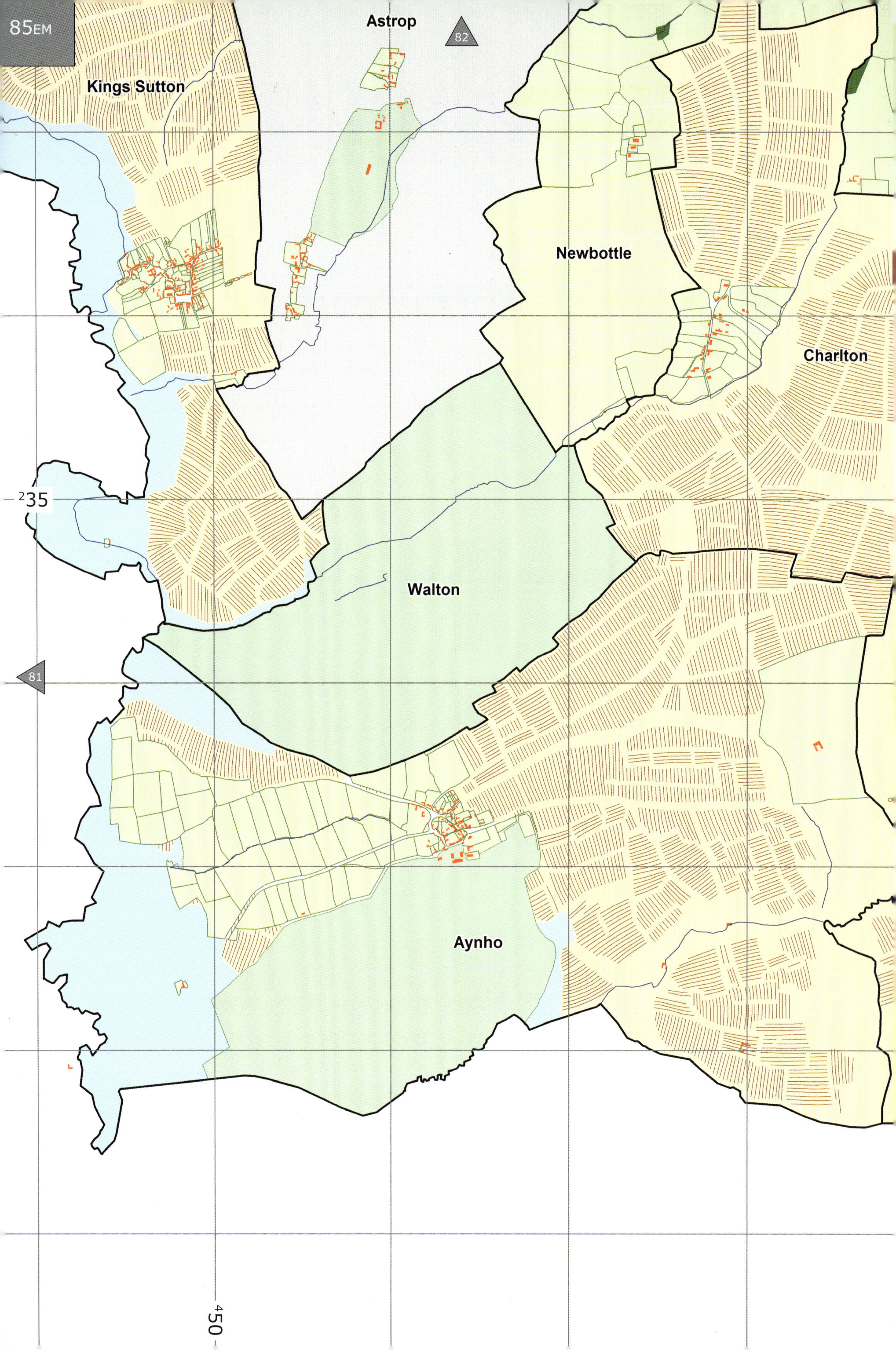
Astrop
82
Kings Sutton
Newbottle
Charlton
235
Walton
81
Aynho
450

83
Brackley
Hinton in the Hedges
Croughton
Astwick
Evenley
84
455

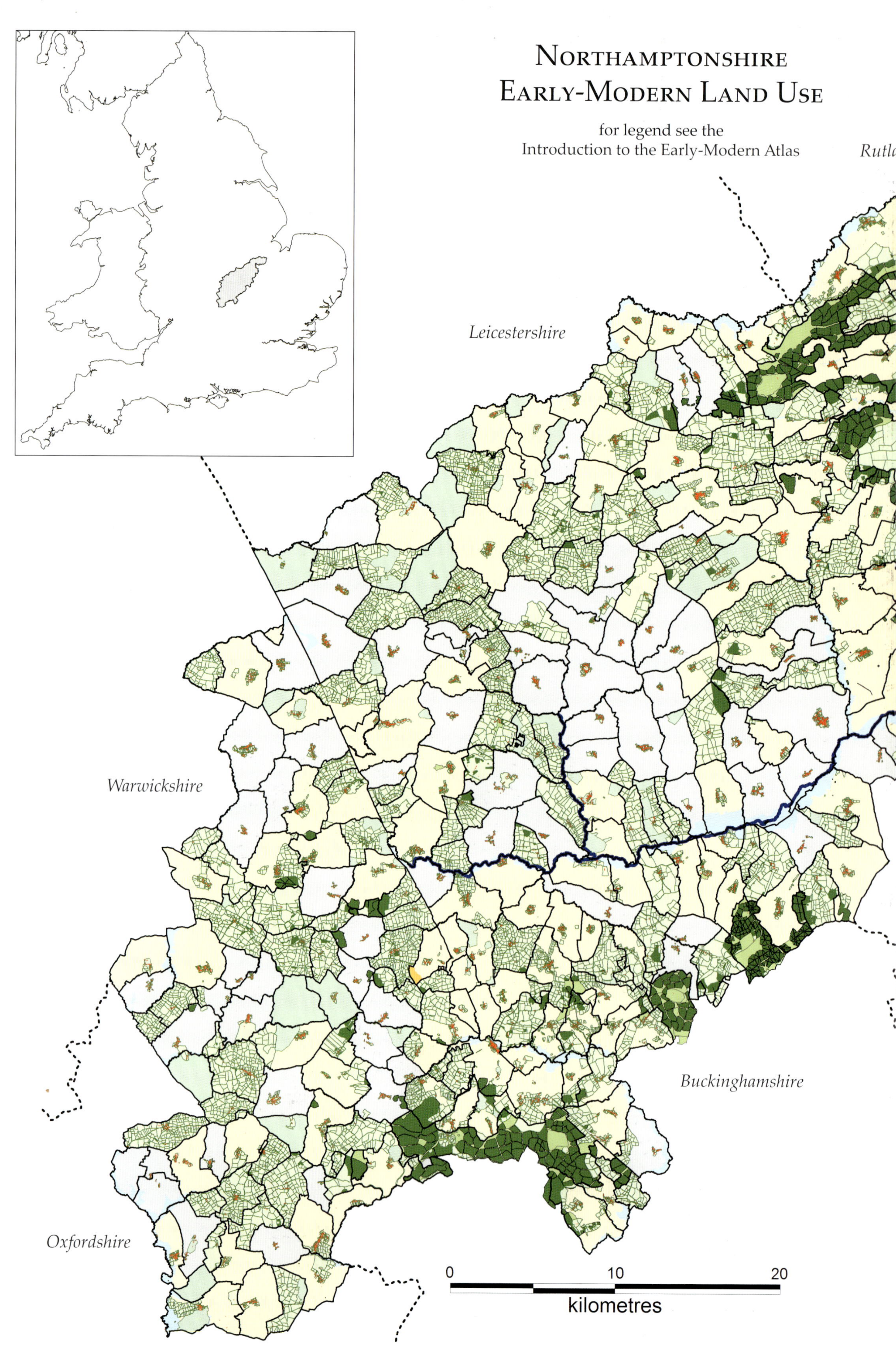
NORTHAMPTONSHIRE
EARLY-MODERN LAND USE
for legend see the
Introduction to the Early-Modern Atlas
Rutla
Leicestershire
Warwickshire
Buckinghamshire
Oxfordshire
0
10
20
kilometres